CATFISH AND CRYSTAL

CATFISH
AND CRYSTAL

Ernest Kirschten

We may be through with the past,
but the past is not through with us.
—BERGEN EVANS.

DOUBLEDAY & COMPANY, INC.
GARDEN CITY, NEW YORK

Library of Congress Catalog Card Number 60–9483
Copyright © 1960 by Ernest Kirschten
All Rights Reserved
Printed in the United States of America

The city is where she is because fate has set her there, and it would be ungracious to complain overmuch, since there is so much beauty in her choice of a site, marked out as a meeting-place of many ways. The rivers called for her, and the open plains. The folk, wandering at first, and later settled on their lands, craved her presence. The people of the mountains found it good that their capital should be builded in a valley low and fruitful.

—Jules Romains.

Contents

Foreword

This is a big book. Yet it would be easy (not for me!) to write a bigger one about St. Louis. In its rather quiet way, this fascinating city has stamped a considerable portion of the United States as "Made in St. Louis." It was the gateway for the adventurers, explorers, traders—the old French called them *négociants*—missionaries, soldiers, and settlers of the trans-Mississippi West. It was their source of supplies, their link with the East. A good part of the cotton-growing South looked to St. Louis for commerce and culture, calling the city "the Mistress of the North." Wisconsin and Iowa sent their lead down to its three-mile levee for fabrication or transshipment. From St. Louis the pelts of Wyoming and Montana went to New Orleans, New York, London, and Paris. To St. Louis came the gold of California and Colorado, and the silver of New Mexico. For a century and a half St. Louisans have been influential in Washington. From St. Louis came the generals and many of the regiments who won the Civil War for Abraham Lincoln, the lawyer from nearby Springfield. Its people once regarded Chicago as an upstart village, and still consider it rather gauche. Indeed, because it dominates the world's greatest river highway, St. Louis once was proposed as the substitute for Washington, D.C., as the capital of the nation.

Today, although it is the country's ninth city—and might stand higher had it not legally confined itself to an area about twenty miles long and seven miles wide—its pace is slower, if not more sedate. After all, Henry M. Brackenridge, writing in 1814 of his travels in Louisiana, said, "St. Louis was always a place of refinement and fashion, the residence of many genteel families, both French and American." They had "in their deportment something of the gravity of the Spaniard, though gay and fond of amusements." He admired their good manners, their hospitality, their classless society, and the virtue and acumen of St. Louis women. But he did say also: "It is to be lamented that no space has been left between the town and the river. . . ." Belatedly, St. Louis has taken his hint. Its riverfront will be superbly transformed in time for the celebration of the bicentennial in 1964.

No matter what the pace, the events of two centuries, if recounted with any pretense of completeness, would fill a bigger book than this one. Much has been skipped or barely suggested. Some fine old names have not been mentioned. Some fine old stories have not been retold. It is lucky for a writer that a "foreword" really is his last word. It offers an opportunity of sorts to make up for some of the omissions. Realizing, for example, that the city's baseball heroes have received rather short shrift, it is possible to stir the reader's memory by rattling off such names as George Sisler, Rogers Hornsby, Grover Cleveland Alexander, the brothers Dean, Marty Marion, Frank Frisch, Hank Severeid, and "Red" Schoendienst. Yet even such amendments are held down by the limits of space, time, and energy.

Of course it may be argued also that this book is too long, that there is too much in it. Is Sherman's march to the sea part of the St. Louis story? Schurz's fight against corruption in Washington? Grant's death, far from the St. Louis he loved? Eads's saving of the port of New Orleans? Lindbergh's flight across the Atlantic? There are no geographic bounds on the St. Louis story. Its citizens never kept themselves within the city limits. St. Louis never was parochial. From the earliest days St. Louisans regarded it primarily as a base for wide-ranging activities, commercial and political. In his day no man, including President Polk, knew one tenth as much about California as did Thomas Hart Benton of St. Louis. The city was—and is—nationally significant. It has been the host of half a dozen presidential nominating conventions, to wit: 1868, Horatio Seymour (Dem.); 1876, Tilden (Dem.); 1888, Cleveland (Dem.); 1896, McKinley (Rep.); 1904, Parker (Dem.), and 1916, Wilson (Dem.). Those who profit by conventions probably wish that St. Louis and Missouri would appear at least once in a while in the "doubtful" column. The Democrats may take for granted voters who steadfastly mark their ballots for Roosevelt, Truman, and Stevenson, and the Republicans may feel that they neither would be rewarding friends nor making new ones by holding more of their conventions in St. Louis. So the city has for some time missed the excitement—or has it been spared the disturbance?—of these super-clambakes. Take the principle, and let the profit go! St. Louisans continue to speak their minds unmistakably about the issues facing a nation which they—to an extraordinary degree—helped to shape. So their story cannot be unwound from the nation's story without diminishing it and somehow falsifying it. So this book at least suggests the relationship—accurately, it is hoped, if not completely and definitively.

St. Louis has not thrown a first-class party since the world's fair of 1904—perhaps because that one was too successful to risk tempting Fortuna with a repeat performance. Or it may be that the venturesome spirit which once supported the Missouri State Lottery has been displaced by an impeccable prudence. Be that as it may, St. Louis raised and induced others to raise a round $45,000,000 for its world's fair. However much that might be in 1959 dollars, it was considerably more than went into Chicago's deservedly famous "White City" a decade earlier. Yet, after 184 days and 19,694,855 clicks of the turnstiles, the directors found a profit on their books. Hence the Jefferson Memorial in Forest Park. But this was not only an eleemosynary success; business in the year after the fair was up twenty-five per cent. Another big fair was suggested after World War II, but the powers that be set themselves against such a massive, self-administered shot in the arm. Unlike New Yorkers, they decided that fairs had had their day. St. Louis no longer has even the annual Agricultural and Mechanical Fair, the fair of which Clark McAdams sang:

> Don't you remember the old Fair Grounds?
>   The arch above the gate,
> The stall and the merry-go-arounds,
>   And the windmills tall and straight
> That spun around at a merry rate
>   When the autumn winds would blow
> And the season was grown soft and late
>   In the long, long time ago?

This bit of verse is a reminder that beyond a passing mention of *Reedy's Mirror*, there is nothing in this book about literary St. Louis. Not that there is not anything to say—Winston Churchill, author of the best-selling *The Crisis,* and James Hosmer, another novelist, Sara Teasdale the poet, Zoë Akins, the playwright, and Fannie Hurst, Rupert Hughes, and Martin Quigley still other novelists, would make a nice chapter even without claiming St. Louis-born T. S. Eliot, Marianne Moore, and Eugene Field as St. Louis poets. But since Max Putzel has a whole book on St. Louis writers in preparation, why flick the froth off a sound potation?

There is another field left to another hand, perhaps for a double-breasted paperback, the field of the scarlet beauties. This may be ungallant to them or to the reader, since some of them were dazzlers. For example, there was Mme. Pierre François de Volsay, daughter of de Noyen of Chartres, niece of St. Ange, and wife of a member of the Royal Order of St. Louis and an officer in the French King's service. She left vivid daubs of scandal on the record. In 1772, saying that she was going to New Orleans to visit her father, she went no farther than Sainte Genevieve, where she carried on so gaudily that after nine months one of the first citizens was deputed to return her to St. Louis. Father Valentin and Governor Piernas had real trouble in bringing about a reconciliation. Maybe they were too persuasive for, in 1774, her husband left her at home while he made a two-year business trip to France. No sooner was he out of sight than the irrepressible de Volsay plunged into "open and shameless debauchery" with one René Kiercereau. The two squandered as much of the absent husband's wealth as they could; and just before his return in 1776, they took as much more as they could find and fled to English territory. This time he went to Governor Cruzat and demanded a dissolution of the marriage. This finally was granted by Governor De Leyba. Another of the St. Louis lovelies was a precoronation favorite of Edward VII. After he ascended the throne, she appeared on the banks of the Mississippi with a husband. Aloof from most of the townspeople, the pair took a house well beyond the city limits. Tongues wagged about more than the lavish marketing of their servants. And there were others. Surely some lively soul will explore this field of scarlet. Maybe Jay Landesman. *Sex and Sin in Old St. Louis.*

It ought to go—big!

There must be a bow, no matter how perfunctory, to those St. Louisans who have been especially devoted to the welfare of others. For instance, David P. Wohl, before he died early this year, had given some $8,500,000 to the universities, hospitals, and municipal health and recreation centers. Young Dr. Thomas Dooley went from the St. Louis University medical school to Southeast Asia to establish badly needed hospitals. He also persuaded others to form teams to carry on this work in half a dozen countries. He tapes a weekly report on life in the hills of Laos. It is heard on Sunday evenings over Radio Station KMOX. Then there is Father Dismas Clark, a Jesuit, who converted an old school building into a "halfway house" for former convicts to help them fit themselves into the life of the community once more. These are typical of widespread, if less spectacular, generosity.

Twenty years ago or so St. Louisans were mildly annoyed by a magazine article headed "A City in Decay." More recently one of the weekly picture books for adults chose St. Louis as the country's most improved city. Perhaps both were wide of the mark. Yet there has been an awakening. There had to be. After World War I St. Louis dozed off. Maybe it was tired. Maybe Prohibition was not only a shock but also a sedative to this beer city. Depression was no stimulant. More than ever, St. Louis turned in on itself, contemplated its communal navel. But now it is out of the trance, out of the coma. There is not much brass-tooting, but St. Louis is tearing out its slums, rebuilding itself. This is a close race between progress and decay. Yet currently the city's symbols might well be the wrecker's heavy iron ball and the builder's derrick. The metropolitan area is awakening to the problem of its balkanization, the confusion and expense of its hundred city halls. St. Louis also is facing economic and industrial problems with new initiative. Ample space and facilities are being provided for new plants. St. Louisans again are writing books, painting pictures, composing music. The city is being heard again in the councils of the nation through the voices of Senator Hennings and Senator Symington. It looks forward to its bicentennial and the sixty-story stainless-steel arch which is to rise from its levee as the symbol of the Gateway of the West.

Nobody need make a door-to-door census to establish that St. Louis has a full complement of plumbers, paper hangers, piano players, painters (plain and fancy), policemen, precinct captains, press agents, painless dentists, psychologists, poker players, prize fighters, panhandlers, process servers, Peeping Toms, petticoat chasers, prudes, publicans, and poltroons. The gamut of the so-called human race, no less. It's a big place, and big places are full of all the kinds of people it takes to make a world. Yet if any Brahmin or B-girl, broker or bondsman, biologist or baseballer, boilermaker or zymurgist finds that he or she has been neglected in this book, may he or she or all of them in their compassion put the blame on that Old Devil Space. May he also be the object of the malediction of any who may feel that they should here be given credit while the author assumes the usual responsibility. No credit without responsibility! Instead, a full unconditional pardon to Adam

Yarmolinsky, erstwhile tempter for Doubleday, whose blandishments started it all.

For regret or rejoicing, according to each reader's private, Fifth Amendment-protected judgment, I add here that this book was almost blown away in last February's tornado. I was working into the early morning of Feb. 10, 1959—it is *work* to write a book!—in that litter of books, magazines, notes, and assorted debris which in our home is known as "that filthy office"—and at the southwest window at that! —when the wind under the eaves raced into overtones of screaming alarm. It was raining hard. The trees bent almost to a breaking point. But instead of contemplating the fury of the storm, I was sorting out the browning, breaking newspaper clippings which told at least part of the story of Nellie Muench. Suddenly the rain slapped against the windowpanes in a solid torrent. Such rain I had never seen before. Two-fifteen A.M. Then the lights went out. No more work tonight, I thought. Then the lights went on again, and my wife was out of bed and offering a cup of coffee.

"You should have seen the rain a little while ago."

"Surely it couldn't have been worse than it is now!"

"Oh, much worse, wild!"

The sound of fire engines, rain-muffled. The house-shaking rumble of the trucks. How long before the city collapses, leveled not by a bomb but by its traffic? The engines apparently stopping nearby, but no youthful chasing into the night to get into the way of the firemen. Back to the clips. Two ladder trucks going by. In this residential neighborhood? For what? But on with Nellie. Then the telephone. Mrs. Graham, as a friend, rather than the city editor's wife, asking:

"Are you all right?"

"Why, yes—and why are you asking at this hour?"

"A tornado. Its path is close to your house. Apparently the same hedgehopping path across the city, from southwest to northeast, as in 1927. Much damage in your vicinity. Some dead. *Are* you all right?"

"Yes, quite all right."

In the morning, the KSD-TV people out early. So downstairs to turn on the bore-box. It does have its moments. Newspapermen may take disaster in stride, like policemen and firemen, but they are nevertheless impressed by grotesquely ruined buildings, debris-clogged streets. And the dead. In the end there were twenty-seven; not as bad as the seventy-two in 1927.* More phone calls. Neighbors unable to drive through the streets. Well, if they will walk over, we will see if we can get out. Glad to give them a ride. So, finally, out of the house.

The rustic fence along the terrace smashed. Windows gone next door. Much worse on the other side of the street and to the east of us. Huge trees uprooted. The stained glass out of City House, the nuns' school. Roofs gone, walls blown out. Had the storm chosen a path less than fifty feet to the west of the one it followed, manuscript and notes for this book would have been gone.

As it is, a bushel or two of more or less unused notes, more or less decipherable, still are available. But the disorder of the notes is almost as bad as if they had been shuffled by the tornado.

E.K.

ITEM: St. Louis still is sometimes called the Mound City. This refers to a group of mounds, believed to have been natural formations, which ancient Indians used as burial places. Despite the protests of antiquarians, all have been removed for assorted unimpressive, mundane reasons. Such mounds, however, may still be seen on the East Side where a number of them seem safe in a small state park.

ITEM: The European tree sparrow is a handsome and very knowing bird. In the Western Hemisphere it is to be found only in St. Louis and its immediate environs.

* Director of Public Safety Joseph P. Sestric reported structural damage to 1179 buildings. Estimated loss: $1,951,435.

CATFISH AND CRYSTAL

I. By Night—

At the turn of the century before last, St. Louis was a small place but a gay one—especially after dark. To the more or less pious disgust of some "Boston" preachers, the habitants danced to fiddle music by candlelight. Why not? Most of the men were deep in the Indian country for half a year or longer. Between fur gatherings in Montana or Wyoming was a time for enjoying family and friends, for feasting, and for lighthearted French gaiety. On the big river or in a mountain camp a man might wear buckskin and subsist on jerked deer meat, but at home he could put on his silk waistcoat with the gold buttons while his wife wore her lace from France. He had adapted himself to survival in the wilderness even more effectively than an Indian, but he was a Frenchman—civilized, not savage. And St. Louis was a bit of France, not an Indian camp.

It was prosperous. Each year a few more stone houses were built, and more good furniture and good cloth came up the river. Often a trapper or trader brought his Indian partner downstream with him for a winter in town. Then he introduced him hospitably to the civilization they had talked about in camp. St. Louis was full of transients—Canadians down from Montreal to become *engagés* of Chouteau or Lisa, "mountain men" in to buy new guns and to spend their pelt money. Always there were Indians, unabashed in their curiosity about the white man. They came to town with birchbark sacks of maple sugar, skins of wild honey, horsehair lariats, moccasins, herbs, buffalo tongues and bear grease—the shortening of the frontier cook—to trade for blankets, horse gear, coffee, tobacco, knives, tin cups and the like. The trappers, who customarily acted as their interpreters, did not try very hard, if at all, to keep them from buying firewater too.

The young braves generally loitered around Chouteau's big stone warehouse, where the "fur rows" smelled to high heaven. When they were bored, however, a band of them would mount their horses and race madly down the main street, shooting blunt arrows at every dog and cat in sight. The Indians never did understand why the white men so sternly forbade these races. There was much they did not understand about the white man. For example, why did Mr. Boujou, the watchmaker, always wave his arms and scream *"Sacré!"* when they sauntered into his shop to examine his collection of glass eyes? In his best blanket and wearing his tomahawk like a dress sword, an Indian brave went where he felt like going. He knocked at no doors. But Negro cooks screamed and sometimes hurled hot water. And their white mistresses screamed and sometimes fainted. There was no such silliness if a brave stayed with the men down near the levee. That's where there were firewater, big talk and, sometimes, a melee.

That is where the "greasers," too, could be found after St. Louis began trading with Sante Fe and Chihuahua. Many of the Spanish merchants came to the city once a year to replenish their stock, especially to purchase the luxuries desired by their Spanish rancher customers. These merchants, respected for their probity, would hitch up a big cart and head for St. Louis with a few oaken cases full of Mexican silver dollars. At the peak of this trade it was not unusual for a merchant to arrive with as much as $50,000, or even $100,000. The money was guarded on the long trek by half a dozen "greasers" under big sombreros, armed with short, big-bored, brass-barreled "escapettes." After steamer service became available, these parties boarded stern-wheelers on the Missouri. Their procession would form again on the St. Louis levee for the parade to Campbell's or some other trading emporium.

Naturally it was time for a little relaxation, time to put into circulation some of those Mexican dollars which replaced pelts as the currency of early St. Louis. For change-making purposes the big dollars were chopped into eight "bits." Any amount smaller than a bit had to be accepted in merchandise—or in a glass. The "bit" became the standard coin. A pound of coffee was priced at, say, two "bits," a load of wood was worth six "bits." "Bits" jingled in the riverfront taverns.

After the Louisiana Purchase came the "movers," the people bound from Pennsylvania or Ohio or Virginia for the Oregon country. There were days when the white-covered "mover wagons" were lined up for a mile or more on the far side of the river waiting to cross on the Wiggins ferry. St. Louis maintained the Spring Campground on the edge of town for these transients. (The site now is the Aloe Plaza with its splendid Milles fountain.) Most of them stopped for a few days before pushing on by steamer or overland. And St. Louis was the "last chance"— not only for hardware and harness. Many of the drivers sauntered from the camp to the more interesting spots along the levee, especially after sundown. In the West there would be time enough for work and sleep. Incidentally, Bill Sublette of St. Louis in 1830 led the first wagon train to the Rockies.

Always there were boatmen. First those who hauled the pirogues up from the sister city of New Orleans. Then the flatboat and keelboat crews who transported not only pelts and produce, but also lead. The soft, gray metal was as important in forming the base of the city's economy as furs. Sainte Genevieve, down the river, got into the lead trade first, but although it was nearer the early Missouri mines it lost most of the business to St. Louis. Further, the best lead came down from Wisconsin and Iowa, where Julien Dubuque took the lead in developing the mines, and this was sent to St. Louis for processing and reshipment. But the metal trade could not be half as glamorous as that in pelts. Who, in a tavern, could boast about mining?

And then came the planters. Before the war and the railroads changed so much, St. Louis on the big river was the natural market and source of supplies for a large part of the South. And it was the city to visit for the company and the pleasures not to be found on a plantation. The old Planters' House—the first one was built in 1817, the second in 1841, and the third in 1892—was not misnamed. It was the city's most elegant inn, although in time the Southern, the Lindell, and the Jefferson became rivals. The old Planters' did not cater to guests in town for only a few days. Plantation families and their personal servants came to spend the whole winter—"the season"—in St. Louis. At the levee they stepped from a new luxury steamer to the Planters' bus, drawn by four horses. Planters' House slaves were on hand to take charge of baggage. Everything was done with a flourish, especially after Judge J. B. C. Lucas and his associates built the second hotel on Fourth Street between Chestnut and Pine. The guests swept up the stairs and were shown to their rooms ($1.25 a day). The management explained that breakfast was served from 7 to 11, dinner at 1:30, tea at 5:30, and supper from 9 to 12, but old guests knew that. The ladies organized their quilting bees and resumed their chitchat just where they had left off at the end of the last "season." The young people were full of excitement about minuets, Virginia reels, and the new waltz. And the men went into the bar where the lordly, yet benign, John King made "a julep like a maiden's kiss, by gad." And it was the chief bartender of the Planters' House and not some sun-torpid West Indian sugar grower who gave the world the Planters' punch. Indeed, the world owes much to St. Louis—especially for the highball. The first Southern Comfort was served at the bar of the Southern Hotel. In the Southern were held the "Assemblies," the dances attended by the best society, and there the politicians gathered until the old hotel on Walnut Street, between Broadway and Fourth, was destroyed by fire on April 11, 1877. At least eleven lives were lost; the number never was firmly established. St. Louis has had only one fire which was worse, the Missouri Athletic Club blaze on March 9, 1914, in which thirty-nine died. Seven were killed in the Buckingham Hotel fire on December 5, 1927, and ten died in the Christian Brothers College fire on October 5, 1926. Twenty bodies were recovered from the Pacific Hotel fire on February 20, 1858. The number of those killed was estimated as high as thirty.

The old Planters' lived on in a new ten-story building until it was converted to office purposes in 1922. One of those perverse shifts in urban geography finished off the hotel favored by Van Buren, Lincoln, Grant, and hundreds of other famous guests—the hotel in which "Cump" Sherman showed old "Brains" Halleck a map and told him how to win the Civil War. New hotels went up on Washington Avenue—first the Lindell, and later the Statler and the Lennox, with the Mayfair nearby. The Jefferson was built on Twelfth Street. The Coronado went up on Lindell, west of Grand. The Buckingham, the Chase, and, finally, the big, elegant Park Plaza were built in the West End on Kingshighway. The outlying hotels are an excuse of sorts for the downtown visitor who exclaims that everybody goes home at five o'clock, that St. Louis has no night life, that it is a nine o'clock town."

But why do the Cardinals play their games at night? Isn't it almost midnight when the *Admiral* docks at the levee after its evening excursions on the Mississippi? Do not patrons of the Municipal Opera insist on a nice long show? It isn't daylight when the bartenders and dancers on the De Baliviere strip are busiest. The blue neon sign atop the Chase is not turned off at 12 P.M. Nor do the Dixieland bands on Delmar Boulevard lower the last tail gate in time to get Cinderella home safely. Indeed, Colonel H. Sam Priest of the Police Board would be quite happy if no raids had to be made on clubs and taverns where the 2:30 A.M. (daylight saving time) closing rule is forgotten. There's night life in St. Louis, but it is not downtown. That's where people work, rather than play.

Of course it is a little hard to say just what could be suggested if

Paderewski were to return and ask, as he once asked George S. Johns in his days as a music critic, if there is "anything novel, anything out of the ordinary, a trifle bizarre, to be seen in St. Louis at night." Johns took the Pole to Babe Connors' place. But Babe isn't here any more. Nobody is importing "the pick of the girls from Louisiana" and advertising them as "Creoles" any more. Nor do the girls, tastefully dressed in stockings, any longer sing Negro songs to the accompaniment of a blind pianist. No stock company is playing the *Mikado* amidst the beer coolers in Uhrig's Cave on Washington Avenue. The gaslight is out and so is the red light. But there still are those Dixieland "combos," on Delmar, and the hotcha Scheherazades and the hey-hey Salomes on De Baliviere. There are the honky-tonks and the burlesque places around Sixth and Market. No, they are not as elegant as Babe Connors' place by a long shot. With the police force as pure as it is today, a B-girl (meaning a girl who will help the house sell you drinks at the bar) has a hard time making a decent living. Even the East Side is not what it used to be. There is nothing left of the notorious "Valley" except a dilapidated old hotel and a store front or two which may go down before a high wind even before the bulldozers get to them. But the police reporters can tell you that some people still do manage to get into trouble. And if trouble means only losing money to the house, it is not too hard to find across the river. There is horse racing, too, at Fairmount and Cahokia. Still, rakes and libertines—contemporary Rochesters and Boswells—must admit stoically that "the changeable world to our joy is unjust." What the police had not closed, the wartime M.P.s did, for the sake of the fighting potential of the young men of Jefferson Barracks, Scott Field, and Fort Leonard Wood. Then all the young men came home and rushed into suburban wedded bliss. So that's how it has been these last twenty years or so . . . and the police not even having to work very hard to keep it so . . . and conventioneers and cab drivers talking less and less about the "old days."

Still, this is not the "night life" St. Louis people have in mind. When they complain that there is nothing to do after dark, they imply that there are no good restaurants, no theaters, no big sports events, no excitement. People who were not born when Tony Faust's restaurant succumbed to Prohibition sigh for it as though they had been habitués. But it is always Faust's that is missed, never McTague's, Schnaider's, Porcher's, or Schweickhordt's Cottage in Forest Park. Which proves that this is a ritual without much real meaning. Such *bons vivants*

about town as Stan Mockler and Bill Feustel can lead a visitor to
good wine and a good meal too. Anybody can find the hotels, with
dining rooms just like those operated by the chains in New York, Houston, and Minneapolis. Each has its "club lounge" in which drinks are
served to the accompaniment of a chanteuse, or a piano player, or a
whole team of "big name" entertainers. There are old restaurants like
Schumacker's and 415 downtown. The 415 serves wonderful catfish by
the pound. Any cab driver will suggest the Italian places on "the Hill."
There are still some more or less German places on the South Side—
for example, the neighborly Bavarian Tavern on Arsenal near Gravois.
The Chase and the Park Plaza are the haunts of plush and semiplush
café society. And there are scores of good eating places farther west—
old ones like Busch's Grove on Clayton Road, and new ones, like the
Nantucket Cove, which are still being "discovered." The location of
many of these places in the West End or beyond, of course, is a sign
of the trek to suburbia. There are people who now live so deep in the
realtor's boondocks that they rarely come downtown after dark, and
in this enterprising world restaurateurs will spread a cloth where they
must to make a buck. But this is no place for a diners' directory with
"recommendations"—one-star to five-star. This is simply an assurance
to all but those connoisseurs ("gourmet" has become a tawdry word)
who write ecstatically dull books about *haute cuisine* and La Tour
d'Argent that appetites need not be overly disciplined in St. Louis. What
is so extra good about numbered pressed duck?

As for Tony Faust's, the old gaffers may have something after all.
Having just come upon an ancient menu, how about blue points on the
half shell for 25 cents? (A dozen of any other variety of oyster or clam
for the same price.) A cup of consommé, 10 cents. The fish we can
skip. Or would somebody like a whole lobster for 60 cents? Or frogs'
legs at 75 cents? The sirloin of beef, Baden-Baden, is good at 50 cents.
Does somebody prefer woodcock at 75 cents? Or both, perhaps? Potatoes are prepared in a dozen ways; let's settle on au gratin, 10 cents.
You would rather have steak? There are more than twenty-five offerings under this heading. How about a sirloin *à la bordelaise* at 50
cents, or a tenderloin with mushrooms at 80 cents, or a porterhouse with
truffles for a dollar? Or would anybody care to share a fillet Château-
briand *à la Parisienne* at $1.60? The tomato salad, Faust style, is very
good at 25 cents. Coffee and dessert later? Well, what about a look
at the wine list now?

No, no more of this make-believe. Talk of the best meal in Faust's for $1.50 verges on subversion, the spreading of that discontent which breeds communism or worse. But Faust's prices do explain why the nineties were gay—at least for those who came by $1.50 without excessive effort. There is one place, though, in the St. Louis area in which $1.50 still is fairly important money. It is the old drovers' hotel in the National Stock Yards across the river. The rains of yesteryear washed away all the baroque glory of the place. Today it is as ugly-plain as a Union News lunch counter in a dilapidated railroad station. Its patrons are overalled cattlemen and farmers who have business in the yards. But what steaks! And on the way home one can stop on the Illinoistown levee and contemplate illuminated St. Louis rising above the Mississippi.

The scene is not an imitation of garish Manhattan after dark. St. Louis hardly has a building which might rightly be called a skyscraper. With the new electronic equipment on its roof, the Southwestern Bell Telephone Building on Pine Street is the highest structure in town. Its 31 floors, not counting that deckload, reach a height of 396 feet, 8 3/4 inches. That was determined in 1929, when F. N. Hatch, for the telephone company, and Rudolph Weinberger, for the city, settled the community-searing question of whether or not the architects and the engineers really had maintained public above private power by building the nearby Civil Courts Building higher than the telephone offices. With scrupulous professional integrity, Weinberger conceded that the new Court House—not ineptly described as a cigar box surmounted by the Mausoleum of Halicarnassus—really is only 386 feet, 1 5/8 inches high. Yet the Court House, with only 13 stories to the telephone building's 31, does represent a semi-heroic bid for supremacy. In the West End, the Park Plaza soars up 310 feet and 30 floors. But downtown there is a dead heat between the Lennox Hotel (25 floors and 268 feet), the Missouri Pacific Building (23 floors and 264 feet), and the Railway Exchange Building, occupied by the Famous-Barr department store (24 floors and 250 feet). On Olive near Grand, the lonely Continental Building rises 23 floors and 310 feet. It has not even occurred to St. Louisans to compare these with the Empire State's 102 floors and 1250 feet—not counting its superstructure. So St. Louis has no façade on which floodlights play. But it is pleasant to watch the trains chugging along the riverfront, to and from the big bridges, and the running lights of passing towboats.

And the river! The river in the night, sensed more than seen, is vast

and majestic. Its current surges by bridge piers and barges almost si-
lently, laps at the cobblestoned levee with a gentle, almost seductive
friendliness. That is seemly to its power. But the Mississippi in the dark
is ominous too. The ripples of reflected light—red, green, gold—look
less like strips of Christmas tinsel than like luminous serpents imagined
by an Ancient Mariner. Here on the unilluminated levee—and perhaps
only here, except on the river itself—one realizes that Huck Finn's voyage really was an adventure with a leviathan. It was as epic as the adventure of Ulysses—greater, in fact, since the voyager to Ithaca sailed
in one of the black-prowed ships. Huck and Jim were on a raft. Those
eager to purge themselves of such poetic notions may cross the Eads
bridge, or one of the three other downtown spans, and stop at an old
river boat tied up at the St. Louis levee and made into a tavern; or
they can rush to one of those night spots in which the master of ceremonies blabs the names of guests into a radio microphone. This publicity
gimmick is said to be a St. Louis innovation. If so, the innovator's heart
was not here but in Madison Avenue. It suits the late Lyman Bryson's
notion that the great American status indicator is having your name
spread around. Vulgar? In the era of the fin-tailed Cadillac?

Maybe the St. Louis Negroes do best of all after dark—at least as
soon as the weather turns warm, which is about May Day. They pour
out onto the sidewalks or sit on front porches and enjoy themselves with
hardly any props at all. The youngsters wait eagerly for the ice-cream
man. (The ice-cream cone was introduced to the world at the Louisiana
Purchase Exposition, held in St. Louis in 1904.) Then comes the water-
melon man, and the pig-meat man. Delicacies at the curb. A tavern door
is open and everybody around can hear "Frankie and Johnny," or "St.
James Infirmary," or W. C. Handy's "St. Louis Blues," but more likely
numbers that are on the current hit parade. Sure there will be a crowd
going to the Riviera or some other spot. Man, the places are jumping,
night after night!

St. Louis is a talking town. That is one reason why there's a little
less dancing and celebrating by night than there might be. An almost
incredible number of the citizenry seem devoted to the Socratic method,
or have opinions which the undaunted insist on voicing even in this
so-called Age of Conformity. Debates ripple and rage on the paying side
of the bar about the more esoteric questions of baseball and football—
e.g., who's going to win? After-dinner chitchat often turns serious. But
St. Louis seems happiest with "organized" talk. In the aggregate, "dis-

cussion groups" outdraw the theater. After all, at a play who can get a word in even edgewise?

The Public Question Club has been meeting weekly for almost half a century. One member is designated to speak on a topic, and the others are restricted to quite brief comments. This discipline is remarkable, since the club has had among its members not only the late Supreme Court Justice Wiley Rutledge, then Dean of the Washington University Law School, but also Branch Rickey, who—Judas Priest!— could talk another manager out of a twenty-game pitcher for a .225 fielder. Gustav Lippmann, Ralph Fuchs, and Hyman Meltzer brought the Clarence Darrows—oh, all the good talkers—to the meetings. Of course the keep-it-brief rule often took a beating, and still does. "Town and Gown" meet regularly at the University Club for food and talk, lest the town grow crass and the faculty esoteric. Frank P. O'Hare started the Dunkers, who take time out of the middle of the day for talking and arguing. So does the Episcopal Cathedral Luncheon Club, a reminder of the years during which Bishop Will Scarlett brought together the Senior Thinkers and the Junior Thinkers, first citizens and first citizens to be, to expose them to provocative and even downright radical ideas. There is another group, formally associated with the Foreign Policy Association, which regularly corrects the mistakes of statesmen. There is the Round Table, at which the excellence of the food and the wine sometimes dims the intellectual sheen of the evening but more often gives it a more luminous sparkle. There is the Cauliflower Ear Club which obviously tells off football coaches and fight managers, a specialized group. There are the Ambassadors, the Sunday nights at the Artists' Guild, and the Toastmasters' Club, at which everybody wields the gavel. The John Marshall Club is made up of lawyers— Republican lawyers, another specialized talking society. The League of Women Voters really belongs in this category, especially since it still reflects the catholic and energetic spirit of Edna Gellhorn, Martha's mother and Walter's.*

The Great Books program is assiduously promoted by William Compton, former public librarian, and by Raymond Wittcoff, a young industrialist who reads and reads. Hundreds of groups of these book discussers are active year after year. The Liberal Forum, made fascinating

* Carrie Chapman Catt suggested the establishment of the League of Women Voters at a Votes-for-Women convention in St. Louis forty years ago. The idea was taken up at once.

by Dr. Major Seelig, brings "outstanding personages" to town as much to argue with them as to listen to them. KETC, the first educational television station on the air, thanks to the two universities, has added greatly to the decibels. Not only does it assemble citizens by the half dozen before its cameras, but it also assembles them in living rooms all over town. These TV parties can get into the show by telephone; their members get their turns under the lights, and they carry on after the show leaves the air. This really is "audience participation." But St. Louisans hardly need such electronic stimulation to form "discussion groups." With them, it's a habit. And it may be a better habit than dropping in at the Elks, the Eagles, the Moose, or the Lions—the good American zoo. The pattern was set probably even before Carl Schurz, Emil Preetorius, William Taussig, Felix Coste, Charles P. Johnson, Gratz Brown, William Grosvenor, Henry Blow, John McNeil, G. A. Finkelnburg, and Enos Clark started the Twentieth Century Club to meet each Sunday at the Planters' House. Nowadays one can get into an informal facsimile of the Twentieth Century almost any evening in Alderman Ray Leisure's tavern on Chouteau Avenue and get a good idea of what's going on in city hall and who is going to win in the next elections. But let's face it: this taste for talk has its drawbacks—especially for teachers, newspapermen, and all who can be introduced on the thinnest pretext as "experts." Such individuals must live in expectation of a phone call from the chairwoman of the speakers' committee of the Upper Glenmore Rose Garden Society. And they know that talk is no more golden than silence.

One night a year—make it two—St. Louis does put on a real after-dark wingding—the Veiled Prophet's parade and ball. The mysterious potentate recently mixed things up a bit, holding his ball on the first night and the parade on the second. For decades and decades he would first arrive and make his progress through the city, and then open his Court of Love and Beauty—in the Merchants Exchange in the early days, then in the old coliseum, and more recently in the new Kiel Auditorium. That did seem logical. But now the V.P.'s Queen also gets into the parade. (It is not lese majesty, by the way, to refer to the Prophet by his initials—just plain V.P.—in his democratic realm.) So the new order of events may be a subtle acknowledgment that what was once a commercial promotion now has become a social rite. The first V.P. parade was held October 18, 1878, after the harvest, to bring farmers and other country people into St. Louis. It was a business booster like the Agricultural and Mechanical Fair, started in 1856 and held annually for almost fifty years. Its biggest feature now is the coronation of the V.P. Queen, a girl who is to "reign over society" for the next twelve months. Just how society is ruled may be a bit mysterious, but this is a "big thing." The Queen's picture not only appears in the newspapers, but it is added to the gallery of V.P. Queens in the Missouri Historical Society to hang there, presumably, forever and ever. For her year, the Queen may give her job a hard whirl and cut just about all the ribbons, open all the charity benefits, and award all the prizes at all the horse shows. Or she may make only an occasional regal appearance. She may even go to college. One thing she may not do: marry, not for a year. The V.P. insists on a virgin Queen, but Love has on an occasion or two blithely ignored the Prophet's command. The V.P. Queen has a ballet of attendants—Maids of Honor and Special Maids of Honor. The distinction is very real, but the reason is supposed to be known only to the Prophet's Krewe—and they will not even tell why or how the Queen was chosen. All of the girls, however, do get jeweled brooches, according to rank, so any knowing St. Louis eye immediately perceives at a party that the handsome woman standing by the fireplace once was a V.P. Queen or a Maid, first class or second.

The identity of the girls is almost as deep a secret as the identity of the V.P. himself. Their names are revealed only when trumpets summon them, one by one, to the Prophet's throne. His name never is disclosed. To this rule there has been but one exception. The first Prophet, back in 1878, was John G. Priest. He helped form the Mysterious Organization of the Veiled Prophets, according to its own records, in "10,842 B.C., some 294 years before the creation of the world." He chose Miss Susie Slayback as the first Queen.

The V.P. ball, of course, is a white-tie affair, and guests attend only by invitation. Yet since the hall is so big, the invitations may be classified as only semiprecious. They are accompanied by a gift, often some piece of coffeetable bric-a-brac such as an ash tray or cigarette box with the initials V.P. and the year on it. Or it may be a telephone-book cover displaying the initials and year. There is a general impression abroad that the V.P. mementos are not quite what they used to be, but this probably is a canard circulated by unscrupulous operators seeking to undermine the market for bonds of Khorassan, the mysterious monarch's realm. Unquestionably, Khorassan will be stoutly defended, especially by the fathers of debutantes-to-be. Also alert are the Prophet's

Bengal Lancers, who guard his Court. In the most magnificent uniforms of the Raj, the Lancers really dominate the ball. The Prophet looks a bit fuddy-duddy in his bejeweled robe, his heavy veil, and a crown hardly approved by the Garter King-of-Arms. The Lancers escort him to his throne. They also escort each girl across the long hall as she answers his summons. The Lancers do an awful lot of marching, and it takes an awful lot of time. As a result, the affair is not much of a ball. By the time the Prophet gives the sign for dancing to begin, there is just time for a turn or two around the floor before hurrying off to the Queen's Supper. This also is a "big thing," but there is champagne—which helps a lot.

The next night comes the V.P. parade, which seems a social anti-climax, but the youngsters of St. Louis don't care about that. And it doesn't make much difference to the hundreds of policemen guarding the route whether they are ordered out for this duty the night before or the night after the ball. It probably does not make much difference either to Frank Neudescher or Siegfried Reinhardt, or whatever other artist may have been commissioned to design the floats. He must start early to have twenty of them ready in time. Incidentally, a few years ago a fire broke out shortly before the big day in the V.P. quarters in which the floats were being given the finishing touches. It was one time that Mayor Tucker made like Mayor La Guardia and hurried to the blaze. But the St. Louis fire department is first-rate. Only a few floats were superficially scorched. Nothing that couldn't be fixed with a quick touch of paint. Still, it was a close thing.

The V.P. parade always has a theme. Back in 1878 it was the legend of Ceres. Floats depicted the barren earth after Persephone's abduction, the chariot of Phoebus, Demeter, Bacchus, and such. All very handsome. The floats of one year may be more "inspired" than those of another. But all make a brave progress through the streets, all the way from Kingshighway to Broadway, and back to the V.P. "temple." The route was not so long when the floats were drawn by horses, yet many would give a half mile or even a mile to have the horses back, especially those of the mounted police. But progress is progress. For instance, the floats now are protected by strong sheets of plastic, because some juvenile delinquents persisted in falling into the ways of boys with sling-shots. Oh, well! The man who has an office window along the parade route is especially popular in early October with those of his neighbors who have children and no advantageously located windows. The curbs

are lined early and the side streets are full of parked cars. The bands
strike up. The parade passes by with the V.P. himself on the last float.
A fine sight, followed by a gradually clearing traffic snarl—just like
getting home from the ball park. It is not half the fun on TV. But jubila-
tion in the streets in Mardi Gras fashion might carry things a mite too
far.

On second thought, the night of the V.P. ball is not the biggest night
of the St. Louis year after all. For almost everybody except victims of
office parties, and especially for South Siders who perpetuate old German customs, the big night is Christmas Eve. It never has been more
impressively celebrated than in the early days. Theophile Papin set
down how it was then:

"The villagers liked their pleasures. . . . But they were Catholics,
and few enjoyments found favor among them equal to those of their
religious festivals. Of these, there being many during the year, the Midnight Mass of Christmas, 'Noel,' was probably the most brilliant and
affecting. . . . There yonder stands the wooden church, not large in
fact, but within the shadows of night mystically imposing. Twelve
o'clock has struck from its belfry of open beams; the inhabitants are
all assembled. Hundreds of lights flood the interior and stream through
the windows on the glistening snow without. The brief, eloquent sermon
has been spoken in French first, then in Indian, and then the elevation,
simultaneous with the tinkling altar bells and the deeper vibrations
out of the tower. There is heard from near the churchyard the booming
of a cannon—that readily loaned by the commandant of the post—
whereupon the inspired choir intones the exultant "Venite Adoremus,"
the swelling strains filling the edifice, and the reverberations from the
huge wooden vault aloft returning in echoes of divine harmony upon
the adoring multitude. There, too, is the high altar, resplendent with
its myriads of lesser lights, and its abounding ornaments of gold, silver,
and fine laces, received year by year from the religious of New Orleans
and Quebec. Again the eye turns to the gorgeous festal vestments of
the priests and deacons (for this year a company of visiting curates had
joined the venerable village pastor) and the long retinue of white-robed
acolytes. All these objects and figures, seen through the haze of the
fragrant incense diffused from the sanctuary, form a soul-stirring
pageant, truly, albeit as adjuncts only, to the overwhelming credence
of the pious worshippers that God, the Redeemer Himself, is there in
person among them . . . not the villagers only, but all the voyageurs

and all the Indians that happened to obtain place that night within the sacred edifice. In the solitude of the swift-flowing Mississippi hard by, through the fast-falling darkness of Christmas Eve, the mountaineer whose pirogue had already borne him hundreds of miles, bethinking himself suddenly, as he neared the beloved village, of the joyous fete impending, a strange, new energy would reinfuse his limbs, his long sweeping strokes, then lifting his trusty craft madly over and through the floating fragments of fast-forming ice—so fearful would he be of tardy arrival for the blessed mysteries of Midnight Mass."

II. —and by Day

From the air, the big rivers make it easy to recognize St. Louis. The city is on the west side of the Mississippi about ten miles below its meeting with the Missouri. The Mississippi at St. Louis is a big bow fitted with an arrow which is the Mill Creek Valley, through which the railroads run across the city to the cobblestoned levee. A lighter arrow is the main street—Olive Street, which continues as Lindell Boulevard to the city's limit. The western end of this arrow is neatly feathered by the campus of Washington University. The string of the bow is Grand Avenue, the chief north-south artery. Beyond the arrow's eastern tip, on the Illinois side of the river, are many of the city's steel mills, electric generating plants, stockyards, and chemical plants. (Most of the crime and racketeering are over there too.)

Like Gaul, from which its founder came, St. Louis is divided into three, tree-shaded, parts, unimaginatively called the South Side, the North Side, and the West End. Suburban subdividers have more than made up for this plain nomenclature. They have lettered the community map with such names as Ladue—swankiest of the dormitory satellites— Creve Coeur, Bellefontaine Neighbors, Town and Country, Frontenac, Huntleigh Downs, and Country Club Hills. The older and larger suburbs carry the more ordinary names of University City, Clayton, Webster Groves, Ferguson, and Jennings. These and the rest of the subdivisions and what open ground is left are lumped together as "the County."

From the air it is easy to follow the Olive-Lindell main stem as it runs from the levee past downtown stores and offices, public buildings grouped around the Memorial Plaza, then apartments and hotels, out to the huge, domed Catholic cathedral, and the two miles of Forest Park to Washington University. Where Grand crosses Lindell, about four miles west of the river, is a concentration of theaters, restaurants, and taverns. Here, also, perhaps not in expected company, are the brown-red buildings of St. Louis University. On North Grand, near Fairgrounds Park, is the home diamond of the St. Louis Cardinals. On South Grand are the St. Louis University medical school buildings and the business centers and used-car lots of the South Side—the once-German St. Louis, which still is the realm of Anheuser-Busch, where beer is not only brewed but enjoyed, and where housewives still scrub the stone steps of their red brick houses six times a week.

About two miles west of Grand is another wide north-south street, Kingshighway. As it crosses the Lindell Boulevard axis, it skirts Forest Park. Here are elegant hotels and the tightly huddled hospitals of the Washington University medical center. Clearly to be seen on its hill in the park is the City Art Museum. Nearby are the big zoo, the terraced seats of the Municipal Opera, and the crowded Steinberg Memorial skating rink (ice in winter, roller in summer). West of the park, the ruler-straight pattern of city streets fades into the horseshoes of the sub-dividers' roads, mews, lanes, drives, and terraces. Beyond the rapidly spreading suburbs are the Meramec Valley and the first bulges of the Ozark foothills.

There is, of course, much more of the Mississippi to be seen from a plane by day than from the levee by night. From on high the river does not create the nocturnal impression of reserved, mysterious strength. Between its green banks it runs to the horizon, and this does suggest its 2500-mile, continent-draining, nation-serving length. By day the river displays its island-dotted beauty, but more especially its utility. Tow-boats, pushing perhaps a dozen barges—the big new *United States* can handle forty or more—are evidence that water transportation still is important to St. Louis. The half-dozen bridges across the Mississippi bring the transcontinental railroads into Union Station, largest in the United States—maybe in the world. The bridges also carry the trains' ubiquitous rivals, the trucks. The modern airport, with its gracefully arched administration building, perhaps the most photographed example of contemporary architecture, shows that St. Louis knows about the air age too.

The East Side's shrinking stockyards are but one indication of the city's farming hinterland—flat, east of the Mississippi, but rolling upward from its west bank. The once air-poisoning factories are suggestions of the Illinois coal fields, but smoke now is illegal in St. Louis. The power lines flow from the generating stations and the more distant hydroelectric dams—one across the Mississippi at Keokuk, Iowa, the other across the Osage in the Ozarks—to provide energy for diversified industry.

South and west of St. Louis, the plane passenger in a clear sky can discern the hills growing into the time-gentled Ozark Mountains. The only range on the continent running east and west instead of north and south, the worn-down, tree-covered mountains are geological ages older than the Appalachians and much, much older than the Rockies. Traversed by fast, spring-clear, fish-rich rivers, they tempt the asphalt angler with smallmouth bass in his salutary intervals away from the labors of the city.

"First in booze, first in shoes, and last in the American League." Any slick-paper writer knows that this is the sure-fire way to start a piece about St. Louis. Garnish with a few paragraphs about packet boats on the Mississippi, Negroes playing the banjo on the levee, and some South Side Germans enjoying beer, rose gardens, and Gemuetlichkeit, and the job is done. The trouble, though, is that what you read about St. Louis "ain't necessarily so."

Take booze. St. Louis does brew foamy seas of beer, more than any other American city. Yet Milwaukeeans are said to drink more—390 glasses a year for each man, woman and child. This shows that St. Louis has lost some of its taste for the golden brew since the *Missouri Republican* reported in 1860 that the average St. Louisan poured down 658 glasses a year. Perhaps there really were giants in those days—or the distillers of scotch, bourbon, and gin may be cutting down the brewers' profits as zealously as prohibitionists. Anyway, beer isn't booze.

As for shoes, St. Louis is America's "shoe capital" still. Its footwear keeps millions of feet dry and warm. The big mass manufacturers, notably the International Shoe Company and the Brown Shoe Company, still have their home offices in the city, but they make a lot of shoes in small-town factories where taxes are low and union organizers scarce. Since its early trade in fur and lead—both still important—the city has grealty diversified its commerce and industry. It has profited by carrying its eggs in many baskets.

St. Louis is not last in the American League; it is out of the league. The only extant St. Louis Brownie fans belong to a club in Chicago which meets periodically to refuse to face the fact that the Browns now are the high-flying Baltimore Orioles.

St. Louis still does have a river packet. It is preserved on the city seal. But there was a movement a few years ago to get rid of this, since nowadays the river is navigated by diesel-powered towboats, perversely so called, since they push their tows of barges. The shells and oarsmen of the old boat clubs have given way to outboard-motor addicts.

As for *Gemuetlichkeit,* I have been told not to use that word at all, which shows how little respect the most time-honored formula can expect from the "beat" generation—which, by the way, feels it has brought St. Louis into step with San Francisco. But St. Louis still is *gemuetlich,* or about as *gemuetlich* as may be in 17 A.M.P. (After Manhattan Project.) St. Louis people are socially friendly, politically liberal, and economically conservative. Most of them are well-behaved traditionalists. They are homebodies rather than expense-account elbow benders. They have given up their picnics for the backyard barbecue.

Gemuetlich may not be quite the word for Stan Musial as he comes up to try to hit one out of the ball park, or for Harry Caray, the Cardinals' radio announcer, as he yells, "It might be! It could be! It *is* a home run!" The fans may not sound *gemuetlich* either, but consider the tolerant good grace with which they have accepted a dozen years without a pennant. Yet the Cardinals do have a pretty ball park under the floodlights, with not an advertisement around except the Anheuser-Busch eagle atop the scoreboard, the bird which flaps its wings in excitement every time a player hits a homer. Most of the time the eagle is *gemuetlich* enough. With the exception of Cardinal baseball and, more recently, Hawks basketball, St. Louis does not care very much about professional sports. Many people prefer to spend a day in the park playing golf, tennis, soccer, rugby or cricket—yes, there is cricket in Forest Park every Sunday. The Davis Cup is the gift of a St. Louis park director. Some, of course, are inveterate spectators, and prefer to go to the zoo to watch the performances of the famous chimpanzees. Others just sit on the grass and bask in the sun, at least until evening comes and they can go to the Municipal Opera to see *The Vagabond King* or *South Pacific* under the stars.

Jim Conzelman, pianist extraordinary and football coach turned advertising executive, once said he liked St. Louis because it is a "big city in which it is easy to know everybody." That's why he would not move to Chicago. Governor David R. Francis spurned the opportunities of New York because, as he said, "St. Louis is a good place to raise sons." General Sherman felt that way too. And Tom Sherman, the music critic, maintains that in St. Louis a young man easily can cut a swath in "society." Few St. Louis hostesses see virtue in a pose of exclusiveness.

Speaking of warmth, there are still some St. Louisans who boast not merely of warmth but of heat. That is why it took the British Foreign Office so long to discover that the city is on the Mississippi and not the Amazon—to the regret of the consulate's staff which, until a few years ago, was granted the extra summer holidays of H.M.'s servants working in the tropics. Oh, St. Louis does have its heat waves— about two each summer, each lasting about ten days. And every twenty years or so may come a real "boiler"—ninety days above ninety. There is nothing *gemuetlich* about such a summer, but the last one occurred in 1936. There was never another like that one, with 375 deaths attributed to the heat.

St. Louis probably is relaxed and self-assured because it stands knee-deep in history. It once hoped to become the nation's first city. Today this notion seems not only fantastic but somewhat distasteful. Yet if the city cannot boast primacy in population, productivity, prosperity, and pushiness, it could—if it were so brash—ask to be regarded as perhaps the most American of American cities, a community which did much to shape the nation. As a melting pot, mingling French, Spanish, Yankee, Irish, German, Polish, Italian, and many other nationalities, St. Louis is not unique. If Americanism is to be measured by the height of sky-scrapers, the length of expressways, the volume of jukeboxes, the circulation of *Reader's Digest,* or admiration for J. Edgar Hoover, St. Louis can be given no more than an average rating. But if measured by the aspirations of the founding fathers—freedom, democracy, equality of opportunity, fair treatment for all—then surely St. Louis ranks very high. It has shown an unusual respect for individual freedom and communal rectitude. There have been some lapses, but time has developed a tradition which has very practical effects. An abuse of public office which might be passed over as a peccadillo elsewhere is in St. Louis a scandal. A Joe McCarthy or a Gerald L. K. Smith may hire a hall in St. Louis, but he can't count on much of an audience. A mere five or six hundred party workers were dragooned into the big auditorium when McCarthy came to St. Louis to wind up the 1952 senatorial campaign against Stuart Symington. St. Louis people are not immune to the more deplorable human weaknesses, yet they have developed a way of doing things which keeps these weaknesses in check instead of exploiting them.

All this is rather abstract—editorial-page copy—until a specific situation brings the St. Louis tradition into play. This happened when the

Dennis case was to be taken to the United States Supreme Court and
the Communists could find no lawyer in the East to present the appeal.
They turned to John Raeburn Green, one of the most eminent lawyers
in St. Louis. He told them at once that he was in utter disagreement
with their doctrine. Since he believed every man is entitled to his day in
court, however, he presented a brief but would accept no fee. So the
justices heard a masterly exposition of fundamental American rights
which in an almost hysterical time were being widely ignored, but not
in St. Louis.

Henry Luce advertises that on the day his magazines appear, St.
Louisans act just like people everywhere else in the U.S.A. Neither the
Better Business Bureau nor the Federal Trade Commission has challenged the claim. But there could be a spot of trouble if anybody said
St. Louisans act just like people everywhere in Missouri. From the beginning, the city's enthusiasm for the state has been limited—and vice
versa. Richard C. Wade is correct in asserting that the "towns were
the spearheads of the frontier. Planted far in advance of the line of
settlement, they held the West for the approaching population." This
was especially true of French-rooted St. Louis. The city was more than
half a century old before Missouri was made a state. So those who
assert, quite legally, that cities are creatures of the state still may be
asked since when parents owe their existence to their children. Earlier
St. Louisans were inclined to agree that Boston was "an incorporated
republic" rather than a subdivision of Massachusetts. In their struggle
to win adequate home rule from their state legislatures, the mayors of
New York, Chicago, and many another city may yet reassert this propo-
sition. Asphalt may yet secede from cow pasture. Certainly the temptation to insurrection must flit through a St. Louis mayor's mind every
now and then as he tries to make ends meet in spite of state-imposed
limitations and exactions. The extent to which the Missouri income
tax is ignored by city dwellers suggests that the idea is not altogether
alien to those who are not overawed by the law and its penalties. The
motivation of such scofflaws may be mercenary, but they could invoke
tradition to pretty up their case.

For all the moccasined Indians padding about its streets, old St. Louis
never regarded itself as backwoodsy. Laclède, the city's founder, was a
graduate of the University of Toulouse and quite suited to the salons of
Paris. He brought a remarkable library into the wilderness. So did
Charles Gratiot, who had studied in Montreal, London, and Switzer-

land. Likewise Silvestre Labbadie, Dr. Antoine Saugrain, Governor
Charles Delassus, and kindred spirits. The ideas of the Enlightenment
were discussed along the Mississippi as well as along the Seine. Although
the territorial legislature authorized St. Louis to establish a public school
board while denying it taxing powers to support schools, families like
the Prattes sent their children to school in Canada or to the Catholic
college in Bardstown, Ky. Two sons of St. Louis pioneers, Auguste
Pierre Chouteau and Charles Gratiot, Jr., were members of the West
Point graduating class of 1806. It was about that time that Father
François Neil and half a dozen other Cathedral priests opened an
academy attended by the sons of William Clark, Thomas Hart Benton,
and Governor Alexander McNair. When the bishop opened this school,
which is now St. Louis University, he emphasized that students of all
faiths were welcome and that "no undue influence will be exercised in
matters of religion." Tuition was free.

Even those early St. Louisans who never learned to sign their names,
or a goodly number of them, cultivated high style. As Henry Brackenridge observed, the Creole women were proud of their small feet, and
one merchant wrote to his Philadelphia and Baltimore suppliers that
"pointed and old-fashioned shoes will never sell" even to those whose
feet were a few sizes larger than petite. A shipment of fur bonnets was
rejected because they were not in the latest mode. No Easterner could
afford to assume that Frenchwomen would wear what their husbands
might carry into the Indian trade. Frenchwomen were as interested
in Paris fashions as Frenchmen were in Paris ideas. And this outward
show was a sign of inward charm. St. Louisans considered themselves
sophisticated—and not merely in the ladies'-magazine meaning of the
word. Indeed, as early as 1787 a poet—or was he a real-estate promoter?
—sang of the city at the confluence of the Missouri and the Mississippi:

> Again shall Athens bid her columns rise;
> Again her lofty turrets reach the skies,
> Science again shall find a safe retreat,
> And commerce here as in a centre meet.

St. Louis, however, never was in danger of becoming too genteel.
The rivers took care of that. Flatboatmen, trappers, and transients
did not read Racine, and the proprietors of grogshops did not quote
Virgil. At least, none are on record as doing so. Brackenridge might
enthuse about the fur trade, which sent St. Louisans from the Rockies

to the trading floors of New Orleans and New York, London, and
Paris, and predict that their city would become "the Memphis of the
American Nile," but few, if any, *engagés,* or drifters, paid attention
to such hifalutin folderol. Their predilections were much simpler—
in fact, downright crude—and they indulged them along the waterfront. It did not bother them a bit that they were giving St. Louis a
reputation as a tough town. The illiterate rough and the literate rich
between them found little favor with the hymn-singing farmers who
followed the trails firstcomers had blazed. It was, in a way, the familiar
story of city slicker against hayseed. Old Tom Benton was a genius because he managed to be popular with both elements.

It was the influence of St. Louis which won admission to the Union
for Missouri in 1821. The state's constitution was drawn up in the
Missouri Hotel in St. Louis. The city became the first capital, and the
hotel the first capitol. Missouri's first governor, Alexander McNair, was
a St. Louisan. The first two Senators, Benton and David Barton, were
St. Louisans. But coolness between city and state set in almost at once.
The depression of 1819, caused partly by western land speculation but
preferably blamed on city banks, touched St. Louis—but lightly—the
next year just as the new state government was being established. Thus
the first frost nipped city-state relations under the first governor. The
capital was transferred to St. Charles, and later to Jefferson City. The
pattern of the relationship also crystallized. The legislators began to
circumscribe municipal powers, especially that of taxation. Yet this
hardly would have happened had not St. Louis merchants felt that it
might be for the best. Their heirs still felt that way when the 1945
state constitutional convention continued rural overrepresentation in
the legislature, and state control over purely municipal functions. Curtis
Betts, formerly political correspondent of the *Post-Dispatch,* once remarked that most legislators could be bought for a chicken dinner,
although the price of a few might run as high as a blue serge suit. Aldermen used to cost more. But why be cynical? Merchants know that
farmers hate taxes.

St. Louis, however, did reassert its strength on the eve of the Civil
War. By that time thousands of Germans and Irish had settled in the
city. They were not enamored of Know-Nothings, bushwhacking, Ol'
Virginny, moonlight and magnolias. They did loathe slavery and admire
Lincoln. So in spite of Governor Clai Jackson, Senator Davie Atchison,
and the other secessionists in Jefferson City, they kept Missouri in the

Union. Then in 1875 St. Louis seceded from St. Louis County. This was meant to gain a larger measure of freedom from the domination of rural senators sitting by their betty lamps composing speeches in praise of hound dogs. Today the wisdom of the separation may be questioned. At least the city's area should have been made much larger than it was. Because of the failure to anticipate how great the expansion of St. Louis would be, it now is enclosed by steel-riveted boundaries. Inside them are almost 900,000 people, and there isn't room for any more, unless more factory-slums are turned into new residential neighborhoods. Meanwhile St. Louis County, which borders the city on three sides, has grown into a Balkan agglomeration of nearly a hundred suburbs with a population of about 600,000, and it still is growing almost as fast as realtor-builders can cover nice farms with un-nice ranch houses. Of course most of the County people come into the city for their paychecks and their culture. They hate to pay the city earnings tax as much as the city hates to lose the taxes of merchants who follow customers into the County. So St. Louis is one big community, but it is not one big, happy family. It has a bad case of galloping schizophrenia. And under the ground rules of the sovereign state of Missouri, this is almost incurable.

Jefferson City sometimes seems to be interested in nothing other than sending tax bills to the urban area—and as little help as possible. Rural legislators seem convinced that it is good for cities to stew in their own juices, and they frequently are willing to turn up the heat a bit. Unfortunately it is easy to get the impression that the victims in city and County prefer the disease to the taste and cost of its remedy. People are that way. Maybe it's more fun to be mad at the legislature and the courthouse than to straighten them out. If that were done, how could a subvillage with an unpaid mayor and a volunteer fire department be spiffy and exclusive?

There is no cause for undue concern, however, since St. Louis learned long ago how to live in such a mish-mash. The first Mayor, Dr. William Carr Lane, complained that "we generally have on our hands a greater number of sick than of right belong to us" (as is still the case) and he believed that "the state itself ought to extend its arm" (as it still is reluctant to do). But Dr. Carr Lane did not sink into the Slough of Despond under the weight of inequities. He also said:

"The fortunes of inhabitants may fluctuate; you and I may sink into oblivion, and even our families may become extinct, but the progressive rise of our city is morally certain; the causes of its prosperity are inscribed upon the very face of the earth, and are as permanent as the foundation of the soil and the sources of the Mississippi."

It would be difficult to argue that Carr Lane was overly optimistic. Slow and shabby-old as St. Louis may seem when compared with a boom-boom Kansas City, it still has the knack of lifting itself by its boot-straps now and then. The great park being developed on the riverfront is but one sign of this. And St. Louis is a "national institution," not just another pea-in-a-pod city like Indianapolis or Omaha or Cleveland or Minneapolis—places where airliners stop so salesmen can call on cus-tomers. Bernard De Voto called it "the splendid city of St. Louis which civilization made her abode long before the Yankees stopped honing their crabbedness on rum." Perhaps that is why even to Yankee ears St. Louis is a warm and exciting name—Lindbergh's "Spirit of St. Louis," the St. Louis Cardinals, the St. Louis Blues, and "Meet me in St. Louie, Louie."

Here's how it got that way——

III. Commoners' King

People who dote on mystery and confusion are happy to explain that St. Louis was not really named for St. Louis. They hint that Charles H. Niehaus's majestic equestrian bronze of the Crusader King overlooking his city, holding forth his sword in benediction over its people, really ought to be replaced by the figure of a later, less heroic monarch. They are not right, yet they do have a point—of sorts.

Auguste Chouteau, the young lieutenant of Pierre Laclède Liguest, the city's founder, set it down in his diary that St. Louis was given the name of the patron saint of the reigning French king to honor that second last of the Bourbons, Louis XV. Yet Laclède surely would have done a turn in his grave, the conventional sign of disapproval among the dead, had the city set up in some glade a figure of the weakling who brought the revolution on his grandson. Such a statue could be decorative, of course, with Pompadour, De Châteauroux, and Du Barry gracefully draped about the royal person—a Watteau in bronze, a *fête champêtre* in stone. But Laclède was a Béarnais, more independent even than his neighbors, the Gascons. His library suggests that he was not given to reading *The Lives of the Saints* or other works of piety. He had a doubt or two about the kings who reigned in Paris, even if they were to be upheld without hesitation against those who reigned in London. This merely meant that Laclède was thoroughly French, that he felt just as Jean d'Arc had felt about the "goddams." So there can be little question that he preferred the ninth Louis to the fifteenth.

Yet, being under the impression that this great-grandson of the Sun King was master of the west bank of the Mississippi, Laclède felt it politic to make a little bow toward his throne. The privilege of trading in furs and lead, after all, depended on the royal favor or on the favor of the royal governor of Louisiana. Naming his settlement for "the good Louis" as patron of "the bad Louis" was insurance bought with a bit of courtly double talk. Much good that did! The franchise was canceled as soon as it reached Paris for approval. Quite aside from this, had Laclède been in France twenty-five years later he might not have been a royalist. It was easier to stand by the old fleur-de-lis in

Quebec or Louisiana or the Indies than in Paris. In the end the best Romans were Britons, Gauls, or Spaniards who had never seen Rome. The latter-day Bourbons had lost less repute overseas than at home, even though their disregard was not entirely unnoticed along the St. Lawrence and the Mississippi. But good Frenchmen had no doubts at all about Louis IX.

This medieval king preferred to call himself simply Louis de Poissy, according to the town of his birth in the valley of the Loire, the most French region of France. A just and able man, he recognized the feudal order chiefly because it offered special opportunities to serve France. But Louis was, above all, the friend and protector of communes and commoners. He entrusted responsible positions to plain citizens who would govern without fear or favor. The French people never forgot this. When subsequent generations were threatened by misrule—and especially by the tax collector—they prayed for the return of "the ways of the good St. Louis." As Tocqueville explained, the French Revolution, for all the veneer and varnish of the Enlightenment, was for many a Frenchman an effort to create a modernized facsimile of those "good old days." Perhaps that is why, in the end, it worked so few fundamental changes in France. Be that as it may, St. Louis built its monument to the right king.

Louis de Poissy was a good model for men building a new city. He was solid and energetic. He preferred a good joke to haughty airs. He was a great embellisher of towns. Currently he must be sorely tempted to pass a miracle or two to speed up some of his city's plans—especially the one for the 610-foot stainless-steel arch on the riverfront as a symbol of the Gateway of the West. Louis was a great one for arches—the pointed arches which were the chief feature of the modern architecture of the thirteenth century. He built the towers and the side chapels of Notre Dame de Paris; he rebuilt Chartres from the ruins of the fire of 1194; he pushed work on Rheims, Bourges, Amiens, Beauvais, and Rouen, and on the incomparable Sainte-Chapelle, the gem of this far-flung garland of stone. So the slow architectural progress of St. Louis, his city, must annoy him at times.

Louis was perhaps the last knight *"sans peur et sans rapproche"*—an able soldier but not really the equestrian statue type. On crusade, he was in the saddle as long as there was an ounce of strength in him, but at home he gave less time to soldiers' work. He built not only cathedrals, but also hospitals—general hospitals in Paris, Compiègne, Pontoise, and Versailles, and some of the earliest specialized hospitals, such as the *Quinze-Vingts* for the blind and institutions for lepers.

He built guest houses for the needy, orphanages, and, everywhere, schools which the Benedictines staffed. Under the direction of his chaplain, Master Robert de Sorbon, he established the college still known as the Sorbonne, and Monte Sainte Geneviève became a neighborhood of lecture halls and student homes.

This king was modern as modern could be. He would spend no time jousting when he might be rebuilding a slum or finding funds for city hospitals. Those who have contrary notions may be misled by pious accounts of his saintliness. Voltaire called him the "crowned monk," but Voltaire did not know his man. Gibbon, who cared no more for the church than did the sharp-tongued Frenchman, saw Louis clearly. According to Gibbon, "he united the virtues of a king, a hero and a man; his martial spirit was tempered by the love of private and public justice; Louis was the father of his people, the friend of his neighbors, and the terror of the infidels."

Bergson wrote that the "great mystics have generally been men and women of action, of superior common sense." And there is old Montaigne's saying that such virtue has a "pleasant and gay quality." Louis' talk was generally gay. If from time to time he admonished and exhorted those about him, he had good cause; and it was generally taken in good fashion. For this we have the word of his biographer, John of Joinville, seneschal of Champagne.

Steven Runciman, the historian of the Crusades, agrees that the King's "character never lacked strength. He felt that he was responsible before God for the welfare of his people; and no prelate, not even the Pope himself, was allowed to come between him and this duty." He respected the feudal rights of his vassals, says Runciman, but "he expected them to play their part, and if they failed, their powers were curtailed." Runciman also testifies that although he was stern, "his standard of honor was high, he never broke his pledged word, and his intimates found his conversation full of charm and gentle humour." A man with a hair shirt, perhaps, but not a stuffed shirt.

Several popes, especially Innocent IV and Gregory IX, learned that with Louis the rights and duties of the French crown came first. Louis was no friend of the agnostic German Frederick II, but he would not attend the council called by the Pope to depose the emperor, and he took no notice of its decree. When a group of bishops asked him to enforce their excommunications, the king told them that their penalties were too severe and too frequently imposed. But when the bishops appealed to him against Rome's high ecclesiastical taxes, they had his support at once.

More appropriate than the figure of the mounted knight is the picture of Louis holding court beneath the oak of Vincennes. He was troubled because his law courts seemed able to administer justice only for those who could afford it. So Louis would hear in the open "without impediment of court procedure" anyone who wanted to state his case. The king was not an indulgent judge. He was ready to carry out the last letter of the law, especially against those in high places who felt that privilege and influence could set it aside. Louis did away with such nonsense as "judicial duels," declaring in 1260 that proof was to be based on evidence, "instead of battle."

He knew he could not try all the law cases of France himself, so he was careful in the selection of judges. He broadened the right of appeal, and he made the provostship of Paris a salaried office, entrusting it to Etienne Boileau, a commoner, who so reformed the courts of Paris that, according to Joinville, people were drawn to them by their fairness.

If Louis were to wander through the streets of twentieth century St. Louis, as he wandered through those of his realm to see how his subjects fared, the Old Courthouse would make him pause. Its connection with the Dred Scott case would remind him of his emancipation of the serfs in 1246. Louis, of course, would not confuse serfdom and slavery. In spite of the nonsense about the lord's bridal-night privilege—*primae noctis*—which poor historians drew from poor translations, Louis knew that a serf's obligations—primarily that of remaining attached to an estate—were matched by his rights. For the security which these afforded, villeins sometimes gave up their freedom of movement. Louis, however, was devoted to the independence and the dignity of the individual. "We have not been fashioned, some of us from gold or silver, others from clay," he believed. "We have not come, some of us from the head, others from the heel. We are all descended from the same man, all sprung from his loins."

Louis was strong enough to suppress the private warfare of his age. He was able to teach Henry III of England a severe lesson, and generous enough to return to him part of the territory conquered by French arms "so that there may be peace between my children and his children." He was so highly esteemed that he was called upon time and again to arbitrate the quarrels of sovereigns.

Louis was born in 1214 and died before Tunis in 1270. That was on his second crusade, which, like the first, ended in disaster. For this it is hard to blame him. Perhaps he should not have allowed his ambitious brother to persuade him to take the African route to the Holy Land, yet this was not altogether unreasonable. The first defeat came largely because the cavalry in his advance guard disobeyed orders. The objective set for them was achieved by a Prince Rupert charge. Then, instead of waiting for the king to bring up the rest of the army, they dashed on—into a trap. In trying to rescue them, the wise were forced to pay the penalty of the foolish. Louis agreed to his ransoming only to be free to find funds for the ransom of his followers. Before returning to Europe he pacified and strengthened the Christian principalities in the Levant. His second crusade was a failure partly because promised reinforcements never sailed from England.

His throne, according to Joinville, "shone like the sun which sheds its rays far and wide." Those rays reach us through 700 years of history and hagiography. They may touch his city with new splendor if it will but follow his example. In any case, it bears a proud name. "In the eyes of posterity," says Daniel-Rops, "St. Louis is not only the type of manhood at its best, according to medieval standards, but one of those transcendent figures which, through generation after generation, vouch for the grandeur of our race."

The city of St. Louis has not been altogether unworthy of its patron. Its citizens—merchants, soldiers, teachers, public officials—have developed a tradition of liberality and responsibility, of good sense and good humor. By this they live.

iv. Bend Sinister

When Pierre Laclède Liguest unfurled
His parti-colored pennant,
He said, "Auguste, I'll tell the world,"
Auguste was his lieutenant,
"That here on this historic ground
Your mother, you and I will found
A city destined to be great
Unless we're out of luck, my mate."

"You see yourself there's ample space,"
He spoke with animation,
"There's nothing lacking in the place
Excepting population;
And every loyal son of France
Will populate with half a chance."
He danced a sprightly little jig,
Then gaily signalled for his gig.

"I'm going South," the Founder said,
"To advertise our city,
To organize and then to head
A Citizens' Committee;
Au 'voir Auguste—Vive St. Louis,
Next Spring we'll plant our family tree,
You build yourself a little shack
And stick around 'til I get back."
                              Louis La Beaume.

A century and a half after its establishment—157 years for those
with an aversion to figures in the round—St. Louis was aroused by
the "big debate" as to who really had founded the city. Until 1921 it
seemed utterly out of the question that this question should be raised.
What was more fully documented by records, personal and official,

than the fact that St. Louis had been established in 1764—its site chosen in 1763—by Pierre Laclède Liguest, the working partner of Maxent, Laclède & Co. of New Orleans? The firm had obtained an exclusive charter for trade with the Indian tribes of the Missouri country, and Laclède had started up the Mississippi in August, 1763, to build a fur-trading post.

Because bothersome delays forced him to leave New Orleans so late in the summer, the foliage had turned red and gold, and the tang in the air threatened to become biting-sharp by the time he reached Fort Chartres, massive French stronghold on the Illinois side of the river in what is now Monroe County, about nine miles north of St. Genevieve, Missouri. It was too late in the year to build cabins and a warehouse, but there was still time to look for a site before winter set in. So Laclède left his stock behind the walls of the fort and set out with his lieutenant, thirteen-year-old Auguste Chouteau, to explore the river as far north as the confluence of the Missouri. Turning south again, he stopped below the high ground which had impressed him while the party was moving upstream. Here was a broad and safe landing. Above it—and easy of access—was a fine, flood-safe building site, and beyond that was prairie which could be turned into ample fields for crops and pasturage. On closer inspection, Laclède saw how advantageously streets could be laid out, and he drew a little map of the town-to-be. With his ax he marked trees, telling his young lieutenant:

"You will come here as soon as navigation opens, and will cause this place to be cleared, in order to form our settlement after the plan that I shall give you."

Chouteau recorded the order in his diary. He wrote also of Laclède's enthusiasm when the exploring party got back to Fort Chartres. To its commander, Neyon de Villiers, Laclède said that he had settled on a site on which would become not merely a trading post but "one of the most beautiful cities in America."

No doubt Laclède would have supervised the spring labors had he not encountered a political situation as alarming as his town site was encouraging. Laclède had been aware, of course, that French territory east of the Mississippi—with the exception of New Orleans—had been ceded to Great Britain in 1763 by the Treaty of Paris, which ended the Seven Years War, known in the eastern colonies as King George's War, the last of the French and Indian Wars. He was alarmed, however, by the determination of de Villiers to lead the French settlers of Notre

Dame de Kahokias and other French villages on the east bank to New
Orleans in a "splendid retreat." Laclède was an ardent Frenchman,
automatically anti-British. He was, in fact, the last of those adventurous
and imaginative men who had gained and tried to hold for France the
fabulous North American domain, reaching from Quebec to Louisiana,
the chief highway of which reached from the Atlantic to the Gulf by
way of the St. Lawrence, the Great Lakes, and the Mississippi—the
highway so important that it justified heavy expenditures on Fort
Chartres and the other French posts in the western wilderness.

If the court of Paris—which never adequately appreciated its explorers and colonizers—had surrendered Fort Chartres to the British,
it would have to be turned over to them. But granting this, Laclède
saw all the more reason for raising a new bastion against British expansion on the west bank of the river. This was no time for withdrawal
to New Orleans, but for resettlement on the far side of the Mississippi.
If half a continent had been given up, there still was half a continent
to be held. So Laclède turned over the work of building his post to
young Chouteau. He was to put up a warehouse first of all, so that
the expedition's cargo could be moved from Fort Chartres before its
surrender. Laclède himself would meanwhile try to persuade the Illinois
French to join him in his new settlement.

Having selected the site in December, Laclède sent his young
lieutenant upstream to start its development in February, even before
the ice was out of the river. A big assignment for a boy, but in those
days boys often did men's work. Young midshipmen commanded naval
batteries, and their brothers led cavalry charges. Young Chouteau had
been in command of one of the boats in Laclède's flotilla on the tedious
trip from New Orleans. Laclède had observed how well the boy did a
responsible man's work. Apparently he did not hesitate to send him
to start the building operations. In any case, Laclède had pressing work
on hand. So young Chouteau might be called the cofounder of St. Louis.
So, in fact, might all of the carpenters, masons, blacksmiths, and boatmen who made up the party, the men known to St. Louis as "the
First Thirty."

It is silly hairsplitting, however, to proclaim the fourteen-year-old
boy to be "the father of St. Louis." It is even sillier to try to wash the
name of Laclède out of the city's history. Yet emotion can rise against
facts. And it was emotion which tried to rewrite history in 1921. A
stonecutter was engaged to alter Chouteau's birth date on his tombstone

in Calvary cemetery to make him ten years older, and also to cut from the stone the acknowledgment: "sent by M. de Laclède." This graveyard huggermugger was one of the more amusing details of a genealogical battle royal which ignored even the testimony of Chouteau's diary that the site and the name of the city had been chosen by Laclède. A revised family tree was circulated. The St. Louis Historical Society, an *ad hoc* organization, solemnly adopted a resolution declaring Auguste Chouteau the founder of St. Louis. Pseudohistorical monographs were concocted. And it all boiled up in the newspapers, where space was not yet pre-empted by the cold war, atomic tests, and summit conferences.

There was a romance behind this storm, the romance of Laclède and young Chouteau's mother, Marie Thérèse Bourgeois Chouteau, wife of René Auguste Chouteau of New Orleans. This was another reason for sending the young man ahead to start building operations—as he did on St. Valentine's day, 1764. Laclède wanted a comfortable home ready for madame and her other children—Pierre, Pelagie, and Ann Marie Louise.

Most historians have taken it for granted that Madame Chouteau and her children accompanied Laclède up the river in 1763, wintering at the fort, and then waiting at Notre Dame de Kahokias until the St. Louis house with the wide veranda was finished. Yet this may be questioned. The cathedral records in New Orleans indicate that madame's fifth child, Victoire, was born there on March 23, 1764, and baptized in May with Pierre and Pelagie as godparents. Perhaps the family accompanied Laclède up the river in the summer and then returned to New Orleans. Perhaps Laclède was with them and brought them north again in the spring. There is no documentary evidence, but there is a deposition which declares that Laclède, on his horse, accompanied the cart in which Madame Chouteau rode from Notre Dame de Kahokias to St. Louis. And it is said that when they reached the new house, he carried her across the threshold quite as though she were his bride. That was in the summer of 1764. And she lived in the same house as he did until her death on August 14, 1814.

During all those years she was regarded as his wife—or as his widow—and he as the father of her four younger children. Just why she insisted on retaining the name of Chouteau, even when her descendants asked to be allowed to use the name of Laclède, is not clear. But there was no mystery for early St. Louisans in the relationship. An amusing bit of evidence was found in the St. Louis Cathedral records. When Pelagie Chouteau, named for one of the Magdalen saints, stood sponsor at the baptism of the child of a slave, Father Meurin with a slip of the pen wrote her name as Pelagie Laclède. But Madame Chouteau never took the name of Laclède. No doubt the shrewd woman wanted no trouble with the laws of church or state.

The man whose name she never used but with whom she lived and whose children she bore was born in the village of Bedous, Valle d'Aspe, at the base of the Pyrenees. The people of this region are rugged as their mountains—consider Foch and Joffre—but dashing and elegant too. Laclède carried a fine sword, carefully wrought pistols, and elegant clothes into the wilderness. His father and elder brother were royal officials. The family was long and honorably known along the frontier of France and Spain. The Laclède coat of arms was blue with a face of gold accompanied in chief with three towers of silver; in the point, a woodcock in silver with two roses of the same color. On the side were two eagles spreading wings supporting the crest. The escutcheon was surmounted with a crown with nine points. When used as a seal, the escutcheon was surmounted by a helmet.

It was not the genteel poverty of a second son, but a hankering for the freer life of the colonies which sent this dark-skinned, dark-eyed young man overseas. Having studied civil engineering, learned to manage the family's mill, and having sat for a portrait by which he might be remembered, he set out from Bordeaux for Louisiana in 1755. His plan was to become a planter. He was financed by his family, and he had persuaded a dozen or more of his countrymen to join him. He did try farming for a while, but the storms and floods of southern Louisiana spoiled his prospects. Anyway life was more attractive in New Orleans than on a swampy plantation. The young Frenchman was soon enjoying the city's gay society. He also was intrigued by its speculative spirit. New Orleans was an outgrowth of John Law's "Mississippi Bubble." Through its port was to flow the silver of Upper Louisiana to enrich the shareholders in the Company of the Indies. In 1720 Law's boom collapsed with a crash as loud as that of 1929—in part because Paris did not realize that Missouri lead might be almost as profitable as silver. But New Orleans did not forget the wilderness wealth of pelts and metals. Laclède made an investment or two, but fighting against the British and their Indian allies was even more exciting. He became an officer on the staff of Colonel Gilbert Antoine de Maxent—and his commander's good friend. Back from the wars, Maxent and Laclède found the authorities greatly in their debt. So in 1762 they obtained the privilege of trade with the savages of the Missouri and with all the nations residing west of the Mississippi for a term of eight years. Maxent, Laclède & Co. was formed. The older man set about raising capital. The young enthusiast set about organizing the expedition to the Missouri country. And his imminent invasion of the wilderness became the prime concern of Madame Chouteau.

The date and circumstances of the first meeting of these two are not in the records; such things rarely are, except in the case of those addicted to a diary even in the days of their youth. Madame Chouteau—who was born Marie Thérèse Bourgeois in New Orleans in 1733, and orphaned when four years old—left her first husband, René Chouteau, shortly after the birth of their son in 1749—six years before Laclède left France. As a girl she attended the academy of the Ursulines, as all proper New Orleans young ladies did, and lived in their convent. She returned to the convent with her baby to escape her husband's brutality. The man seems to have been the proprietor of one of the eight cabarets —or restaurants—then, as now, a feature of New Orleans. His cuisine was better than his conduct. His child bride came back to the Ursulines with a scar which she carried the rest of her life. She still was more schoolgirl than mother. There is, in fact, a delightfully improbable story about the awakening of her maternal instinct.

She had left her baby in a cradle on one of the convent's long, New Orleans-style balconies while she played in the yard with the other girls. Suddenly a monkey—it must have been a big one—appeared on the balcony, seized the child, and clambered with it to the convent roof, sitting there and fondling the baby. The young mother was horror-stricken. So were the other girls, naturally. But while they screamed, she ran up the stairs. The monkey, meanwhile, climbed down to the balcony and put the baby back in its cradle. Thereafter, Marie Thérèse watched over young Auguste with more concern than a mother hen. How a baby-fondling monkey got to the Ursuline convent is not part of the story. The animal may have escaped from an African slave smuggler or from one of those pirates who infested the Mississippi Delta, waiting for the time to help Andrew Jackson beat the British. The reader is free to make his own guess, but there is no point in being prosaic about this detail. There is nothing in the records to refute any fantasy.

The births of Marie Thérèse's other children are all inscribed in the

New Orleans Cathedral's baptistry records. And all of the children are listed as Chouteaus, not as Laclèdes. Much was made of this in 1921. It was one of the big arguments of the Chouteau-Chouteaus against the Laclède-Chouteaus. There is no official record of a separation, civil or canonical. Yet the trustees of the Missouri Historical Society politely deplored the Chouteau-Chouteau claims. The Reverend Lawrence Kenny, S.J., professor of history in St. Louis University, after a study of all available material, asserted that Laclède undoubtedly was the father of Madame Chouteau's younger children; that he had taken the boy, Auguste, up the river with him, and that to regard the boy, rather than his stepfather, as the founder of the city is preposterous. There are many concurring opinions. For a time, however, the dispute excited St. Louis. The *Post-Dispatch*'s star World War I correspondent, Clare Kenamore, launched a search of the records—from those in the Cabildo in New Orleans to those in the Colonial Office in Madrid. Documents were photographed and depositions taken. The "revisionists" were repulsed. Only a few of them still hold forth over teacups. More widely than ever, Laclède is recognized as the founder of St. Louis.

Poignantly, not one participant in the "great debate" was named Laclède. Hundreds of St. Louisans, however, claim Pierre Laclède Liguest as an ancestor. (He dropped the Liguest in later years.) Like good medievalists, they prefer an escutcheon with a bend sinister to no escutcheon at all. As for other St. Louisans—and this means most of them—in their equally broad-minded way, they were amused for a while by the ancestral hurly-burly. They were glad to be reminded again of a man whose memory had been on occasion neglected. But they had insurance against such neglect in the future, since the directors of the Louisiana Purchase Exposition had commissioned a fine bronze statue of Laclède, which now stands on the city hall lawn. They were relieved not to be under the necessity of finding new names for streets, utilities, and everything else called Laclède.

v. The First American Revolution

Laclède probably had more of the good soldier in him than of the ambitious fur trader. To attract settlers to a new French bastion in Upper Louisiana, he gladly shared his trading rights with others. He was unaware that Paris had withheld approval of the monopoly. He also set up a simple democracy. And after his friend, St. Ange, had turned Fort Chartres over to the British, Laclède invited him to St. Louis and persuaded him, as an officer of the king, to become its official governor. St. Ange, a guest in Laclède's home, simply confirmed with his signature what Laclède and the other citizens decided. St. Ange was respected, but a government of the people and not of the king was established, and this was reported to D'Abbadie, the French governor in New Orleans.

D'Abbadie hardly could assert royal authority, since he knew—as Laclède did not—that St. Louis really had not been established on French territory. News of the transfer of French possessions west of the Mississippi to Spain by the secret treaty of San Ildefonso reached New Orleans only after Laclède had started north. It was this transfer which led to the first American revolution, almost a decade before the shots at Lexington and Concord were heard round the world. Had Laclède been in New Orleans, he might well have been one of the signers of the first American Declaration of Independence, holding: "Without liberty there are few virtues. Despotism breeds pusillanimity."*

The leader of this rising was Nicholas Chauvin de Lafrenière. In the summer of 1765, on hearing that a Spanish governor, Don Antonio de Ulloa, was on his way from Havana, Lafrenière called a secret meeting of patriots in the outlying plantation home of Madame Pradel. Instead of immediately proclaiming the Republic of Louisiana, they sent to France one of their number, Jean Milhet, to persuade the king to reassert French sovereignty over the province. When Ulloa arrived in 1766 and attempted to assert Spanish authority, he was so intimi-

* If Laclède returned to New Orleans early in 1765 to bring Madame Chouteau to St. Louis, he must have heard of the transfer of Louisiana to Spain, but he might have been ignorant of the subsequent movement for independence.

dated by these citizens that he postponed the flag-raising and retired to the mouth of the Mississippi to set up winter quarters. Meanwhile, Milhet returned to report the unconcern of Paris. Ulloa was allowed to occupy a house in the city so long as he did not exercise authority. He sent a report to Madrid which aroused utmost consternation. There Aranda said to the Royal Council:

"A republic in Louisiana would be independent of all European powers. It would then become the interest of all to keep on terms of amity with her and to support her existence. The favorable position in which Louisiana would then be placed would not only increase her population, but also enlarge her limits, and transform her into a rich, flourishing and free state in sight of our provinces, which would present the melancholy contrast of exhaustion and want of cultivation. From the example under their eyes, the inhabitants of our vast Mexican domains would be led to consider their utter want of commerce, the extortions of their different governors, the little esteem in which they are held, the few offices they are permitted to fill. These things will weight the great inducements they have to hate still more the Spanish domination and to think they can brave it with more security, when they shall see that a province, weak compared with their extensive and populous country, can make good her position with impunity and secure her prosperity."

In New Orleans the Supreme Council, with Lafrenière as president, exercised virtually independent authority. On learning that Spain was sending a strong expedition under the Count O'Reilly, the forty-one men who had met in the home of Madame Pradel decided on even more positive action. On the night of October 27, 1768, the rebels took over the cannon at the city gates. Captain Noyan marched into the city with a company of Acadians recently arrived in Louisiana. A company of the Germans who had settled east of New Orleans marched in under Captain Villare. Farmers also came in from their scattered plantations. In the morning the declaration of independence was adopted and the Republic of Louisiana proclaimed. Ulloa was given three days to leave the city, but he did not need that much time. He sailed on October 31. Then Lafrenière was elected "Protector." New Orleans was as free in 1768 as Philadelphia in 1776—and technically so was all of Louisiana, including St. Louis. The following July, O'Reilly reached the Mississippi with 24 vessels and 2600 soldiers. Soon he was ready to attack the city. The patriots were in poor position to resist such a force. There were only 1398 men in the city capable of bearing arms, and some of these were royalists who felt that if they could not live under a French king, a Spanish king would be preferable to no king at all.

Under the circumstances, the patriot leaders were ready enough to parley. They were induced to go aboard O'Reilly's flagship. No sooner had the last of them stepped on deck than all were arrested. Spanish troops were landed immediately. Taken by surprise, and with virtually all of their leaders already prisoners, the resistance of the rebels was confused and futile. Villare was bayoneted to death. But the harsh O'Reilly had him tried and condemned posthumously. Lafrenière and six others also were condemned "as chiefs and principal movers of the conspiracy aforesaid to the ordinary pain of the gallows which they have deserved by the infamy of their conduct and *ipso jure* by their participation in so horrible a crime; and to be led to the place of execution on asses and each one with a rope around his neck, to be then and there hanged until death ensues and to remain suspended on the gallows until further orders, it being hereby understood that anyone having the temerity to carry away their bodies without leave or contravening in whole or in part of the execution of said sentence shall suffer death."

Other patriots were sentenced to imprisonment for life, and still others for shorter terms. The people of New Orleans, however, clamored in protest, and the public hangman refused to carry out the sentences. So on October 25, 1769, the men were led to the Place des Armes and shot by a platoon of Spanish soldiers. The declaration of independence was publicly burned.

On May 20, 1770, Don Pedro Piernas, whom O'Reilly had appointed Governor of Upper Louisiana, arrived at St. Louis with a charming French wife and 20 soldiers. The casual disregard of his authority is indicated by the continued issuance of land titles despite contrary orders from New Orleans. Piernas was treated as a guest rather than as a governor in the home of the Spanish-speaking Laclède. By accepting things largely as he found them, and by his affability, the Spaniard gradually won acceptance. Piernas was not the first Spaniard to come to St. Louis. In 1767 a small force had been sent north by Ulloa to build two forts at the confluence of the Missouri and the Mississippi, but these men gave up the effort and made no attempt to assert authority in the town. After all, they did not have with them so rare a creature as Madame Piernas, a woman who charmed other women. Her chitchat about Europe, especially about the latest Paris fashions, did more to establish the Spaniards than any writ from Madrid or New Orleans.

Captain Philip Pitman, a British engineering officer who had been sent by General Gage to gather information about the Mississippi Valley, was in St. Louis in 1767, reporting:

"This village is one league and a half above Kaoquias . . . for the security and encouragement of this settlement a staff of French officers and the commissary were ordered to remove there, upon the rendering of Fort Chartres to the English; and great encouragement was given to the inhabitants to remove with them, most of whom did. The company has built a large house and stores here, and there are about 45 houses and as many families. No fort or barracks are yet built."

Apparently Pitman did not learn that most of the garrison of Fort Chartres, as well as many settlers, had gone to New Orleans. In any case he was not overly impressed by St. Louis, writing that: "Cascasquias is by far the most considerable settlement in the Illinois country," and that it is regarded as "the Paris of America." There were at this time several other French settlements in the area, notably St. Genevieve, which was prospering in the lead trade and was slow to regard St. Louis as a rival.

Carondelet, established a few miles south of St. Louis, soon became part of the community, although not officially annexed until 1870. It held out forty years longer than North St. Louis, which was founded by "Bostons" only after the Louisiana Purchase. One of the chief attractions of Carondelet was horse racing. The younger men soon called it *Vide Poche*—empty pocket. About this time St. Louis acquired the name of *Pain Court,* or scanty bread. That was because although men had come to the settlement as bakers or carpenters most were tempted by the profits of the fur trade and abandoned their original occupations, preferring to depend on the other settlements for supplies.

The small town was an exciting place, ringing with the songs and the brawling voices of the *chasseurs de bois* and the *engagés* back from fur-trading trips up the wide Missouri. Departing from the aristocratic European pattern of land tenure which prevailed in the eastern colonies, Laclède had granted freeholds to all, with only one condition: that they begin the improvement of the land within a year. Disturbed by the town's nickname, the Béarnais miller helped Joseph and Roger Taillon to dam the little stream which ran through what is still known as Mill

Creek Valley. They built their dam and their mill where the big Cupples Station freight terminal now stands. Where the railroad tracks now run westward to the Union Station, the dam formed a beautiful body of water long known as Chouteau's Pond. This mill and the crops which Laclède induced at least a few of the settlers to raise in the common fields south and west of the settlement as early as 1765 were the beginnings of the community's self-sufficiency.

Unhappily, Laclède did not share to any great extent in its early prosperity. On June 20, 1778, he died in one of the boats in which he was bringing a cargo of merchandise from New Orleans, and was buried on the shore near the mouth of the Arkansas. It was at approximately this point that the body of De Soto, the discoverer of the Mississippi, was consigned to its waters 236 years earlier. And it was at the mouth of the Arkansas that Marquette and Joliet turned back in their exploration of the Mississippi in 1673. Thus the site of Laclède's grave, long since swept away by floods, linked him with the great names of the Mississippi. Like De Soto and Marquette and Joliet and La Salle, he was one of its explorers.

After his death, De Leyba, the third Spanish governor, and Auguste Chouteau made an inventory of Laclède's possessions, including his library. Among his books were the works of Locke, Descartes, Petronius, Bacon, Corneille, and some 150 other volumes on history, politics, commerce, geography, science, mathematics, agriculture, law, and even on anatomy and surgery. In the cargo he was bringing up the river at the time of his death was a history of the Roman emperors in twelve volumes. Such a collection in the wilderness is a key to Laclède's mind. So, also, in his copy of Rousseau's *Social Contract*. The quality of his furniture and of his clothes, the wines, honey, chocolate, olive oil, and "odor water" among the more ordinary items of his cargo are evidence enough of a desire to live in his pioneer village as graciously as in New Orleans or in France.

"I wish I could see you again," Laclède, anticipating death, wrote to his family in St. Louis. "It is painful to die in debt," he added, asking his stepson to give first consideration to his obligations to his partner, Maxent. His old commander was as just and as fair as Laclède had expected him to be. Auguste Chouteau was able to buy out Maxent's interest in the trading firm in 1779, but another ten years went by before he paid Maxent for the house in St. Louis. By this time the young man had fully succeeded to Laclède's role as first citizen of St. Louis.

He was an active and successful trader, and he had as much authority, though unofficial, as the Spanish governor. His brother, Pierre, was also on the way to success. Their fortune was based on a deed of gift, dated May 12, 1768, in which Laclède "in consideration for the faithful service which he has received from M. Auguste Chouteau during the several years in which he has worked for him as his clerk, also Pierre Chouteau, his brother, Pelagie Chouteau, Marie Louise Chouteau, Victoire Chouteau, brothers and sisters, through the affection which he bears them has voluntarily made a gift to them unreservedly and irrevocably in the best manner possible without hope of revoking same, and for their greater security" of his property. This deed specified that the enjoyment of this property was to be Madame Chouteau's for life. Thereafter, it was to go to the children. Thus the name of Laclède faded from the records of St. Louis and that of Chouteau became increasingly prominent.

After the Spanish governors decided to build a "Government House" of their own, Chouteau remodeled, enlarged, and embellished Laclède's old home. Now called the Chouteau mansion, it continued to be the place where citizens made their decisions, taking them across the street to the Spanish "Government House" for official confirmation.

VI. A Spanish Benedict Arnold

St. Louis had seven Spanish governors between 1770 and 1804, if you count one of them twice, à la Grover Cleveland. Piernas, with his friendship for Laclède and only the mildest exertion of authority, set the pattern for them all. During the entire period no more than twenty Spanish families settled in St. Louis. The community grew more slowly in numbers than it did in wealth and influence. At the turn of the century its population was about 1000. Like Laclède, the Spanish governors feared attempts to extend British powers to the west side of the Mississippi. To guard against this, both Piernas and Cruzat invited French-Canadians to settle in Northern Louisiana, especially in St. Louis. The settlers built primitive fortifications, little more than palisades and ditches. They gave all the help they could to the rebellious American colonists. St. Louis sent men, money, and munitions to help George Rogers Clark in his campaign against the British at Vincennes. And the town finally became one of the battlefields of the revolutionary struggle.

In 1780 the British governor of Fort Michilimackinac organized an Indian expedition against St. Louis under the command of three renegade Frenchmen: Langlade, Calde, and Ducharne. The last of the three had once lived in St. Louis. The force reached the east bank of the Mississippi, somewhat north of the settlement, on the Feast of Corpus Christi, May 25. Since this was a day for religious processions through the fields, and then for the gathering of the first strawberries of the season, the city might have been taken easily by a well-timed attack, but the Indians and their leaders decided not to move until the next day, when their full force should be on hand. On the afternoon of the twenty-fifth a settler named Quenelle crossed to the east side of the Mississippi to angle for catfish, a delicacy appreciated in St. Louis since the earliest days. Suddenly he heard a familiar voice. Looking up from his skiff, he saw his former fellow citizen, Ducharne. The turncoat urged him to come ashore, saying that he had important news for him, but Quenelle noticed several Indians in the brush.

"I am sure your news is important," he cried, "but not good news for me." He crossed the river as rapidly as possible and hurried to the Spanish governor, Don Fernando de Leyba, telling him that an Indian attack was imminent. De Leyba scoffed at this, and had him put in the calabozo lest he alarm the citizens—and on a feast day.

During the night the Indians crossed the river north of the city and, moving west and south, encircled it, remaining in the woods beyond the cultivated fields. Very early in the morning they encountered two men in what is now Fairgrounds Park, killing one and holding the other a prisoner. Then they waited for the workers to come into the fields but, perhaps because there had been a ball the night before, only relatively few appeared, and these chiefly to gather strawberries. Deciding to wait no longer, the Indians launched the attack with a loud shout. About forty of the villagers were killed in the fields. Some put the figure at a hundred or more. More would have escaped had not so many of them fled toward the upper city gate, which was closed— by De Leyba's orders. Citizens had opened the lower gate.

The first man to die that morning was Jean Marie Cardinal. He had been one of the early trader-explorers on the head waters of the Missouri but, having acquired a wife and a brood of children, he had settled to a more pastoral life. His wife, a Pawnee named Careche-Caranche, was the mother of his seven daughters and one son. The eight children were baptized in the little Catholic church in St. Louis on May 30, 1776; then the father and mother were married. (Many of the fur traders had Indian wives. Some left these women behind in the wilderness, but others proudly brought them to St. Louis.) All of Cardinal's daughters married Frenchmen, and Cardinal Avenue honors his name, rather than a Prince of the Church or a baseball team.

Among those surprised in the fields was a man named Chancellor. He had gone out in a cart drawn by two horses with his wife and two daughters and an American whose name seems to have been lost, although he is said to have been the first American to live in St. Louis. When the savages attacked, Chancellor leaped into the driver's seat while the American took his position in the back of the cart to protect the women. Chancellor was struck in the right arm by two balls. A bullet went through his wife's hand. His elder daughter was shot through the shoulder and his younger daughter received a grazing blow on the forehead. The American was killed and fell from the cart. Chancellor reined in his horses, leaped to the ground, threw the body of the American amidst the women and shouted:

"Those Indians shall not get the scalp of my American." He whipped up his wounded horses and just reached the city gate as they collapsed.

Julian Roy was fortunate enough to have a pistol when he was caught in the field. Pursued by a big Indian who was rapidly overtaking him, Roy turned and fired. The ball struck the Indian's jaw and broke it, also inflicting a nasty wound. Instead of continuing his flight, Roy tended the Indian's wound. He could have done nothing more calculated to insure his safety. For the grateful Indian escorted him across the field of carnage to the safety of the city gate.

At the onset of the attack, Governor de Leyba took refuge in his stone house. He ordered all citizens to take shelter, and—most strangely—he commanded that the cannon at the city gates be filled with sand. When, instead, the men brought one of the guns into action against the Indians, De Leyba ordered that another gun be trained on them. But his handful of Spanish soldiers already had taken refuge in the upper part of the tower recently added to the city's scant fortifications. Frustrated, De Leyba again fled to his house. With the cannon giving the townsmen the advantage in firepower, the Indians fled the field.

The most conspicuous heroine of the day was Marie Josepha Rigauche, the young schoolteacher. Dressed in an old coat and armed with pistols and knives, she rushed to one of the gates, rallying the men fighting there and making a number of sallies into the field to help those seeking safety.

Father O'Hanlon, the historian-priest of the Old Cathedral, was able to interview many of the participants in this affair in their later years. Of the governor, he wrote:

"There can hardly be a doubt that De Leyba had been seduced into defection from his duty, and that it was only the unflinching heroism of the St. Louis people that saved their infant outpost from utter destruction. Their defense against this attack and that bold spirit manifested on that occasion were in keeping with the deeds of their brethren, the French, who took part in the American Revolution."

St. Louis was so enraged by the governor's conduct that a protest was sent to New Orleans at once. De Leyba made his will on June 10, 1780. He died and was buried on the 28th. Many believed that he had poisoned himself, perhaps out of shame and remorse.

The case against the Spanish governor seems all the more black because he had so strongly opposed the building of the new fortifications which the citizens had put up at their own expense.* He called the builders old dotards, saying there was no danger to be guarded against, and he scoffed loudly when they placed in position the old guns which St. Ange had brought over from Fort Chartres. De Leyba could not help being aware of the danger of Indian trouble, since bands of Osages camped near the town almost constantly and braves strutted through the place at all hours.

The previous Spanish governors had asserted their authority most strongly when it came to defense against the Indians. They had insisted that all able-bodied men form a militia company for regular drill, and they forbade the sale of liquor to the natives. Yet the Spaniards were not as vigorous as the French in punishing Indian depradations. On one occasion a band of Osages descended on St. Genevieve and drove off every horse in the village. Instead of pursuing them, the Spaniards simply sent word to the Indians that unless the horses were returned they would no longer trade with them. Captain Amos Stoddard, who took over Louisiana for the United States, gives another example of this Spanish conduct:

"One instance, among many others, may be of use to explain the character of the Missouri Indians. While a kind of predatory war raged in 1794, between one of their tribes and the whites, a peace was concluded in a singular manner: A war chief, with a party of his nation, boldly entered St. Louis and demanded an interview with the Lt. Governor, to whom he said: 'We have come to offer you peace; we have been at war with you many moons, and what have we done? Nothing. Our warriors have tried every means to meet yours in battle, but you will not, you dare not fight us: You are a parcel of old women. What can be done with such a people but to make peace, and to bury the hatchet?' The Spanish government was obliged to bear this insult with patience, and to grant the desired peace."

This supine attitude, however, was not the result of cowardice—or not of cowardice alone. From the very first, the Spanish authorities in St. Louis were under orders from O'Reilly and his successors in New Orleans to observe the strictest economy. Almost all the expenses of their administration were charged against their personal salaries, which were none too munificent. On one occasion, when a windstorm wrecked the

---

* The fortifications of St. Louis ran westward from the river roughly along what is now Biddle Street, turned south along Third Street to Chouteau Avenue, and ran from that point back to the river. They were supplemented early in 1780 by a round tower at approximately Fourth and Walnut streets.

barracks in St. Louis, message after message had to be exchanged with New Orleans before the repairs were authorized. But even then the governor was severely upbraided for incurring the expense of four pounds of nails. So it may have been pride which urged De Leyba to scoff at the building of the fortifications, a function taken over by the citizens from the governor because he simply could not carry it out. And it may have been the parsimony of his superiors which led him into temptation.

Indignation at his treason (or cowardice) caused Jean Baptiste Trudeau, the schoolmaster, to write the chanson which became the "Yankee Doodle" of St. Louis. Here is a verse of it as translated in 1845 by J. M. Field, editor of the *Reveille,* a literary journal of that time:

> When the enemy first appeared,
> To arms we ran, no one afeared;
> Townsmen, traders, grave and gay,
> Bravely to battle and win the day;
> But by command we were forbid
> To quit the trench where our ranks were hid.

This one day of fighting caused 1780 to be remembered in St. Louis as *L'Année du Coup.* It was the only direct impact of the Revolutionary War on the city, but it gave St. Louis its Benedict Arnold.

The story of the Battle of St. Louis depends at least as much on tradition as on history, and tradition often means exaggeration. The most exciting, and so the most popular account was set down in 1831 by Judge Wilson Primm. Like a number of others who wrote after the event, he did have opportunities to interview some of the participants. Nevertheless, it is difficult to accept fully his story of an assault by an army of 1400 Indians and their British and renegade French leaders on a town defended by hardly more than 100 able-bodied men—and those betrayed by their own drunken governor. That should have ended in a massacre. Yet the testimony of Auguste Chouteau, Pierre Chouteau, Jean Baptiste Rivière, Laurent Reed and others—all preserved in Hunt's *Minutes*—leaves no doubt that there was an attack in some force.

Thomas Hart Benton wrote that "on the approach of so formidable an enemy, the inhabitants, despairing of successful resistance, deputed one of their most respectable citizens, the late Charles Gratiot, to solicit the aid of Gen. G. R. Clark, then encamped with his men on the American Bottom. Gen. Clark, although having but 400 men, led them to the ferry opposite the town, and made a demonstration of crossing, while 200 more were sent to cross under the bend of the river. The Indians were disconcerted and hastily retired."

Captain Amos Stoddard in his *Sketches of Louisiana* wrote: "The commandant of Michilimackinac, in 1789, assembled about 1500 Indians and 140 English, and attempted the reduction of St. Louis, the capital of Upper Louisiana. During the short time they were before the town sixty of the inhabitants were killed and thirty taken prisoner."

Nicollet in his topographical report said: "There were not more than 150 males in the place, of whom not more than seventy could be relied upon as efficient to repel an enemy numbering, according to the best authorities, 900 combatants. It is said that sixty were killed and thirteen made prisoners."

Frederick Billon and J. Thomas Scharf, careful but not always quite correct writers, in 1880 and 1883 respectively debunked the *grand coup*. There was no reason for a British attack on St. Louis, they maintain, although there was good reason to attempt to retake Cahokia and Kaskaskia just as they had retaken Vincennes from the Americans. Clark had made preparations for the defense of Cahokia, but when word reached the town that the enemy was coming down from Prairie du Chien, he was near the mouth of the Ohio. That is why Gratiot, then living in Cahokia, was sent to find him. Gratiot, according to Billon and Scharf, had transferred merchandise from Cahokia to St. Louis for safekeeping. Clark did not get to Cahokia in time, but the Indians were discouraged by the town's defenses. These two writers concede that some of the Indians, under a renegade trapper who had a grievance against the authorities in St. Louis, did cross the river in the hope of easy scalps and loot.

The affair seems to have been more serious than that—even if nobody kept a careful record of it. Trudeau's song and the readiness of the whole town to sing it in defiance and disdain of De Leyba at least suggests his deep unpopularity. Considering that the wilderness was rife with the intrigues of British, Spanish, and American agents, the charge against De Leyba is not an utterly unacceptable improbability. The townsmen must have believed that they had good grounds for suspicion. And what a community chooses to believe is, after a fashion, part of its history—just as is that which it fails to record.

VII. Pianos and Pirates

St. Louis never was really primitive. The settlers from Kaskaskia and the other French towns on the east bank of the Mississippi were beyond the pioneering stage by the time of Laclède's arrival. Cahokia was founded by French Canadians in 1699, and Kaskaskia in 1703. They had acquired furniture and some finery from France by way of Canada or New Orleans. So a new home for them meant more than just shelter. Even so, it was subject to frontier limitations and often was a log structure, but built with the logs set up vertically rather than in the American horizontal style. And the more prosperous built even their first houses of stone. Within a quarter century St. Louis had grown into a city of fifty blocks and its population was nearing one thousand. It had thirty or so fine stone mansions along its three main north and south streets—the Rue Royale, the Rue de l'Eglise, and the Rue des Granges. The "Bostons" later changed Laclède's street names to Main, Second, and Third. All three have now disappeared in the cleared space which is to become the riverfront national park. The hundred or more frame buildings had elaborate verandas and considerable additions. Some of the houses occupied a whole block, with beautiful flower gardens, cultivated fruit trees, and the inevitable *potager,* or vegetable garden. Almost always there was a separate kitchen. New and handsome furniture had come from New Orleans, San Domingo, and from France. There were a few pianos in the town, and also billiard tables. The tree-shaded village was cheerful and prosperous.

The Indians roundabout dispelled any illusion that this was a little town in Brittany. The natives were strange, worrisome, and hard to control. When Pontiac, no longer the leader of his great confederation, came to visit his old friend, St. Ange, it was impossible to persuade him not to visit cronies on the east side of the river, and there he was murdered. St. Ange recovered the body (not without some trouble) and conducted a full military funeral.

The frontier had its drawbacks: sickness without doctors, children to be educated without adequate schools, families and homes to be maintained with supplies uncertain. But comfortable, congenial St. Louis took its hardships in stride. On Sunday morning everybody went to the church built in 1770 where the Old Cathedral now stands, and heard Père Valentin, the Capuchin missionary, or his successor, Père Bernard, read mass and preach the sermon. Then everybody went home to a feast. From the kitchen a well-trained Negro cook sent gumbo soup, turkeys roasted on a spit, and stews flavored with the onions, garlic, pepper, and morelles from the kitchen rafters. There were wines and liqueurs and pralines—all the delicacies of a fine French meal. After dinner there was dancing to the fiddling of Tardif and Chevreuil. Manners were good, and the ever-present chaperones might divert themselves with a game of loo or bezique.

There was much singing in early St. Louis and a great talent for turning hard work into fun. For example, the family washing was done along La Petite Rivière (Mill Creek) in little cabins very much like those along the Eure in Chartres. This work, of course, was the occasion for much gossip and chatter. There were good hunting and fishing a stone's throw from home, but men who lived by the paddle, the rifle, and the ax were not disposed to hunt and fish for mere sport. They caused great excitement as they set off from the riverfront on those expeditions up the Missouri to build forts in far Wyoming, and there was even greater excitement when they returned—almost as much as that of a charivari on a wedding day. But the most joyful times came with the celebration of Noël and Jour de l'An, New Year's Day. Some of that French jollification is still to be encountered in the St. Louis area in villages like Prairie du Rocher, Portage des Sioux, and Mine la Motte.

Ordinarily the Creole mothers and daughters of St. Louis might be content to go about in freshly laundered calico, but on feast days they brought out their silks and their laces and their silver buckles. Ordinarily the men might go about with a capote over a gay shirt, and *bottes sauvages,* but for the feasting days they donned coats of white satin embroidered with gold, or coats of red or blue with gold buttons. They kept up—as M. Laclède did—with the Spaniards. For a grand holiday they even powdered their hair and tied it with bows of silk—after some urging by the womenfolk.

If Governor Piernas had some unfavorable opinions about the people of St. Louis, he kept them in his own mind, and in his letters to his superiors. Throughout the Spanish regime of thirty-four years no taxes, except some light duties on imports and exports, were imposed. When the administration was short of funds because of the military drain on the treasury in Madrid, it was suggested to the leading citizens of St. Louis that they might make contributions. This they did cheerfully enough. Even Indians brought gifts for "our Spanish father."

There was trouble in those days with the Hudson's Bay Company. British traders and trappers often trespassed on Louisiana territory and made trouble with the Indians. The attack on St. Louis showed how bold they could be. Cruzat, the most energetic of the Spanish representatives, succeeded the beclouded De Leyba, and decided at once on a counterstroke. In 1781 he organized a military expedition, made up entirely of Frenchmen, which marched across winter-quiet Illinois and seized the British fort at what is now St. Joseph, Michigan. The men brought the English flag back to St. Louis. Their feat later became the basis for Spanish land claims to the east and north of St. Louis, which Madrid, however, was unable to maintain.

Also troublesome were the pirates on the Mississippi. Under Jamie Colbert they preyed on river traffic. Chouteau's friend, Labbadie, once lost a cargo to them, and they even dared to hold a Spanish governor's wife and daughter as hostages. These murderers and freebooters were forerunners of Mike Fink, the legendary desperado. Later, even the United States Army found it difficult to drive these characters out of their lairs in the wild and unsettled country which now is eastern Arkansas and western Tennessee. This meant that the pirogues on the river had to be prepared for defense. So when Pedro Vial, *dit* Manitou, arrived in St. Louis, having traced the long route from Mexico which was to become the Santa Fe trail, some St. Louis traders were ready enough to ponder trade with the Spanish Southwest. It would be safe at least from the depradations of river pirates. But there could be no thought of giving up profitable business in pelts which had to be sent to Europe by way of New Orleans. So Chouteau and some of the other merchants decided on naval action. Instead of sending a cargo down the river whenever it was ready, they held up their boats until a flotilla was assembled. The boats were well armed, and the river rats were given a good dose of shot. That was in 1788, the year which went into the old St. Louis chronology as *L'Année des Dix Bateaux*.

Another threat, if threat it may be called, developed in 1796 when Citizen Genêt sent General George Collot from Philadelphia to St. Louis on behalf of the French revolutionary government. Collot formed a small group of sans-culottes, to the alarm of the Spaniards in New Orleans. Governor Trudeau, however, seems to have smiled at their meetings, their balls, their singing of revolutionary songs, and their celebration of New Year's Eve on September 22. But most of the St. Louis French, like the Quebec French, were loyal to the crown rather than to the revolutionary regime. They may have tried a revolt in Louisiana against Spain, but they were shocked by news which *émigrés* brought from France.

The "Bostons," as St. Louis French called the Americans, were becoming more of a menace than the harmless sans-culottes. As common enemies of the British, some of them had been encouraged to settle in the Missouri country. For example, Governor Trudeau had granted Daniel Boone a large tract of land in St. Charles County, northwest of St. Louis, and Governor Delassus, the friend of William Henry Harrison of Vincennes, had made Boone commandant of the Femme Osage district. The famous frontiersman, immortalized in the George Caleb Bingham painting, attracted settlers from Kentucky, Tennessee, and Virginia. Established in the big house with the beautifully carved mantels which the tourist may still visit, Boone was loyal to the Spanish, from whom he had derived land and authority. Moses Austin of Connecticut, however, was a different bird. He had been granted permission to mine lead at Mine à Breton near Potosi, Missouri. Soon he was defying the governor's surveyor, Soulard, and carrying on as though he were a law unto himself. The Spaniards were to have more trouble with him and his son in Missouri and in Texas. Austin's conduct ended the welcoming of Americans. The offer of David Wilcox to develop the iron mines south of St. Louis was politely declined. Yet more and more Americans did cross the Mississippi. They came mostly from "the American Bottoms," the fertile land along the Illinois side of the river to which they had been attracted some years earlier by Shadrach Bond. They were, on the whole, enterprising, but bossy too. Thus John Mullanphy, the first St. Louis millionaire, offered to build a suitable courthouse if the seat of government were removed to St. Ferdinand, a village which he was seeking to develop. It was in such places in the environs of St. Louis that the Americans first settled. According to a census made in 1789 by Delassus, the last Spanish governor, who, like several of his predecessors, was a Frenchman in Spain's employ, there were 681 white persons in St. Louis, 50 free mulattoes, 6 free Negroes, and 268 slaves. But there were 1203 white persons living in stockades or "forts" outside the city, and almost all of them were Americans. When Captain Amos Stoddard took over after the Louisiana Purchase, he reported that the city was four-fifths French and the adjacent territory three-fifths American.

VIII. The Two Napoleons

The American community growing up beside the French was becoming aggressive, and Delassus was preparing to discipline the obstreperous "Bostons." But a much stronger hand was poised to make St. Louis and the trans-Mississippi West thoroughly French—not Spanish—not only in manners and customs but also in government. Napoleon had accepted Talleyrand's grand plan to pacify Europe and to build a new French overseas empire. This was to enrich France, offset England's colonial realm, and check the growth of the United States, the republic despised by Talleyrand and hated by Napoleon. Once the Corsican accepted the former Bishop of Autun's scheme, it took less than two years to establish peace on the continent. Then he brazenly offered Spain the Duchy of Parma for Louisiana. The king and queen were eager to make this fantastic bargain. They wanted their son-in-law to wear a crown so that their daughter might be a queen. After Hohenlinden, it was easy to take Parma from its grand duke and to install Spain's son-in-law as the King of Etruria. The treaty was signed March 21, 1801. On October 1 an agreement was reached in London which ended the war of England and France on the high seas.

France had regained the eastern part of San Domingo from Spain in 1795, but did not take possession. There had been two obstacles: the British fleet and Toussaint L'Ouverture. Now there was only Toussaint. He was to be crushed and slavery re-established. And vast Louisiana was to be occupied and fortified, so that it might feed San Domingo. For this, Napoleon assembled a large fleet and a powerful army at Brest. It was commanded by Leclerc, his brother-in-law and one of the most competent of his generals.

Spanish rule over Louisiana and Florida was galling to the Americans west of the Appalachians because it threatened their use of the great Mississippi highway, and at New Orleans blocked the outlet to the sea. How much worse to have the territory in the hands of the ruthless Napoleon! Yet what could the few western militiamen Jefferson might raise do against French veterans? These were not troops to be turned back by hunters with squirrel rifles. They were, however, stopped by Toussaint. Contemporary statesmen, glad to see Napoleon's gaze turned across the Atlantic, hardly grasped Toussaint's importance, and few historians have recognized it as clearly as did Henry Adams in his history of the administrations of Jefferson and Madison. "The story of Toussaint L'Ouverture has been told almost as often as that of Napoleon," Adams wrote, "but not in connection with that of the United States, although Toussaint exercised on their history an influence as decisive as that of any European ruler. . . . Before Bonaparte could reach Louisiana he was obliged to crush the power of Toussaint. If he and his blacks should succumb easily to their fate, the wave of French empire would roll on to Louisiana and sweep far up the Mississippi; if San Domingo should resist, and succeed in resistance, the recoil would spend its force in Europe, while America would be left to pursue the democratic destiny in peace." Had Napoleon reconquered the Mississippi Valley, St. Louis inevitably would have become the capital of this second New France.

With Canada and India gone, San Domingo was the richest of France's colonial possessions. No less than 700 ships and 80,000 seamen were kept busy carrying its sugar, coffee, indigo, and cotton to French ports. Even though France owned only part of the West Indian island, two-thirds of its commercial interests centered there. Henry Adams estimated that in 1789 its trade was worth $240,000,000. San Domingo's Creole aristocrats were frequently seen in Paris, and at home they lived with almost Parisian luxury. But San Domingo was even more dangerously volcanic than its less prosperous neighbor, Martinique. Of its 600,000 inhabitants, five sixths were Negro slaves. More privileged were the less numerous mulattoes. But all were ruled by the small Creole aristocracy of planters, merchants, and officials. When the French Revolution broke out, the mulattoes offered the National Assembly in Paris one fifth of their possessions to be relieved of caste distinctions. The Creoles turned Royalist. And, in utter madness, both sides took up arms. This was the great opportunity for the Haitian Negroes. In August of 1791 they spread blood and fire across the colony. Spain and England tried to take advantage of preoccupied France by attempting to quell the revolt and seize the French part of the island. They were repulsed, however, when Toussaint, the redoubtable Negro Royalist in Spanish pay, raised the French Republican banner and cleared the island of foreigners. In 1794 the French National Assembly abolished slavery on

Haiti, and in 1797 it proclaimed L'Ouverture General-in-Chief. Not content with these rewards, Toussaint demanded that he be regarded as the equal of Napoleon. He declared Haiti independent, and promulgated a constitution. This invited the lightning. Leclerc was ordered to San Domingo.

For three bloody months the Black Napoleon more than held the French at bay. Then his lieutenant, Christophe, treacherously surrendered a large part of the Negro army. Through trickery, Toussaint was arrested and sent to France. He was incarcerated in the fortress of Joux in the high Jura. There, in the damp and the cold, he died April 7, 1803, of pneumonia.

Leclerc was trying to carry out Napoleon's order to "rid us of these gilded Africans." Yet Christophe and Dessalines, another of Toussaint's lieutenants, had no more taste for slavery than had the man they betrayed. They renewed the war. Yellow fever turned the tide against the French. Leclerc himself died of fever. Rochambeau, son of the Rochambeau who had fought in the American Revolution, was penned up in Port au Prince. Occasionally he sallied forth with 1500 Jamaican bloodhounds—worth $100 each—to shoot or hang every Negro he could find. Christophe and Dessalines shot or burned every white man they could find. San Domingo was utterly ruined. The army which was to fortify the Mississippi was wasted, unit after unit, in the West Indian war.

The death of Leclerc was announced in the *Moniteur* in Paris on January 7, 1803. Although Napoleon pretended that everything was as before and issued orders for the reinforcement of the army, this really marked the end of his interest in San Domingo, Louisiana, and an overseas empire. (The islanders again declared their independence in 1804, and it was finally recognized by France in 1825.) The fighting had been enormously expensive. To continue it would cost even more. Napoleon turned again to Europe, where war could be more glorious and more profitable. Europe's statesmen did not realize how close he had come to bleeding himself white—indeed, ending his whole adventure—in the West Indies. Even Jefferson and his associates did not fully appreciate what had happened. As for those who had more time to realize the significance of events, Henry Adams wrote:

"The prejudice of race alone blinded the American people to the debt they owed to the desperate courage of 500,000 Haitian Negroes who would not be enslaved."

Livingston and Monroe were in Paris bargaining for New Orleans and West Florida, apparently with less and less hope, when Talleyrand asked that seminal question:

"What will you give for the whole?"

The question was forced by Toussaint L'Ouverture, the Black Napoleon of the Antilles.

Was Napoleon himself more fully aware of the import of his defeat? Did he acknowledge it by disposing of the vast, vaguely bounded Louisiana Territory for 60,000,000 francs ($15,000,000) which he soon sank into preparations for an attack on England which was never made? To complete the transaction he violated the treaty of retrocession under which France had promised Spain "not to sell or alienate in any manner the prosperity or enjoyment of Louisiana." He had ridden harshly over his family's protests against the transfer. Was he rationalizing when he said he had established a counterpoise to England? He cried to Talleyrand, "Sixty million francs for an occupation that will not perhaps last a day!" Did he really believe that the American states would quarrel over the territory? When he refused to make its boundaries more specific, was he planning one of those territorial claims which served him for an excuse for war in Europe? If so, Talleyrand saw more clearly that the hope for a French empire in America had been dashed. By way of farewell, he told Livingston:

"You have made a noble bargain for yourselves, and I suppose you will make the most of it."

Jefferson's bargain—made possible by Toussaint L'Ouverture—was indeed a noble one. It may have kept St. Louis from becoming the Paris of a French America, but almost overnight it made St. Louis into an American city, the most important city of the westering nation, a city which now could dream of becoming the capital of the United States.

ix. Up the Wide Missouri

The American flag was raised over St. Louis on March 10, 1804, by Captain Amos Stoddard. Since Upper Louisiana had not been taken over by France from Spain, Stoddard performed that transfer ceremony on the previous day, acting as the deputy for the French Governor in New Orleans, who had no desire to make the trip up the river. He drew up his small party of American soldiers facing the Spaniards under Delassus. The Spanish flag was lowered and the tricolor was run up. The cheers of the inhabitants were so fervid that they almost drowned out the blare of the bugles, the roll of the drums, and the salute of the guns.

This was not the royal lily-banner under which Laclède had meant to establish the town and under which its settlers had meant to live, but it was the flag of France. So they asked Stoddard to let it fly all night. They formed a guard of honor around it. There were toasting and dancing. No Frenchman in St. Louis slept that night. The next day, the 10th, the French flag came down and the American flag, with its 17 stars, was pulled to the top of the staff. Again the bugles blared, the drums rolled, and the volleys were fired. Delassus made a little speech to the assembled Indians:

Delawares, Abenakis, and Saquis and others:
Your old fathers, the Spaniards and the Frenchmen, who grasped by the hand your new father, the Chief of the United States, by an Act of their Good Will, and in virtue of their last treaty, have delivered up all of these lands. The new father will keep and defend the land and protect all of the white and redskins who live thereon. You will live as happily as if the Spaniard was still here.

I have informed your new father, who here takes my place, that since I have been here, the Delawares, Shawnees, and Saquis have always conducted themselves well; that I have always received them kindly; that the chiefs always restrained their young men as much as possible. I have recommended thee, Takinosa, as chief of the natives; that thou hast always labored much and well to maintain a sincere friendship with the whites and that, in consequence of thy good services, I recently presented to thee a medal with a portrait of thy great father, the Spaniard, and letters patent reciting thy good and loyal services. For several days past we have fired off cannon shots that we may announce to all the nations your father, the Spaniard, is going, his heart happy to know that you will be protected and sustained by your new father, and that the smoke of the powder may ascend to the Master of Life, praying him to shower on you all a happy destiny and prosperity and always and always living in good union with the whites.

The cheers were not quite as gay and enthusiastic as the day before. Still, the affair went off with dash and smoothness, thanks to Meriwether Lewis, who had been in and out of St. Louis in the previous months and who had been of great help to Stoddard in arranging the transfer ceremonies. Yet this day did not become the regularly celebrated holiday which, for example, Patriots' Day is in Boston. No doubt the St. Louisans were happier to be under the American flag than under the Spanish. Still, it took a while for them to regard it as their own and not as another alien banner. And the Americans were too busy to commemorate the day. That was done, of course, a hundred years later at the great Louisiana Purchase world's fair. And fifty years after that a handful of St. Louisans, inspired by John Raeburn Green, again went to the riverfront to celebrate the occasion. Dickson Terry, licensed for the day by the federal and municipal authorities as a fireworks expert, also became the chronicler of this event in the *Post-Dispatch:*

A small but dedicated group of men met at a spot on the riverfront, which had once been First and Walnut streets, Wednesday afternoon and raised their glasses in a solemn toast. The glasses contained champagne. The toast was in commemoration of an event which had taken place on that site 150 years ago to the day.

It was on March 10, 1804, that the American flag was raised and formal possession taken by the United States of the upper portion of the Louisiana Territory. This terminated the formalities in connection with the Louisiana Purchase, an event about whose celebration there has been a great deal of talk in the past five years, but no results.

So Wednesday's celebration sprang from a determination on the part of the group that the anniversary would not go completely unrecognized and unsung. Present for the occasion were John Raeburn Green, lawyer; Julian Spotts of the National Park Service and superintendent of Jefferson National Expansion Memorial, and Ernest Kirschten, editorial writer for the Post-Dispatch—three who had been trying for several years to arouse the city to some kind of celebration of the event. Present as interested spectators were Arthur Ross, superintendent of MacArthur Bridge and James Knowles, a drug company executive, and your correspondent.

The group met at Schumacker's restaurant hard by the Old Courthouse where they picked up two bottles of champagne, donated for the occasion by Green, and some fireworks. They then moved in solemn procession down Market street and to the spot on the riverfront which Spotts had previously marked out. They opened the champagne and in glasses which Schumacker's had loaned for the occasion, drank a toast to the Louisiana Purchase. Some teen-age boys playing ball nearby paused momentarily to watch, and then went on with their game.

It was now time for the fireworks, which consisted of three buzz-bombs and three skyrockets, a bomb and a rocket for each 50 years. One of the buzz-bombs fizzled and another turned over. But the third one went off with a resounding bang. The ball players turned to see what was going on. Two of the skyrockets performed as they should, but since it was daylight they weren't effective. It was agreed, however, that it was the spirit that counted.

When Superintendent Spotts completed his narrative of the events which took place on the spot 150 years ago, a toast was proposed to him. But it was discovered that the champagne was all gone, so the group repaired to Schumacker's to talk about old times and changing scenes. The celebration too had joined history.

The American flag meant for the French of St. Louis the invasion of "the Bostons." That was their name for the Yankees and for all Americans from east of the Mississippi. Jefferson had told Stoddard to make as few changes as possible, and, on the whole, things went smoothly enough. Less ambitious than the new fortune seekers, most of the French were inclined to maintain their old pace, to enjoy life, and to wonder why the newcomers did not also do so. But the leaders among the French—men like Auguste Chouteau and his brother, Pierre—held their own.

For all his concern about the constitutionality of his real estate purchase, Jefferson was eager to discover in detail what he had acquired for the United States. He wanted to know just what lay between the Mississippi and the Pacific. So he authorized an exploring expedition under his secretary, Meriwether Lewis, a good soldier with seeing eyes. Of him the President said, "We cannot in the United States find a person who to courage, prudence, habits and health adapted to the woods, and some familiarity with the Indian character, joins a perfect knowledge of botany, natural history, mineralogy, and astronomy. He will readily seize whatever is new in the country he passes through and give us account of new things only."

Lewis accepted the commission eagerly. He bought scientific instruments, a new-fangled air rifle, ordered the Harper's Ferry arsenal to build a collapsible iron boat called the *Experiment*. He read science, and even crammed medicine under the famous Dr. Rush. But most important, he asked his old friend, Lieutenant Billy Clark, who was "as brave as Caesar," who knew the wilderness, and who was good with a drawing pencil, to join him in leading the expedition. Clark's brother, George Rogers Clark, encouraged Billy's desire to sign up. So the young officer wrote to Lewis:

"This is an amence undertaking fraited with numerous dificulties, but my friend, I can assure you, that no man lives with whome I would prefer to undertake and share the Dificulties of such a trip than yourself. My friend, I Join you with hand and Heart." Thus these two embarked on an adventure which was to make them prominent in St. Louis for years.

Even though without a Pentagon full of red tape, the old War Department did its best to make pointless trouble. Lewis had promised Clark a captain's commission. They were to be of equal rank. But the Secretary of War decided "no appointment above that of a Lieutenant in the Corps of the Artilleriests could with propriety be given him." It was one of those decisions which only military minds can make and understand. This stupidity hurt Clark, but Lewis told him to forget about it. He would be Captain Clark, War Department or no War Department, and it was as Captain Clark that he took command of the expedition's base at Rivière du Bois—it is Wood River now—even before Lewis arrived there and before Louisiana became part of the United States.

St. Louis, of course, was the only possible base for such an expedition. It was the gateway of the West, the place to find "mountain men" like Fontenelle, and Indian traders like the aggressive Manuel Lisa, men full of information gathered on trips up the wide Missouri, not to mention Dr. Antoine Saugrain,* who scraped the mercury from his wife's mirror to make the thermometers Mr. Jefferson wanted. Lewis found St. Louis a pleasant place to gather information. He was fascinated by its young ladies. Both officers were entertained by the leading

---

* Dr. Saugrain was a nephew of Dr. Guillotin, inventor of the French instrument of capital punishment.

citizens. Lewis and Clark supplied Captain Stoddard with tobacco and whisky for the Indians who came in "to see their new 'White Father.'" With St. Louis under the American flag, there were even more parties for this pair. But spring was running toward summer. Everything was green and fresh, and it was time to be off. At 4 P.M. on Sunday, May 14, 1804, Clark launched the "Corps of Discovery" and "proceded under a jentle brease up the Missouri."

The expedition covered its first twenty miles to St. Charles in two days. Clark wanted to reload the three boats there after trying them on the water. He also wanted a last talk with Daniel Boone, whom he had consulted frequently in the last few months. And it was at St. Charles that Lewis was to join the company. He had been in St. Louis officially to see some Osage Indian chiefs being escorted to Washington by Pierre Chouteau, and unofficially to say good-by to the beautiful St. Louis girls who had helped him to forget his infatuation with Theodosia Burr Alston, who had dazzled him while he served Jefferson in Washington. A party of citizens accompanied him to St. Charles, where there were another ball and a farewell dinner. Private Cruzat, one of the members of the Lewis and Clark corps, helped entertain by playing the fiddle which was to cheer the explorers so often in the wilderness. But, finally, at 2 P.M. on May 21, an hour and a half late, the two commanders and their thirty-seven men got under way to the cheers of a friendly crowd on the riverbank.

The adventures and the hardships and the discoveries of these men on their way to the Pacific and back to St. Louis are not a proper part of this story. The Lewis and Clark venture was only one of many such based on the city, which very quickly became the capital of the West. The new acquisition having been divided by Congress into the District of Orleans and the Louisiana Territory, the latter came briefly under the governorship of William Henry Harrison and received a peculiarly harsh code of laws, largely ignored and not long kept in force. General Wilkinson—the man who was to make so much mischief in the west with Aaron Burr—took over in St. Louis on September 30, 1804, from Captain Stoddard, who was to become a wealthy owner of western land. Wilkinson sent Lieutenant Zebulon Pike to discover the true source of the Mississippi. After a winter in what is now Minnesota, Pike was back in St. Louis on April 30, 1806. Wilkinson then sent him to explore the headwaters of the Arkansas and the Red rivers. Pike left St. Louis on July 15, 1806. It was on this expedition that his name

was given to Pike's Peak. Henry Adams said that these expeditions
"added little to the stock of science or wealth. Many years must pass
before the vast reaches west of the Mississippi could be brought within
reach of civilization. The crossing of the continent was a great feat, but
nothing more. The French explorers had performed feats almost as
remarkable long before; but in 1805 the country they explored was still
a wilderness." But only in the very short run was Adams correct in
saying that the explorations had "little immediate bearing on the interests of commerce and agriculture."

The Chouteaus, Sublettes, Sarpys, Prattes, and other St. Louis French
already had developed a profitable trade in buffalo, deer, beaver, fox,
otter, muskrat, and other skins and furs. This now grew rapidly. Traders
exchanged strouding, a cloth the Indians used for breechclouts, as well
as blankets, knives, kettles, tin cups, scarlet cloth, beads, earrings,
brooches, and bracelets for pelts at the various trading forts they established on the Missouri and its tributaries.

The one Spaniard in fur trade was Manuel Lisa. He came up from
New Orleans to build the stone warehouse which still stands on the
riverfront, the only relic of the early city. In 1807 Lisa employed John
Colter of the Lewis and Clark corps as his guide and built the first St.
Louis trading post in the West at the mouth of the Big Horn in the
Crow country. Lisa was by turns the partner and the competitor of
the Chouteaus. In the beginning, St. Louis men banded together only
for one year's venture. But Auguste Chouteau had the mind of a
nineteenth-century trust builder and sought to dominate the trade. Lisa
—who later married Mrs. Mary Hempstead Keeney, a Connecticut
woman, widow of John Keeney, a sea captain—gave them a run for
their money.

John Jacob Astor naturally was attracted to the fur trade. He sent an
expedition to the Pacific Northwest by sea. Washington Irving wrote
the story of Astoria. But when this disappointed Astor's expectations,
his agent, Wilson Price Hunt, organized an overland expedition in
St. Louis. Russell Farnham of St. Louis, another of Astor's agents,
crossed not only the Rockies, but also the Pacific and Siberia, paying his
respects en route to Czar Alexander in St. Petersburg before reporting
to Astor in New York.

Of course Astor was regarded as an interloper by the St. Louis junta
when his men began trapping and trading east of the Rockies. Yet it
seemed wiser to Chouteau to join him than to fight him. Thus the

"Western Department" of the American Fur Company was established in St. Louis in 1822. Its operations were directed by Pierre Chouteau, Jr. Associated with him were such famous mountain men as Lucien Fontenelle, Andrew Drips, and Kenneth McKenzie, the "King of the Missouri." At the company's fort at the junction of the Missouri and the Yellowstone, McKenzie dealt with the Indians like a sovereign. A copy of one of his treaties was made by Prince Maximilian, the seventy-year old German scientist who rambled through the western wilderness with such gusto. Here it is:

We send greetings to all mankind. Be it known unto all nations that the most ancient, most illustrious, and most numerous tribes of the red-skins, lords of the soil, from the banks of the great waters unto the tops of the mountains upon which the heavens rest, have entered into a solemn league and covenant to make, preserve and cherish a firm and lasting peace, that, as long as the water runs and the grass grows, they may hail each other as brethren and smoke the calumet in peace and friendship. On the vigil of St. Andrew, in the year 1831, the powerful and distinguished nation of the Blackfeet, Piegan, and Blood Indians by their ambassadors appeared at Fort Union, near the spot where the Yellowstone River unites its current with the Missouri, and in the Council Chamber of the Governor, Kenneth McKenzie, and the principal chiefs of the Assiniboine Nation, the Man-that-holds-the-knife, attended by his chiefs of Council, Bechu, Le Borne, the Sparrow, the Bears's Arm, La Terre qui Tremble, and L' Enfant de Medicin, conforming to all ancient customs and ceremonies, and observing due mystical signs, enjoined by the Great Medicine, the Treaty of Peace and Friendship was entered into by the said high contracting parties, and it is testified by their hands and seals here-unto annexed, hereafter and forever to live as brethren of one, large, united and happy family; and may the Great Spirit who watches over us all, approve our conduct and teach us to love one another.

Done, executed, ratified, and confirmed at Fort Union, on the day and year first written, in the presence of James Archdale Hamilton.

In competition with the American Fur Company—generally called imperiously "The Company"—was the Rocky Mountain Fur Company, the outgrowth of an expedition undertaken in 1822–23 by General William H. Ashley of St. Louis. This seemed to be without the favor of the gods, white or red. At the very outset a wagonload of powder exploded at what is now Washington Avenue and Ninth Street, killing several men. Yet a series of disasters did not keep Ashley from discovering the Great South Pass through the Rockies, and reaching the Great Salt Lake. The company eventually did prosper, but Ashley sold out to William Sublette (old Cut Face) and Jedediah Smith and David Jackson. After he sold out, he was elected to Congress for the unexpired term of Spencer Pettis, who had been killed on Bloody Island, the St. Louis dueling ground, by Major Thomas Biddle, brother of Nicholas Biddle of the Bank of the United States. These three in turn sold out to the Rocky Mountain Fur Company, formed by Broken-Hand Fitzpatrick, Jean Baptiste Gervais, Milton Sublette, Jim Bridger, and Henry Fraeb. Since Ashley's first expedition, this was the most venturesome outfit. It profited accordingly, drew the attacks of the American Fur Company, but also attracted the most able of the mountain men. Among them, in addition to the partners, were Joe Meek, Kit Carson, Louis Vasquez, Doc Newell, and Moses (Black) Harris, each one legendary.

Foreseeing a decline in the demand for beaver pelts with the introduction of the silk hat, Astor quit the fur trade in 1834. Chouteau and the others prospered for a while longer. Also on the cautious side were William Sublette and Robert Campbell. The latter's home, incidentally, is now a St. Louis museum. These two former Ashley lieutenants formed Sublette & Campbell as a carrying and outfitting firm for the Rocky Mountain Fur Company. General Clark's brother, Reuben, was a partner in the Missouri Fur Company, and there were, of course, numerous free trappers who sold their pelts at an annual company rendezvous, and later at the company posts, or even brought them to St. Louis. For most of them it was an unprofitable business. Often the fur harvest did not meet the expenses of an expedition. The big money was made by the Chouteaus, the Astors, and their partners who sold the pelts on the markets of London and Paris, New Orleans and New York. But it was the mountain men, the harvesters of the pelts which were piled high in the stinking "fur rows" above the levee, who made St. Louis the primary fur center of the United States.

This it continues to be, even though the uncounted buffalo and beaver have all but vanished. The fur crop was as ruthlessly exploited as were the forests of virgin timber, and the trade declined accordingly. The railroads also helped to change it. First, St. Louis fur merchants sent out buyers by train. Later they took to advertising, urging trappers to ship their furs to St. Louis and promising a check by return mail. Today the Fouke Fur Company still holds the government contract

for the killing of Alaska's Pribilof Islands seals and for the auction of
the skins in St. Louis.

The fur trade was started by St. Louis Creoles and other West-
wandering men who became hardened children of Nature, tougher than
the Indians. They were the hunter-trappers who went into the wilderness for pelts. Most of these *engagés* came down-river to St. Louis in the
fall and set out again with the fur company boats in the spring. But
some of the mountain men rarely came nearer civilization than the forts
which the Chouteaus and Lisa built far up the Missouri, or the big
rendezvous held once a year in the Indian country. Joseph M. Field
(1810–1856) recalled one of these "independents," old Jean Tisan,
who was asked at a rendezvous whether Madame Tisan of St. Louis
was his wife.

"Oui, Madame Tisan, St. Louis," said the trapper. "I was no see
her more zen fifteen year,—St. Louis, too, bidam! St. Louis all Yankee,
and Madame Tisan all hell, vat you call, an' I say good-bye to all de
two! I was make St. Louis myself, wis' Laclède, mais, first ting, I marry
and bring Madame over from Caho', and next ting, contree belong to
Yankee doodle, and we have freedom, bidam, wis' de constable and de
jury, and tax, and de all help Madame Tisan to faire come ze debbil
in my maison. She make balls for de stranger, and I stay way hunt and
nevare come back. . . ."

After that the men at the rendezvous could only sing:

> Adieu to St. Louis, I bid you er-dieu;
> Likewise to the French and the mers-qui-ters, too,
> For of all the nations I do you disdain. . . .

There were fantastic bouts of eating, drinking, singing, fighting, and
squaw-wenching when the trappers sold their pelts and bought their
supplies at these gatherings. When they were alone again, the men
could make a breakfast of lye corn hominy. They might have a bite of
fat pork and a biscuit at midday. And they supped more often on tallow
than they gorged on buffalo hump. They swam the coldest streams
and exposed themselves to the wildest storms in pathless country. If
they were stricken by the ague, endurance was their only medicine
unless there was an Indian squaw to comfort them instead of an Indian
brave to scalp them. It is estimated that two fifths of them were killed
by Indians or died in wilderness accidents. Despite their scars, they
were a handsome, athletic lot, colorful with red sashes around their
beaded buckskin coats. They were great singers—anyway, loud and

lusty ones. An old French chanson or a ballad of their own improvising drove all thought of hardship from the campfire.

Just about as rugged were the boatmen on the rivers, especially the keelboatmen. Flatboats or broadhorns—so called because of their protruding oars—made only downstream floats. At their destination they were sold, usually for what they would bring as lumber. But the keelboats also made the tedious upstream trip. Sail helped against the current. So did poling. Often they were "bushwhacked," the crews working them along by pulling on tree limbs which extended over the water. As often as not, they were pulled along by men who had gone ashore with one end of a hawser. Stumbling in and out of the water, the men proclaimed themselves to be "half horse and half alligator." These were linsey-woolsey rather than buckskin types, but they were as full of bravado as the mountain men. Crews of from 20 to 36 men brought keelboats upstream as much as 15 miles a day—and the boats were from 40 to 120 feet long and from 7 to 20 feet in the beam, carrying from 15 to 50 tons of freight as well as passengers. Of course it took only half as many men to shoot the chutes downstream. The best fighter on each boat wore a red feather in his hat. Inevitably frontier writers glamorized the keelboatmen, and they made one of them, Mike Fink, the Paul Bunyan of the western waters.

The Reverend Timothy Flint and the Reverend Peter Cartwright, doughty wilderness preachers, pictured the rivermen more or less accurately. The *St. Louis Reveille,* after it was established in 1844, published stories by Joseph M. Field, Morgan Neville, Emerson Bennett, John S. Robb, and Colonel Charles Keemle. They knew their characters, but many of their accounts were out-and-out romances. Jared Sparks, Mark Twain, John G. Neihardt, Constance Rourke, Vernon Parrington, and Bernard De Voto sifted some of the facts from the fiction. Walter Blair and Franklin J. Meine still are at the job. Even the London *Times Literary Supplement* in 1933 carried an article on Mike Fink.

There really were two Finks, one composed of the more or less sheer stuff of fancy and the other of all too common clay. The feats of the legendary Mike outdid even those of Jessie Benton Fremont's mountain man hero, Kit Carson. This Fink was "kind-hearted as a Connecticut grandmother but rough as a Rocky Mountain bear." He was a better man with a quick-loading, far-shooting, hard-hitting Kentucky rifle than old Daniel Boone himself. He never missed his fillee (ration) of whisky, and when he "gasconaded" in the Green Tree Tavern in St. Louis he swore by "corn-cobs, painters and catermounts." Despite drinking bouts and rough-and-tumble fights, he was the able, river-wise master of his craft and crew. Utterly fearless, he "walked tall" into gangs of river pirates and other assorted doers of evil, never coming out of such a "caterumpus" second best, always maintaining virtue triumphant. Ready for fight or frolic when he and his boys set out to "regulate" New Orleans at the end of a trip, he was more than a match for the Johnny-be-damns, as the boatmen called the *gens d'armes*.

He loved and was loved by pretty Mary Benson, but while he was taking a boat down the river her sinister father, Deacon Benson, married her off to a river pirate named Talbot, "the ugliest white man yet." Mary could only pine and die. Mike raised her son, Carpenter, as his own. His loyalty to dear, dead Mary, however, did not prevent him from being a conquering Casanova too. Some contradictions are inevitable in the legend of a man who was compared with Apollo, Hercules, Jason, Galahad, Roland, the Lionheart and Davy Crockett. And always there are belittlers around—for example the character who started the story that Mike and his boys once tried to break up a camp meeting being conducted at Alton by the Reverend Cartwright and that the backwoods preacher licked the last ounce of starch out of Mike in a no-holds-barred, catch-as-catch-can, everything's-fair battle. Cartwright himself repudiated that canard.

Mike Fink began to lose fights only when Dr. Menra Hopewell, a colleague of the redoubtable Dr. McDowell, and the Sunday School writers went to work on his story. About 1860 they began to pit him against another keelboater, Jack Pierce, who killed rams by butting heads with them. Jack had promised his mother to stay out of the doggeries on the bluff above the St. Louis riverfront. In him, Mike met not only a strong boy but also a good boy and, naturally, his match. The prohibition preachers just had to have it that way. And they were near the truth, at least, when they sent him West to die in a brawl among the mountain men. But no epic whimpers out that way. Down on the Cowskin River in the Ozarks, the fishing guides—no mean boatmen themselves—will tell you that, disgusted with prohibitionists and steamboats that came up the river "without hand, hoss or hawser," the greatest of the keelboaters turned himself into a giant catfish. And whenever he remembers the attempts to degrade him, he swishes his tail and lashes **up** an awful powerful storm.

The story of the genuine Mike Fink—he Frenchified his name by spelling it Miche Fincke or even Finque—also is on the incredible side, but sordid. Born a Pennsylvania German near Fort Pitt about 1775, he became one of a band of Indian scouts that got into trouble with the army. In fact, he was a loud-boasting frontier hoodlum on the prowl for trouble—which was easy enough to find in the wilderness, which had a natural attraction for lawless characters, many of them fugitives from courts east of the mountains. Fink took to river-boating and worked his way down the Monongahela and the Ohio to the Mississippi. He became a notorious habitué of the St. Louis riverfront saloons, the hiring halls for keelboatmen. That he ever was the "patron" of such a boat seems doubtful. It is more likely that he pirated property than that cargoes were entrusted to him. But he was a crack rifle shot. In his cups—which were big ones—he would on a small wager shoot a can of whisky off the head of a companion. He varied this William Tell game when he tested the devotion of his women by blazing away at a can held between their thighs.

His favorite partner in these touching displays seems to have been Mira Hodgkins, a Kentucky woman whose infatuation stood on no ceremony. She followed Mike up and down the river, utterly at the bully boy's disposal. She got him out of some serious scrapes, once saving his life in New Orleans. She was not the Mary Benson of the legend, yet there was a limit to the spells of abuse and disdain which she would endure. When her passion turned to hate, she married another keelboater, a rival of Fink's named Talbot, in sheer spite. According to the legends, the steamboats drove Mike off the river, but there still were hundreds of keelboats on the Mississippi a quarter of a century after he died. Perhaps Mike's last fight with his woman turned him from *la belle rivière*. More likely, his reputation had become so bad that he found it difficult to get a job on a boat. Gone were the days in which Mike could

> Dance all night, till broad daylight,
> And go home with the girls in the morning.

Or sing:

> Oh, some call me rak-ish, and some call me wild,
> And some say that I have pretty maids beguiled;
> But they are all liars by the powers er-bove,
> For I'm guilt-i of nothing but innercent love.

On March 20, 1822, the following notice appeared in the Missouri Republican:

To enterprising young men. The subscriber wishes to engage one hundred young men to ascend the Missouri River to its source, there to be employed for one, two or three years. For particulars enquire of Major Andrew Henry near the lead mines in the County of Washington, who will ascend with, and command, the party; or of the subscriber near St. Louis.

(Signed) William H. Ashley.

As a man with scorpions in his heart, Mike Fink joined General Ashley's Rocky Mountain Fur Company expedition to the juncture of the Missouri and the Yellowstone. Also on the scene were his rival, Talbot, and his friend, Carpenter, the legendary son of Mary Benson. Others present were Jim Bridger, Jedediah Smith and Hugh Glass, the grizzly fighter. It was hard to cheer Mike out of his ill humor. He quarreled even with Carpenter. But one day, as the whisky can was going from hand to hand, Mike begged Carpenter to let bygones be bygones and to set the can on his head once more. Mike stepped off 70 yards and took aim, then he deliberately lowered his rifle and killed Carpenter. Talbot immediately shot Fink—some say to revenge Carpenter, whom he had befriended, and others say because Fink had accused him of stealing a blanket. Talbot himself was drowned in a mountain torrent a few days later. Such were the simple facts as reported to St. Louisans on July 16, 1823, on the authority of "a letter received in town from one of General Ashley's expedition." Few tears were shed in St. Louis where, as Charles Cist wrote, "Fink's character was worthless and vile." Before long, more elaborate stories gained circulation. As Joseph M. Field, later a Fink adulator, said, this was "the first gathering of the mythic haze." But life as lived in the mountains and on the rivers generally was more stark than mythic.

x. Treason in the West

The cult of the pioneer is one of the most romantic items in American folklore. It was spread by schoolmasters who abused history to inculcate an overweening patriotism. The pedagogue-patriots taught that the men and women who crossed the Appalachians were, all of them, strong, noble souls, determined by their labors and privations to transform the wilderness into a new utopia of wealth, culture, and high-minded living. They were the sturdy descendants of sturdy, liberty-loving, God-fearing English yeomen. And never a word about how these yeomen, ignorant and bigoted, enlisted in Cromwell's New Model army and ran cold steel through the breasts of the women of Drogheda. The character of many a pioneer was beyond reproach, but the frontier also was a natural magnet for fugitives from courts, jails, creditors, and wives. Adventurers were attracted to the life of hatchet, knife, and rifle. Speculators saw fortunes to be made by claiming the lands of Indians, Spaniards, and Frenchmen, whom they held almost equally in contempt. Some of the rapacious plundered travelers on wilderness roads and rivers. The more imaginatively avaricious schemed against the tramontane government and perfidiously accepted the pay of foreigners. Men as prominent as George Rogers Clark, Senator William Blount, and Andrew Jackson were involved in conspiracy and filibustering. But the most grasping and most devious surely was James Wilkinson, commanding general of the army of the young republic.

Wilkinson was at the Cabildo in New Orleans with Governor William C. C. Claiborne on December 20, 1803, for the transfer of Louisiana to the United States. When it was divided the next year along the 33rd parallel into the District of Orleans and the Territory of Louisiana, he became governor of the northern section, with his capital in St. Louis. Jefferson, despite his settled principle that civil and military authority should not rest in the same hands, made this appointment on the plea of Wilkinson's old friend, Vice President Aaron Burr. He erred further by appointing James Brown, brother of Mrs. Burr's sister, territorial secretary in St. Louis, and J. B. Prevost, Burr's stepson, judge in New

Orleans. The preposterously proud and pompous Wilkinson was far less fit for the post in St. Louis than the crude but honest Claiborne was for authority in New Orleans. The former French prefect, Pierre Clement Laussat, perceptively reported to Paris:

It was hardly possible that the Government of the United States should have made a worse beginning, and that it should have sent two men (Messrs. Claiborne, Governor, and Wilkinson, General) less fit to attract affection. The first, with estimable private qualities, has little capacity and much awkwardness, and is extremely beneath his place; the second, already known here in a bad way, is a flighty, rattleheaded fellow, often drunk, who has committed a hundred impertinent follies. Neither the one nor the other understands a word of French or Spanish. They have on all occasions, and without delicacy, shocked the habits, the prejudices, the character of the population.

Born in Maryland in 1757, Wilkinson served in the Revolution under his friend, Benedict Arnold. After Saratoga, Horatio Gates sent him to report the victory to Congress. In doing so, Wilkinson magnified his role by claiming credit for a feat actually performed by Colonel John Hardin. He was involved in the Conway Cabal, the plot to depose George Washington as supreme commander. The intrigue came to light through a leak by Wilkinson, another example of his duplicity. He was in trouble because of his accounts after serving from 1779 to 1781 as clothier general. Leaving the army, he tried farming in Kentucky. There he indulged in land speculations and was involved in the several conventions called to separate the western territory from Virginia. To the Spaniards, worried about possible war with the United States, Wilkinson said he was promoting separatism to weaken Washington. After he took an oath of loyalty to Carlos IV, Jean Ventura Morales, the intendant at New Orleans, designated him as Agent No. 13. Wilkinson received a Spanish pension of $2000 a year for twenty years. When Morales suspended the right of Ohio and Mississippi valley farmers to deposit their produce at New Orleans for transshipment, it was extended to Wilkinson as a personal privilege. He profited accordingly. His speculations, however, were unsuccessful. So he re-entered the army, and fought in the Indian War under "Mad Anthony" Wayne. This general accused Wilkinson of plotting to displace him, but the schemer managed to clear himself; and when Wayne died in 1796, Wilkinson succeeded to the command of the army. Congress, however, did not raise his rank from Brigadier to Major General. (Even the

vainglorious, gold-laced Wilkinson never dreamed of five stars!)
Wilkinson's military career culminated in the fiasco of the invasion
of Canada, in the War of 1812. This meant another court martial.
Yet while poor old General Hull was condemned to death for the
surrender of Detroit—a sentence never carried out—Wilkinson was ac-
quitted once more. Always officially innocent, in the words of Thomas
Perkins Abernethy: "the Commanding General of the United States
Army went into a niche of infamy unique in American history."

Wilkinson reached the lowest depth of shame by participation in
the Burr Conspiracy while serving as governor in St. Louis. This scheme
to make Aaron Burr the ruler of a vast western empire had two immediate objectives. The first was to separate the trans-Appalachian territory—especially western Pennsylvania, Ohio, Kentucky, Tennessee,
and all of the Louisiana Territory—from the United States. To this,
the conspirators hoped to add Mexico, Florida, and other Spanish
possessions by conquest and revolution. Thus Wilkinson was a traitor
both to the United States and to the Spanish king who employed him.
Nor was he a dupe of the persuasive Burr. In fact, the murky evidence
strongly suggests that he originated this grandiose scheme.

The bonds of the Union then were not as strong as they were half a
century later on the eve of the Civil War. Secession was not the unpardonable political sin to men who had rebelled against the English
crown. The New England Federalists also contemplated separation in
their bitterness over the national expansion which threatened their
supremacy. The Creoles, abandoned by Napoleon, felt no deep loyalty
to the republic to which their territory had been sold. And in New
Orleans and St. Louis they had just cause for complaint when, contrary
to the terms of the Louisiana Purchase, they were treated more like
conquered people than like fellow citizens. They resisted the setting
aside of their laws and institutions. They made a saint of the troublesome Spanish Capuchin, Antonio de Sedella, when the Irish-American
vicar-general, Father Patrick Walsh, suspended him. Despite the
austerity and good works of Père Antoine, he once had been sent back
to Spain by Governor Esteban Miro. But now the Creoles appealed on
his behalf through France to Rome, and were angered when they were
upbraided for this by Secretary of State Madison.

The free Negroes, too, were alarmed by the racial prejudice of the
Americans. Under the Spaniards they had maintained a militia company. This was immediately disbanded by the American authorities

who, in a slave economy, saw a threat in Negroes under arms. Exposed to intensified discrimination, the disarmed freemen developed their own fears.

"Thus, my dear sir," wrote Jeremiah Brown, "this territory appears to me at length on the eve of eternal alienation from the American Union. . . . One would suppose us rather in preparation to form a department of France than an American state." The only hope Brown saw was that the rising Creole opposition might "be conciliated by indulgence and consideration."

Wilkinson deviously intensified Creole grievances in the hope of exploiting them later in furtherance of the conspiracy, yet the only support he and Burr received came from the so-called Mexican Association of New Orleans which, under the leadership of Daniel Clark, hoped to foment revolution in Spanish territory—purely for mercenary reasons. No Creole in New Orleans or St. Louis joined in the plot to dismember the nation. Yet it enmeshed such "Bostons" as Senator John Adair of Kentucky, Senator Jonathan Dayton of New Jersey, Senator John Smith of Ohio, Representative Matthew Lyon of Kentucky, and that romantic Irishman, Harman Blennerhasset. His wife dreamed of becoming lady-in-waiting to Burr's brilliant daughter, Theodosia, who was to be the crown princess of the new realm. Theodosia's husband, Joseph Alston of Charleston, probably the richest planter in South Carolina and later governor of that state, poured money into the scheme. Andrew Jackson entertained Burr in Nashville and built boats for him. Nobody knows how deeply Old Hickory was involved. The plot naturally attracted speculators in dubious land titles which were to be validated by the new government. It also was made attractive and given a gloss of patriotism by the imminence of war with Spain. Western feeling ran high after the Spanish authorities in 1802 withdrew the right of deposit at New Orleans. Americans overlooked the provocation they had given by their illicit money exchanges and widespread smuggling— not to mention, as Thomas D. Clark acknowledged, the way they "caroused, played practical jokes, swarmed into bordellos, gawked in the churches, cluttered up the already filthy city with their rubbish, blustered through crowds shouting lusty oaths, and in general disrupted life." The Louisiana Purchase opened up the port of New Orleans, but new provocations arose from the dispute over the boundary of Louisiana and the Spanish territory, the American desire for West Florida and Mobile, and the intensified Spanish fears of the growing power of the United States.

It was of this bouillabaisse of greed and resentment that Burr and Wilkinson proposed to make their feast. Out of the vice presidency on March 4, 1804, Burr needed to replenish his fortune, and his old friend Wilkinson talked glowingly of the opportunities in the West. For months before Wilkinson left for St. Louis the two were closeted over maps, hatching their plans. In addition to raising forces in the western states, it would be necessary to have naval support at New Orleans and for the contemplated Mexican invasion. So Burr remained in Washington temporarily to involve the British ambassador, Anthony Merry, and to try to obtain through him the help of the Royal Navy. Wilkinson, meanwhile, assumed his office in St. Louis. He arrived early in 1805.

The French of the city had made common cause during the Revolution with the Americans, but they were not happy at the prospect of being inundated by them. Major James Bruff, who had been in command since the departure of Captain Amos Stoddard and who continued to serve under the new governor-general, soon observed that it seemed to be Wilkinson's purpose to make the French dissatisfied, but he alienated Americans too. The latter armed themselves with knives and pistols, while the French made no secret of their disappointment in the change of regimes. The people who had happily entertained Lewis and Clark were annoyed by the loud talk and heavy drinking of Wilkinson, whom they regarded as a vulgar popinjay. He sought to ingratiate himself with Chouteau, Manuel Lisa, and other well-to-do traders for profit's sake. They were politic but avoided undue intimacy. As for the Americans, Wilkinson favored the few Federalists rather than the Democratic majority. Thus was the community made factious and rebellious. Wilkinson's appointment as governor was confirmed only with the help of Jefferson's Federalist adversaries, and by just a few votes. But this did not chasten the general.

When in January of 1806 a messenger arrived in St. Louis with news of his confirmation, the general immediately ordered a public celebration. A large quantity of wood and several barrels of tar were set afire. As reflections of the festal flames reddened the Mississippi, church bells were rung and cannons boomed out a "federal salute." The band was lined up to play for the crowd. Corks were drawn and kegs were broached so that all might toast Wilkinson with wine and whisky. Although a storm broke shortly after the celebration started, it went on

until after midnight. A few days later a banquet was given by the leading townsmen. Chouteau at this affair proposed a toast to the General:
"Dollars to his friends, and lead for his enemies."

The St. Louis Creoles probably were never better disposed toward
Wilkinson than on this occasion. They loved festivities, dancing, and
parties, as Captain Stoddard had quickly learned. "Nothing ever re-
strains them from amusement," he wrote rather complainingly—perhaps because he had spent $622.75 of government money to return
the hospitality shown him after he raised the flag on the riverfront. Wilkinson had no such scruples, but the hospitality shown him was discreet.
He made no friends in St. Louis. The merchants may have been unwilling to risk the harassments of official disfavor but, like their friends
in New Orleans, they were eager for free and easy self-government
such as they had been accustomed to since Laclède's time. Less wealthy
citizens disagreed more openly with Wilkinson's notion that Creoles were
unfit to run their own affairs and needed military government.

Suspicions were aroused even more quickly among the officers of
the American garrison. In feeling out these men, Wilkinson necessarily
revealed at least the Spanish aspect of the conspiracy. He pushed preparations for a campaign against Mexico under cover of defending the
disputed Sabine River boundary between Louisiana and Texas. Zebulon
Pike was sent on his mission of exploration to give Wilkinson a "peek"
at the route to Santa Fe and Mexico which, the general wrote to Adair,
"I have reserved for my own triumphant entry, that I have been rec-
onnoitering and exploring for years." Meanwhile he advised his Spanish employers to arrest any members of the Lewis and Clark expedition
who might fall into their hands! Far from the schemers, the explorers
had spent the winter of 1804–1805 at Fort Mandan, a St. Louis outpost
fifty miles north of Bismarck, North Dakota, where an intensely cold
season was warmed by voluptuous Indian celebrations.

In the spring Burr followed Wilkinson west, enlisting support for his
imperial design. The general met him at Fort Massac, near the mouth
of the Ohio. They had their heads together for four days, from June 6
to June 10. Wilkinson gave Burr letters to Daniel Clark and others
in New Orleans, and, as Burr wrote to Theodosia, "The General and
his officers fitted me out with an elegant barge—sails, colors, and ten
oars—with a sergeant and ten able, faithful hands." Full of confidence
and optimism, Burr returned by way of St. Louis, arriving on September 11. He remained with Wilkinson almost two weeks. He strutted

about town, asking injudicious questions of citizens as prominent as Judge Rufus Easton. Burr was just as brazen when he got back to Washington. This was the high tide of the conspiracy; it soon began to ebb. Hope of British aid ended with the death of Pitt. The new prime minister, Fox, wrote to Merry accepting his resignation, which the envoy had not tendered. Burr and Dayton now demanded help from the Spanish minister, Yrujo, against whose country they were plotting. The desperate conspirators even considered a raid on Washington—on the Treasury and the Navy Yard. But they lacked that kind of boldness. Instead they began to deceive and cheat each other.

Instead of being intimidated, Yrujo started a backfire, giving the press such details of the plot as he had learned. Soon after Burr left St. Louis, Wilkinson received a letter from Daniel Clark saying that Burr had talked too much in New Orleans and Tennessee. Joseph H. Daveiss, the federal attorney at Frankfort, Kentucky, went to St. Louis to investigate, and sent a letter of warning to President Jefferson. Similar letters reached the President from General William Eaton and Major Bruff. Articles appeared in the United States *Gazette* of Philadelphia and the Richmond *Enquirer*. Daveiss started the *Western World* to expose the scheme, while poor Blennerhasset published a series of articles in the Marietta, Ohio, *Gazette* which advocated it. John Randolph of Roanoke thundered in Congress. But President Jefferson remained strangely silent.

Rebuffed by his officers and alarmed by the publicity, Wilkinson also fell into silence. Burr sent him a long letter in cipher on May 31, 1806, announcing that everything was ready for the expedition of conquest. Wilkinson was to rank second only to Burr. British naval support was assured. Orders already had been given contractors to furnish Wilkinson with provisions for six months. Burr's forces would rendezvous at Blennerhassett's island in the Ohio on November 1. He would reach the Mississippi with 500 to 1000 men, with more to follow. "The people are ready to receive us. The gods invite us to glory and fortune; it remains to be seen whether we deserve the boon." A second letter with more detailed plans came to Wilkinson late in July by a confidential messenger. In it Burr asked, "Are you ready? Are your numerous associates ready? Wealth and glory! Louisiana and Mexico!"

Wilkinson was not taken in by these blandishments. Burr's egregious conceit had become a menace. The general did not propose to go down to ruin with him. Instead he would turn developments to his own advantage. So he informed his Spanish friends that he meant to protect their interests; and, to have the necessary freedom of action, he obtained a truce along the Sabine, where a border war was imminent. Then he sent a carefully edited version of Burr's revealing letter to Jefferson. It reached the President on October 21. Action no longer could be put off. A Cabinet meeting was held October 22. John Graham was named to replace Wilkinson in St. Louis, and the general was given sweeping powers to defend New Orleans, Burr's ostensible objective. Graham was sent westward to rouse the governors of Ohio, Kentucky, and Tennessee against the conspiracy. Burr's second westward progress became that of a fugitive rather than a conqueror. He managed to escape from Cincinnati and from Nashville, and with a handful of men he got by Fort Massac before orders to apprehend him reached that post. Others of his followers, however, were seized on the Ohio. When Burr heard that Wilkinson had virtually taken over New Orleans from Governor Claiborne, that he was tyrannizing over the city in the name of defending it against a mighty army, and that he had seized Adair and other Burr agents, the conspirator could only attempt to escape into the Indian country. But he was captured, and so the scene was set for the famous trial, conducted by Chief Justice John Marshall in the Eagle Tavern in Richmond. Burr was arraigned on March 30, 1807. The actual trial started on August 3, and Burr finally was acquitted on October 20 because, as the now disillusioned Blennerhassett said, "Mr. Marshall, at last, has delivered an elaborate opinion purporting that he cannot commit any of us for treason; not because we did not have it in our hearts, but because we did none with our hands."

Wilkinson perforce was the government's chief witness against Burr, although he himself escaped indictment by the grand jury by only two votes. On December 31 John Randolph, having declined Wilkinson's challenge to a duel because he would not treat the general as an equal, introduced a resolution in the House calling for an investigation of his conduct. It was tabled, but in self-defense the general was forced to request a court martial. It was convened in Morin's Tavern in Washington, January 11. The evidence, especially regarding his role as Agent No. 13, was damning, but his Spanish employers, still trusting him, supplied documents of a sort which enabled the court to let him go.

XI. Death on the Natchez Trace

On September 23, 1806, while Wilkinson was on the Sabine negotiating his truce with the Spaniards, the Lewis and Clark Corps of Discovery, after an absence of two years and four months, and 6000 miles in the wilderness, again was in St. Louis.

The welcoming festivities outdid those of the departure. For more than a week there were daily dinners and balls. The ladies composed poems and songs in honor of the heroes. The men proposed toasts. The bitter taste left by Wilkinson was forgotten in the joy of greeting the gallant Captain Lewis and his friend Billy Clark once more. But the celebrating had to end. The men were mustered out, and Lewis took off for muddy little Washington to make sure they would receive proper recognition. Clark agreed to join Chouteau in escorting some Mandan chiefs to Monticello a little later.

Lewis again was made warmly and intimately at home in President Jefferson's family. He had no trouble with the War Department or with Congress about recognition for his men. Each was given extra pay and a grant of thirty-two acres of land. Lewis himself was given 1500 acres and Clark 1000. Lewis was appointed Governor of the Louisiana Territory, and Clark was appointed its Indian agent and promoted to the rank of brigadier general, the third of the Clarks to wear a general's stars. The President hardly could have made better appointments to placate the ill will aroused by Wilkinson. But he had a more immediate assignment for the explorer.

Lewis found Jefferson in a troubled mood. There was danger of war with England or France or both, and even with Spain. Many Americans were still hankering for the Floridas. England was seizing American sailors at sea. And Napoleon was seizing American ships—in the end more than 200, worth at least $10,000,000—in most of the ports of Europe, not without justification, since many of them were smuggling for the British. At the same time, Randolph of Roanoke was leading the attack on the President in Congress, and John Marshall was sniping at him from the bench. Most irritating, however, was the Burr affair. The "veneered profligate" was about to be brought to trial in

Richmond. The proceedings would be almost entirely in the hands of the anti-Jeffersonians, and they were determined to turn them against the President, chiefly by attacking his star witness, Wilkinson. Yet Jefferson could not demean himself by personally entering the Richmond arena against the man who had battled him for the presidency. Under the circumstances, he wanted a trusted friend on the scene. His former secretary postponed his departure for St. Louis to accept the frustrating mission.

In Richmond Lewis again saw Burr's daughter, Theodosia, the brilliant woman who had charmed him years earlier in Washington. Now, as then, her husband was on his plantation in South Carolina. She was as attractive as ever. Lewis took her to dinner and talked with her through a long, long evening. She was as engaging as when he had taught her to ride. Her pleasure in the company of the dashing young officer then did not mean that she loved him. She might enjoy the talk of the gallant explorer now, but that meant no more. Since the outcome of the trial was foregone, she was leaving at once for the South. Gaily she told Lewis that they would meet again. But he knew the promise was meaningless. Melancholia enshrouded him. About the only news that cheered him came in a letter from Clark, announcing that he had married Julia Hancock in Kentucky. As a wedding gift the dejected Lewis sent the couple his favorite pair of ivory-handled dueling pistols.

Then he hurried back to St. Louis to assume his duties as governor and to find a home for the Clarks. They, too, were soon in St. Louis. The newly-wed general invited the bachelor governor to share the house. But Lewis refused to impose on the Clarks. He would move in with Auguste Chouteau; it was better for "two wayward bachelors" to live together. Meriwether Lewis found himself behind a desk, as he never had been, except in those few years with Jefferson. But those had been different. His duties had been stimulating and exciting. His work in St. Louis was drudgery, distasteful to a man who cared so much for hunting and soldiering. As governor he had to concern himself with politics, which he did not like. Then there were Indian troubles. Unlike the French, the Americans were not tactful with the Indians—as if the British were not causing enough trouble by supplying them with arms!

There were abuses of the fur trade. Worst of all were the troubles about land titles. Each day seemed to bring more of the frontier riffraff: the squatters, who settled where they would, the developers, who sold what they would, and the shysters, who claimed what they would. The

President's land commissioners would adjourn to the Oak and Acorn saloon, and the controversies were brought to Lewis.

His distasteful occupations depressed him. Gradually he became careless about his clothes. He began to drink too much. Wandering along the riverfront one night, he was approached by a Creole derelict named Piernea, who did not recognize the governor. Lewis took him home and made him into a sort of body servant, giving him clothes, whisky, tobacco, and an allowance. Lewis also had the services of a Negro, simply named Jim. Both retainers were grateful and faithful, but they could not lighten his burden or cheer him in his dark moods. Clark and his wife tried to do that, but they also found it difficult. Letters from the busy President were few, and most of them urged Lewis to prepare his journals for publication; science should have had the benefit of them long ago. But Jefferson also sent cheering words. He announced the naming of a grandchild, Meriwether Lewis Randolph. The name of Meriwether Lewis would be carried into a new generation. The Clarks named their first son Meriwether Lewis too. The bachelor would go to their home and lift the child out of its cradle, hold it high. The Clarks were filled with hope when they saw this, but the smiles were too rare.

A new administration took over in Washington. Vouchers which Lewis had signed for medicine for the Indians were returned unpaid. He emptied his own purse and he borrowed from his army friend, Stoddard, now a major. But he also ranted and fumed at those in Washington who had questioned his word and impugned his Virginia honor. Clark told him not to become so wrought up about stupid clerks far away; these were petty annoyances, not matters of life and death. But Lewis was sure that lies were being told about him. He became quite sick, physically. Clark doctored him, and Piernea nursed him. They both told him to stop worrying, that worry was making him sick.

Then, in the midst of deepening melancholy, Lewis announced that he was going to Washington to defend himself. There was no dissuading him. Accompanied by Piernea and Jim, he boarded a flatboat that was to take them to New Orleans. From there they were to go to Washington by sea. But on reaching Chickasaw Bluffs, now Memphis, the party heard reports of hostile British action at sea. Lewis could not risk being captured. He could not risk losing his all-important records. So he decided to make his way to Washington by land—over the Natchez Trace, the crude wilderness trail over which Burr had ridden a few years earlier. Officers at the army post told him that he was not in condition for so many days in the saddle. But he bought two pack mules for his records. Then he borrowed three army horses for himself and his servants. Major John Neely, the Cherokee Indian agent at the Bluffs, decided that since he could not stop Lewis, he would accompany him. As they rode through the forest, now displaying the first lapidary touches of autumn, Lewis complained of terrible headaches. Neely worried about what would happen to him when the weather turned bad.

On October 10, 1809, thunder and torrential rains broke upon them. The two pack mules stampeded into the forest with the precious records. Piernea and Jim took after them. Major Neely begged Lewis to ride to the house of the first white settler along trail. He promised that he would help recover mules and records. So a thoroughly wet, distraught, and frightening man reined up at the door of John Griner, seventy-two miles from Nashville, and asked the farmer's wife for shelter. The Griners accommodated travelers along the Trace, so she opened the door to him, but not before taking her children to the adjoining kitchen house. Somewhat later, the storm having passed, the two servants rode up with the mules. They reassured the woman somewhat. She prepared a meal. But Lewis would eat very little. He raved and roared; then he became quite calm:

"Madame," he said, "this is a very pleasant evening." He lit his pipe and paced up and down in the yard. Then he began to rant again about his enemies in Washington. The woman had prepared a bed for him, but he spurned it. Accustomed to wilderness life and sleeping on the ground, he had his servants spread his buffalo robe on the floor. Mrs. Griner retired to the kitchen house and her children, telling the servants they could sleep in the barn, a hundred yards away. But here is more of the story as it was first set down in detail by Dr. Alexander Wilson, the ornithologist, who had it directly from Mrs. Griner and published it in the *Philadelphia Folio* in November, 1811:

The kitchen is only a few paces from the room where Lewis was: and the woman being constantly alarmed by the behaviour of her guest, could not sleep, but listened to him walking backwards and forwards, she heard him for several hours, talking aloud like a lawyer, she then heard a report of a pistol and something fall heavily on the floor and the words, "Oh, Lord!"

Immediately afterwards, she heard another pistol shot, and in a few minutes she heard him at her door calling out "Oh, Madame, give me some water and heal my wounds."

The logs being open and unplastered, she saw him stagger and fall against the stump that stands between the kitchen and the room. He crawled for some distance, raised himself by the side of the tree, where he sat for about a minute. He once more got to the room, and afterwards he came to the kitchen door but did not speak. . . . She heard him then scraping the bucket with the gourd for water, but it appears this cooling element was denied the dying man.

As soon as day broke and not before, the terror of the woman having permitted him to remain for two hours in the most deplorable situation, she sent two of her children to the barn, her husband not being home, to bring the servants. On going in they found him lying on his bed. He only said, "I am no coward. But I am so strong, so hard to die." He begged the servants not to be afraid of him, because he would not hurt them. He expired in about two hours. Or just as the sun rose above the trees.

The death of Lewis in the wilderness at the age of thirty-five recalls the death of Laclède on the Mississippi. What perversity denies such men the enjoyment of their laurels?

Major Neely rode up in the morning. He took charge of Lewis's papers and carried them to Washington. There all the protested vouchers were promptly paid by the Treasury. The journals were turned over to Jefferson, and other records were placed in the custody of the State Department. A year later, on October 7, 1810, John Griner, the Tennessee backwoods farmer, was brought before a grand jury in Savannah, Tennessee, and accused of having murdered Lewis. The charge was dismissed. It was held that there was neither evidence nor motive. His friend Jefferson wrote:

He was in a paroxysm of one of those seizures of hypochondriac affliction when his affairs rendered it necessary for him to come to Washington. About three in the night he did the deed which plunged his friends into affliction. He deprived his country of one of her most valued citizens, whose valor and intelligence would have now been employed in avenging the wrongs of his country, and in emulating by land the splendid deeds which have honoured her arms on the ocean.

To this melancholy close of the life of one whom posterity will declare not to have lived in vain, I have only to add that all of the facts I have stated here are known either to myself, or communicated by his family to others. For its truth I have no hesitation to make myself responsible. *

* Jefferson's introduction to *Lewis and Clark*, Biddle edition, 1812.

Did Jefferson make himself responsible for the true facts? Surely this suicide, if suicide it was, was a strange affair. There is the failure of the shots to be more directly effective. There is Lewis's appeal for help and the refusal of Mrs. Griner to give him even a drink of water. And why didn't the servants hear the shots? Were they prevented from going to the aid of a man to whom they had been loyal? Were they involved in a crime which was passed off as suicide? Was a murder perpetrated by some robber of travelers along the Trace, or by an Indian? In any case, the body of Meriwether Lewis, dead on his way from St. Louis to Washington, was buried beside the Natchez Trace.

XII.   From Village to City

General Clark eventually succeeded his lifelong friend, Meriwether Lewis, in the governor's office in St. Louis. Open, cheerful, and simple when compared with his dark-meined, brooding companion, Clark could be taken as a sign of the change coming over the city. Its tempo quickened with the arrival of the "Bostons." The Americans had long had their eyes on this western territory. In 1789 Henry Knox, Washington's Secretary of War, had ordered Josiah Harmar to "devise some practicable way for exploring that Branch of the Mississippi called the 'Messorui' to its source." And then in 1792 Washington, Jefferson, Hamilton, and others had, in the name of the American Philosophical Society, sent André Michaux on a similar mission, but he only made off with their money. Even the Lewis and Clark expedition had been planned before the Louisiana Purchase. Jefferson had hoped to send the men up the Missouri as civilians and had obtained French passports for them. But now the Gateway to the West was wide open.

On July 5, 1808, the leading citizens informed the Court of Common Pleas of their desire that St. Louis be incorporated as a town under a recently adopted act of the Indiana territorial legislature which provided for such incorporation on the request of two thirds of the citizens and the approval of the court. An election of town trustees was held on July 23, 1808, and the first ordinances were adopted the next month. This was somewhat premature, since the three judges of the court—Silas Bent, Louis La Beaume, and Bernard Pratte—did not record their approval until November 9, 1809. Yet one of them, Judge Pratte, had been elected a town trustee more than a year earlier. Obviously St. Louis never was very meticulous about observing the authority of Vincennes. And in 1812 the Missouri Territory was organized, with St. Louis as its capital.

Because he anticipated war with Great Britain and hoped to serve under arms, Clark at first did not want the governor's position. He helped to get it for a Kentucky congressman, Benjamin Howard, who held the post from 1809 to 1813. Disappointed in his hopes of a military

command, Clark accepted the governorship, and was reappointed for
three-year terms until Missouri became a state in 1821. Urged on by
his friends, he then made a feeble campaign for election as the new
state's first governor, but his heart was not in it. His wife was in her
last illness in Virginia, and Clark could not put his mind on politics.
So he was defeated by Alexander McNair.

The general, however, remained in St. Louis as Indian commissioner.
This meant a smaller salary, but he had made a modest profit from
the sale of western lands—not nearly so big as that made by his friend,
Major Stoddard, but enough to enable him to live in ample comfort.
So he continued to be a bit more prominent than even his good friend,
Chouteau, and even more respected than McNair. Personal charm,
more than official position, made him the first citizen of St. Louis.

His patience and his easy ways were fruitful among the Indians. "A
lot of time and a lot of smoking" was his formula for negotiating a treaty
with them; and he signed treaties with at least twenty-nine tribes. The
British, especially during the War of 1812, worked constantly to turn
the Indians against the Americans. In 1814 they organized a large
Indian expedition against St. Louis. The warriors assembled at Prairie
du Chien in what is now southwestern Wisconsin. When word of this
reached the city, Mrs. Clark exclaimed,

"God only knows what our fate is to be!"

Her husband immediately rode north. He defeated the British and
their allies without great difficulty. The British did recapture Prairie
du Chien shortly after Clark started back to St. Louis. In 1815 Auguste
Chouteau, General Clark, and Ninian Edwards, Abraham Lincoln's
friend, as United States Commissioners signed a treaty with nineteen
Indian nations at Portage des Sioux, a few miles above St. Louis. (Here
a monumental figure of Our Lady of the Rivers now watches over boatmen.)

Clark worked hard to carry out the policy of Jefferson and Jackson
in settling all the tribes west of the Mississippi in what was to be forever
Indian territory. But white men, poor soil, and bad weather made many
an Indian wish he were back in his old happy hunting ground. Although Black Hawk, chief of the Sauks and Foxes, denounced such
treaties, he finally was induced in 1831 to leave his native haunts near
the mouth of the Rock River in Illinois. Yet when his people faced
famine the next year he recrossed the Mississippi with between 500 and
1000 braves, seeking a prairie in which they might plant crops. At once

the Illinois militia turned out, Abraham Lincoln commanding one company. They pursued the Indians up the Rock River Valley into southern Wisconsin in a shameful orgy of slaughter. Black Hawk, of course, had even less of a chance than Pontiac and Tecumseh. He was captured by Winnebagoes and turned over to Lieutenant Jefferson Davis, who, to his credit, showed the chief courtesy and consideration as he conducted him to St. Louis. There Black Hawk was locked up at Jefferson Barracks. Clark also was kind. He brought distinguished visitors to see the chief and persuaded George Catlin to paint his portrait. (A very fine book about these Western painters—Catlin, Charles Bodmer, and Alfred Miller—the Indians, the trappers, and the traders is Bernard De Voto's *Across the Wide Missouri,* based largely on research done in the Missouri Historical Society in St. Louis.) The portrait was barely finished before Black Hawk was taken on an exhibition tour of Washington and other eastern cities. He was released in 1833.

After Black Hawk's war, serious Indian fighting never again occurred within hundreds of miles of St. Louis, but General Clark still had to cope with Indian troubles. The agents of the Hudson's Bay Company were active among the tribes. For the sake of trade they strove to keep them hostile to the Americans. They told the Indians that Lewis and Clark were "children of the Pope," and that the western lands, therefore, were not the lawful property of the United States, no matter what treaties the chiefs had signed around the council fire. Irresponsible traders and young braves caused more trouble, almost for the fun of it. As frequently as not, the younger Indians would resent the stealing of a pretty wife or sister, no matter how willing she might be. Kioway, a Fox chief, explained it all to Clark:

"Your work is hard and my work is hard. Among all nations the young men are foolish and will not be governed by their chiefs."

Whisky, as Clark well knew, was the most dangerous of the troublemakers. The Jesuits and the Hudson's Bay Company had tried in vain to keep it out of the Indian country. Since all western trading was done by license of the United States Government, it would seem that Washington could keep out firewater by denying or withdrawing trading licenses. As a matter of fact, it always was illegal to give or sell whisky to Indians, and in July, 1832, it was made illegal to take whisky into the Indian country. Yet American trade with the Indian was based on whisky. Traders always tried to get their customers drunk before bargaining. So, as in the noble days of Prohibition, federal agents were bribed. The law allowed trading parties to take up to twenty gallons a head for medical purposes on the summer expeditions westward from St. Louis. Whisky, carried in curved tin "kegs," was worth from $24 to $32 a gallon, so it was not often poured to quiet the ague, but to acquire pelts at a profit of at least 200 per cent. Clark said he could stop most of the abuses with a thousand good men; but, of course, he never got the thousand good men. General Ashley, representing the opponents of the American Fur Company in Congress, naturally blamed the company for the trouble, but it had fairly stout defenders in Thomas Hart Benton and Daniel Webster.

The small independent trader had the least trouble in bootlegging because he carried less of the contraband and his operations were not as easily watched as those of the big outfits. When the ban was imposed, Clark gave the company permission to take in 1400 gallons of medicinal alcohol, but this was seized by the army. Then company agents seized a small trader carrying 250 gallons with Clark's permission. He had escaped the military, but the company men took his whisky and put him in irons. This caused more trouble than Benton and Webster could smooth over, and the Chouteaus almost were put out of the fur trade for the first time since Laclède brought young Auguste into it. It would not do to send out whisky from the St. Louis headquarters for a while. Fearing that Sublette and Campbell had managed to bring some west, "King" McKenzie, the company agent at Fort Union, bought corn from the Mandans and set up a still. But a report by Nathaniel Wyeth, a trader from Cambridge, Massachusetts, who had not lost all of his Puritan background in the West and who had no love for the company, led to the discovery of the still. The "fix" had to be put in according to the approved manner of the 1920s. For good measure, McKenzie was called from Fort Union to St. Louis for a year.

Clark was distressed to see good friends in such difficulties, but he was concerned for the Indians too. He asked his friend, Bishop Rosati, to send out missionaries, but there were no clergymen, Catholic or Protestant, available as yet. Agriculture might have an influence as settling as that of religion, so Clark lectured about it to every chief who came to St. Louis, even though he knew the odds against making the braves into farmers, of persuading them to do squaws' work. But Clark did gradually move the tribes westward. By emulating French tact and discouraging American aggressiveness he became popular with the Indians. Said one chief:

"When I go to St. Louis I go to see Chouteau or Clark. He say 'Hello' and Negro comes in with great plate of cake, wine, and so forth. He say 'Eat, drink!' If he want anything else he say 'Hello.' Three, four, five, six Negroes come in and do what he want. That I call happy. He no plow. He no work. He no cut wood." The general's hospitality and Chouteau's, too, were famous. When Lafayette visited St. Louis, Governor Edward Bates, a rather surly character, said that he would not entertain him because he had no authorization from the legislature. Clark and Chouteau immediately took over the function in the grand manner. Clark, incidentally, presented the Revolutionary hero with a grizzly cub which Lafayette tried to make into a pet, but a letter from Paris confessed failure. As the animal grew larger, Lafayette wrote, he was forced to turn it over to the Jardin des Plantes. George Catlin's notes, written like a painter's memorandum, present a picture of how Clark and other prominent St. Louisans lived:

Drove out to Gov. Clark's—across prairie—flowering & fragrant shrubs —the Gov.'s farm—small cottage—orchard bending & breaking with loads of fruit—Negroes with tables under trees preparing meal—fine sitting room in open air—little Negroes whispering and laughing—civil Negro Major Domo who asks to take horses out—invites us to walk in the orchard & spreads table with additional cover—sitting room—rifle & game bag in corners—Indian calumet over fireplace—remains of fire on hearth, showing that morning has been cool—lovely day—golden sunshine—transparent atmosphere—pure breeze.

Fine nut-trees, peach trees, grape-vines, catalpas, &c. About the house —lookout over rich, level plain or prairie—green near at hand—blue line at the horizon—universal chirp and spinning of insects—fertility of country —grove of walnuts in rear of house—bee hives—dove cotes—canoe— General arrives on horseback with dogs—guns. His grandson on a calico pony, hallowing, & laughing—Gen'l on horseback—gun on his shoulder— cur—housedog—bullying setter. . . .

Dinner plentiful—good—but rustic—fried chicken, bacon and grouse, roast beef, roasted potatoes, tomatoes, cakes, bread, butter & . . .

The "transparent air" which Catlin enjoyed already was being threatened by the development of coal in southern Illinois just east of St. Louis by Peter Lindell and several associates. They already were beginning to sell it in the city. Eventually it was to make the air thicker than the waters of the Big Muddy and more sulphurous than the pit. Not for a century, not until 1941, was this smoke pall to be banished.

But in those early days, just after St. Louis became the first city of the new state of Missouri, it was a pleasant place—well, that depends on one's point of view. A traveler from the East said that "in one section you find it built up entirely with the broad, steep-roofed stone edifices of the French, and the Spaniards' tall stuccoed dwellings raising their tiers of open corridors above them, like a once showy but half-defaced galleon in a fleet of battered frigates; while another will present you with the clipper-built brick houses of the American residences, light as a Baltimore schooner, and pert-looking as a Connecticut smack." Others found the new American row-houses, built one against the other, dark and inhospitable, and not nearly as cool in summer as the old French houses with their shaded porches. Another traveler reported:

Since this part of the continent became subject to the United States, the City of St. Louis, over-run by the speculative New Englanders, has begun to spread over a large extent of ground on the bank of the river, and promises to become one of the flourishing cities of the West. A new town has in fact sprung up by the side of the old one, with long well-built streets and handsome rows of warehouses, constructed of excellent grey limestone, quarried on the spot. The inhabitants, of French extraction, are however still numerous, both in their part of town and in the neighboring villages; and it is amusing to a European that beside the hurry and bustle of the upper streets, full of pale, seamed faces, depressed brows, and busy fingers, are the quiet quarters of the lower division where many a characteristic sight and sound may be observed. Who can peep into the odd little coffee-houses with their homey billiard tables—see those cozy balconies and settees—mark the prominent nose, rosy cheek, the contented air and civil demeanour of the males, and intelligent eye and gossiping tongue of the females—listen to the sound of the fiddle, or perchance the jingle of the harpsichord, or spinet, from the windows of the wealthier *habitant,* crisp and sharp like a box of crickets—without thinking of scenes in the province of some other country?

Still another observer, however, complained:

Twenty years ago (1802) the fashions of the town were simple. The natural dimensions of a belle were not screwed by the aid of a milliner into a decanter-like shape possessing neither comeliness or gentility. False hair did not decorate the head, false teeth did not fill the mouth, nor was the vinegar barrel exhausted to reduce them to the proper size. Females appeared as nature made them, and were not less loved for being so. In those days it could not be said that the tailor made the man, for he did not dress in tight unmentionables surmounted by a blanket capote. It is true, that people had vague notions of morals and religion which were easily set aside when opposed to their pleasures or interest. In the short period of twenty years the rich have become poor, and the poor rich, while the names of the old inhabitants but serve to point a moral and adorn a tale.

Sir William Drummond Stewart, a great admirer of "the venerable and hospitable General Clark," was a better reporter. He wrote:

I lived with a vast variety of society, as well as food, that presented itself at the City Hotel and stumbled my way down to the market place to have an evening glass of eggnog with Mr. Bennet, that worthy compounder of cherry cobblers and hail storms . . . the reckless mountain boys who had returned from their summer campaigns were the life and terror of the place; and in the intervals of debauch, told the tales of the wilds with graphic and inspiring enthusiasm.

This Scotsman had a very special fondness for St. Louis and St. Louis men. A veteran of Waterloo, he succeeded his brother in 1838 as baronet of Grandtully and proprietor of Birnam Wood, the boughs of which once moved to Dunsinane to signal Macbeth's bloody end. But before that he spent six years in the American West, making five trips to the mountains with the St. Louis men. Although he went for buffalo and grizzly hunting and for trout, rather than for pelts, the best of them considered him their peer. He was all the more popular for always managing somehow to carry very good wines, canned delicacies, and candied fruits into the wildest wilderness. He relished the succulent meat from the buffalo's hump as they did—and it is said that beef never was half so good—but a bottle never spoiled a feast. He was the friend of Bracelet de fer, old Iron-Cuff, and other Indian chiefs, as well as of Prince Maximilian of Wied-Neuwied, another veteran of the Napoleonic wars, who, having studied the Indians, the fauna and the flora of South America, rode westward from St. Louis to study those of the northern continent. Stewart got along after a fashion even with that unspeakable missionary and malicious hankerer, William H. Gray. He was baptized in St. Louis by Bishop Rosati with Dr. Simon Bruté, the bishop of Vincennes, as his godfather, "returning to the faith of his illustrious ancestors" at a time when he felt he might soon join them. He was too tough to be carried off prematurely by a touch of illness, but life on the estates of his ancestors lacked its full savor. Antoine Clement, the St. Louis hunter, went to live with him. Alfred Miller, who had gone West with him to paint Indians and buffalo, paid him a long visit, and the three talked much of adventure-bright western days as they sat under Miller's pictures or gazed at the deer and the buffalo which Cut-Face Bill Sublette had shipped across the ocean to graze on the banks of the Tay. Barely a year passed before Stewart wrote to Sublette in St. Louis, asking about Clark's health and announcing that "if it pleases God, I shall be in New York in the fall of 1840 with a view of going to the Mts. in Spring following," and urging him to make preparations. It was 1843 before Stewart started on his last expedition, the first "dude" affair of this kind. He had sold one of his estates for more than $1,000,000, so he was ready to do things in the really grand manner, but the West and the fur trade had changed, the surviving mountain men had changed into prosperous city merchants, and St. Louis also had changed.

There was nothing left for Stewart to do but to go home again to write two very melancholy and very bad novels. It's too bad he did not simply tell of his adventures as the "reckless mountain boys" told their stories in Mr. Bennet's tavern, or of the town's festivities as they were described by Theophile Papin:

"The most animating day of all the year in this, our curious French village, was undoubtedly the Jour-de-L'An, New Year's Day. This was the day for interchanging presents and for social visiting—the calls beginning in the morning, and among families generally before daylight. The Jour-de-L'An did not entail a church fete—not an obligatory mass was celebrated in its honor. Strangely enough, however, there were certain ethical observances of the inhabitants, which, mingling with their light pleasures, inculcated most effectively the gentlest, sweetest precepts of our common Christianity. The Jour-de-L'An was the day for restoring impaired friendships, for drawing closer the ties of family, for generous atonements, for good resolutions."

The St. Louis which enjoyed dancing and sleighing in winter—as General Clark did—in summer went to Chouteau's Pond for picnics, bathing, boating and fishing. James Cartwright Essex, who came to St. Louis in 1825, admitted that he was not nearly as good an angler as John Shade. Yet he told of catching a string of twenty or thirty fine bass in the early morning, before his eight o'clock breakfast.

General Clark's wife and his young daughter, Mary, died in Virginia in 1820. On November 1821, he married Mrs. Harriet Kennerly Radford, an old family friend. After she died in 1831, his days must have been empty now and then. But he could always pride himself, quietly, on the splendid record that his son, Meriwether Lewis Clark, was making in the army. The young officer left the service in 1838 to come to St. Louis to keep his father company, but that was only a few months before the old general died.

Every now and then Clark must have mused and marveled at what he had seen in his three decades in St. Louis. When he first set up camp at Wood River, St. Louis was a village with less than a thousand inhabitants. In his last years, it was a city of about 16,000 with an assessed property value of $8,682,000. When he first walked its streets the total property value was a scant $100,000. He had seen the dedication of the Catholic Cathedral in Walnut Street, a gem of eighteenth century architecture. He had seen the building of churches of other denominations, and the beginning of his own Episcopal Christ Church. In his latter years St. Louis had half a dozen newspapers, among them the St. Louis *Evening Gazette,* founded in 1836; the *Anzeiger des Westens,* established in 1835; the *Herald,* the city's first daily, established in 1834, and the *Missouri Republican,* which took that name in 1822 after having been established as the *Missouri Gazette* in 1808. (In 1809 it was briefly the *Louisiana Gazette.*) He had congratulated Chouteau and Lucas in 1826 when they gave a city block for the Court House. Between 1808 and 1818 he saw the opening of the first post office, the creation of a public-school board, the arrival of the first steamer, the beginning of St. Louis University, and he attended the first performance of *She Stoops to Conquer* in the Thespian Theater. He probably lost money in the first bank, the Bank of St. Louis, which closed in the panic of 1819, the same year that the Wiggins Ferry Company put its first steamer into service. The first waterworks were started in 1830; gaslight was introduced in 1837—five years after the arrival of the first Germans, the people who were to do so much for this city of his. Quicker, oh much quicker than a man might believe, St. Louis the trading post, the jumping-off place for the Wild West, was fulfilling Laclède's prediction by becoming "one of the fairest cities of America," one of the most important, and one of the largest. The big boom was beginning.

XIII. Altar and Pulpit

The Roman Catholic religion, introduced here by the early French settlers, prevails extensively." So Charles Dickens wrote in the account of his visit to St. Louis in 1842. According to a census announced in 1959 by Archbishop Joseph E. Ritter, there were 481,202 baptized Roman Catholics in the Archdiocese of St. Louis, which includes the city and ten surrounding counties. This is more than thirty per cent of the area's population. For the city alone the percentage is probably somewhat higher.

St. Louis antiquarians certainly may put up a sign reading "Père Marquette Passed Here," just as they may boast that T. S. Eliot and Eugene Field were born here, or that Louis D. Brandeis spent his first six months as a lawyer in St. Louis—and think of all the eminences and excellencies who "slept here," especially in the river-boat days when St. Louis could not be avoided in a "grand tour" of the United States! —but it would be stretching too far to count the ardent Marquette as the first priest in St. Louis.

More than a hundred French-Canadian *coureurs de bois* were wandering up and down the Mississippi and the Missouri in the last half of the seventeenth century. Marquette in 1673 and La Salle in 1682 simply made a deeper impression on document-loving historians. Other missionaries also visited the Illinois Country, notably Jacques Garvier and Julien Binneteau. Their reports encouraged the Jesuit superiors in Quebec to establish a mission on the site of St. Louis in 1699 to serve the woodsmen and the Indians, especially the Tamaroas. It was built on the bank of the Mississippi at the mouth of a little saline stream, the River des Peres. Had the mission had a longer existence, the city might well be called Des Peres instead of St. Louis.

Sloppy Parson Weems school histories say that the Jesuits abandoned the place out of fear of wolves in a cold winter, because a crop failed, because the Indians moved their village. Nonsense! Desiring to share the western missionary activities, the Seminary of Foreign Missions in Quebec obtained from the Bishop in 1698 letters patent granting "The Superior and the Directors of the Seminary . . . ample power to establish themselves and to found missions among all the nations which are on both sides of the Mississippi River as well as the length of the river and all rivers which flow into it." The Bishop also made it clear that he wanted no interference from "other missionaries not of their body." With the popular Henri de Tonti as their guide and with the Sieur de Vincennes keeping them company part way, the gentlemen of the Tamaroa Mission started that long canoe trip against the current of the St. Lawrence in early May of 1698. They were Francis Jolliet de Montigny, the Superior, Jean Buisson de St. Cosme, Antoine Davion and a layman, Thaumur *dit* La Source. Several workmen also joined the flotilla. They passed the fading piasa bird, an Indian symbol painted on the bluffs above Alton, and arrived at what now is Cahokia on the Feast of the Immaculate Conception, December 8, 1698. In the third week of the following May, they raised the cross which signified the completion of the Mission of the Holy Family of the Tamaroa. So when the Jesuits opened their mission on the right bank of the Mississippi, they really were trespassers. Tonti wrote to Quebec from Michilimac-kinac in the summer of 1699 that "there has arisen some difficulty be-tween M. Montigny and the Reverend Jesuit Fathers concerning the mission at Tamaroa . . . A dispute will have a very bad effect on the savages who are clever enough to seize the advantage when they per-ceive that the French are at odds among themselves." But the Jesuits set up their mission on the River des Peres. And neither winter nor wolves nor Indians budged them. Church bells rang on both sides of the river while the dispute was taken all the way to Versailles. There, in 1701, the issue was decided in favor of the Seminarians and against the Jesuits. The order reached the River des Peres in 1702. And that is why Laclède found no white men on the site he chose sixty years later for his city.

Tonti, like his Jesuit-educated former commander, La Salle, disliked this order of black robes. He was eager to have the Western Jesuits supplanted by the Recollets or the missionaries from Bishop Laval's seminary. One of the more successful Jesuit missions was that at Kaskaskia. It was established by Père Marquette* for the Illinois Indians, for whom he had a special fondness. "When one speaks the

---

* It was Pere Marquette who discovered the Piasa bird on the Alton bluffs, the dangerous Chain of Rocks reach of the Mississippi at St. Louis, and, above all, the river's famous catfish, "monstrous fish, one of which struck our Canoe with such Violence that I thought it was a great tree, about to break the Canoe to pieces."

word 'Illinois' it is as if one said in their language, 'the men,' as if the other savages were looked upon by them as merely animals," he wrote in a letter which became part of the *Jesuit Relations*. "It must also be admitted that they have an air of humanity which we have not observed in the other nations that we have seen upon our route. They are of a gentle and tractable disposition." After LaSalle's influence waned, Alloüez led the Jesuits back to their work among the Kaskaskias, Cahokias, Peorias, and Tamaroas.

But the abandonment of the mission on the River des Peres, served by Father Jacques Gravier and Father Julian Bineteau, foreshadowed the banishment of the Jesuits not only from the Illinois country but also from all those missionary endeavors which, as Parkman has shown, were so important to the exploration of North America. Their success, envied by other orders, and their controversies with the Jansenists aroused keen hostility against the followers of Loyola in France. Jean Poisson, Marquise de Pompadour, and the Duc de Choiseul as well as the freethinkers were among their enemies. In 1762 the Parliament of Paris closed the Jesuit schools in the capital. Most of the provincial parliaments followed suit, and on December 1, 1764, Louis XV, against his will, issued a decree dissolving the order throughout his realm. The Superior Council of Louisiana already had expelled them from the colony by a decree dated July 9, 1763. How rigorously this was enforced even against priests at distant wilderness posts was described by Francis Philibert Watrin, one of those exiled:

"It was said that the Institute of the Jesuits was hostile to the royal authority, the rights of the bishops, and the public peace and safety; and the vows uttered according to this institute were null. It was prohibited to these Jesuits, hitherto thus styled, to take that name hereafter, or to wear their customary garb, orders being given them to assume that of secular ecclesiastics. Excepting their books and some wearing apparel which was allowed to them, all their property, real and personal, was to be seized and sold at auction. It was ordained that the chapel ornaments and sacred vessels of New Orleans should be delivered up to the Reverend Capuchin Fathers; that the chapel ornaments and sacred vessels of the Jesuits living in the country of the Illinois should be delivered up to the Royal procurator for that country, and that the chapels themselves should be demolished; and that, finally, the aforesaid Jesuits, so-called, should return to France, embarking upon the first ships ready to depart—prohibiting them, meanwhile, to remain together . . .

"The courier despatched to the Illinois to bear the decree, arrived on the night of September 23, at fort Chartres, distant six leagues from the residence of the Jesuits. He delivered to the procurator of the King the commission which charged him to execute the decree; and on the next day, about eight or nine o'clock in the morning, that officer of justice repaired to the house of the Jesuits. . . .

"As soon as the savages learned that he had arrived among them, they came to show to . . . Father Meurin, and his associate, the share which they took in the distress of their Fathers; the news of their condemnation already had caused many tears to be shed in the village. They were asked why they were thus treated, especially in a country where so many disorders had been so long allowed. The old missionary, after several repeated interrogations, finally replied: '*Arechi Kiécouègane tchichi ki canta manghi* [It is because we sternly condemn their follies].' . . .

"The Christian savages proposed to send their chief men to Monsieur Neyon, commandant, and to Monsieur Bobé, sub-deputy commissary of the country, to ask at least that Father Meurin, their missionary, be kept in his mission. The two Jesuits told them plainly to do nothing of the kind, because this proceeding would be scoffed at and ineffectual, as having been suggested . . .

"The auction was finished . . . after the sacred vessels and the pictures had been taken away, the shelves of the altar had been thrown down; the linings of the ornaments had been given to negresses decried for their evil lives; and a large crucifix which had stood above the altar, and the chandeliers, were found placed above a cupboard in a house whose reputation was not good. To see these marks of spoliation in the chapel, one might have thought that it was the enemies of the Catholic religion who had caused it."

But the company of Marquette, de Brebeuf, Jogues, and Lemoine was a brave company. Worthy of it was Sebastian Louis Meurin, a native of Champagne who came to Canada in 1741 at the age of twenty-two to be sent the next year to the Illinois missions. Decree or no decree, he still had work to do. Father Watrin also reported this:

"Father Meurin asked the Gentlemen of the Council (in New Orleans) for permission to return to the Illinois. This was a brave resolution, after the sale of all the property of the Jesuits; he could not count upon any fund for his subsistence, the French were under no obligations to him, and the savages have more need of receiving than of giving. His request was granted . . ."

So Meurin made the wearying journey up the river again. He established himself as the curé of Cahokia, and he also ministered to the new settlement of St. Louis across the Mississippi until it had a permanent priest. Meurin, who died at Prairie du Rocher in nearby Randolph County, Illinois, on August 15, 1777, had no easy time. He wrote to Jean Oliver Briand, bishop of Quebec who had appointed him Vicar General in the West, why he had not exercised the powers of that office:

"On the 26th of last august, 1767, I received your first letter by which you did me the honor of appointing me your vicar-general in This part of your diocese. . . . On the 29th of january, 1768, I received your second letter, confirming the first. I would almost wish that my self-esteem might prevent me from telling you, Monseigneur, that I am as unworthy as anyone can be of the honor which you confer on me; and more than ever incapable of such an office, of which I know but the name. I have never been acquainted with any jurisprudence, either notarial, pontifical, or any other. I have been too long left to myself, and I barely know the duties of a simple priest. It is no longer possible for me to learn anything else.

"My letters of last spring must have omitted to inform you of my age, and of my weakness of body and mind. I retain only a small portion of weak judgment, have no memory, and possess still less firmness. I Need a guide both for the soul and the body; for my eyes, my ears, and my legs are likewise very feeble. I am no longer good for anything but to be laid in the ground. I trust, Monseigneur, that you will be good enough to forgive me for having neither carried nor sent your graces and favors to new orleans, according to your letters and instructions . . . How would I have been received there after having stated over my own signature (in order to obtain permission to return to the Illinois) that I would always act as vicar of the Reverend Capuchin Fathers,—subject to their visits, their reprimands and corrections, and to their jurisdiction, etc., which was to be the only one throughout the mississippi country? . . . As soon as they heard, through the voyageurs, that you had honored me with the appointment of vicar-general, a warrant of proscription was issued against me; and it would have been executed had I not, on being warned thereof by a friend in authority, escaped from it by withdrawing to english territory. There, on at once taking the oath of allegiance as a former resident, I secured myself against the spanish persecutions,—which declare that I am a criminal because I have received jurisdiction from quebec, which is opposed to the intentions and interests of spain, etc. . . ."

Thus Father Meurin was forced to leave St. Louis and return to the Illinois side of the river, where General Gage and the British authorities were almost as reluctant as the Spaniards to recognize his ecclesiastical function. It does seem that the latter were willing to overlook his occasional visits to conduct religious ceremonies, but he got little help from those he served. "I have received naught but what was given me out of charity," he reported to Bishop Briand. "They, I mean the rich ones, always claimed that they owe nothing when there is no resident pastor." But he added that "I have always the poor on my side." Over sixty and low in vitality after more than a quarter of a century in the wilderness, he hoped for "a corner in one of the clergy-houses of the country," but was uncertain even of this since "Father harding, the superior in Philadelphia, wrote me last autumn that they (the Jesuits) were about to be treated in england as in france, spain, portugal and prussia and he bade me farewell, fearing that he would have no other opportunity of doing so. Why am I not a great enough enemy of the devil to deserve such treatment for the 3rd time?" On that very human note ends the story of the Jesuits in the West.

Father Meurin's place in Cahokia was taken by Father Pierre Gibault, the patriot who gave his life savings of $1000 to George Rogers Clark for the expedition against Vincennes. The first priest regularly assigned to the seventy-six families who made up "the parish of St. Louis, in the Country of the Illinois, Province of Louisiana, Bishopric of St. James of Cuba" was the Capuchin Father Valentin. He arrived in 1772, and completed the first church near the site of the Old Cathedral in 1776.

For the church in St. Louis, the French Revolution was a boon. It brought cultivated *emigrés* to the frontier settlement who would not otherwise have left the colleges and salons of Paris. Laclède's library suggests that the early French leaders may have been more inclined to freethinking than to piety. In the *emigré* clergy, however, they found men of sophistication and culture, especially Louis Guillaume Valentin Du Bourg, first Bishop of St. Louis. He had been rector of a Paris school before the Revolution caused him to seek a haven in Baltimore, where he began an extraordinary Sunday lecture course for Negroes. Bishop Carroll made him president of Georgetown College in 1796. He was a popular preacher. After several years in New Orleans, he came to St. Louis in 1817 following a visit to Europe. He brought an 8000-volume library and other gifts for the St. Louis church. He found that the Vincentians had established a seminary at The Barrens, near Perry-ville, Missouri, from which young priests rode out to the scattered settlements and forts of *Haut Missouri*. The Jesuits had a school for Indian boys in Florissant. It now is St. Stanislaus Seminary. Mother Duchesne had opened the first of her schools for girls. Du Bourg made plans for a college. He spent three years in St. Louis and then set out for New Orleans. There Père Antoine, who had challenged his authority, was ready to submit. Du Bourg persuaded the Italian Vincentian, Joseph Rosati, to become his successor in 1825. Then he returned to Europe to serve for seven years as Bishop of Montauban, and later became Archbishop of Besançon. There he died December 12, 1833.

Circumstances sent Du Bourg to the frontier and he served it well, but Joseph Rosati became a genuine frontiersman. He loved the town in the wilderness as much as did his friend, General Clark. He was not an exile pining for Europe. Rosati, born at Sora, near Naples, in 1789, joined Vincent de Paul's Congregation of the Missions, and studied theology under Andrew de Andreis, who preceded him to America and soon was urging him to come over too. So in 1816 Rosati followed him to Bardstown, Kentucky, and then to The Barrens, where he and his followers established the first seminary west of the Mississippi. When De Andreis died on October 15, 1820, Rosati succeeded him as superior of the Vincentians in Louisiana. The development of The Barrens became largely Rosati's work.

Rosati probably smiled quietly when Rome named him Bishop and Vicar Apostolic of Mississippi and Alabama. The appointment was made by men looking at a map—and not a very good map. He thought the appointment premature, and said so. But Rome only changed his title to Bishop of Louisiana, and bade him make no more protests. Since he was to be a frontier bishop, he saw to it that he was consecrated in Donaldsville, Louisiana, on March 25, 1824, rather than in a big cathedral. He continued for some years to make his headquarters at The Barrens, on the fringe of the Ozarks, and spent much of his time in the saddle. He was not a prelate in the grand manner, but a missionary riding trails, rather than roads, through the forest from clearing to clearing. Willa Cather should have told his story.

When the vast diocese was divided into two, St. Louis and New Orleans, Leo XII asked Rosati to become Bishop of New Orleans, but he preferred St. Louis. Actually, he administered both until June 24, 1830, when Leo de Neckere was installed in New Orleans. De Neckere, incidentally, was the first of a number of bishops elevated from the St. Louis clergy. Among these were Timon of Buffalo, Lefebre of Detroit, Odin of New Orleans, Feehan of Chicago, Hennessy of Dubuque, Duggan of Chicago, Hogan of St. Joseph, and Ryan of Philadelphia.

Rosati was a civilizer. He opened the first hospital west of the Mississippi—in 1828. He saw to the erection of St. Louis College in 1829. In 1831 he began the construction of the handsome Old Cathedral of St. Louis of France. It was completed in 1834. Like most frontier churchmen of whatever denomination, Rosati sought help in the East and in Europe. He died while on such a mission in Rome on September 25, 1843.

St. Louis became an archdiocese under Peter Richard Kenrick on July 20, 1847. Kenrick, adviser of immigrants, was one of the foremost "Americanizers" of the Church. The influx of Irish and Germans, the flurry of Know-Nothingism, and the Civil War created tensions which he eased with tact and uncommon good sense. He quietly told his clergy to ignore the Drake test oath, and the United States Supreme Court agreed with him. He discouraged inordinate ties with the "old country" and set an example of sterling patriotism. With Lord Acton, the Cambridge historian, Kenrick was among those who opposed the promulgation of the dogma of papal infallibility by the Vatican Council in 1870. He deemed it unnecessary and inexpedient. Like Acton, he quietly accepted the decision when it went against him. Archbishop Kenrick, a scholarly man as well as an administrator, had been brought from Philadelphia to St. Louis by Bishop Rosati. Tenure of this Dublin-born, Maynooth-trained churchman extended from 1843 to 1896, almost from frontier days to the modern era. The tiny park at Lindell Boulevard and Vandeventer Avenue perpetuates his name.

Man of the Morning, a Flathead war chief, Black Eagle, a Nez Percé chief, and two young Nez Percé braves, No Horns on his Head and Rabbit-Skin Leggings, arrived in St. Louis in the early fall of 1831 to ask the Big Red-Headed Chief—as most Indians called General Clark—to send to their tribes men who would teach them the magic of the white man's religion. At least that is how Bishop Rosati set it down when he wrote their story. Among the "fur rows" of St. Louis were men who understood almost every Indian language, but the Nez Percés had come from the far side of the mountains, the area, beyond the Continental Divide, in which the St. Louis mountain men had not seriously challenged the agents of the Hudson's Bay Company. In fact these

Indians, who had made an especially favorable impression on members
of the Lewis and Clark expedition, had heard of white magic from
Spokane Garry, a Nez Percé who had been half civilized by Robert
Simpson at the company's headquarters on the Red River of the North.
But Spokane Garry, whatever else he told his tribesmen, had not given
them enough words of English or of French to be understood in St.
Louis. So they had to speak largely in the sign language, by which,
perforce, the red man and the white man first exchanged ideas. Having
fallen in with Lucien Fontenelle, the redoubtable brigade leader
of the American Fur Company who guided them to the city, they must
have picked up an extra word or two, but in the city they were confused and confusing.

Clark, who had a spark of the missionary in him, talked to them
after a fashion about Christianity. He took them to his friend, the
Bishop, asking that he send priests across the mountains with them.
Bishop Rosati, however, did not have enough priests in the saddle at
the time to serve the settlements, trading posts, and forts being built
in the less distant West, and zeal was only a limited substitute for man
power. This was difficult to explain to these Indians who, incidentally,
arrived in poor health because they were unaccustomed to the summer
heat through which they had traveled. But before Black Eagle died,
on October 31, he was baptized by Father Saulinier. Man of the Morning, who died a few days later, was baptized by Father Rous. Both
were buried in the Catholic cemetery. The other two braves, disappointed because no missionary-magician had been assigned to their people, left St. Louis before the year's end.

George Catlin met them aboard the little steamer Yellowstone, buck-
ing up the Missouri, and painted them at the feast given in their honor
in March of 1832 by the Sioux at Fort Pierre. No Horns on his Head
died shortly thereafter near the mouth of the Yellowstone River. Rabbit-
Skin Leggings met a wandering band of his tribesmen and reported the
failure of the mission. But while still out of the Nez Percé country,
this band was attacked by Blackfeet in the autumn of 1832. These
barbarians of the plains tomahawked Rabbit-Skin Leggings and took
his scalp as a trophy.

The Nez Percé-Flathead journey, however, was not to be altogether
fruitless. William Walker, a half-breed Christian Wyandot from Ohio,
had crossed the Mississippi to investigate the Indian Country in which
the government proposed to settle his tribe, and while calling on Clark

in St. Louis he heard the story of the four. He immediately elaborated it in a letter to his benefactor, G. P. Disoway, a pious and wealthy New York merchant who had become the secretary of the Methodist Church's Board of Foreign Missions. Walker wrote touchingly—and with no factual justification—of how the skulls of Flathead infants were malformed by bandaging, but also that they were earnest seekers of the truth. That was enough for Disoway. He wrote a letter, published in the *Christian Advocate and Journal* of New York for March 1, 1833, in which he repeated Walker's story and urged "the Church (to) awake from her slumbers and go forth in her strength to the salvation of those wandering sons of our native forests." Others took up brands from the fire Disoway had kindled. Soon the text of the appeal of the four Indians—all changed into Flatheads by now, but also into orators —was published:

"I came with an eye partly open for my people who sit in darkness. I go back with both eyes closed. How can I go blind to my blind people? . . . My people sent me to get the White Man's Book of Heaven. You took me to where you allow your women to dance, and the Book was not there. You took me to where they worship the Great Spirit with candles and the Book was not there. . . ."

A real tearjerker! Yet the Indians had escaped papist bonds. Would not all good Protestants come to their aid?

Actually the Protestants never had much luck with the Indians, as Bernard De Voto pointed out. When they met "the noble savage" beyond the coasts of the Nebraska, they found him and his ways and his smells hard to take. Some of the missionaries were full of "a self-righteousness which was as much dyspepsia as spirituality." Some became the vanguard for the settlers and the land boomers, especially in the Oregon Country. But others unselfishly carried on their difficult work. And almost all of them, of course, went westward through the gateway of St. Louis.

De Voto's dim view of missionaries reflects that of the mountain men, who were understandingly reluctant to conduct tenderfeet, and especially their women, into the Wild West. Broken-Hand Fitzpatrick, Cut-Face Sublette, and their friends felt strongly that the Indian Country was not the place for a white woman, and they had no ear for preaching. Joe Meek used to tell a story that summed up this attitude. De Voto retold it in *Across the Wide Missouri:*

"Joe Meek was having wife trouble. Joe had married a Nez Percé. Mrs. Meek failed somewhat in subordination and got sore at Joe. Exercising her perogative under Indian marriage laws, she started home for her father's lodge. Connubial rage boiled up in Joe. Hanging what he describes as a kettle of alcohol from his saddle horn, he lit out after her. He cursed his pack mules to the Sweetwater and into South Pass, camped, and woke with a head four times lifesize. The specific for that was in his kettle, and he rode into the sagebrush plain singing and envisioning the consolation of lodgepoling his Nez Percé girl. It was a July day, burning-glass sun and your skin sandpaper. Joe needed water but, quartering northwest from the Sandy, he would get none till he reached the Green. Alcohol parched his throat and he treated it with more alcohol, which parched it some more. Hell of a fix to be in over a squaw.

"Then he saw a couple of horses ahead of him and when he came up to them a man was stretched out on the ground and a distracted woman was watching his agonies. The Reverend Asa Bowen Smith had given up here and was so he reported, dying of thirst. His wife Sarah recognized Joe as the agent of Providence, and mastered her sobs long enough to plead for water. The angel of the trail had no water but would share his liquor with the reverend. No sale; Smith resigned himself to death. The mountain ethics did not recognize holy dying; they held that you fought back against this country. Joe loosed his vocabulary on the missionary. We may be confident that what he said exceeded [a contemporary] report of it.

" 'You're a——fellow to be lying on the ground here, lolling your tongue out of your mouth and trying to die. Die if you want to, you're of no account and will never be missed. Here's your wife, who you are keeping standing here in the hot sun: why don't she die? She's got more pluck than a white-livered chap like you. But I'm not going to leave her waiting here for you to die. Thar's a band of Indians behind me on the trail and I've been riding like——to keep out of their way. If you want to stay here and be scalped, you can stay; Mrs. Smith is going with me. Come, Madam, let me help you to mount for we must get out of this cursed country as fast as possible.'

"He shouted down Sarah's protests and got her on the horse. To the dying Christian he must have been a demoniac figure—thick beard, cheeks caked with dust, red-eyed from alkali and hangover, bass voice shouting blasphemies. 'Mrs. Smith can find plenty of better men than you,' he said, quirted her horse, swore at his mules, and was off. Sarah wept, pleading to die with her beloved. Not with Joe Meek on the job. A mile farther into the sagebrush he looked back and it had worked—the Reverend Asa was sitting up, one scalp the Indians whom Joe had extemporized would not get."

The first to respond to the appeal of the four braves were the Methodists. With the generous backing of the Methodist Mission Board, Jason Lee arrived in St. Louis from New York in 1833. Sublette, Wyeth, and Stewart were headed for the Platte, and agreed to let his party join their wagon train. He met the Flatheads, but immediately turned his back on them. He had heard of the lush land of Oregon and lost no time in getting there. It did not disappoint him as Indian squalor had, and Lee soon became more real estate promoter than missionary.

Others, however, were heroically devoted. The Reverend Samuel Parker of Middlefield, Massachusetts, set out from St. Louis with Lucien Fontenelle on behalf of the American Board of Commissioners for Foreign Missions, a joint Presbyterian-Congregationalist organization. With him were Dr. Marcus Whitman, a medical missionary, and his charming bride, the blond Narcissa Prentiss, and also the Reverend Henry Harmon Spalding and his wife, and the envious W. H. Gray. Parker was old, fifty-six, for the arduous undertaking, yet his intelligence carried him through. His journal reveals that he understood the Indians about as well as a white man could. And the Whitmans were loved by mountain men and Indians alike. Dr. Whitman nursed Fontanelle's company through an epidemic, so the brigade captain gallantly refused his fee when they reached the rendezvous on the Laramie plain. There Whitman cut an arrowhead out of Jim Bridger's back and made another firm friend. Indeed, as news of the "sawbones" spread, a dozen or more mountain men lined up for repairs. There were Flatheads and Nez Percés at the rendezvous with the story of how Lee had disappointed them the year before. They would not be disappointed again, Parker promised. The missionaries consulted with Tom Fitzpatrick, who was to take them farther west, and especially with Captain Stewart, who told them all about the Nez Percé country. So it was decided that Parker should return East—by ship from California—to recruit needed help. Spalding was to go into the Nez Percé country, and Whitman elected to go on to the Cayuses, although warned by the Nez Percés that these cousins of theirs were not overly friendly and even less trustworthy. The party suffered hardship after hardship before Mt. Hood stood on the horizon, blue and white. They might well have accepted the offered hospitality of Fort Vancouver, a Hudson's Bay Company post, but they would not be dissuaded from their mission.

The Indians, especially the Nez Percés, sincerely tried to understand and to live according to the white men's religion no matter how it conflicted with their Stone Age beliefs. Spalding baptized an old chief named Joseph, who set an example of ardor. But his son, the one the white men still call Chief Joseph but whom the Indians called Thunder Coming from the Water up over the Land, finally denounced the preaching as part of the magic by which the white men were taking the Indians' land.

The doctor and his wife worked themselves to the bone for truculent Cayuses. What success they had also was undermined by the nation's expansion into Indian territory. Religion and Manifest Destiny were working at cross-purposes. Then, in November, 1847, an epidemic of amoebic dysentery spread among the Cayuses. Whitman's mission was full of sick and dying men, women and children, red and white. On November 29, Whitman buried three children of a chief—children who had been killed by the white man's sorcery. For this the Indians would be avenged. Whitman was brained with a pipe tomahawk. Narcissa was shot and scalped. Fourteen of the mission company were slaughtered. A few escaped to Walla Walla. A handful of women and children were held by the Cayuses against the arrival of avenging white men. Spalding, on his way to visit Whitman, was warned of the trouble and turned back in time. This, then, was the outcome of the mission of the two chiefs and the two braves to the Great Red-Headed Chief in St. Louis.

The missionary who understood the Indians best was the first one sent out from St. Louis by Bishop Rosati. He was Pierre Jean de Smet, a sturdy, stocky, round-faced Belgian who had been given the name of "Samson" in his seminary days in Malines. He came to the new Jesuit novitiate at Florissant, a suburb of St. Louis, in 1823, and was ordained there in 1827. Eleven years later he started his career among the Indians with the Potawatomis at what is now Council Bluffs. After two years he was in the Oregon country. De Smet saw as much, or more, of the Great Plains, the mountains, and the Pacific Northwest as any mountain man. He covered more than 180,000 miles. He also made frequent trips to the East, to New Orleans, and to Europe to solicit support for his missions. He crossed the Atlantic sixteen times. De Smet mastered the languages of the Sioux, Blackfeet, Flatheads, Pend d'Oreilles, and other tribes.

In 1868, when he heard that Sitting Bull had sworn to kill the first white man he saw—and every other one thereafter—De Smet rode into his camp in the Big Horn Valley and persuaded the chief to smoke the peace pipe. He was the guiding spirit of the great council at Fort Laramie in 1851, at which a general understanding was achieved on the rights of Indians and the westward-moving immigrants. He settled the Mormon War and the Yakima War of 1858–59, and was everywhere recognized as the mediator between the whites and the sorely goaded red men. De Smet was a keen observer. His journals—the originals are preserved in the library of St. Louis University—are among the most important firsthand accounts of the opening of the West. He died May 23, 1873.

Another distinguished western missioner from St. Louis was the Episcopalian, Daniel Sylvester Tuttle. Although only twenty-nine years old, he was elected bishop of Montana, Idaho, and Utah in 1866. The next year he went into western territory never before visited by an Anglican clergyman. He stopped in Salt Lake City to call on Brigham Young, and then moved on to a cabin in Virginia City, which makes the West a little less wild than TV would have it. There he received a telegram from the Reverend Montgomery Schuyler of St. Louis: "Elected Bishop of Missouri at Kirkwood May 29th, on first ballot." Tuttle, however, declined the honor, preferring to continue his ministry in the West.

He was to have succeeded Cicero Stephens Hawks, who had come to St. Louis as rector of Christ Church in 1843 and who had been elected Bishop of Missouri in 1844. The present Christ Church Cathedral, incidentally, was started in 1859, and the first service was held in it on Christmas Day, 1867. The tower was added in 1911. The beautiful stone reredos, carved in England, was dedicated Christmas Day, 1911. Schuyler succeeded Hawks as rector. He was of New York stock, a convinced anti-slavery man. Yet despite its many pro-Southern members, the congregation refused to accept his resignation. When the old church was sold before the Civil War, he conducted services in the Mercantile Library hall. He selected the site of the present Cathedral at Thirteenth and Locust streets. During the war he was chaplain of army hospitals in St. Louis. Nineteen years after he sent his first message of notification to Tuttle, Schuyler sent a second telegram. This time the missionary did accept the election to the Bishopric of Missouri, returning to St. Louis from a Utah mining camp. He later was elected Presiding Bishop of the Episcopal Church. The Christ Church Cathedral Annex is a memorial to Bishop Tuttle. The second St. Louis bishop to be elected to the church's highest office was the Right Reverend Arthur C. Lichtenberger. He was chosen in 1958. His predecessor as

Bishop of Missouri was William Scarlett—fondly remembered as a liberal churchman and humanitarian. The present bishop is the Right Reverend George Cadigan.

Bishop Tuttle in 1898 alluded to the Catholic beginnings of St. Louis, and deplored the absence of Episcopal missionary endeavour. This began only with the organization of Christ Church in 1819—fifteen years after the Louisiana Purchase removed all obstacles. By way of extenuation, Bishop Tuttle pointed out that the American branch of the Anglican Church, while based on Episcopal government, simply had no bishop available for the frontier. It had been for 177 years subject to the Bishop of London. There was no Episcopal bishop on American soil until 1784, and there were only six in 1804. Furthermore, the close connection with the English Crown left the Church in poor repute after the Revolution. Accustomed to praying for the king in the Prayer Book formula, and for the most part dependent on the English Society for the Propagation of the Faith in Foreign Parts, many of its priests were Tories who preferred exile in Nova Scotia, or at least kept their churches closed. These were the new recusants. The church in America emerged only slowly from its torpor.

The Reverend John Ward undertook the organization of Christ Church through misadventure. On a visit he fell sick in St. Louis. While he was recuperating in 1819, several persons asked him to remain as the minister of a St. Louis parish. An Episcopal service was held in rented quarters at Second and Walnut streets, and forty-seven individuals subscribed $1714 for a church building. After two years Ward went back to Lexington. Four years later the Reverend Thomas Horrell, a Virginian, held Episcopal services in the Methodist, and sometimes in the Baptist church. In 1829 an Episcopal church, seating 250, was built at Third and Chestnut streets. The parish, however, attracted no more than thirty communicants in a dozen years. Genuine missionary zeal was kindled only by the 1835 General Convention in Philadelphia, according to Bishop Tuttle.

Then Jackson Kemper was appointed missionary bishop for Indiana and Missouri. He labored in St. Louis for nine years. Perhaps his zeal outran his prudence. With a gift of $20,000 from the East, he bought 100 acres of land adjoining the County Poor Farm, and in 1836 obtained a charter for Kemper College, which was opened in 1838 with the Reverend P. R. Minard as its president. Dr. McDowell's medical school was affiliated with it in 1840, but the college was forced to close in 1845. At the time, Christ Church parish was the whole Episcopal

Church west of the Mississippi, and it was too small to provide the primary support of a college.

So when Bishop Hawks came to St. Louis from Buffalo in 1844 he found his first problem in an unmanageable debt. The college was closed four months after his arrival, and its property was sold by the sheriff. The church was sold to the Baptists. But Hawks still had an economic problem, since a new church at Fifth and Chestnut, which was supposed to have been built for $40,000, eventually cost $75,000. So until his death in 1868 he found his hands tied by debts. And his spirit was saddened by slavery and war. His burdens were eased, however, when Schuyler came to Christ Church as rector in 1854. He served forty-one years—until his death in 1896. In 1859 the second church building was sold for $80,000, and work on the present building was started. Again the diocesan architect had a poor head for figures. His calculated cost of $125,000 actually became $235,000. Nevertheless the parish was out of debt by 1881, and the church became the diocesan cathedral in 1888. By this time more than a dozen other parishes had been established. An orphan's home and a hospital, St. Luke's, also had been opened.

The first Presbyterian church in St. Louis was opened by the Reverend Salmon Giddings, a graduate of Williams, who came 1200 miles from Connecticut on horseback to do so in 1816. The broad tolerance which has been characteristic of St. Louis—with a few lamentable, emotional exceptions—was displayed when the Catholics of St. Louis subscribed generously to the First Presbyterian building fund. A gift of twenty-five dollars also came from John Quincy Adams. Giddings eventually organized twelve Presbyterian churches in the area. He also established a school for girls opposite the Old Courthouse.

Officially, Protestantism was not tolerated in the territories of His Catholic Majesty of Spain, but Governor Trudeau wanted settlers who could be relied upon against the British. So when the Reverend John Clark, a Methodist who later turned Baptist, began making pastoral visits in the St. Louis area, the governor reminded him of the law and also remarked that only loud church bells could be heard. Apparently the Americans in town could be more hostile to ministers than were the subtle French and the tolerant Spaniards. As late as 1817 the Reverend John Mason Peck complained that in St. Louis there were "infidels of a low and indecent degree" given to "orgies of drunkenness and profane revelry." These were the drinkers and wenchers and fighters who boasted that "God will never cross the Mississippi." Joseph

Charless, on the other hand, complained in 1816 that many of the Protestant missionaries "are taught to propagate the doctrine of union of church and state, and to discountenance republicanism." Some of the missionaries did hold church trials on charges of immorality, gambling, profanity, working on the Sabbath, and other "sins" not discountenanced by the state. Such Protestant discipline, however, was sporadic.

Much missionary effort was devoted to rural areas reached only by the circuit riders. For a long time only the Methodist Church insisted on a regular salary, although a small one, for its itinerant preachers. Many of them supported themselves by peddling books. These men had a hard time on the frontier, where people did not even pay taxes and left reading to the city dwellers. But the preachers did have at their disposal that frontier institution, the camp meeting. Men like Charless probably had their doubts about these gatherings. As Charles van Ravenswaay observed, "the early camp meeting left the worshipers in an argumentative and belligerent state of mind." The Abolitionist views of many of the preachers also rubbed some Missouri hair the wrong way. In fact the issue divided some of the denominations more enduringly than it split the Union. In the 1840s Southern proslavery adherents of the Presbyterian, Methodist, and Baptist religions broke away from their national churches to establish regional groups. Segregation still does not stop at some church doors. No sect, however, unleashed as much turbulence as did the Mormons.

While he was abiding at Kirtland, in the burned-over land of Ohio, it was revealed to Joseph Smith by the angel Nephi—or Moroni— that his apostles must go "speedily to the place which is called St. Louis." So the Mormons came to the levee in 1833—some by "mover wagon" and ferry, others by steamer. But for most of them St. Louis was only a stop on the way to Independence, and then to Nauvoo— which also proved to be only stops on the way to Deseret, the land of the honeybee. The Mormons did not have a happy time in Missouri, and they got into worse trouble in Illinois. Neither their religious nor their political notions were particularly acceptable on the frontier. Their communal land holdings and mass voting, according to the dictates of leaders, were a threat to free-and-easy ways. Charges against them of thievery and unfriendliness toward "gentiles" made them even less popular. Governor Lillburn Boggs was determined to drive them out of Missouri. When he was shot and wounded, they were blamed—guilty or not. The story of the westward trek of this "holy and peculiar people" is clouded by prejudices. Yet some of the Latter-day Saints, a group which rebelled against the sanction of polygamy by Smith, did settle in St. Louis. They were among the first to mine coal in what now is Forest Park.

St. Louis has been the center of the orthodox Lutherans, represented by the Missouri Synod, since 1839. That year about 700 members of the denomination arrived from Saxony by way of New Orleans on the steamers *Rienzi, Clyde, Knickerbocker,* and *Selma,* under the leadership of Martin Stephan. They were strict subscribers to the unaltered Augsburg Confession of Martin Luther. This had brought them into conflict with European authorities. Like so many others, they sought freedom of worship in America and were made welcome in St. Louis— especially by Bishop Kemper. In March 1839 he read the following notice to the congregation of Christ Church:

"A body of Lutherans having been persecuted by the Saxon Government because they believed it their duty to adhere to the doctrines inculcated by their great leader has arrived here with the intention of settling in this or one of the neighboring states, and most respectfully requested the use of our Church that they may again unite in all the ordinances of our holy religion. I have, therefore, with the entire approbation of the vestry, granted the use of this church for this day from 2 P.M. until sunset."

Some of these immigrants settled in Perry County, but many of them remained in the city. They used Christ Church for three years, until they built Trinity, the first of the many German Lutheran churches in St. Louis. Disappointed in Bishop Stephan, they turned to the Reverend Carl Ferdinand Wilhelm Walther, the thirty-year old brother of Pastor Otto Walther of Trinity. He restored discipline and founded a score of churches and parochial schools. The group established Concordia Seminary in 1839 at Altenburg, Missouri, and moved it to St. Louis in 1849. Today the school consists of a group of about twenty buildings, Gothic in spirit, on an ample campus, dedicated in 1926. The Missouri Synod also maintains a score of other schools in various parts of the world.

Walther was a theologian, a strict one. He called on other Lutherans in the United States to return to Augsburg orthodoxy, publishing the *Lutheraner* to reach them more effectively. He was always ready for a doctrinal disputation. He was the leader in the establishment of the Missouri Synod at a convention in Chicago in 1847, and became its first president.

These Saxon Lutherans came to the United States because at home they had feared the rising influence of their liberal coreligionists and the Catholics. In the United States the more liberal Lutherans were determined not to come under the domination of Walther's conservatives. Many of them had settled in Missouri. In 1840 they met in Mehlville, now a St. Louis suburb, and formed the *Deutscher Evangelischer Kirchenverein des Westens,* the German Evangelical Church Association of the West. To assure a liberal clergy, they opened Eden Seminary in 1849 in Warren County, fifty-four miles from St. Louis. The school later was moved to suburban Webster Groves. One of its best known alumni is the theologian-journalist, Reinhold Niebuhr.

Among the major religious groups, the Jews were the last to establish themselves in St. Louis. In spite of the official view of the Louisiana Spaniards, there probably were some Marranos, or secret Jews, in the territory. Several are said to have been with Columbus when he discovered America. Perhaps the first Jew settled in St. Louis about 1816. He was Wolf Bloch—the name later became Block—a native of Bohemia. He came to Baltimore late in the eighteenth century. When he went back to Europe for his wife, she decided she preferred a divorce to crossing the ocean. But a number of Bloch's kinsmen, especially younger cousins, were persuaded to make their fortunes in Missouri. Of course there were no synagogues for them to attend, and no Jewish families with Jewish daughters for them to marry. So some of them "fell away." Levi Bloch married a Catholic. And Eliezer Bloch twice married Presbyterians. He attended Dr. Post's Presbyterian church. Yet on his deathbed he declared he had never given up his faith, and asked to be buried in the new Jewish cemetery. His request was granted. Dr. Post conducted the burial rite, avoiding any specific Christian expressions. Yet half a century later Rabbi Louis Sale indignantly repudiated such "cemetery Jews."

The first Jewish service in St. Louis was held in 1836 above a grocery store at Second and Spruce streets. Abraham Weigel, Nathan Abeles, a younger Eliezer Bloch, and some itinerant Jewish peddlers formed the minyan, the minimum of ten men required for an orthodox service. A year or so later, a Know-Nothing gang desecrated their improvised sanctuary. A group of outraged Masons offered their temple for the Jewish rites. Weigel and his friends declined with thanks. They would stand their ground. Furthermore, they said that they believed a repetition of the outrage would not be tolerated in St. Louis. They were right.

In 1839 this group, now augmented by new immigrants, met to organize the city's first Jewish congregation. With Weigel as president, it became *Achduth Israel,* better known as the United Hebrew congregation, with a place of worship at Sixth and St. Charles streets. Abeles officiated as mohel and as shochet. In the same year, the first Jewish relief agency, *Chesed W' Emeth,* or "Mercy and Truth," was formed, and in the next year a Jewish cemetery was laid out. A temporary synagogue was maintained and the Polish orthodox rite was observed.

Younger Jews, determined to adjust themselves to their new surroundings instead of setting themselves apart, were repelled rather than attracted by strict observance of old-world customs. While the older St. Louis Jews were Henry Clay Whigs almost to a man, many of the younger ones were avoiding political commitments lest they alienate part of the community. With nativist demagogy, and worse, in the air, their caution was natural enough. But the '48ers—chiefly from Germany and Austria, but with a slight sprinkling from the French West Indies —were a less timid sort. They had no taste for Polish orthodoxy, but they would not hide their religion for fear of political hooligans. Their temper abetted a breakaway from United Hebrew and the formation of a more liberal congregation, *Emanu-El.* The early records of this congregation unfortunately were lost in the fire of 1849. Meanwhile a Bohemian congregation had been formed under the name of *B'nai B'rith.* Out of these two in 1869 came the reformed congregation of *Shaare Emeth,* with its first synagogue at Seventeenth and Pine, but now in University City. There was one more major breakaway which resulted in the formation of Temple Israel, now handsomely housed on Washington Boulevard and Kingshighway. The United Hebrew congregation, long served by Rabbi Samuel Thurman, now occupies a handsome temple on Skinker Road, opposite Forest Park. *B'nai El* is presently located on Delmar Boulevard at Clara Avenue. *Shaare Emeth* was served by Rabbi Samuel Sale from 1887 until 1927, when he was succeeded by Rabbi Julius Gordon.

Each Jewish congregation is a law unto itself, united with others by a common tradition but not by an episcopacy, synod, or other form of church government. There still are conservative groups like *B'nai Amoona,* but the reformed groups have the larger membership. They also have produced such notable leaders as the Reverend Dr. S. H. Sonnenshein, who left *Shaare Emeth* to help in the establishment of

Temple Israel, and that congregation's widely respected leader, the
late Rabbi Leon Harrison. The latter was succeeded in 1929 by Rabbi
Ferdinand Isserman, who laid the cornerstone of Temple Israel House
and considerably enlarged the congregation's educational activities.
After several years of litigation, supported by Archbishop Joseph Ritter
and the Protestant Metropolitan Church Federation, the congregation
overcame zoning restrictions designed to keep churches out of residential
suburbs, and Rabbi Isserman now has plans for a new temple in the
County.

Many of the Jewish congregations grew from small beginnings and
only with great difficulty. A favorite story in the Jewish community is
that of *Chesed Shel Emeth,* an organization formed in 1888 by three
immigrants from Eastern Europe—Chaim Albert, Yacow Leibel, and
John Helman—primarily to establish a Jewish cemetery. In October
1892, with exactly $162 in the treasury, a plot was purchased for
$3100. It was a struggle to pay off this debt because, as Dr. Z. Abrams
wrote, "in those days a nickel spelled 'money'." Even after the cemetery
had been acquired, more nickels had to be found for a proper Jewish
hearse. So great was the rejoicing when this was accomplished that
the whole Jewish community was invited not to a *Sium Hatorah,* the
traditional feast celebrating a scribe's completion of a copy of the
Scriptures after years of labor and its delivery to the congregation,
but a *Sium Havogen,* a feast of the wagon.

First formed to help those Jewish victims of the Chicago fire of
1871 who sought refuge in St. Louis, the United Jewish Charities, a
community-wide organization, now aids the Jewish Hospital on
Kingshighway, adjacent to the Barnes group, the Jewish Home for the
Aged, the Jewish Orphans Home, and similar undertakings.

Aside from their primary religious function, the congregations of
St. Louis—Catholic, Protestant, and Jewish—are reflections of the
larger community. The history of almost all of them is the story of three,
four, and five churches, each one built farther from the heart of the
old city. The churches have been following their parishioners to new
neighborhoods. This may mean that the difference between old St.
Louis and the new suburbia is not as great as it sometimes seems to be.
It is heartening, nevertheless, to see some of the old churches—St.
John's Basilica near the Memorial Plaza, for example—being refur-
bished while the bulldozers are demolishing the surrounding slums. The
old churches are ready to serve new congregations. Here is renewal
rather than escape.

xiv. Cheap Land and the Union

General Clark had as sharp an eye for men as for mountains. So he was quick to notice a young Southerner attracted to St. Louis in 1815, Thomas Hart Benton.

At thirty-three Benton had already wound up a frustrated military, career in the Indian Wars and had served in the Tennessee Legislature. He also had been hounded by reports of thefts from his classmates and his early expulsion from the University of North Carolina. Much worse, he had incurred the enmity of Andrew Jackson in a tavern brawl.

As a young protégé of Jackson, Benton had been in Washington on business for "Old Hickory" when his brother, Jesse, became involved in a ludicrous duel. Benton felt Jackson should have prevented this. Quick to assert family pride, Benton spoke sharply to Jackson and some of his followers. Frontier blood boiled fast. That night the two Bentons were set upon in a tavern by Jackson and four or five other men. Swords, knives, and pistols were drawn. Jackson came out of the affray with a bullet in his arm which he carried there for years. The two Bentons were lucky to be alive.

So, with one thing and another, Tom Benton decided to lay the foundations of "character and fortune" in St. Louis. He was looking for lodgings and wishing he had more than just a few hundred dollars in his pocket when he was met by a friendly French-American, Charles Gratiot, who asked whether he could be of service.

"Lodgings? Why not stay at my house?"

The invitation was not so unusual as it may seem in the Statler-Hilton era. It was a year or so before Mrs. Charless, wife of the editor of the *Gazette,* put out a sign inviting guests—and that was almost a year before the Missouri Hotel, the first in St. Louis, was built. It was because there were no inns that a mansion as handsome as Gratiot's was built with so many rooms. A man as well known in Washington as he was and who was, furthermore, the husband of Victoire Chouteau and the business associate of her brother and her rising young nephew, as well as of Jean Cabanne and Silvestre Labbadie, was accustomed to entertaining guests.

He was as influential a sponsor as Benton could have in St. Louis. Gratiot introduced him to the French traders, and almost as soon as he had gone to the courthouse on October 2, 1815, to be admitted to the bar, Benton became the attorney of this dominant group which Charless called the Junta. Naturally he was introduced to Clark, ex officio a member of the Junta, and was soon defending Clark and the old French against attacks by Charless. He began to make small investments in real estate. And he also made his first enemy in St. Louis, Jean Baptiste Charles Lucas.

Lucas and his wife were Normans who came to America determined to make a fortune after the manner of Benjamin Franklin. They did not particularly like Philadelphia, so they set out for Duquesne, now Pittsburgh, because it had a French name. Although they did not find the French community they had expected, Lucas remained in Pennsylvania long enough to be elected to the legislature, to serve as judge, and to be sent to Congress in 1803. Still hankering for French surroundings, he obtained an appointment as one of President Jefferson's commissioners for the adjudication of Louisiana land titles. So he resigned from the House and set out for St. Louis. Yet he and his wife did not hit it off too well with most of the St. Louis French. When his wife died in 1811, Lucas built a new house at what is now the corner of Seventh and Walnut streets, despite warnings, so his daughter wrote, "that he was not doing a prudent thing in taking me, a fourteen-year old girl, so far away; that the Indians might carry me off sometime when he was downtown attending to his business." One reason he moved to the "suburbs" probably was that he owned so much land there. His daughter, Ann Lucas Hunt, explained in a memoir written for her descendants:

On the advice of my mother, he invested his salary in the purchase of land. He bought mostly out-lots, facing on what is now Fourth Street, each being one arpent wide by forty arpents deep. By purchasing a lot at a time, he at length came to own all the land from Market Street to St. Charles Street, and from Fourth Street to Jefferson Avenue. He did not buy it as a speculation, but for what it would produce; it turned out, however, to be an immense speculation, for the whole seven arpents front did not cost him over $700, and that property is now worth, I suppose, seventy millions! A hundred dollars was what he usually paid for an arpent in width by forty deep, though sometimes he got it for less. The heirs to this vast estate need not thank my father for it; he was too much of a politician to think of investing his money in land; it was my mother's fore-sight that suggested the investment which turned out so well. [An arpent was about 192 feet long.]

As a partisan of the Chouteau clan and a protégé of General Clark, Benton became a target of Lucas's barbs. One of the Lucas sons, Charles, was an attorney. He opposed Benton in a circuit court case in October 1816, and Benton obviously was irritated by the young man. Suddenly Benton interrupted him:

"I contradict you, sir!"

"I contradict you, sir!" Lucas shouted back.

After the altercation Benton challenged Lucas to a duel, but the young lawyer refused to take personal responsibility for what he had said in court on behalf of a client. The matter did not end there. Soon Benton challenged Lucas again. In time, the pair met on Bloody Island in the Mississippi. (This now is part of the Illinois shore.) Benton shot young Lucas through the neck, barely missing the jugular. While Benton refused to declare himself satisfied on the "field of honor," the affair probably would have cooled off had not the elder Lucas made inflammatory remarks all over town. Benton then insisted on a second meeting and killed the young man. The affair was hardly a glorious one—but other times, other ways! Benton had been in St. Louis less than a year when he had been asked to serve as a second for Edward Hempstead, a new friend and fellow lawyer. Men lived by "the code." Among most of his contemporaries, except those of the Lucas family, the killing of the young man was not regarded as a blemish on Benton's record. General Clark appointed him a member of the first school board, and the Chouteaus made him a director of their Bank of St. Louis. In 1817 Benton brought his mother and sister to St. Louis, and he was well on the way to becoming one of the most important men in the community.

More than a dozen of these "affairs of honor," involving citizens of the first rank, have been described by McCune Gill, historian and vice-president of the Title Insurance Corporation of St. Louis. One of the earliest and most peculiar occurred in 1810 and involved Dr. Bernard G. Farrar, the city's first American surgeon, and James A. Graham, a young lawyer. The doctor's brother-in-law was involved in a card players' dispute. He asked Farrar to act as his second, and then failed to appear on Bloody Island. Under the code, the doctor had to take his place even though he was not involved in the quarrel and was a close friend of young Graham. Both men were wounded. Dr. Farrar ignored his own injury to treat that of his adversary, but the young man died several days later.

A year before the Benton-Lucas meeting, Henry S. Geyer fought a duel with George H. Kennerly, a merchant. Both were wounded, but not seriously. In 1818 Captain Ramsay and Captain Martin of Fort Bellefontaine met on the island. Ramsay died of his wound. At least once a duelist was prosecuted for murder—and hanged. He was William Bennett, who in 1820 had met Alphonse Stewart near Belleville. Their seconds had humanely agreed to remove the bullets from the dueling pistols. Bennett detected this and secretly dropped another ball into his weapon and killed Stewart. This treachery rather than the duel was resented.

A duel which closely touched Benton was fought in 1823 between Thomas C. Rector and Joshua Barton, brother of Judge David Barton, author of Missouri's first constitution. Rector was the brother of William Rector, a Virginian who served as United States Surveyor-General in St. Louis. Barton, who was the federal District Attorney, wrote an article in Benton's *Missouri Enquirer,* accusing William Rector of employing an unusual number of relatives as deputy surveyor. Thomas Rector challenged the writer, and killed him.

Names even more prominent were involved in the Biddle-Pettis duel in 1831. Again the challenge was provoked by an article in Benton's paper. Major Thomas Biddle, paymaster at Jefferson Barracks, was the brother of Nicholas Biddle of the Bank of the United States in Philadelphia. The closing of the bank was a prime objective of Benton and the Jacksonians. Spencer Pettis, who was seeking re-election to the House of Representatives as a Jacksonian, wrote an article in the *Enquirer* reflecting on the Biddles. The major, who had just married Ann Mullanphy, daughter of John Mullanphy and sister of Bryan Mullanphy, published an even sharper reply. A day or so later he stormed into the house in which Pettis was lying on a sickbed. He horsewhipped the man until outsiders pulled him away. The code called for a challenge, but Benton pointed out to Pettis that if he were killed there would not be time enough to bring forward another strong candidate against David Barton, who was seeking his seat in the House. He advised Pettis to have Biddle arrested on a peace warrant, and to vindicate his honor after the votes were counted. On the day before the election, Judge Ferguson deemed it wise to put both men under restraint. The disgraceful whipping aroused much sympathy for Pettis, and he was re-elected by a much wider margin than had been expected. For a month both men attended to business, but on August 22 Pettis challenged Biddle to a duel.

They met at 5 P.M. on August 27 on Bloody Island. Because of the time of day and the widespread knowledge of their quarrel, several thousand persons lined the levee and the riverfront housetops to watch the meeting. Since Biddle was nearsighted, the duelists took positions only five feet apart. Their pistols, when lowered, overlapped. Both mortally wounded, they exchanged pardons. Biddle was given a splendid military funeral, and Benton arranged an even more elaborate one for Pettis.

Ann Biddle thereafter devoted her time and her fortune to Catholic charities. Throngs attended her funeral in January, 1846. She is believed to be the first American woman to have been mentioned for canonization. Her body and her husband's were placed in a common grave on the grounds of the Widows' and Infants' Asylum which she had established at Tenth and Biddle streets. The monument was simply inscribed: "Pray for Thomas and Ann Biddle" (The bodies later were removed to Calvary.)

Abraham Lincoln almost fought a cavalry saber duel with James Shields on the Illinois side of the river because of a newspaper article derogatory to Shields. The men came down from Springfield and stopped for breakfast in an Alton hotel, where friends persuaded them to abandon their bloody plan. Herndon's account of Lincoln's plan to take advantage of the short-armed Shields does not brighten the Civil War President's conception of a fair fight.

Frank Blair, ally of Benton and of Lincoln, also almost fought a duel. He published an article in the *Enquirer*. Loring Pickering regarded this as insulting and challenged Blair to a running fight with bowie knives or a pistol battle at the corner of Fourth and Pine streets. Blair naturally spurned anything so fantastic. The men did belabor each other on the street with umbrellas on one occasion, but nothing more came of the challenge.

But Blair's friend, B. Gratz Brown, was wounded in a duel in 1857 with Thomas C. Reynolds, a lawyer. Fought near Kimmswick, south of

St. Louis, this encounter also grew out of political newspaper articles.
Reynolds, an ardent pro-slavery man, challenged Brown.

Probably the last Bloody Island duel was that of General D. M. Frost,
the commander of Camp Jackson, and Edward B. Sayers, the engineer
who laid out the camp. Sayers criticized Frost as a tactician. On the
island he missed Frost, and the general fired into the air. With the nation
involved in a war of brothers, men found less cause and time for
private wars.

Since the killing or wounding of another always was prohibited by
law, duels really were illegal. The Missouri Legislature passed laws
against the custom in 1822 and in 1835, yet these were not effective—
especially since there was a question whether Bloody Island was within
the jurisdiction of Missouri. The Drake constitution of 1865 finally
provided an effective legal prohibition. With an eye to the politicians
who had engaged in duels, it provided that anybody who should
"hereafter" participate in a duel in any manner or leave the state to do
so could not "hold any office in the state." This remained part of the
basic law of the state until 1945. Incidentally, it underscores the fact
that politicians and lawyers were peculiarly inclined to invoke "the
code."

Benton in 1818 became editor and part owner of the *Enquirer,* the
weekly through which a number of his friends found their way to
Bloody Island. In itself, journalism could no more satisfy Benton than
did the practice of law, or those little real estate deals in which he
made or lost a few hundred dollars. While he regarded the press as the
"great school of instruction," he was interested in it primarily because
he saw it as "the most powerful lever which can be applied to the
human mind." Benton was above all else a politician. "It is time," he
said, "that Western men had some share in the destinies of this
Republic." He used the *Enquirer* to tell his readers what their share
should be.

Almost from the beginning he was a "hard money" man. Eventually
he would be known as "Old Bullion." The frontier was flooded with
worthless paper—shinplasters—with which farmers, laborers, and
soldiers were paid, only to discover that the paper was all but worthless.
"Banish paper," proclaimed Benton, "and you introduce gold and
silver. Where gold and silver is the standard, the price of everything is
reasonable, and a dollar stands for a dollar." This was accepted
doctrine in St. Louis, where the old French had no faith in paper

money. Their favorite coin was the big Spanish-Mexican dollar, worth a tangible, tactile eight "bits." This was the only currency preferable to shaved pelts.

In 1820, on the eve of Missouri's admission to the Union, Benton's enthusiasm and his views brought him a letter signed by Auguste Chouteau, Manuel Lisa, Charles Gratiot, Alexander McNair, and David Barton. It was nothing less than a proposal that he should be one of the state's first two senators. Barton would be the other senatorial candidate. General Clark would stand for governor; and Benton's friend John Scott, who lived in St. Genevieve but spent much time in St. Louis, would be the nominee for the House of Representatives. Benton wasted no time on mock surprise or false modesty. He joined the party. John Lucas, naturally, headed an opposing slate.

The legislature, which would name the senators, met in the new Missouri Hotel in September 1820. The electioneering was intense. One delegate, Marie Philippe Leduc, was kept up all night in the Chouteau mansion while Benton's virtues were explained to him. He finally was persuaded. Another member, Daniel Ralls, was carried to the hotel on his sickbed—against his doctor's orders—so that he might cast his vote for Benton. At three o'clock on October 2, Jesse B. Boone, a son of Daniel Boone, rose to nominate Thomas Hart Benton for the United States Senate. In addition to Benton, Barton, and Lucas, the other candidates were Henry Elliott, Nathaniel Cook, and John Rice Jones. On the first ballot Barton received 34 votes, Benton 27, Lucas 16, Elliott 11, Cook 8 and Jones 8. Barton and Thomas Hart Benton had been elected to the Senate, Benton to a seat which he would hold for thirty years. As the antagonist of Calhoun, Webster, and Clay, he was to play a role second only to that of Andrew Jackson.

Benton knew that a statesman must be, first of all, a politician. So in Washington he never forgot the interests of his supporters in St. Louis. Most important was the confirmation of their land titles, many of which were technically questionable. The French and Spanish authorities made concessions, usually based on the occupation and cultivation of the land or the performance of some service, military or civil. Once these conditions were met, a formal grant could be issued. Many St. Louisans did not bother to perfect their titles in this way. Everybody knew they had met the conditions and nobody questioned their claims, so why make a tedious, expensive trip to New Orleans? The records as left by Laclède and St. Ange and the Spaniards after them were good enough—but not for the hair-splitting Lucas, who dominated the title commissioners. The Board could validate a title; it could also throw it out, and Lucas was taking a very strict view. This often was unfair, and it certainly did not please Benton and his St. Louis law partner, Luke E. Lawless. David Barton, John Scott, and other lawyers were no more happy. Almost as soon as they were seated in Congress, Benton, Barton, and Scott had authority over titles transferred to the United States District Court for Missouri and its first judge, James H. Peck. To their consternation, Peck asked the advice of Lucas when Lawless presented the claim of Antoine Soulard for land given him by the Spaniards for his services as surveyor. It was a good claim in all but the most technical sense, yet Judge Peck denied it. He published his decision, and Lawless rushed into print with a criticism of his "assumptions of fact and doctrine." Whereupon Peck summoned the lawyer, sentenced him to twenty-four hours' imprisonment for contempt of court, and disbarred him for a year and a half.

No wrongheaded judge could do this to Benton's partner, his clients, and his friends. John Scott in 1826 asked the House to impeach Peck, and the representatives got around to doing so—by a vote of 123 to 49—in 1830. The Senate organized a High Court of Impeachment with James Buchanan as one of the prosecutors. William Wirt, who had prosecuted Aaron Burr, was Peck's defense lawyer. Buchanan held forth on the tyranny and oppression of judges, Wirt on their need of independence and freedom from the constraint of possible impeachment. Wirt and Judge Peck won on January 31, 1831, when twenty-one votes were cast for conviction and twenty-two for acquittal. But Benton and his friends persuaded Congress to enact a law limiting the power to punish for contempt, the law which still is in force. And the Supreme Court, John Marshall presiding, reversed Judge Peck's rulings on the claims of Soulard, Delassus, Chouteau, Mackay, and other St. Louisans. In 1832 Congress also created a new Board of Land Commissioners. Benton—as well as Barton and Scott—had served their constituents well.

Benton pleased them, too, when he persuaded the government to give up its fur "factories" and to turn the trade over entirely to private enterprise. He questioned the system of having Missouri's lead mines worked under contracts granted by the War Department. Here at the very outset of his senatorial career he antagonized John Calhoun, then the Secretary of War, by suggesting that the contracts were not profitable, that they were the cause of inefficiency and probably of corruption as well. Much as Benton's stands might accord with the interests of his backers, they were not parochial. They were, after all, opening the way to the Pacific and the Orient. They worked in the national interest as Benton saw it, and usually he saw it clearly.

Benton was to show time and again—as in the fight against Nicholas Biddle and the Bank of the United States—that he would not sacrifice principle to please wealth, let alone to acquire wealth. He did not hesitate to oppose the more speculative element in St. Louis by advocating the "currency of the constitution, not the currency of the corporations." Majority sentiment in St. Louis, in fact, turned for a time against him. He had to count for support on the rural counties rather than on the city until the German and Irish immigrants again made it a Benton stronghold. As a follower of Jefferson and Jackson, his strength was with the farmers, the working man, and those of "middle wealth." Yet he never broke completely with the old St. Louis fur traders. He felt that they, unlike the speculators seeking only a quick profit, were working for the sound, long-range development of the West, not its exploitation. But Benton always was much more than an errand boy for his constituents. He soon was advocating a change in the method of electing the President and the Vice-President. "The people," he said, "can vote as easily for a President as for an elector."

Benton entertained Henry Clay ("Harry of the West") in St. Louis, and transacted legal business for him there. In 1822 he campaigned for him against Andrew Jackson. Yet Benton's democratic convictions made a reconciliation with "Old Hickory" inevitable. It came in 1823. After that he was Jackson's floor leader in the Senate, and the battles of the Giants—Clay, Calhoun, Webster, Benton—really began. Benton campaigned for Jackson in Missouri in 1828, predicting that he would carry the state two to one. He did better: 8372 to 3407. This was one of Benton's many Missouri campaigns, all conducted with almost super-human energy and enthusiasm. What he called a "flying ride" from Washington to St. Louis meant ten days and a good part of ten nights on horseback. During the hottest months of the Missouri summer, July and August, he would be in the saddle day after day, riding from one end of the state to the other, stopping at every courthouse to talk for two or three hours, to confer with local leaders, and to shake hands. Benton had most of his important speeches published in pamphlet form and widely distributed, but he insisted that there was no substitute for meeting the people, for letting them see their candidate. Short, but flagstaff-straight and dapper-dandy neat, his head always thrown back, he really made it easy for his admirers to talk of "glorious Tom Benton." He had a strong voice. His direct and mordant wit cut deep into opponents. Yet Benton preferred to explain the issues. Facts and more facts were for him the great weapons. He astounded many by his learning and his marvelous memory. These were the fruits of enormous efforts. Until the last days of his life, he never retired before midnight, and was always up at 4 A.M. Then after a brief walk he began his desk work. Few men came into the Senate chamber or to the hustings so well prepared. Even the great dinners and demonstrations in the Planters' House in St. Louis, which concluded his campaigns, Benton would not accept as tributes but as opportunities to explain the issues.

Benton supported "Old Kinderhook" Van Buren with almost as much enthusiasm as he had supported Jackson. Under O.K., he continued to exercise great influence in the Senate. The New Yorker was in tune with the expanding West. As a practical politician, Benton always tried to be a good party man. Yet he could muster only limited enthusiasm for Polk, Pierce, and Buchanan. After Jackson's retirement began the "Benton for President" booms. They came regularly every four years, but always "Old Bullion" stopped them: "Everything for the cause; nothing for the man." Perhaps he was wrong—he feared his candidacy might divide the Union. Yet his outlook was less sectional than he sometimes believed it to be. He was, in fact, a unifying force. He saved Missouri for the Union—or made it possible for Frank Blair and the St. Louis Unionists to do so.

As important for Benton as the battle for hard money against soft was the proper and speedy development of the West. He supported his son-in-law, Charles Frémont, in his five explorations of the western country. In his house on Laurel Street in St. Louis he entertained Kit Carson, Broken-Hand Fitzpatrick, and most of the explorers, traders, and Indian chiefs who came to St. Louis and could tell him of the mountains and the land beyond. He felt that Webster's treaty of 1819 had lost Texas to the United States, and he opposed joint British-American occupation of the Oregon country. Yet on these territorial questions he was a moderate. He felt, for example, that the 49th parallel was the proper border between the United States and Canada, and he refused to follow the extremist demand of "54–40 or fight." He was against sending a military force into Texas and across the border into Mexico. He knew that the Americans were the real aggressors, that they had provoked the Mexicans to attack them. Some of Benton's followers denounced him for abandoning his own Western Doctrine. To the extent that he did so, he sacrificed it to a greater cause.

In the later Texas and Oregon schemes, he saw a Southern plot to extend slavery and to undermine the Union. Benton told the Senate that he was a Southerner by birth, affection, interest, and connections. He owned a few slaves himself, but he declared, "I will not engage in schemes for slavery's extension into regions where it was never known." If it did not exist in Missouri, he would oppose its introduction. If it did not exist in the United States, he would oppose its introduction anywhere. It was the great divisive curse upon the land, and it was uneconomic too. One day he turned to former President Adams, a political adversary, and said: "Mr. Adams, you are passing off the stage, and I am passing away also, but while we live, we will stand by the Union."

Benton showed a statesmanlike respect for Mexican sensibilities, and urged Polk to negotiate with Mexico in 1848. Yet when the war resolution was before Congress, he voted for it—reluctantly and only because of compelling belief in the necessity of national unity. Benton urged a quick end to the war. He was willing to accept command of the armies in the field so that a civilian rather than a soldier would deal with the Mexicans. He urged a landing at Vera Cruz, and an immediate march on Mexico City. This strategy, belatedly adopted, brought victory.

The new American imperialism was a further sign of the change in the political climate which had really started with the campaign of "Tippecanoe and Tyler, too." Benton regarded that as a campaign waged not on principle and platform, but on vilification and violence. His own friend, Andrew Jackson Davis, editor of the St. Louis *Argus*, was murdered on Market Street after a Whig "jollification." Writing of the "log cabin and cider" campaign, William Chambers, Benton's biographer, said:

"Never again was a conservative party like the Whigs to fight a major, national election with the same candor that had characterized Henry Clay when he chose the Bank of the United States as an issue in 1832. From bitter experience, the conservatives had learned that in a democratic political system such candor could not serve them half so well as Hoorah, and the appeal of an attractive candidate."

Benton was even more disturbed by the advent of the Know-Nothings.

He hoped, however, that the new poison might be overcome in St. Louis and in Missouri. In 1842, his protégé, Montgomery Blair, had been elected judge. Blair's brother, Frank, and such other young men as B. Gratz Brown, the editor of the *Missouri Democrat,* were fighting vigorously for the liberal cause. As the national leaders of his own Democratic party weakened, Benton grew more firm. When his old friend, Roger Taney, handed down the Dred Scott decision, Benton wrote and circulated a 190-page pamphlet criticizing it severely. Benton was personally interested because old friends had helped the momentous proceedings in St. Louis, but that was a minor consideration compared with the fact that, if not challenged and reversed, the Dred Scott decision would mean the extension of slavery into free territory. With Texas, Oregon, and California—not to mention Nebraska and Kansas —coming into the Union, this decision must not be allowed to stand.

Benton's opponents, the proslavery Democrats, were gaining strength in Missouri. Under the leadership of men like Claiborne Fox Jackson, Sterling Price, and Senator David Atchison, the border ruffian, they persuaded the Missouri Legislature to instruct Benton to follow the proslavery line. Benton felt sure that John Calhoun had urged them to "instruct" him out of his seat. Here there was no room for moderation. Between him and them, Benton proclaimed, there would be "a high wall, a deep ditch." There would be "no communication, no compromise, no caucus." And so came the great Missouri campaign of 1850. A salute of 100 guns greeted the old senator as he stepped onto the levee from the steamer on which he had made the last part of his trip from Washington. His St. Louis friends had won a great liberal victory over the Know-Nothings the previous April, and they cheered him as he pleaded for "family harmony and fraternal affection."

The white-haired "tribune of the people" again climbed into the saddle—for his famous "forty-days' campaign." Benton crisscrossed the state, speaking everywhere to large throngs. In St. Louis the Courthouse was not nearly large enough to hold all of those who wanted to hear the closing speech, so Benton delivered it in Washington Square, the open block on which the City Hall now stands. But the opposition also had been drawing big crowds, and on Election Day the proslavery element strengthened its hold on the Missouri Legislature. The balloting for senator started in Jefferson City on January 17, 1851, and it did not end until the twenty-second. On the first ballot, Henry Geyer, a proslavery Whig, received 54 votes and Benton received 55—not enough to elect. On the last ballot Benton still commanded 55 votes, but Geyer received 80. After thirty years, the giant had been unseated. But he would not bow. His head was still thrown back. He would fight—as he had always fought—for the cause, not the man.

By March 1851 he was home again after a brief trip to Washington. There he had refused to sell his house in C Street, explaining that he still would need it. In his seventy-first year he moved into a new house in St. Louis at Sixth and Walnut streets. Here he made plans for a grass-roots fight for party control. At a rally in the Courthouse rotunda, he agreed to run for a seat in the House of Representatives. Like old President Adams, he would go back to the battlefield to fight those who were "converting the government into an oligarchy instead of a democracy." Campaigning in a district which embraced the twenty counties of southeastern Missouri, running from St. Louis to Arkansas, he spoke about railroads and homesteads and other immediate interests of the voters, but always his main theme was the preservation of the Union. On Election Day, August 2, 1852, he defeated the combined Whig and proslavery Democratic opposition. It was, he said, a "triumph for direct election."

In the House, Benton was as busy a politician as he had been in his early days in the Senate. He did not merely make statesmanlike speeches against nullification. He introduced a bill for the removal of St. Louis Arsenal to Jefferson Barracks so that its site might be made into a city park. He asked for an appropriation of $100,000 to complete the Customhouse. His chief interest, however, was the admission of "bleeding Kansas" and Nebraska as free states. Elected as a Democrat, Benton was opposing the chief measures of the Democratic administration, but he was willing to disregard party labels for the cause. In men like Seward he found new allies.

In May 1854 he was renominated for his seat in the House and also proposed for the Senate. The primary election, held on Saturday, June 24, found Benton unopposed. (This, incidentally, was probably the first American primary in which the voters named the nominees of their parties at the polls.) As the campaign got under way, Benton explained that he hoped for "an interval of repose before I die," but that he could not give up the fight against nullification. It was a campaign of confused and divided parties. Election Day, Monday, August 7, 1854, was a day of violence and riots in St. Louis. A mob stormed the offices of the *Anzeiger des Westens,* a German paper loyal to Benton, and troops had to be called to restore order. Once again Benton was defeated, and once again he refused to give up the fight. The old man now evolved new tactics.

He made only a superficial campaign when his friends nominated him for governor in 1856. Instead, he made a series of lecture tours —in New England, in New York, and in the Middle West—in which he spoke for national unity. Old adversaries like Horace Greeley now acclaimed him. At Harvard he was sponsored by Jared Sparks and George Bancroft. Perhaps Benton had risen completely above partisan strife. Perhaps he was disappointed that he could no longer cheerfully support his own party. He had advised his son-in-law, Frémont, against becoming the first Republican candidate for the presidency. But by 1858 his friends, Blair, Brown, and the rest, all were for Lincoln. Benton could only say that if Buchanan proved to be as weak as Pierce had been "the Union will approach its last days." He would deliver more lectures to prepare people for 1860.

Benton's private life was almost as serene as his public life was stormy. Shortly after his election to the Senate, he married Elizabeth McDowell of Cherry Grove in Lexington, Virginia. He was conspicuously fond of his children. Adams said he was almost disarmed by the man's parental affection. The famous Jessie's elopement when only eighteen with Lieutenant Frémont was a shock, but in her way she was a chip off the old block, and Tom Benton could not help admiring the western explorations and the California adventures of his son-in-law, "the Pathfinder." Benton's family generally accompanied the senator from Washington to St. Louis, especially after canals and river steamers made the trip less arduous. They lived for years in a house at Laurel Street and Washington Avenue. This was almost constantly mortgaged. Benton cared so little about personal gain that he was forced to borrow $1000 on his deathbed. Only the posthumous royalties on his books paid his debts. Much as he was away from the city, Benton always regarded St. Louis as his home. He had the bodies of all the members of his family brought together on a lot in Bellefontaine Cemetery. Yet he was to spend his own last days in Washington, not at home.

Toward the end of May, 1857, he was injured in a railroad accident while on his way to give a lecture in Pittsburgh. He made his speech and went on to Washington. There he was confined to his home for three weeks, but the man could carry on in bed as well as at a desk. He was working on the second volume of his autobiography, *Thirty Years' View*.

In doing so he had to rely on his prodigious memory, since a fire on February 27, 1855, had destroyed all his papers in the C Street house. He was also working on the *Abridgment of the Debates of Congress —1789–1856,* which Bancroft called the "monument of the age."

Early in September of 1857 Benton developed cancer of the bowel. By October he was pronounced "out of danger." He began taking brief walks and then short rides. In March 1858 the pain returned, but he kept on working. He would finish what he had started. Benton was by this time almost alone. His wife had died on September 10, 1854, after eight years of invalidism. His son, Randolph, had died in St. Louis on March 17, 1852, after having been admitted to the Catholic Church by the western missionary, Father De Smet, a good friend of the young man and of Benton too. "I intended to do it long ago," the dying man told his father, "but I did not know whether you would like it." The Benton family was Presbyterian. The other children, except Susan, were married and far away. So he was alone with her in the Washington house. Their conversation turned once to the fire. The old senator said:

"It makes dying easier, there is so much less to leave."

On April 8 he asked his old friend Sam Houston to make sure that no notice of his death was taken in Congress. The next day, Friday, April 9, President Buchanan called, at his request. Benton could say only one thing, "Preserve the Union!" That evening he said, "I am comfortable and content."

On Saturday, April 10, at 7:30, he died. On Thursday, April 15, his body arrived in St. Louis. It was solemnly carried to the Mercantile Library hall. The Merchants Exchange closed its new building. Long lines of his fellow citizens passed the bier. On April 16, Thomas Hart Benton was buried in Bellefontaine Cemetery—in that lot to which he had brought his family—on the western bank of the great river which to him was a symbol of a united nation.

xv. Fire, Plague, and Flood

One of the silliest campaign mistakes ever made by Thomas Hart Benton's opponents was to accuse him of squandering the taxpayers' money in traveling by river. He should have made his homeward trip from Washington to St. Louis by horse and by the shortest possible route, they said. Instead Benton had brought his family home by way of the Ohio and the Mississippi—by canalboat and river boat—and had collected for every mile of this longer route! Such whomped-up implications of turpitude and pocket-lining are ancient campaign weapons, but this smear was a boomerang. Any reasonably bright public-relations counselor would have known from the beginning that it could be nothing else. Travel by horseback or stage across unpaved forest trails and unbridged rivers was an ordeal a man did not impose on his family, if it could be avoided. The trip by river might be more expensive, but why should not "Old Tom"—who spent time enough in the saddle—travel first class after a wearing session? And should not a St. Louis man patronize the steamboats? The boats were making St. Louis rich. Indeed they might make it the capital of the United States. There was serious talk of ceding it to the nation so that Congress might meet in this rapidly growing metropolis instead of in slow, mosquito-black Washington. And accessibility by steamer was one of its big attractions.

Double-decked, tall-stacked, curlicue-bedizened, white-painted packet boats, the favorites of the Currier and Ives engravers, were changing St. Louis from a wilderness settlement into a city dreaming of national and world importance. They made possible the sensational boom of the 1840s and 1850s, checked only temporarily by the Civil War.

When Laclède first came up the Mississippi, and for sixty years thereafter, river travel was by pirogue or flatboat. These pirogues, built rather like barges, were 35 to 60 feet long and 12 to 15 feet wide. They carried from 30 to 40 tons of freight at a penny a pound. Much of the time they had to be poled through shallow water or towed like a canalboat by men tugging on long lines. Such travel was arduous for crew and passengers alike. The trip from St. Louis to New Orleans took from four to six weeks, and the trip up the river from New Orleans to St. Louis might take three months. The arrival of the first steamboat, the *Zebulon M. Pike*, at the St. Louis levee in 1817 may be set down as the false dawn of the new era. True, as early as 1810 Nicholas Roosevelt of New York had come to St. Louis on behalf of his partners, Robert Fulton and Robert R. Livingston. If granted a monopoly, they would provide transportation on the inland rivers. John Fitch, another steamboat builder, had first insisted that steamers could not be operated competitively on a river. Westerners realized how wrong he was. The Mississippi and Missouri and their tributaries, according to an estimate made by Senator Benton and Governor Clark, consisted of "50,000 miles of boatable water." So St. Louisans had no notion of granting a monopoly—least of all to strangers. In fact Louisiana is the only state along the Mississippi which ever extended such a privilege. Fulton, Roosevelt, and Livingston, however, went a step farther and asserted patent claims against Henry Shreve, Daniel French, and other western boatbuilders, claims dismissed by the courts as the West developed its fabulous river traffic.

This traffic grew rather slowly, not because of eastern litigation but because of the snags and other navigational perils of the big river. It flourished only after young James B. Eads of St. Louis devised an ingenious double-hulled boat for clearing streams of wrecks and hazards. Even so, the claims of the New Yorkers added another drop of bitterness to the resentment the West was developing against the East.

St. Louis, however, did not miss the significance of the *Pike*. Her captain, Jacob Reed, collected one dollar each from the curious who wanted to come aboard, and made a fine thing of this. The next year, 1818, the *St. Louis*, built on the Ohio, tied up at the city for which it was named. "The company on board was large and genteel, and the entertainment very elegant," reported the *Missouri Gazette*. In May 1819 the *Maid of Orleans*, built in Philadelphia, came up from New Orleans, and that year the *Independence* went up the Missouri as far as Franklin, now Boonville. But it was not until 1825, when two stern-wheelers, the *Brown* and the *Magnet*, laid over for repairs, that St. Louis really became a river port.

With the swelling and quickening of the westward flow of explorers, traders, adventurers, soldiers, and settlers, came the days when the St. Louis levee was lined tightly for a mile or more with packets, often two- and sometimes three-deep. The bustling confusion of "the bully boats, the bully crews, and the bully captains, too," is still the favorite subject of St. Louis muralists. River steamers could not be built fast enough. Incidentally, it took eight months to build a fine and fast boat, and it cost between $100,000 and $150,000—more for the big ones. Yet such a handsome craft—one of those floating palaces with which Mark Twain was infatuated—had a life expectancy of only five years.

In two years there were 103 wrecks in one bend of the Mississippi. The first disaster was the explosion of the *George Washington*, with a loss of nine lives. Perhaps the worst was the explosion of the *Sultana* in 1865 with the loss of 1647 lives, all Civil War prisoners on their way North. Disasters, each of which took more than fifty lives, included those of the *Ellen McGregor* in 1836, the *Blackhawk* in 1837, the *Orinoco* in 1838, the *General Brown* the same year, the *H. W. Johnston* in 1847, the *Edward Bates*, also in 1847, the *Louisiana* in 1849, the *Anglo-Norman* in 1850, the *Glencoe* in 1852, the *Ben Sherrod* in 1861, the *Pennsylvania* in 1858, the *H. R. Arthur* in 1871.

The first of the steamers frightened the Indians. They called it "the big thunder canoe." Later steamers frightened at least some of the whites. In the early days of steamboating there were no rules and no aids to navigation. The boats had no whistles. There were no signals for passing. For that matter, there were no fixed schedules, no load limits. There were no restrictions on engines and boilers. It was common to carry a pressure of 180 to 220 pounds to the square inch in a boiler made of iron only three-sixteenths of an inch thick. Racing added to the dangers, although Mark Twain, in *Life on the Mississippi,* said a "slow boat was more dangerous than a fast one with an alert pilot." In some of the famous river races, the boats carried no passengers because they were regarded as a nuisance under the circumstances, but passengers often did urge captains to race a passing boat.

Captain Joseph Brown, veteran St. Louis steamboat man, said that the builders "never entirely mastered the science of building boats suitable to the trade." By way of evidence he cited the big *St. Louis*. Built for Captain George R. Taylor at St. Louis, this boat was 360 feet long, with a 45-foot beam and a 10-foot hold. She was powered by seven engines. Captain Taylor, backing his experience on the river with his money, hoped to make the New Orleans–St. Louis run in three and one-half days, carrying a payload, but the best time the big boat ever made was seven days. When loaded, she was nose-heavy. In their famous race in 1871, the *Robert E. Lee* made the 1200 miles between New Orleans and St. Louis in three days, eighteen hours, fourteen minutes to beat the *Natchez,* which took three days, twenty-one hours and fifty-seven minutes. Today's towboats take an average of six days to push a tow of barges upstream. They make the downstream trip in half the time. They don't race; they work.

Captain Brown himself invested in a big triple-decked paddle-wheeler, 310 feet long. Seven boilers powered her 40-foot stern wheel. After only seven months he lost her by fire at Memphis. She was tied up at the wharf when the burning *George Collier* came alongside at one o'clock in the morning. "In fifteen minutes what cost me $220,000 was a smoldering wreck that sold for $1500," Brown said. That was in 1854. He also recalled the explosion of the *Moselle* at Cincinnati, which "littered both shores with arms and legs." Of the *Moselle*'s 250 St. Louis-bound passengers, 100 were killed. But freight rates were profitable. A steamer might pay for itself in three or four trips. But the railroads ended the era of the fancy boats.

Mark Twain, revisiting the levee, bewailed the change:

Half a dozen sound-asleep steamboats where I used to see a solid mile of wide-awake ones! This was melancholy, this was woeful. . . . Half a dozen lifeless steamboats, a mile of empty wharves, a Negro, fatigued with whiskey, stretched asleep in a wide and soundless vacancy, where the serried hosts of commerce used to contend! . . . The towboat and the railroad had done their work, and done it well and completely. The mighty bridge, stretching over our heads, had done its share in the slaughter and spoliation. . . .

The pavements along the riverfront were bad; the sidewalks were rather out of repair; there was a rich abundance of mud. All this was familiar and satisfying; but the ancient armies of drays, and struggling throngs of men, and mountains of freight, were gone; and Sabbath reigned in their stead. The immemorial mile of cheap, foul doggeries remained, but business was dull with them. . . . St. Louis is a great and prosperous and advancing city; but the river-edge of it seems beyond resurrection.

For a long time it was hard to disagree with Mark Twain. The towboats rarely tie up at the downtown levee. A magnificent national memorial is now abuilding there, but Mark Twain might not accept it as a substitute for the glory departed. Hear him argue against Charles Dickens and hear, too, in what surroundings our grandparents and great-grandparents lived:

Mr. Dickens declined to agree that the Mississippi steamboats were "magnificent," or that they were "floating palaces." . . . If Mr. Dickens was comparing these boats with the crown jewels; or with the Taj, or with the Matterhorn; or with some other priceless or wonderful thing which he had seen, they were not magnificent—he was right. The people compared them with what they had seen; and, thus measured, thus judged, the boats were magnificent—the term was a correct one, it was not at all too strong. . . . The steamboats were finer than anything on shore. Compared with superior dwelling-houses and first-class hotels in the valley, they were indubitably magnificent, they were "palaces." . . .

Every town and village along that vast stretch of double river frontage had a best dwelling, finest dwelling, mansion—the home of its wealthiest and most conspicuous citizen. It is easy to describe it: large grassy yard, with paling fence painted white—in fair repair; brick walk from gate to door; big, square, two-story "frame" house, painted white and porticoed like a Grecian temple—with this difference, that the imposing fluted columns and Corinthian capitals were a pathetic sham, being made of white pine, and painted; iron knocker; brass door-knob—discolored for lack of polishing. Within, an uncarpeted hall, of planed boards; opening out of it, a parlor, fifteen feet by fifteen—in some instances five or ten feet larger; ingrain carpet; mahogany center table; lamp on it, with green paper shade . . . several books, piled and disposed, with cast-iron exactness, according to an inherited and unchangeable plan; among them . . . "Album" full of original "poetry" of the Thou-hast-wounded-the-spirit-that-loved-thee breed; two or three goody-goody works—*Shepherd of Salisbury Plain,* etc; current number of the chaste and innocuous *Godey's Lady's Book,* with painted fashion plate of wax-figure women with mouths all alike—lips and eyelids the same size—each five-foot woman with a two-inch wedge sticking from under her dress and letting on to be half her foot. . . . On each end of the wooden mantel, over the fireplace, a large basket of peaches and other fruits, natural size, all done in plaster, rudely, or in wax, and painted to resemble the originals—which they don't. Over middle of mantel, engraving—Washington Crossing the Delaware— which would have made Washington hesitate about crossing, if he could have forseen what advantage was going to be taken of it. Piano—kettle in disguise—with music bound and unbound piled on it, and on a stand nearby: "Battle of Prague"; "Bird Waltz"; "Arkansas Traveler"; "Rosin the Bow"; "Marseillaise Hymn"; "On a Lone Barren Isle" (St. Helena); "The Last Link Is Broken"; "She Wore a Wreath of Roses"; "The Night When Last We Met"; "Go, Forget Me, Why Should Sorrow o'er That Brow a Shadow Fling"; "Hours That Were to Memory Dearer"; "Long, Long Ago"; "Days of Absence"; "A Life on the Ocean Wave, a Home on the Rolling Deep"; "Bird at Sea"; and spread open on the rack where the plaintive singer has left it, "Rolholl on, silver moo-hoon, guide the trav-el-err on his way," etc. . . . Frantic work of art on the wall—pious motto, done on the premises, sometimes in colored yarns, sometimes in faded grasses: progenitor of the "God Bless Our Home" of modern commerce. . . . In big gilt frame, slander of the family in oil: papa holding a book (Constitution of the United States); guitar leaning against mama, blue ribbons fluttering against its neck; the young ladies, as children, in slippers and scalloped pantalettes, one embracing toy horse, the other beguiling kitten with ball of yarn, and both simpering up at mama, who simpers back. . . . Under a glass French clock dome, large bouquet of stiff flowers done in corpsy-white wax. Pyramidal what-not in the corner, the shelves occupied chiefly with bric-a-brac of the period. . . . Horsehair chairs, horsehair sofa which keeps sliding from under you.

That was the residence of the principal citizen, all the way from the suburbs of New Orleans to the edge of St. Louis. When he stepped aboard a big fine steamboat, he entered a new and marvelous world: chimney-tops cut to counterfeit a spraying crown of plumes—and maybe painted red; pilot-house, hurricane-deck, boiler-deck guards, all garnished with white wooden filigree-work of fanciful patterns; gilt acorns topping the derricks; gilt deer-horns over the big bell; gaudy symbolical picture on the paddle-box, possibly; big roomy boiler-deck, painted blue, and furnished with Windsor armchairs; inside, a far-receding snow-white "cabin"; porcelain knob and oil-picture on every stateroom door; curving patterns of filigree work touched up with gilding, stretching overhead all down the converging vista; big chandeliers every little way, each an April shower of glittering glass drops; lovely rain-bow light falling everywhere from the colored glazing of the sky-lights; the whole a long-drawn resplendent tunnel, a bewildering and soul-satisfying spectacle! . . . Every stateroom had its couple of cozy clean bunks, and perhaps a looking-glass and a snug closet, and sometimes there was even a wash-bowl and pitcher, and part of a towel which could be told from mosquito-netting by an expert—though generally these things were absent, and the shirt-sleeved passengers cleansed themselves at a long row of stationary bowls in the barber shop, where were also public towels, public combs, and public soap.

The *Golden Eagle,* one of the last of these river boats, made excursion trips down to New Orleans and also up the Tennessee until World War II days. But no matter how hard the feature writers tried to embellish her, she was no "floating palace." So it is barely possible that Mark Twain, infatuated with the Mississippi and everything about it, may have looked on the town mansion with one pair of eyes, and on the packet boats with quite a different pair. Certainly the crews of today's towboats in their fine quarters are not overly impressed by a recitation of the old splendors; but towboats carry no passengers, except an occasional friend of the company. And all-steel towboats do not go up in a quick flash of flame, as did Captain Brown's pride at Memphis. Nor does St. Louis live in fear of such a great fire as the steamboats brought to the city in 1849.

The volunteer fire companies—the Phoenix, St. Louis, Central, Union, Washington, Liberty, Franklin, Mound, Laclede, and Missouri —in their gold-braided, sailor-collared merino shirts and stiff-brimmed hats had just held their annual May parade. The people of the city, now numbering more than 60,000, were impressed; they felt safe. Then at 9 P.M. on May 17 fire was discovered aboard the packet *White Cloud,* tied up at the foot of Cherry Street. It was soon out of control. The boat was cut loose from her moorings. Pushed by current and wind, she bumped into one vessel after another along the crowded levee. The volunteer firemen responded to the alarm bells quickly enough, but with thirty boats ablaze, the heat became too intense for the men to work at the water's edge. They fell back, trying to protect the stores and warehouses along Front Street. But the flames leaped to a building at the corner of Front and Locust streets. Then the fire ran rapidly southward along Front Street; a shift in the wind sent the flames westward to Main Street, and then to Second Street. The fire jumped Second Street at its intersection with Olive. Then the wind again spread it southward, toward the Cathedral. Sparks leaped to an old cooper's establishment three blocks away, and there the fire consumed two more city squares.

Blocked from access to river water where it was needed most, equipped with only primitive fire engines, the volunteers were dead-tired after a night of fighting to check the spread of the flames. On that grim morning Thomas B. Targee, auctioneer and leader of the Christ Church choir, decided that extraordinary methods would have to be used to overcome the holocaust. He was captain of the Missouri volunteer fire brigade. The leaders of the other companies deferred to him. He proposed to blow up enough buildings to form a firebreak. That, incidentally, was how the Cathedral was saved. Targee sent a wagon to the United States Arsenal, on the southern edge of the city, for a load of gunpowder. While this was being brought to Third and Market streets, Targee hurried to his home at Fourteenth and Market for a quick cup of coffee and a word of reassurance for his family. Back at the fire, he threw a tarpaulin over the powder kegs, lest they be set off by sparks. Then he volunteered to carry the kegs into the buildings to be demolished. After safely blowing up three of these, Targee picked up a keg of powder and carried it into Phillips' Music Store on Market Street, two doors east of Second. He had barely entered the door when there was a terrific explosion. Subsequent investigation suggested that somebody else had already placed a powder keg in the store. Targee's was one of three lives lost in the fire. The flames destroyed thirty-three river craft and 430 buildings, including the post office, three banks, and the three principal printing shops. A dozen city blocks were reduced to ruin. Property loss was estimated as high as $10,000,000. So devastating a fire had never before occurred in the United States. And it occurred in the midst of the worst of the city's cholera epidemics.

It was in the fire of '49 that the volunteer fire companies for the last time covered themselves with glory. The rivalry between them was becoming so keen that they were turning into a serious public nuisance. Not content to vie with each other in uniforms, equipment, and parades, they were turning conflagrations into contests. The men were more intent on beating out a rival company than in beating down the flames. The rowdyism of the b'hoys became notorious, especially as they fought for fireplugs. These had two outlets, but the water pressure was too low to make the upper one of much use if a hose had been attached to the lower outlet. So the first company on the scene would attach short lengths of hose to the lower outlets of as many plugs as possible to frustrate those arriving a little later. This became more important to the volunteers than speedily playing a stream of water on the flames. Rather than accept frustration, the late-comers sometimes would cut the hoses of their rivals. Then the two companies would fight each other instead of the fire. The only answer was a regular, paid fire department, yet the volunteers had enough political influence to prevent the formation of such a force under Mayor Washington King, and again under Mayor John M. Wimer. But Ordinance No. 3871 finally was adopted on September 14, 1857, on the insistence of Mayor John How.

Then the volunteers closed ranks against the new force. Those that owned their own buildings and equipment—some of the volunteer stations had been paid for in whole or in part by the city—for a long time resisted selling them to the city, as they were required to do by law. For a time they even persisted in answering the alarms sounded by the two fire watchmen, John Leonard and Pat Creary, from the belfry of the College Church at Ninth and Lucas. John and Pat indicated the approximate location of a fire by the number of strokes they tolled on the big bell. (The first telegraphic fire alarm system was not set up until 1858.) But the regulars were determined to show that they were real "pros," not to be beaten to the plugs. So Mike Dressell and Henry Marquis hitched Mike, a fine gray trotter, to the Mound City Belle, a light rig. They were in the streets at all hours, often backed into some alley. As soon as they heard the fire bell of the College Church, they were off to the plugs. They held them until the other equipment, including the city's first steamer, arrived.

This was not always easy. Even the volunteers who gave up answering the alarms would be in the streets to howl at the firemen, calling them "hirelings" and "Hessians," and jeering them as traitors. One volunteer group broke out a banner lettered "Not One Cent for Protection." Stones were thrown at the men. Hoses were cut. Horses were stabbed. Once even shots were fired. Nice sport while it lasted!

The first cholera epidemic broke out in October 1832. It raged for five weeks. It carried off five per cent of the population. The epidemic which began in the spring of 1849 was worse. Before it ran its course it claimed 4317 citizens' lives. While it was raging more than 4000 deaths were ascribed to other causes. Yet when the first deaths occurred people tried to ignore them. Eight years later the *Sketchbook of St. Louis* reported:

The general cry was "hush up, don't alarm the people, you'll frighten them into disease, it is all humbug, this is only a slight sickness among deck-hands and poor laborers who eat poor food and live in ill-ventilated houses." But the formidable and insidious malady would not consent to be ignored. All the while, it was furtively and gradually disseminating its poison, filling up the wards of the city hospital and thinning the crowds of laborers on the levee. The very small number of our citizens who ever took the trouble to examine the statistics of mortality began to be alarmed, but they were frowned down as panic-makers, and the disease was pronounced to be ship fever, which threatened only sailors and steamboat men.

The disease in 1849 assumed a more bold and formidable appearance, and instead of stalking through dirty lanes and filthy alleys, it walked boldly in the streets. It was proclaimed in a thousand forms of gloom, sorrow, desolation and death. Funeral processions crowded every street. No vehicle could be seen except doctors' cabs and coaches passing to and from cemeteries, and hearses, often solitary, making their way towards those gloomy destinations. The hum of trade was hushed, the levee was a desert, the streets, wont to shine with fashion and beauty, were silent. The tombs, the homes of the dead, were the only places where there was life, for there the incessant rumblings of carriages and the tramping of feet and the murmur of voices were heard. Physicians were kept continually on the move, on visits of mercy, going hither and thither with no hope of a fee or reward except that which may follow them to the after world. Some reeled through the streets like drunken men, from sheer fatigue and exhaustion. Many did not touch a bed for weeks. To realize the full horror and virulence of the pestilence, you must go into the crowded localities of the laboring classes, where the poor immigrants cluster together in filth, sleeping half a dozen in a room without ventilation and having access to filthy yards which have never been filled up. Here you can find scenes of woe, misery and death which will haunt your memory in all time to come. Here you can see the dead and dying and the sick and convalescent in one and the same bed. Here you could find the living babe clinging to the pallid breast of a dead mother. Here you will find whole families swept off in a few hours. Offensive odors frequently drew neighbors to such awful spectacles. What a terrible disease! Terrible in its insidious character, in its treachery, in the quiet serpent-like manner in which it gradually wound its folds around its victim, beguiling it by its deceptive wiles, cheated his judgement and sense, and then consigned him to grim death! Not like the plague with its red spots and fever and wild delirium, but with a guise so deceptive that none feared the danger until too late.

While the disease apparently was described as early as the fifth century B.C., the great pandemic broke out in India in 1816 and took ten years to reach Calcutta and the ships of the seven seas. By 1830 it reached the Near East and Russia. In the next two years it ravaged Europe. Ships brought it to Canada from the British Isles in 1832. By way of Lake Champlain and the Hudson it came down to New York. It also came directly across the ocean. Cholera reached New Orleans in the same year. It descended on St. Louis from the Erie Canal and the Great Lakes, by way of the Ohio, and up the Mississippi. There were serious outbreaks that year in the great inland valleys. General Winfield Scott lost a detachment of troops on the way to the Black

Hawk War. Travelers took circuitous routes to St. Louis, but in vain. In 1833 the American Fur Company's steamer, *Yellowstone,* carried the disease up the Missouri as far as Fort Union. Its ravages among some of the Indian tribes were especially terrible. The survivors swore eternal enmity against the white man and his evil "medicine." Actually the men on the steamer and in the forts tried in vain to keep the Indians away. They simply were accused of refusing to distribute the gifts the Great White Father had sent from Washington. They isolated the sick, but even in the cities there was little to be done. The disease survived in pockets along the Mississippi. And cases also were brought to the city year after year by the steamboats. Some of the outbreaks were relatively mild, but not that of 1849.

Belatedly, a mass meeting was held at the Courthouse on June 25. A Committee on Public Health was formed. Mayor James G. Barry called a special session of the City Council on June 26. The Council gave the Committee almost unlimited emergency powers. It was authorized to make "rules and regulations" and to impose fines for their violation. It also was given an appropriation of $50,000. The members of the committee were T. T. Gantt, R. S. Blennerhasset, A. B. Chambers, Isaac Hedges, James Clemens, J. M. Field, George Collier, L. M. Kennett, Trusten Polk, Lewis Bach, Thomas Gray, and William Clark. They established hospitals in each of the city's six wards and appointed physicians to attend them. The most prominent doctors in the community rendered heroic services. The committee also appointed "block inspectors" and put them in charge of a thorough cleaning of the city.

On Saturday, June 30, at 8 P.M., heaps of stone, coal, resinous tar and sulphur were burned at every street intersection. It was hoped that the smoke would "dissipate the foul air which has been the cause of so much mortality." Monday, July 2, was declared a day of fasting and prayer. A quarantine was placed in effect against all steamboats from the South. Yet not one case of cholera occurred among the student body of St. Louis University, then at Ninth and Washington in one of the worst cholera areas. This circumstance strongly suggested that the city's water supply had as much to do with the epidemic as steamboats. The university drew its water from wells which obviously were not contaminated. (There is a votive statue in the present College Church, commemorating the escape of students and faculty.)

On August 1 the committee proclaimed the epidemic at an end and returned $16,000 of its $50,000 appropriation. Just as the fire led to the establishment of a paid fire department in 1851, so did the cholera outbreak lead to the establishment of modern public health methods. But for at least another decade cholera was a recurring scourge in the cities along the Mississippi and the Ohio.

Steamboats might bring fire and the plague; they also could save lives—especially when the Missouri and the Mississippi floods raged by St. Louis. The city itself was safe from inundation, thanks to Laclède's eye for high ground. But the "American Bottom" on the Illinois side could become a churning brown lake. The worst flood, even worse than that of 1947, came in June of 1844. There then was no levee system to protect settlers. The Missouri rose steadily in late May and early June, and the Illinois was swollen by heavy rains. By June 16 the water was high in the streets of Illinois Town, as East St. Louis was then known. By the eighteenth loss of life and property were becoming catastrophic. Crowds came to the St. Louis waterfront to see the turbulent yellow stream, still rising, pitching uprooted trees and flinging houses past the levee. St. Louis suspended much of its business activity to be of help to the flood victims. Bernard Pratte called on the steamboat captains to volunteer for rescue work. Preparations were made to shelter refugees in the huge new tobacco barn and in warehouses elsewhere in the city. Clothing and food were made available. On June 24 the flood reached its crest at St. Louis, setting an all-time high-water mark.

During these days river boats steamed far inland across the Illinois countryside. The *Kaskaskia,* for example, tied up at Colonel Menard's door in Cahokia to rescue pupils of the Sisters' Convent who had found refuge there. And the pilot of the *Indiana* followed the Illinois wagon roads to rescue stranded farmers. The river was 38 feet above the low-water mark at St. Louis, and water was 10 to 20 feet deep over the streets and roads of the East Side. The *Indiana* alone brought almost 200 refugees to the city.

The steamboats also brought color, entertainment, and excitement to St. Louis. One of the very few old boats still tied up at the St. Louis levee is the *Goldenrod,* a showboat. It is a reminder of the first floating circus, which came to the city in the spring of 1853. Under the management of George R. Spalding, this showboat had an amphitheater which seated 1000 persons. It offered bareback riding and all the customary circus thrills. Crowds as large as 2500 crowded to the gangplank for the performances. After selling all his seats, Spalding offered—at $1 each—"permissions" to look through the boat's windows.

The river pilots, dapper and independent, sometimes were something of a circus themselves. Men like Captain Sellers, Horace Bixby, the chief pilot of the Union fleet in the Civil War, George Ritchie, John C. Swon, and John S. McCune of the Keokuk Packet Company, as well as Mark Twain, generally stayed at the Barnum Hotel. Ashore, as in the pilothouse and on texas deck, they were elegant dressers and free spenders.

Sellers, it was said, knew every house, barn, shed, and dead tree in the 1200 miles between New Orleans and St. Louis. He knew where state lines came to the river. He could tell his position in the dark. He made no less than 109 consecutive New Orleans–St. Louis trips on the same boat. St. Louis people still visit his monument in Bellefontaine Cemetery, the figure of a pilot at the helmsman's wheel with a river map, inscribed "Sellers Is at the Wheel." Only a little less spectacular were Bart and Dan Able. Dan took the *Anthony Wayne* 160 miles up the St. Peter's, now the Minnesota River. And the two brothers could boast that not a single life was lost on the boats which they piloted in their long careers.

The crews were even more devil-may-care than the captains and the pilots. They had their favorite poolrooms in St. Louis, where they inspired many a youngster with an irresistible desire for life on the river. A boy could hardly resist joining the company of Mark Twain's riverman, who proclaimed with no inhibiting modesty:

Whoo-oop! I'm the old original iron-jawed, brass-mounted, copper-bellied corpse-maker from the wilds of Arkansas! Look at me! I'm the man they call Sudden Death and General Desolation! Sired by a hurricane, dam'd by an earthquake, half-brother to the cholera, nearly related to the small pox on the mother's side! Look at me! I take 19 alligators and a bar'l of whiskey for breakfast when I'm in robust health, and a bushel of rattlesnakes and a dead body when I'm ailing. I split the everlasting rocks with my glance, and I squench the thunder when I speak! Whoo-oop! Stand back and give me room according to my strength! Blood's my natural drink, and the wails of the dying is music to my ear. Cast your eyes on me, gentlemen! And lay low and hold your breath, for I'm about to turn myself loose! Look at me, gentlemen! Whoo-oop! I'm the bloodiest son of a wild cat that lives! Whoo-oop! Bow your neck and spread, for the Pet Child of Calamity's a-coming!

No riverman, with the exception of Mark Twain, ever was quite so flamboyantly eloquent—and Twain probably was a little better on paper than on deck. But why quibble about exaggeration where exaggeration is the essence of the matter? Surely the Child of Calamity was reasonably typical of these "reckless fellows, every one elephantinely jolly, foul-witted, profane, prodigal of money, bankrupt at the end of the trip, fond of barbaric finery, prodigious braggarts; yet in the main, honest, trustworthy, faithful to promise and duty."

Then there were the river gamblers—perhaps never as many as may be found between the covers of a double-breasted historical novel or in a grade-B movie, but enough to cause Mayor John Darby and a number of his successors to start periodic antigambling drives in St. Louis. They added their touch to deck and levee. And they were not too much resented by the muttonchop men in Wellington boots and tall hats and their ladies in princess dresses and cashmere shawls who made their way through the confusion of loading and unloading to the cabins of the river boats. After all, to travel on these luxurious vessels in such romantic company was to realize the thrill of every boy who waited on the bluff above a river town for the chance to cry, "Steamboat a-comin'."

"Steamboats plied all the western streams wherever there was water enough to float them," wrote Thomas D. Clark in *Frontier America*. "Some reckless pilots said they asked only for heavy dews to speed them on their way across country. Lower decks of these vessels were crammed with freight; animals, wagons, plow tools, furniture, and household plunder in general, millstones, stocks of peddlers' goods, clocks, gadgets, and even coffins. Settler, merchant, Yankee speculator, land hunter, preacher, European traveler and government official all were going westward. As Robert Baird wrote:

Whilst above, in the deck cabin, there is everything that may be called human—all sorts of men and women, of all trades, from all parts of the world, of all possible manners and habits. There is the half-horse and half-alligator Kentucky flatboatman, swaggering and boasting of his prowess, his rifle, and his wife. One is sawing away on his wretched old fiddle all day long; another is grinding a knife or razor; here is a party playing cards; and in yonder corner is a dance to the sound of a jew's harp; whilst few are trying to demean themselves soberly, by sitting in silence or reading a book. But it is almost impossible—the wondrous tale and horrible Indian story they are telling; the bottle and the jug are freely circulating; and the boisterous and deafening laugh is incessantly raised, sufficient to banish every vestige of seriousness, thought and sense.

Amidst this confusion, and even in the minds of those lank and laconic men who sat astride piles of freight leaning their chins forward on long, bony, calloused hands, there worked the silent factor of the great American dream . . . everybody . . . dreamed of the rich lands of the West.

There was a time when old boatmen had cause to wail about the decline in river traffic. But men like Mark Twain and Captain Brown were poor prophets. "The glory of steamboating on the Mississippi is past," said Brown; and Mark Twain complained that "the government has taken away the romance of our calling." Maybe so, but Dick Bissell's *A Stretch on the River* is as up-to-date as can be, and it makes even better reading than parts of *Life on the Mississippi*. True, the railroads and the trucks became the great freight haulers, and the fancy firetraps rotted away at their moorings while travelers took to Pullmans and planes. But there has been a spectacular revival of river traffic since the advent of the steel towboat. A modern river boat, like the *United States* or the *Allied-Ashland,* among the latest to be built in Captain Eads's Carondelet Yards in St. Louis, has three times the power of the *Sprague,* which when built in 1901 was supposed to be the mightiest stern-wheeler of them all. The new towboats are powered by safe diesel engines instead of explosion-prone boilers. They have finger-tip steering control, ship-to-shore telephones, and radar. Their galleys, all handsome stainless steel, are the envy of hotel chefs. Living quarters of their officers and crew are air conditioned, walnut paneled, and furnished with leather sofas. The occasional guest who travels on such a boat wastes no sighs for "the good old days." He finds it evidence enough that river traffic always has been important in the economy of St. Louis, although it declined sharply in the early part of this century.

By 1850 St. Louis owned more river shipping—24,955 tons—than any other port. Three years later, St. Louis owners had doubled this tonnage, and over the years they have consistently maintained their lead. The excitement of a dozen arrivals a day at the downtown levee may have "gone to the catfishes," but the volume of freight handled at the fifty-three river terminals in the St. Louis harbor area has grown sensationally—especially in the last ten years. In their offices in the Boatmen's Bank Building, the army engineers maintain a year-by-year tabulation of commercial tonnage on the Mississippi between the Ohio and the Missouri rivers. Beginning with the estimates for the earlier period, this now covers 134 years. That means too many figures for this book, but here are the highlights:

1824—	90,000	tons	1884—	1,275,590	tons
1834—	174,000	″	1894—	1,003,710	″
1835—	439,000	″	1904—	421,607	″
1844—	716,000	″	1914—	204,118	″
1854—	1,370,000	″	1924—	738,728	″
1861—	800,000	″	1925—	1,003,569	″
1862—	950,000	″	1934—	1,858,011	″
1864—	1,650,000	″	1944—	4,775,489	″
1865—	2,251,523	″	1947—	5,746,160	″
1874—	1,440,090	″	1948—	9,464,196	″
1880—	2,129,700	″	1954—	17,663,048	″

1957— —23,647,777 tons

These figures really are worth a second glance for the fascinating story they tell. When set down on graph paper—and it must be a big sheet—they produce a curve beyond the happiest dream of the bulls of Wall Street. It climbs steadily until the first two years of the Civil War, 1861 and 1862, bring a bit of a dip. Yet by 1865, still a war year, the previous high has almost been doubled. In that year the tonnage rose to 2,251,523. The next decade brought a severe setback, the figure for 1874 being only 1,440,092. This reflects the South's economic depression in the postwar decade. By 1880 the river tonnage again was above the 2,000,000 mark. After that, however, came the really breathtaking slide to a low of only 204,118 tons in 1914—almost as low a figure as that of a century earlier.

From nothing to nothing in a hundred years! This dive was so traumatic that some St. Louisans have not yet recovered from it. They are still in shock, in coma. They turned their backs on the Mississippi once and for all, and they will not be told that it is not the chief tributary of the Dead Sea. The sensational fall-off was caused chiefly by the competition of the railroads, but it also must be attributed in part to a peculiar blindness along the big river. Many towns had fallen into the habit of charging wharfage fees so high that boats could not afford to stop at their levees. Owners were charging all the traffic would bear. They hoped to stop the railroads by lobbying against them—a hopeless business. Many spurned the plebeian barge and joined in Mark Twain's lament for the gilded, gingerbread boats which never did have enough space for freight. Worst of all, the waterways were neglected.

Men like David R. Francis of St. Louis, however, were unwilling to abandon the great national artery which from the beginning had been the source of the city's strength and wealth. They started the deep-waterways movement, especially the campaign for a 6-foot channel from the Great Lakes to the Gulf. This gained real momentum after World War I. By 1925 river tonnage again was over the million mark. By 1944 it was twice as great as ever before—4,775,489. Within three years it was well above 5,000,000. And this figure was virtually doubled in another year! River freight figures were rising faster than a flash flood. Today the tonnage on the engineers' chart is well above 25,000,-000. There has been an increase of more than 300 per cent in the last ten years—and roughly one third of this tonnage is handled at St. Louis.

The long, low barges pushed along by towboats carry chiefly petro-leum products, coal, cement, sand, gravel, iron and steel, chemicals and grains. They are, of course, most economical for such bulky car-goes. But the tows to and from St. Louis also carry more items than may be found in the most varied mail-order catalogue: automobiles, bamboo, shoes, wine, beer, paper, sugar, bicycles, glass, catsup, honey, coffee—oh, name it! And now there are the St. Lawrence Seaway and the new Calumet Harbor, offering even more freight for transfer from economical steamer to more economical tow and vice versa.

Truly the Mississippi has been more loyal to St. Louis than many St. Louisans have been to the Father of Waters. It used to be said that St. Louis people simply sat on the bank of the great river and watched it bring them wealth. Now it may be said that a good many—but not all of them—turned their backs on the river and it brings them more wealth!

The Mississippi Valley Barge Line and the Federal Barge Lines, the nation's No. 1 and No. 3 inland water carriers, have their headquarters in St. Louis. Mississippi Valley operates more than twenty towboats and about 500 barges. Its two newest towboats, the 3600-horsepower *Missouri* and the *Lackland Mackay,* are built especially for operation on the Missouri River. On that stream they follow the course of the fur traders, explorers, and Western settlers to the Chouteau outposts which now are Kansas City and St. Joseph, and to the trading "forts" even farther upstream, stockades which have grown into such thriving prairie cities as Omaha, Council Bluffs, and Sioux City.

Federal Barge Lines, incidentally, is a subsidiary of the St. Louis Shipbuilding and Steel Company. This is the world's largest builder of inland towboats and barges. It still operates the Carondelet yard of

Captain James B. Eads at the foot of Davis Street in South St. Louis. Here the company has made many innovations in inland marine architecture. It has built the largest all-welded steamboat, the first streamlined river craft, the first air-conditioned towboat, the fastest towboat, and many special-purpose boats such as suction dredges and derrick boats. Two other St. Louis yards, the Barbour Metal Boat Works and the Humboldt Boat Service, specialize in the building of barges and small craft.

The 13,494-mile inland waterways system by which St. Louis cargoes reach major mid-continental cities in twenty-seven states and also ten ocean ports, exists today because of consciousness of the importance of the Mississippi. Long ago St. Louis at its own expense joined Bloody Island to the Illinois shore, lest the river cut a new channel and leave the city high and dry. General Charles Gratiot of St. Louis, when he was Chief of Engineers, sent young Lieutenant Robert E. Lee to join City Engineer Henry Kayser in developing the dikes and revetments which force the Mississippi to dig its own channel, and which still are the backbone of its harbor.

Today certainly it is not true—as tourists just back from the Rhine are inclined to say—that Europeans use their rivers while we neglect ours. While passenger traffic hardly is to be expected on the rivers in the jet age, St. Louisans more than ever use the Mississippi for excursions and pleasure-boating. The *S.S. Admiral,* a huge all-steel excursion boat, carried most of the 643,378 water passengers recorded in St. Louis in 1955. Except during the winter, it makes a daily trip of about fifty miles downstream and back—far enough to afford an idea of Mississippi scenery—and an evening excursion during which most of the passengers enjoy its dance floors rather than the scenery. Of course, some do prefer seats on the moonlit deck, but it is a question whether they are interested in the scenery. Excepting the towboat men, those who see most of the river and its bluffs, of course, are the owners of thousands of small craft—motor cruisers and sailboats—on the river, especially on the big pool above the Alton dam. There more and more St. Louisans spend halcyon summer holidays. Some suburbanites, preferring golf courses to the city's bustle, may not see the Mississippi very often. They probably are corporation *Wandervoegel* just waiting to serve another hitch in another town. To a genuine St. Louisan the river is as important as the sea is to a Gloucesterman. He can stay away from the levee just so long; then he must have another contemplative look at the Father of Waters.

xvi. With Scalpel and Sword

St. Louis is one of the outstanding centers of medical training in the United States. Over the years more than a dozen medical schools have flourished in the city, but not since Dr. Joseph N. McDowell's college was closed on the eve of the Civil War has there been a school like his. It was protected by cannon, and its students armed with worn-out rifles—a thousand of which the good doctor got from the government at a bargain price. In the 1840s and 1850s medical schools had not yet won the worshipful respect they now claim. A doctor might be jeered in the streets as "Old Sawbones," and rumor might spread stories about diabolical activities of medical students which today are beyond the wildest imagination of the antivivisectionists. Dr. McDowell was not one to take chances. He had his cannon; and having them, he used them.

On the Fourth of July, George Washington's birthday, and just about every other patriotic holiday, he had his students carry the guns into the field in front of the school on Seventh Street. He put on a handsomely decorated three-cornered hat and strapped on a cavalry saber. After marching his students back and forth for a while and then giving them a patriotic harangue, he would issue the order to "make Rome howl." That was the signal for loading the cannons and firing them across the empty field in the direction of Mill Creek.

Brother Jasper, in charge of the playground of the Christian Brothers College, next door to the medical school, also was a man who took no chances. Whenever Dr. McDowell began his cannonading, Brother Jasper got all his pupils indoors as quickly as possible. Those guns were supposed to be aimed across an empty field but, since they were mounted only on sawhorses, one could never be sure. Dr. McDowell regarded the Christian Brothers as good neighbors and fellow educators. He always was somewhat annoyed when Brother Jasper ordered a retreat. So half in anger and, perhaps, half in amusement, he would rush to the Brothers' door to protest against such an unpatriotic retirement.

"You run a good school," he would shout, "so good that I would send my own boy to it—if I had a boy. There is only one thing wrong with you. You retire from the celebration of your country's glories." Then he would return to his own students, and again they would "make Rome howl."

Although Dr. McDowell was on good terms with the Christian Brothers, he had grievous doubts about the Jesuits. Had not their St. Louis University absorbed one of the earlier medical colleges? And under the auspices of the university, was this not being transformed into a school which required years of study before it would grant a student a diploma as a physician and surgeon? Had it not built up a considerable faculty, many of whose members were trained abroad? Was it not a breeding place of dangerous innovations?

Dr. McDowell was even more disturbed over the medical school established by Dr. Charles Alexander Pope. Dr. Pope was a handsome man, trained in Europe, with high professional standing in the community. He had married Caroline O'Fallon, the daughter of wealthy John O'Fallon. Immensely proud of his son-in-law, O'Fallon had built an architecturally handsome school for him at Seventh and Spruce streets. People were saying it was without equal in the United States, outside of New York and Philadelphia. Dr. McDowell's school was connected with a college opened by Episcopal Bishop Kemper. Dr. Pope's college was for a time associated with St. Louis University and finally became the medical school of Washington University. But long before that it became the one institution Dr. McDowell could not tolerate. He never failed to refer to it on commencement day. That celebration was almost as splendid as his patriotic commemorations. There never were any empty seats in the amphitheater. Dr. McDowell, playing his violin, would lead his students in academic procession. He would play a few tunes and then put aside his fiddle to begin his oration:

Now gentlemen, we have been together five long months. Doubtless, some of these months have been very happy months, and doubtless some have been very perplexing ones. Such is the eternal fate of workers and students. But now, gentlemen, the saddest of all sad words must be uttered, namely, farewell! Here, retrospection takes her sway, either gladdened or saddened, as idiosyncracies hold the mind. We have wandered in the labyrinthian way of anatomy. We have floated in the ethereal atmosphere of physiology. We have waded knee-deep, nay, neck-deep, into a sea of theory and practice; ground, filtered, pounded and inspected elements of materia medica, and slowly pounded in the endless crucible of chemistry.

As we say farewell, it is needless for me to say that I hope God may in His infinite mercy, bless you as you deserve. But remember that labor *omnia vincit*. No man under God need hope that success can come or will come without labor, for God has ordained that all of us must earn our living by the sweat of our brow. Nature only recognizes the laborer, and eternally damns the rich man, by satiety and disease!

Doubtless, one of your number in this class, will come back to the great city of St. Louis with the snow of many winters upon his hair and walking upon three legs instead of two, as Sphinx has it. As he wanders here and there upon its streets amidst the crowded and eager throng, noting the wondrous improvement here and change there, suddenly, gentlemen, it will occur to him to ask one of the eager passers-by, "Where is Dr. Mc-Dowell?" "Dr. McDowell? Dr. McDowell?" he will say, "What Dr. Mc-Dowell?" "Why," he will tell him, "Dr. McDowell, the surgeon!" "Oh, yes, Dr. McDowell, the surgeon. Why he lies buried close to Bellefontaine."

Slowly, gentlemen, he will wend his way thither, and there amidst the rank weeds, he will find a plain marble slab inscribed "J. McDowell, Surgeon." While he stands there contemplating the rare virtues and eccentricities of this old man, suddenly, gentlemen, the spirit of Dr. McDowell will arise on ethereal wings and bless him, thrice bless him. Then, gentlemen, this spirit will take a swoop and as he passes McDowell's College, he will drop a parting tear. But, gentlemen, when he gets to Pope's College he will spit upon it. Yes, I say he will spit upon it.

Dr. McDowell had eccentricities enough. His college building had eight sides, and it was to have been eight stories high, although finances never allowed it to rise to its full height. It had a domed roof supported by a central pillar of brick. In this pillar were recesses in which Dr. McDowell hoped to install the remains of his family. The bodies were placed in copper receptacles filled with alcohol and then tightly sealed. Pending completion of the niches, they were carried to a cave in back of the school by students carrying torches. When Dr. McDowell thought he was on his own deathbed, he called Dr. Charles W. Stevens and his son, Dr. Drake McDowell, and made them promise solemnly that they would place his body in a similar receptacle and suspend it in Mammoth Cave, Kentucky. With the passing of the years, he had come to prefer caves to his pillar niches. Indeed, he had purchased a cave near Hannibal, Missouri, to make it the last resting place of his family. The people of the Mark Twain country, however, seemed benighted and lacking in respect to the medical profession. The iron door was pried off the cave, and the "coffin" of one child interred there became an object of idle curiosity. So, when his wife died, Dr. McDowell purchased a mound across the river, near Cahokia, and had a tomb built on it. This he could watch with a telescope from the cupola of his college. Years later the doctor and his wife were buried in Bellefontaine Cemetery. Meanwhile, at the outbreak of the Civil War, he had gone south with his cannons, which he contributed to the Confederacy.

Dr. McDowell's eccentricities—and even the possibility that his cannons were turned against St. Louis troops under Grant and Sherman —could be forgiven, and were. In spite of his odd notions, he was regarded as an exceptionally able physician and surgeon in a community in which medical standards were relatively high. In fact many of the graduates of the other medical colleges attended his lectures for half a year as a sort of graduate course. During the cholera epidemic no medical man was more selfless and more tireless than Dr. McDowell.

Perhaps St. Louis University should have acquired Dr. McDowell's cannons for the protection of its medical school. There was one tense day in 1849—the year the Know-Nothings sat in City Hall—when it seemed that guns might be needed. Ignorant and malicious reports of abuses, cruelties, and profanations perpetrated in hospitals and medical schools, especially in dissection rooms, were fodder for prevailing prejudices, especially in connection with a Roman Catholic institution. So it took only an act of unpardonable carelessness—and if it was a callow prank, it was worse—to precipitate an ugly affair. Parts of a cadaver were left on a table in a yard adjoining the school. Although the yard was surrounded by a high fence, these were seen. Soon a menacing and muttering crowd gathered in Washington Avenue in front of the university. Some of the bolder rioters broke into the building. Furniture, books, and scientific collections were damaged. As reports of the attack spread, crowds of Irish and Germans—many of them Catholic and all of them anti-nativist—hurried to the scene. A bloody fight was averted by the commanding coolness of Judge Bryan Mullanphy. Mounted, he rode into the street between the two crowds where a line of sorts had not yet been crossed. Although a leading political opponent of the nativists, his appeal for order was respected. It soon was supported by the mayor and other authorities. Some of the mobsters proposed attacks on the other medical schools, but the crowd slowly dispersed. After this affair, several faculty members appealed for a separation of the medical school from the university on the ground that the prevailing anti-Catholic spirit handicapped its work. This was rejected by the university trustees. Nevertheless a separate charter eventually was obtained, but the independent medical school languished.

St. Louis became the first medical center west of the Mississippi as inevitably as it became the region's trading and industrial center. The importance of its location was apparent to Europeans who studied a map with migration in mind. They had learned that Philadelphia, Boston, New York, and Charleston already were much like the cities they knew in the Old World. The new, beckoning America of opportunity was the West. And the West was St. Louis. Such thoughts had been in the mind of Dr. André Auguste Condé even before there was a St. Louis. They led him to Fort Chartres. When that post was abandoned, he, like St. Ange, accepted Laclède's invitation to the new French outpost. He practiced there from 1766 to 1776. Similar thoughts were suggested to Antoine François Saugrain, born in Versailles, by his fellow scientist, Benjamin Franklin. Persuaded to go to the United States, he nevertheless was drawn to Gallipolis, the French settlement in Ohio. He remained there for more than half-a-dozen years before being attracted to St. Louis in 1800 by the Spanish governor's offer to build a small hospital for him. He was not the first, but certainly the most eminent European medical man brought to the settlement by the Spaniards. Saugrain was not only a doctor but also a good botanist. He planted a large herb garden and made careful studies of the usefulness of plants in the treatment of diseases.

A dish of Father Didier's tea generally was adequate to cure the ills which afflicted early St. Louisans who, for the most part, lived a vigorous outdoor life. What St. Louis really feared was an epidemic. When smallpox broke out, Dr. Saugrain undertook a campaign to persuade everybody to be vaccinated. Through the *Gazette* he informed "such physicians and other intelligent persons as reside beyond the limits of his accustomed practice that he will with much pleasure upon application, furnish them with vaccine injection." He also let it be known through the *Gazette* that "persons in indigent circumstances, paupers and Indians will be vaccinated and attended gratis."

The first American doctor to settle in St. Louis was Bernard Gaines Farrar. This Virginian came to the city two years after the Louisiana Purchase. His ability as a surgeon was extolled throughout the West by a man named Shannon, a member of the Lewis and Clark expedition.

On a subsequent exploring trip Shannon was shot by a Blackfoot Indian and brought back to St. Louis in what was considered a hopeless condition, but Dr. Farrar amputated a leg and nursed the man back to health. Shannon later served as a judge in Kentucky. Dr. Farrar's repute, however, was based even more on the respect of his colleagues in the medical profession. He died in the terrible cholera epidemic of 1849. Another doctor who died in this epidemic was William Carr Lane, the city's first mayor. Respect and gratitude of Dr. Carr Lane's patients helped him to win nine successive terms in office. Here was a "Boston" for whom many of the French were glad to vote. Immediately after his first election he organized a public health system.

The establishment of a military post, Jefferson Barracks, brought army doctors to St. Louis, and many of them settled in the city. Best known among these was William Beaumont. After twenty years in the army he set up practice in St. Louis in 1834. Even laymen still know him for "building a window in a man's stomach." While serving near the Canadian border, he treated Alexis St. Martin for a gunshot wound. Since the wound would not close, Dr. Beaumont took advantage of the opening to study St. Martin's digestive system. St. Martin lived with him for years, and Beaumont conducted a lengthy series of experiments described in an internationally circulated book, *Experiments and Observations on the Gastric Juice and the Physiology of Digestion.* Dr. Beaumont was one of the founders of the first medical school west of the Mississippi at St. Louis University in 1836. He was its professor of surgery. As related, that school, went out of existence in a few years. The present medical school of the university traces its beginnings to Dr. Pope's institution.

The city's first really modern hospital—St. Louis now has more than fifty—was established by Mother Seton's Sisters of Charity in 1828 on Spruce between Third and Fourth streets. John Mullanphy, who had given the nuns a convent in 1827, built a new four-story hospital for the nuns in 1832, which became known as the St. Louis Hospital. In 1874 this hospital was moved to Montgomery Street near Grand Avenue, and in 1930 it moved into the large and architecturally impressive De Paul Hospital buildings, since enlarged, on North Kingshighway. About twenty years after the establishment of the original hospital, the Sisters persuaded Dr. Louis C. H. Boislinière, a native of Guadalupe, to make his home in St. Louis and help them in opening the first lying-in hospital and foundling asylum in the United States. Dr. Boislinière became the city's first coroner in 1858.

Another notable institution was the Free Clinic established by Dr. F. Gratz Moses, who came to St. Louis in 1841 after having been the personal physician of Joseph Bonaparte. He was persuaded to open the dispensary by Mrs. Vital M. Garesche, who raised the necessary money with the help of the Reverend William G. Eliot. He also made the basement of his church available as the dispensary's first office. Associated with Dr. Moses were Dr. William M. McPheeters, Dr. J. B. Johnson, Dr. George Johnson, Dr. J. L. Clark, and Dr. Pope. They operated the place on a volunteer basis for seven years. It was then taken over by the city. Dr. Simon Pollak, who came from Prague in 1845, opened the dispensary's department of ophthalmology. In 1852 he solicited subscriptions to establish the Missouri Institution for the Education of the Blind. This was taken over by the state after five years of private operation. Its present buildings are one of the features of the South Side.

Construction of the first City Hospital was begun in 1840 on a two-block site bounded by Lafayette and Carroll avenues and 14th and Grattan streets. It was opened in 1846 with ninety beds. Thus it became the nucleus of the present group of municipal hospitals on the same site just south of the business district. This includes the large Max C. Starkloff Memorial, more prosaically known as City Hospital No. 1, and the Malcolm A. Bliss Psychopathic Hospital, and their connected facilities. The city also maintains the outlying Robert Koch Hospital for contagious diseases, the St. Louis Chronic Hospital on Arsenal Street, not to be confused with the St. Louis State Mental Hospital on the same street, which with its high red dome dominates the Mill Creek skyline, and the Homer G. Phillips Hospital, City Hospital No. 2, on Whittier Street on the North Side. The relatively new Homer G. Phillips Hospital—with its wings arranged so that it has only "outside" rooms—was built originally for Negro patients. Largely through the efforts of the late Dr. Robert Elman, professor of surgery in the Washington University medical school, who made it into the nation's outstanding training center for Negro doctors, this hospital and City Hospital were desegregated. In case of an accident, for example, the police now take the victim to the nearest hospital, regardless of race. The high quality of care afforded by the municipal hospitals is assured because they are staffed largely by the city's two medical schools. Their chief handicap stems from a chronic shortage of funds made inevitable by the city's lack of adequate taxing powers.

Patent medicines and bizarre systems of treatment followed the American flag to St. Louis. In 1845 the *St. Louis Medical and Surgical Journal* reported that the city had "146 persons who are endeavoring to obtain a livelihood by the practice of the healing art, which includes homeopaths, botanics, Thompsonians, etc." This meant some kind of doctor for every 274 persons. Today the St. Louis Medical Society has 1267 members, and the County Medical Society has 450 members. This means roughly one doctor for every 835 persons.

Another notable medical immigrant was Dublin-trained Dr. Thomas O'Reilly. One of the most indefatigable crusaders for higher standards of practice was a Kentuckian, Dr. Moses L. Linton of the St. Louis University faculty. He founded the *St. Louis Medical Journal* in 1843. He also was the author of a widely used text, *Outlines of Pathology*.

The arrival of the émigrés of 1848, including a goodly number of doctors trained in German universities, helped considerably to raise the standards of medical education in St. Louis. They were astounded by the inadequacies of Dr. McDowell's half-year course, and said so. Dr. Adam Hammer was especially outspoken. He attended all Medical Society meetings, and regularly—and scathingly—denounced one or another procedure of the local practitioners. In self-defense they closed their gatherings to newspaper reporters and prayed that Dr. Hammer would go back to Europe—which, eventually, he did. But not before he and some of his colleagues, notably Dr. F. Ernst Baumgarten, Dr. J. Fischer, and Dr. Ernst Schmidt, founded the Humboldt Medical College across the street from City Hospital.

Dr. Schmidt, as professor of anatomy, was almost as colorful as Dr. Hammer or, for that matter, Dr. McDowell. At the outbreak of the Civil War he immediately joined one of the St. Louis regiments, the Second Missouri, with the rank of major. But he was given only $66 for medical supplies and equipment for 1800 men. Well, Dr. Schmidt was not a surgeon who would march off to war without even enough lint and bandages. So he quietly made his plans with some of the soldiers. They would go to the outskirts of the city and hold up a train! As they collected money from the passengers, they would explain that this was a forced levy for war purposes. And so Dr. Schmidt went off to war, prepared to care for the victims of battle. He and his son, Dr. Louis Schmidt, the eminent urologist, for years told the story of the "forced levy." The still rough-and-ready St. Louis of 1861 was rather proud of Dr. Schmidt. For the moment it was willing to concede that the end justified the means. In 1879 Dr. Schmidt ran for mayor of Chicago against Carter Harrison on the Socialist-Labor ticket after having refused both the Republican and Democratic nominations. That was in the days of Altgeld and the Haymarket riot excitement. He was defeated, but seven of his partisans were elected to the city council.

Today the hospitals and medical schools set the community's professional standards. The largest aggregation of private hospitals is the Barnes group, associated with Washington University. This includes Barnes, Barnard Free Skin and Cancer Hospital, McMillan, Renard, St. Louis Children's, St. Louis Maternity and Wohl, located with the medical and dental schools and their dormitories at Kingshighway and Euclid avenue. Nearby are Shriners Hospital for Crippled Children, Central Institute for the Deaf, St. John's, and Jewish hospitals. Directly affiliated with St. Louis University are Firmin Desloge Hospital, which soars high above Grand Avenue opposite the medical school, the adjacent new Cardinal Glennon Memorial Hospital for Children and the St. Mary's group. Other outstanding hospitals are Alexian Brothers, DePaul, Deaconess, Lutheran, St. Luke's, St. Anthony, Missouri Baptist, and the Missouri-Pacific and Frisco, as well as the Cochran Memorial Veterans' Hospital.

The Washington University medical school now ranks with Harvard, Johns Hopkins, and Chicago; and St. Louis University sends well-trained practitioners to all parts of the country. The late Dr. Evarts A. Graham of the Washington University faculty, the first surgeon to remove a human lung and the first to associate cancer with the smoking of cigarettes, was a towering figure among latter-day medical school teachers. Outstanding teachers today are Dr. James O'Leary and Henry Schwartz, the neurosurgeon. Medals and awards sometimes tell more about those who give them than about those who receive them. Some even may be regarded as the rewards of effective "public relations" rather than as acknowledgments of professional eminence. But surely the Nobel Prizes are beyond such doubts. In the last two decades no less than five St. Louisans have received them: Dr. Edward A. Doisy of St. Louis University, and Drs. Joseph Erlanger, Herbert Gasser, Carl F. Cori and the late Gerty T. Cori of Washington University. It is well that their standards are so high, since today's medical schools are not prepared to ward off attacks with swords and cannons.

XVII. Lovejoy Against Slavery

In spite of the compassionate and courageous Spanish friar, Bartolomé de Las Casas, slavery spread under every flag raised in the New World. Slavery was sanctioned in the Louisiana territory by French, Spanish, and American law. The French brought a few slaves to St. Louis from New Orleans. There was a larger influx when the Spaniards welcomed slave-owning American settlers. Yet in 1860 Missouri, with a population of 1,182,012, had only 114,931 slaves and 24,320 slave-owners—909 of them in Lafayette County. Two thirds of the slaves were owned within a few miles of the Missouri River—in the tier of counties still known as "Little Dixie." There slavery bred the same attitudes that it did in the South: a cavalier pride of caste, unthinking loyalty to established customs, and a partisan political arrogance which fed on economic weakness instead of being curbed by it. The Missouri "planter" could not help being at odds with the homestead farmer and the city worker. Slavery was a cause of the continuing coolness, if not antipathy, between St. Louis and the rest of Missouri.

There never were very many slaves in St. Louis. Oh, Madame Chouteau kept a few. There are the usual stories of how kindly she treated them, and there is a record of a suit she carried to the Spanish governor against a son-in-law who accidentally killed one of her slaves in the pursuit of two others bent on running away. If the law regarded slaves as property, the Church, with Gallic practicality, discouraged their sale. The first French priests insisted on the baptism of Negro children, and they introduced the custom of having the master or a member of his family as a sponsor. This established a spiritual relationship and a genuine responsibility for the Negro infant's welfare and education. Personal servants often were given their freedom, if not for the reason given by Louis Villars, lieutenant of infantry, when he petitioned for permission to emancipate a "Negress named Julie . . . the zeal and attachment she exhibited in his service having completely ruined her health, he desires to see her at liberty with a view to her recovery."

The condition of many a slave also was eased by the practice of allowing him to "hire his own time." This permitted him to take a job, provided that he paid part of his earnings to his owner, often a very small part. Some owners allowed slaves to purchase their freedom with such earnings. Slaves in St. Louis were entitled to trial by jury as early as 1811. Since they could not be expected to pay fines, they were punished with the lash at a rough approximation of one stroke for $2. Since a $10 fine was regarded as verging on the excessive for any-body, the whipping post was not inordinately cruel. Slaves were not supposed to be abroad after 9 P.M. in winter and 10 P.M. in summer without their master's permission. But there were after-curfew regula-tions for whites as well, especially those caught by the watch in "gardens not their own." There were restrictions on balls and entertainments given by free Negroes for slaves. But there seems to have been little excessive severity until slaveowners felt compelled to protect their prop-erty against Abolitionist slave snatchers. The first police board, ap-pointed by secessionist Governor Claiborne Jackson, abrogated the privilege of "hiring time," and restricted the other liberties enjoyed by slaves by custom if not by law. But that was in 1861, and very shortly the police were not taking orders from Jefferson City but rather from an anti-slavery mayor, the Committee of Public Safety, or a Union general. The largest number of slaves in St. Louis at any one time probably was not much over 1500. There really was little to be gained by owning slaves in the city. The fur trade called for men more independent and venturesome than easygoing Negroes. A few slaves could be used in a warehouse or to drive drays. A little money might be made by hiring out Negroes as teamsters or laborers. But since cotton did not grow in the streets of St. Louis, slaves were most useful around the house as cooks and servants, and only in limited num-bers. Slavery did not fit into the pattern of a growing commercial and industrial community. Quite aside from its moral aspect, it made the city unattractive to enterprising immigrants. Henry Boernstein said this time and time again in the *Anzeiger des Westens.* Tom Benton, Ed-ward Bates, the Blairs, Gratz Brown, Thornton Grimsley, Mayor Filley, Henry T. Blow, John How, John Stevenson, and many others down the years felt the same way. Many of those who owned slaves in the city did so largely out of tradition. To a man from a Virginia plantation it seemed part of his way of life, and he automatically resented those who criticized him.

Others put up with slavery in spite of their dislike of it because of the hard questions raised by emancipation: How would the free Negro earn a livelihood? What would be his social status? How would he be educated? Housed? And what of the slaveowners? How would they be compensated? Placated? Frank Blair thought it might be best to pay the owners and return the Negroes to Africa or send them to Central American colonies. Yet he knew that the American Colonization Society was no success. (Up to 1872 it helped only 13,598 back to Africa.) And many an American Negro, of course, could not and would not go home again.

St. Louis never could work itself into an Abolitionist frenzy. It was not edified by the New Englanders who cheered William Lloyd Garrison while New Bedford slavers were landing contraband "black ivory" on the reefs and the sea islands off Georgia and the Carolinas. Yet in general it was as ready on the eve of the Civil War for emancipation as it was a century later for desegregation in the schools. In the very years when feeling was most inflamed, slaves were being freed more and more frequently. Although he could hardly afford it, U. S. Grant, a man who agreed with Douglas in his debates with Lincoln, freed his farm hand when he gave up his farm. Frank Blair freed four slaves. So the records run, including the story of Colonel William B. Mason, who in his youth had been tutor to the children of Edward Bates. He bought Jane Waters to save her and her children from being "sold down the river."

Jane was the property of a Colonel James B. Crockett, who left her in St. Louis when he joined the 1849 gold rush. While Crockett was in California Jane married George Waters, a slave who "hired his own time" and was employed by a group of professional men to tidy up their offices. Crockett came back from California in 1858 to wind up his affairs, to "turn everything into money." So he had Jane and her three children locked up in Lynch's slavepen on Locust Street between Fourth and Fifth streets, and offered them for sale. In this extremity George Waters went to Mason for help.

Mason called on Crockett at the Planters' House. A bit surprised at Mason's indignation over routine business, Crockett explained that Jane was "a likely breeding woman" and that he had been offered $1800 for her.

"Since you take this matter so much to heart," he said, "I will sell Jane and her children to you for $1000." Mason made out a check and then immediately went to court to free the woman and her children.

This meant giving adequate assurance that they would not become public charges.

Another slave fared better as the result of the '49 gold rush. He accompanied his owner, Robert Lewis, to California. On their return Lewis divided half the gold he had found between his wife and the slave.

St. Louis accepted the 1820 compromise, which made Missouri a slave state and Maine a free state, to avoid further delay in being admitted to the Union, but also because it prohibited the extension of slavery elsewhere north of 36° 30'. This meant that the North and the West had "snatched the scepter from Virginia forever." Yet the compromise brought an invasion of the Missouri Valley by Virginians and other Southerners who believed that its bottom lands invited cultivation by slave labor. About the same time the South turned to a one-crop economy. King Cotton pushed his realm into Texas. Wasteful methods caused the planters to clamor for more land—and for more slaves. There was agitation for a revival of the slave trade. Thomas Hart Benton perceived the shift and recognized the dangers. He wanted western land made cheap for homesteaders. He wanted railroads to speed the settlement of the West. And he set himself more and more firmly against the slave power.

Yet even in 1860 Lincoln said, "We must not interfere with the institution of slavery where it exists." The first Republican candidate, Benton's son-in-law, was defeated as an anti-slavery candidate. The country rejected "Free-Soil, Free Speech, and Frémont." When Frémont issued his premature emancipation proclamation, Lincoln repudiated it. Neither Lincoln nor St. Louis went to war primarily for the Abolitionist cause. The armies of Grant and Sherman did not march to "The Battle Hymn of the Republic," but to the tune of "The Union Forever."

In the anxious years before the war, people and politicians were not blind to the tragedy of slavery. St. Louisans were not edified by the slave auctions on the Courthouse steps—held on New Year's Day when the courts disposed of assets of estates in their charge. "How could the free laboring man ever get $2 a day," they wondered with Boernstein, "when a black slave cost his master but 10¢ a day to keep?" They saw through the pretense which made fashionable society in New York and Philadelphia as ardently proslave as the fashionable society of Charleston and New Orleans. They could agree with Senator James

H. Mason of Virginia when he said of the Civil War, "I look upon it then, sir, as a war of sentiment and opinion by one form of society against another form of society," pseudo aristocracy, if you will, against the worker and the homesteader. In 1820 and 1830 St. Louisans were not holding their ears to the ground to hear each premonitory rumble of "the shocks and throes and convulsions" that Lincoln heard in his debate with Douglas, but they were increasingly aware of the divisive forces threatening the Union. Charleston might be willing to "let the Union slide," not St. Louis.

The Union meant everything to western men. They had explored the region between the Mississippi and the Pacific. They had disproved the myth of the Great American Desert. They wanted a unified nation to exploit that region. They were tired of hotheads. They knew, as Lincoln did, that slavery was "a moral, social and political wrong," but they would not be surprised to hear him say that, given the power to work a radical change, "I should not know what to do." They were ready to see some merit in the Douglas "Freeport Doctrine" that every state should mind its own business. In the 1830s and 1840s they were busy building a city and half a nation. They did not want a nation-rending crisis. The problem of slavery would have to be worked out gradually. "Squatter sovereignty" ought to end the evil instead of spreading it.

When young Elijah Parish Lovejoy came to St. Louis in 1827 to teach school, he was welcomed. Education also would work against the slave power in the West. Lovejoy was born in Albion, Maine, the son of the Reverend Daniel Lovejoy, a Congregationalist minister. He was a graduate of Waterville College (now Colby). In St. Louis he soon began to make something of a name for himself by writing first for the *Missouri Republican* and then for the *Times,* the first of five St. Louis papers to carry that name. The *Times* championed Henry Clay—Harry of the West, the expansionist who even wanted Canada—and was popular with St. Louis Whigs. Pleased by the paper's new contributor, they said Lovejoy would go far in politics. Then, in the winter of 1831–32, Lovejoy attended a revival, one of those religious affairs characteristic of frontier Protestantism. He was converted and joined the First Presbyterian Church of Dr. W. S. Potts. Education and politics now seemed unworthy activities. Lovejoy wanted to preach. On the advice of Dr. Potts he went in 1832 to the seminary at Princeton, New Jersey. In April of 1833 he was licensed as a preacher by the Second Presbytery of Philadelphia. And in the fall he was back in St. Louis—and again welcome.

Some readers of his *Times* articles suggested that Lovejoy start a Presbyterian weekly. They offered to finance it. So the first issue of the *St. Louis Observer* appeared on November 22, 1833. Its sponsors were pleased until the paper took an extreme position on emancipation. They expostulated with the editor. Slavery was an evil, they agreed, but Missourians were of two minds about the institution which, after all, was ancient and lawful. It ought to be opposed by reasoned argument, they said, rather than by harsh denunciation. Lovejoy listened until they had finished; then he reminded his patrons that the Missouri Constitution declared that "the free communication of thoughts and opinions is one of the inalienable rights of man." Again they agreed, but argued that a man might be prudent about the manner in which he published his opinions. Lovejoy's ultimate rejoinder was a public protest against "these attempts to frown down the freedom of the press." He said:

"I have appealed to the constitution and the laws of my country; if they fail to protect me, I appeal to God."

Lovejoy antagonized not only proslavery men in the city, but also the moderate opponents of the system. On top of that, he denounced "popery" and preached prohibition. St. Louis was not a temperance town, and so many of its people were Catholics that it was called "the Rome of the New World." Lovejoy, of course, was under no obligation to conform to the standards of the majority. He had every right to his ideals and his opinions. In voicing them, however, he hardly was the lowly, meek, and humble man described by Dwight Lowell Dumond in *Anti-Slavery Origins of the Civil War*. Nor was he the only man in St. Louis outraged by the lynching of the Negro, McIntosh, or by the man's brutal killings. St. Louis had had a taste of violence and it wanted no more, least of all Abolitionist violence intensified by social and religious prejudices.

The city was, on the whole, an easygoing place. But it had taverns full of rivermen accustomed to encounters with Indians and grizzlies, fearing neither man nor beast, and ever ready for a brawl. Vindictive slavery men might buy trouble for Lovejoy at the price of a few drinks. Respectable citizens whom he had offended might not rush to his defense at the first alarm in the middle of the night. His backers concluded that it would be best to move him and his press across the river to the free soil of Illinois. Their decision was confirmed when plug-uglies poured out of riverfront saloons into the *Observer* office. Furniture was broken, but the press was not seriously damaged. Desiring none of the rioting that was going on in New England, in Pennsylvania, in Ohio, and elsewhere in the East, St. Louis was not unhappy to see Lovejoy leave. The man had too much of the agitator in him.

In Alton, then the largest city in Illinois, Lovejoy established the *Alton Observer*. In its very first issue he advocated the Abolitionist doctrine of immediate freedom for the slaves and no compensation for their owners, the straight Garrison line. He was joined by Edward Beecher, David Nelson, and Gideon Blackburn, also refugees from violence precipitated by their Abolitionist preachings. But a doctrine which would not go down in Boston—where Channing denounced it as the source of "bitter passions and a fierce fanaticism which have shut every ear and heart against argument"—would not go down in Alton more readily than in St. Louis. Trouble followed Lovejoy across the Mississippi. His press arrived in Alton on a Sunday. A strict observer of the Sabbath, he left it unguarded in a warehouse. After nightfall it was dumped into the river. A public meeting was called to protest against the outrage. The vandalism was denounced and funds were raised for a new press, but Lovejoy's extreme views were repudiated. His fervor was disturbing on free soil too.

Yet Lovejoy was not intimidated even when his second press was destroyed on the night of August 21. A new one was obtained. His friends again implored him to be discreet. They even exacted a promise that he would devote the *Observer* exclusively to Presbyterian church news. He gave his promise, but he could not keep it. He and his friends were in correspondence with zealous Abolitionists in all parts of the country. They had issued a call for a meeting on July 4, 1837, for the establishment of the Illinois Anti-Slavery Society, the state auxilliary of Garrison's rather loose organization. So Lovejoy again was committed to go against the dominant sentiment in the community. Another mass meeting was held. Resolutions condemning his conduct of the *Observer* were adopted. A committee was appointed to call on Lovejoy. He told its members that he intended to continue without change. So Press No. 2 was dumped into the river.

The Ohio Anti-Slavery Society sent a third press. It was taken from the warehouse and thrown into the Mississippi the day it arrived, September 3. Lovejoy's Abolitionist friends immediately promised him

still another press. In Alton anger had simmered through the heat of
the summer. Now it came to a boil. An indignation meeting was held
on November 3. Again strongly worded resolutions were adopted. This
time they called for discontinuance of the *Observer*. In fairness, Lovejoy
was given the floor. He began with valiant defiance:

"My rights have been shamefully, wickedly outraged; this I know
and feel, and can never forgive. I can and do freely forgive those who
have done it. But if by compromise is meant that I shall cease from
doing that which my duty requires of me, I cannot make it. And the
reason is that I fear God more than I fear men. Think not that I
would go lightly contrary to the public sentiment around me. The good
opinion of my fellow-men is dear to me, and I would sacrifice anything
but principles to obtain their good wishes—I know I am but one and
that you are many. My strength would avail but little against you all.
You can crush me if you will: but I shall die at my post, for I cannot and
will not forsake it."

Lovejoy could be provocative too. He mixed bigotry with his anti-
slavery crusading. He hardly helped his cause when he proclaimed:

"These mobs will cease as soon as some of the mobites are hanged by
the neck, and not before . . . Mercy no less than Justice calls for a
summary execution of some of the wretches as an example to the rest."

This sounded like an invitation to a lynching! It was inevitably resented by those who felt that slavery was sanctioned not only by the
law, but also by religion. While the Catholic and Episcopal churches—
although not all their members—were neutral on the issue, many ministers of other denominations defended slavery. Lovejoy enraged the
hotheads. He told a committee—which asked him to end his activities
for his own safety—that he was ready for martyrdom.

Elijah and his younger brother, Owen, organized some of Lovejoy's
followers into bands of six to defend the fourth press. Mayor John M.
Krum, later also a mayor of St. Louis, authorized them to carry
firearms. The press from Ohio arrived on the Alton riverfront
November 7, 1837, a day made grim by a chill premonition of more
than winter. Stores were closed and people remained off the streets as
Lovejoy and his friends moved the new press to a warehouse. After
nightfall a mob did attack the place. There was gunfire from both sides.
A man named Bishop was killed. Some of his friends tried to set fire
to the roof of the building. Lovejoy rushed out and was shot. He
staggered back into the warehouse, up to its second floor, and fell

dead, five bullets in his body. The other defenders, all wounded, escaped along the dark riverfront. The press was thrown into the water. The Abolitionists had a martyr, and by and by it dawned on American journalism that it had one too. A shaft of stone now towers above the Mississippi in memory of the man from Maine.

Owen Lovejoy, over his brother's body, dedicated his life to the Abolitionist cause. He became its leader in Illinois. He was elected to the state legislature in 1854 and to Congress in 1856, serving until his death in 1864. In the House, he was a firebrand. In the spring of 1860 he made an unbridled attack against slaveowners. Anger turned to rage as he advanced toward the Democratic side, his arms in the air, fists clenched. A melee broke out, and for a time it seemed that the Capitol would be disgraced by bloodshed.

The Lovejoy affair was one more demonstration of the deep passions aroused by the slavery issue. The young crusader's extreme arguments obviously did not persuade his fellow citizens. Yet the destruction of his presses and the taking of his life were not justified by his provocations. Those who were angered by his writings would have been wise to ignore them. He had the right to plead his cause. Freedom of the press is guaranteed to make controversy possible. It is not to be opposed by violence. But the question of slavery carried many men beyond reason. St. Louis saw all too much of this turbulence. Responsible politicians refused to exploit it. Abolition came in spite of the Abolitionists.

Shortly after the dirty night by the river, Mayor Krum was in New York, where a friend took him to an Abolitionist rally. Krum, originally a New York State man, heard himself denounced as worse than the most rabid slave driver. His friend finally announced that the Mayor of Alton was present and suggested that he be given the floor. So Krum began to speak. Quietly he outlined all aspects of the Lovejoy affair. He did not blame and he did not exculpate; he explained. He was against slavery himself; but as the first mayor of a river town without police, he was sure that moderation was essential to public peace. Soon he was being cheered. If the Civil War could have been prevented, it would have been by men like Krum.

His residence in Alton, incidentally, was only temporary. While in the East he married the daughter of Chester Harding, and in 1839 he was back in St. Louis, where he had first settled in 1833. From 1843 to 1848 he was judge of the Circuit Court. In the latter year he defeated Mayor Luther Kennett, becoming the first Whig to beat a Democrat for the office. Krum built the Bloody Island dike, which kept the Mississippi from shifting its channel and leaving the St. Louis levee high and dry. He was more proud, however, of obtaining the first mill tax for the support of the public schools. Education would show the way out of the jungle. So he served ten terms on the school board, and also was on the first board of Washington University. Those who put up a column for Lovejoy might consider putting up a plaque for Krum.

A few years after Missouri's admission to the Union, men who realized that slavery could only mean trouble for the new state met in St. Louis to consider its early abolition. John Wilson, a lawyer of Fayette, Missouri, was at that meeting. Years later in a letter now in the archives of the Missouri Historical Society, he wrote:

In 1827 (I believe it may have been 1828), I was one of those who attended a private meeting of about twenty of us claiming at least to be party leaders, about equally representing every district of the state, of about equal numbers of Democrats and Whigs. Colonel Benton and Judge Barton were present, the two latter, however, not being on speaking terms. One object that brought us together was to consider how we should get rid of slavery in Missouri. We unanimously determined to urge action upon all candidates at the approaching election. Resolutions were drawn up and printed (in secret) and distributed amongst us, with an agreement that on the same day these resolutions, in the shape of memorials, were to be placed before the people all over the state, and both parties were to urge the people to sign them. Our combination, too, then had the power to carry out our project. Unfortunately, before the day arrived, it was published in the newspapers generally that Arthur Tappan of New York had entertained at his private table some Negro men, and that, in fact, the Negro men had rode out in his private carriage with his daughters. Perhaps it was not true, but it was believed in Missouri, and raised such a furor that we dared not let our memorials see the light . . . But for that story of the conduct of the great original fanatic on this subject we should have carried, under the leadership of Barton and Benton, our project, and begun in future the emancipation of the colored race that would have been followed by Kentucky, Maryland, Virginia, North Carolina, Tennessee, etc. Our purpose, further, after we got such a law safely placed on the statute books, was to have followed it up by a provision requiring the masters of those who should be born to be free to teach them to read and write. This shows you how little a thing turns the destiny of nations.

If Lovejoy was too impetuous, were these men too timid?

XVIII. Scott vs. Sandford (19 How. 393)

If the Dred Scott decision started the Civil War, this enormous implication was not foreseen when the litigation began in the Old Courthouse in St. Louis in 1845. The charge of the New York *Tribune,* made in 1856 after the *cause cèlèbre* reached the Supreme Court, that it had been fabricated by proponents of slavery never made any sense. Since the Kansas-Nebraska Act effectively repealed the Missouri Compromise and its ban on slavery north of 36° 30', the slave power would have risked reversal by the Court of the victory won in Congress over the Free-Soilers.

When he filed his suit in the Missouri Circuit Court, Scott was simply a St. Louis Negro seeking to establish his freedom. He was a fine figure of a man, dignified, well-mannered, liked by those who knew him, especially those who chatted with him as he carried his shopping basket along Third Street. Later a reporter for the *Missouri Republican* called him "another Thornton Grimsley done in ebony." This was saying a lot in parade-loving St. Louis, which considered no turnout first-class unless its grand marshall was the impressive, public-spirited army saddle maker, Grimsley, who, incidentally, also introduced the ten-hour day for St. Louis workmen.

Scott was brought to St. Louis in 1827 from Virginia as the slave of Captain Peter Blow, the father of Henry T. Blow and Taylor Blow, both prominent in the anti-slavery movement in the city. He was left to an unmarried daughter of Captain Blow so that he might support her by doing odd jobs. When this did not work out he was sold to Dr. John Emerson, an army surgeon stationed at Jefferson Barracks. When the doctor was transferred to the Arsenal at Rock Island, Illinois, he took Scott with him as his body servant. Scott married in Illinois and when Emerson was again transferred—this time to Fort Snelling in what is now Minnesota—he purchased Scott's wife, Harriet, and took the family with him. The Scotts had two children, Eliza and Lizzie; the first was born aboard the river steamer *Gypsy* on the way upstream to Fort Snelling. Dr. Emerson returned to St. Louis in 1837 and died in 1842, leaving the Scott family as part of his estate. The executors were his widow and her brother, John F. A. Sandford, formerly Indian agent to the Mandans. He had married a daughter of Pierre Chouteau and moved to New York.

Scott sought to buy his freedom and that of his family, offering $500 in cash and the guarantee of a St. Louis army officer that the remainder of the price would be paid. The rejection of this offer decided Scott to assert his freedom in court—on the theory that he had ceased to be a slave by residence in Illinois, where the state law forbade slavery, and at Fort Snelling, in territory where slavery was forbidden by Congress. Scott filed suit in Circuit Court against Mrs. Emerson late in 1846. The case was tried in one of the graceful, elliptical court chambers recently restored by the National Park Service. The verdict went against him, but a second suit, also tried in the old building, brought a verdict in his favor in January 1850. This was appealed, and in 1852 the Missouri Supreme Court, sitting in the St. Louis Courthouse, reversed the lower court, holding that Scott resumed his status as a slave when he returned to Missouri, no matter what he was while he was out of the state.*

In November 1853 Scott's cause was carried to the United States Circuit Court by Roswell M. Field, father of Eugene Field, the newspaper poet. Mrs. Emerson having married Dr. Calvin C. Chafee, a Massachusetts Abolitionist congressman, control over Scott was transferred to Sandford. Scott lost this suit against Sandford, but on May 15, 1854, the case was carried to the United States Supreme Court. Taylor Blow, whose sister had sold Scott to Dr. Emerson, undertook to pay the expenses of this appeal. Montgomery Blair, former mayor of St. Louis, agreed to argue the case. Opposed to him were Senator Henry S. Geyer of Missouri and former Attorney General Revery Johnson. The constitutional and political implications of the case were clear by now and Scott had backers.

* Prof. Harold Schwarz says that the Dred Scott case had a political coloration virtually from the beginning. He agrees that it was not a friendly suit arranged for Scott's benefit. His owner hired an expensive lawyer to protect property of value. Political motives seem to have been involved once it reached the Missouri Supreme Court. Judge James H. Birch and Judge William B. Napton were anti-Benton men displeased by the old senator's advocacy of the Wilmot Proviso, which barred slavery in territory acquired from Mexico. Since both judges were defeated in the November, 1850, elections before deciding the case, it had to be reargued. Judge William Scott, who wrote the two-to-one verdict, also was an anti-Benton man and a strong defender of slavery. According to Schwarz, he conferred at length with Napton before writing his decision.

Once the Dred Scott case attracted national attention, it was exploited, twisted and misrepresented. It was argued before the Supreme Court on Monday February 11, 1856. James S. Pike of the New York *Tribune* at once began to "report" what the judges thought and what their decision would be. He was only one of the correspondents who wrote as if the Court's deliberations were being held in public. Most of this "news" was incorrect, but for the New York *Tribune* it was justification enough to denounce "the five slave-holders and two or three doughfaces on the bench." The New York *Courier,* on the other hand, said the Court "is not prepared—to ruffle its ermine in the strife of politicians and the squabbles of demagogues." The Abolitionist press, which had been warring on the Court for half a dozen years, was not inclined to wait for the verdict before condemning it. It was said that Buchanan was told what the decision would be, and that it was not handed down until March 6 so that at his inauguration March 4, 1857, the President might say that "to the Court's decision, in common with all good citizens, I shall cheerfully submit whatever this may be. . . ." Actually the decision was delayed by the illness of Chief Justice Taney.

Taney was regarded as just another instrument of the slave power. Gone was the esteem in which Andrew Jackson's old ally had been held by both parties. Forgotten, General Zachary Taylor's request that Taney administer the oath of office at his inauguration to "give expression to the high respect I entertain for the Supreme Bench and its august presiding officer." Forgotten the praise of Daniel Webster, who at the Pilgrim's Festival in New York said, "We are Protestants, but a Roman Catholic is Chief Justice and no man imagines that the administration of public justice is less respectable or less secure."

On January 12, 1857, with the case still pending, Benjamin Stanton of Ohio introduced a bill in the House to eliminate the South's disproportionate representation on the Court. "Without such a change," he said, "its decisions have no moral power and cannot command the confidence of the people." He especially warned that nothing could weaken the Union more than a ruling by the Court that Congress does not have the power to exclude slavery from the territories. If the Court went into the question of Scott's citizenship, such a ruling was a possibility. But the reargument of the case on May 12, 1856, indicated the judges were divided, five to four, as to whether the issue of citizenship was before them. On this narrow point they could have dismissed the appeal. The Justices first agreed to say simply that whatever

Scott's status had been when away from Missouri his return made him again subject to Missouri law, and that the Missouri Supreme Court had declared him to be a slave incapable of maintaining a suit.

Justices McLean and Curtis, however, decided to write long opinions sustaining the Missouri Compromise, and Scott's freedom by virtue of living in a free territory. This convinced Justice Wayne that it would be well for the majority to "quiet" the issue of slavery in the territories by saying that it was not in the jurisdiction of Congress. He persuaded Taney, Campbell, Daniel and Catron. When Grier hesitated, Catron wrote to Buchanan, suggesting that he persuade his fellow Pennsylvanian to join in deciding the question, "one way or another." Grier then told Buchanan that he would join the majority because he was anxious that it should not appear "that the line of latitude should mark the line of division in the Court." Thus the historic decision was handed down because two of the nine Justices insisted on raising the broader issue. On Friday, March 6, Chief Justice Taney took two hours to read his opinion. It was 125 pages long. Nelson and Catron read separate opinions. On Saturday McLean and Curtis read elaborate dissenting opinions. Separate concurring opinions were read by Daniel, Grier, Campbell, and Wayne. Thus in a case decided 7 to 2, every member of the Court read an opinion.

Back in St. Louis, Dred Scott was amazed and amused, according to the *Republican,* by "de fuss dey made dar in Washington." The litigation had cost him $500 in cash—and a good deal of labor in lieu of cash. There had been times when he felt that he would not have filed the suit had he known "it was gwine to last so long." He had become something of a star in the vicinity of the Courthouse, where he liked to talk about his case. The Springfield, Illinois, *Argus* created a further sensation when it revealed that Scott's real owner was the former Mrs. Emerson, the wife of the Abolitionist Congressman, rather than Sandford. She then arranged a sale to Taylor Blow so that he, as a Missourian, could ask a Missouri Court to free Scott.

The former slave preserved his dignity in the midst of all the excitement. He received offer after offer to go on tours, to exhibit himself in "museums," and even to lecture. But he would have nothing to do with such exploitation.

The details of the decision in Scott vs. Sandford (19 How. 393) are as dead as the dust on Helen's eyes. Charles Warren, historian of the Supreme Court, wrote, "It will suffice to say that six of the judges—

Taney, Wayne, Catron, Daniel, Grier and Campbell—concurred in holding, that not only a Negro could not be a citizen of the United States but also that Congress had no power to exclude slavery from the territories. . . . Nelson decided only that the Court was bound to follow the law laid down by the Missouri Supreme Court, with reference to the appellant's status as a slave; McLean and Curtis in dissenting, delivered very long and elaborate opinions taking the contrary position on all three points involved."

With the case decided, "the fateful lightning" crackled about the heads of the nine men who, as Warren said, did not "comprehend the intensity of feeling in the North on the subject of slavery was such that it would not tolerate the settlement of the issue by 'judicial decision'; and that such an attempt would only serve to inflame rather than extinguish." One sentence especially was torn out of Taney's opinion and maliciously perverted, the statement that "the Negro has no rights which the white man is bound to respect." The old champion of individual rights did not hold that opinion at all. He had merely said, historically, that this view had been held in the eighteenth century. Not until 1866 did the New York *Independent,* one of the chief spreaders of the falsehood, admit that "it is but justice to the memory of Chief Justice Taney as well as to the Supreme Court to note that . . . Justice Taney did not say it and the Supreme Court did not say it. What Chief Justice Taney said was by way of narration, relating to a period prior to the adoption of the Constitution." Doughty old Taney took the abuse philosophically. In 1856 he vote to former President Pierce:

"You see I am passing through conflict. . . . At my time of life when my end must be near, I should have rejoiced to find that the irritating strifes of this world were over, and that I was about to depart in peace with all men and all men at peace with me. Yet perhaps it is best as it is. The mind is less apt to feel the torpor of age when it is thus forced into action by public duties."

Taney's mind was yet to perform some of its greatest public duties. Two years after the Dred Scott decision he upheld the authority of the national government against interference with its rightful functions by the states. That was in the Booth cases when Wisconsin, rather than South Carolina, was spouting nullification. And in 1861, after the attack on Fort Sumter, the eighty-four-year-old Taney, in his most valiant ruling, clashed directly with Abraham Lincoln. In Baltimore a man named Merryman had been arrested by the military. Taney issued a writ of habeas corpus. The officer in charge of Fort McHenry, where Merryman was held, declined to honor the writ. He said he had been authorized by the President to suspend habeas corpus. Taney immediately cited the officer for contempt. When military force was used to prevent the service of his citation, Taney filed an opinion that the suspension of habeas corpus was illegal. He ordered a copy of this to be transmitted to the President. Once more the storm broke. "The Chief Justice takes sides with traitors," screamed the New York *Tribune.* In St. Louis he was denounced for "his meddling and traitorous efforts to thwart the efficiency of the Government in its hour of peril." But even some of Taney's enemies, for example, the *Cincinnati Commercial,* now applauded him: "Let us have no dictation from the army, so long as we can have justice administered from her customary seat." In *Great American Lawyers,* William E. Mikell wrote, almost half a century later:

There is nothing more sublime in the acts of great magistrates than this attempt of Chief Justice Taney to uphold the supremacy of the Constitution and civil authority in the midst of arms. . . . There is no sublimer picture in our history than this of the aged Chief Justice, the fires of civil war kindling around him, the President usurping the powers of Congress, and Congress itself a seething furnace of sectional animosity, serene and unafraid . . . interposing the shield of the law in the defense of the liberties of the citizens.

St. Louis would have cause to regret that Taney's writ was flaunted. It was to get a taste of military rule, arbitrary taxation, exilings, and unwarranted arrests. Meanwhile a reconstituted Court timidly waited for the war's end to uphold Taney. Then it said, in the Milligan case, that it was illegal for the President to establish military law where civil courts were open. It is a poor tribute to Lincoln to forget Taney.

Benton and his St. Louis followers denounced the Dred Scott decision—and rightly. Yet disappointing as the ruling was to all who wanted to limit or abolish slavery, it was not judicial usurpation of the legislative function. The Court ruled in accord with the prevailing sentiment in Congress. And it did not make the President unhappy. In the Dred Scott case it really "followed the election returns." In December 1853, while the case was still far from adjudication, Stephen A. Douglas from the free-soil state of Illinois introduced the Kansas-Nebraska bill in the Senate. It was signed into law the following July by

President Pierce. And it was the Kansas-Nebraska Act rather than the Dred Scott decision that repealed the Missouri Compromise. This legislation was suggested by Benton's archenemy, Senator David Rice Atchison of Missouri, and pushed by the obtuse Douglas as part of his plan to build a railroad from Lake Michigan to the Gulf, and another from St. Louis to the Pacific. The admission of Kansas and the organization of the territory beyond would speed the line to the ocean, Douglas believed. Nobody wanted that railroad more than the Benton men in St. Louis, but they knew that men like Jefferson Davis supported the bill not to build a railroad but to open the West to slavery. The Kansas-Nebraska Act legalized "squatter sovereignty." Whether a given territory was to be slave or free was left to the settlers. The Missouri Compromise as well as the Compromise of 1850, under which California was admitted, had drawn a line against slavery. That line was gone now. The West—which meant primarily Kansas—was disputed territory to be bought with blood.

XIX. From Carbarn to the Sea

"Cump" Sherman was a distraught, worried man in the early months of 1861. He was president of the Lucas horsecar line in St. Louis. With his sharp mind and nervous energy he had cut the line's expenses 20 per cent almost overnight, but he had more than enough time on his hands to ponder his own concerns and the nation's danger.

This man with the half-cropped, reddish truculent beard who was to become America's greatest general—in fact, one of the greatest in all history—felt perversely frustrated at the age of forty. On the death of his father, Judge Charles R. Sherman of the Ohio Supreme Court, he had been taken into the home of a neighbor, Thomas Ewing, to relieve his mother of part of the burden of a large family. (It was the Catholic Ewings who added the William to the name of Tecumseh Sherman.) He stood high in the West Point class of 1840. He served in Florida, in Charleston, South Carolina—where he danced at all the parties and painted on Sundays—and at Jefferson Barracks, where he became so enthusiastic about St. Louis that he decided it should be his home. Yet when other young officers were sent to the easy glory of the Mexican War, he was assigned as adjutant to Persifor Frazer Smith, commander of the Division of the Pacific. It was a clerk's job. It gave Sherman only one possible claim to fame—his announcement of the discovery of gold at Sutter's Fort, and apparently he was the only man utterly immune to the fever he kindled.

After long wooing—having grown up in the same home, it took them time to realize that they really were not brother and sister—he married Ellen Ewing on May 1, 1850. The responsibilities of a family made army desk work less and less attractive. So he resigned September 6, 1853. Through his friend, Major Turner, he became the manager of Lucas, Turner & Co., the San Francisco branch of the St. Louis banking house of James H. Lucas & Co. When it was closed in the depression of 1857, he was sent to the New York branch. But soon the parent bank also failed. Sherman practiced law briefly. Then in October, 1859, he accepted the presidency of the new military school at

Alexandria, Louisiana, which was to become Louisiana State University. There he showed himself to be an administrator and teacher of high quality. He formed friendships with men of perception and sensibility, and was willing to forget even St. Louis for the quietly stimulating life of the campus. But talk of secession was growing louder and louder. He would not grant for a moment that the Union might be dissolved. So he resigned on January 18, 1861, and left seditious Louisiana.

"Cump" Sherman went to Washington to see his brother, John, the mischievous Kenyon College boy who now was a United States Senator from Ohio and who still was to become, as Secretary of the Treasury, the mainstay of his college friend Rutherford B. Hayes, as well as author of the Sherman Anti-Trust Act, Secretary of State, and almost President. With prophetic foresight, "Cump" tried to tell his brother, who also was his best friend, how terrible civil war would be. John took him to Abraham Lincoln. To Sherman, even the President did not seem to be sufficiently concerned. He told Lincoln he was sure that Louisiana would secede, and he was shocked to hear him reply in an almost offhand manner that he "guessed we will be able to keep house." His brother, the politician, urged "Cump" to go back to Ohio and raise a regiment of volunteers; but "Cump" said that Ohio had neglected and then forgotten him. Actually, Governor Dennison offered Sherman the command of the state's troops. He had to turn instead to a Cincinnati railroad president, George B. McClellan. Sherman also rejected Montgomery Blair's appeals to accept an appointment which probably would have made him Secretary of War within a few months. Back in St. Louis, he spurned Frank Blair's request that he take charge of Missouri volunteers. The war could not be fought with "three-month" men, civilians who elected politicians as their commanders. A thorough reorganization of the regular army was absolutely necessary. In any case, he could not afford a few precarious months as a volunteer. He had a wife and six children to support, and he was almost out of money.

As Sherman walked to the carbarn day after day, he felt that St. Louis was in that electrically ominous hour before a storm. The sunshine of the city's easygoing tolerance had changed to that sulphur-green atmosphere, half light and half dark, that agitated stillness which is a warning of the lightning and the thunderclap to come. Northern merchants and Southern cotton growers had been drinking together at the Planters' House bar for years, deploring abolition and nullification alike. The Germans and the Irish had been made welcome in the city, and the Know-Nothings had been rupulsed. Men acknowledged that all was not well, but they believed in moderation and compromise. They were annoyed by hotheads. But now they began to feel—with a touch of fright—that they might be unrealistically optimistic, that great forces do not meet quietly, but in terrible collision. For all their hope and good will, the grapes of wrath were ripening into a terrible vintage. Sherman saw blood in the sky.

On December 30, 1860, the Missouri Legislature met in Jefferson City. On January 4, 1861, Claiborne Fox Jackson took the oath as governor. His inaugural address left hardly a doubt about his design to lead Missouri into the rapidly forming Confederacy. State conventions were being held for the formalities of secession. Governor Jackson and the legislature in mid-January called for the election of delegates to such a convention to be held in Jefferson City on February 28. The campaign to elect them began at once. Many of the outstate Democrats were known to be Jefferson Davis men, and there were some Southern sympathizers in the city.

Former Mayor Darby, Wayman Crow, Thornton Grimsley, Lewis V. Bogy, James Yeatman, P. B. Garesche, Luther Kennett, Henry Overstolz, James Lucas, and other moderates called meetings of the Constitutional Union party. They wanted to preserve the Union and also the peace of the state and the nation. Frank P. Blair, Jr., political heir of Thomas Hart Benton, had given up hope for a compromise and was advocating a "thorough" policy. He was the leader of the Lincoln forces in Missouri. He was for supporting the President and ending the threat of secession once and for all. Allied with him were the four Filleys—Mayor Oliver D. Filley and his brother, Chauncey, and their cousins, Edward A. and Samuel R. Filley—B. Gratz Brown, who had embarked on a political career in alliance with the St. Louis Germans, James O. Broadhead, who as District Attorney was to expose Governor Jackson's conspiracy and eventually become the first president of the American Bar Association, John How, and those other Lincoln men who, on the verge of war, were being called the Black Republicans.

Sherman's friends—and his inclinations—turned him toward the Constitutional Unionists. In Blair, at first, he saw only the leader of a political faction determined to rule at any cost. Closer association, especially on the battlefield, would induce mutual respect—but that was still in the future. Meanwhile it was Blair and the Germans and the Kerry Patch Irish who had their eyes on what was going on in clear sight. They knew that the Jefferson City secessionists were moving slowly only because they wanted to get a firm grip on Lincoln-voting St. Louis and its resources, military and economic, before raising the Stars and Bars. They knew that the Democratic Broom Rangers, street fighters who had been checked in the 1860 pre-election campaigning by the Republican Wide-Awakes, were being armed as state militiamen with headquarters in the Berthold Mansion—Fort Berthold, the secessionists called it—at Fifth and Pine streets. Over it flew the Missouri seccessionist banner with its single bar and crescent. That is why on January 11 Mayor Filley urged members of the Common Council in each ward to "select from their best citizens such a number of men as the exigencies of the case may seem to require and organize them to be ready for any emergency." The Union men had their headquarters in the Turner Hall. They also were drilling openly. Governor Yates of Illinois sent them 2000 muskets in a load of beer barrels. Both factions had their eyes on the fifty-four-year-old Arsenal, a group of buildings—barracks, shops, and storehouses—near the river at the southern extremity of the city. At least 60,000 guns, 200 barrels of powder and other munitions were stored there—lightly defended, if at all.

Governor Jackson was to complain a little later that "if his advice had been taken, the Arsenal would have been seized when he could have walked in with ten men and taken it, as it had no protection, but to do so now would cost the lives of a great many men and probably the destruction of the city." For the moment, however, he was reassured by General D. M. Frost, a former West Pointer in command of the state militia in St. Louis, who reported that Major Bell at the Arsenal "is with us. . . . He recognizes the right of Missouri at the right time to seize the place as being on her soil." There was no need for the action urged by the "sensationists," he said. "I intend to look after it."

Isaac Sturgeon, federal assistant treasurer in St. Louis, also was concerned, not only about the Arsenal but also about the funds in his charge. With only two bodies of United States regulars west of the Mississippi, he felt compelled to report his fears to Washington. Shortly thereafter a small detachment was sent to strengthen the contingent at Jefferson Barracks, and on January 11—the day Mayor Filley urged the councilmen to make defense preparations—Lieutenant Thompson and a few soldiers marched into the city, took over the Customhouse, and removed the government's money. It was the alarm of those early days of 1861 which later caused a new Customhouse, now known as the Old Post Office, to be built like a fort, complete with moat and steel window shutters with slits for the use of riflemen. (Indeed, the massive construction of the building may frustrate the current campaign for its removal.)

The chief military commander in Missouri at this time was General William Selby Harney, the handsome, athletic friend of Jefferson Davis. Harney had served gallantly in the Indian wars and against Mexico. He had seized the island of Juan de Fuca from the British, and he had just written a book about that exploit. Married to a Mullanphy, he was prospering in St. Louis and saw no cause for alarm. But Major (later General) David Hunter, who conferred in the city with Sturgeon on February 9, was not so confident. On the 13th Harney received a telegram from the War Department asking whether it would not be wise to bring soldiers up from Jefferson Barracks to guard the Arsenal. Shortly thereafter Captain Nathaniel Lyon was sent from Fort Riley to St. Louis with a detachment of troops. Blair at once asked Washington to put Lyon in charge of the Arsenal. On March 11 Lyon was ordered to take over. He found himself in complete command when Harney was summoned to Washington, ostensibly to answer some questions about that book about Juan de Fuca.

In the midst of these moves and countermoves, which Sherman followed with ever more foreboding, the pro-Union ticket of delegates to the state convention was elected on February 18 by a majority of more than 80,000 votes. The convention opened in Jefferson City on the twenty-eighth. On the first day former Governor Sterling Price (later to command the Confederate troops in Missouri) was elected chairman. On the second day the delegates voted to adjourn and to reconvene in the Mercantile Library hall in St. Louis on March 4. The fifteen delegates from St. Louis helped to carry Hamilton R. Gamble's resolution on federal relations:

"That while Missouri cannot leave the Union to join the Southern states, we will do all in our power to induce them to again take their place with us in the family from which they have attempted to separate themselves. For this purpose we will not only recommend a compromise with which they ought to be satisfied, but we will endeavor to procure an assembly of the whole family of the states in order that in a general convention such amendments to the Constitution may be agreed upon as shall permanently restore harmony to the whole nation."

This was a declaration of loyalty, yet it was conciliatory. Missourians still were trying to prevent the division of their state as well as that of the country. They persisted in this hope for three weeks after the temporary adjournment of the convention—until April 12 and the firing on Fort Sumter. That first act of aggression stiffened their tone. When President Lincoln called for four regiments of Missouri volunteers, Claiborne Jackson denounced the call as "illegal, unconstitutional and revolutionary." Meanwhile the Committee of Public Safety was formed in St. Louis. Although an orderly election was held that spring and Daniel G. Taylor, a moderate Unionist, had been elected mayor over John How, the committee was organized under the chairmanship of former Mayor Filley. Its other members were Samuel T. Glover, a Kentucky man, Francis P. Blair, Jr., also born in Kentucky, John How, a Pennsylvanian, J. J. Witzig, a native of Germany, and James O. Broadhead, a Virginian. These men were chosen at a mass meeting of Republicans and pro-Union Democrats pledged to "unalterable fidelity to the Union under all circumstances." They met daily in the Turner Hall.

Four days after Governor Jackson refused to obey the President's call for troops, Lyon was ordered to "muster four regiments into the public service." Before nightfall he had them at the Arsenal, supplied with arms and ammunition. By April 30 Washington had fully recognized the committee, informing Lyon: "You will, if deemed necessary by yourself and by Messrs. O. D. Filley, James How, James O. Broadhead, Samuel T. Glover, J. J. Witzig and F. P. Blair, proclaim martial law in the City of St. Louis."

Sherman watched all this with skepticism. Were Blair and the German politicians really soldiers? Sigel, perhaps. Sherman knew that the rebels would field well-officered armies. Had not West Point and the army itself been virtually Southern institutions for thirty years? Old General Winfield Scott believed that only Southern gentlemen made good officers. That is why so many Northern officers had put away the uniform—even "Sam" Grant, the St. Louis wood peddler who was cut out to be a soldier and nothing else. Sam—that was the name a man was bound to be given at the Point if his initials were U.S.—was happy to be sent, as a young lieutenant, to Jefferson Barracks. It was the biggest army post in the country, garrisoned by sixteen infantry companies. Nearby was White Haven, the plantation of Colonel Dent, father of his classmate, Fred Dent. It was a pleasant place to visit, since Grant did not mind the Colonel's vituperation about Abolitionists. Grant disliked them himself. And there was the Colonel's daughter, Julia, a belle who liked horses as much as he did. They were engaged before he went off to the Mexican War, and married when he came back. He loved her and always depended on her.

In 1852, however, his luck changed. He was assigned to the Oregon frontier and Julia had to stay in the Middle West. Like Sherman, he learned that army life on the Pacific coast was grim—especially under an unfair commander. Everything was expensive and soldiers' pay was low. Yet all his efforts to make a bit of extra money—investments in a farm, hogs, chickens, in a cargo of ice, in a boardinghouse—resulted in losses instead of gains. So lonely Sam Grant took to the whisky bottle, not very surprising in a hard-drinking army. He got into a scrape, nothing serious, but his commander, Colonel Robert C. Buchanan, told him in the spring of 1854 to face a court martial or resign. The court probably would have cleared him, but he quit in disgust, took ship, and arrived in New York stone broke. A West Point friend, Simon B. Buckner, let him have some money, which he repaid as soon as he had a draft from his father, Jesse. But Grant remembered the friendly favor extended in a dark hour. When Buckner surrendered Fort Donelson to him not so many years later, Grant handed him his billfold, saying, "You will need it now." A war had to be won before Buckner could repay him.

Back in St. Louis, Colonel Dent turned over sixty acres of woodland southwest of the city to Grant. When cleared, it would make a fine farm. So Grant began to cut the trees, to build a house (still standing) and to sell wood in the St. Louis streets. He and Julia called the place "Hardscrabble Farm." But he had no luck with it. Unfavorable weather spoiled his first crop, and the panic of '57 took the profit out of the second one. So Sam Grant gave up farming. He might have sold his slave for $1000—and he certainly needed money—but he freed him instead. He applied for the job of County Engineer, but it was given to another. Then, briefly, he went into the real estate business in St. Louis, but could make no money. He had always vowed that he would never work in his father's tannery, but in 1860 he was not keeping such promises. Actually he did not have to go into the tannery. Galena, Illinois, was thriving in the midst of a lead-mining boom, and Jesse Grant had opened a leather store there. He gave Sam a chance to work in it with his two brothers. Perhaps the half-dozen years in St. Louis were not as bad as they are said to have been. In the White House, Grant once exclaimed, "Those were the happy days!" But a man's memory can be selective. In any case, he had not outgrown the need for the solace of John Barleycorn.

Whisky? Why not? Grant was a soldier, not a farmer, not a storekeeper. It was natural that he should be eager to drill the Illinois volunteers for Governor Yates. Sherman, however, was more convinced than ever that the regular army must be reorganized; so many of its best officers had put on the Southern uniform. Robert E. Lee, Albert Sidney Johnson, William J. Hardee, Earl Van Doren, E. Kirby Smith, John B. Hood and Fitzhugh Lee—those seven from just one regiment, the Second Cavalry! Sherman's West Point friend, George H. Thomas, Virginia-born though he was, had remained loyal—and some in Washington were asking why, suspiciously watching a fine soldier instead of trusting him. Secretary of War Cameron was screaming that West Point was a "breeding ground for traitors." Even Lincoln was talking of officers "false to the hand that had pampered them while the common soldiers remained loyal." Almost 300 graduates of the academy, a score of Northerners among them, had gone over to the Confederacy. So had roughly a quarter of the Navy's officers. Well, that still left a good many Southern-born officers loyal, and Cameron would need every one of them. Sherman was sure of that. Again, he told Ellen that he was not going to this war until the politicians realized that it was a job for regulars. But in St. Louis the war was not waiting for Sherman.

On May 2 the secessionists still in Jefferson City held a special legislative session to enact such measures that might be deemed "necessary for the more perfect organization of the equipment of the militia." The state troops were ordered into camp. The two St. Louis units obeyed this order on May 6. They marched to Camp Jackson, formerly Lindell Grove, on the east side of Grand Avenue between Olive Street and Laclede Avenue, where St. Louis University is about to extend its campus. One regiment, under Lieutenant Colonel Sam Bowen, was made up mostly of "full Confederate men" and Broom Rangers. The other was for the most part loyal. It is doubtful that the rank and file knew much about Governor Jackson's plans, but the police of the Committee of Public Safety had learned that the governor had asked Jefferson Davis to send cannons for a siege of the Arsenal. Saying that the South was looking "anxiously and hopefully for the day when the Star of Missouri shall be added to the constellation of the Confederate States of America," Davis gave Jackson's agents several 12-pound howitzers and 32-pound guns. On May 8 the *J. C. Swon,* flying a Confederate flag, reached the St. Louis levee with the guns— crated and marked "Tamaroa Marble." Major James A. Shaler of the Minute Men took this "stone" to Camp Jackson, not realizing that he was being watched.

Captain Lyon, a dramatic man, on May 9 disguised himself in women's clothes and drove through the encampment. As soon as he returned to the Arsenal, he called a meeting of the Committee of Public Safety. The United States flag still was flying over the camp. Nevertheless, he said, General Frost, a West Point classmate, was preparing to attack the Arsenal. It was decided that Lyon should strike first, that he should disarm and disband the militia companies. So early the next morning six volunteer regiments marched toward the camp. Blair's regiment marched out Laclede Avenue; Boernstein's went out Pine Street; Schuttner's men used Market Street; Sigel's followed Olive Street; Gratz Brown's regiment took Morgan Street, and McNeill's went out Clark Avenue. The troops surrounded the camp and unlimbered half a dozen artillery pieces on the Grand Avenue ridge and on a hill near Olive Street and Garrison Avenue. Lyon then demanded Frost's surrender, telling him:

"Sir, Your command is regarded as evidently hostile to the government of the United States. It is for the most part made up of secessionists who have openly avowed their hostility to the general government, and who have been plotting the seizure of its property and the overthrow of its authority. You are openly in communication with the so-called Southern Confederacy, which is now at war with the United States, and you are receiving at your camp from said Confederacy and under its flag large supplies of the material of war, most of which is known to be the property of the United States. These extraordinary preparations plainly indicate none other than the well known purposes of the Governor of this state, under whose orders you are acting, and whose purpose, recently communicated to the Legislature, has just been responded to in the most unparalleled legislation, being in direct hostility to the United States and co-operation with its enemies."

Frost denounced Lyon's demand as unconstitutional, but he said that he was in no position to defend the camp against a superior force and so had no other choice than to surrender. Lyon offered immediate parole to all who would take the oath of allegiance. Eight or nine of about 800 men agreed, but the others protested that they already had taken the oath and that to repeat it now would be to confess that they had violated it and had been enemies of the nation. Lyon gathered up all weapons, and the militiamen were formed in line as prisoners to be marched downtown between Union soldiers. The troops, of course, had brought a big crowd into the streets. Many of the spectators were unfriendly, and some of them were armed. They shouted insults, especially at "the d—— Germans." The taunts grew sharper during the long delay in the camp's evacuation. Part of the crowd got into the place, actually moving between the soldiers and their prisoners in the southwestern part of the grove. The column had just started to move, marching north in Grand Avenue and then east in Olive Street, when a pistol shot rang out and stones and rubble flew through the air.

The targets were the men of Captain C. Blandowski's Company F, Third Missouri Volunteers, guarding the west gate. Several soldiers fell. Then came the order to wheel, load, and fire. The recruits shot directly at the onlookers, many of whom were running for cover. At almost the same time there was a less serious exchange of shots near the head of the column at Olive Street and Garrison Avenue. Major John Schofield, who was with those in charge of Frost and his officers in the middle of the camp, spurred his horse toward the gate. He found that ninety persons had been shot. Twenty-eight of them died. Several men in Sigel's regiment also had been wounded. Despite the excitement and the confusion, Blair's men held their fire. Colonel Peckham later reported:

"Not until one of his men was shot dead, several severely wounded, and himself shot in the leg, did Captain Blandowski feel it his duty to retaliate. As he fell, he commanded his men to fire."

Expecting a parade rather than a battle, "Cump" Sherman walked out Grand Avenue that spring afternoon with his son, Willy, and his young brother-in-law, Charles Ewing. As the bullets clipped the first young leaves from the sycamores, Ewing fell on the boy to protect him. When Sherman saw that the soldiers were preparing to fire again, he pulled Willy and Ewing into a gully. Also in the crowd that afternoon was U. S. Grant. Governor Yates had sent him to Belleville, near St. Louis, to raise more men. So he happened to be on the scene. What if Sherman and Grant, the forgers of Union victory, had been killed early in May of 1861 by Union volunteers?

As fast as a mountain stream boils around rocks, anger spread among the Southern sympathizers in St. Louis. Inflammatory speeches were made from the steps of the Planters' House and in front of "Fort Berthold." The streets were not safe that night for a Union man. Police Chief James McDonough's men had much trouble keeping mobs under control. They lined up shoulder to shoulder in the street in front of the *Anzeiger* offices to prevent an attack on that paper, and later they had to drive back a mean crowd moving toward the *Democrat* offices. Threatening crowds were abroad again the next day, Friday. The windows of H. E. Dimick's gun shop in Main Street were broken, and fifteen or twenty guns were stolen before the police could stop the looting. That evening a newly armed German volunteer regiment marched from the Arsenal up Third Street, turning west up Walnut Street. As the first recruits reached Seventh Street, shots were fired from the steps of the church on that corner. A soldier fell dead. Almost in panic, the untrained troops stopped and fired down the street—actually at their fellow soldiers as well as at their tormentors. Six were killed, four of them soldiers. Again the "dead carts" rolled. All day Saturday the curious gaped at the bullet-pocked walls. That day the legislature, which already had put the St. Louis police under the governor's control, passed a military bill which was virtually a declaration of war. Throughout Saturday and Sunday people packed trunks and got ready to leave the city. On Sunday Mayor Taylor rode among the omnibuses which took passengers from the Planters' House to the East Side railroad depots. He made a little speech:

"I am sorry to observe such a stampede of citizens from the city as I am convinced myself that you need not fear danger from any quarter."

There were cheers, and the strain was eased a bit. But there was to be one more exchange of shots between citizens and soldiers. On June 17 a detachment of home guards, which had been guarding railroad tracks beyond the city, marched downtown from the railroad station and turned into Seventh Street. This time the spectators seemed obviously friendly. They cheered the men. But between Olive and Pine streets, bullets suddenly tore into the center of the column. The soldiers were halted and soon were firing at the balcony of the recorder's court on the second floor of the Missouri Engine House. Four persons were killed and two were seriously wounded. Captain J. W. Bissell was accused by some of being too drastic, yet the most experienced officers would have found it necessary to defend their men. The "murderers," if that word must be used, were the cowardly malcontents who mingled with crowds, hoping perhaps that this would enable them to fire with impunity. In any case, the soldiers made it clear that they would shoot, and there was no more shooting at soldiers.

General Harney returned to St. Louis a few days after the Camp Jackson affair. In rather lukewarm fashion he said that it would be improper for him to comment on Lyon's action, but he did add that the fact that the main streets of the camp were named for Jefferson Davis and General Beauregard revealed the purpose of the militia mobilization. On May 21—seemingly in contradiction to this statement —he held a most unusual conference with General Sterling Price. At its close, the Northern and Southern commanders issued a joint statement, which follows in part:

General Price, having by commission full authority over the militia of the State of Missouri, undertakes, with the sanction of the Governor of the State, already declared, to direct the whole power of the State officers to maintain order within the State among the people thereof; and General Harney publicly declares that, this object being thus assured, he can have no occasion, as he has no wish, to make military movements which might otherwise create excitements and jealousies, which he most earnestly desires to avoid.

We, the undersigned, do therefore mutually enjoin upon the people of the State to attend to their civil business, of whatever sort it may be; and it is to be hoped that the unquiet elements which have threatened so seriously to disturb the public peace may soon subside, and be remembered only to be deplored.

This was a strange truce for a United States general to sign with the military representative of a governor who had defied the President and raised the banner of rebellion. Yet Hamilton R. Gamble and James Yeatmen, representatives of the moderate and still hopeful element in St. Louis, went to Washington and tried to persuade President Lincoln to accept Harney's policy. Blair, however, was of a different mind. The truce could mean the loss of Missouri to the Union. He obtained an order, dated May 16, for Harney's removal; and the President, disturbed as he was about St. Louis, authorized him to serve it on the general if deemed necessary. Blair did deliver the order on May

31, and thereafter Harney waited in vain for another military assignment. Lyon, who had been made a brigadier general, took over command in Missouri until Frémont's arrival in July. Early in June, Governor Jackson and General Price called upon him at the Planters' House to propose that all regiments be disbanded and strict neutrality maintained in the state. Lyon, however, was no Harney. Pointing at the governor and then at each man in his party, the general exclaimed:

"Rather than concede to the State of Missouri for one moment the right to dictate to my government in any matter, however unimportant, I would see you, and you, and you, and every man, woman, and child dead and buried." Turning especially to Governor Jackson, he said:

"This means war. In an hour one of my officers will call for you and conduct you out of my lines."

Jackson countered by calling for 50,000 troops to "repel this invasion." On June 14, hearing that troops under Lyon and Sigel were on the way to the state capital, he left Jefferson City. His office was declared vacant, and the convention named Gamble as provisional governor. Trusten Polk and Waldo P. Johnson were expelled from the United States Senate as members from Missouri. They were replaced by Robert Wilson and John B. Henderson, a friend of Sherman. On June 17, Jackson's forces were defeated at Boonville, but they got the better of Sigel in an engagement at Carthage and escaped from the state. Jackson went through the motions of bringing Missouri into the Confederacy, but he was able to do no more than establish a pseudo capital in Neosho in the southwestern corner of the state. Lyon, hearing that a Southern army was moving up from Arkansas in an attempt to take Springfield, met it on August 10 with an utterly inadequate force which Frémont refused to reinforce in the battle of Wilson's Creek. Already twice wounded, he rallied an Iowa regiment and led it back to the attack. A ball struck him above the heart, killing him in his first battle of the war. He left $30,000, almost his whole estate, to the government for the prosecution of that war.

Lyon had given his life to save St. Louis and Missouri for the Union. The real victory, of course, was a political one—and the chief credit for that belongs to Francis P. Blair, Jr. As editor of the Washington *Globe,* his father had been the most trenchant defender of Andrew Jackson and Thomas Hart Benton. "Old Bullion" had persuaded Blair's two boys, Montgomery and young Frank, to move to St. Louis. Montgomery soon became a prominent lawyer and served for a time as a judge, but he returned to Washington to practice before the Supreme Court. In 1852 Frank Blair was elected to the Missouri Legislature as a Benton man, but in 1856 he was elected to Congress on the Free-Soil ticket. His political philosophy was essentially that of Benton, but he did not agree with the old man that the formation of a new political party would only intensify the threat of secession. So he took a prominent part in the nomination of Benton's son-in-law, John Charles Frémont, for the presidency in 1856, helping to make him the first Republican candidate for the office. Later he did return to Benton's Democratic party, and in 1868 he was its candidate for Vice-President, Horatio Seymour and Blair being nominated in St. Louis to run against Grant and Colfax. Blair was no more an all-out Abolitionist than Benton had been but, like most men of the West, he was a staunch Unionist. He became an early supporter of Abraham Lincoln. While his brother, Montgomery, served as Postmaster General in Lincoln's cabinet, Frank put on a uniform as colonel of volunteers in 1861 and served under Sherman. He rose to major general, and after the war represented Missouri in the Senate. Yet he performed his greatest service to the nation in the period just before the Civil War when he organized the anti-slavery, anti-secessionist elements in Benton's Democratic party together with the Free-Soilers, the new Republicans, and groups otherwise so disparate as the German and Irish immigrants into a solid, determined, effective pro-Union, pro-Lincoln bloc.

Lincoln, meanwhile, was deluged by demanding messages from Frémont and disturbed by reports of favoritism and corruption. As the President's representative, Blair called on the Pathfinder. With him went General John M. Schofield, the West Pointer who had returned to the army from the Washington University faculty. Later Schofield wrote:

"To my great surprise, no questions were asked, nor mention made, of the bloody field from which I had just come, where Lyon had been killed."

Frémont apparently was interested only in lecturing the two men on how gloriously he would win the war.

"We walked down the street for some time in silence," wrote Schofield. "Then Blair turned to me and said, 'Well, what do you think of him?' I replied in words rather too strong to print. Blair said, 'I have been suspecting that for some time.'"

Blair and the President soon were even more outraged by the grandiose Frémont. On August 30 the man who had been so reluctant to fight for full possession of the state declared martial law throughout Missouri. He threatened to shoot suspected Southern sympathizers caught carrying arms, and ordered the confiscation of their property, real and personal, "and their slaves, if any they have, are hereby declared freemen."

At the time, this was even more impolitic than the still remembered General Order No. 11 under which General Thomas Ewing evacuated all residents from guerilla-infested areas of Missouri in an effort to overcome these rebels by depriving them of support. Equally unfortunate was the order, by coincidence also numbered 11, which Grant issued at Holly Springs:

"The Jews, as a class violating every regulation of trade established by the Treasury Department and also department orders, are hereby expelled from the department within twenty-four hours of the receipt of this order. Post commanders will see that all of this class of people be furnished passes and be required to leave, and anyone returning after such notification will be arrested and held in confinement until an opportunity occurs of sending them out as prisoners, unless furnished with permit from headquarters. No passes will be given these people to visit headquarters for the purpose of making personal application for trade permits." The bad effect of this order hardly was mitigated by the fact that it was occasioned by Grant's own father, Jesse, and three Cincinnati friends of his who had sought preferred treatment in purchasing captured cotton. Lincoln countermanded the order within two days.

Lincoln also ordered Frémont to countermand his emancipation order. If he shot a secessionist, "the Confederates would very certainly shoot our best man in their hands in retaliation." As for confiscating property and emancipating slaves, "this will alarm our Southern Union friends and turn them against us—perhaps ruin our rather fair prospect for Kentucky."

Lincoln wrote to Frémont on September 2. Only on the 8th did Jessie Frémont leave St. Louis for Washington with her husband's reply. As soon as she reached the White House, the President saw old Tom Benton's energetic, ambitious daughter, the woman who was being called "General Jessie." Although she seems to have started her expostulations mildly enough, before she had finished Lincoln needed all the tact and control at his command. (According to Jessie, this was not enough.) The President told her that Frémont had exceeded his authority, that he should have consulted Blair in political matters, that he should not have dragged the Negro into the war. She asserted that the emancipation proclamation was a military device, that wars are won by ideas as well as guns. She was full of anger at the Blairs, at Lincoln himself. She asserted that Frémont could make the proclamation effective despite Lincoln's order that it be withdrawn. The President said that the army had no independent generals; all were under the War Department. Hard tried, he even exclaimed:

"You are quite a female politician!"

She burst into fervid, frantic argument, and cried out:

"Sir, the general will try titles with you. He is a man and I am his wife."

Even Jessie's admirers—or most of them—admit that this was a sad, bad business. She and her husband must have known how the Abolitionist press would cheer and exploit this premature attempt to free the slaves. They must have had more than an inkling, those two, of how divisive its effect would be in the North, how it would anger and stiffen the South. But Frémont and Jessie, it seems, had their eyes on the presidency even more than on war and glory. They had made one bid for the White House and would make another before the war's end. Venting his frustration on Blair, Frémont accused him of having solicited a crooked contract for a crony. The General suppressed his former friend's pro-Lincoln paper, and twice clapped him behind bars in Jefferson Barracks.

Blair was to be falsely accused once more. While he was with Sherman and Grant before Vicksburg, his adversaries charged, he had speculated in whisky, wine, and candied fruit. An invoice in the amount of $8651 was produced by an employee of the St. Louis customhouse. Blair by this time had proved he was not the political general dreaded by Grant in the early days of the war. He had shown bravery and military competence in half a dozen battles, and Sherman had promoted him to the command of the 15th Corps, 30,000 men whom he handled to the satisfaction of that demanding commander. But Secretary of War Stanton tried to get him out of the army, and in January of 1864 Blair returned to Congress to defend himself. He blamed Secretary of the Treasury Chase for the false charges and proved that the customhouse document was a forgery. In a speech which filled ten columns in the *Congressional Globe,* he virtually called Chase a liar, falsifier, and scoundrel. Blair said that "these dogs have been set on me by their master" because in a St. Louis speech he had revealed that Chase had given his son-in-law a permit to trade in contraband cotton "by which he will probably make $2,000,000." (It was this trade which led to Grant's unfortunate order against Jews. Naturally enough, this profiteering annoyed Sherman and other fighting men as well.) As soon as Lincoln heard of Blair's speech, he "knew that another beehive was kicked over." And the President was indeed accused of having prompted his St. Louis friend to make the attack on Chase. This was not true. The speech simply showed that "when the Blairs go in for a fight, they go in for a funeral."

Frémont should have kept this in mind when he crossed swords with Frank Blair in St. Louis. Even before Jessie Frémont got back to the city, Montgomery Blair and Meigs appeared to look into irregularities. Meigs made a blunt report to Lincoln and the Cabinet. On September 20 came the news that Colonel James A. Mulligan and 1600 men of Chicago's Irish Brigade had surrendered Lexington on the Missouri River, after defending it for eight days against 20,000 Confederates. Again Frémont had failed to support fighting men. But Frémont finally did take the field against Price. Jessie, at headquarters in St. Louis, intercepted a message from Washington that her husband was to be replaced unless "he shall then have, in personal command, fought and won a battle, or shall then be actually in a battle, or shall then be in the immediate presence of the enemy, in expectation of battle." She raced frantically across the state to Frémont's headquarters outside Springfield with the purloined order. After commanding that no messenger should be allowed to approach him, he prepared to attack. But before this desperate strategem could be started, Lincoln's message was delivered officially. Frémont had been in command in Missouri exactly 100 days.

Although a Congressional committee exonerated him of personal responsibility for the corruption of his quartermaster, Frémont had done mischief enough. He had weakened the North's support of Lincoln. Henry Ward Beecher, Wendell Phillips, Bryant, Greeley, and other Abolitionists praised his premature emancipation proclamation, and they condemned its repudiation by Lincoln. Strongly against slavery, the St. Louis Germans long were loyal to Frémont. So were other Radical Republicans. When General Schofield took over in St. Louis, he had his hands full. Because of Frémont's sins of omission and commission, Missouri was full of bushwhackers, raiding, robbing, and burning. He had to organize ten regiments against these guerrillas. Governor Gamble was not overly co-operative. While loyal to the Union, he was a reluctant recruit against slavery. His attitude inflamed the Radicals.

Under Charles Daniel Drake, they organized the "Committee of Seventy," one member from each county, which called on Lincoln on September 30, 1863. The seventy—actually, they were more than eighty —demanded, above all, immediate and unconditional emancipation in the loyal border states. They also protested against Schofield's measures against the malcontent press, his suspension of habeas corpus, and his dispatch of militia regiments to support Grant at Vicksburg. Schofield had been acting strictly according to Lincoln's desires, and the President supported him. He wanted no quarrel at the moment with Union men who might still have proslavery leanings.

"If a man votes for supplies of men and money," said the President, "encourages enlistments, discourages desertions, does all in his power to carry the war to a successful issue, I have no right to question him for his abstract political opinions."

Lincoln did not believe that, in sending militiamen to Vicksburg, Schofield had wronged loyal Missourians. Yet at the end of the two-hour interview Drake told the President that danger threatened the committee members:

"Many of them, Sir, in returning home do so at the risk of their lives, and if any of those lives are sacrificed by reason of the military operations of this government, let me tell you, Sir, that their blood will be upon your garments and not upon ours."

Schofield probably was glad when the opportunity came for more active service. Lincoln, familiar with southern Illinois, wedged between the slave territory of Missouri and Kentucky, knew better than a Frémont or a Drake what he was up against. He understood the deserters who announced that they had enlisted to save the Union and not to end slavery. He understood men like the Reverend Dr. McPheeters of St. Louis, who belligerently baptized an infant with the name of a Confederate general. When the provost marshal arrested him and took over the church, Lincoln wrote:

"I tell you frankly, I believe he does sympathize with the rebels; but the question remains whether such a man of unquestioned good character can be exiled."

Ready as he was to suspend habeas corpus and to crack down on those who were guilty of treason, he agreed with Blair that only moderation could win over those inclined toward the Confederacy. Radical policies would only produce more Copperheads, and the government had troubles enough on its hands. Perhaps he also was aware that the objectives of a war change as it is waged. He was patient when many of those who had elected him were impatient. Except for its radical Germans, St. Louis understood Lincoln and the problems of the war far better than did Boston or Chicago.

A few days after the Camp Jackson affair, on May 14, 1861, "Cump" Sherman received a telegram offering a commission in the regular army. His old St. Louis friend, Major Turner, had gone to Washington to urge that he be made at least a brigadier general. Yet when he reported to President Lincoln, Sherman asked for no higher rank than that of colonel. He was given the command of the new 13th Infantry. This refusal to accept a higher rank was another sign of Sherman's dark mood ever since his return from Louisiana. It is not altogether surprising that some in Washington feared that Sherman would go over to the South. He had indeed been offered a Confederate general's stars.

Turbulent crosscurrents were agitating Sherman's mind. He had, first of all, a genuine affection for the South. On his return to the North he had gained a false impression of Lincoln. Then there was his disgust and despair at the unmilitary preparation for what he knew would be a terrible war. To have thrown up his position with the car line would have left Ellen and the children to charity. Yet his strongest motive probably was a not fully conscious reluctance to assume responsibility for the slaughter of boys unprepared for war.

Working against all this was his devotion to the Union. And he was reminded of the Union every time he looked at the Mississippi. He shared Benton's enthusiasm for the river. He agreed with Judge Edward Bates that "the great valley of the Mississippi is not a section, but conspicuously the body of the nation, and large as it is, it is not capable of being divided into sections, for the great river cannot be divided." He agreed with his brother John's "unwritten law" that "the Mississippi River, gathering all the rivulets of the Northwest into one current, must be permitted to float our commerce, uninterrupted, untrammeled to the sea, for thousands of men will float down its waters to make it free." The Mississippi had been a powerful magnet for Sherman ever since he first saw it as a young soldier. It had brought him back to St. Louis, and it was to bring him back again after the war.

Sherman had seen so much of America that he could not be a narrow sectionalist. In a final letter from St. Louis to one of his friends on the Louisiana Military Seminary faculty he wrote he would teach his children that "there are fine, good people everywhere, that a great God made all the world, that He slighted no part, that to some He assigned the rock and fir, with clear, babbling brooks, but cold and bitter winters, to others the grassy plains and fertile soil, to others the rich alluvium and burning sun to ripen the orange and sugar cane, but everywhere He gave the same firmament, the same gentle moon, and to the inhabitants the same attributes for good and evil. If the present politicians break up our country, let us resolve to re-establish it." So on May 8, the day Lyon heard of the guns' coming to Camp Jackson, Sherman wrote to the Secretary of War, and a week later he was on his way to Washington once again to put on the uniform of a regular army officer.

Sherman got his baptism of fire at Bull Run in the middle of July. In that confused clash of two untrained armies he skillfully covered the Union retreat, and on August 3 he was promoted to brigadier general of volunteers. But in the battle he had seen what he had dreaded, the unreadiness of Northern troops. This made him so cautious that when he was sent to free loyal West Virginia, the Cincinnati *Commerical* called him insane. Even back in Missouri his conduct aroused such doubts that Mrs. Sherman felt it necessary to explain to President Lincoln that "Cump" was sick. He had suffered a nervous breakdown. But soon enough he was back in the Planters' House with Halleck, standing before a map and pointing to the Mississippi. There was the river. It must divide the South and unite the nation. Almost at the war's beginning, Sherman was outlining the strategy which was to bring victory.

The Southerners had cut the Mississippi artery by throwing up fortifications at Vicksburg, but they had neglected the Tennessee and the Cumberland, except for the belated construction of Fort Henry and Fort Donelson. Here was a route into the heartland of the Confederacy. The quick, decisive Sherman told the bookish Halleck— "Old Brains"—what must be done. Grant should command the advance. Sherman would keep him supplied. The two were to find Halleck as troublesome, in his way, as Frémont had been. Halleck was a man of petty jealousies and agonizing slowness. Sherman gradually lost much of his respect for him. Grant never had much. Halleck insisted on fighting a war according to points on a map, whether held by the enemy or not. Sherman believed that wars were won by beating the enemy in the field, cutting off his supplies, demoralizing his supporters. But in spite of hesitations in St. Louis, Fort Henry was taken, and then Donelson. Gladly yielding seniority to Grant, Sherman saved the field for him at bloody Shiloh. There Sherman was twice wounded —in the hand and in the shoulder—but not seriously. Three horses were shot under him. There were bullet holes in his hat. Sherman was no longer nervous. Corinth was taken. Vicksburg surrendered the day after Gettysburg. With Eastern generals fighting inconclusively, the St. Louis pair—Grant and Sherman—moved into Tennessee and avenged Chickamauga. Then Sherman gave the order for "marching through Georgia." Grant, meanwhile, went East and undertook his dogged campaign against Lee and Richmond. "I will fight it out along this line if it takes all summer." Sherman's lean, fast-marching Westerners besieged Atlanta. Then, abandoning their communications, they disappeared for thirty-two days on their "march to the sea."

This was war as chess. Sherman fought no unnecessary battles. He maneuvered Joe Johnston out of one position after another. Lee never left hopeless Richmond—and this Sherman could not understand—to join Johnston and make a war of it where the South still had a chance.

Kennesaw Mountain and Peach Tree Orchard were the only major engagements Sherman had to fight; and in the one he beat The Fabian Johnston, in the other Thomas beat Hood, the gambler who would "bet $2500 with nary a pair." After the first battle one of Sherman's lanky Missouri soldiers asked a Confederate prisoner whether he still believed that one rebel could beat five Yanks.

"Oh, we don't mean you Westerners," came the frank answer. "We never saw such big men in our lives. You looked like giants."

But Johnston was not thinking particularly of the size of Sherman's soldiers when he said, "There has been no such army since the days of Julius Caesar."

This also was psychological warfare. Sherman was the first modern general. As his "bummers" advanced, fading confidence depleted the rebel ranks. Ravaging deserters became a greater plague than Union troops. Sherman occupied Savannah, and offered it to Lincoln as a Christmas gift. With incredible swiftness his men marched northward through the Carolina swamps. Charleston was abandoned. Columbia was burned—not by Sherman, but because romantic Wade Hampton dreamed of a second "retreat from Moscow." There was no retreat. All along the route were scattered "Sherman's hairpins," iron rails torn from their ties, heated and twisted around trees. They symbolized Sherman's destruction of the South's power to carry on the war. The magnificent march was, as Lincoln said, a matter of Grant's holding the bear by the hind foot while Sherman skinned it.

News of the victories of Grant and Sherman thrilled St. Louis. On hearing of the fall of Fort Donelson, the men of the Merchants Exchange stopped to sing "The Star-Spangled Banner," and then paraded to Halleck's headquarters to cheer the army. The only real threat to the city came during Price's foray into Missouri in 1864. And that was ended by General Tom Ewing, Sherman's brother-in-law, at Pilot Knob in the St. Francis Mountains. But as it was the great base for the exploration of the West, so St. Louis became the great base for the war in the West. Armies and supplies went out by river, rail, and wagon road. The wounded, the refugees, and the prisoners came in by wagon road, rail, and river.

Since 1827, when Jefferson Barracks replaced Fort Bellefontaine, established by General Wilkinson on the site of the old Spanish Fort of St. Charles the King, north of the city, this post just south of the city had been the heart of the army in the West. From the Barracks troops set out for the Mexican War and all the Indian wars. Most regular army men lived for a while in the pleasant quarters built for them by General Atkinson on the site selected personally by General Jacob Brown when he was commander in chief. Mrs. Atkinson and her three elegant sisters made connections with the polite society of St. Louis which brought invitations for young officers to all the balls and fetes of the city. It seemed almost a part of the regulations that these lieutenants should find their brides here. Jefferson Barracks, abandoned by the army only after World War II, was a show place. Edmund Flagg, coming from Louisville by boat, was thrilled by his first sight of the post in 1837:

It was a bright morning, on the fifth day of an exceedingly long passage, that we found ourselves approaching St. Louis. At about noon we were gliding beneath the broad ensign floating from the flagstaff of Jefferson Barracks. The site of the quadrangle of the barracks enclosing the parade is the broad summit of a noble bluff, swelling up from the water, while the outbuildings are scattered picturesquely along the interval beneath. Passing the village of Carondelet, with its whitewashed cottages crumbling with the years, and old Cahokia buried in the forests on the opposite bank, the gray walls of the Arsenal next stood out before us in the rear of its beautiful esplanade. Sweeping onward, the lofty spire and dusky walls of St. Louis Cathedral, on rounding a river bend, opened upon the eye, the gilded crucifix gleaming in the sunlight from its lofty summit; and then the glittering cupolas and church domes, and the fresh aspect of private residences, mingling with the bright foliage of forest-trees, recalled vividly the beautiful "Mistress of the North."

In a century, industry has sadly changed those few beautiful miles.

Serenity pervaded the peacetime post and city. During the Civil War, however, the building of cantonments and hospitals made Jefferson Barracks a much busier place. Frémont also built the Benton Barracks, a camp of instruction for 25,000 men, on 150 acres of farm land made available by John O'Fallon for a nominal rental of $150 a year. The 721 wounded from Wilson's Creek in the summer of 1861 crowded City Hospital and the Hospital of the Sisters of Charity. New hospitals were quickly built or improvised—one at Benton Barracks, another at Jefferson Barracks, one in Hickory Street, the Marine Hospital and Lawson Hospital, the Good Samaritan on O'Fallon Street at Pratte Avenue, the Receiving Hospital on Fourth Street between Morgan and Franklin, the remodeled Pacific Hotel, the five-story City General Hospital at Fifth and Chouteau Avenue, and the Gratiot Street Prison Hospital in the McDowell medical college. The Contagious Disease Hospital on Duncan's Island was remodeled, and a 2500-bed institution was made of the Fairgrounds amphitheater, one of the brightest and airiest of all. In all, 61,744 patients were treated in these hospitals. There were 5684 deaths.

The immense task of staffing and supplying these institutions led to the formation in the summer of 1861 of the Western Sanitary Commission, the volunteer organization which assumed almost total responsibility for the military hospitals in Missouri, Illinois, Iowa, Indiana, Kentucky, Tennessee, Arkansas, Louisiana, and the Indian Territory —in fact, throughout the western states—as well as for the accommodation of refugees from the war zones. Additional facilities had to be established especially for the slaves who came north, first as contraband and then as freemen. Five schools for Negroes were opened, the first of their kind in St. Louis. An asylum was established for soldiers' orphans. Accommodations also were provided for wounded and discharged troops, and for wives and other relatives coming to visit soldiers or to seek missing ones. And there was the usual wartime work of sending to the front blankets, sheets, pillows, bandages, hospital gowns, gloves, socks, and underwear, as well as canned vegetables, fruits, jellies and homemade wines.

And nurses. Through the influence of Dorothea Dix, the army reluctantly accepted female nurses. In charge of the new Army Nursing Corps, Miss Dix frowned on all applicants who were young and pretty. She made that clear on her visit to St. Louis. Yet many unqualified women were accepted. Perhaps that is why Dr. Joseph Brinton, who went down to Cairo with Grant, complained so sharply:

"They defied all military law. There they were and there they would stay, entrenched behind their bags and parcels, until accommodations might be found for them. This female nurse business was a great trial to all the men concerned, and to me . . . it became intolerable."

Dr. Joseph Cooper, who also had accompanied Grant from St. Louis, muttered about preachers who shipped off "the most troublesome old maids in their congregation" as nurses and then wrote daily letters about their "ewe lamb . . . a schoolmarm whose only experience in nursing was of the wrath of the boys whose ears had been warmed too often because their fathers had overlooked her." But if Doctor Cooper did not like the women Miss Dix brought to camp, he was enthusiastic about the Catholic Sisters recruited by Dr. Brinton. To the joy of the doctors, they asked for nothing more than a sleeping room. They were ready for hardships.

James Yeatman, C. S. Greeley, S. J. Johnson, M.D., George Partridge and the Reverend William G. Eliot were the organizers of the Western Sanitary Commission. Yeatman set up its office in his bank, moved in a bed, and gave the organization almost all of his time, day and night. He punctiliously handled $4,270,998.50

The military commanders in St. Louis—Halleck, Rosecrans, Schofield and Dodge—had a simple way of raising needed funds: a levy on those in the city suspected of sympathizing with the South. An individual might not know that he was thus suspected until he was assessed, and he was given little opportunity to protest. Even men as ardently pro-Union as Blair and his friends felt that this was as unwise as it was unfair. Hearing of one of these levies, Lincoln told Halleck in Washington, "Stop the thing at once by telegraph." When another assessment was planned nonetheless, James B. Eads, the man who built the ironclads of the river navy, on March 14, 1865, wrote to General G. M. Dodge that the banks of St. Louis would contribute the needed money "rather than have old animosities and feelings revived." He enclosed a check for $1000 from the Third National Bank, of which he was a director, and he offered a larger sum, if needed.

While there undoubtedly were war profiteers in St. Louis, businessmen such as the Ames brothers furnished large quantities of food, clothing, and other supplies without assurance as to when, how, and if they would be paid. Charles Chouteau, who was once denied the right to vote because he might be disloyal, promptly supplied troops, especially in the northwest, and eventually presented for payment only those bills which he himself had paid in procuring matériel for the army. As they demonstrated at the big Western Sanitary Fair, held in the spring of 1864, St. Louisans were generous in supporting the war and its victims.

It might be necessary in wartime to arrest foolish women who promenaded in front of a military prison and waved the enemy colors, just as it was necessary to exile spies and even to hang one, and to execute six Confederate prisoners, as General Rosecrans did on October 29, 1864, in retaliation for the killing of Major James Wilson and six members of the Third Missouri Militia near Washington, Missouri. Yet most St. Louisans could not feel vengeful, let alone bloodthirsty. They knew Southerners too well. There were too many families in the city with members in both armies. However much justification there might be for civil disabilities in wartime, many St. Louisans were uneasy about the test oaths demanded by the military and by the state convention, especially of ministers of religion. Archbishop Kenrick did not forget the injunction which he issued amidst the rioting of 1861:

"In no case is a Christian justified in forgetting the precept of universal charity. . . . Listen not to the suggestions of anger, but banish from your thoughts as well as from your hearts every feeling incompatible with the duty of subjecting it to the dictates of reason and religion. Remember that any aggression by individuals or bodies not recognized by the laws from which the loss of life may follow is an act of murder of which everyone engaged in such aggression is guilty, no matter how great the provocation may have been. 'Dearly beloved, let us love one another.'"

Yet this conciliator quietly told his clergy that they need not sub-scribe to the obnoxious oath. Two of them, the Reverend D. H. Murphy of Cape Girardeau and Father Cummings of Pike County, were con-victed and fined $500 for continuing their ministrations after refusing to take the oath. The Cummings conviction was overturned by the United States Supreme Court, which held the oath requirement to be ex post facto as well as an unconstitutional bill of pains and penalties. In the Murphy case, the Missouri Supreme Court handed down a lengthy vindication of the United States Supreme Court ruling. The decisions were acclaimed in St. Louis. Yet under the dom-ination of Senator Drake, the state convention carried the oath re-quirement and other disabilities into the harsh Missouri Constitution of 1865. St. Louis rejected this, two to one. When it was announced that the constitution had been adopted by a bare 1862 votes, the *Republic,* arguing that it really had been defeated, said:

"However the returns may be figured in Jefferson City, there is no escape from the fact that the vile thing has not the sanction of the people."

So some of the causes of wartime bitterness were given new life—to the distress of many Missouri Unionists. Their attitude, however, by no means betokened lukewarm support of the Northern cause. St. Louis sent more men into Lincoln's armies than any other city of its size. No less than 199,111 Missourians fought under the Stars and Stripes. Only four states, New York, Pennsylvania, Ohio and Illinois, had more men in blue. Missouri's contingent was larger than those of nine other Northern states combined. There were no draft riots in St. Louis.

Sherman meanwhile went to City Point to join Lincoln and Grant. There he learned the President's terms for peace. Essentially they were the terms Grant gave Lee at Appomattox. Sherman granted the same terms, considerably elaborated, to Johnston. Three men who trusted each other had won the war—Lincoln and Grant and Sherman. They were Westerners—two of them from St. Louis and one from Spring-field, not far away. Sherman was the military genius. Grant made no bones about that. He feared that the war might not be ended until Sherman "mopped up" in the East, leaving not a bit of respect for its dapper-dandy, oft-defeated armies. That was not necessary. Yet as they were encamped in the outskirts of Washington the Westerners, full of oats, almost started a new war, this one against the East. The only contest, however, was one of parades. The Easterners, all spit and polish, marched on the first day of the grand review. Could Sherman's tatterdemalions put on such a show? Lloyd Lewis tells how they marched like the lords of the world:

The Capitol was blooming with flags. The morning was bright and soft. A cannon boomed. Nine o'clock! Sherman shook a spur; his horse stepped forward, drumsticks made the air flutter like flying canister or wild-geese wings. Bands blared into "The Star-Spangled Banner." Around the corner of the Capitol the Westerners came.

Stage fright stuck in plowboys' throats. The roofs and trees were black with people. Pennsylvania Avenue stretched like a long, long river between human banks. White handkerchiefs waved like apple blossoms in an Indiana wind. Boys' eyes caught blurred sights of signs spanning the avenue—"Hail, Champions of Belmont, Donelson, Shiloh, Vicksburg, Chattanooga, Atlanta, Savannah, Bentonville—Pride of the Nation."

Sherman, riding ahead, his old slouch hat in hand—the sun on his red hair—was listening to the tread of his men. Sometimes in sudden hushes he could hear one footfall behind him. The hushes came when ambulances rolled by with bloodstained stretchers fastened on their sides.

Sherman hoped, as perhaps he had never hoped anything in his lifetime, that his men were marching well. They sounded all right, but he couldn't be sure in the roaring current of noise. They must show the East that they were not "an undisciplined mob."

Sherman's horse walked up the avenue slope before the Treasury Building. In a minute it would swing to the right and come into view of the stand. Behind him he heard the tumult growing louder. Were his wild young fellows behaving? He dared not look back; he had ordered everybody to hold eyes front.

He was on the crest of the rise now. He could hold his nerves no longer. He spun in the saddle and looked. A blissful thrill ran to his finger tips. His legions were coming in line, every man locked in steady formation— formal for perhaps the first and last time in their lives. "They have swung into it," said Sherman to himself. Long afterwards he said, "I believe it was the happiest and most satisfactory moment of my life."

The whole army was thin. Carl Schurz, in the stand, felt his heart leap as the Westerners wheeled into view—"nothing but bone and muscle and skin under their tattered battle-flags." Their flags were thin, too, from winds and bullets—many were nothing but shreds of faded red and white and blue. Cheers drowned the bands. The street in front of the stand was ankle-deep in flowers—worn heels, bare heels, kept step among the roses.

Of the three shapers of victory, Lincoln and Sherman had much in common. Lincoln appreciated Grant, the soldier, and gave him no orders. Grant appreciated this respect and confidence. He respected the President. Yet the two had little to say to each other. But Sherman and Lincoln talked at City Point by the hour. They looked to the future, and the President was happy that his most ruthless soldier had the most generous sentiments about peace and reconstruction. But Lincoln was assassinated.* The Radical Republicans were against "charity for all and malice toward none." The politicians howled when Sherman's step-brother, Tom Ewing, undertook the defense of three of those accused of a part in Lincoln's murder—Dr. Samuel A. Mudd, Samuel Arnold, and Edward Spangler. Sherman resented this. Had not Tom Ewing been made a major general for his desperate defense of Pilot Knob? Had not Hugh Ewing also risen to the rank of major general, and had not Charles Ewing served as a brigadier general? Tom Ewing saved the lives of his three clients, and Sherman cursed the politicians. The Radicals already were attacking him. He was ready to go back to St. Louis.

And St. Louisans, who had bound up the wounds of friend and foe while their generals and their regiments were winning victories for the Union, were glad to have him back. They too were tired of wormwood. As soon as news of the surrender of Richmond had been received, they had decked the city in flags. And when word came that Johnston had surrendered to Sherman as Lee had to Grant, Mayor Thomas C. Fletcher proclaimed April 15 a day of thanksgiving. Then committees got busy planning a welcome for Sherman's returning veterans, and a big dinner in the Lindell Hotel for the general. A purse of $30,000 was given to him for the purchase of a house; eventually he chose one at Garrison and Franklin avenues. Meanwhile he wrote to the committee, a little stiffly for a man so good with words:

"I deem it a most fortunate accident that events have led me back to the very point whence I sallied at the beginning of the tremendous struggle now happily ended. And if the good citizens of St. Louis account me one of them, I accept the title with honor and satisfaction. I feel

---

* When the time came to bury Abraham Lincoln, Jesse Arnet of St. Louis, the only undertaker in this part of the country who had a four-horse hearse, took it and his horses across the river and onto the cars for Springfield. There he drove the President's remains to the cemetery. Incidentally, he knotted his reins so that he could drive the four horses with one hand, and he tied a similar knot in his tie, the knot now known as the four-in-hand.

sure that St. Louis as a city is more than any other interested in
maintaining a firm government and a united people, and therefore
though my efforts in the past have tended especially to your welfare
so may it be in the future, and no man will rejoice more than I will
to see your city again enter upon the path of progress and wealth that
was temporarily interrupted by a struggle begotten by ambitious and
designing men."

Maybe there's a rule which demands such a style in replies to committees.

General Dodge told Sherman that some Union men in St. Louis
—those of the Drake faction—were "concerned" because he had accepted an invitation to a dinner at which some of the guests would
be "unreconstructed rebels." Dodge was troubled about the effect on
Sherman's chances in politics.

"Don't worry, General," said the man who had marched from
the carbarn to the sea. "I will settle that question at the dinner."

In his memoirs, Dodge set it down that at the Lindell on July
20, 1865, Sherman said that "since the war was over he did not feel
it necessary for him to refuse any attentions . . . but when it came
to a question between loyal men and rebels, everyone knew where his
heart was. . . . 'Let us all go to work and do what seems honest and
just to restore the country to its prosperity.' As to its political prosperity,
he knew nothing of it and cared far less."

Sherman returned to St. Louis as soon after the war's end as he
could. As commander of the army's new Division of the Mississippi,
he made St. Louis his headquarters. He did so again a decade later
as Commanding General. The army's work was in the West, pacifying
the Indians and opening the way for the railroad builders. Riding
across the prairies in a Dougherty wagon drawn by four mules, Sherman
told chief after chief that "you can no more stop a locomotive than
you can stop the sun or the moon." Again he was the prophet of grand
strategy: the Indian problem would be overcome not by fighting, but
by the advance of the iron horse. Of his part in that advance he
said, "I honestly believe in this way I have done more good for the
human race than I did in the Civil War."

Sherman also had more intimate reasons for returning to St. Louis.
For one, he liked the city on the great river, and still had good friends
there. It was a place where he and his family could comfortably make
ends meet on his army pay. His wife and children were devout

Catholics. (His son, Tom, after graduation from Yale and the Washington University Law School, joined the Jesuits.) So Sherman deplored the decline of religious tolerance in the Midwest. He attributed this to the fact that Westerners had made common cause with the New England Abolitionists during the war and had become infected with Eastern prejudices. But in St. Louis, Catholics were respected. He wrote to James G. Blaine: "My children will grow up in contact with an industrious and frugal people."

His strongest motive was his detestation of politics. He begged Frank Blair, who had become a good friend, not to return to politics, but to make a career in the army instead. After Blair died on July 8, 1875—a frustrated man after being defeated for the vice-presidency in 1868, and for re-election to the Senate in 1874—Sherman dedicated his monument in Forest Park. Privately he said that Blair "was noble and intelligent as a soldier, but as a politician he was erratic and unstable. He admitted this many a time to me." Carl Schurz could murmur: "How true!"

Sherman had not been a friend of Grant in St. Louis. Their years at West Point had overlapped, but the school's aristocratic discipline had kept Sherman, the upperclassman, and Grant, the plebe, far apart. The war changed that. Now that the fighting was over, Sherman urged his friend to have nothing to do with the politicians coming into power. Sherman's fine mind was set against revenge and carpetbagging. Grant, by comparison, was naïve.

Here again Sherman was prophetic. He respected Grant's personal integrity, but he knew the man's limitations. As the years went on, Sherman lamented, "I have been with General Grant in the midst of death and slaughter . . . and yet I never saw him more troubled than since he has been in Washington." Sherman deplored the ostentatious entombment of Grant in New York. He believed that he should have been buried simply and modestly in St. Louis. But he was personally loyal to him for life, and visited him in his last illness. When Grant's administration was in dark disgrace, Sherman refused offers to write magazine articles about him. "As to money in this connection," he exclaimed, "the very thought is revolting." When a British writer disparaged Grant to praise Lee, Sherman said in the *North American Review* that Grant was "the greatest soldier of our time." Lee fought "like a gallant knight," Sherman wrote, "but he never saw the grand problem . . . his Virginia was to him the world. . . . As an aggressive soldier he was not a success, and in war that is the true and proper test."

Even though Julia Grant was so entranced by the White House that she urged her husband to seek a third term, both of them long had planned to return to St. Louis to live out their lives. But the scandals which broke around the careless, lazy President made this impossible. Grant himself was called a "complaisant accomplice," although congressional investigations exonerated him. So far as St. Louis was concerned, the worst of the scandals was the Whisky Ring. Distillers evaded federal taxes with the connivance of the collectors. They blackmailed other distillers into complicity. Newspapers were "bought" and silenced. Treasury agents in Washington acted as spies for the ring. Whisky Ring money poured into the Republican campaign coffers. When Grant visited St. Louis to inspect the Eads Bridge, an assistant collector of revenue in the St. Louis office said to him,

"Mr. President, I suppose you know what we are doing in St. Louis, and it's all right?"

A little later, the poor man shot himself, fearing that he would be called to testify against the President. When the scandals were exposed, Grant instructed Attorney General Bristow:

"Let no guilty man escape if it can be avoided. Be especially vigilant —or instruct those engaged in the investigation of the fraud to be— against all who insinuate that they have high influence to protect them." Yet Grant did realize the effect of the scandals. In a sad message to Congress he said:

"The responsibility is mine, I know it. My name will carry it long after I am dead—but people who have been my friends and associates are not blameless. No one else will remember that—Remember it yourselves."

So the dreams of Julia and Ulysses Grant for old age at White Haven, the old Dent estate near St. Louis, guttered out. The Grants moved to New York instead. And there Grant became involved in the scandal which touched his name most closely. A fast-talking adventurer made him a partner in the investment firm of Grant & Ward. The firm promised "high interest and no risk." It was, of course, an out-and-out swindle, but Grant's credulity and indifference kept him from discovering anything wrong. He was paid frequent, large dividends, and they were enough to satisfy him. It was different when some of Sherman's army friends came to him in the bank in San Francisco, asking him to invest their small savings. When the panic closed the bank's doors, Sherman lost more than they did. Yet he held himself personally responsible and eventually made good every lost dollar. When old friends tried to suggest to Grant that he was being duped and was being used to dupe others, he smiled. When the crash came, Grant & Ward had liabilities of $17,000,000 and assets of only $67,000—and Ward had disappeared. It was a harsh eye-opening for the former President, but he did make a gallant, if hopeless, effort to assume the debt. The farm in St. Louis and the fine house in New York were sold. Contributions from friends saved the Grants from poverty. And the family received handsome royalties on the memoirs he wrote in the pain that preceded his death. If only he had listened to Sherman!

President Johnson summoned Sherman to Washington and tried to use him as a foil against Grant, but Sherman preferred to act "the peacemaker" instead. Of Johnson he wrote in his vivid, almost poetical prose:

He attempts to govern after he has lost the power to govern. He is like a general fighting without an army . . . he is like Lear roaring at the storm, bareheaded and helpless. And now he wants me to go with him to the wilderness. I do want peace, and do say that if all hands would stop talking and writing, and let the sun shine, and the rains fall for two or three years, we would be nearer reconstruction. . . .

When Grant was elected to the presidency and Sherman succeeded him as the nation's first general, he again asserted his preference of St. Louis. Probably this was unwise because it gave Belknap, Rawlins, Boyd, and other faithless presidential advisers greater freedom for their intrigues against him. They resented Sherman especially because he opposed the employment of soldiers for police duty by the Reconstruction regimes of the South, and accordingly bypassed him in issuing orders. His command became rather a farce. So he settled down in St. Louis to writing his memoirs. When they appeared, Boyd gave Grant a "review" in which he said the President had been traduced. Grant believed this until he read the work. His anger passed and, in 1876 when scandals forced Belknap to resign as Secretary of War, Grant asked Sherman to come to Washington to clean up. Sherman also served there after his brother's friend, Rutherford B. Hayes, became President in 1877. Sherman was glad to help, yet he returned once more to his home on Garrison Avenue. Again politics had much to do with his decision.

Although Sherman missed no opportunity, public or private, to declare that he did not seek public office, "Sherman-for-President" booms were started even before the war was over. The first one was launched in August, 1864, by the Democrats, especially those in the border states. Sherman pretty well killed that with a letter advocating universal emancipation. He also wrote Halleck from Atlanta:

"If forced to choose between the penitentiary and the White House . . . I would say the penitentiary, thank you." That also took care of the New York *Herald*'s call on Lincoln to retire as the Republican candidate in favor of a ticket headed by Grant and Sherman. The Radical Republicans, however, feared the popular general. In their irrational bitterness against the South, they had repudiated his peace terms. With Stanton in the lead, they accused him of disobeying Lincoln's orders, of plotting the escape of Jeff Davis, of planning to arrest Grant while marching through the East to establish a dictatorship, and even of complicity in the assassination of the President. Sherman was so angry that Salmon P. Chase had a hard time persuading him not to resign from the army to live in some foreign country as an exile. This affair caused much of the bitterness between Sherman's soldiers and Halleck's paper-collared Easterners on the eve of the grand review in Washington. It caused Sherman to write to his wife: "Washington is as corrupt as hell. . . . I will avoid it as a pest house."

The Democrats, however, started a "Sherman in '68" boom. Of this he wrote to Grant: "I would like Mr. Johnson to read this letter, and to believe me that the newspaper gossip of my having Presidential aspirations is absurd and offensive to me, and I would check it if I knew how."

When the Grant administration foundered in its corruption, the New York *Herald* and the Republicans started another drive to put Sherman in the White House. This, too, was promptly discouraged by the general. The biggest boom of all was launched in 1883 when Sherman retired from the army. Convinced that he could not be nominated himself, James G. Blaine started a movement to draft Sherman. The general explained to Blaine, to his brother, to J. B. Henderson of St. Louis, and to other party leaders that experience since 1865 had shown soldiers to be unfit for the presidency; that his devout Catholic family would not be wanted in the White House. Nevertheless, the pro-Sherman activities were carried into the convention, and it was a wire from Chicago which elicited his most categorical refusal. His son, Tom, told the story:

I was at his side in his library on Garrison Avenue when he received the telegram. . . . "Your name is the only one we can agree upon, you will have to put aside your prejudices and accept the Presidency."

Without taking his cigar from his mouth, without changing his expression, while I stood there trembling by his side, my father wrote the answer: "I will not accept if nominated and will not serve if elected."

He tossed it over to me to be handed to the messenger and then went on with the conversation he had been engaged in. In that moment I thought my father a great man.

Would Sherman, many-talented and sharp-minded, have been a great President? Or would Washington only have spoiled his children as it spoiled Grant's children? Would Sherman have "become tempest-tossed by the perfidy, the defalcation, the dishonesty, or the neglect of any one of a hundred thousand subordinates utterly unknown to the President?" Was he right when he said to Philemon Ewing, "I lead a peaceful life here and if I ran for President I'd wake up some morning and find all over the newspapers that I'd poisoned my grandmother." Was this again the almost fatal caution he displayed in the first year of the war before he found audacity equal to his prophetic vision? Did he serve the nation by withholding his service?

"The last twenty-five years of Sherman's life were one long chicken dinner." Did Lloyd Lewis say that? The general had a fine time in St. Louis with Blair, Turner, Lucas, and other friends—and with the ladies. He was especially popular with them and rarely left one without a friendly kiss. But he was almost constantly packing a bag for a quick trip. He had become the nation's most popular speaker. Between trips he enjoyed his family. On the door of his study there was the sign: "The Office of General Sherman." Behind it he enjoyed Burns, Dickens, and Scott, and his cigars. But always there were politicians—even those in City Hall. They kept sending him tax bills. He became involved in a first-class altercation with Water Commissioner F. W. Mott after a woman in the neighborhood complained that he wasted water by sprinkling the street. She probably was the same one who tried to warm up a "scandal" by whispering that the general patronized massage parlors which employed female attendants. And Joseph B. McCullagh, former war correspondent, never missed a chance to take a pot shot at him in the *Globe-Democrat*. Nevertheless Sherman had a quick enough answer for the president of the Chicago Board of Trade who asked him, "Why do you live in such an old, played-out town as St. Louis?"

Yet he finally decided to move to New York. That was in 1886. His daughter and son-in-law and their children had moved East the year before, and "Cump" had written to John Sherman: "I confess the move of Minnie and her children will change the aspect of St. Louis. . . . I will soon be isolated—but I deem it best to end my years here." But when Tom went to Yale the next year, Sherman wrote again: "I know Ellen well enough to conclude that she will be at New Haven or on the road half her time. . . . We shall be in New York next September. . . . My neighbors and friends will make a big fuss over this and I am very fond of some of them, though Turner, Lucas, Patterson etc, etc, are dead and gone." So Sherman, his outlook still young-bright, moved to New York. There he was soon boasting:

"Here in this great city I am subjected to dangers greater than those of the march or battlefield, or, as Chauncey Depew said a few evenings ago after Howard, Schofield, and Slocum had boasted of following me to Atlanta, Savannah, and Raleigh midst danger and triumph—he had followed me for an equal if not longer time through these campaigns of New York dinners."

The grand strategist, however, was not to be defeated by chicken croquettes. He made it a rule not to eat more than 15 per cent of the banquet food set before him. He enjoyed the theater and its people as they could not be enjoyed in St. Louis. But Ellen, who always straightened his tie and reminded him which invitation he had accepted for the evening, died in 1888. Sherman died just a little more than two years later on St. Valentine's Day, 1891. Old Joe Johnston came to New York to accompany the body to the St. Louis train. Bareheaded, he caught the cold that led to his death within the fortnight. One-armed Howard issued the command which started the military parade to the station, the bands playing in dirgetime "Marching through Georgia." In Calvary Cemetery in St. Louis, his son, Father Tom, read the Roman Catholic Office of the Dead:

> Grant unto him eternal rest, O Lord,
> And may perpetual light shine upon him.

"Cump" Sherman was buried beside the great national river which he called "the spinal column of America." And for St. Louisans—

half Northern, half Southern; half old stock and half immigrant—there is special significance in the inscription William Tecumseh Sherman chose for his monument:

Faithful and Honorable

xx. Perseverance Builds a Bridge

Even though it has not yet been enunciated by the eminent Professor Parkinson, it is safe to assume that there is a law of bureaucracy which holds that second-rate men—always in the majority—will fight almost to the death to block the first-rate.

If a case history is needed to establish this principle, there is the story of James Buchanan Eads of St. Louis. Eads studied the frustrated current of the Mississippi and made the stream naviagable. He built its boats and salvaged its wrecks. He spanned its width with one of the world's most daring and most beautiful bridges. And at the end he was trying to give the Mississippi's commerce easy access to the Pacific. Yet each achievement was accomplished only in the face of opposition even more stubborn than stupid. In the process Eads came to the verge of bankruptcy half a dozen times, and his health was broken as often. Yet the little square-jawed, self-trained engineer had the fighting qualities of his friend, General Sherman, and a thicker skin. He knew that his projects were sound and, somehow, he carried them through.

Born in Lawrenceburg, Indiana, May 23, 1820, Eads arrived in St. Louis in 1833—aboard a burning steamboat. The family was destitute when it reached the safety of the levee. Since Eads's father was a man of large ideas rather than large deeds, his mother opened a boardinghouse, and the boy sold apples in the street—a century before almost everybody seemed to be doing it. One of the boarders was Barrett Williams, partner in a dry-goods store at Main and Locust. He employed Eads as an errand boy at $3 a week. More important, Williams allowed Eads to use his library of technical books. A brief career as second clerk aboard the *Knickerbocker,* a steamboat in the Galena, Illinois, and Dubuque, Iowa, lead trade came to an end when the boat was wrecked on a snag at the mouth of the Ohio. Out of the wreck and the books came his plan for salvaging steamboats. He outlined this to Calvin Case and William Nelson, St. Louis boatbuilders. After looking at his drawings of a double-hulled boat equipped with derricks, pumps, and a diving bell, they became the partners of the twenty-two-year-old Eads and built their first "bell boat," the *Submarine*. Since it was difficult to find men willing to use the diving equipment, Eads himself walked the bottoms of the Mississippi, the Cumberland, the Tennessee, the Ohio, and the Missouri. For the better part of four years he spent four hours a day below the surface. Insurance made this profitable enough, and a diver was entitled to 100 per cent of any cargo under water for five years.

On October 21, 1845, Eads married his cousin, Martha Dillon, in the Old Cathedral, and decided that henceforth he should work on dry land. So he opened the first glass factory west of the Mississippi. But in 1847 the Mexican War dried up his sources of credit and also the market for glass. So at twenty-seven, bankrupt, he was forced to return to salvage work. *Submarine No. 2* and *Submarine No. 3* were built in 1848. Eventually Eads and Nelson were to have a fleet of a dozen of these boats, each one larger than its predecessor. Mrs. Eads died of cholera October 12, 1852, and on May 2, 1854, he married Eunice Eads, the widow of a cousin, in old St. Vincent's Church. By this time he had so prospered that they made a honeymoon trip to Europe before returning to a new brick house in St. Louis.

Eads was not content to profit by river wrecks; he wanted to prevent them. Like Captain Henry Shreve before him, he realized that the steamboat had conquered the Mississippi current. Without engine-driven paddle wheels, Bird's Point or earthquake-ravaged New Madrid—or *L'Anse à la Graisse,* as the French first called it—in the Missouri boot heel near the mouth of the Ohio might have become the most thriving town on the river. The strong current would have kept most of the Ohio traffic from turning north toward St. Louis. But there was another handicap for boats whether they went with the current or against it: snags, the big, flood-uprooted trees which were swept along by the current or settled to the bottom to become upreaching menaces to any pilot who unwittingly floated a hull over them. With inadequate help from Congress, Shreve worked for years to remove these snags. But he finally got tired of spending as much energy on a reluctant government as on menaces to navigation. Eads wanted to take up this work. In 1856 he submitted to Congress a proposal to keep the river channel clear for five years. This was approved by the House but defeated in the Senate, where Jefferson Davis argued that a civilian could not possibly do what the army engineers found impossible.

That winter Eads learned that ice could do even more damage along the levee than fire. Steamboats were frozen solid for twenty blocks along the St. Louis riverfront. Then came a thaw on the upper reaches of the Missouri and the Mississippi, but not at St. Louis. The floodwater swept huge ice blocks toward the still-solid ice sheet along the levee. Some of the river bergs were forced under the sheet. More of them slid along its surface. Like an avalanche they hit the steamer *Federal Arch*. Then they slid and smashed along the whole line of immobilized boats. Forty steamers were wrecked. A wall of ice twenty to thirty feet high crashed into *Submarine No. 4*. To a salvage operator the ice meant more gain than loss. But Eads was frustrated. He seemed condemned to leave the river. His doctors warned him that he must retire at the age of thirty-seven. It was not for this that he had built a new suburban home on Compton Hill.

But by 1860 Eads, now forty, found himself in good health again, or what he considered good enough health. The threat of civil war rather than the concerns of business preoccupied him. He aligned himself with the St. Louis anti-secession liberals—his cousin Benjamin Gratz Brown, Blair, Bates, and James Rollins. "Missouri," he said, "cannot be a peninsula of slavery in a sea of freedom." Poor prospect that he was, he drilled with a volunteer company. He thought about the war, however, as of everything else, in terms of the river: the government should have a fleet of ironclad gunboats. Eads was a magnet for scoffers; now they wanted to know who had ever heard of a river navy. But Bates, who had become Lincoln's Attorney General, wrote to him: "Be not surprised if you are called here suddenly by telegram." The telegram reached Eads almost as quickly as the letter, and he started at once for Washington. He suggested that a few strong steamboats be converted into ironclads while his proposed ships were being built.

Secretary of War Cameron immediately took scoffer's role, but Gideon Welles, the Secretary of the Navy, and other Cabinet members, as well as President Lincoln, approved Eads's plan. He hurried back to St. Louis with Captain John Rodgers, assigned by the navy to keep an eye on the work. These two, however, had not reckoned on Cameron's style of interservice rivalry. The Secretary claimed jurisdiction over this inland work for the army. The navy assignment was canceled and no army orders were forthcoming. The strongest intervention by Welles, Bates, Blair, and others seemed in vain. Then suddenly the Quartermaster General advertised for seven iron river gunboats. Eads considered the plans inferior to his own, but he did not argue. He pared his bid to the bone, and pledged delivery in sixty-five days. On August 7, 1861, he signed a contract which did permit him to incorporate some of his own ideas in the vessels.

Eads and his partner, William Nelson, immediately plunged into an intense struggle for men and materials. Because illuminating gas had been available in St. Louis for more than a dozen years, it was possible to put 4000 men to work in shifts seven nights as well as seven days a week. After dark, the Union Marine Works in Carondelet was turned into a reasonable facsimile of a fundamentalist's hell. During the hot nights of August and September, half-naked men worked by the light of the blue-yellow gas flares and amidst the clangorous din of iron on iron. From the Illinois bank, the light of flares and furnaces, reflected by the river and sometimes also by low-hanging clouds or banks of fog, was as vivid as red war itself. Before very long Eads was the driving demon of other such infernos. To speed the building of a river navy, some of the work was done by Morse & Daggett at the East St. Louis Dry Dock Company, by McCord & Steel at the National Iron Works, and in the Mound City yard above Cairo, all under the direction of Eads. Government red tape, especially failure to make payments in time to meet payrolls, bedeviled the work, but on October 12, Columbus Day, the first gunboat was launched at Carondelet.

She was turned over to Commander Andrew Hull Foote, who named her the *St. Louis*, and made her his flagship. The first of her class, all named for river cities, she was 175 feet long, 51 feet in beam, drew 5 feet of water. Her speed was nine knots. She carried 13 guns— 32 to 42-pounders—and two 9-inch Dahlgren guns in her bow. Most of the gunboats built subsequently were even larger. The *Fort Henry*, a ram designed by Commodore Porter and launched at Carondelet on September 22, 1862, was 280 feet long. Several Ericsson-type monitors also were built for river duty. And the last vessels of the river navy— the *Milwaukee*, *Chickasaw*, and *Winnebago*—were propeller-driven, and, so, faster and more maneuverable than the early boats. But Eads —and Foote, too—were most proud of the first of them, the *St. Louis*. Eads sent a picture of her to Lincoln with a note in which he said, "The *St. Louis* was the first ironclad built in America. It was the first armored vessel against which the fire of a hostile battery was directed on this continent and, so far as I can ascertain, she was the first ironclad that ever engaged naval forces in the world."

The one other gunboat which meant almost as much to Eads as the *St. Louis* was the *Benton*. He had bought this vessel, originally a government snag boat, and rebuilt it as one of his *Submarines*. To get warships on the Mississippi as rapidly as possible, Eads had urged Washington to armor the *Benton* and similar boats for service while the ironclads were being built. He urged that an impartial board of examiners be appointed to underapprise her. He was willing to accept $28,850, considerably less than she was worth, but Quartermaster Meigs professed to see in this offer not patriotism but trickery. Yet after a while the *Benton* was changed into a ship of war. She was 200 feet long and 75 feet wide, considerably wider than seagoing warships of the time, and encased in armor three and one-half inches thick. When Foote saw her, he changed flagships, saying, "The *Benton* is greatly superior—she is the best gunboat in the Union." Eads never disappointed this enthusiast. He built better and better vessels. But instead of paying promptly for the *Benton*, Meigs sought to claim a forfeit. Eads meanwhile was recruiting a crew, since Foote had been unable to do so. But he was most exasperated because the gunboats, ready for action, still were idle.

On December 13, 1861, however, the ironclads left St. Louis to rendezvous at Cairo. And early in February, 1862, came the news that the river navy had gone up the Tennessee, fishing mines out of the river, bombarding Fort Henry, and forcing beseiged Fort Donelson to surrender to Grant. Eads was sent a copy of a letter in which a Confederate soldier had written that the gunboats "exceeded in terror anything that the imagination had pictured of shot and shell, plowing roads through the earthworks and sandbags, dismantling guns, setting on fire and bringing down buildings within the fortifications."

But all was not glory. At Fort Henry a Confederate shell passed through a gun port on the *Essex*, killing a young officer and then entering the flue of the ship's center boiler. Twenty men were killed, including two in the pilot house. That was known on all the gunboats as "the slaughter pen." It had to be the highest and most prominent point on a boat so that pilot and captain could see what they were doing. But it could not be as well protected as other parts of the boat even though it was a prime target for the enemy, since to disable a pilot was to disable his boat. Two St. Louis pilots, Marsh Ford and James McBride, were killed at Fort Henry. Two more, Frank Riley and William Hinton, were killed at Donelson. That helped to stop the unfair talk that Mississippi pilots, almost to a man, were Southern sympathizers. A few, including Mark Twain, did go south. But from the day that John Scott stepped into the pilothouse of the *St. Louis* as her sailing master, many times the required number of pilots were ready to serve on the gunboats.

There were many other victories ahead for "de Linkum gunboats" built in St. Louis—Island No. 10, Vicksburg, Mobile Bay. At the launching of the *Winnebago* Eads, not a meek man, could jibe at his scoffers. "The Secretary of War, Mr. Cameron, told me, somewhat sneeringly, that the putting of gunboats on the Mississippi was Mr. Bates's hobby," he recalled. "Mr. Cameron, who at first thought so lightly of the conception of Mr. Bates, then claimed that the execution of the scheme properly belonged to his department. . . . But the Attorney General rode his hobby so energetically that the Secretary of War had no peace until he had undertaken to put armed gunboats on this river." Edward Bates picked up his hobby from Eads, but that makes little difference. In any case, it was the civilian rather than the military mind which brought forth a battle-winning innovation.

The launching of the *Chickasaw* was not quite so happy. Some of the civilians on the top of the gunboat had not learned a fundamental sailor's rule: Stand clear of the bight of a line. When the boat hit the water, the anchor went overboard. Its line snapped across the deck, hurling Jenny Eads, the builder's daughter, Mary McGuire, and Mr. and Mrs. William P. Bradley into the river. Mrs. Bradley struck her head on the ship's side and drowned. Skiffs put out and rescued the three others.

When Captain Eads received his first payment on the Benton, he promptly sent the check to Commodore Foote, requesting him to use the money, if he could, for the gunboat's Confederate victims. This was characteristic of the man who, busy as he was, found time to raise money for the relief of the wounded, the refugees, and the prisoners of war in St. Louis. Unhappily the bureaucrats in Washington were not equally liberal in spirit. Eads's irritating difficulties with them again brought his health to the breaking point in 1864. But he could foresee victory for the Union, and so undertook a recuperative voyage to Europe. There he was besieged for advice on naval matters, but he wanted to forget about war and warships.

On February 2, 1867, he was back in St. Louis addressing a large "river convention" in the Mercantile Library hall—as he was ever ready to do—on the importance of the Mississippi and its tributaries, and on the nation's neglect of its waterways. "Not a dollar should be voted by the representatives of this valley for any public works," he said, "while these great rivers are neglected."

Eads had set his heart on the bridging of the Mississippi. Ever since 1797, when Captain James Piggot, a veteran of the Revolutionary War, had obtained permission of Governor Trudeau to operate a ferry, the city had depended on such service for its connection with the eastern half of the country. The ferry service had been improved, especially in 1828, when Samuel Wiggins first provided a steamboat for the cross-river traffic. Wiggins' ferry line, as a matter of fact, remained in business until after the turn of the century. In 1897 it carried 673,275 passengers, 364,000 vehicles, 51,400 head of horses, cattle, and sheep, and 123,011 railroad cars in 62,000 trips, although at that time three other ferries were in operation and two bridges had been built. By 1856 the Baltimore and Ohio had reached East St. Louis, and soon other railroads would arrive on the far side of the river. Passengers and freight could not be stranded indefinitely opposite the city to the inconvenience of all but the ferry operators. Furthermore, Eads argued, if a bridge were not built at St. Louis the city would lose the advantage of being on transcontinental lines. The railroads would cross the river upstream. Indeed, the uncertainty about Missouri's loyalty to the Union on the eve of the Civil War already had caused the government to move the first transcontinental line northward to a route running from Chicago to Omaha. St. Louis must bridge the Mississippi.

The scoffers again said that the Eads proposal was fantastic. Who built bridges a third of a mile long? But Eads insisted that nothing was impossible simply because it had not been done before. So a small bridge company was organized in 1866 and chartered by the state of Missouri. The Wiggins Ferry Company successfully opposed the granting of a charter in Illinois. Even the Missouri charter, despite the hard work of Gratz Brown, was loaded down with amendments which seemed to make it worthless. For example, the company was forbidden to build a suspension bridge or drawbridge, and any other bridge must have at least two spans 350 feet wide or one span of 500 feet. Eads was not disturbed by these restrictions. He presented drawings of his beautiful bridge with two spans, each 502 feet wide, and a central span of 520 feet.

While the drawing was being admired, L. B. Boomer, a Chicago bridge contractor, appeared as a rival. Somehow he had obtained an "exclusive" contract to build a bridge. But Eads's Missouri charter made an exclusive contract impossible. Boomer actually won some supporters for the Eads plan. He was from Chicago, wasn't he? And Chicago's population was growing at a faster rate than that of St. Louis. So on May 1, 1867, the *Missouri Democrat* editorialized: "Chicago, that Babylon of houses that fall down, is reaching after trade to support its fast horses, faster men and fallen women. Beware, you Chicageese!"

Eads and his company offered to employ J. H. Lindille, president of the Keystone Bridge Company of Pittsburgh, as a consultant, but he said he would have nothing to do with a plan so fantastic. So Colonel Henry Flad and Charles Pfeiffer were engaged to assist Eads. By August 1868 pile drivers, work boats, derricks, and materials were assembled at the foot of Washington Avenue. But Boomer's voice had not been stilled. He called a convention of twenty-seven engineers, many of them in his employ, in St. Louis for August 21. Noting the date, Eads started work on the cofferdam on August 20. The Boomer convention, of course, found the Eads plan wanting in every detail. As it was meant to do, this report raised some doubts in St. Louis. Boomer was even more effective when he appointed St. Louis men as officers of his bridge company, thus giving a bit of color to his denial that he represented Chicago interests. On top of that he threatened litigation. Then the work on the cofferdam ran into trouble and this, too, was exploited by the adversaries of Eads. St. Louis banks became reluctant about credit, and several persons withdrew from the bridge company. These machinations and futile litigation in Illinois wasted almost a year's time and interest. The *Missouri Republican* began to scoff: "How much will the bridge cost? Seven million dollars. How long will it take to build the bridge? Seven million years."

When the rivalry of the two companies was carried to Washington, Eads realized that his work might be delayed indefinitely unless a compromise were reached. Reluctantly, he consented to a merger of the two companies. Things looked better when, after a while, Boomer's friends withdrew, but this financial byplay had been expensive. And it was hardly out of the way before the northern railroads, rival river cities, and steamboat interests took up the fight. They tried to induce Congress to forbid this bridge over a navigable stream. But jibes at the plan helped it along: if the thing couldn't be built, what need for legislation prohibiting it? Again Eads paid for a victory with a breakdown of his health. His resignation, however, was refused by the bridge company. He was granted a leave of absence for another voyage to England. Milnor Roberts, his choice, was put in charge of the work, and Eads made the best of adversity by raising fresh capital in London. Inspection of a number of European bridgebuilding projects also induced him to abandon the cofferdam method of construction in favor of caissons. These huge devices were built by his old partner, Nelson, in the Carondelet yard. The first one was lowered to the river bottom in 1869. Now 1500 men on two dozen boats were at work in earnest.

That winter a sudden and extreme drop in the temperature filled the river with ice. Workmen could not come ashore, but they carried on cheerfully enough on the boats. Remembering his experience with river ice, Eads had anticipated the situation. So the men were well supplied with food and other necessities from stocks on the boats. On Christmas Eve, 1869, they were still marooned. Late that afternoon they noticed a tug pull away from the levee. Wondering about its purpose, they watched it make its dangerous way through the ice. For all his delight in family celebrations, Eads had insisted on cheering his workmen first of all and in person. After the risk he took to say "Merry Christmas," no man ever heard anything but praise of him from the bridgebuilders. Worse troubles than ice came with the New Year. The first symptoms of the "bends," an unknown disease at this time, appeared. Early in 1870 the first death occurred. Eads equipped a hospital boat and brought out his personal physician, Dr. Jaminet, to watch over the men. The work day was reduced to three one-hour shifts, and finally to two shifts of only forty-five minutes each.

So far as its engineering aspects were concerned, the project was carried through without a hitch. This was because Eads and his assistant, Colonel Henry Flad, made all their calculations with the utmost exactitude. To be even more certain, they submitted them to Chancellor Chauvenet of Washington University for careful checking. Flad had been trained at the University of Munich and gained his early experience on various projects along the Rhine. The uprising of 1848 brought him to St. Louis, where his competence soon was recognized. He built much of the Iron Mountain, and stretches of other railroads. He also built the Bissell's Point waterworks. When the Civil War broke out he entered the Union Army as a private, but he soon was raised to the rank of colonel of engineers. He worked with Eads not only on the bridge, but also on the tunnel which linked the span with the approach to the Union Station. Later he devised the plan for bringing all St. Louis trains into and out of the one huge depot. Others concerned with the building of the bridge, however, were not so co-operative. Almost a year before the great stone piers were completed, Lindille and his partner in the Keystone Bridge Company, Andrew Carnegie, had agreed to produce and install its steel. But on December 1, 1871, they served notice that they were abrogating the contract. Eads had violated the agreement, they said, by adopting an unspecified quality of steel for his bridge. This was nonsense. True, Eads's specifications had been demanding, but the Butcher Steel Company of Philadelphia had undertaken to produce the steel under a subcontract. Eads himself had been helpful beyond all contractual obligations. He had spent the summer in Philadelphia installing a testing machine devised by Colonel Flad. Through his friend, President Grant, he had borrowed Henry W. Fitch, a navy engineer, to supervise the work in Philadelphia. The St. Louis bridge company had paid for all the special machinery. A quantity of acceptable steel had been produced. Why, then, this belated, one-sided cancellation of the contract?

At a meeting with Carnegie in New York it must have become clear to Eads very quickly that this was nothing less than a shakedown—the first of half a dozen to which the St. Louis men would be forced to submit. Two of those came even before the steel work was started. Eads was compelled to modify his design, and also to accept iron bolts because the contractor had "forgotten" to make the specified steel bolts, and then said it could not be done. Twice Eads had to go to England for money, in 1872 and 1873. As the arches neared completion, the contractor demanded a bonus for closing them by January 1, 1874. Then he said they could not be joined. Eads and Flad had to do this difficult work themselves and under a blazing summer sun which expanded the steel. This, however, was another of the difficulties Eads had anticipated. Meanwhile there were more exactions, including bonuses for finishing the railroad deck by March 1, 1874, and another of $1000 a day for every day the railroads could use the bridge before June 1. A demand even was made that these should be paid in advance! The St. Louis men would have been glad to be rid of Carnegie but for his influence with the railroads. After all, only their payment for its use could justify the mounting investment. The vehicular level was complete on April 15, with a ceremonial opening planned for April 18.

But before that came another "cancellation." On the eve of the celebration, workmen suddenly began tearing up the east approach to the
bridge, and the next day they started wrecking operations at the west
end. Almost resigned to such highhandedness, Eads again went East
and came back with an agreement that the bridge sidewalks would
be opened on May 23 and the roadway on May 24. This word was
not broken.

General Sherman "drove the last spike," and Eads tested his bridge
with fourteen locomotives—he had hoped to line it with engines from
end to end, but he could only borrow fourteen. And so at long and
bitter last, in the presence of President Grant and half a dozen governors, with a hundred-gun salute, a fifteen-mile parade, a procession
of steamboats and a grand show of fireworks, a tourist-crowded city
celebrated the completion of the magnificent bridge which still serves
and adorns St. Louis.

Other troubles had to be overcome before the flags were unfurled.
In 1873, as the steel work got under way, the Keokuk Steamship Company carried a formal protest to Grant's shady Secretary of War, William W. Belknap, an Iowa man and a personal friend of company's
officers. The arches of the bridge were only fifty-five feet above the
river, they said; how were steamboats like the *Great Republic,* with
smokestacks more than 100 feet high, to pass under the bridge? It
would be outrageous, of course, to expect the steamboats to lower
their fantastic stacks. General A. A. Humphreys, chief of the army
engineers, convened a committee of engineers which preposterously recommended that a canal be built around the bridge! Eads had to go to
Washington to see President Grant—with some embarrassment, since
he had opposed his friend politically in the last campaign—but the
President was helpful.

Despite an unprecedented engineering feat, and despite perseverance
through seven years of outrageous provocations, the bridgebuilders in
the end were not to reap the rewards of their triumph. While Carnegie
strutted and claimed all credit for the accomplishment, his railroad
friends refused for a solid year to use the bridge! (He had sold his
bridge bonds in London long ago—and at a profit.) In 1878 the bridge
was sold under auctioneer's hammer!

The Eads Bridge eventually made St. Louis a railroad center second only to Chicago. But for a long time it stirred St. Louis to anger as
readily as it evoked pride. There was the "bridge arbitrary." Refusing

to assume the cost of transporting passengers and freight across the river or to charge for this service at the usual mileage rate, the railroads—which eventually became the owners of the bridge—imposed an arbitrary charge on each passenger and on each ton of freight. But there was the long, graceful sweep of the bridge. James B. Eads had given St. Louis one of the world's great architectural beauties—simple, clean, and useful.

Bridging the Mississippi for the railroads did not imply hostility to the steamboats. Eads proved this by his next great Mississippi River accomplishment: saving New Orleans as an ocean port. The three "passes" by which shipping passed through the Mississippi River Delta were being obstructed by a rapidly growing sand bar in the Gulf of Mexico. On a typical day in 1859 thirty-five ships were held up inside the bar, seventeen were anchored outside, and three were grounded —all waiting for high water to sail or be dragged across the barrier. The Civil War had stopped even the ineffectual "raking" to keep the passes open. But as the South began to recover, the army engineers proposed to cut a canal through the bar. Having learned much about the ways of the river in the years he walked its bottom, Eads said such a channel soon would fill up. Jetties should be built, he said, which would force the powerful current to scour out a really deep channel. Again the scoffers laughed—especially the engineers.

Nettled, Eads went to Washington in February, 1874, and offered to provide and maintain for ten years a jetty channel, 28 feet deep and 350 feet wide. His price was $10,000,000. This was $5,000,000 less than the estimated cost of a canal. The House of Representatives, nevertheless, passed the engineers' canal bill. But Carl Schurz of St. Louis stopped that scheme in the Senate. "For thirty-seven years," Schurz said, "they have been planning and reporting, scratching and scraping at the mouth of the Mississippi, and today the depth of the water is no greater." The Senate committee asked to be discharged from further consideration of the canal bill. The Eads plan finally was accepted, but not until it was loaded down with discouraging conditions and restrictions. All over again, this was the scheme used in vain to make the Missouri bridge charter self-defeating. Again Eads was confident that he could overcome unreasonable handicaps. Joseph Pulitzer was one of his backers.

So in May 1875, Eads—with James Andrews and William Nelson —began driving piles and sinking willowbrush mats along one of the

silting "passes." Long before the jetties were completed, they began to
guide the current and the channel began to deepen. The army engineers
continued to scoff, to protest, and to obstruct. Looking for deep water
rather than debates, the master of the coastal steamer *Hudson* took
his ship through the Eads channel, which by October 5, 1876, had
attained a depth of twenty feet. Others soon followed. In 1877 the
channel was used by 587 ocean-going ships. The old main "pass," still
in charge of the engineers, now was used only by fishing smacks.

Foreigners who had been impressed by the Eads Bridge were
even more impressed by the jetties. Don Pedro II, Emperor of
Brazil, came in person to Port Eads, the neat little village which
had been built for the channel workers in the midst of swamp
and Spanish moss, to ask Eads to undertake similar work on Brazilian
streams. Even if Eads had been so inclined, it would have been impossible for him to accept commissions at the time. Yellow fever struck
Port Eads. Eleven men died, including his old friend and partner,
William Nelson. At the same time, General Heywood of the engineers
was using his influence in Washington to hold up payments to Eads.
It was like the gunboatbuilding days when Eads found he could not
meet the payroll—yet all but two of the seventy-six workers agreed
to remain on the job and to wait until the government paid Eads.
Praising these men, Elmer Corthill, an Eads associate, later said:

"Little did the great valley realize that its vast commercial interests
were being advanced by a few laboring men at the mouth of the
Mississippi to whom great credit should be given for their devotion
to duty and faith in the ultimate success of the jetties."

By July 10, 1879, the Gulf approach to New Orleans was deeper
than the Sandy Hook approach to New York. New Orleans was impressed. The square at the foot of Canal Street was named for Eads.
Finally he did get his money. Over four years, the work cost the
government $5,250,000, a little more than half of what had been asked
to start the engineers' canal.

Eads had preserved an outlet to the Atlantic for the commerce of
the inland waterways. His services now were solicited for river and
harbor work in Toronto, in Florida, in California's Sacramento Valley,
and in a dozen countries abroad. At most he would study and advise;
he would not take charge of any of these projects. His mind was still
on the Mississippi. He felt that its commerce should have a short cut
to the Pacific. Count de Lesseps was promoting his sea-level canal in

Panama. Others were urging a canal across Nicaragua. Eads came forward with a more unorthodox proposal, the Tehuantepec marine railway. Ships would be lifted from the waters of the Gulf of Mexico, placed on special railroad cars, and pulled across Mexico to be launched again in the Pacific. He built a working model, which was applauded by engineers and bankers in New York. He went to Mexico and was granted a right of way. But the voice of the scoffers and the obstructionists was heard again in Washington.

This time Eads left the field to them; he died March 8, 1887, in New York. Funeral services were held in Christ Church Cathedral in St. Louis on the 18th, and he was buried in Bellefontaine Cemetery —on the same Mississippi River bluff on which stand the monuments of Governor Clark, General Sherman, and so many others who had been as sure as Laclède that the Mississippi would make St. Louis "une des plus belles villes de l'Amérique."

XXI. Romantic Reformers

The Age of Metternich brought revolution to Germany and the culture of Germany to St. Louis. A goodly number of Germans, attracted by the lyrical praise of the Missouri country which Gottfried Duden spread through the press of the Fatherland, had settled in the city or on nearby farms before the arrival of the '48ers. Outstanding among them were the Latin farmers of Belleville, called so by their neighbors either out of respect or in derision of the devotion of these yeomen to the classics. Virgil was a best seller on the frontier. But most of the *Dreissiger*—those who came to America in the 1830s—were plainer people than the university men who tried to topple the thrones of Prussia and Austria.

In the three years of 1848, 1849, and 1850, 34,418 Germans arrived in St. Louis. By 1860 the city and county had 50,510 German-born citizens. The earliest Germans came as farmers. They settled in the rich bottom land of the Missouri Valley. They established villages like Herman, Missouri, famous for its annual *Maifest,* planted vineyards, and introduced scientific agriculture. They did have their eggheads. For example: Friederich Muench, philosopher, poet, journalist, and farmer; Friederich Adolph Wislizensus, fur trader and founder of the St. Louis Academy of Science; Anton Eickhoff, who came from Westphalia to teach at St. Louis University; Wilhelm Weber, librarian of the Mercantile, who in 1836 became editor of the *Anzeiger des Westens,* founded the year before, and soon made it one of the most exciting of St. Louis German publications, and Max Oertel, *bon vivant* and editor of the Catholic *Kirchenzeitung*. But most of the early St. Louis Germans were unspectacular workers who drank their beer and endured nativist contempt. But the *Vierundachtziger,* the '48ers, would not be brushed aside as "damned Dutch."

These Germans were rather like Hilaire Belloc's Normans—men who emerged in history for a brief interlude of scene-changing power, "a very lucky freak . . . the only body of men who all were lords, and who in their collective action showed continually nothing but genius."

Some of the '48ers would not have disclaimed comparison with the men who "awoke all Europe," who suddenly created a new society. Their stage was smaller and their time shorter than the Normans', but there were no other immigrants like those who arrived within a few years in the middle of the nineteenth century, and who had finished their work by the century's end. Defeat abroad did not dim their libertarian ideals; they did not abandon them in the forest; they brought them to fruition amidst the alien corn.

Perhaps the zeal of some of them bordered on the arrogant. But as heirs of a thousand years of culture, these men from Jena and Bonn and Heidelberg were shocked to find Americans hanging out doctors' shingles after attending Dr. McDowell's lectures for less than a year. They were disgusted by the patois of their *Landsleute,* by the mediocrity of the press, by the condition of politics, by the low estate of the arts. But they were appalled, above all, by the contradiction of slavery in the land of the free. It took them two generations, according to Carl Witte, to raise musical taste from "Yankee Doodle" to *Parsifal.* They helped to accomplish greater reforms in less time.

Radical in ideas and in speech, advocating reforms in school and church as well as in politics, the '48ers were by no means welcomed everywhere and by everybody. Among the least friendly were the German Lutherans and Catholics of St. Louis. In fact, many of the earlier German settlers resented the newcomers as "riders of moonbeams." The German community soon was divided into two groups—the Grays, the early settlers, and the Greens, the newcomers. The latter also antagonized some of the natives, especially the temperance advocates, whom they regarded as Puritans more dour than Cromwell himself. They were outraged by the depredations of the Know-Nothings, the Secret Order of the Star-Spangled Banner. Ranks were closed only when the bugles sounded. Then Greens, Grays, and "Bostons" marched in step to the battlefields of the Civil War.

First, however, Grays and Greens had to fight their own civil war, an echo of the German *Kulturkampf.* As rebels against authoritarianism, the '48ers were for the most part freethinkers. Blaming them for having fought in "bloody Kansas" and for John Brown's raid on the arsenal at Harper's Ferry, the *Missouri Republican* called them "Red Republicans—all Robespierres, Dantons and Saint-Justs, red down to their very kidneys." Well, it was a time of political acrimony, and these men could give as good as they took. In celebrating May Day, 1858, with a big parade and picnic, the speakers of the St. Louis Gambrinus Society inveighed against the "barbarians and the Methodists" who would forbid the drinking of beer. But the Grays were most offended by the establishment of the *Freimaennervereine* and *Freie Gemeinden* —freemen's societies and free congregations—the precursors of the Ethical Societies as alternatives to the orthodox churches. The Missouri Lutherans were deeply offended, and Philip Schaff in 1855 was quite bitter about the "so-called educated immigrants floated over by unsuccessful revolutions." They were atheists and agnostics who preached doubt instead of faith. They were "not only estranged from all Christianity, but even from all higher morality, and deserve to be called pioneers of heathenism and a new barbarism. . . . This godless German-American pest" is a "reproach and shame" to the German element in the United States.

The Catholic reaction was equally vigorous. Not content with denunciations, the bishops established parishes for German immigrants to save them from the freethinkers. They also favored the publication of papers and periodicals to carry on a great debate. Thus Father P. Martin Seidel, a St. Louis Jesuit, edited the *Katholisches Sonntagsblatt*, later called the *Herold des Glaubens*, to hold the line against the *Anzeiger des Westens*. The Central Verein was established to counter the '48ers' Immigrant Aid Society. There was work enough for both, since many immigrants were duped abroad by agents of the shipping lines and fleeced during the steerage crossing, arriving with empty pockets. Unable to speak English, even a learned Ph.D. found it difficult to earn a living. The United States was not necessarily a land of milk and honey for the greenhorn. Some men of standing in the Fatherland even were driven to suicide in inhospitable America.

The difficult period of adjustment was eased for many an immigrant by a *Turnverein*. The first in St. Louis, called *Bestrebung,* Endeavor, was formed in 1850. The Turner movement was started by Friedrich Ludwig Jahn—Turnvater Jahn—while Germany was under the domination of Napoleon. He adopted Juvenal's prescription: *"mens sana in corpore sano."* These were more than physical-culture clubs, open also to women in bloomers. They sought to foster the ideal of political liberty and a morality centered on the love of one's neighbor. They maintained libraries, schools, lecture courses, and dramatic programs. There also was much parading and pageantry, singing and feasting. Eventually they became chiefly social clubs with gymnasiums attached.

But to Hecker, a Turner was "the carrier and developer and apostle of the free spirit." The Turners naturally defended the Union and the new Republican party. So did many of the nativists, and to gain Turner support, ironically, they organized a Know-Nothing branch for Germans, the *Sag Nichts!* This, somehow, didn't get very far.

Closely associated with the Turners were the singing society, the sharpshooter's club or *Schuetzenbund,* and the workmen's association. As the immigrants prospered, they held more and more folk festivals, turkey shoots, singing contests and parades of brightly uniformed militia companies, known as the German Hussars or the Steuben Guards. Most celebrations wound up with a performance at a *Volkstheater,* the open-air theaters which were features of most beer gardens. Seidel after seidel was served as the lieder of the *Heimat* were played on one of Heinrich Steinweg's pianos and everybody joined in the chorus. But at least one *Landsmann* prayed the Lord to guard us against these celebrations as against war and plague:

> *Behuet uns, Herr, vor Krieg und Pest*
> *Vor Schuetzen, Turn' und Saengerfest.*

One of the most popular leaders of the German revolution was Friedrich Hecker of Mannheim. Sympathizers of the liberal cause even in the United States wore Hecker hats, green Tyrolean hats with a red feather, and sang the Hecker lied. After defeat, he came to the United States, raised a little money, and returned in a vain attempt to renew resistance in Germany. Frustrated, he came back and settled on a farm near Belleville. This German Cincinnatus announced that "the German Fatherland now lives on in the Far West." Not overly ambitious for wealth and fame, he was loyal to the cause of democracy as it came to be represented by Lincoln, and he served it well as an orator in English, German, and French.

Almost Hecker's opposite in temperament was Henry Boernstein. He had an amazing variety of interests and the vitality adequate to all of them. He had been president of the *Société des Démocrates Allemands* in Paris and one of the leaders of the German Legion which marched from France to the aid of the rebels. He and his wife reached New Orleans in 1849 with dozens of trunks and chests—enough clothes for years—and soon boarded a steamer for St. Louis. They had been on the Vienna and Paris stage and had made several successful tours of Italy. In St. Louis Boernstein ran a hotel, a brewery, and a few saloons. He organized an amateur theatrical group, the *Philodrama-tische Gesellschaft,* and after a year or two became the proprietor of the St. Louis Opera House, the city's earliest first-rate professional theater. No showboat entertainment was offered, but *Hamlet, Wil-helm Tell, Faust,* and *Maria Stuart.* Schiller and Heine, rather than Goethe, admired by princes, were the favorites of the '48ers who, it is said, bought more copies of the German classics than were being sold in Germany. Another of Boernstein's projects was the *Leseverein,* a library and reading room in the pattern of a Parisian *cabinet de lecture,* which he established above a drugstore. Here, for five cents a visit, one could read books and publications of all kinds, study maps and consult reference works.

The versatile Boernstein, however, made his deepest impression on the community as editor of the *Anzeiger des Westens.* He offered prizes for novels and plays in German on American themes and, in-cidentally, raised eyebrows by himself writing a novel rather too daring for the times. He commissioned and published a translation of Benton's *Thirty Years' View.* Having been the Paris and Vienna correspondent of a number of European and American newspapers, he was able to improve the paper's news coverage, but he regarded it principally as a political organ. He waged an aggressive campaign against the Know-Nothings, during which the police with difficulty kept a mob from burning down his building. He took a strong free-soil stand, and was an early supporter of Frémont. He regarded Lincoln as too conserva-tive on emancipation. Yet he joined Blair in the fight to keep Missouri in the Union, and was one of the first to put on a colonel's uniform and raise a regiment for the Civil War, the Second Missouri.

Franz Sigel, another refugee of '48, took a more prominent part in the war. A graduate of the military academy at Karlsruhe, he left the army for the cause of German liberty and conducted with skill what were bound to be losing military operations. Before the Civil War, Sigel was on the faculty of the St. Louis *Realschule,* one of the private schools established in the United States by '48ers along the lines of the French lycée and the German gymnasium. Their hope was to educate a bilingual people—good American citizens who would preserve Ger-man cultural interests. Perhaps this was impossible in the long run, but St. Louis had a German theater until World War I, and a German press until World War II. Associated with the *Realschule* was a German boarding school for girls, conducted by Emma Poesche. The Germans also emphasized adult education and organized many evening classes. Full of the ideas of Froebel and Pestalozzi, they were far in advance of American educators, and had a considerable influence on them. Mrs. Schurz, for example, had studied under Froebel and interested many American women in the *Kindergarten*. The first one in an American public school was opened in St. Louis in 1873.

Sigel, however, was to make a reputation not as an educator, but as a soldier and politician. Like Boernstein, he raised a German regiment in St. Louis and marched with Lyon to Camp Jackson. He distinguished himself at Pea Ridge, but his support of Frémont got him into trouble with Halleck. He was to have difficulties with McDowell and others, too. He was so popular among German-Americans that when, as a major general, he was assigned to serve under Pope and Banks, a delegation from St. Louis called on Lincoln to protest. It was backed by Blair and Trumbull. Some of the St. Louisans believed that the war could be shortened by giving Sigel full command of the Union armies. A wiser '48er exclaimed:

"Sigel can handle his enemies. God protect him from his friends."

Those friends, organized in a number of cities, in November 1862 presented him with a $2000 sword. His initials were set into it with diamonds, and there were seventy ounces of silver in the blade. The women of St. Louis gave him a big silver cup, very useful in the field. All criticism of Sigel was blamed on the nativists. In fact, he became the symbol and almost the idol of the German-American victims of this prejudice. To his credit, he kept his head. In 1863 he strongly urged the defeat of the Copperheads, and in 1864 he condemned those Germans who wanted to displace Lincoln. A Democratic victory would be "a national calamity," he said, "and an immortal shame to this Republic." The cause of the North, he said, was the cause for which the '48ers had fought in Germany.

German-Americans were by no means the only wartime critics of Lincoln. Thaddeus Stevens, Sumner, Joseph Medill, Wendell Phillips, Wade, Chandler, and others believed he was too "soft" toward the slave power. McClellan ran against the President. And there was a boom for Frémont as the Republican candidate. This had considerable support in St. Louis, where Benton's son-in-law had not lost all his popularity. The *Westliche Post,* not stridently anti-Lincoln, nevertheless was disappointed when Frémont withdrew. But, despite his friendship with Frémont, Sigel supported Lincoln. He encouraged George

Hillgaertner to start a German paper in St. Louis to support the President for a second term. Whatever mistake Sigel made in the field, he was loyal to his commander in chief.

Perhaps the best German soldier in the Civil War was the little-celebrated Peter Joseph Osterhaus of St. Louis. He enlisted as a private. At the war's end he was a major general. He had been under fire in thirty-four battles. He was a man after the heart of his commander, "Cump" Sherman.

It was understandable that in the postwar era many of the '48ers should have followed the lead of the Radical Republicans in the reconstruction of the South. Not only slavery but also nativism turned them against the Southern *Junkers*. Fortunately, rigid German logic yielded to unrigid German manners and customs. Singing and beer drinking were not conducive to sustained bitterness. *"Durst macht Lustig."*

The '48ers, of course, were not without their rivalries. Boernstein's *Anzeiger des Westens* for a time towered above the half-dozen German newspapers in St. Louis, thanks to editors like Charles Bernays and Carl Daenzer. But in 1857 Daenzer founded the *Westliche Post,* and it soon provided serious opposition for the older paper. The *Anzeiger* suspended publication when Boernstein and many of its employees went to war, but Daenzer revived it in 1864, the year Dr. Emil Preetorius, a native of Hesse-Darmstadt and a Heidelberg doctor of law, became editor in chief of the *Westliche Post*. He was joined by Carl Schurz in 1867, and for more than half a century the paper was distinguished and influential throughout the Mississippi Valley. Preetorius was prominent in St. Louis until he died in 1905.

Carl Schurz, "the tremendous Dutchman," towered an historical head above all the other '48ers. He was so well known on both sides of the Atlantic before he settled in St. Louis after the Civil War that he was elected United States Senator from Missouri two years later over the opposition of one of the state's most powerful politicians, Charles D. Drake, by whose name the punitive, anti-Confederate state constitution was known.

Like Sherman, Carl Schurz was a *Wandervogel*. His life was tied to causes, not places. Wherever men struggled for freedom and integrity, he was at home. He learned English by reading newspapers. Six months after his arrival in America he spoke the language with only that trace of an accent which he never overcame. Carl Schurz was a St. Louisan for only fifteen years, and the greater part of ten of those years he spent in Washington as senator and as Secretary of the Interior. Yet the political morality of St. Louis is to a considerable degree a reflection of the political morality of Carl Schurz. He was the epitome of *Buergerlichkeit.*

St. Louis and Schurz took the lead in the fight against Grantism and in the campaign for civil service. He was a national rather than a local figure, yet in the exultation of political victory he could say to his wife that he was the "most powerful man in Missouri." Even though St. Louis politicians frustrated his most ambitious project for good government, it was the spirit typified by Carl Schurz which enabled St. Louis to reclaim its self-respect at the turn of the century after Lincoln Steffens had denounced it as one of the most shameful cities of America.

Schurz was a romantic, a *Glueckskind* or, in rock-and-roll talk, a glamour boy. He was born in a castle—but only because his grandfather was the overseer of a Rhenish estate. Schurz was hard pressed for funds to go to the university in Bonn. Nevertheless he distinguished himself and was accepted as a member of the Franconia student society, an exceptional group which, instead of fighting the customary student duels, fought for German liberty. The society's colors—red, gold, and black—now are the national colors of the German Federal Republic.

His mother solemnly handed him the sword he carried in the German uprising. He fought under Franz Sigel. Captured by the Prussians at Rastatt July 23, 1849, Schurz escaped through a sewer and made his way to Switzerland. But he found it impossible to resume a student's life so long as his friend and teacher, Gottfried Kinkel, was in Spandau prison in Berlin. Determined to rescue Kinkel, Schurz made his dangerous way across Germany. One plan and another went awry. Finally he induced a guard to smuggle a rope to Kinkel and to leave a prison window open. He had a coach waiting when Kinkel reached a dark street, fortunately empty, and the two started a wild ride to the sea. In two nights they reached Warnemuende. Despite a heavy storm, they set out in a small ship to cross the North Sea. It took them eleven days to reach Leith in Scotland. The story of the *Befreiung* spread around the world, and Schurz was famous before he was twenty-one years old. When he went to Paris in the spring of 1851, Louis Napoleon asked him to leave France. Schurz could hardly expect to be welcomed by a man who was preparing to change his title from President to Emperor. So he joined the 1848 refugees in London. There he met

Kossuth, the Hungarian, and Mazzini, the Italian. He married Margarethe Meyer, eighteen-year-old daughter of a banker, in the parish church of Marylebone. And he watched the grip of reaction tighten on the continent. Louis Blanc, refugee from France, met Schurz one day in Hyde Park.

"*Oh, c'est vous, mon jeune ami!*" he exclaimed. "*C'est fini, n'est-ce pas?*"

Schurz and his young wife arrived in the United States on September 17, 1852. His name had gone before him because:

> *In youth he braved a monarch's ire*
> *To set his people free.*

His instinct for politics drew Schurz to Washington. There two things shocked him: slavery, which he knew about, and the spoils system, which was a surprise to him. Here were "causes," freedom and reform, to fill a whole life. Schurz met Jefferson Davis, Seward, Sumner, and others. He was told that if he went to one of the western states he soon would be back in Washington as a member of Congress. In 1854, as a representative of a Philadelphia street-lighting firm, he made an extensive tour of the West. He was welcomed in St. Louis by Hecker, but he did not like the shadow of slavery over the city. Soon after his return to Philadelphia he spent an evening at the home of his friend, Dr. Tiedeman. Spiritualism and thought transference, the half-amusing, half-serious dabbling in the occult, was a parlor vogue at the time. Dr. Tiedeman's daughter was regarded as a talented "reading medium." So Schurz found himself participating in a seance. With curiosity, and perhaps with a touch of seriousness, he asked the girl:

"What will I become?"

"A United States Senator."

"From what state?"

"Missouri."

"Who knows this?"

"Abraham Lincoln."

If he felt that his destiny had been made manifest, Schurz hardly co-operated with his occult guide. Instead of moving to Missouri at once, he decided in March 1855 to join an uncle in Watertown, Wisconsin, and he took to that place with all the enthusiasm of a Chamber of Commerce booster. He bought real estate which was going to make him rich. (He lost it and his shirt, too, in the panic of 1857.) He was elected alderman. He was defeated as a candidate for lieutenant governor, the only loser on his ticket, and was appointed a regent of the University of Wisconsin. But in his politicking he did get to know Abraham Lincoln and was asked to campaign for the Republicans in 1860. He had made one of the great speeches of the convention in the Chicago Wigwam when he said:

"We defy the whole slave power and the whole vassalage of hell!"

Schurz was credited with lining up the million and a half German-American votes solidly for Lincoln, and the President appointed him Ambassador to Spain. The firing on Fort Sumter made Schurz reluctant to depart for Europe. He offered instead to enlist German regiments, but Lincoln persuaded him that for the time being he would be of greater service abroad. That is how the former rebel came to be closeted with Bismarck. The Iron Chancellor smiled at the incongruity, but he was friendly toward Schurz as the revolutionary-turned-diplomat explained the Union position. Like most busy men, Bismarck had devices for getting rid of a caller who stayed too long. An aide had orders to enter the room after a given length of time to remind the Chancellor of an engagement. When the man came in, Bismarck said:

"Never mind, please get us more cigars."

"Your cigars are good," said Schurz.

When the aide appeared a second time, he was told, "Yes, yes, but please bring us a little more brandy."

"Your brandy is good," said Schurz.

The aide did not interrupt a third time.

In Madrid Schurz realized how much Bull Run had hurt the government's prestige abroad. He urged Lincoln to offset this by making a positive statement on emancipation. Schurz was back in Washington early in 1862, and on June 2 he was made a brigadier general, attached to Frémont's command. After Frémont's resignation he served under his old friend, Franz Sigel, and in the final phase of the war under another St. Louisan, Sherman, the one genius, in Schurz's eyes, among all commanders of the Civil War, North and South.

Tall and thin, his beard carefully trimmed, Schurz was handsome in uniform. In action he was brave to the point of foolhardiness. Still, the gods of battle did not smile on him and his men. They were cruelly tried in half a dozen engagements: Manassas, Chancellorsville, and Gettysburg among them. Although only about one third of the men in his division were Germans, they were cursed by the nativists as "cowardly Dutchmen" when they were forced to give ground. Schurz was a better officer than some of his stupid commanders. He was fully justified in writing in one of his reports:

I am far from saying that on May 2 everybody did his duty to the best of his power—but one thing I will say, because I know it, these men are no cowards. . . . I have seen with my own eyes troops who now affect to look down on the 11th Corps with sovereign contempt behave much worse under circumstances far less trying.

These incidents may explain at least in part why, after the war, Schurz never used his military title—useful as it could have been in politics—and why he refused to join the G.A.R. or any other veterans' organization. They also explain why he fired off one letter after another to Lincoln about men like McClellan, Halleck, and Buell, whose incompetence was losing lives. During the campaign of 1864 Lincoln had more use for Schurz, blunt and outspoken as he was, on the hustings than in the field. Schurz worked with heart and soul for Lincoln's re-election. Of the President, he wrote to a friend:

He is a man of profound feeling, and firm principles, and incorruptible integrity. One can always rely on his motives, and the characteristic gift of this people, a sound common sense, is developed in him to a marvelous degree. He is the people personified.

Schurz returned to Sherman's headquarters shortly before the end of the war. The romantic and the intellectual in Schurz both were captivated by Sherman's brilliant innovations and his rapid, relentless performance. When the drums beat in march time for the last review in Washington, Carl Schurz was full of pride for "Cump" Sherman. Peace meant for Schurz the extirpation of slavery. He was slow to appreciate the tolerance and the charity of the Second Inaugural. He disapproved of Sherman's generous terms of surrender. Maybe he had been listening too much to Seward and Sumner. Like most of the anti-slavery Germans, Schurz for a while was in step with the Radical Republicans. Perhaps it was just as well that his immediate need was a job. In November 1865 he became a correspondent for Horace Greeley's *Tribune,* but he didn't care much for Greeley and was glad to take the editorship of the Detroit *Post,* a German newspaper. Then came his big opportunity. In April 1867 Dr. Emil Preetorius, an old

'48er, offered him a half interest—on easy terms—in the *Westliche Post,* and its editorship. He had been in the United States for fifteen years. He had been an ambassador, a general, a politician, a popular lecturer, a spokesman for the German-American against the nativists. Approaching his forties, Carl Schurz was about to exert his greatest influence on America.

He made friends easily during that first hot summer in St. Louis. But the paper meant politics. And politics meant firing away at President Johnson and the Temperance agitators. The President, he wrote, "now bites at all about him like a wounded and anger-crazed bear." Prohibition, Schurz denounced as Puritan interference in personal affairs. Let the Republicans have no part of it if they expected votes from Germans who drank beer and wine in moderation—and were better for it. Schurz was asked to run for Congress and was assured that he would be elected—just what he had heard on his first visit to Washington. But he declined; he would like to learn a little about Missouri first.

On May 20, 1868, Schurz made the keynote speech at the Republican Convention in Chicago. As a delegate-at-large from Missouri, he helped to nominate Grant. His work on the resolutions committee showed that his Radical views were changing. He spoke for leniency toward the South. Although Schurz "stumped" for Grant, he quickly lost enthusiasm for the man.

That summer the La Grange, Missouri *American* suggested him as a senatorial possibility. Senator Drake of St. Louis set himself against Schurz from the start. It was and is a tradition—not always observed— that one Missouri senator should come from the eastern, the other from the western part of the state. So Drake backed General Benjamin Loan of St. Joseph, Missouri. Schurz's ambition grew even faster than his boom. He had no false modesty. But Drake's organization also worked hard. Schurz was denounced as an infidel, a drunkard, a foreign upstart, a coward in battle. These charges angered the St. Louis Germans. They had battled the Know-Nothings before the war. They had helped Lyon and Blair keep Missouri in the Union. Thousands of them had fought in Lincoln's armies. They counted themselves as Republicans and they were aroused by the old attacks now repeated by the Republican "boss."

Schurz was in Jefferson City when the legislature convened on Janurary 6, 1869. He challenged both Loan and Drake to public debates. The Senate seat was at stake for the one, the party leadership for the other. They could not decline to meet so popular an orator. Poor Loan was heckled and laughed at. The next night Drake, full of anger, made the fatal mistake of repeating the most outrageous charges against the Germans. His violent emotion destroyed him. He left Jefferson City within the hour. At a joint session the next day, Schurz was unanimously elected. Not quite overnight, he had become the leader of the Republican party in Missouri. In the Senate, the state again had a voice as strong as Benton's. In St. Louis people marveled. Which man had made the more sensational advance? Grant, the ne'er-do-well woodpeddler who was now President? Or Schurz, the editor who was elected senator almost as soon as he settled in Missouri? These two by now, however, had little more in common than their association with the same party and the same city.

Schurz was an idealist, but a practical one. Having paid for his interest in the *Westliche Post* and having agreed with Preetorius to continue as editor, he now was financially independent. "I recorded a vow in my heart," he wrote later, "that I would at least honestly endeavour to fulfill my duty; that I would conscienciously adhere to the principle *salus populi suprema lex*. [The motto of Missouri.] That I would never be a sycophant, a fawner or a flatterer of the multitudes; that, if need be, I would stand up alone for my conviction of truth and right; and that there would be no personal sacrifice too great for my devotion to the Republic."

Schurz was not unworldly, yet he was shocked by the corruption typified in the Senate by Administration leaders like Roscoe Conkling of New York, Oliver H. P. Morton of Indiana and Zachariah Chandler of Michigan, not to mention the boodlers in Grant's cabinet. He was amazed by the extent to which the government was "honeycombed with whisky-rings, customhouse frauds, assessments on officeholders, nepotism and general uncleanness." He was especially shocked by Grant's perhaps unwitting part in the gold conspiracy of Jay Gould and Jim Fisk. Still Schurz was slow to find fault with the President. His early complaint was mild: "He seeks to run the government like an army."

What worked inexorably for a break between the two men was their change of attitude toward the South. Grant, generous to Lee at Appomatox as Lincoln wanted him to be, had turned. He backed the carpetbaggers with federal bayonets. Schurz, at the war's end inclined toward the irreconcilables, had gradually changed his attitude on Reconstruction. He was more and more inclined to forgive and forget. He recognized the problem created by the freed Negroes and the rising of the Ku-Klux Klan. He saw the remedy in moderation. This change in outlook was hastened by his residence in St. Louis, where contracts with the South were more intimate than in the Boston of Charles Sumner. However Schurz's lasting break with Grant came when the President tried to force Congress to approve treaties negotiated by his aide, General Orville E. Babcock, for the annexation of Santo Domingo. Schurz joined with Sumner to beat the President on this issue, and thereafter the doors of the White House were closed to him. But this left him all the more free to conduct his crusades for civil service, sound money, and lower tariffs—all, of course, opposed by the dominant Grant faction. Schurz's leadership made it inevitable that the revolt against Grantism should begin in Missouri.

Many Missourians who had carried a rifle for the Confederacy came home after the war. The Democrats naturally welcomed the return of the errant, and the Republicans had promised the removal of political disabilities as soon as the rebellion was put down. By 1870 Schurz felt the time had come to make good this promise. The party's state convention at Jefferson City, however, was dominated by Radicals, so Schurz and 250 liberal delegates organized a rump convention. They nominated Benjamin Gratz Brown for governor. Brown, as a Benton Democrat, had served as senator from 1863 to 1867. The regular Republican convention nominated Joseph W. McClurg, and Grant gave him his full support.

Schurz knew that he had been read out of the Republican party by Grant and that the President was bent on having his head and those of all who sided with him. So he buckled up for battle. This was his fight as much as anybody's. And when Brown was elected by more than 40,000 votes, he wrote to Schurz: "In this great victory in Missouri you were the true hero, and for our success we were more indebted to your prudence, sagacity, and indomitable canvass than to all other causes." He also said that the fight had been for "state reform, revenue reform, and civil service reform."

The victory meant that Schurz could no longer expect anything from the Grant Republicans in Washington, but to him principle was all-important and the party only a means to an end. He said as much in the Senate on December 12, 1870, when he introduced a resolution for the removal of "disabilities imposed upon persons lately in rebellion against the Government of the United States." He explained that this issue had split the Republican party in Missouri. "I recognize objects in political life superior to the immediate advantage of the party," he said. "The only way to preserve the vitality of the Republican party is to make it the party of progressive reform." If this were not done, he would lead a revolt.

This audacity reflected the views of many St. Louis men, especially the group with which Schurz lunched regularly to discuss reforms. Yet Brown, who owed his election to Schurz and who shared his eagerness for reform, defeated the attempt to do on a national scale what had been accomplished in Missouri—and after he had helped Schurz launch the national effort. On Janurary 24, 1872, the Liberal Republicans of Missouri in their state convention called for a national convention in Cincinnati in May. Senator Lyman Trumbull of Illinois, Senator Orris Ferry of Connecticut, Thomas W. Tipton of Nebraska, Horace Greeley of New York, Samuel S. Bowles of the Springfield, Massachusetts, *Republican,* Murat Halstead of the Cincinnati *Commercial,* Horace White of the Chicago *Tribune,* E. L. Godkin of the *Nation,* and others backed the movement. Schurz himself made speeches and helped to form Liberal clubs in many parts of the country. As a program for the convention he suggested a general amnesty for Southerners, home rule for the South, civil-service reform, resumption of specie payments, and regulation of corporations. Above all he wanted the defeat of Grant, because he was convinced that the Administration was utterly corrupt. Schurz hoped that the Cincinnati convention would nominate Charles Francis Adams of Massachusetts for the presidency.

Grant men turned all their strength against Schurz. In the Senate his quick wit readily repelled their attacks. A more formidable adversary was Thomas Nast, the cartoonist of *Harper's Weekly.* Over the protests of the magazine's political editor, George William Curtis, Nast began a campaign of ridicule against the anti-Administration leaders. Himself a German-American, he labeled Schurz "the Dutchman." He certainly made the public more familiar with Schurz's bearded face. When the Liberal Republicans opened their convention in Cincinnati, Schurz was the most popular man in the big *Saengerfest* Hall. He could have been nominated for the presidency by acclamation had he not been disqualified by his birth abroad.

The convention, not confined to regularly chosen party representatives, attracted all sorts of crackpots, from Prohibitionists to Lucy Stoners. The most ambitious were Horace Greeley and his claque. The New York editor, whose white chin whiskers and white coat were famous, was honest but erratic. In Cincinnati he was a protectionist among free traders. He was a Prohibitionist to boot. But Lincoln's old friend from Illinois, Judge David Davis, already nominated on a Labor ticket, seemed a greater threat and, when his boom was deflated, the "Quadrilateral"—Bowles, Halstead, White, and "Marse Henry" Watterson—felt that they could turn back Greeley too. Either Adams or Senator Trumbull would be nominated and go on to beat Grant. But they did not attach nearly enough importance to the sudden arrival of B. Gratz Brown and Frank Blair from St. Louis.

Schurz and Brown had disagreed when Senator Drake received a federal judgeship, leaving his Senate seat to be filled. Brown proposed a coalition of Missouri Liberal Republicans with the Democrats to elect Blair. Schurz was against the alliance, but it was formed, nevertheless, and Blair became the state's junior senator. Of course he was cool toward Schurz, and succeeded in weaning away Brown. Now they appeared in Cincinnati with only one purpose: to reduce Schurz's political influence. Quite openly they went to work for the erratic Greeley, the man least likely to fulfill the hopes of the reformers and least likely to defeat Grant. It is a puzzle why Schurz and the other strong men in the convention did not move at once to check the Brown–Blair scheme. Joseph Pulitzer, one of the Missouri delegates, probably explained this as well as it could be explained when he said, "Carl Schurz was the most industrious and the least energetic man I have ever worked with."

On the first ballot Adams, who was on his way to Geneva to arbitrate the *Alabama* claims, got 205 votes, Greeley 147, Trumbull 110, and B. Gratz Brown 95. Then Brown made a bold speech, trying to stampede the convention to Greeley. His man did get 245 votes to 243 for Adams on the second ballot. On the third tally Adams was ahead again. Had Trumbull withdrawn in his favor, Adams still could have been nominated. Or Trumbull might have been put over with Adams' votes. Schurz saw this clearly enough, but both men were respected friends. He would not suggest that either name be withdrawn. Schurz was not a manipulator. So on the sixth ballot the manipulators won. Greeley got 482 votes to 187 for Adams. Brown was speedily nominated for the vice-presidency. As the Cincinnati *Commercial* said: "It was understood that the Blair and Brown party, having handed over the goods, were to receive their pay." Ironically, Grant, the St. Louis wood peddler, was saved by the division of his Missouri opponents. The inept Greeley, of course, had no chance. He carried only six of thirty-seven states. The campaign was tragic. Mrs. Greeley died a week before election day; Greeley himself died on November 29.

As the prime mover behind the call for the convention which nominated Greeley, Schurz felt compelled to support him. Grant's backers charged that he did so on orders from Bismarck, that he would be awarded the Iron Cross if Greeley won. The '48ers—Germans like Muench and Hecker—had been crying out for a cleansing of the "Augean stables" of Washington. Others, naturally enough, had resented the Administration's pro-French attitude during the Franco-Prussian war. With Sumner's help, Schurz had exposed the sale of war materials—through the avaricious Belknap—to the French in violation of the neutrality law. All wanted a strong candidate against Grant. Most of the '48ers had been for Adams, and they did not like the hobby-riding Greeley. Yet Hecker and most of the German press, including the *Westliche Post*, "choked down" the nominee. The *Anzeiger des Westens* and a few other German papers refused their support. Sigel campaigned for Grant. Many Germans simply did not vote in 1872.

In the Senate, Schurz was punished for his revolt as his friend, Sumner, had been for blocking Grant's Santo Domingo scheme. He lost his most important committee appointments. Yet, as scandal followed scandal, Schurz spoke up—especially for civil service reform. He did not quit the field, but he found he had much more time to write for the *Westliche Post*. He refused to support Blair for election for a full term in the Senate in 1873, thus contributing to a Democratic victory. In view of this sweep, he refused to stand for re-election himself the next year. The Bourbon Democrats, who had cheered him and carried him on their shoulders when he fought for the removal of their political disabilities, now fulfilled the prophecy he made at the time:

"Oh, yes, you are wonderfully fond of me now; but you will soon choose a Confederate brigadier to succeed me."

They elected Brigadier General Francis M. Cockrell of Warrensburg for five consecutive terms, from 1875 to 1905.

Schurz continued to be a power in liberal circles. He lost none of the regard of the German-Americans, and he became a great favorite in Beacon Hill Boston, where he was a friend of the Adamses, the Eliots,

the Lodges, and the Lowells. Harvard gave him an honorary degree.
An effort was made to buy the Boston *Post* and to make him its editor,
but that fell through. When the Democratic National Convention in
St. Louis in 1877 nominated Samuel J. Tilden for the presidency,
Schurz backed the Republican candidate, Rutherford B. Hayes.
Schurz had been impressed by the fundamental decency of the little
group of Kenyon College men—John Sherman, Stanley Matthews, and
Hayes, but not Stanton—among the Ohio Republicans. Whatever may
be said of Hayes's election, Schurz was not disappointed in his man.
He had integrity and courage. By immediately withdrawing federal
troops from South Carolina and Louisiana, Hayes ended carpetbag
government in the South. He named a Southerner to his cabinet. He
cleaned up much of the mess left by Grant. Hayes also asserted
presidential authority against a Congress which had all but ignored the
White House in Grant's day. In doing this he clipped the wings of the
Conklings and the Mortons. Hayes is the least appreciated of the
Presidents.

As Secretary of the Interior, Schurz had a big part in the cleanup
and in the establishment of higher standards for government service.
The American Indians at last received a measure of justice, and a
beginning was made on conservation. A little bitterly, Henry Adams
said of Schurz in 1877, "Lumber and Indians are his sole mental food
just at present."

When a third term was proposed for Grant, Schurz called a meeting
in St. Louis to organize the opposition. The movement was stopped.
Schurz, at the request of Missouri independents, asked Hayes to
reconsider his earlier decision against a second term, but in vain. In the
end the Republicans nominated Garfield, who had come to the convention to press the candidacy of John Sherman. Schurz was not very
happy, but for the first and only time in his life he went as far as the
Pacific Coast on a campaign tour. When Garfield was elected, Schurz
wrote to him: "I congratulate you. . . . Your real troubles will now
begin." In 1881 Schurz, at the age of fifty-two, retired from official
Washington.

Schurz made a trip or two to the "new" Germany and reported its
progress to the readers of the *Westliche Post*. In 1873 Hecker also
had gone over to see what changes had been wrought. He was given
rousing welcomes, and the crowds even sang the Hecker lied. He
applauded the enterprise of his Fatherland but was disturbed by "so

many uniforms." Soon he was making speeches in which he praised the Bill of Rights and said that immigrants from Germany to the United States had made the better choice. Hecker sent reports to the *Westliche Post* in which he deplored military conscription. After a while the police stopped further demonstrations in his honor. On his return to the United States he exclaimed:

"Thank God, I am again on free soil and can say what is in my heart, without the gag of imperial penal statutes."

He and Schurz had a cultural and sentimental attachment to the *Heimatsland,* but they had become thoroughly democratic Americans. So had the rest of the '48ers. Indeed they had made an unrivaled contribution to the country in which they had found a haven.

The 50s are said to be a man's most productive decade—he is old enough to mature and young enough to be energetic. Schurz still had his interest in the *Westliche Post,* but editing a German-language paper in St. Louis was not as attractive as the suggestion of Henry Villard, another '48er, that he become editor in chief of the New York *Evening Post* with Edwin L. Godkin and Horace White as his associates. With Godkin's *Nation* as the *Evening Post*'s weekly edition, this meant a national readership. Schurz, however, could not tolerate Godkin's reactionary views on labor and farm problems. When Godkin violently denounced the railway telegraphers' strike in 1883, Schurz resigned. He later became an editorial writer for *Harper's Weekly.* He became president of the Civil Reform League in 1892. He was the unofficial leader of the Mugwumps. Convinced that the Republican party had "sold out body and soul to the money powers," he supported Cleveland. But like his former reporter, Joseph Pulitzer, he preferred McKinley to Bryan. Yet he was so disgusted by Teddy Roosevelt's Roughriderism that he decided there were "worse things than free silver and Tammany." Incidentally, seven of the eleven candidates he supported won the presidency—and he backed some of the losers reluctantly.

Bernard Baruch was a rank and diffident outsider compared with Schurz when it came to advising Presidents. Once Cleveland sent him a mild note of protest, saying: "I take up my burden every morning and carry it as well as I can until night." But Schurz set up his own standards for men in high office and, as his biographer, C. M. Fuess, wrote, "he sincerely believed that in the long run, honesty, unselfishness, and efficiency would triumph over greed, corruption, and inertia." He was no fool. "Ideals are like stars," he said. "You will not succeed in touching them with your hands. But like the seafaring man on the desert of waters, you chose them as your guides, and following them you will reach your destiny." With his last breath this man could say, "It is so simple to die." After his death in 1906, Pulitzer's New York *World* said of him, "How far his life of devotion to ideals outshone the trumpery success of a regiment of overprosperous money-grubbers."

Schurz went to St. Louis two years before his death for German Day at the World's Fair. He was almost a stranger to a new generation of St. Louisans. Yet St. Louis had given him the opportunity to further his ideals in the Senate and the Cabinet. Gratz Brown lived to regret his disloyalty to Schurz. He lived to see the degeneration of St. Louis politics. But other men, notably Joseph Folk and Herbert Hadley, demonstrated that the spirit of Schurz really was the spirit of St. Louis.

XXII. Pulitzer and the Press

Joseph Pulitzer—like his friend, Carl Schurz—also was one of the St. Louis *Wandervoegel*. Yet he made an even more lasting impression on the community through the establishment of the *St. Louis Post-Dispatch,* the newspaper which Senator George Norris of Nebraska once called the *"Manchester Guardian* of America." The paper and its staff have won no less than thirteen Pulitzer prizes. The "unlucky" thirteenth came to William Mauldin for his first year's work as the successor to Daniel R. Fitzpatrick, whose powerful cartoons for thirty-five years supported *Post-Dispatch* editorials. Fitzpatrick, incidentally, was given two of those Pulitzer prizes. But the reputation of the paper is best attested by the readers who give it their confidence—and by those who dread it.

Joseph Pulitzer also was a *Wunderkind*. He had completed the St. Louis chapter of his story and left for New York and his exploits as publisher of the *World* by 1883, when he was only thirty-five years old. He then had spent almost eighteen years in the city, and the *Post-Dispatch* was in its fifth year. Incidentally, with one interruption of sorts, the paper always has been in the control of the Pulitzer family, its present publisher being Joseph Pulitzer, Jr., who took over after the death of his father in 1955. The first Joseph Pulitzer early adopted as his own one of Goethe's maxims: "Mut verloren, Alles verloren"—"Courage lost, all lost." This really is the keynote of the "platform" he wrote for his successors on his sixtieth birthday, April 10, 1907. It appears each day at the paper's masthead:

"I know that my retirement will make no difference in its cardinal principles, that it will always fight for progress and reform, never tolerate injustice or corruption, always fight demagogues of all parties, never belong to any party, always oppose privileged classes and public plunderers, never lack sympathy with the poor, always remain devoted to the public welfare, never be satisfied with merely printing news, always be drastically independent, never be afraid to attack wrong, whether by predatory plutocracy or predatory poverty."

Joseph Pulitzer was born in Mako, Hungary, April 10, 1847. At the age of sixteen, the tall, rather gaunt boy decided he wanted to be a soldier. But his physique impressed neither Austrian or French recruiting officers. American agents in Hamburg, seeking volunteers for the Union Army, were less fussy. After all, they received a bounty for each man they enlisted—but not for Pulitzer; he went over the ship's side in Boston and then collected his own bounty in New York, joining Company L of the 1st New York Cavalry, the Lincoln Cavalry, one of the German-American regiments organized by Schurz. The boy saw more hazing than fighting, but he rode in the great review in Washington at the war's end. Back in New York in 1865, he discovered that veterans were not regarded as heroes when they applied for jobs. So he decided that it would be indeed wise for a young man to go West—especially since getting away from New York's German immigrants would facilitate his mastery of English. Some prankster sent him to St. Louis. Oliver K. Bovard once called this the most fortunate of historical accidents—for St. Louis. Pulitzer arrived in East St. Louis October 10, 1865. It was a cold, sleety day. He was without an overcoat and without money. He himself told the story of how he worked his way across the Mississippi on one of the Wiggins ferries:

There was no bridge across the Mississippi. Passengers had to cross on a ferry boat for which an extra charge was made. I don't remember how much the charge was, but it made no difference for I had not a cent. I was hungry, and I was shivering with cold. I had no dinner, no overcoat. The lights of St. Louis looked like a promised land to me. But how to get across the river was a problem. A ferry boat came into the slip. I edged my way down to the gates, hoping something might turn up to help me. Two deck hands of the ferry boat came to the end of the boat near the gates. I heard them speak in the German language. I ventured to call out to them in German. What I said I don't recall, but one of them came up to the gate and I got to talking with him, finally asking if there was any way I could get aboard and across the river. He said that one of the firemen had quit and they might need a man in his place. He went to the engineer, who came and asked whether I could fire a boiler. I said I could. In my condition I was willing to say anything and do anything. He said he would take me and opened the gate, letting me on the boat. The boiler was on the open deck. He put a shovel in my hand and told me to throw some coal on the fire. I opened the fire box door and a blast of fiery hot air struck me in the face. At the same time a blast of cold driven rain struck me in the back. I was roasting in front and freezing in the back. But I stuck to the job and shoveled coal as hard as I could. I don't remember how many trips back and forth across the river I made that night, but the next day I went ashore and walked the streets of St. Louis.

Through an advertisement in the *Westliche Post,* he got a job as a mule hostler at the old Benton Barracks, but the food at the army post was worse than Missouri's stubborn beasts. The friendly ferry engineer got him a job on a river packet. On a run to Memphis during an outbreak of cholera this consisted almost exclusively in caring for the dying and the dead. Back on the levee, Pulitzer went into the stevedoring business for a while. He also kept books for a lumberyard. Then he went to work for some lawyers. He became a citizen March 6, 1867. This led to his admission to the bar—in those days largely a matter of being introduced to a judge and giving him a box of his favorite cigars. A decade earlier, Federal Judge Lecompte had admitted Sherman to the bar on the ground of "general intelligence." Pulitzer learned something about outstate Missouri when, as a representative of the Atlantic and Pacific Railroad, now the Frisco, he filed copies of its charter and land claims in the courthouses of a dozen counties through which the line was to be built. During this business, a Negro assistant was drowned, and Pulitzer almost lost his own life in swimming the flooding Gasconade.

During these early years in St. Louis, Pulitzer's favorite haunts were the Mercantile Library, the *Deutsche Gesellschaft,* the Jones and Sibley drugstore at Market Street and Broadway, and Fritz Roeslein's book-store at 22 Fourth Street. In them he met Ugo Brachvogel, the Mercantile's librarian; Dr. McDowell, who called him "Shakespeare" and got him the job of warden of Arsenal Island during the 1866 cholera outbreak; Schurz, who got him the job of secretary of the *Deutsche Gesellschaft;* Dr. and Mrs. Preetorius, who especially befriended him; Keppler, the cartoonist and publisher of *Puck;* Thomas Davidson, the high school teacher who shared his great knowledge with Pulitzer and became a lifelong friend, and Louis Willich, the city editor of the *Westliche Post,* who persuaded Schurz and Preetorius to give Pulitzer his first newspaper job. They had a more experienced reporter in mind, but it probably was easy enough to persuade them to try the ambitious young man with whom they played chess at the Mercantile.

Pulitzer took to reporting as whisky takes to branch water. Because he worked for a German paper, he was sent on more than his quota of wild-goose chases by other newspapermen, but that friendly nonsense stopped when he beat them on story after story. "His chief ambition at that time seemed to be to root out public abuses and expose evildoers," said a contemporary. If this reflected the influence of Schurz, it also reflected his own character. The *Westliche Post* soon sent him to Jefferson City to cover the legislature, and there Pulitzer set the pattern of uncovering skulduggery which came to be characteristic of *Post-Dispatch* coverage of the state capitol. Like Schurz and unlike later correspondents, he got into politics up to his neck. Late in 1869 John H. Terry, a Democrat, resigned as representative of the Fifth District in St. Louis. Because the Republicans believed they had no chance of winning the seat, Pulitzer was nominated for it. To the surprise of the "regulars," he was elected over the Democratic candidate, Samuel A. Grantham. Not old enough to qualify, he was seated nevertheless when the session opened on January 5, 1870. As the correspondent of an influential newspaper, he carried more weight than an ordinary freshman member, and he put every bit of it behind a bill to unseat the members of the St. Louis County Court. He and his paper were convinced that these men were grafters and corruptionists. Evidence of this was the premature granting of a contract for a new poorhouse—a million-dollar deal—to Captain Edward Augustine, county supervisor of registration.

Adoption of the Pulitzer bill would wreck the whole setup. So Captain Augustine took off for Jefferson City, announcing that he meant to humiliate Pulitzer publicly and to force him to stop pressing for the legislation. The two men met in Schmidt's Hotel. Augustine called the young legislator a "liar." Pulitzer told him to be more careful about his language. Augustine rejoined by calling him a "damned liar." As Pulitzer stalked out of the hotel, a reporter for another St. Louis paper told him he should have knocked the man down.

"Come back to the hotel in a little while and you will have a real item," said Pulitzer. He did not tell the reporter that he was going to his room in High Street to get a revolver.

The resumption of the altercation in Schmidt's was angry, short, and slightly bloody. As Pulitzer re-entered the place, Augustine called him a "puppy." Pulitzer pushed his revolver at Augustine, but the politician grabbed the barrel just as the trigger was pulled. Wounded in the right leg, superficially, he hit Pulitzer over the head—apparently with a derringer—and knocked him into a corner. That was the end of the scuffle. Somebody called Pulitzer's roommate, Tony Ittner of St. Louis, and he went with him to the police station and put up bail.

One politically hostile newspaper all but called Pulitzer a murderer. However Wallace Gruelle of the St. Louis *Dispatch,* while differing politically with Pulitzer and saying that it was impossible to condone his action, insisted that it not be distorted. "I have stood by him," he wrote, "and I will stand by him." Support also came from more unexpected quarters. A lobbyist, no friend of the St. Louis reformer, nevertheless declared that "if this young man goes to prison, he will not go alone." He threatened to reveal all he knew about goings on in Jefferson City.

A motion for a legislative investigation was tabled by a vote of fifty-eight to forty-two after some of the more responsible members warned that it could become the precedent for a long series of investigations into the personal affairs of legislators. In Police Court, Pulitzer was fined $5 for violation of a city ordinance. Several well-established lawyers came to his aid when he was arraigned by the state on a charge of assault with intent to kill. After a few continuances, he finally was fined $100 on November 20, 1871. Don Seitz, his co-worker and biographer, wrote that "he was plainly guilty of felonious assault." This young man had spirit, and temper, and a hot head. His bill was adopted, and the Augustine contract was annulled.

Pulitzer threw himself into a bigger fight when his editor, Schurz, sounded the bugle against Grant and his cronies. That battle started with B. Gratz Brown's gubernatorial campaign. When elected, Brown appointed Pulitzer to the police board. The job paid $1000 a year and was a real help to the reporter-politician. It did involve him in a vigorous—and, let's face it, not altogether popular—drive against the gaslight-and-riverboat era gamblers on South Broadway. But the man from Mako had a touch of Puritan rectitude in his make-up. So almost inevitably he was one of those who signed the call for the independents' convention in Jefferson City on January 24, 1872, which, in turn, issued the call for the Cincinnati convention which nominated the Greeley-Brown ticket. Like Schurz, Pulitzer went campaigning, making more than sixty speeches in German, mostly in Missouri and Indiana. When the Republicans re-elected Grant, Pulitzer quit the party. Greeley's defeat brought on a conference—as Pulitzer years later explained in a letter:

"About forty years ago, when I was only twenty-five, some of the proprietors of the *Westliche Post,* in St. Louis, became nervous, wanted to retire, thought the paper was ruined by the Greeley campaign, and sold me a proprietary interest in that paper on very liberal terms."

It was nice to be part owner of a good newspaper—even one which had just suffered a political setback. It meant more money in pocket, more friends, and a more pleasant way of life. Young Pulitzer had fun—but he also had ideas about how to run the paper, ideas too sweeping for Preetorius and Schurz. So after a few months they bought out their new partner for $30,000. Pulitzer felt that this was a good time for an ocean voyage and a visit with kith and kin in Hungary. But he was soon back in St. Louis.

The St. Louis press was in the midst of one of those epidemics of shake-ups and consolidations which marked the change from a multiplicity of poorly financed, often ephemeral, partisan papers to the present pattern of financially solid, if less colorful and less strident, publications. George W. Fishback in 1872 had gained control of the old St. Louis *Democrat*—paradoxically a Republican organ—and the next year, with the help of J. B. McCullagh and D. M. Houser, he had established the *Morning Globe*. The new paper had talent, but it lacked an Associated Press franchise. The tottering *Staats-Zeitung* had one. Pulitzer bought this German paper, published it for one day, and then sold the A.P. franchise to the *Globe* for $20,000. This gave the *Globe* such an advantage over the faltering *Democrat* that on May 18, 1876, the proprietors combined the two papers as the *Globe-Democrat*.

At the time of the consolidation, Pulitzer's interest in newspapering was confined to the quick profit he realized from his shrewd purchase of the *Staats-Zeitung*. His passion was for politics. He strode into a bitter battle to defeat William R. Gentry, the Republican candidate for governor, the battle of Bourbons against the Tadpoles. This was another reflection of his opposition to Grantism and Reconstruction. His strong feelings caused him to break with Schurz and his old political friends when they returned, for the time being, to the Republican ranks to back Rutherford B. Hayes. Yet Pulitzer and Schurz did not differ on fundamental principles.

Nothing showed this more clearly than the 1873 Missouri Constitutional Convention, to which Schurz went as a delegate. Charles D. Drake, the Republican boss, was extremely bitter against South-

erners. This was understandable enough when brother was fighting
brother. Missouri got a taste of his severity under the provisional state
constitution of 1863, and a heavier dose under the constitution of 1865,
both strongly influenced by Drake. But the time had come to bind up
wounds and to end the disqualifications based on "guilt by association."
On this, Pulitzer, Schurz, and all men of good will agreed. The result
was the adoption of the state constitution of 1875, which stood until
1945. The 1875 constitution was a further triumph for Pulitzer, since it
made possible the separation of St. Louis and St. Louis County—the
issue which, in effect, had involved him in the Schmidt's Hotel affray
five years earlier.

During the next few years Pulitzer was more or less at loose ends.
Charles A. Dana proposed a German edition of the New York *Sun*,
but the scheme fell through. So did a proposed partnership with Keppler,
who had moved *Puck* to New York. Pulitzer was considering the practice
of law in the District of Columbia when on June 19, 1878, in Washington's Church of the Epiphany he married Kate Davis. Opportunity,
however, called him to St. Louis. At a sheriff's sale on the steps of the
Old Courthouse on December 9, 1878, he bought the bankrupt St.
Louis *Dispatch* for $2500. He had another $2700, which Daniel M.
Houser of the *Globe-Democrat* told him was enough to run the paper
for seventeen weeks.

The *Dispatch* was founded in 1862 (as the *Union*) by Frank Blair,
O. D. Filley, John How, Barton Able, and others, to oppose the
Democrat, which was supporting Frémont. These men won their battle
against the Pathfinder, but despite various mutations of ownership the
paper never made much headway. It was finally taken over by the
proprietors of the St. Louis *Journal*, but they managed only to bankrupt
both papers. In this extremity the *Journal* was merged with the old
Times. The *Dispatch* was knocked down by the sheriff to the only
bidder, Pulitzer.

The paper was in such sad shape—physically and in every other
way—that few newspaper people believed Pulitzer would attempt to
keep it alive. They rather expected a quick liquidation such as that of
the *Staats-Zeitung*. John A. Dillon, who had left the *Globe-Democrat* in
January of 1875 to establish a new evening paper, the *Post*, headed his
comment on the sale with the question: "What Will He Do With It?"
The question really betrayed his own concern about the unprofitable
state of the *Post*, heightened by the fact that the *Dispatch* had an

Associated Press franchise, while the *Post* did not. Dillon called on Pulitzer at once, and on December 12—three days after the sheriff's sale—came the announcement of the consolidation of the two papers, which henceforth were to be the *Post and Dispatch,* a name which was shortened two weeks later to *Post-Dispatch.* The paper was making money before Pulitzer's $2700 was gone, and its books never again showed red ink. The platform of the new paper declared that it "will serve no party but the people; will be no organ of Republicanism but the organ of the truth . . . will oppose all frauds and shams wherever and whatever they are; will advocate principles and ideas rather than prejudices and partisanship. . . ." This voice clearly was Pulitzer's.

The implementation of these pledges took forms now familiar to St. Louis newspaper readers: a drive to clean up abuses in the city government, an exposé of wealthy tax dodgers, a successful crackdown on the lottery racket, and vigorous advocacy of a park system and other municipal improvements.

For some time the *Post-Dispatch* was printed on the presses of the *Globe-Democrat.* A clairvoyant might have seen in this an omen of the purchase of the *Globe-Democrat* plant by the *Post-Dispatch* in 1959 and the contract under which the *Post-Dispatch* undertook to print the *Globe.* And when in 1881 the *Post-Dispatch* took over the subscription list of the old *Star,* the same soothsayer might have predicted the purchase in 1951 of the assets of the *Star-Times.* Pulitzer, however, was concerned not with prophecy but with politics. And politics brought trouble—tragic trouble. Pulitzer brought Colonel John A. Cockerill, formerly managing editor of the *Baltimore Gazette* and then of the *Cincinnati Enquirer,* into the editorial office of the *Post-Dispatch.* Publisher and editor were ardent partisans. Pulitzer even ran for the Democratic nomination for a seat in Congress, but was defeated by Thomas Allen, president of the Iron Mountain Railroad. Both he and Cockerill used biting language. Pulitzer was bodily assaulted on one occasion by Colonel W. B. Hyde, the editor of the old *Republican.*

Anger mounted even higher when, in a paradoxical clash of personalities, Cockerill, once associated in Dayton, Ohio, with V. L. Vallandingham, opposed the congressional candidacy of Colonel James O. Broadhead. The editor asserted that the lawyer had accepted a $10,000 retainer from the city, which was engaged in litigation with the Laclede Gas Company, and that he had subsequently switched clients and defended the utility. Broadhead's partner was Colonel

Alonzo W. Slayback, who had taken the Confederate side in the Civil War and had lived for a time as an exile from St. Louis. He regarded Cockerill's statement as a slur on the law firm. In the Elks Club one day he accosted General Sherman and asked him what kind of a man Cockerill was.

"His father served with me in the war, and he was a fighter," said Sherman, "and I am sure the son is a fighter too."

But instead of heeding the warning Slayback continued his ominous talk about "that blackmailing sheet." Finally he announced that he would "have it out." On October 5, 1887, a week after his conversation with Sherman, he asked William H. Clopton to go with him to the *Post-Dispatch* office on Broadway. There they found Cockerill in conference with John B. McGuffin, the business manager, and Victor T. Cole, the pressroom foreman. There are conflicting stories about what happened when the two men confronted each other across the editor's desk. Certainly Cockerill reached for a revolver. A bullet pierced Slayback's chest, and the lawyer died within a few minutes.

Cockerill said he fired when Slayback pointed a revolver at him. It was a case of shoot or be shot. Clopton said that Slayback was unarmed. A coroner's jury said it was an "affair between gentlemen" and therefore returned no verdict, leaving judgment to the courts. No court inquiry was held. But, as might have been expected, some of the public found no problem in the apportionment of guilt. A mob even threatened to burn down the *Post-Dispatch* building. The paper lost circulation and was denounced for the "personal character" of its campaigning. Joseph Pulitzer stood by his editor, but he was profoundly affected by the reaction to the Slayback affair. According to Seitz, he came to the conclusion that "neither owner nor editor could hold his former standing in the community, that the paper required another pilot."

John A. Dillon took the helm at Pulitzer's request. A nephew of Captain James B. Eads and the husband of a descendant of Auguste Chouteau, Dillon had the position in the community as well as the ability necessary to check the paper's decline. The Slayback affair undoubtedly was an added handicap to that of the stiff competition of the *Globe-Democrat* under J. B. McCullagh. But both gradually were overcome. By the turn of the century, the *Post-Dispatch* stood first in St. Louis in journalistic prestige and in business enterprise. In 1882 the *Post-Dispatch* made $85,000. Today it has an annual operating budget of almost $27,000,000—almost half as much as the operating budget of the City of St. Louis.

In the spring of 1883 Joseph Pulitzer suffered a decline in health, premonitory of the affliction which was to make his later years so trying. With the *Post-Dispatch* in shape to ride out the storm, he decided to go to Europe for a while. Yet, on arriving in New York, he learned that Jay Gould was ready to sell the New York *World*. So the Atlantic crossing was put off. Pulitzer earlier had shown some interest in the old New York *News* and in the Tammany Hall-subsidized *Star*. He also was impressed by the success of his brother, Albert Pulitzer, with his penny paper, the New York *Morning Journal*. So his purchase of the *World* for $346,000 was no surprise. Accumulated profits of the *Post-Dispatch* were more than ample for the first payment. He was as successful in New York as he had been in St. Louis. On October 10, 1889, the twenty-fourth anniversary of his arrival in St. Louis, his four-year old son, Joseph, laid the cornerstone of the *World* Building in Park Row. From a sickbed in Germany, the elder Pulitzer sent a message:

> God grant that this structure be the enduring home of a newspaper forever unsatisfied with merely printing news—forever fighting every form of Wrong—forever Independent—forever advancing in Enlightenment and Progress—forever wedded to truly Democratic ideas —forever aspiring to be a Moral Force—forever rising to a higher plane of perfection as a Public Institution.

The story of the *World*, however, is not a St. Louis story.

Pulitzer control of the *Post-Dispatch* was threatened only once. In 1895 Joseph Pulitzer sold a one-sixth interest in the paper to Colonel Charles Howard Jones, who had come from the St. Louis *Republic* to the New York *World*. Jones went back to St. Louis and ran the *Post-Dispatch* to suit himself. Old Pulitzer hands were swept aside as Jones rushed to the support of William Jennings Bryan's "free silver" policy, which the *World* was opposing with every line of type at its command. In 1896 Pulitzer went to court to try to regain control of his paper, but he lost. The next year, however, Jones offered to sell out for what he had paid plus one sixth of the profits earned while he was in charge. The old crew returned. Since then the *Post-Dispatch* has never been closely associated with organizations, political or otherwise. Any handicaps involved in this aloofness were offset by independence of decision and action.

The policy left the paper free to support Democratic Joseph Folk in his cleanup of the St. Louis plunderbund, just as it later left the paper free to expose Democratic Boss Tom Pendergast of Kansas City and his influence in the state government. The *Post-Dispatch* was equally free to expose the Democratic vote frauds in St. Louis in 1936 and the Republican corruption in Illinois in the days of Governor Dwight Green. It had a leading part in the revelation of the Teapot Dome scandal in the Harding administration, and a quarter of a century later it turned the spotlight on Ed Pauley and the offshore-oil grabbers. It was just as free to expose the corruption of Missouri legislators by the officers of the Union Electric Company of St. Louis and to pave the way for their conviction by a Democratic administration. It hesitated no more to expose the misuse of funds by School Superintendent Henry J. Gerling in St. Louis than it did to dig into the influence-peddling of State Auditor Orville Hodge of Illinois.

It supported the Tennessee Valley Authority and other New Deal projects, and a few years later it criticized the cronyism of the Truman administration. It twice advocated the election of Franklin D. Roosevelt, but it also supported Governor Landon and Governor Dewey. If there is a "key" to the paper's policy, it is to be found not in partisan politics, but in a demand for integrity in public life and in respect for constitutional guarantees. There never was a question regarding its position on Senator Joseph McCarthy of Wisconsin or Governor Faubus in neighboring Arkansas. It has been indignant about James Hoffa's Teamsters, but it held no brief for Kohler of Kohler. It is not intimidated by slurs of "Afghanistanism" when it interests itself in the affairs of Europe, Asia, and Africa.

If one accepts the democratic verdict of election returns—and that is not always easy—the *Post-Dispatch* made its mistakes. But they were held down by keen competition in the gathering of news. Typical of this were the three managing editors celebrated by Charles Sherman in the silver anniversary edition of the St. Louis Newspaper Guild's *Page One:*

At the *Post-Dispatch* there was O. K. Bovard, one of the great m.e.'s in the history of American journalism. Joseph J. McAuliffe of the *Globe-Democrat* was known as a brilliant political analyst. At the *Star-Times* Frank W. Taylor performed minor miracles with a sparse staff. These men were distant, demanding, autocratic. They could and frequently did provoke members of their staffs to mumbled profanities.

Gruffest of the three editors, yet perhaps the softest touch, was Mc-Auliffe. A heavy-set man of medium height, he walked in a half-shuffle, half-waddle, eyes downcast to discourage attempted conversation by underlings. McAuliffe was at his best as a political forecaster, and his formula for success as a prognosticator was simple. He prowled the city listening to persons in every walk of life—cab drivers, plumbers, barbers, mechanics; civic, business, and professional leaders.

He gambled everything he had, in addition to loans from relatives, that Alfred E. Smith would be elected President in 1928. For several months after the election, the editor was near nervous collapse. Eventually Mc-Auliffe paid his debts, but intimates feel that never again in his thirteen remaining years with the newspaper did he regain his old-time fire.

To feel the pulse of the common man and to obtain news tips—or even to find out what readers thought about a new comic strip—McAuliffe toured saloons during the day. (He did his drinking at night, usually in establishments where he would not be pressured by acquaintances.) The little man he met in these places sometimes sought his help. During Prohibition, the distraught owner of a small speakeasy in South St. Louis got word to McAuliffe that his place of business had been demolished by policemen, with whom he would have no dealings. McAuliffe called the police chief and suggested that his minions of the law would have a more profitable evening raiding the plush Racquet Club, the M.A.C. or the University Club than by picking on such a two-bit operation as the speakeasy. The lawman interpreted the message correctly and dispatched some policemen to repair the damage.

After spending most of the day feeling the pulse of the city's little people, McAuliffe would head for the *Globe-Democrat* about 4:30 in the afternoon and immediately isolate himself in his private office. (In contrast, Bovard made himself accessible to his staff by keeping his desk out in the newsroom.) He would let his staff get out the first two editions, then would take charge in midevening. Proofs would pour out of his office as he slashed through the overset, until he felt he had the essential news in the paper.

He would rather lay off a man than fire him. When the late Harry LaMertha, assigned to photograph every move Charles Lindbergh made on his triumphant return to St. Louis, discovered at the end of the memorable day that he had neglected to load his holders, McAuliffe dropped him from the payroll for two weeks.

Similarly, when the late Harry Burke failed to disembark before the showboat on which he was writing a feature pulled up anchor, McAuliffe again used the suspension ritual. However, this time it took a while to put into effect. It was nearly three weeks before Burke, an admirer of the skipper's taste in bourbon, wired McAuliffe from a remote landing in Iowa that his mission was accomplished but that he needed funds to return to St. Louis.

The three managing editors had diverse views about the Newspaper Guild. Bovard, whose *Post-Dispatch* staff was among the highest paid in the country, felt that the Guild would benefit both the writers and their newspapers. McAuliffe, who was paying his city editor and sports editor an estimated top of $70 a week in the middle '30s—and college graduate cub reporters $16 a week—was outspoken against the Guild.

Somewhere in between the stand of Bovard and McAuliffe was Frank Taylor, who is described by Ted Link, a former *Star-Times* staffer now with the *Post-Dispatch,* as perhaps the only man in the newspaper game who could get $100 worth of work out of a $20-a-week reporter.

He has been called egocentric, ruthless and other things by those who knew him, but even his detractors concede he was a fine trainer of men. This may explain how Taylor, with a staff of less than one-half the size of his competitors, could jab, harass and occasionally outmaneuver his rivals.

In a hail-and-farewell editorial in a special edition observing Taylor's departure in 1941, Reed Hynds described his boss as a man of "gorgeous and rowdy audacity." Taylor would not scold staffers, Hynds reported. He would lacerate them.

Sports writers were Taylor's frequent targets. He felt that many of them were semi-literate, a view shared in lesser degree by McAuliffe. (The *Globe-Democrat* editor believed that sports reporters did not have to be writers, but merely assemblers of phrases understood by most sports fans.)

Taylor became personally involved in happenings of the day. "During the breaking of a story," Hynds relates, "there was nothing in the world for him but that story, and he attacked it with a fiercely burning inward fury. He was consumed with a fighter's joy in licking his opponent. This resulted in a certain lack of perspective . . . but some fine jobs came from it."

Oliver Kirby Bovard was an austere man. He was tall, had the figure of an athlete and steely eyes that gave him a judicial air. Everything about his staffers was of immediate concern to Bovard—even their walk, their talk, their clothes. A cub reporter whose manner of speech offended Bovard was discharged with the statement, "If a man can't talk English, he can't write it." That is the arbitrary side of Bovard. But there are *Post-Dispatch* men who recall his kindnesses during their personal misfortunes. And even men fired by Bovard could speak of him with admiration.

An editor of monumental standards, Bovard was the editor who looked askance at comics and the other entertainment features of newspapers, and who sought to make the newspaper into a daily "people's university." He held himself aloof from the business office. On one occasion the advertising manager of a downtown store protested the lack of enthusiasm in a story by Richard L. Stokes on a new type of phonograph. Bovard ushered him out with: "Anything Mr. Stokes writes is okay with me."

Familiarity by a subordinate was rare. Bovard set the pattern for staff behavior the first day he became city editor in 1900. When Harry James, a colleague who was unaware of Bovard's promotion, phoned and called him Jack—as he was known to his intimates—the iceberg response was, "This is Mr. Bovard, the city editor. Please keep that in mind, James."

He disciplined Joe McAuliffe, then on the *Post-Dispatch* staff, in a similar manner a few weeks later. The two had been out on the town, and when Bovard cut his forehead in a streetcar mishap, McAuliffe solicitously escorted him home. When McAuliffe checked in late at the office the next morning, Bovard laid him off for a week but did not carry out a threat to deduct his salary.

Had he chosen to remain at the *Post-Dispatch*, McAuliffe, with his political acumen, might have made more as a writer there than he did as a managing editor at the *Globe-Democrat*. His top salary at the *Globe-Democrat* was about $18,000. Bovard's peak at the *P.D.* was $75,000.

In a strange parallel, Bovard and McAuliffe each withheld a story in a manner that focused national attention upon them. In the presidential election of 1916, when virtually all morning newspapers went in with what appeared to be an obvious victory for Charles Evans Hughes, McAuliffe—despite a threat of dismissal by publisher E. Lansing Ray—insisted the returns were too incomplete and held out the story. Hughes himself retired for the night believing he was the next President. McAuliffe's hunch, of course, was right.

Two years later, when the false armistice was flashed four days prematurely from France, Bovard, in an astute analysis, felt that the wire story "bore no inherent mark of truth." Even though angry readers stormed the *Post-Dispatch* and newsboys were stoned in the streets, Bovard refused to retreat and in a matter of a few days was vindicated.

Bovard, who retired in 1938, died in 1945 at the age of 73. McAuliffe retired in 1941 when 64 years old, and died the following year. Taylor, at last report in poor health, is living with a daughter in the East. Journalism in St. Louis under their stewardship was at times painful, occasionally pleasurable and, in retrospect, always memorable.

The *Globe-Democrat*, Major Albert Bond Lambert, and a few other businessmen backed young Charles A. Lindbergh in 1927 when he wanted $10,000 for a plane to fly the Atlantic. When Ray Knabenshue made the first successful dirigible flight in America at the world's fair in 1904, St. Louis had become air-minded. In 1907 the first international balloon race was held here. The first Middle Western airmail route was based on St. Louis in 1911. It was here that former President Theodore Roosevelt was persuaded by Major Lambert to go up in one of the kite-like machines of the day. (Lambert's pharmaceutical firm, incidentally, made "the jazz age" conscious of halitosis and gave it the cure for that terrible blight on social intercourse in Listerine.) In the early days of flying, the *Post-Dispatch* offered a prize to the pilot who would fly along the river from one end of the city to the other and pass under one of the arches of the Eads Bridge. With the increased interest in aviation after the first world war, the paper put up the Pulitzer trophy which was won by the Navy's Lieutenant Al Williams at the 1923 international air races in St. Louis. But when Roy Alexander, then a *Post-Dispatch* reporter and now editor of *Time,* brought Lindbergh to Bovard, his editor would have no part of a promotion stunt which would imperil a young man's life. Lindbergh had better luck at the *Globe,* but neither he nor his backers could have realized how really "lucky" he was to be.

After all, the Atlantic already had been crossed by aircraft. A British dirigible had accomplished the feat twice before the Navy's NC-4, with a crew of five, flew from Long Island to Plymouth, England. A month later, English Captain John Alcock and American Arthur W. Brown made the first heavier-than-air nonstop flight from Newfoundland to Ireland to win the London *Daily Mail*'s $50,000 prize, twice as much as Lindbergh won. And in 1927 almost a dozen aviators had a better chance than the St. Louis airmail pilot to win the New York-to-Paris test—Commander Richard E. Byrd, who already had flown to the North Pole; Floyd Bennett, a member of his crew; Clarence Chamberlin, who held the endurance record of more than fifty-one hours in the air; Commander Davis, who was being backed by the American Legion; Captain René Fonck, the French war ace who had come to the United States to fly the Sikorsky entry, and the French team of Nungesser and Coli, whose *White Bird* was lost after starting west from Le Bourget. Yet disasters, major or minor, overtook all of them. Indeed Lindbergh was fortunate to get his overloaded Ryan, *The Spirit of St. Louis,* into the air the night of May 19 from a muddy Roosevelt Field runway and with an adverse wind. The New York *Herald Tribune* said he lifted the plane "by his indomitable will alone." This was the first note of the wild adulation which surprised Lindbergh 33 hours and 30 minutes later at the Le Bourget Aerodrome.

By flying his Ryan across the country with a stop only at St. Louis, "Lindy" had convinced himself that the machine would carry him across the ocean. Now Paris, London, New York, St. Louis—the whole world—foamed up in excitement over what he had done. In Paris he told the reporters that they were not saying enough about his wonderful motor, but Ambassador Herrick took over: "This young man from out of the West brings you better than anything else the spirit of America . . . the high purpose of our people." Editorialists, high and low, took up the theme of the young Lochinvar who came alone out of the West. A poem in the New York *Sun* called him "The Flying Fool":

> . . . no kingly plane for him;
> No endless data, comrades, moneyed chums;
> No boards, no councils, no directors grim—
> He plans alone . . . and takes luck as it comes.

To Lindbergh this must have been horrible guff, but he was now the "pioneer" of a new "frontier," the bold and lonely Viking, "the lone eagle," "the trail blazer." Colonel Theodore Roosevelt compared him with Daniel Boone and the men who "played a lone hand and made America." The New York *Times* was a little bit puzzled, observing that "there has been no complete and satisfactory explanation of the enthusiasm and acclaim for Captain Lindbergh." Years later John W. Ward reviewed the almost hysterical upsurge in *The American Quarterly* and concluded:

Lindbergh's flight came at the end of a decade marked by social and political corruption and by a sense of moral loss. The heady idealism of the First World War had been succeeded by a deep cynicism as to the war's real purpose. The naïve belief that virtue could be legislated was violated by the vast discrepancy between the law and the social habits of prohibition. A philosophy of relativism had become the uneasy rationale of a nation which formerly believed in moral absolutes. The newspapers agreed that Lindbergh's chief worth was his spiritual and moral value. His story was held to be in striking contrast with "the sordid unhallowed themes that have for months steeped the imaginations and thinking of the people." Or as another had it: "There is good reason why people should hail Lindbergh and give him honor. He stands out in a grubby world as an inspiration."

So Lindbergh was to wash out "the jazz age" of the '20s? That was done two years later as the tolling bells of Old Trinity carried the message of tabular doom from Wall Street to the nation. Lindbergh, transformed into something utterly unreal, could not bring back the salvation of the frontier. Ward explained this too:

Rather than escape into the self-sufficient simplicity of the American past, the machine which made Lindbergh's flight possible represented an advance into a complex industrial present. . . . The world had changed from the open society of the pioneer to the close-knit, interdependent world of a modern machine-oriented civilization. . . . By calling Lindbergh a pioneer, the people could read into American history the necessity of turning back to the frontier past. Yet the people could also read American history in terms of progress into the industrial future. They could do this by emphasizing the machine which was involved in Lindbergh's flight. . . . In Lindbergh, the people celebrated both the self-sufficient individual and the machine. Americans still celebrate both.

Lindbergh certainly did—if he thought of his exploit in such philosophical terms. He knew about the engineer behind the aviator. Yet, in its conception, this crossing of the Atlantic was little more than the super-stunt of the "flying-circus" era. It could not have been much more to most Americans in the days of Channel swimmers, flagpole sitters, Babe Ruth, Jack Dempsey, Red Grange, and ticker-tape parade after ticker-tape parade. We were perhaps more innocent than we seemed, more eager for a binge than an examination of conscience. Tumultuous as Lindbergh's reception was in New York and in Washington, nowhere did people turn out to cheer him as they did in St. Louis. Martin Schweig made a newsreel of his arrival at the airport, his appearance at the base of the St. Louis monument of Art Hill, and of the parade down Lindell Boulevard and through the downtown streets. Everywhere every bit of available space—and there was a lot of it in Forest Park—was packed with people. Motorcycle police and mounted officers had constant trouble in clearing a quickly closing path for Lindbergh's car. There were the ticker tape, the confetti, and the telephone directory pages, too, but there also was something special about this demonstration which set it apart from so many others. Perhaps Lindbergh's mother was somehow right when she said that this welcome was tender. But from Bovard there never came one word of regret that he had refused to take a chance on a life to sell a few more papers,

St. Louis at the end of World War II still had three newspapers, the prosperous *Post-Dispatch* at Twelfth and Olive, the reasonably flourishing *Globe-Democrat* at Twelfth and Franklin, and the *Star-Times,* with a modern plant at Twelfth and Delmar. All were locally controlled and directed: the *Post-Dispatch* by the Pulitzers, the *Globe-Democrat* by E. Lansing Ray, and the *Star-Times* by Elzey Roberts. The *Globe* was alone in the morning field, and also was, although officially independent, closest to being a party organ. It generally supported Republican policies and candidates. The two afternoon papers were liberal in outlook with the *Star-Times* somewhat more inclined to back the Democrats. Each had its "faithful readers" and "loyal subscribers," who provided comfortable circulations.

At the war's end—in September 1945—the *Globe-Democrat* actually had a slight edge on the *Post-Dispatch* in daily circulation, 281,709 to 271,057, but the *Post*'s Sunday circulation was 352,172 to 320,650 for the *Globe*. The *Star-Times* had a daily circulation of 192,155. By September of 1958, the *Post*'s daily figure was 380,495 compared with the *Globe*'s 332,823, and the *Star-Times* was out of the field. The *Post-Dispatch* Sunday lead was even greater—510,145 to the *Globe*'s 373,939. By January 1960 the *Post*'s Sunday circulation was 580,541, and its daily circulation was 414,437. It announced that it had published 41,500,000 lines of advertising in 1959, a new record. It had been first in advertising for 59 consecutive years.

In 1945 the *Post-Dispatch* and the *Star-Times* also owned radio stations. The *Post*'s NBC-affiliated KSD began transmission of radio broadcasts on March 7, 1922, and put its first TV program on the air on February 8, 1947. The radio and television outlets are the first to be operated by a newspaper. The *Star-Times* had Radio Station KXOK, which for some years was the St. Louis ABC affiliate, but it did not get into television. The *Globe-Democrat* acquired an interest in KWK.

Without the advertising revenue of a Sunday publication, the *Star-Times* was hardest hit by the postwar rise in operating costs. In 1951 Elzey Roberts decided that competition was becoming too difficult, so he sold the paper—but neither its building nor its radio station—to the *Post-Dispatch*.

The *Globe-Democrat,* the only remaining competitor of the *Post-Dispatch,* takes a more complicated view of history than does the Pulitzer paper, which reckons its age from the combination of the

Dispatch and the *Post*. It does not associate itself with the prior history of either of those papers. Yet if it were so minded, it could claim kinship of sorts with some famous old-timers. The *Globe-Democrat*, on the other hand, puts its founding date back twenty-three years before a paper bearing its name came off the presses—but not without logic. Of course it might set the date all the way back to 1808, the year Joseph Charless founded the *Missouri Gazette*, which became the *Republican*, which finally was absorbed by the *Globe-Democrat*. Several intermediate dates also might be claimed, since the morning paper's lineage also can be traced to the *Workingman's Advocate*, the *Signal*, and the *Argus*. Merger after merger make a bewildering family tree.

S. I. Newhouse of New York, who bought the *Globe-Democrat* in 1954, has accepted 1852 as the year of its foundation. That was the year William McKee merged the *Argus* and the *Signal* into the *Democrat* to support Thomas Hart Benton. Frank Blair and his friends bought an interest in the paper, and Blair became its editor. Within a few years, however, the *Democrat* was lashing at stockholder Blair and he was lashing back from the editorial chair of the *Union*—which, by the way, is one of the antecedents of the *Post-Dispatch*. In those a man could be less than moderately rich and start a paper or two, and he did not have to be overly worried by a failure, even if it did not become a tax credit. Political candidates then could establish a newspaper as readily as they now subsidize a campaign biography. Newspapering was fun, but rugged. Opposing editors caned each other in the streets. Even a non-journalist could get into the act. Consider this item which Joseph Charless, an Irishman from Westmeath, published about Judge Carr in the *Gazette* for July 22, 1814:

A Medal for the Brave: Yesterday evening, when I was conversing with some gentlemen near the Post Office of St. Louis, William C. Carr approached close to me, without my observing him, spit in my face, and at the same instant drew a pistol and presented it towards me. Being altogether unarmed, not even a stick in my hand, I had no other resort than stoning him, from which I was soon prevented by individuals, who interfered and laid hold of me, which gave Carr an opportunity of retreating to his house, no doubt exulting in his own brave and manly management of the affair, and at the strong proof he had given of being a gentleman.

Who says sentences must be Flesch-short to tell a good story?

Newspaper life is more pleasant in St. Louis nowadays. Rival gentlemen of the press meet over a martini, and confine their aggression to baiting each other into betting on Old Siwash against Oklahoma. Of the assorted owners of the old *Democrat,* William McKee was closest to the modern school. The paper was supporting the Charcoals against the Claybanks—as the rival factions were known in the saloon English of the day—but he was not really mad at anybody. The *Union* was for Lincoln, and the *Democrat* was for Frémont. But after Lincoln won, McKee could see that it was his clear duty to support the nation's leader. And by and by, he got a note from the White House which said: "You have been of more service in saving Missouri from secession than would have been twenty regiments of troops." No doubt the President got a sharp word from Blair about that, but nobody could say that Lincoln was not a politician.

McKee's associates at this time were George W. Fishback, who became a partner in 1857, and Daniel M. Houser, who became a one-sixth owner of the *Democrat* by buying out Blair. After a while these three could not even agree on how to break up their partnership. So the Circuit Court sold the paper at auction, only the three owners being allowed to bid. Fishback won with an offer of $456,100. That was in 1872, and on July 18 of that year McKee and Houser started a new paper, the *Globe,* on the proposition that "in the prevalence or overthrow of Republican principles is wrapped up the thrift and glory or the ruin and disgrace of the American people." Over the years the paper has been fairly faithful to that proposition, allowing the fact that in Missouri it is necessary to support a Democrat now and then to get in out of the cold for a change.

McKee and Houser had brought J. B. McCullagh, a Civil War reporter of repute in almost all eyes except those of General Sherman—who did not like reporters and least of all McCullagh—to the *Democrat* as managing editor, and in the fall of 1873 he moved into the same position at the *Globe.* It seems that the breakup with Fishback stemmed from the first hiring of McCullagh. Yet this Dublin-born Irishman had distinguished himself during the Civil War as the correspondent of the Cincinnati *Commercial* and later as its Washington representative. One of his notable scoops was an interview with President Johnson about his impeachment trial. This helped him to land the job of managing editor of the Cincinnati *Enquirer.* A little later he went to Chicago to start a paper—just in time to be burned out in the big fire of 1871. So he came to St. Louis. But if Fishback was happy enough to have him go over to his former partners, he was perturbed when Joseph Pulitzer sold them the press association franchise of the *Staats-Zeitung*. The *Democrat* had no such franchise, and therefore was at a serious disadvantage. So on May 18, 1875, Fishback sold the paper to McKee and Houser for $325,000—or $131,000 less than he had paid for it three years earlier. The two papers now were merged as the *Globe-Democrat*.

William McKee died December 20, 1879. His death did not precipitate another major realignment of partners, since ownership of the paper had been transferred to a corporation several years before. This was capitalized at $500,000 with McKee holding $300,000 in shares; Houser, $160,000; McCullagh, $20,000; Henry McKee, $10,000, and Simeon Ray, $10,000. On McKee's death, Houser, who had started as an office boy at the *Union,* was named president. He saw to the business side of the *Globe-Democrat,* while McCullagh lifted it above the level of the average, short-lived paper of the last century. McCullagh was interested in controversy—preferably political, but even a religious debate would do in a dry political season. The news columns became lively while Caspar Yost for fifty years kept the editorial page properly sedate. McCullagh died in a fall from his apartment window in 1896.

By this time E. Lansing Ray had gone to work for the *Globe-Democrat*. He became its cashier in 1903, and its publisher in 1918. The next year he bought the old *Republic*—the last syllable of the name had been worn away by time—and thus consolidated the position of the *Globe-Democrat* in the morning field. When E. Lansing Ray, Jr., died prematurely, after having recovered from serious injuries suffered in World War II fighting in North Africa, his father sold the paper to Newhouse, operator of a string of papers from New Jersey to Oregon. For the first time in a century and a half an important St. Louis newspaper came under absentee ownership.

Although Newhouse makes relatively infrequent visits to St. Louis, he is represented in the city by Richard Amberg as publisher of the *Globe-Democrat*. Charles Pierson was brought from the Scripps-Howard Pittsburgh *Press* to become its executive editor. Amberg did not follow the *Post-Dispatch* rule of non-involvement. He immediately set out to be more Roman than the Romans, more local than the locals. Joining organization after organization and committee after committee, he undertook to build up public relations. Awards—including an award to "the legislator of the year," fashion shows, and contests—brought some gains in circulation and in advertising. But the *Post-Dispatch* showed that it could play the contest game, too, if necessary.

Newhouse has something of a reputation as an efficient and economical manager. He sold the paper's interest in *KWK*, and cuts in the staff were made. On the whole the paper maintained reasonably good relations with its employees, signing contracts with the various unions which were comparable with those in force at the *Post-Dispatch*. But negotiations with the American Newspaper Guild came to a standstill early in 1959 over the issue of suitable guarantees for pensions. On February 21 a strike was called. The issue was complicated by the announcement that the *Globe-Democrat* plant had been sold to the *Post-Dispatch*, and that the paper would be printed by the Pulitzer Publishing Company. The *Post-Dispatch* made it clear that this was strictly a matter of contract, that the papers would remain separate, the *Globe-Democrat* was to have no office space in the *Post-Dispatch* building. The strike was settled after 99 days—just one day short of the expiration of the *Globe-Democrat*'s strike insurance, according to the Guild. The Newhouse management then agreed to back pensions with $25,000,000 of the chain's assets.

Meanwhile office space was leased for ten years in the Illinois Terminal Building, which was renamed the *Globe-Democrat* Building. Returning employees were greeted by a rather sharp editorial, and the paper soon announced that it had "decided upon a new and daring operational change which has been successful in some other cities and may be the pioneering of a new trend." It is something of a novelty for a paper to own neither its printshop nor its offices. The high capital investment represented by a newspaper plant certainly has militated against the establishment of new papers, yet few in the profession seem to believe that the *Globe-Democrat* pattern will reverse the decline in the number of newspapers in the United States.

Shortly after the end of the *Globe-Democrat* strike the *Post-Dispatch* was closed down for more than a week by a contractual dispute with its stereotypers. Of course neither paper could be published during this shut-down. Needless to say, these two strikes, unprecedented in St. Louis newspaper history, raised the question of whether something new in publisher-employee relations might be in the making. Joseph Pulitzer, Jr., answered that in a signed editorial:

The interruption of publication was costly in inconvenience to the public, in economic losses suffered by merchants, by employes and by the publishers of the two dailies.

"Despite these dislocations, the *Post-Dispatch* returns to its readers with no bitterness, no spirit of vindictiveness or reprisal. The strike will not affect by one iota this newspaper's opinions on trade unionism, which has contributed incalculably to the American way of life. On our part we are resolved that collective bargaining in future shall be conducted with such forthrightness, patience and resourcefulness that mutually satisfactory arrangements between the company and its employes will be obtained without the destructive influence of a work stoppage.

JOSEPH PULITZER, JR.

St. Louis newspapermen have been especially loyal to their papers, and St. Louis publishers to their staffs. The "tramp" copy-reader, once familiar in many newspaper offices, always was a rarity in St. Louis. There never was much staff turnover. And Ben Reese, managing editor of the *Post-Dispatch* from 1938 to 1951, used to boast of those staffers who had left the *Post-Dispatch*, the alumni. He had cause to do so since among them were Frederick Hazlitt Brennan and Jack Alexander of the *Saturday Evening Post;* Roy Alexander and Otto Fuerbringer, respectively editor and managing editor of *Time;* Lawrence Laybourne, who is in charge of the magazine's Canadian edition; Robert Lewis Taylor and Berton Roueché of *The New Yorker,* Homer Croy, writer of novels about Missouri; Jacob Burck, the Pulitzer prize-winning cartoonist of the Chicago *Sun-Times,* and Roy Howard of the Scripps-Howard newspapers. When the second Joseph Pulitzer celebrated his sixtieth birthday, former as well as current employees were invited to a big dinner at the Jefferson.

Times change, and they change newspapers. Reporters who in their younger days covered gang wars found themselves after a while writing about depression and relief. They became war correspondents, and then they told their readers about Joe McCarthy, his followers, and his victims. Now they find themselves trying to measure the "missile lag," or passing along reports on what should be done about "the exploding city," and about juvenile delinquency. There is a fair chance that Eric F. Goldman of Princeton hit the nail on the head—and hard—when he wrote in *Harper's Magazine;*

We've grown unbelievably prosperous, and we maunder along in a stupor of fat. We are badly scared by the Communists, so scared that we are leery of anybody who even twits our ideas, our customs, or our leaders. We live in a heavy, humorless, sanctimonious, stultifying atmosphere, singularly lacking in the self-mockery that is self-criticism. . . . Never in history has a nation been more ripe, more begging for mockery, for satire, for wit. . . . The American civilization which we all cherish could go down either with a whimper or a bang, as the poet's phrase suggests. It could also end with us just sitting solemnly on our lawn chaises, overfed, over-sanctified, and overbearing, talking a suicidal stuffiness.

If newspapers perforce reflect their times, the *Post-Dispatch,* like a well-established plant, has shown itself remarkably immune to the weakening effects of a dry season. Raymond L. Crowley, now its managing editor, is as pachydermatous as any predecessor. With Robert Lasch, who succeeded Irving Dilliard, in charge of the editorial page, with Evarts Graham Jr. on the city desk, and with Julius Klyman editing the paper's distinguished Sunday "Pictures" section, and Raymond L. Brandt as chief of its big Washington bureau, the paper has grown in circulation and in repute. According to the 1960 Bernays survey as well as a poll of American editors, it still ranks among the nation's papers second only to the New York *Times.* If it is not overly devoted to wit, it maintains a saving sort of seriousness, which is seemly in "a people's university." It is determined to do right by its city, laughs or no laughs.

XXIII. Erin Mavourneen

Cold is the heart that does not love
Its own dear native land,
When her sons are far beyond the sea
All on a foreign strand.
—Irish Street Baddad.

Old St. Patrick's, at Sixth and Biddle, had been in use for more than a hundred years. It was dedicated in 1845. On a Catholic holy day, downtown workers crowd the church for the noon mass. Its regular parishioners now are mostly from the nearby Cochran Apartments, one of the larger subsidized housing groups in St. Louis, but once it was the largest parish in the city and the pride of Kerry Patch. Father Edward Dowling, former baseball player, newspaper reporter, and Jesuit editor, used to describe the Patch, a little to the north of the business section, as "the Irish ghetto." He would explain to a stranger that "there the Irish specialize in drinking, fighting, politics, and religion. All fine, lovable people." And so they are, although most of them left the Patch long ago and no longer have much occasion for fighting.

The Irish, of course, got into the way of fighting long before they came to St. Louis. And it's an everlasting wonder that they did not come, most of them, long before they did, considering the harsh domination under which they were in their own country. Like the Chinese, the Irish absorbed the earlier invaders of their island. But once the Protestant ascendancy became established in Dublin Castle, a man was sure of being rack-rented by an absentee landlord and not nearly so sure of the seven pounds of potatoes needed for a sustaining meal. To be sure, the Celt loved the singing names—Galway, Killarney, Tipperary, and the Ballyhouras. He saw the beauty in the red rowan trees and in the peat smoke lazing from a cottage chimney into the sky where eagles screamed. He had loyalty to his family, and extraordinary devotion to his church and the priests, who counseled obedience to worldly authority. But he could be rebellious, too. He might join the White Boys or the Ribbon Men, the secret organizations which met in "midnight legislatures" to send warnings to landlords and bailiffs, and who had their "enforcers" for those who did not heed. (Similar groups—the Molly Maguires, for example, sprang up among the Irishmen who built the canals and railroads of America.) Nor did all Irish opposition remain underground.

Edmund Burke, Irishman and British imperialist at the same time, had cause for concern. The French tumult threatened trouble in Ireland even if the Jacobins and Napoleon were no friends of the Pope. That is why he worked for the establishment of the Royal College of St. Patrick at Maynooth for the training of priests in Ireland, lest a foreign-educated clergy spread foreign ideas. With Fitzwilliam, Grattan, and Bishop Hussey, he also strove for Catholic emancipation, since an Ireland without civil rights was a weak link in the imperial chain. But when the Irish were quiet, Pitt saw no point in concessions. When they were rebellious, concessions were out of the question. So even though Daniel O'Connell won emancipation in 1829, events followed their tragic course through the 1916 Easter week to eventual independence.

A century earlier, the wind from France did touch Emmet, Wolfe Tone, and Sarsfield. But the 1798 revolution was put down, and Ireland enjoyed a boom of sorts while feeding the armies England sent against Bonaparte. But peace put an end to profit, and the owners began to clear their land of peasants. Many found it cheaper to pay their tenants' passage to America—$12.50 to $25, depending on the port of embarkation and on whether the destination was Canada or a more distant harbor in the United States—than to support them in the shabby asylums established under the Poor Law of 1838. Then the potato famines of 1845–50 carried the emigration to its crest.

In Boston especially, the Irish again were regarded as "hewers of wood and drawers of water." Emerson talked of "guano." Lyman Beecher preached against popery as though the armada were off Cape Cod. He repeated his sermon on the perils of the increasing Irish migration to the Mississippi Valley in three Boston churches on Sunday, August 10, 1834, the day before the Charlestown louts—without official hindrance—burned down the academy of the Ursulines. Worse outrages occurred in Philadelphia and elsewhere. In one sense, the Irish brought bad treatment on themselves. Poor and clannish, they settled in the slums of the seaboard cities, where they were the easy prey of nativists. Too few of them took the advice of Bishop John Timon, the

St. Louisan from Bishop Rosati's seminary at The Barrens. Timon wrote:

"In years past, ministerial duties forced me to travel widely over the West and the South of our country. From the facts there noted, I feel convinced that the Irish Catholic emigrant of sober, industrious habits but modest means, can find no *safer*, and perhaps no *better*, location than in some of the districts I have mentioned. There indeed, life will be less of a lottery; few great prizes can be drawn, but then *also there need be no blanks.*" Timon, Edward Gillan of Notre Dame, and Thomas Mooney, the itinerant peddler of his fantastic history of Ireland, invited the immigrants to the farmlands of the Middle West just as Gottfried Duden had invited the German settlers, but most of the Irish preferred the cities in which they could live with their own, build their churches, and save their money to bring kith and kin to the new country. But in their search for employment, from which they were often barred by the curt notice "No Irish need apply," many went to work on the canals and the railroads. The building of the Illinois Central—once called "the St. Louis cut-off" because it gave Chicago direct access to New Orleans and the Gulf of Mexico—brought a goodly number of them to St. Louis. There the men found jobs on the levee and on the steamboats. And more Irish landed at New Orleans than at Boston, although not nearly so many as arrived in New York, and some of these came up the river to find some of their countrymen already well established in St. Louis.

As early as February 9, 1818, the Irish Immigrant and Corresponding Society was organized in the home of Jeremiah Conner, the merchant who gave the city the original stretch of Washington Avenue and also gave the Bishop land for his college. Thomas Brady was chosen chairman, and Thomas Hanley was named secretary. John Mullanphy, James McGunnegle, Alexander Blackweell, and Arthur McGuiness formed the resolutions committee. The initiation fee was set at $5.

The first Hibernian Relief Society was founded in Boston on April 16, 1827, to raise funds for O'Connell's Catholic Emancipation movement. The second one was established in St. Louis in July of the same year. Philadelphia's Liberty Bell was cracked in 1829, celebrating O'Connell's success. Festivities were as jubilant in St. Louis, where Irishmen were ever ready to cheer such speakers as President Tyler's son, Robert, who said, "All I know is that I love Irishmen and hate tyranny in any form," or Colonel Richard M. Johnson, hero of the

War of 1812, who proclaimed that, despite his years and enfeeblement, he would "rather display zeal in behalf of Ireland by charging upon her foes at the head of gallant columns than by pleading her cause in words."

Thus early did politicians solicit the Irish vote. Abraham Lincoln was among those who sat on the stage at Irish rallies. The clergy frowned on bloc voting; yet as long as the poorest and least educated were packed into a river ward, it was almost inevitable. It did not help much that the Irish considered themselves superior to other immigrants because they spoke the language of the country. Their first interest was in their own. Thus they sent funds to O'Connell, Parnell, James Stephens, or whoever at the moment was fighting for their great cause. And they were always forming organizations, such as the Robert Emmet Monument Association,* which were closely connected with groups in Ireland.

As in the case of the German Grays and Greens, there was a cleavage between the earlier Irish settlers and Thomas D'Arcy McGee and the other Young Irish refugees of 1848. But while the German radicals fitted more easily into the American scheme of things than did those who came earlier, it was the early Irish who were most readily assimilated. Robert McKnight, for example, went with Chouteau and De Mun to Santa Fe, where they were imprisoned for forty-eight days. The celebration of their return in Major Christy's tavern on September 13, 1817, hardly was an exclusively Irish affair. Nor did only Irishmen participate in the first big St. Patrick's Day parade and dinner in St. Louis in 1820. Captain May always had his steamer, the *Shamrock,* at the levee on March 17 to fire a salvo which was an invitation to one and all to join in the celebration. This was fully publicized by Joseph Charless, a native of Westmeath and a fugitive rebel who had founded the city's first newspaper, the *Gazette.* He added the extra "s" to his name in the hope that it would help the French to its proper pronunciation. Perhaps because the Chouteaus never did manage this, he set himself the more firmly against their "junta."

Then there was John Mullanphy, the father of Bryan Mullanphy, and a sharp one the old man was. He had been a member of the Irish Brigade in France, a sort of royalist foreign legion. When it was broken up by the Revolution, he crossed the ocean and became a frontier

* On the gallows, Robert Emmet begged that no monument be built to his memory so long as Ireland was not free.

trader. During the War of 1812 he went to New Orleans to buy, for not much more than a song, the cotton that could not be shipped to England. It was Mullanphy's cotton that Andrew Jackson seized to shield his men against the fire of General Packenham's troops in the Battle of New Orleans. When Mullanphy protested, Jackson pushed a rifle into his hands, saying:

"If it is your cotton, you are just the man to defend it."

Mullanphy waited below Natchez for news of the outcome of the war, already ended by the Treaty of Ghent. As soon as the first rider brought this information over the Natchez Trace, Mullanphy hurried to New Orleans by boat. Starting by night while the messenger slept, he got to New Orleans two days ahead of the news, and bought as much more cotton as he could. He paid as little as four cents a pound. Then he chartered a ship and sent the cotton to Liverpool, where it brought thirty cents a pound.

Two towns near St. Louis, one in Missouri and the other in Illinois, are named for Protestant John O'Fallon, who became almost as rich as the Catholic Mullanphy. Jeremiah Conner, John Timon, and McKnight also were among the city's prosperous merchants. Luke Lawless, brother of "Honest Jack" Lawless, the O'Connellite, was a fiery lawyer and a fierce judge. He was the law partner and good friend of Thomas Hart Benton. He acted as Benton's second in the duel with Lucas. With David Barton, Lucas's second, he tried to prevent the second meeting of the two on Bloody Island. He was zealous in looking after Benton's interests while the senator was in Washington. Religious and political lines could be ignored by these Irishmen. Lawless and O'Fallon, for example, joined Edward Walsh in 1841 in establishing the Friends of Ireland for the solicitation of funds in every ward of the city for the Irish cause. A decade earlier, in July of 1832, Matthew Kerr and R. H. McGill joined Edward Bates, William Carr Lane, Thornton Grimsley, and Henry Geyer in organizing a mass protest against the veto of the charter of the Bank of the United States. Not all of the Irish were Jacksonian Democrats. Several of them joined the Masons without feeling that they were unfaithful to their church (so did Daniel Carroll, brother of John Carroll, the first American bishop). The Masons contributed to the building of the Old Cathedral, and Catholics subscribed to the building funds of early Protestant churches. Protestants got up a send-off dinner for Father Neil before he left for Europe to seek money and books for the cathedral school.

It was all very sociable. Later arrivals, however, were confronted by the upsurge of an odious nativism which contaminated even tolerant St. Louis.

European wars all but stopped immigration for more than a generation after the American Revolution. Many of the earlier settlers developed an indigenous feeling, forgetting their European origins. When foreigners began arriving by the thousands, these people regarded them as an engulfing plague. "Our naturalization laws were never intended to convert this land into the almshouse of Europe," exclaimed Samuel Finley Breese Morse. "No, we must have the law amended that no foreigners . . . shall ever be allowed to exercise the elective franchise." The foreigner who also was a Catholic was doubly suspect. The more fanatical nativists actually believed there was a plot to move the Vatican to Cincinnati or St. Louis. The battened on such insanely bigoted books as *Awful Disclosures of Maria Monk,* the alleged confessions of an ex-nun, which became the *Uncle Tom's Cabin* of Know-Nothingism. This spirit brought about the organization of the Native American Democratic Party in New York in 1835, the Supreme Order of the Star-Spangled Banner and other societies of the wild-eyed who insisted that only native Protestants could be allowed to hold public office.

Nativism struck the nation in three great waves which crested, roughly, in 1835, 1845, and 1855. Politically it was helped by the disintegration of the Whigs after the defeat of their presidential candidate, General Scott, in 1852, and by the split of the Democrats on the slavery issue. Its anti-Catholic aspect undoubtedly was stimulated by the fact that while there was only one bishop in the United States in 1800, by 1850 there were six archbishops, 26 bishops, 1245 Roman Catholic churches, and 1303 priests, many of them Irish. The clergy also had taken to wearing the Roman collar and to being addressed as "Father" instead of plain "Mr." The quiet statesmanship of Bishop Carroll and Bishop England gave way to the more assertive leadership of Bishop Hughes. Indeed the Catholic Irish of St. Louis might have fared worse but for the calmness and patience of Archbishop Kenrick. (His memory deserves its commemoration in the name of the little park at Lindell and Vandeventer.) While the nativist spirit burst out again in the form of the American Protective Association in the Populist era—and who will say that even now it is extinct?—its impact on St. Louis largely was confined to the decade that began with the attack on the St. Louis University Medical school on February 25, 1844. (About that, there is more elsewhere.)

This was followed by a fight at the Fifth Ward polling place in April of 1844, and a worse one that night at Maher's Tavern on Franklin Avenue. The place was wrecked, and one Joseph Jones was shot. That such fighting was hoodlums' work is made clear by the wholehearted response of leading citizens—James Yeatman, Henry von Puhl, Thornton Grimsley, and John O. Filley, for instance—to the 1847 appeal of the Friends of Ireland on behalf of the potato-famine victims.

It was hoodlumism more than anything else which precipitated the disturbance on the levee on July 29, 1849, a much more serious affair. Fire broke out on the *Algoma* and spread to several other steamers. Even in the early morning hours a crowd gathered to watch the firemen. At 5:30 A.M. one of them became involved in an altercation with a bystander. Blows were struck. The firemen always were ready for a fight—with each other or with anybody else. This one spread more quickly than the flames. It was the firemen on one side and the bystanders, mostly Irishmen who lived near the levee, on the other.

Soon the Irish were forced to take refuge in O'Brien's coffee house at 89 Levee Street. There the firemen were repulsed by shots from an upper window. Two or three of them were slightly wounded. As they retreated, fifteen or twenty men sallied out of O'Brien's. Most of those who took up the pursuit were boatmen. But the tide turned against them, and they fell back into Morgan Street. The mayor and the police were on the scene, but they could not restore order. O'Brien's was stormed. Windows and furniture were smashed. Completely out of control, the firemen and their partisans attacked the boardinghouse of Dennis Murphy at 104 Battle Row. Then they wrecked another boatmen's lodging place, Shannon's, at 14 Green Street. They also demolished the coffee house of James Gilligan in Cherry Street, and that of Terrence Brady at Fifth and Morgan. Fifty citizens were deputized, and the St. Louis Grays were called out. So the afternoon was quiet.

At about 9 P.M., however, between 200 and 300 firemen and their friends gathered on the levee at the foot of Morgan Street. They had a six-inch howitzer taken from the steamer *Missouri*. This they loaded with punchings and slugs of boiler iron. Then they turned it on the boardinghouses of Battle Row. At about 10:30 a heavy rain did what the authorities had been unable to do: it dispersed the mob. The howitzer was taken to the Missouri fire-engine house. There, in a sudden raid, the police seized it.

Another political riot occurred on April 5, 1852, election day. This was the culmination of a bitter mayoral campaign which was won by Bentonite John How. It began with an attempt in the First Ward, largely German, to keep the anti-How Whigs from voting. Mayor Kennett drew only groans and hisses when he appealed for fair play. Joseph Jecko, the Democratic candidate for city attorney, was more successful when he warned the troublemakers that they could not expect to escape the consequences of their conduct. But early in the afternoon word got around that the Germans had seized the First Ward ballot boxes. At about 3 o'clock an angry crowd of Whigs approached the polling place in the Soulard Market. The Germans in the vicinity of Fifth and Park Avenue were determined to repel the "invasion," but an armed group took over the polling place. Order of a sort was restored. A Whig politician named McDonough invited all who had been unable to vote to come foreward and mark their ballots. A man of the neighborhood, named Abele, repeated the invitation in German.

Desultory fighting soon broke out again. Enraged, the "invaders" set out to wreck all the Beer Stuben in the vicinity. Joseph Stevens, a fighting fireman, was shot and killed while trying to break down the door of Neumeyer's Tavern at Seventh and Park. The mob stormed the place, made a shambles of it, and then set it on fire. It was utterly destroyed. Some of the rioters broke into the Armory and seized two brass six-pounders. At about 10 P.M. a howling throng of more than 1500 men marched on the offices of the *Anzeiger des Westens,* but it was repulsed by the St. Louis Grays. By midnight Marshal Phelps had restored quiet in the streets, but scores of broken heads were being bandaged.

The worst election riot broke out on August 7, 1854. That day the nativists did just about everything they could to keep the foreign born from voting against their mayoral candidate, Washington King. They concentrated most of their efforts against the Irish in the Fifth Ward. There a boy, an overgrown juvenile delinquent, was stabbed by an Irishman in a polling-place affray. The man ran to the Mechanics' Boarding House at Second and Morgan with a crowd at his heels. The ruffians broke into the place and soon were pitching furniture out of the windows. In half an hour, it is said, at least 5000 men and boys had gathered. They wrecked other Irish workingmen's boardinghouses in

Morgan, Cherry, and Second streets. They seemed bent on wholesale extermination.

At Morgan Street and the levee, a band of Irishmen lined up in almost military formation to keep the rioters out of Battle Row. As the mob was repeatedly repulsed, several men were killed. Then the mobsters pried heavy cobblestones out of the pavement. Each man armed himself with two of these skull crushers. The blockade was broken. The Irishmen sought cover in the boardinghouses and the shebeens. Gunfire from second-story windows, however, did not stop the assailants. The defenders had to run for their lives. Every Irish establishment between Morgan and Locust streets was wrecked.

Late in the afternoon, just as the violence seemed to be dying down, a boatman-bystander was killed by a shot from a window. Passions flared anew. The wreckers went to work again in Battle Row, in Morgan, in Cherry, in Fifth, and in Green streets. At about 10 P.M. came an attack on Draymen's Hall at Eighth Street and Franklin Avenue; others carried their depredations farther along Green and Morgan streets. Mayor Howe had a posse in the streets, but the deputies found it impossible to restore order. Finally three companies of militia overcame the rioters. It was a bloody job. Even then, small groups spread sporadic terror through the night.

The next morning was calm enough. A large number of Irishmen gathered in Morgan Street near the levee, but the police were given no trouble. Then a rumor made the rounds that companies of reinforcements had gathered outside the city and were marching to the assistance of the Irish in St. Louis. This was a cock-and-bull story, but the Mayor ordered the militia to be prepared for emergencies. As night fell, ominous groups clustered at street corners. Militiamen patrolled the levee neighborhood. At about 10 o'clock they heard firing uptown. Their officers marched them in that direction. The Continentals encountered a mob at Fifth and Green streets, but its ranks opened to make way for the soldiers. The Grays followed up the street. At Sixth and Green, rioters fired on the Continentals, and the fire was effectively returned. Shooting, the Grays cleared hoodlums out of an alley between Sixth and Seventh. The police made many arrests.

About midnight several citizens tried to disarm a man at Seventh and Biddle, near St. Patrick's church. In the attempt, E. R. Viollett, a well-known businessman, was shot three times. He died in the street.

Another man was killed and three were wounded in an affray in front of the Humboldt House at Broadway and Ashley Street. Similar isolated incidents occurred all night long, especially in the Fifth Ward.

More trouble was threatened on Wednesday morning as nativist agitators called on Americans to protect their homes against "foreigners." Bands of fifteen to twenty men roamed the streets. The Mayor called a citizens' meeting at the Courthouse for noon. At 11 A.M. the members of the Merchants' Exchange, with James Lucas presiding, adopted resolution calling on Mayor How to ask people in all parts of the city to remain in their homes. The Mayor also was asked to replace the obviously inadequate police by a temporary citizen's patrol. At the Courthouse meeting a resolution offered by Joseph Charless was adopted. It proclaimed "the duty of every good citizen . . . to support the Mayor in preserving the peace and quiet of the city." Edward Bates called for a thousand volunteers, agreeing with Charless that "the spirit of disorder must be quelled at whatever cost, that the fair name of our city may no longer be disgraced by bloodshed and murder." N. J. Eaton was put in charge of the patrol. At the Courthouse alone, seven hundred men volunteered. They were divided into companies of twenty, each under a captain and lieutenant on horseback. Thus was order restored, but not before ten men had been killed and thirty very seriously wounded. The city eventually paid ninety-three damage claims.

The 1854 riot was the last anti-Irish violence in St. Louis—unless it is necessary to count the eighty-six round, bare-knuckles fight on May 10, 1859, between "Bendigo" Smith of Philadelphia and Pat Curley of St. Louis for stakes of twenty-five dollars a side. Curley was forced to "throw up the sponge." But Pat later married gay and gaudy Ada Izaaks Mencken, and she favored St. Louis with her last—positively her last—and final appearance in *Mazzepa's Ride*.

If Carl Schurz was a born senator, almost every Irishman was a born alderman. That helped. Persecution had turned the Irish into rebels, but not into radicals. They had a hunger for authority. To them, a policeman's uniform had symbolic importance. Their conservatism was deepened when they came under the influence of Orestes A. Brownson, the most distinguished American Catholic convert of the time. The *Boston Pilot,* read by Irishmen everywhere in the United States, followed the straight Brownson line in saying: "Your European democracy is a cut-throat affair, it is blood-thirsty, it is Red, it is socialist, it *aims* only to destroy, never to build up, it is atheistical, it is develish, it is criminal *per se*." The Irish clergy had no kind words for a Kossuth or a Mazzini, and turned even against O'Connell when he unequivocally denounced slavery. Most of the Irish were Democrats. They found Jeffersonianism more acceptable than anti-foreign Federalist views. They made much of Jackson's Irish antecedents. And they cheered Stephen A. Douglas, "the little giant," for his denunciations of nativism. The Abolitionists also had much to do with Irish politics, since they talked as much against popery as against slavery. The bishops were reluctant to split the church on the slavery issue as a number of major Protestant denominations were split. And the politicians did the rest with a bit of praise for, say, Colonel Bennet Riley, who raised a St. Louis Irish brigade for the Mexican War, or for Tom Fitzpatrick, the army's chief guide in the Southwest, who, after all, was a County Cavan man. And there were the jobs on the force.

Ed Butler's river-ward machine had much in common with the organizations built by Irish bosses in other American cities in the second half of the nineteenth century. Yet it achieved less power and was shorter-lived than most of them. Archbishop Kenrick quietly sought to deprive bosses of the strength of greater numbers. So did Archbishop Kain. Like Gibbons of Baltimore and Spalding of Peoria, he was sure that the Catholic interest was not served by political factionalism. So Butler really was more of a political broker and arranger of deals than the commander of an always deliverable bloc of votes.

The St. Louis Irish, both "lace-curtain" and "shanty," were great railroad builders. Mullanphy and O'Fallon were leaders in the Internal Improvement Convention of 1835. Since the eastern roads were approaching St. Louis, these men were convinced with Loughborough that St. Louis must extend the tracks westward. Just the same, they joined a few other St. Louisans in becoming directors of the Ohio & Mississippi, part of the Baltimore & Ohio system, to make sure that its terminal really would be in Illinoistown. Ground was broken for its East Side depot on April 25, 1853. Their chief interest, however, was in the Pacific Railroad, now the Missouri Pacific. And their enthusiasm was exceeded, if possible, by that of Edward Walsh. Born in Ireland on December 27, 1798, he established himself in St. Louis in 1818. From flour milling he branched out into steamboating. But he realized that the railroads could reach vast regions inaccessible by steamer. So he pushed the sale of Pacific Railroad shares* while Tom Benton worked for the project in Washington. Congress in 1852 made a grant of land extending from St. Louis to Kansas City. The year before, the Missouri Legislature had voted $2,000,000 in 6 per cent bonds to match funds put up by the investors. James P. Kirkwood, who had been brought from New York to become the road's first chief engineer, chose a route running from Fourteenth Street through the drained Chouteau Pond, the Mill Creek Valley, and the valley of the River des Peres to the Meramac Valley, a distance of thirty-five miles, for its first division. Mayor Luther Kennett turned the first spade of earth on July 4, 1851. There probably never was another Fourth of July parade in St. Louis such as the one held that day. Everybody marched through the flag-draped streets, but nobody with more spirit than the Hibernian Benevolent Society and Father Matthew's Catholic Total Abstinence Society. The building of the road was the work of many of these men. And Walsh could exclaim with a County Cork man who had speculated in Pennsylvania petroleum:

"Bejabbers, yesterday I wasn't worth a cent, and today I'm worth thousands and thousands."

On May 12, 1852, the road received its first locomotive, the Pacific, from Taunton, Massachusetts, and by the following May it was in operation as far as Kirkwood, fourteen miles from the Union Station. Then came disaster.

On November 1, 1855, a fourteen-car special train left St. Louis for a trip through the autumnal foliage to mark the inauguration of service to Jefferson City. The Mayor, the City Council, Company A of the Grays, the militia band, and more than 600 guests were on board. There had been a very heavy rain during the night, and when the locomotive ran out onto the huge wooden bridge across the Gasconade —the river in which Joseph Pulitzer almost lost his life as a representative of another railroad a decade later—the structure collapsed. Ten of the fourteen cars plunged down the 30-foot bank. T. S. O'Sullivan, who had succeeded Kirkwood as chief engineer, was riding on the locomotive and was killed. Twenty-five others also were killed. Many

---

* Incorporators of the Pacific Railroad, March 12, 1849, were: John O'Fallon, Lewis V. Bogy, James H. Lucas, Edward Walsh, George Collier, Thomas B. Hudson, Daniel D. Page, Henry M. Shreve, James E. Yeatman, John B. Sarpy, Wayman Crow, Joshua B. Brant, Thomas Allen, Robert Campbell, Pierre Chouteau Jr., Henry Shaw, Bernard Pratte, Ernst Angelbrodt, Adolphus Meier, Louis A. Benoist, Adam L. Mills. Thomas Allen was the first president, and Louis A. LaBeaume, secretary.

more were injured. Dr. McDowell, who was among the passengers, attended them.

The panic of 1857 slowed down the building of the Missouri Pacific. In 1861 Confederate raiders burned the depots at Rolla and Sedalia. General Price, in his invasion of Missouri, tore up some of the track. But the railroad reached Kansas City in September of 1865. The Wabash, originally the Toledo & Illinois, reached East St. Louis in 1853. The Pennsylvania came to the river's edge in 1869. Much of the St. Louis & Iron Mountain, the Chicago & Alton, and the Burlington had been built, mostly by Irish laborers. They made St. Louis a railroad center second only to Chicago.

Working on the railroad, living in the slums, mobbed by the nativists, and sharing less than most in the boom that came after the Civil War, it is a wonder that the Irish were not more reform-minded. Yet one of the reasons why Blair and Brown wrecked the hopes of Schurz and the liberals in 1872 was their fear that the nomination of Charles Francis Adams on a reform ticket would be offensive to their Irish supporters in St. Louis. But it may be that the depression of 1873, which brought Henry George's *Progress and Poverty* and also a revival of such nativist sneer words as "dago," "wop," "kike," "bohunk," and "paddy," turned the Irish away from the prejudice-tainted Populists of the nineties. Times were as hard for the workingmen, who banded together as the Knights of Labor, as they were for the farmers, who formed the Grange, the Western and the Southern Farmers' Alliances. Delegates of the last two groups as well as representatives of the Colored Farmers' Alliance held a big "unity" convention in St. Louis in December 1889. Although Kansas and the two Dakotas joined the Southern Alliance, a merger was not achieved because the other northern groups were reluctant to be absorbed in the much larger Southern Alliance. But the convention did launch "hayseed socialism."

Since co-operative stores, cotton gins, grain elevators, and insurance plans so often failed for lack of capital, the convention demanded federal crop loans, public operation of the railroads, the subtreasury plan as a check on national banks, the abolition of the gold standard, and the coinage of silver. With such demagogic politicians as "Pitchfork Ben" Tillman of South Carolina, James S. Hogg of Texas, and Thomas E. Watson of Georgia on their band wagon, the farmers captured eight legislatures, elected five governors, and gained a strong voice in Congress. Awakened to the power of the farm vote, the 1892

Alliance convention, also held in St. Louis, made more demands: direct election of senators, the initiative and referendum, the secret ballot, and a postal savings system. Then a convention was called for Omaha to put a national ticket in the field. This eventually was headed by General James B. Weaver of Iowa. The farmers adopted the advice of Mary Elizabeth Lease "to raise less corn and more hell."

Even though Ignatius Donnelly, one of the most colorful of reformers, became an outstanding figure in the Populist movement, few of the St. Louis Irish were stirred. They were not farmers. They were left cold even when the reformers called for an eight-hour day, and a law against strikebreakers. Like most St. Louisans, they stood by as spectators while a prairie fire burst out of the city's convention hall. Yet St. Louis was not altogether stony ground for the seeds of radicalism and reform. Perhaps because they were railroad workers, some of the Irish were more attentive when Eugene Debs began to preach his depression-bred socialism. At least two St. Louisans joined the cause—and ardently. Frank O'Hare and his wife, Kate Richards O'Hare, stumped the country. In fact, they spent their honeymoon in 1902 on a speaking tour of the North and the East. And both were on the staff of the *National Ripsaw,* the socialist paper which was published in St. Louis. Mrs. O'Hare, a born crusader, campaigned for many causes, including woman suffrage, and she was a candidate for offices—local, state and national.

Her most prominent newspaper headlines, however, resulted from the crude passions to which so many Americans surrendered themselves, as Woodrow Wilson feared they would, during World War I. A pacifist as well as a socialist, Mrs. O'Hare was accused of saying in a speech at Bowman, North Dakota, on July 17, 1917, that "mothers who raised their sons to be cannon fodder were no better than a farmer's brood sow," and that "young men who are foolish enough to enlist or volunteer are only good enough for German fertilizer."

Mrs. O'Hare disclaimed this language. W. E. Zeuch of Clark University interviewed thirty-seven persons who were in the hall. All said that they did not hear those words. The government called five witnesses; two of them said they were in the hall and heard her speak as charged; three others said they were outside the hall but heard the words. Judge Martin Wade made a speech from the bench, saying that "the nation did not propose to be shot in the back by cowards and traitors." He sentenced Mrs. O'Hare to five years in the penitentiary at Jefferson City, Missouri. Things like that happened in a time when states and even municipalities enacted espionage and sedition laws as though those of the national government were not enough. Cabinet members, vigilante Liberty Bond peddlers, college trustees— all sorts of 100 per cent Americans went Hun-hunting. It was not a pleasant time for the German South Side of St. Louis. But by and by, most people recovered their senses. America may have gained a little by the debauch. There was nothing as bad during World War II. Even the worst McCarthyites showed a little more restraint.

A big farewell demonstration was held for Mrs. O'Hare in the fashionable old Odeon, the city's favorite concert hall, before she went to prison. Several hundred persons could not get into the hall. There was another big demonstration for her in the Odeon when she came home after Woodrow Wilson freed her on May 20, 1920, after fourteen months in prison, on the ground that she had been punished sufficiently.

"I went to prison as a sort of pale, pinkish, cream-colored pacifist," she said. "I came out of it a downright red-blooded absolutist on that question. I preferred going to prison to losing my self-respect. I could not agree that war was the best way to settle disputes. I don't agree yet."

Apparently Judge Wade forgot that the first woman to sit in either branch of Congress, Representative Jeannette Rankin of Montana, also had found it impossible to vote for war.

Kate O'Hare told the welcoming audience that she still was a socialist, but that she had found a new cause: prison reform. Had she not been sent to a penitentiary, she never would have realized the shortcomings of these institutions. The politicians had been in charge of them long enough; it was time to turn them over to the educators and the psychiatrists. But, above all, she wanted to thank St. Louis for its kindness:

"There never was an unkind thing said to my children (she had four) at school or anywhere else. The trial took all we had, even our furniture and wedding silver, and my husband and babies had to go down and live on the edge of the slums, but the kindness, the tenderness, and the sympathy of our friends in St. Louis was the finest thing they ever encountered."

The very first task this woman undertook was an appeal on behalf of fifteen fathers of young children, all men imprisoned under wartime laws. She and her husband—with the support of Jane Addams, Roger Baldwin's American Civil Liberties Union, and several labor organizations—set out for Washington with the children of the prisoners. This was the Children's Crusade for Amnesty. Before they left St. Louis on April 16, 1922, the youngsters paraded up Olive Street. Mayor Henry Kiel greeted them at City Hall. There was a send-off meeting at the Sheldon Memorial. The New York Central helped with transportation. There were receptions along the way, an especially warm one in New York by the owners and employees of the finest restaurants and night clubs.

The "crusade" arrived in Washington on April 29. President Harding refused to see the O'Hares and their charges, mumbling about "publicity." Attorney General Daugherty promised somewhat vaguely to look into the cases. Members of Congress were more friendly. Senator Caraway of Arkansas took the floor to rebuke the President for his refusal to hear the children's request that their fathers' sentences be "put on a peace-time basis." Then began the picketing of the White House. This continued for almost a month. The O'Hares were back in St. Louis early in June. Of the fifteen fathers, fourteen had been freed; the release of the fifteenth was expected imminently. Irish persistence had paid off.

Far and away the most popular St. Louis Irishman was Cardinal Glennon—even though the city never saw him as a prince of the church. The red hat was conferred on him in his eighty-third year. He broke his return journey from Rome by a visit to Ireland, and there he died in the residence of the President in Dublin on March 9, 1946, a month after his departure from St. Louis. His cardinal's hat came home on his casket. It now hangs above his crypt in All Souls' chapel in his cathedral.

The big Byzantine church in the West End, one of the most impressive in the United States, is one measure of the man. Archbishop Kain had the cathedral in mind when he brought John Joseph Glennon from Kansas City April 27, 1903, to make him his coadjutor. In October, at the age of forty-one, Glennon succeeded him. Kain already had acquired the cathedral site, but Glennon waited until after the close of the world's fair to raise building funds. The cornerstone was laid October 18, 1908. The church was opened October 18, 1914, but it was not dedicated until June 29, 1926. Not yet completed in every detail, its great dome is a principal landmark of the city, and its gold-gleaming mosaics are one of its most beautiful adornments.

Archbishop Glennon lived in the shadow of the cathedral, but it was by no means his only concern. He consecrated eighty-five churches in the city and the County. He opened almost as many schools, and built half a dozen new high schools. He opened the new Kenrick Seminary in 1915, and pushed the construction of a number of hospitals and colleges. Fittingly, the new children's hospital in the St. Louis University group is named the Cardinal Glennon Memorial. Yet all this may be no more than is expected of a competent ecclesiastical administrator.

What is more interesting about Cardinal Glennon is that he bridged the gap between Father Dowling's Kerry Patch "ghetto" Irish and those who have realized Brownson's promise: "Out of these narrow lanes, blind courts, dirty streets, damp cellars, and suffocating garrets will come forth some of the noblest sons of our country, whom she will delight to own and to honor." He covered the emotional span of the immigrant from despair through disillusionment to integration, acceptance, and achievement. Born near St. Finian's Abbey, in Joseph Chariess' Westmeath, on June 14, 1862, he began his education at Mullingar but was able to complete it only by volunteering for the American ministry. He was ordained in Kansas City on December 20, 1884. Much changed in the ensuing years.

His arrival in St. Louis on the eve of the world's fair and his hearty participation in that great civic project quickly brought Glennon to public notice, but so gallant a gentleman would not have gone unrecognized for long. As it was, he fell at once into the company of Rolla Wells, Chancellor Hadley, Adolphus Busch, George Johns, David Francis, William Marion Reedy, Frederick Lehman, Festus Wade, Rabbi Leon Harrison, and the other "lights" of the world's fair city. These friendships were deeper than the banquet-table kind, yet mellowed by Irish wit. Thus when the Archbishop had listened long enough to an argument between Hadley and Lehman about a text from Mark's gospel, he said:

"Why don't you two go down to Twelfth and Olive, and get the gospel according to Johns?"

Perhaps nothing flattered the Archbishop more than the way parents named their boys for him. From time to time he held open house for these youngsters. Many of them were on hand when he celebrated his golden jubilee in December 1934. From his residence at Taylor Avenue to the cathedral at Newstead Avenue, Lindell Boulevard was spanned by electrically illuminated arches. The streets were so thronged that they became impassable to traffic. Archbishop Glennon surveyed all this, and promised not be around for another jubilee. The thousands who turned out for his funeral jammed the streets even more thickly.

When Cardinal Glennon's will was read, it became known that he had made no personal bequests, that he had left his estate "for the general religious, educational and charitable purposes of the Catholic Archdiocese of St. Louis." Gallant and generous, too.

XXIV. The Millionaire Blacksmith

After the election of 1888, John Sherman said that the United States had "reached the last stages in the history of the Roman Empire, when offices were sold at auction to the highest bidder." The last glimmer of the "fiery gospel writ in burnished rows of steel" had guttered out. The new light came from the putrescent glow of boodle and swag. This was the "get-rich-quick" era. Business and politics were in corrupt alliance. The man who didn't get "his" was, well, not sharp, not up to date. Half of a continent was being looted—as quickly, it seemed, and as shamelessly as possible. The corruption which Schurz fought in Washington also was rampant in St. Louis and in other big cities. New York had its Boss Tweed, and St. Louis had Butler's Indians.

Bribery would come to little more than a free drink and a free cigar for the policeman on the beat if the silk-stockings did not find it profitable. What would a ward boss do with a stolen franchise? It takes a Fisk or a Gould to raise the ante, to play for table stakes and, having won the pot, to try to fix the rules to avoid the risks of losing it again. And never try to steal less than a railroad, unless you want to get into trouble.

Ed Butler was on his way to brigandage in the grand manner, but he really never raised his sights high enough. He knew elections were not stolen for fun, but he had so much fun stealing them that he never did become more than the boldest of the mercenary captains for hire by the Missouri Medicis. Lincoln Steffens made quite a story of all this in *The Shame of the Cities*. He should have written about Chicago in the days of Al Capone. Its 3,000,000 citizens might complain that not all of them were gangsters, yet how deeply disturbed were they by the machine-gun massacres, by election-day shootings, and by the rackets and pay-offs which led to the gunfire? They were fascinated by lurid newspaper accounts of gang wars and gang funerals, just as they were fascinated by gangster novels and gangster movies. Here was color and excitement, no matter how right the preachers and reformers might be. The city was booming. Big Bill Thompson was shouting, "Throw away your hammer and get a horn!" Who wants to be a knocker? Be a booster!

Take a look at Kansas City or San Francisco or any other city in its boom days. The town is "wide open." Smart people are on the make, doing fine. Business men are cutting corners and politicians are helping them. Everybody profits by a "deal." Taxes are "adjusted." Franchises and privileges bring a fair price. Campaign contributions are generous. It is just "common sense" to regard political power as a saleable commodity. The man who can "deliver" is worth his price. He may be an amusing and exciting character to boot. Sure, saloon-closing regulations are ignored. "Live and let live." Of course there are howls now and then about "lugs" and "sandbagging," but why should suckers get a break? The virtuous are told that grafters are good for a town; their price may be a bit high but, unlike the budget trimmers, they "get things done." Whoopee!

St. Louis after the Civil War still was a boom town. Its banks were paying in specie, and that could be said in only one other city in the whole country. The outbreak of war had checked the city's prosperity only momentarily. Dislocations in its trade with the South were offset by the new railroads. In 1860 St. Louis had been a city of 160,000. By 1900 it had a population of 600,000. It was the "Fourth City," sure that in a decade or so its population would be more than a million. It was preparing for the great Louisiana Purchase Exposition in 1904, which would make Chicago's 1893 World's Fair look like peanuts. Oh, there were some growing pains. By the 1880s the city budget ran to $6,000,000 a year. Well, it could be worse! Meet me in St. Louie, Louie!"

Cities are tangled skeins of human activity, diverse individuals and diverse groups working diversely toward diverse ends. A citizen living comfortably in the West End or on the South Side at the turn of the century might know little of what was going on in the river wards. He might dismiss newspaper alarms. Some Romans didn't know or didn't care that "offices were sold at auction to the highest bidder."

The chief auctioneer—the dependable "deliverer" in St. Louis—was Colonel Edward Butler, a millionaire blacksmith. The *Post-Dispatch* described him as a "prodigy of physical and mental strength." He was a broad, brawny man, not too good at reading but sharp as a Swedish knife when it came to figuring a deal. He had a bluff, gruff presence. He stood out. He saw to that with an actor's instinct. His

$1200 diamond stickpin and a derby were props for the cartoonists. To him they were symbols of wealth and dignity, the evidences of power won the hard way.

Ed Butler was born poor in Ireland in 1838. He was twelve years old when he arrived in New York. There he got a job as a stableboy and learned the blacksmith's trade. Having saved a few dollars, he came to St. Louis shortly before the Civil War and opened his own horse-shoeing shop. He multiplied his profits by shrewd investments. One of these was the St. Louis Sanitary Company, which had the city garbage-disposal contract that, in the end, got him into trouble. What first got him into politics was the desire for the shoeing contracts of the horse- and mule-drawn street railways. As a cunning man, he felt that a low bid might not be the easiest way to get the business. The car lines were beholden to the politicians for their franchises, so Butler set out to make the politicians beholden to him. He quickly mastered the "queer trick" of delivering votes. Six months after he first adventured into electioneering, he had his first contract—and also the nucleus of Butler's Indians. He was a boss. By the 1890s he was The Boss, and worth four or five million dollars. In his line of work his reputation was well established.

By way of evidence, here is an anecdote which Orrick Johns, son of George S. Johns, the *Post-Dispatch* editor, told of his father's days as a reporter—complete with quotations perhaps improvised for verisimilitude's sake:

On the night of an election victorious for the Butler forces, after the returns had been made ready for publication in the paper, a small group of newspapermen were gathered in the marble and mahogany bar of the Southern Hotel, decorated with sculptures and oil paintings. Ed Butler walked in, marched up to the bar, and swept all the highballs off the counter with his cane. He was a big, square-headed Irishman, smooth-shaven, with large, deep eye-sockets and flat cheek-bones which gave him the look of a gorilla.

"We'll drink champagne tonight, Jim," he said to the bartender.

Butler could be as taciturn as any other man with a thousand secrets, but tonight he evidently felt like talking; and he knew that anything he said to newspapermen over a bar would be respected and held confidential. There were a few post-mortems about the election, and he asked:

"Have you ever heard how I saved the Democracy from defeat in a Pres-idential election? I was a poor blacksmith then, just beginning to get a notion about politics, and I knew a few of the boys in two wards who would generally do what I asked 'em. Two fine looking men in high hats, kid gloves and long-tailed coats came into my forge. They told me that Indiana was a doubtful state and had to be carried by the party in order to win the election.

"They said, 'Ed, we want you to help us carry Indiana.'

"It flattered me to have these fine gentlemen ask me to help save the Democratic party, but I said Nix, I was only a poor blacksmith and couldn't do a big job like that.

"They said, 'Colonel (that made me feel still more stuck up), Colonel, couldn't you get together about a thousand men and take them to Indianapolis on election day?'

"I said, 'I might do that, but where is a poor blacksmith to get the expense money?'

" 'We'll fix that,' one of them said. He put his hand in his pocket and pulled out a roll of bills. He peeled off a number of big ones and handed them to me.

" 'Here's money enough to take you all to Indianapolis,' he said. 'I'll write the State Committee to give you instructions; and when you're through, go to the president of the First National Bank and he'll give you enough to pay the boys and cover the rest of your expenses.'

"Well, I gathered up about a thousand good boys and took them over to Indianapolis, got my instructions at committee headquarters, and we went to work. We worked hard all day—you see the boys had to vote about ten times each—and in the afternoon when we were tired out, I went back to headquarters.

"I said, 'Now, we have all done our duty and I'd like to see the president of the First National Bank.'

"They said, 'There ain't no First National Bank.'

" 'Well,' I said, 'the Second National or the Third National Bank— maybe I made a mistake.'

"They said, 'There ain't no Second and there ain't no Third National.'

"When I said I wanted my expense money, they told me they didn't have no instructions to pay me anything. So I was out. I took my boys home. I was madder than a burned mule, and if I'd met them slick gentlemen I'd have wrung their necks. I finally charged the expense to service for the Democratic party. But I carried Indiana, and saved the Democracy."

That is how Johns told the story in *The Time of Our Lives*.

Butler was not one for holding public office; he preferred to hold officeholders in his control—and never mind about party regularity; that can be a handicap. Bulter was a Democrat, but he could work smoothly with a Republican. Only once did he take a stand on a political issue: he came out against the Democrats' free-silver plank just as that other sound businessman and Democratic leader, former mayor and former governor, David R. Francis, did. Ed Butler built his machine on personal loyalty. He kept his word and he rewarded his followers. It's an old formula. But he expected others to remain "regular" as long as it paid him. That was explained to George Johns on an occasion when he expostulated with Butler about an attack on the City Charter, the 1876 Charter, adopted after St. Louis was allowed by the 1875 State Constitution to secede from St. Louis County. Orrick Johns also dramatized this in his interesting book:

"Ed," Johns said, "you know that that ordinance you are trying to jam through the City Council is against the City Charter."

"Damn the Charter," grunted Butler.

"Damn the Charter? That's going too far. You oughtn't to speak disrespectfully of such a sacred object as the City Charter—the palladium of municipal rights and liberties! It's sacrilegious."

"Palladium be damned," said Ed. "It's a sacred fake. I've got a right to cuss it. I carried it." They all laughed at him, but Ed went on: "I'm the man that gave that Charter to the city. The city was in the county at that time and was governed by a county court of three judges, who did what they damned pleased. Some of these leading fine gentlemen I was telling you about wanted a change; they wanted a municipal government separate from the county, with a constitution and all that, so they took steps to draft and pass a charter. I wasn't very smart on constitutional law, so when I met Stils Hutchins, a good politician, I asked, 'Stils, what do you think of this charter business?'

" 'Well, Ed,' he said, 'if judges of the county court will do right by us in the future, I think the charter would be a good thing to defeat. Suppose you have to talk with the judges and find out what they are willing to do.'

"I dropped in on the county judges and had a talk with 'em. I said to 'em, 'Gentlemen, if this charter's carried, there won't be no county court governing St. Louis, will there?' They allowed that the charter would shut up their political shop in town. 'It would be a bad thing,' I said, 'for the city to be deprived of the services of such able and honorable men as you three gentlemen, wouldn't it?' They agreed that the loss of their services would be a bad thing for the city.

" 'Now,' I said, 'if this charter should be defeated, and I should come in here the day after with some good Democrats—real high-up Democrats— suppose I should bring Thomas Jefferson, James Madison, Andy Jackson, and Sam Tilden, would you recognize them as good and deserving Democrats? Recognition of Democrats by Democrats, as you know, gentlemen, is the lifeblood of the party.'

" 'Would we recognize 'em?' said the judges. 'Of course we'd recognize 'em. We'd be glad to recognize good Democrats who are in good standing with the party.' I never met gentlemen in official positions who seemed so anxious to promote the interests of the party and to see that its deserving members were well provided for. When I met Stils again, I told him what the judges had said and how they had acted.

" 'Do you think they mean it?' Stils asked.

" 'I ain't a mind-reader,' I said, 'but I didn't see anything but square marks on 'em.'

" 'It looks like interfering with a kind Providence,' said Stils, 'to turn such good Democrats out of office. It seems to me the charter is a bad thing. It's a dangerous experiment and ought to be defeated.' What he said seemed to be words of wisdom to me, too, so we put the boys to work and snowed the charter under.

"Well, after the returns were all in, I dropped in on my friends, the county judges. I brought along a few prominent Democrats. They were thoroughbreds, pedigreed and branded with Stils' special brand. What do you think! Those honorable judges didn't know one of 'em—not one— and they hardly knew me. They bowed and gave me two fingers, haughtily. They couldn't remember where they met me; they had forgotten all about our little talk; they had never heard of Thomas Jefferson or Andy Jackson. They gave the whole bunch of distinguished Democrats the marble heart and clammy hand. When I met Stils again he asked me if it was all right.

" 'All wrong,' I said.

" 'Didn't they do the right thing?' he asked, pulling a face as long as this bar.

" 'Not a thing,' I said.

" 'What!' he said.

" 'Froze us,' said I. 'The office was cold storage; it gave us the chills. We'd be stiffs if we'd stayed a minute longer. Don't go near the place if you don't want to catch pneumonia.'

" 'So they don't know good Democrats, eh?' he said.

" 'Not from Adam's off ox,' said I. Stils had a way of rumpling his hair with his fingers when his tank was boiling with deep thought, and pretty soon his head looked like the trail of a Kansas cyclone.

" 'Look here, Ed,' he asked, 'do you think that election was straight?'

" 'Straight?' I said. 'Don't kid me, I can't stand it.'

" 'No, I'm in earnest,' he said solemn as an old owl. 'Was it straight?'

" 'Straight as a rail fence,' said I, 'and you know it.'

"He sorter winked and asked me, 'How many surplus votes were cast?'

" 'What's the voting population of the city cemetery?' I asked.

" 'Five thousand, isn't it?'

" 'Five or six.'

" 'Ain't that enough?' he asked, looking at me hard, 'to more than cover the majority against the charter?'

" 'Two thousand more than enough,' I told him.

" 'Ed, do you think you could produce any of those voters?'

" 'I ain't the angel Gabriel,' I said.

" 'But could you lay hands on the workers who brought out the cemetery vote?'

" 'I might be able to identify most of 'em.'

" 'Would they testify in court that the voters were dead men?'

" 'Testify in court!' I yelled. 'Are you crazy?'

" 'No, I mean it; could *you* induce 'em to do it?'

"I seemed to see a light somewhere, and I told him they might be induced to face a judge on two conditions—if it was worth while and safe.

" 'How safe?'

" 'Why, if the prosecuting attorney said it was safe,' said I.

" 'If I show you a letter from the prosecuting attorney saying it would be a patriotic act, worthy of the gratitude of the community, to expose election frauds, would it be satisfactory?'

" 'I think that would be satisfactory, Stils,' I said.

"So we got up a contest and swore 5000 votes out of the ballot boxes. All of them dead went back to their graves. Then another election was held, and when the benefits of the charter were explained to the boys they carried it by six thousand majority. The city got its charter—your palladium of municipal rights and liberties."

Bipartisanship kept Ed Butler in business even if it made him some Democratic enemies. In 1889 his opponents in the party elected a mayor, E. H. Noonan. Butler was annoyed but not too perturbed. He immediately started a build-up for the Republican City Collector, Henry Ziegenhein. He won with him in the next election, giving St. Louis its most quoted mayor. Whenever ardent public improvers feel that St. Louis is letting the snail set the pace, they remember Mayor Ziegenhein. A citizen's committee called on him to demand better street lighting. Unimpressed, the mayor asked:

"We got a moon yet, ain't we?"

With Democrat Butler's help, the Republicans won city elections in 1893, 1895, and 1897. He was especially zealous in 1897 because his party had nominated an out-and-out anti-Butler man, Edwin Harrison, for mayor. Butler fought Harrison in the primaries preceding the Democratic city convention. He backed his old opponent, former Mayor Noonan. But Noonan ran third to Harrison and Lee Meriwether, a reform candidate. Although not a delegate, Butler went to the convention and tried to win the nomination for Meriwether by throwing Noonan's strength to him. These brash tactics turned the convention into a Donnybrook. The Harrison forces refused to have it stampeded by a man who had no right on the floor. They called the police to bring the meeting back to order. Members of the barely formed Butler-reform coalition were ejected. The Colonel led the way to another hall. There Meriwether was duly nominated—and two Democrats in the field assured the re-election of Butler's Republican ally, Ziegenhein. It also helped Republicans to win twenty-five of the twenty-eight seats in the Municipal Assembly.

What made graft and corruption easy in St. Louis was the bicameral city legislature, consisting of a House of Delegates and a Council. The Assembly was dominated by "the Combination" which could threaten to pass an undesired ordinance—say, a special tax on some business or industry—unless it was paid its price. The "Combination" may have been so effective because its members were bound by a thieves' oath. Here is part of the pledge:

"I do swear before Almighty God that . . . I will vote and act with the Combination . . . that I will not at any place or any time reveal the fact that there is a Combination . . . that I will not communicate . . . anything that may take place at any meeting. . . .

"And I do solemnly agree that, in case I should reveal the fact that any person in this Combination has received money, I hereby permit and authorize other members of this Combination to take the forfeit of my life . . . and that my throat may be cut, my tongue torn out, and my body thrown into the Mississippi River. . . ."

If written in blood, that would be in the best Missouri style of Huck Finn and Tom Sawyer. But this game was being played by big boys, grown men.

Occasionally there were mavericks, men in key positions who would buck "the Combination"—also for a price. So the buyer of privilege was in double jeopardy. Generally mavericks were retained only by those who felt that a bargain might be had by bypassing Ed Butler.

The blacksmith's fee might be high, but his "Combination" was well forged. He might hold party affiliations lightly, but he knew the sort of men to be elected and relied upon. A grand jury once described them as "utterly illiterate and lacking in ordinary intelligence, unable to give a better reason for favoring or opposing a measure than a desire to act with the majority. In some, no trace of mentality or morality could be found; in others, a low order of training united with base cunning, groveling instincts, and sordid desires."

A man with so crass a notion of public office, no matter how shrewd, was bound to make some mistakes. Ed Butler made a big one when he helped to elect the circuit attorney who prompted the grand jurors to frame this indictment. The man was Joe Folk. He drove Butler out of politics and, in doing so, became Governor of Missouri, and for a decade or more a presidential possibility.

xxv. Wiping Out the Shame

Joseph W. Folk—the name given to him when he was born, October 28, 1869, in Brownsville, Tennessee, was Joel Wingate Folk —was a small-town boy eager to make good in the big city. He was the seventh of the ten children of a quietly prosperous, ardently devout Baptist railroad lawyer. He grew up to be a round-faced young man with a cleft chin, who wore a pince-nez and properly conservative suits. He was expected, like all the other Folks, to go to Baptist Wake Forest College and to settle down as a solid citizen of Brownsville, perhaps to represent the district in the legislature. Instead he worked in Memphis until he had saved and borrowed enough to go to the Vanderbilt University law school in 1888. Even after he began the practice of law in Brownsville, he was a mild rebel. His abandonment of an old family name and his unwillingness to attend church with his family, even after his father had become a Baptist minister, showed this. He eagerly accepted the invitation to join the St. Louis law firm of his uncle, Frank M. Estes,* in 1893. On visits to Brownsville after that, Joe Folk walked down the street like a drum major. The visits stopped after he married the druggist's daughter, blue-eyed, piano-playing Gertrude Glass in 1896.

"Folk was a professional man," says his biographer, Louis G. Geiger, "and paradoxically, in view of his small-town background and pro-Bryan leanings, essentially a city man." Perhaps this is not so paradoxical after all. Being a city man is somewhat like being a religious man. The "cradle citizen" takes much for granted, but the convert can be fanatically enthusiastic about his adopted city. St. Louis alone could never have engaged all the interests and energies of Carl Schurz, but for a long time it did hold Joe Folk's attention exclusively. These two, however, had one characteristic in common: no matter how ambitious, they could not abide corruption.

Being a young lawyer with a name to make in St. Louis, it was

* Joseph Folk and Estes Kefauver have a somewhat distant kinship.

natural enough that, only a year after his arrival in the city, Folk should have joined a group of young Democrats in forming the Jefferson Club. Touched by the Progressive spirit of reform and attracted by William Jennings Bryan, the Commoner, they refused to join the bolt of David R. Francis and the Gold Democrats. Their idealism and their interests made most of them natural opponents of Butlerism.

But Harry Hawes, the real spirit behind the club and its president after Folk, worked closely enough with Butler until Folk destroyed Butler's usefulness. Hawes picked Rolla Wells, president of the American Steel Foundry Company, for mayor, and enlisted Butler's help to elect him. No admirers of Butler, these men nevertheless were more ready than Folk to grant that "politics makes strange bedfellows." In 1897 the Jefferson Club had backed Lee Meriwether for mayor. He was defeated. Governor Lon Stephens, nevertheless had appointed Hawes president of the St. Louis Board of Police Commissioners. Hawes at once enrolled every policeman in the Jefferson Club. He was machine-building. He also switched the club's support from the reforming Meriwether to the honest but more conservative Wells. His friend, William Marion Reedy, publisher of *Reedy's Mirror,* the amazing St. Louis periodical which ranged from the verge of blackmail to the launching of some of the best contemporary writers, said of Hawes in 1901:

The heart of his strength in the Jefferson Club is the crowd of young men of education and professional standing and Southern sympathies and distinctive gentlemanliness, as opposed to the crap-game, bar-tending, touting, sporting characters that heretofore have had such a sway in politics. He has them to put up a respectable front. And at the same time, Hawes takes special pains to ingratiate himself with the elements that come up from the groggeries.

Reedy had something of the snob in him, but he was right enough about Hawes, even when he puffed his friend as far superior to the traditional political bosses because he had "higher intelligence, a measurable culture, and appreciation of finer things that they can never attain." Striped trousers meant a lot to Reedy—more than a $1200 diamond stickpin.

In 1900 the peace of St. Louis was disturbed by a series of prolonged and bloody strikes, started by the new Amalgamated Association of Street Railway Employees in a vain attempt to win the recognition of the troglodyte transit lines. Strikebreakers were recruited and armed.

By midsummer at least fifteen men had been killed. Mayor Ziegenhein did nothing; but Hawes, as president of the police board, armed a posse of about 2000 men to protect property. Not all of these citizen-guards, incidentally, were unfriendly to the strikers. Joe Folk was among them, and he had been one of the two lawyers who won an agreement of sorts for the men which brought the strike to an end on July 3. But it broke out again on July 9 when the company did not live up to its pledge to reinstate union members. In the manner of the times, money won over men. Folk, however, had gained enough prominence to be slated for circuit attorney on the ticket the Democrats were putting together to take over City Hall from Ziegenhein and the Republicans. After all, the strikers and their sympathizers had a lot of votes—and Folk with his pince-nez, his sober lawyer's suit, his deadpan manner and his obvious ambition hardly struck Hawes as irregular. Certainly Ed Butler saw no danger in the man. Some years later he explained to William Allen White how Folk was slated a few days before the nominating convention:

"I was going to nominate a man named Clark—good fellow, and all right, far's I know, when in comes Harry Hawes to my office one day an' says: 'Colonel, how bad do you want that man Clark?' an' I says, 'I dunno; I've promised it to him.' Well, Harry says, 'I got a young feller named Folk who wants to have it.' That was Harry's way. He wanted to be a leader an' he knew he couldn't beat me fair; so he done it the other way. I said, 'Well, I'll see Clark and see what he says.' And I seen him and he says he didn't need the office particularly, and I says, 'Well if you don't, Harry Hawes's got a young feller named Folk that's been attorney for the union labor fellers and settled up their strike for 'em, and Harry kind o' wants to name him.' So the next time I seen Harry I says, 'Bring your little man around,' and he done it and I looked him over, and there didn't seem to be anything the matter with him, so I says all right, and he was nominated. An' look what he done—spent four years tryin' to put me in the penitentiary—that's the kind of man Harry Hawes is. He's a leader now and I'm out. An' that's how he done it."

The story was not nearly so simple, and Butler knew it. He accommodated Hawes because, after two failures, he wanted to send his son, James, to Congress in November under silk-stocking auspices. And Hawes and the business community wanted Butler's help to insure the election in April of a "World's Fair mayor" who could wear a Prince Albert and shake hands with foreign potentates. That Folk was elected with Butler's help is incontrovertible. How eager he was to get this help is moot. Some who knew him very well say that the candidacy was forced on him as a duty to his party—as part of the cleanup for the fair. Be that as it may, the frauds in the November general election and in the municipal election the following spring smelled to high heaven. (St. Louis still elects its municipal officials the year after the presidential elections. This now is a safeguard against the obscuring of important local issues by a national contest. It makes it impossible for local officials to ride into office on presidential coattails. But the boodle boys favored the separation because local elections generally brought out fewer voters and so were more easily controlled by the "regulars.") In November and in April Butler's Indians worked hard. The number of "repeaters" was scandalous. Voters and election officials were intimidated. Enough precinct returns were held out until the last by the Indians to make sure the Democrats would be counted in.

Jim Butler was elected to Congress while William Jennings Bryan and Alexander Dockery, the Democratic candidate for governor, lost the city, although they carried the state. Folk beat his Republican opponent 61,419 to 59,064. In April the Democrats won all the city administrative offices, with Mayor Wells in the lead. They also won a plurality in the Municipal Assembly, with twenty-one seats to the Republicans' eighteen, and the Public Ownership party's six. There were protests against the frauds, but the victors went into the state courts and prevented the opening of the ballot boxes. They were in. But poor Jim Butler, his father's pride, celebrated a sham victory. The House Committee on Elections heard the St. Louis story and investigated. Both parties had been guilty of fraud, the committee concluded, but the Democrats were the worse. Jim Butler was denied his seat.

All in all, an odd way to bring a crusading, reforming prosecutor onto the stage.

Folk took office on January 2, 1901. He uttered a premonitory growl when he refused to appoint the assistants chosen for him. A louder one was his announcement that he would ask the grand jury to look into the election irregularities. To the party faithful, this was worse than kicking sleeping dogs. But Folk had seventeen Democratic and fifteen Republican election officials indicted for neglect of duty. Since this charge was a misdemeanor, the cases went to the Court of Criminal Correction, in which the Circuit Attorney did not act as prosecutor. There had been a roll of thunder but no storm. The first big bolt of lightning illuminated the summer sky in July 1902. Then came the first of a series of investigations to expose the corrupt alliance of business and politics, the investigations which made Folk famous and which would have put Ed Butler into the penitentiary but for the crass intervention of the Missouri Supreme Court, an undistinguished bench.

On July 21, 1902, James Gavin of the St. Louis *Star* reported a quarrel between the "Combination" and officers of the St. Louis and Suburban Street Railway Company over an unpaid bribe. Folk summoned those involved before a grand jury. By a bit of bluffing, he induced Charles H. Turner, the society-page president of the streetcar company, and Philip Stock of the Brewers' Association, the go-between in dealings with the "Combination," to tell the whole story. The Suburban Company wanted a franchise to extend its tracks to the Union Station. Apparently there was less desire to build the extension than to force a rival company, the St. Louis Transit Company, to buy out Suburban for about $6,000,000, approximately twice its real value.

Ed Butler offered to deliver the desired franchise for $145,000. Turner thought this too high and turned to Charles Kratz, a member of the Assembly's House of Delegates, who made a bid of $135,000. Turner got the money on a note signed by himself and two Suburban directors, Henry Nicolaus and Ellis Wainwright. The $135,000 was turned over to Stock. He met with representatives of the "Combination" and put $75,000 for the House of Delegates into a safe deposit box in the Lincoln Trust Company, keeping one key and giving a duplicate to delegate John K. Murrell. In the same way $60,000 was put into a deposit box in the Mississippi Trust Company for the Council, a duplicate key being given to councilman John G. Brinkmeyer. In each case it was agreed that the bank would allow the box to be opened only if both keys were produced.

A bill authorizing the franchise was sent to the Council's Railroad Committee on October 9, 1900. There it was held up for thirty-two consecutive meetings by Emil Meysenberg, a respected stockbroker but a maverick politician. Finally Stock paid Meysenberg $9000, borrowed on another note signed by Turner and Nicolaus, for some worthless shares. The Council passed the bill February 5, 1901, Meysenberg voting "No" to cover up his sandbagging. On February 9 the Circuit Court, on petition of "adjacent property owners"—and this looks like the bossy hand of Ed Butler—forbade the House of Delegates to approve the bill. Suburban had no franchise and would not pay. The "Combination" said it had done its part; payment had not been made contingent on court action.

With this information, Folk seized the telltale safe-deposit boxes. Within a week of Gavin's story the newspapers had all the details and the first arrest had been made. Within another three days the grand jurors adjourned, after indicting Wainwright, Nicolaus, Meysenberg, Kratz, and Murrell. Perjury indictments were voted against Julius Lehman and Harry A. Franklin of the House of Delegates. Turner and Stock had been let off for giving state's evidence. The grand jury praised Folk. Reedy said the exposé had made Folk a national character. But old Adolphus Busch defended Nicolaus, saying, "He has the entire sympathy of the best element in St. Louis." Then Reedy, with his predilection for "gentlemen," also defended Nicolaus. He said Folk ought to go after men like Butler. The Circuit Attorney made the wry observation that he was learning that the prosecution of bankers was "bad for business . . . gave the city a bad name . . . and should be dropped." But he went on, although Nicolaus was exonerated on the plea that he did not know the purpose for which the $144,000 had been borrowed. Butler had a brazen last laugh: "There wouldn't have been any safe-deposit boxes if I had handled the matter. I am not a cheap man but when I get my fee the delivery of the goods is certain and expeditious."

With information supplied by another reporter, Oliver Kirby Bovard, Folk produced another sensation, the Central Traction case. Consolidation of the city's streetcar lines into a single system had been for some time an inviting possibility. An attempt to do this was stopped in 1897 by Mayor Ziegenhein's veto. But fine fruit draws flies. The next year Robert M. Snyder, a flashy Kansas City promoter, came to St. Louis to give it a try. He applied for a franchise for what he called the Central Traction Company and opened negotiations with the "Combination." St. Louis interests, however, closed ranks against the outsider. They "insured" themselves through Ed Butler. Through him, seven of the thirteen members of the Council were put on a salary of $5000 a year—$4700 more than the city paid them. Councilman Frederick Uthoff was given $25,000 a year to keep this majority in line. The arrangement was businesslike, with an apparently adequate margin of safety, and not a penny for one extra vote. But this defense fell apart when Uthoff sent back his $25,000, explaining that it was against his principles to accept payment for services not rendered.

Snyder was bidding not for a bare majority in one chamber but for enough to override a mayoral veto. He was putting out a round $250,000—$3000 for each of twenty-five delegates and $10,000 for each of seven councilmen. He wanted a monopolistic transit franchise, for which he would pay the city $1,000,000 over fifty years. He got it on April 12, 1898. But he never used it. He sold out to the local streetcar lines for $1,250,000, a profit of $1,000,000 for outmaneuvering them and Ed Butler. Still, they had the franchise they wanted.

Again Folk got the full story by offering immunity to a key witness, George J. Kobusch, a St. Louis streetcar manufacturer whom he had cited for perjury. To escape trial, Kobusch testified against Snyder. Because the Missouri statute of limitations blocked the prosecution of bribers after three years if they remained in the state during that time, the grand jury returned only one indictment, that against Snyder. He had been living in New York. As to the others involved, Folk could only parade prominent witnesses before the grand jury and let the community form its own conclusions.

Ed Butler had escaped twice. He was more contemptuous than ever of Folk. He was on the stage at political rallies with Hawes and Wells while Folk was treated almost as a pariah. Then on March 14, 1902, Folk had Butler arrested on a charge of attempting to bribe two members of the Board of Health, Dr. Albert Merrell and Dr. H. H. Chapman. This was a real wall-shaker. Butler had long been the major stockholder in the St. Louis Sanitary Company, the only firm equipped to reduce garbage by the Merz process as required by city ordinance, and therefore the perennial holder of the municipal garbage disposal contract. This was to expire in November 1901. There seemed to be no ground for concern about its renewal, since a similar plant would cost at least $300,000 and take six months to build. The Council had delayed until September 17 in authorizing the Board of Health to advertise for three-year bids, so the possibility of competition had been blocked. The only bid actually received was that of Sanitary, a bid of $130,000 a year, double the annual charge made from 1891 to 1901. Perhaps there was a bit too much of the "arranger" in Ed Butler. He loved to "fix" things. With a fat new contract virtually in his pocket, he called on both Dr. Merrell and Dr. Chapman.

"The city rather owes it to us to throw it our way if possible," he said to the doctors, speaking of the contract. Then he offered $2500 for a favorable vote. Both men turned him down indignantly. They were forced to approve the contract, however, since there was no alternative. They went to Folk to report Butler's attempt to bribe them. They offered the corroborating testimony of members of their families and trusted servants. At last the grand jury trap closed on the Boss. The reformer prosecutor no longer could be scorned.

The pace of Folk's investigations slowed down as those indicted came to trial. In conducting the prosecutions, he ran into almost as many difficulties as he did in laying the groundwork for them. Outstanding legal talent was employed by the boodlers. Every effort was made to put the Circuit Attorney at a disadvantage. For example, he hoped to begin with the cases of Kratz and Murrell, but defense maneuvers forced him to start with that of Meysenberg, for which he was not fully prepared. As this trial got under way—on March 24—Kratz and Murrell jumped bail and fled to Mexico. Meysenberg's lawyers argued that the $9000 stock transaction was not a bribe, but Folk overcame this contention. In summing up for the jury, he brushed aside technicalities and stressed the necessity of law enforcement in a democracy. Bribery is a crime against a democratic community, he argued, because it takes government out of the hands of the people and makes it an instrument of the privileged. The jury was out for less than an hour. It found Meysenberg guilty and recommended a three-year prison term. (Later the Missouri Supreme Court ordered a new trial on technical grounds.)

Lehman and Franklin also were convicted and given two-year terms. Butler's attorneys asked for a postponement and a change of venue. So his trial, the biggest of them all, was set for Columbia, Missouri, in the fall. By the time Folk took a ten-day vacation late in the summer he had examined almost 900 witnesses and had brought to light many details of the operations of the "Combination."

Snyder was brought to trial on September 29. Again Folk was willing to let a lesser boodler go to catch a bigger one. Uphoff told about being offered $50,000. The most damaging evidence, however, was given by Kobusch, who testified against his friend to save himself. Snyder's defense was that he never had been a fugitive. But Henry S. Priest, chief defense attorney, may well have lost the case when he told the jurors: "There are worse crimes than bribery; bribery is, after all, not such a serious crime. It is a conventional offense, a mere perversion of justice." Folk's answer was: "Bribery is treason." In less than an hour the jurors returned a verdict of guilty. They recommended a five-year prison sentence.

Folk's drama moved toward its first big curtain scene when Boss Butler was brought to trial in the ramshackle courthouse in the university town of Columbia. The newspapers of the country had sent enough reporters to cover a presidential convention. The senior class of the University of Missouri law school attended each court session. Butler was defended by a regiment of lawyers, including some of the best in St. Louis as well as politically influential members of the outstate bar. The Mayor of St. Louis and most of the city's politicians were in the audience. Butler himself arrived the Sunday before the trial with his wife, his three sons, a daughter-in-law, and her little girl. For the occasion he was dressed like a prosperous Missouri cattleman, wearing a black broadcloth coat and a wide-brimmed black hat. But he spoiled some of the effect of the costuming when he asked what people in Columbia did for a living. On being told that this was the seat of the state university and two other colleges, and that most of its citizens were educators, Butler exclaimed, "That's a hell of a business!"

The courtroom was not nearly large enough for the crowd. Witnesses and spectators spent much of their time in the fall sunshine on the courthouse steps. There, not so strangely, the chief witness for the prosecution, Dr. Chapman, became the very good friend of Butler's little granddaughter, who liked to sit on the doctor's knee.

The approaching election must have been in the minds of Butler's defenders as they obtained a continuation to November 10, but Folk knew something about timing too. On October 20, a week after the opening of the proceedings in Columbia, a St. Louis grand jury under his direction created yet another sensation by indicting Butler for bribing delegate Charles Kelley in connection with a 1898 street-lighting deal. The subsequent victory of the Butler-Hawes Democratic candidates would be one of the deep mysteries of Missouri politics but for the tacit acknowledgment that the election was stolen.

When Butler's trial finally got under way, his lawyers simply could not overcome the impressive testimony of Dr. Merell and Dr. Chapman. The farmer-jurors gave no weight to the argument that there could be no motive for bribery, since only Butler's firm possibly could get the contract. But emotional references to Butler's age had some effect. While the jury decided on the first ballot that the Boss was guilty, two of its older members held out until his penalty was reduced from five to three years.

The street-lighting exposé was based largely on the evidence of John K. Murrell. Sick and lonely, he was found in Mexico by Frank McNeil, a *Post-Dispatch* reporter, and persuaded to come back to St. Louis. (Folk had to seek the help of President Theodore Roosevelt and an amendment to the extradition treaty with Mexico before the debonair Kratz was returned.) Folk kept Murrell's presence in St. Louis a secret. One day he was questioning George H. Robertson, a member of the House of Delegates. The man denied all knowledge of the "Combination." Folk quietly walked across the room and opened a door. There stood Murrell. Robertson broke down and admitted his complicity.

The pattern of the street-lighting deal was somewhat similar to that of Snyder's Central Traction operation. It was another case of one company's trying to get the business shared by several smaller ones. On October 27, 1899, a bill was introduced in the Council authorizing a ten-year, city-wide franchise. The delegates at once suspected a deal on which they had not been "cut in." So on November 21 they killed the bill, eighteen to eight. That flushed the birds. A week later, delegate Charles Gutke appeared with $20,000 and a promise of $27,500 more after passage of the bill. The "Combination" held out for $75,000, even after Ed Butler said it was $47,500 or nothing. At a session the same night the Boss appeared on the floor and passed word that "everything was all right." So Julius Lehman moved for reconsideration, and the bill passed unanimously. Then the delegates adjourned— to attend Lehman's "birthday party." Tables were set up in his parlor. Charles J. Kelley laid out a stack of bills. With Edmund Bersch and John Helms at his side to check off the names, he gave each man present $2500.

The new exposé made Folk less popular than ever with the "regular" politicians—especially since after the "birthday party" Kelley had been chosen Speaker of the House of Delegates with the backing of Hawes and Wells. Folk's life was threatened, and for a time he accepted the protection of a police detective. Kelley, meanwhile, managed to slip off to Europe, and did not return until the statute of limitations ran out. When he landed at Philadelphia on November 28, 1902, Jim Butler, the blacksmith's son, was on the pier to greet him.

Folk's name by now was regularly on the front pages of most American newspapers. The *Outlook, Literary Digest, Independent,*

McClure's, and other magazines carried stories about him. The St. Louis *Globe-Democrat* was the only St. Louis paper hostile to him, although Reedy, the friend of Hawes and Wells, also grumbled: "What this city needs at present is less advertisement of the sort that is involved in the widespread exploitation of its corruption and more of the spirit of showing up the good that is here." But Finley Peter Dunne's sagacious Mr. Dooley approved:

"Folk is the noblest chaser iv thim all. Set him on a boodler's trail an' he's a whole pack iv trained bloodhounds. With tireless energy an' exalted enthusiasm he chases a boodler up hill an' down dale, into th' woods, across th' pasture, around th' barn, back iv th' pig pen an' into th' hin house, where he pins him to th' wall with a pitchforruk. 'Villain,' says Folk to th' boodler, 'Villain, confess now an' I'll be lenient with ye. Confess to all yer infamies an' all yer thousand-dollar bills, an' all yer associates in fraud and corruption, an' so help me, I will ask the coort to give ye not more than 40 or 50 years!' says Folk as he deftly wiggles th' pitchforruk in the boodler's vitals. . . . 'I do confess,' says th' boodler. . . . And now that I have confessed will ye have th' kindness to pull th' harpoon out iv me vitals an' let me take me chances with the Missouri Supreme Court.' Thus th' Missouri boodlers confess to Mr. Folk, Hinnissy. He's th' champion prober iv Missouri boodlers."

By the end of 1902 Folk had obtained thirteen convictions to one acquittal. The next year brought verdicts of guilty in each of five cases, and in 1904—the world's fair year—he won five out of six. All in all, sixty-one indictments—forty-three for bribery and eighteen for perjury —were obtained. But in the end only eight persons went to prison. The verdict that went against Folk came in the second trial of Ed Butler, this one held in Fulton, Missouri. It seemed that Folk was not to get Butler into a prison on the green side of the turf. The Missouri Supreme Court set aside Butler's Columbia conviction on the rather fantastic grounds that the conditions for bribery had not been established at the time Butler approached the doctors because the ordinance authorizing bids for garbage collections had not yet been signed by the mayor, and even after it was signed the authorization was illegal, since garbage disposal was in the jurisdiction of the Board of Public Improvements and not the Board of Health, though the Board of Health had been awarding those contracts for years. Altogether the Supreme Court reversed thirteen convictions. Years later, Orrick Johns wrote rather angrily:

Folk had scared prominent men in the community out of their skins, but apparently they did not know their own power. The wonder was that men like Charley Turner could be intimidated into making confessions. He and the others were still invulnerable. The machine whitewashed them in the highest court of the state.

Geiger, Folk's biographer, acknowledged that on occasion the Circuit Attorney and some judges were careless about technicalities and that the slow pace of the law let witnesses get away and indignation cool. Yet in view of the uncontroverted evidence piled up by Folk, he finds it difficult to avoid the flat conclusion that the reversals were political. Many commentators found the Supreme Court judges as scandalous as the boodlers.

Lincoln Steffens said that "the machinery of justice broke down under the strains of boodle and pull." Judge James Gantt, a machine Democrat, criticized Folk outrageously from the supreme bench. By this time Folk was running for governor—and so was Gantt. But the reversals helped Folk more than they hurt him. People were not happy to see the boodlers escape. And they knew that, no matter what the Court did, Folk had broken the sway of Butler and the "Combination." In 1914 a new city charter established a unicameral Board of Aldermen and a strong mayor. This did not end all graft—only a few years ago two aldermen were sent to the workhouse on South Broadway for picking up $200 in "campaign contributions"—but the pickings are far from what they used to be.

Folk had a hand in the investigations of the Cole County grand jury which in 1903 began to clear crooked lobbyists out of the state capitol in Jefferson City. Asked for help by the foreman, Folk advised him to call J. J. McAuliffe, then a *Post-Dispatch* reporter and later managing editor of the *Globe-Democrat*. McAuliffe had discovered that Lieutenant Governor John A. Lee had passed bribes to legislators in the Laclede Hotel in St. Louis in 1901. Lee resigned. The money had been paid to prevent the repeal of a "pure food" law which prohibited alum baking powder in Missouri. This gave the cream-of-tartar "trust" a monopoly. Folk, meanwhile, put out of business a group of fraudulent insurance companies which had settled in St. Louis as a "safe town." Evidence which he developed led to the conviction in Federal Court of Senator Ralph Burton of Kansas for accepting money to protect a company against prosecution. An Assistant Attorney General of the United States resigned. Folk meanwhile went after policy games, vice, gambling, police corruption, and other irregularities, the run-of-the-mine stuff which had been somewhat neglected while he wiped out the shame of St. Louis.

XXVI. A Great Governor, Too

If the Democrats had been hostile to Joe Folk, he could afford to be cool and cautious in his relations with the party—especially since reform was rampant and the Democrats were in trouble. Yet even in those days of the first Roosevelt, Bob La Follette, Albert Cummins, Tom Johnson, and other Progressives, Folk could not afford to bolt the party. But in spite of the city bosses, outstate papers started a Folk-for-governor boom. Friends in St. Louis began to raise campaign funds. John C. Roberts, cofounder of the Roberts, Johnson & Rand Shoe Company, supported his fellow Tennesseean. Former governor Lon V. Stephens, Judge Thomas C. Hennings, Champ Clark and others filled the band wagon.

Opposed to Folk in the 1904 Democratic preprimary campaign were James A. Reed, mayor of Kansas City, Judge Gantt, and Harry Hawes. The three attacked Folk; they never assailed each other. This has been called the most bitter campaign in Missouri history since the 1850 fight against Tom Benton. But if the organization was against him, most of the nation's press was advising Missouri to vote for Folk. Bourke Cochran of New York launched a presidential boom for him on the floor of the House. President Roosevelt let it be known that he hoped Folk would be elected.

The day the delegates to the nominating convention were chosen was a rough one at the St. Louis polls. Folk charged that Governor Dockery either could not control the police—under state, not city control in St. Louis—or was implicated in vote stealing. In an angrily unguarded reply, Dockery shouted that he had ordered his appointees in St. Louis and Kansas City to work for Hawes and Reed. But those two dropped out of the fight before the votes were counted. Folk, not yet thirty-five years old, won the Democratic nomination by a wide margin. The Republicans nominated Cyrus P. Walbridge, St. Louis Telephone Company president and veteran politician. Folk beat him by 30,100 votes. He ran far ahead of everybody on the ballot, including the President. Every other Democratic candidate for a major office was defeated, and the Republicans elected nine of Missouri's fifteen congressmen. They also won control of the legislature. Folk piled up his lead in the big cities in which the machine politicians had been most hostile to him. Ed Butler took a look at the returns and said he was through:

"I have been stealing elections from the Republicans for thirty years, and I have decided to quit. . . . I'm like them boodlers who got conscience-stricken and confessed. I've put in many a queer lick for the Democratic party, but I ain't going to do it any more. In other words, I've got conscience-stricken, too."

So Joe Folk moved from the Circuit Attorney's office to the executive mansion. Even some of his most enthusiastic backers wondered whether "an expert thief-catcher" would make a good administrator. The doubts were not warranted. With the help of a Republican legislature, this Democratic governor in his first year in office got rid of the "baking-powder law," lengthened the statute of limitations on bribery from three to five years, and provided more help for circuit attorneys—the things a prosecutor would be expected to do. But he also signed a maximum freight rate bill which cut railroad freight rates from fifteen to forty per cent. Ten other laws regulating railroads were adopted. The eight-hour day was established in mines and smelters. Statutes curtailing the labor of women and children were adopted. Missouri got its first compulsory school attendance law. Two new teachers' colleges were established. It was the most productive session in a decade.

Folk filled appointive offices with energetic young men who agreed to serve out of a sense of duty and not because they were professional office seekers. In fact, Folk neglected the better politicians who had supported him—a serious mistake for a man who was feeling the one insect bite that is enjoyable, the bite of the presidential bug.

He told lobbyists that they could not stay in Jefferson City more than thirty hours, and that they must report their business to him first of all. He began a cleanup of the St. Louis police by forbidding their enrollment in the Jefferson Club, a galling blow to Hawes.

In the spring of 1905, Attorney General Herbert Hadley and Folk discovered that the Standard Oil Company of Indiana and the Waters-Pierce Oil Company had divided Missouri between themselves, that both were under the same management in New York, and that they had formed the Republican Oil Company to get the business of customers dissatisfied with the other two. Standard fought arrogantly and stubbornly, but the state won in the Missouri Supreme Court in 1909 and was sustained by the United States Supreme Court in 1912. This was the basis for similar action in Ohio, Arkansas, Oklahoma, and Texas and for the celebrated federal antitrust action against Standard Oil of New Jersey.

But the governor from St. Louis went against the grain of St. Louisans when he attempted strict enforcement of an 1855 Sunday closing law. It had been a dead letter for years, and it would have been repealed but for the rural drys. St. Louisans always like their wine and beer, and there was no better time for a man to enjoy them than on a Sunday afternoon when he could take his whole family to the beer gardens—those graveled walks and green tables under shade trees which were so popular in preprohibition St. Louis. Here Folk, a self-centered and unimaginative man, displayed more zeal than good sense. Apparently his wife never played on the executive mansion piano a song that became a favorite in the old Delmar Garden:

> *If Folk don't stop, I greatly fear,*
> *You'll never get a million people here*
> *Starlight, star bright, tell me is this so?*

The least offensive places were, of course, the first to bow. It didn't occur to their proprietors to defy the police. But "private clubs" sprang up in St. Louis County, where the sheriff and his deputies did nothing about them. Here was a preview of Prohibition. Folk used the St. Louis police to raid places open on Sunday until the Supreme Court told him he couldn't send the city police beyond the city limits. The governor couldn't take a hint when 30,000 or 40,000 people crossed the Mississippi on a Sunday afternoon or when the sheriff of St. Charles County, which adjoins St. Louis, in a gesture of protest closed everything on a Sunday—even livery stables and penny-candy stores. The governor also seemed to skip the editorials which deplored his intolerance. The law was the law. The drys began to claim him as a hero. But Folk was no dry. He refused an invitation to preside at the 1906 convention of the Anti-Saloon League. On a trip to Kansas he ostentatiously took a drink from a reporter's bottle. Then he was in trouble with Carrie Nation too.

Since Missouri governors may not succeed themselves, they generally lose influence as their terms run along. Folk had his troubles with the legislators. Yet an extraordinary number of progressive measures were adopted in the second half of his term, many of them giving substance to what he called the "Missouri idea." A state banking department, bureau of labor statistics, and mine inspection service were established. More laws regulating railroads, insurance companies, and monopolies were put on the books. The pure-food laws were strengthened. The direct primary was established for state offices. A preferential primary for candidates for the United States Senate also was established. Rules governing lobbyists were tightened. The child-labor laws were stiffened, and the school year was lengthened from six to eight months. The eight-hour day law was extended. The state's mental hospitals were improved. Highway bills helped to take Missouri out of the mud and gave people a chance to drive the newfangled automobiles. (The Moon, the Dorris, and half a dozen others were being built in St. Louis.) The initiative and the referendum were submitted and approved by the voters. Yet Folk did not get everything he asked for. His recommendation of a graduated income tax for the support of the state university, for example, was rejected. Few legislatures, however, have been as constructive as those of his administration.

This record, of course, was exploited by Norman Hapgood, William Allen White, Lincoln Steffens, and all who were pushing the Folk-for-President band wagon. But Folk was sensible enough not to buck Bryan in 1908. He probably wanted to wait until 1910 and then run for the Senate against William Walker, a weak Republican. The clamor of his Progressive followers, however, forced him to run at once against Senator William J. Stone, the boss of the state Democratic organization. This race made it transparently clear that Folk had neglected Missouri politics—partly because he had to spend spare time on the lecture circuit to supplement a salary inadequate even for his simple way of life, and partly because he had little talent for practical politics. Folk was an effective orator, a resourceful prosecutor, and a good administrator, but he was too cool, too formal, too self-centered, to be a first-rate vote getter. Men like Hawes, meanwhile, had regrouped and strengthened their forces. This told on primary day. After a strenuous campaign, Folk carried fifty-seven counties to forty-seven for Stone, but Stone got 159,512 votes to only 144,718 for Folk. The opposition of Hawes in St. Louis and Reed in Kansas City made the difference. There was solace of sorts in the election of Folk's Republican attorney general, Herbert Hadley, as governor. Folk could say quite sincerely, "Let the work go on." Probably nobody realized that Folk never again would win an elective office. "There are men who have talked more of modern democracy," said Reedy; "there is none who has done more." But there was truth, too, in the remark of Folk's friend, Judge Hennings, that "few people ever threw their hats in the air for Joe Folk."

Four years later Woodrow Wilson appointed him to the Interstate Commerce Commission. In Washington he became the crony of Joseph Davies, Mark Sullivan, and Joseph Tumulty, the President's secretary. They lunched almost daily at what they called "The Cockroach Table." Then in January 1918 Folk agreed to conduct a legal campaign for the St. Louis Chamber of Commerce, then known as the Business Men's League, which promised to be almost as popular as that against Ed Butler. For years St. Louis had been victimized by the railroads under what was called the "bridge arbitrary," a scheme cooked up by Jay Gould while he was milking the Missouri Pacific and owned the Eads Bridge. The gouge was continued by the Terminal Railroad Association —formed by fifteen railroads for the operation of the Union Station, switching facilities, and the like—after it acquired the bridge. Trains from the east could come into the city only by way of the bridge and had to pay a stiff arbitrary toll. This amounted to twenty cents a ton on Illinois coal, so many industries—especially the big steel and meat-packing plants—were built on the Illinois side of the river, where their smokestacks contaminated the city's air but where they paid no St. Louis or Missouri taxes, and no "bridge arbitrary." Enterprises conducted on the Missouri side of the river had to submit to the holdup. Many a factory or warehouse which normally would have been built to take advantage of the city's location went up elsewhere—in Chicago or Kansas City—because the owners refused to face the gun of the "kid-glove bandit," as the railroad combine was called. David R. Francis promoted a second bridge to break the monopoly, but this span was sold to the Terminal Railroad Association almost as soon as it was built. Subsequently the city built the Free Bridge—now called the MacArthur Bridge, and no longer free—but for a long time the railroads simply would not use this span. They gave the city the same "absent treatment" that was used to bankrupt the builders of the Eads Bridge.

Negotiations to end or modify the "bridge arbitrary" failed. When William Gibbs McAdoo was named as railroad administrator in World War I, the city looked to him for relief but did not get it. So Folk was retained. On March 19, 1918, he petitioned the Interstate Commerce Commission to order the Terminal to end its arbitrary charge. Hearings were held in June and July. The petition was denied in May,

1919, but in the meantime Folk had made a final plunge into politics. (Frederick W. Lehman, who had served as Solicitor General under Taft, finally won a decision in the Supreme Court.)

Colonel Edward House, the gray eminence of the White House, had urged Folk to run for governor as early as 1916, and Folk had exchanged letters about the Missouri political situation with his old Kansas City friend and supporter, Frank P. Walsh, chairman of the War Labor Board. Tentative plans were crystallized by the death of Senator Stone on April 14, 1918. Missouri's most prominent Democrats at the time were in positions which caused them to decline an appointment by Governor Frederick D. Gardner to take Stone's place in the Senate until it could be filled by the voters. Champ Clark was Speaker of the House. Reed was in the Senate. David R. Francis was Ambassador to Russia, and about to witness the Bolshevik Revolution. Gardner finally appointed Xenophon P. Wilfley, a lawyer who had never sought public office. There was a widespread feeling that Wilfley was to be an interim senator who would step aside to let Gardner run for the office in 1920. In any case the circumstances seemed propitious for Folk, and he was eager to wage the League of Nations battle for Wilson against Jim Reed. Folk was no prairie isolationist.

He entered the Democratic primary. Even though Wilfley had the support of Kansas City's burgeoning Kemper-Pendergast machine, Folk beat him 107,690 to 80,000. The Republicans nominated Selden P. Spencer of St. Louis, a former circuit judge and chairman of the district draft appeals board. Both men pledged full support of the war. Both favored votes for women. Both pussyfooted on Prohibition. They had not really come to grips when Woodrow Wilson made his politically costly appeal for a Democratic Congress. There was no campaigning during the fourth Liberty Loan drive. Folk lost a few more days because of food poisoning. Then the epidemic of Spanish influenza canceled all but a few outdoor meetings. There was nothing to inspire the voters. Folk's worst political enemies—men like Senator Reed—were in his own party and barely gave him token support. The appeal for votes simply petered out. On election day the intimation of the extremely light Democratic primary vote was realized. Spencer got 302,680 votes, while Folk polled only 267,397.

Folk blamed his defeat on "booze and flu." Perhaps the election was a first sign of the reaction which was to put Warren G. Harding into the White House. Politically, it was the end for Joe Folk, a dreary anticlimax.

Until his sudden death of a heart attack in New York on May 28, 1923, Folk practiced law in Washington—and profitably. He and his wife enjoyed a pleasant social life, for which there had been neither time nor means in the furious years in St. Louis and Jefferson City. His biographer sets down Folk's career as a failure because he was not a bigger man. Surely this is too harsh. The failure to go to the Senate, let alone the failure to win the presidency, must be the fate of most men who reach for so much. Nor should it be held against Folk that he did not come from Tennessee to St. Louis with a fully developed political philosophy. Great men rarely come ready-made. They seize opportunities and put them to good use. Folk did that when he went after the boodlers. He did it when, as one of Missouri's best governors, he opened the state to the clean winds of reform and progress. Never in St. Louis had public morality fallen lower than Joe Folk found it. In giving the city self-respect once more, he was far from the least of the shapers of the St. Louis tradition.

XXVII. Bears and Billikens

The Unitarian church is represented in this remote place as in most other parts of America by a gentleman of great worth and excellence." So Charles Dickens wrote in his report on St. Louis. The gentleman to whom he referred was the Reverend William Greenleaf Eliot, pastor of the Church of the Messiah and president of the first board of Washington University.

Eliot was a small, rather frail, yet amazingly energetic New Bedford man who came from the Harvard Divinity School in 1835 to organize the first Congregational Society in St. Louis. The step from Congregationalism to Unitarianism was a short one. Eliot was popular among the "Bostons," and an assiduous money raiser for all good causes. And to him there was no better cause than education. Here he was completely in accord with Wayman Crow, one of his most loyal supporters. Of North Irish stock, Crow had interests as broad as those of Eliot and he, too, had the energy equal to their demands. With his cousin, Joshua Tevis, he established the dry-goods house of Crow & Tevis. Although a self-educated man, Crow steadily advocated the advantages of formal education to a man of business. By way of example, he would point to his young partner, David Davis Walker, a Beloit graduate from Bloomington, Illinois, who in 1880 with Frank Ely formed the great St. Louis dry-goods firm of Ely & Walker.

Eliot and Crow talked much about the need for a new school in St. Louis. So after he was elected to the State Senate, Crow carefully drafted the charter of Eliot Seminary, originally a grammar school with two teachers and thirty pupils. The first board of directors under the charter was organized on February 22, 1854, with Eliot as president, Crow as vice-president, Seth A. Ranlett as secretary, and John Cavender, treasurer. It was at this meeting that the name of Washington University was chosen, and three years later the charter was amended accordingly. At that time another amendment was added:

No instruction either sectarian in religion, or partisan in politics, shall be allowed in any department of said university, and no sectarian or party test shall be allowed in the election of professors, or in the admission of scholars thereto, or for any purpose whatever.

Eliot explained both the name and the purpose of the new institution:

"Under a happy coincidence, the charter had been approved on the 22nd of February, 1853, and the first meeting of the incorporators, at which the organization of the institution was accomplished, was held on the 22nd of February, 1854. By this coincidence of birth, the name of Washington University was suggested. It is also a name admirably adapted to the plan proposed, namely, the establishment of an American university, upon the broad foundation of republican and Christian principles free from the trammels of sect and party; a university for the people, whom Washington served; to educate the rising generations in that love of country and of our whole country which the Farewell Address of Washington inculcates, and in that faithfulness to God and truth which made Washington great."

Crow persuaded business associates to help in the establishment of the school. The largest individual donor during the early years was James Smith, who had come to St. Louis from New Hampshire in 1833. Other early benefactors were Phocian McCreery, William A. Hagadine, William Barr, Gottlieb Conzelman, John How, John O'Fallon, Hudson E. Bridge, George Partridge, the sons of George Collier, Mrs. Mary A. Hemenway of Boston, John R. Shepley, William K. Bixby, the Liggett and the McMillan families. Not least among them was Professor Sylvester Waterhouse. He gave $25,000 on condition that it be invested until it had increased to $1,000,000.

Washington University had its real beginning in the evening classes which were conducted in the old Benton schoolhouse in the winter of 1854–55. These were the nucleus of the O'Fallon Polytechnic Institute, which eventually became the university's engineering department. In September, 1856, Smith Academy, a high school for boys, was opened at Seventeenth Street and Washington Avenue. The university was formally inaugurated on April 22, 1857, with ceremonies in the Mercantile Library hall. As at Gettysburg, the orator of the occasion was the popular Edward Everett. Besides much, much more, he said:

"It is because I appreciate the severity of the struggle, and deeply sympathize with those who have forced their way to eminence, in the face of poverty, friendless obscurity, distance from all the facilities for improvement, and inability to command their time, that I would multiply the means of education, and bring them into as many districts of the country, and as near the homes of as large a portion of the population as possible. . . ."

On May 11, 1859, Mary Institute, a school for girls, was opened with Professor Edwin D. Sanborn in charge. The school still flourishes but now is independent of the university. The St. Louis Law School was organized on March 19, 1860, but because of the Civil War it was not opened until 1867. The first collegiate class of Washington University was graduated in June of 1862. The diplomas were handed out by Chancellor Hoyt. He was succeeded by Dr. William Chauvenet. Dr. Eliot became acting chancellor in December of 1870, and he was inaugurated as chancellor in February 1872.

The first campus of the university was developed under Dr. Eliot with the very substanital help of Crow. An addition to the university building on Washington Avenue was put up in 1871. A new building for Mary Institute was located at Beaumont and Locust streets—next door to the home in which T. S. Eliot, the poet, lived as a boy—in 1878, and Smith Academy, was moved into a new building at Washington Avenue and Nineteenth Street in 1879. In that year also the building of the St. Louis Institute of Fine Arts was begun. This $135,000 structure, which housed both an art school and the city's first important art museum, was a gift of Wayman Crow.

There are those who feel that Washington University is not as widely known as it should be. Yet matters were more or less planned that way. It was established as a school for poor boys, poor St. Louis boys—and girls, since they were admitted to the college shortly after the Civil War—who could not pack a carpetbag and go to Transylvania. Its objectives were practical. More emphasis was put on "manual training" than on Greek (but Professor Waterhouse did teach Greek). Dr. Eliot, speaking of those who disapproved of the school's "practical department," said:

"A carpenter's shop and blacksmith's forge seemed to them a singular appendage to the college humanities and the schools of philosophy and advanced learning which dignify the university career. It seems to have been forgotten that the word university was itself borrowed from the guilds of trade associations which were known as universities two or three hundred years ago, as the university of bakers, of smiths, of watchmakers, etc., in Rome and London. Already the prejudice is passing away. . . ."

In its engineering departments Washington University has realized the ambition described by another of its pioneers, John How: "Our desire is to establish an institution that shall have all the advantages of the mechanic institutes of our country, with those of the polytechnic institutions of Berlin, Vienna and the other cities of Europe." Many of the early graduates of the school who distinguished themselves did so as engineers.

Washington University is a big school and a good school. Its campus —two miles of Tudor Gothic with recent intrusions of "modern"—is handsome, or was until so much of it had to be sacrificed to asphalt accommodations for Detroit's space-covering repudiations of the functional. Even F. Scott Fitzgerald's wealthier Princeton classmates must still wonder how cars came to the campus in such numbers. How many members of the good old class of '20 had even a "tin Lizzie?" At Washington University the automobile indicates that more of the students live at home than in the dormitories and fraternity houses. On the theory that a community of scholars should live together and that it should represent many geographical areas, Chancellor Ethan Allen Shepley in 1959 began the construction of new residential buildings on a wooded, rolling section of university property previously enjoyed only by the bird walkers. Yet, with the exception of its distinguished medical school, Washington University may be slow to lose its predominantly local character.

Of course a football team—Oklahoma or Notre Dame style—could put the school's name on the wires of the press services regularly, but not many want that. Washington University does have teams—and they have been coached by such "immortals" as Jim Conzelman, Glen Dobie, and Carl Snavely—but they are strictly amateur, with relatively little time for practice. Under the likable Conzelman, the school did attempt "big-time" schedules. His teams regularly defeated those of the University of Missouri and held "powerhouses" like Notre Dame and Illinois to one-touchdown margins Saturday after Saturday.

"Most of the boys had to play a full sixty minutes against those bruisers," Conzelman explains with a twinkle in his eye, "but when they got home, all they would hear was: 'Well, we see that you lost another game!'"

Washington University now plays opponents such as Butler, Wabash, Kalamazoo, and the Missouri School of Mines—and every reader of the sports section knows that's no way to get into the "first ten," even if it does give coeds and fraternity brothers an opportunity to indulge in the tribal rituals of cheerleading, drum-majoring, and decorating "homecoming" floats. Still, not so long ago the former chairman of the university's music department got his hair on end at the suggestion that his department should be interested in a marching band. Such a man simply is not "big time!" He probably nodded in approving agreement when Robert M. Hutchins drove the footballers out of the University of Chicago.

Washington University made a great stride toward eminence under Robert Somers Brookings, a second Wayman Crow. He was born January 22, 1850, in Cecil County, Indiana. At the age of seventeen he joined his brother, Harry, as a clerk in the woodenware business of Samuel Cupples in St. Louis, but soon took to the road as a salesman. Brookings was so successful that after four years he and his brother proposed to establish their own firm. Rather than have them as competitors, Cupples made them partners. At twenty-two, Robert became virtual head of the firm. In 1895 he built the big Cupples Station at the eastern end of the Mill Creek Valley. This freight terminal systematized the handling of merchandise and contributed greatly to the efficiency of the city as a distributing center. The blocks of massive red brick warehouses now are the property of Washington University.

Brookings soon was a multimillionaire, yet business was not nearly enough to occupy his mind and his time. He plunged into books methodically. He became an active supporter of the Choral Society, the Symphony, and the Mercantile Library. By 1896 Brookings had enough of money-making. Having been elected president of Washington University's trustees, he decided to devote all his energy to the development of the school. He was surprised when he read in the famous Flexner report on American medical education, issued in 1910 by the Carnegie Foundation, that the university's medical school was mediocre. Instead of defending the school, he convinced himself that Dr. Flexner's verdict was just. Then he raised $15,000,000 for the school, giving generously himself. With the help of Dr. William Henry Welch of Johns Hopkins, he recruited outstanding men for its faculty. Three years after the Flexner report was published, the Carnegie Foundation found the medical school "unexcelled by any in the country."

During World War I Woodrow Wilson called Brookings to Washington to control prices through the War Industries Board. Having devoted himself to business and then to education, he now turned to public affairs, especially their economic aspects. In 1916 he helped to raise funds for the Institute of Governmental Research in Washington, and became its board chairman. In 1922 he induced the Carnegie Foundation to establish the Institute of Economics, and he provided funds for a graduate school of economics and government in the capital. In 1928 these three were combined in the Brookings Institution, "devoted to the public service through research in the social sciences." Brookings lived in Washington the last eight or nine years of his life, but after he died on November 5, 1932, he was buried in St. Louis. He was, as Harold Moulton said, "a constructive liberal."

Washington University was again quickened in 1946 by the return of Arthur Holly Compton, formerly professor of physics, as chancellor. He invigorated the spirit of academic freedom, bringing Martin Kamen, and Edward U. Condon, first-rate scientists, to the school after they had been harassed by an overly suspicious government. This was part of a program of strengthening the faculty. The university was getting more than $4,000,000 from the government, so the scientific departments naturally flourished. But the importance of the humanities was kept in mind, especially after Compton, the scientist, was succeeded by Ethan A. H. Shepley. A lawyer and businessman of the Brookings pattern, he gave special attention to the liberal arts while pushing an extensive building program—the new John M. Olin Library, another building for the school of fine arts, more laboratories and lecture halls, and a group of new dormitories. Since the capital funds of the medical school rose from $9,000,000 to $20,000,000 in the last ten years, its status was assured. The library, with its microfilm collection of rare books and documents, and a $1,000,000 endowment for a school of music, received in 1945, were in the mind of Thomas S. Hall, dean of the College of Liberal Arts, when he summed up the present state of the school: "The University has secured a toe hold on heights from which the peaks of true greatness may be discerned."

Washington University now consists of fifteen schools and colleges. It has more than fifty buildings and a campus of 155 acres. The enrollment in its college of liberal arts is about 1800; the over-all enrollment is about 13,000 students. Many of these attend evening classes, considerably improved by Dean Frank Debatin, in accordance with the founders' desire to help those whose educational opportunities are limited.

St. Louis University also entered a period of expansion after the war, largely under the Reverend Paul C. Reinert, S.J., who became its president in 1949. Father Reinert, an alumnus of the school, has served as president of the North Central Association of Colleges and Secondary Schools, and of the Association of Urban Universities, and as a member of President Eisenhower's Committee on Education Beyond the High School, the Educational Advisory Committee of the International Cooperation Administration, and the Executive Committee of the American Council on Education. He holds the Alumni Medal of the University of Chicago, from which he received his Ph.D. in 1944.

He is energetically directing plans for the expansion of the St. Louis University campus in the Mill Creek Valley redevelopment area—across Grand Avenue from DuBourg Hall, the university's main building, and the College Church of St. Francis Xavier. The community is grateful to the university for the educational opportunities it has provided for a century and a quarter, as well as for its decision not to abandon its accessible midtown location, a decision of major importance in the campaign against neighborhood blight. This gratitude is being shown in the support of a ten-year campaign to raise $46,000,000. Announced April 18, 1959, by a committee of 180 citizens headed by August A. Busch, Jr., the drive is non-denominational. The new campus is to be devoted primarily to the sciences and technology.

Of the half dozen or so university buildings put up since the end of World War II, the most impressive is the $4,500,000 Pius XII Memorial Library. This houses not only some 700,000 bound volumes and 42,000 pamphlets, but also the Knights of Columbus Vatican Film Library, consisting of 11,000,000 pages (30,000 volumes) of manuscripts in the Vatican Library in Rome, reproduced on 873,400 feet of 35 mm microfilm, and more than 6000 color slides. This is one of the most unusual and valuable scholarly collections in the United States. Ranging from the fourth to the nineteenth centuries, it covers every field of human knowledge—religion, philosophy, history, science, medicine, law music, and invaluable letters of statesmen, monarchs, and prelates—and makes these works more conveniently available on a glass screen in the Middle West than they are in their big tomes in Rome. The entire collection is contained on 8734 spools in fourteen steel cabinets a handsome 43×43-foot room. The negatives, of course, are kept in a specially protected vault.

This collection was conceived in 1950 by the Reverend Lowrie J.

Daly, S.J., professor of history at the university, as he thought of what would have been lost had the Vatican Library been bombed. The co-operation of Vatican authorities was obtained, and the Knights of Columbus underwrote the cost of the project, originally estimated at $50,000 but finally running to $340,000. (Some films were lost on the Andrea Doria.) The microfilming took four years. Only the manuscripts, not the books, in the Roman library were filmed, and an effort was made to eliminate the unimportant. Since this leaves the Vatican catalogues a somewhat misleading indication of the contents of the St. Louis collection, *Manuscripts* is issued three times a year. This publication contains scholarly articles as well as check lists of the films. The St. Louis University Library also has been made a depository of the Jesuit Historical Institute—and that would have pleased Father De Smet, who, when not working with the Indians, avidly collected books for the university. He brought some of the most valuable items to its shelves.

The university has about 12,000 students, including those in the evening division, in its twelve schools. It has a faculty of about 1200, full time and part time. Only thirty-five of the hundred Jesuits assigned to the university actually teach. Most of them have administrative duties. With the exception of medicine, dentistry, philosophy, and theology, the schools are housed—some not very elaborately—on the Grand and Lindell campus. But as new buildings go up, this gradually is being transformed. Quonset huts and old mansions are being replaced by spots of grass and trees. As its library indicates, the university, like others, seeks to accommodate all the knowledge of mankind, but it is even more earnestly devoted to the training of the doctors, lawyers, teachers, engineers, and social workers needed by the community. In 1944 the university was the first institution of higher learning in Missouri to lift the barrier against Negroes.

St. Louis University has given up football. Walsh Stadium on Oakland Avenue was torn down to make way for the new Merchants' Exchange. Some alumni, and all sports writers, still miss the Thanksgiving Day game between the St. Louis Billikens and the Washington Bears. Regularly, they recall the St. Louis teams developed by Eddie Cochems of Wisconsin and boast of how he introduced the forward pass in 1906. Of course John Heisman, Harry Williams, John Bell, and Lieutenant Paul Dasheill had some notion about that innovation because they fought Walter Camp for several years before the pass was legalized in the 1906 rule book. A. A. Stagg probably was right when he said, "all of us were working with it that year." But Cochems did send the first sensational passing combination, Bradbury Robinson and Jack Schneider, onto the Sportsman's Park field in 1906. They broke open the game against Kansas, a team expected to "outweigh, outplay, and outclass" St. Louis, with a 48-yard pass, and St. Louis scored a 34 to 2 upset. That team also beat Iowa 39 to 0, Drake 32 to 9, Marquette 30 to 0, and Hugo Bezdek's Arkansas team 24 to 0. St. Louis University students, however, are not likely to care too much about the absence of football as long as their Billikens continue to do as well in basketball as they have in the last dozen years. Soccer was introduced in 1959, and the St. Louis team won the national collegiate championship.

There are half a dozen other colleges in the St. Louis area. The Board of Education's Harris Teachers' College; Maryville, Fontbonne, Webster, Lindenwood of St. Charles, and Monticello in Illinois, all women's schools, the Alton branch of the University of Southern Illinois, and the Principia on the Mississippi River bluffs at Elsah, Illinois, should be listed without going farther afield. There is not a football power in the lot.

Harris Teachers' College is a monument to William Torrey Harris, who, as Superintendent of Schools from 1868 to 1880, made the St. Louis system pre-eminent in the country. This Connecticut schoolmaster was a philosopher, but a very practical one. He agreed with Calvin M. Woodward of Washington University and other advocates of practical education—"manual training"—but never would accept this as the ultimate purpose of schooling. He summed up his ideal: "Philosophy can bake no bread, but it can give God, Freedom and Immortality." He was for bread, but not bread alone.

Harris brought Henry C. Brockmeyer, a sickly Prussian veteran from a farm in Warren County, which was no place for the man, to St. Louis and set him to work translating Hegel. These two were the core of the St. Louis Philosophical Society, which Harris organized in 1866 and which, in turn, became the core of "the St. Louis Movement," one of the significant American contributions to philosophy. Harris and a small group met at least once a week in the Tivoli, a Bohemian beer garden in Fourth Street opposite the Southern Hotel. To the beer-garden music they discussed the correlation and conservation of forces, appraised the latest philosophical ideas from Europe, and launched the *Journal of Speculative Philosophy*. Harris also edited a more popular magazine, *The Western*. The *Journal* published Hegel, Fichte, Schelling, and other Europeans, as well as such Americans as William James, Josiah Royce, and the young John Dewey. In its field, it was even more impressive than *Reedy's Mirror* was as a literary organ. Harris, naturally, was a regular contributor. The man wrote 479 books! More than many Americans read in a lifetime. His annual reports as superintendent of schools still are valued by the profession.

Others active in the Philosophical Society in addition to Harris and Brockmeyer, erstwhile lieutenant-governor of Missouri, who served as president, were Denton J. Snider, author of a system of psychology, Dr. Alexander De Menil, compiler of *The Literature of the Louisiana Purchase Territory*, Adolph E. Kroeger, St. Louis correspondent of the New York *Times*, George H. Howison, J. Gabriel Woerner, William C. Jones, C. F. Childs, Jr., Britton A. Hill, Dr. John W. Waters, and the redoubtable Dr. Adam Hammer. The remarkable awakening of interest in metaphysics which they brought about attracted Emerson, Alcott, Julia Ward Howe, and other "big names" to their meetings in St. Louis.

Born Yankee that he was, Harris always dreamed of Concord, Massachusetts, as the home of American philosophy, and he made it his home after his retirement in 1880. His Society and his *Journal* died out. The last issue appeared in 1893. Perhaps their standards were too high to be maintained indefinitely. The spirit of Harris, who died in 1909, prevailed for a long time in the schools. It prepared the way for such great teachers and administrators as Frank Louis Soldan, Robert Rombauer, Avis Blewitt, and Susan Blow, who established her famous kindergarten in 1873 in the Des Pères school.

Brilliant as they were, these teachers owed a good part of their success to the intense interest of the St. Louis German element in public education. (German, incidentally, was a required subject in the schools until 1888.) But now educational policy has fallen into the control of school board members who are as likely as not to regard their position as an aid in selling merchandise or services to teachers, or who want to distribute the jobs in the building and maintenance department as rewards for political workers. It takes a "politician" to live with such a board. Men less diplomatic than Philip J. Hickey, the present superintendent, served only a short time. To his credit, Hickey has been able to introduce innovations, especially for bright pupils. It is probably too much to expect him to avoid all traces of the blight which has so seriously watered down American primary and secondary education. After all, it is difficult to maintain standards when the truant officer brings to school those unwilling or unable to learn, when teachers can be employed only if they present the state-required teachers' college credits no matter what they really know, when parents want safe-driving and "life-adjustment" courses, and when the nation generally pays only lip service to education, regarding high school diplomas merely as aids to employment and college as a desirable path to the altar or as offering "contacts" to be used later in selling stocks and bonds.

Yet a St. Louisan about to conclude that there is an educational Gresham's law at work will pause when he thinks of Dr. Samuel Shepard, Jr.—if he has heard about him. He is a Negro and a district director of schools—about twenty-five of them in backward neighborhoods. Had he been one of the factotums in the Board of Education offices when the schools were desegregated, he might have joined in the mutual adulations. But he had grown up in an impoverished Kansas City home, had worked his way through the University of Michigan, and had come up in the St. Louis school system as a teacher, coach, and principal. There were 13,000 Negro and only 1000 white pupils in the schools under his charge. He knew those pupils, and he knew, too, that desegregation would not be an unmixed blessing—at least at the outset.

He is a teacher without illusions, and contemptuous of pretense. The "culturally handicapped" were not youngsters he had heard about only in teachers' college courses. They were those youngsters in his schools who were a year or more behind the average in public school performance. And he knew why. They did not care. Their parents did not care. They were not encouraged to work. Why study? What good will it do you? Who will give you a job in which you can use anything you may learn? Two years after desegregation, tests showed that Negro eighth-graders were indeed a year behind in reading, spelling, arithmetic. Only 7 per cent of them were ready for "top track" work in high school.

"Integration did not put us in a good light," Shepard told parents' meetings. "We have been too satisfied to be low man on the totem pole. We cannot blame others. We cannot make excuses."

School is important, he told his pupils, their parents, and their teachers. It calls for work, drive, ambition. The children must be made to work, helped to work. No skipping of homework; instead more should be done than is assigned. Weekends and vacations must be used to study, to learn. No excuses. Shepard has been holding meetings, writing letters, outlining extra work schedules. He has been encouraging the young, goading their elders. No excuses. Opportunities are coming. Be ready for them. Don't be content with ignorance. Thirst for knowledge.

After a few years of this, Dr. Shepard is getting results. In a school in which reading ability was only 28 per cent of the national norm, it rose to 57.8 per cent. Those ready for "top track" high school work rose to 14.8 per cent. There is much still to be done. But Dr. Shepard will hear no more of discouragement than of excuses. Keep at it. Inculcate the desire for excellence. Study! Work! Study!

St. Louis does have a genuine teacher, an ardent educator.

XXVIII. Under the Anheuser-Busch

Adolphus Busch was a magnifico. The high forehead, the long nose, the steady eyes, and the grand mustache and goatee in the Anders Zorn painting in the City Art Museum portray a masterly man—portly, a *bon vivant,* but resourceful and firm. A latter-day Medici, or Sforza, or Malatesta. President Taft called him "Prince Busch." He had his barony on South Broadway, a brewery which now numbers 150 buildings and 70 city blocks, and is worth about $150,000,000. Grown larger than most St. Louis industries, it nevertheless is the prime example of home-grown individualism. Although its beer goes to all parts of the world, nobody has ever dared to suggest that its home office be elsewhere than in St. Louis. Ownership has been held more nearly within the family than is generally the case with corporations so large, even if it is no longer quite the one-man show it was under the first Busch. He built it by salesmanship, according to his biographer, Roland Krebs, but his selling expeditions—whether to downtown St. Louis by carriage or to San Francisco in his private car, *The Adolphus*—always had a touch of a royal progress.

He ruled his domain and some 6000 retainers with paternal benevolence. Like earlier barons, he lived among his people at No. 1 Busch Place, the mansion set on a landscaped plot among the red-brick brewery buildings which billboards made famous to all America. In the heavily ornate style of his time, the place was lavish with Aubusson rugs, stained-glass windows, crystal chandeliers, parquet floors, and massive furniture. Still it was a home, not a palace. He built No. 2 Busch Place for his son. He prized family—children—above all. There was a place in Anheuser-Busch for all his sons and grandsons. It was theirs to maintain and to enhance. And that they have done with a profitable fidelity. Time has not done much to loosen Busch family ties, or to change the Busch way of life.

There really is a Busch way of doing things. It does not always conform to the patterns of the country club or the downtown banks. The Busches were South Siders. They long favored a bank near the brewery.

They came to its aid in the depression, and helped reorganize it as the Manufacturers' Trust Company, naturally without the loss of a penny by anybody. They built their own Manufacturers' Railroad to provide better service than the Terminal would give, and they ran it across the Municipal Bridge to break the Terminal's monopoly on handling rolling stock across the Mississippi. They acquired their own coal mines and built their own bottle factory, engine works, wagon shops, and other industries to be sure of the quality and the adequacy of the brewery's supplies. They still pay the top price for hops, barley, rice—everything they buy. Their beer costs more than other beers, but that is because it is the best beer they can make.

Even in the exceedingly difficult years of Prohibition—Mr. Hoover's "noble experiment"—the family closed ranks rather than look to others for help. And Anheuser-Busch was kept going. Such independence breeds a certain imperiousness. The Busches are not humble folk. But they have an earthy friendliness which overcomes arrogance and anger. The Busch estate on the Gravois Road is—well, fantastic. But its gates are open. Thousands visit the place every year, and there are people waiting to show them through buildings and grounds. St. Louis took note, when No. 1 Busch Place and No. 2 Busch Place were torn down in 1929 to make room for another factory building, and switch tracks, that August A. Busch did not follow the path of fashion to the West End or Ladue, but that he went out Gravois Road, the South Side's favorite street, to General Grant's old Hardscrabble Farm. The son of the magnifico had gone to a South Side public school. During the "dry" years he got up before sunrise to sell yeast in South Side bakeries. The Busches labor, and the Busches enjoy the fruits of their labor in their own way. Their taste runs to horses rather than Picassos. But they know what they want, and they don't care too much about what others want.

All this goes back to the first Adolphus. He was a great entertainer. Often he brought as many as twenty men from the brewery to the house for lunch. And the meal there was as elaborate as the one he ordered when he took customers or business associates to Tony Faust's. On December 6, Sankt Nikolaus with his sack of nuts and candy started out from No. 1 Busch Place to visit all the children of the neighborhood. With him walked his *Knecht* with a switch for those who had misbehaved, but somehow he never found them. On Christmas Eve there was a candle-sparkling Christmas tree, and a man standing by with a bucket of water just in case——. None of your hanging up stockings and coming down into an early-morning-dreary room to see if they had been filled in the night. This was a romantic German Christmas. In South Side homes, a room was closed off a week or two before the feast to give the Christ Child ample time to bring gifts and prepare a tree—and to heighten the childrens' anticipation. Then, on Christmas Eve, family, relatives, and friends assembled in a festooned house to sing carols and wait for the splendid moment. Suddenly, to the tinkling of a little silver bell, the doors would open to reveal the tree, the crèche beneath, and the presents all around. Gasps of awe, and a rush to pull off ribbons and wrappings. Then thanks all around, and an evening full of cookies, candies, and new toys.

On Easter Sunday morning there was an egg hunt in Busch Place until it no longer afforded enough hiding places for the ever increasing number of eggs. Then the search was transferred to Forest Park. But the park was not "home" and the fun was not as keen as it used to be.

The biggest of all Busch parties was the one to celebrate the fiftieth wedding anniversary of Adolphus and Lilly. All the brewery employees and their families, as well as many friends—1400 in all—were invited to the old Coliseum, the block-long hall built over Uhrig's Cave at Jefferson and Washington. Even for the Busch family it was a feat to make food and drink available for those who filled so large a hall. It was done, but Adolphus and Lilly were not at their party. He was sick and Lilly was with him in their garden in Pasadena. From the brewery workers, they received a congratulatory telegram etched in gold. Now that relations with employees are conducted by "human engineers," the ways of Adolphus Busch may seem ostentatious, if not insincere. There is no better refutation of that notion than what his granddaughter wrote for members of the family:

Then came the dining room, a huge, narrow, long affair with a bay window at the end. It had to be long to seat the House of Busch. Off this room came my favorite spot, because I could find my dearest friends and the sweetest people I ever knew: Wenzel, the butler, who ushered me in and always made me feel that I was a Princess out of my favorite Grimm's fairy tale; Babette, my grandmother's maid, who never failed to tell me that I was getting to be quite a young lady—music to my ears; little Barbara, the waitress, whom I loved; and Struzie, the cook, who made the most delicious cinnamon waffles in all the world with huge waffle irons with birds printed on them.

St. Louis, of course, brewed good beer before there was a Busch in the business. The St. Vrain brewery was in operation as early as 1810, offering "strong" beer at $10 a barrel, and "table" beer at $5. These were cash prices; if payment was made in merchandise, the charges were $12 and $6, respectively. Jacob Philipson was a competitor of Vrain, offering his beer at "12½ cents a quart at the stores of Silvestre Labbadie and Michael Tesson and at various other convenient places." Ezra English opened a brewery on the South Side which was the first to utilize the natural caves underlying the city for the storage of beer. With the exception of the old Cook's Champagne Company caves, now used by a vinegar firm, the caverns have been sealed. They once were summer recreation places but lost out to the beer gardens about the turn of the century. The influx of Germans gave St. Louis brewing its big lift. Adam Lemp made his first lager in 1840 in a little place on Second Street, between Walnut and Elm. Lemp's beer hall became popular enough to be called "famous."

In 1860 the Missouri *Handels Zeitung* reported that St. Louis had forty breweries, producing 23,000 barrels of beer a year.

Anheuser-Busch really is an accident. The first Eberhard Anheuser in St. Louis came from Germany and started a soap factory. He soon had a prosperous business. In 1852 a man named Schneider opened a brewery which produced 3000 barrels of beer in the first year of its operation. Schneider, however, was a poor businessman, and after three years sold out to a competitor, Urban & Hammer. To buy the brewery, this firm borrowed $90,000 from Eberhard Anheuser. The name was changed to the Bavarian Brewery, and production was increased to 8000 barrels a year. But in 1857 Urban & Hammer failed, with Eberhard Anheuser as its principal creditor. Rather than liquidate the brewery, he bought out the other creditors. For eight years he managed it as well as his soap factory.

It was also in 1857 that Adolphus Busch, the youngest of the twenty-one children of Ulrich Busch, a wine merchant of Mainz, came to St. Louis. Having been a raftman on the Rhine, he worked on Mississippi steamers for a while, and then got a job as salesman for Anheuser's brewery. In 1861 the young man married Anheuser's daughter, Lilly. The ceremony was a double one, his brother, Ulrich, being married to Lilly's sister, Anna, at the same time. Adolphus went off to the Civil War with one of the South Side regiments and fought in southern and western Missouri. With him as a chaplain went the man who had officiated at his wedding, the Reverend Dr. Hugo Krebs, an old friend of Carl Schurz. He had escaped from the Prussians in 1848 by swimming the Rhine. After the war, Anheuser decided that the soap factory was enough work for one man, so he turned over the management of the brewery to his son-in-law. In five years Adolphus Busch had production up to 18,000 barrels a year.

In 1873 he was made a full partner, and the name of the firm was changed to the E. Anheuser Brewing Association. It was incorporated in 1875 under the name of Anheuser-Busch Brewing Association. Its 480 shares had a par value of $240,000. They were held by Eberhard Anheuser and Adolphus and Lilly Busch. Production was up to 34,797 barrels. That year Adolphus Busch perfected his system of re-icing refrigerator cars, and sent his first carload of beer to Texas. That shipment was the basis of the transformation of Anheuser-Busch from a local brewery into an international business. So the Busches always had a kindly feeling toward Texas. When the businessmen of Dallas wanted somebody to build a grand hotel in the city, Adolphus Busch put up the Hotel Adolphus. Busch was a great one for advertising. In the early days he gave away pocketknives, watch fobs, chinaware, trays, and other novelties. One of the trays was especially popular. It was embellished with a picture of the many-buildinged brewery with flags flying from every cupola and crenelated tower. Sitting on a rather arbitrary crag, a large-breasted, luscious lovely, a wisp of veil across her lap, contemplated the busy Busch barony, ready to praise it to the tones of her harp.

There were many Budweiser girls, dressed and undressed, and they sold a lot of beer—but not nearly as much as General Custer in his last fight against Sitting Bull. Adolphus Busch bought Cassilly Adams' detailed picture of the Battle of the Little Big Horn for $35,000. Millions of people have been intrigued by reproductions, for which the brewery still receives requests. The original was presented to Custer's regiment, the Seventh Cavalry, for its mess hall at Fort Riley, Kansas. By the standard of popularity, it is one of the world's most famous paintings—much more popular than the more competent Oscar E. Berninghaus oils depicting the growth of the nation. These were widely displayed as posters and also are still sought in smaller reproductions. The star-crowned A and the eagle of Anheuser-Busch have appeared in all other forms of advertising—even on sheet music. "Under the Anheuser-Busch" really is a song. The words are by Andrew B. Sterling and the music by Harry von Tilzer. In the days when five-and-ten cent stores had sheet-music counters, the girl at the piano gladly "demonstrated" the number. But whether in newspapers or magazines, neon or radio, there never was an ad like "Custer's Last Fight." Displayed between potted palms in front of the velvet half curtain of an old saloon window, it was the ace of trumps.

In 1876, the year Budweiser was first brewed, Anheuser-Busch made sixteen beers, most of them available in old-fashioned bottles with wired-down, foil-covered corks. August A. Busch introduced the metal bottle cap while his father was in Europe. Old Adolphus caught the first ship to America to stop this meddling nonsense, but by the time he got to St. Louis he was ready to say "well done." Budweiser—brewed with rice rather than corn grits for natural carbonation, subjected to a second fermentation process, and aged as true lager must be—was a premium beer brewed first for the restaurant of Adolphus Busch's friend, Carl Conrad. Despite its higher price, this beer soon was in such demand that Anheuser-Busch could not get enough bottles from its suppliers. So the brewery built its own glass factory. Old Adolphus decided to make only Budweiser, and by 1901 the brewery was turning out 1,000,000 barrels a year and still rationing Budweiser. Until a few years ago the brewery made only one other beer, Michelob, a superfine lager which is not bottled. Then it put "Busch Bavarian," a standard-priced beer, on the market. But Budweiser still is the pride and prop of the house.

After he got his son, August A. Busch, over the notion that he wanted to be a cowboy and sent him to Germany to learn the brewers' art, old Adolphus took things a little easier. August A. showed ability in running the business, so Adolphus and Lilly could spend longer vacations at their summer place at Cooperstown, New York. Both of them delighted in flowers, so they also built a house in Pasadena and started their famous flower garden there. They also built a villa, Villa Lilly, at Langenschwalbach, overlooking the Rhine. It was there that Adolphus died October 10, 1913, at his desk, of a heart attack. He was seventy-six years old. He was buried from No. I Busch Place. The 20-mile route to Bellefontaine Cemetery was solidly lined by St. Louisans. Mayor Henry W. Kiel asked that all business in the city be halted for five minutes during the burial. The Jefferson Hotel and the Planters' House turned off all lights for that interval, and all streetcars were stopped. A committee of employees asked permission to carry the casket through the brewery along the route that Adolphus had followed to make sure his own "pure food laws" were being observed and to chat with his men. This may have been more paternalism, but Adolphus Busch was a defender of labor unions—first of all for his own employees. They were not expected merely to accept what he chose to grant. He signed a contract with the old Knights of Labor. The men had a right to speak up. His grandson, August A. Busch, Jr., remembered this one day when he was particularly angry about a mishap at the brewery. Gussie sounded off, and it was impossible for anybody to get in a word. Suddenly he became aware of this:

"Look," he exclaimed, "you shut up while I blow my top. Then you can blow yours."

Charles Nagel, one of the first citizens of St. Louis, spoke the eulogy at Adolphus Busch's funeral. He had been Secretary of Labor in President Taft's cabinet as well as a member of the legislature, president of the City Council, a law lecturer at Washington University, president of its board of trustees, and a power among Missouri Republicans. But he could remember how Adolphus Busch had furthered his career when he was a retiring young man. Nagel's father, a doctor, was another of those 1848 Germans who made the old St. Louis South Side. He had first settled in San Bernardo, Texas, near Houston, where Nagel was born in 1849. Then the doctor joined other Germans in the little anti-slavery settlement of Millheim, Texas. They were not very popular —least of all outspoken Dr. Nagel. When, on the eve of the Civil War, Millheim voted ninety-nine to eight against secession, the doctor was held responsible. He fled to Mexico with young Charles. From there they made their way to St. Louis, where they were joined by the rest of the family. Young Charles Nagel got his law degree in St. Louis in 1872 and then went to the University of Berlin.

Adolphus Busch took an interest in the young man after his return, and soon turned to him for legal advice. Busch was not a litigious man. He would rather take the short end of a bad bargain than become involved in acrimony, but he did not want to be anybody's fool. Nagel proved to be a good counselor. Indeed, the Busch grandsons still turned to Nagel when he was ninety years old. He died in 1940. Nagel's son, Charles, now is director of the City Art Museum. He had taught at Yale and then practiced architecture in St. Louis. World War II stopped that, so he became acting director of the museum. After the war he went to the Brooklyn Museum and drew much attention by his revitalization of that institution. Back in St. Louis, he is a quiet but effective worker for better race relations.

August A. Busch was allotted a double share in the $50,000,000 trust left by old Adolphus to his family. He also was left in control of the Anheuser-Busch Brewing Association, the Manufacturers' Railway, the American Bottle Company, and the Busch-Sulzer Diesel Engine Company. He had been primarily responsible for the development of the subsidiary companies; now he also assumed responsibility for the big brewery. Beer sales had risen to 1,530,085 barrels in 1913, but there was trouble ahead as the new president took over. World War I broke out within a year, and in 1917 the United States entered the conflict. Lilly Busch was in Germany at the time, and it took former senator Harry Hawes seven and a half months to bring her home. This ordeal included a personal examination by the Immigration Service at Key West, Florida, which Hawes denounced as "unexcelled in brutality," and for which Washington eventually apologized.

A direct handicap to the business was the talk that the Busch family was pro-German. Malicious tongues were not silenced by large purchases of Liberty bonds by the family and by the brewery. But much worse was Prohibition, a "war baby." Busch had tried to offset the propaganda of the Anti-Saloon League by devoting all advertising to appeals for personal liberty. Meanwhile he had asked the brewery staff to work on a non-alcoholic "beer." The result was "Bevo," a name derived from *pivo*, the Bohemian word for beer. This was an astounding success and an even more astounding failure. It was introduced in 1916, and the sale of 2,250,000 cases that year justified the construction of a $10,000,000 building to increase production. The sale of 5,000,000 cases in 1918 brought Anheuser-Busch $6,000,000. By 1919 Bevo was being sold in all parts of the world. There seemed to be no cause for concern at Anheuser-Busch when the brewing of beer was stopped in October 1918. Nobody realized at the time that the disappearance of beer would largely destroy the demand for near-beer. But Prohibition brought more than the hip flask, the speak-easy, the rumrunner, the hijacker, and bathtub gin. It also brought a taste for sweet, mixed drinks. The flavor of illicit liquor was so bad that it had to be disguised. Palates accustomed to these concoctions lost their taste for the tart flavor of beer and near-beer. By 1923 the sale of Bevo had fallen to almost zero. The product was kept on the market until 1929 in hope of a comeback. In the end it represented a $15,000,000 investment and a $4,000,000 loss.

These were grim years on South Broadway. The William J. Lemp Brewing Company, neighbor and chief competitor of Anheuser-Busch, went out of business in 1920, selling its huge plant for ten cents on the dollar. But August Busch would not quit. He told the members of the family—Eberhard Anheuser, Adolphus Busch III, young Gussie Busch, Leicester Faust, and Adalbert von Gontard—to put on their "thinking caps." Anheuser-Busch began to produce truck bodies and refrigerator cabinets. Then the company entered the bakers' yeast business. Here it was up against a near-monopoly, but a superior product eventually won a share of the market large enough to necessitate the building of a yeast plant at Old Bridge, New Jersey. All kinds of soft drinks were bottled, including Busch Extra-Dry Ginger Ale. But the most successful product of the era was canned malt syrup, used to make home brew. Anheuser-Busch did its best to keep its syrup out of the hands of bootleggers, selling instead to makers of pharmaceuticals, cereals, specialty foods, textiles, dairy products, flavoring agents, candy, and vinegar. Yeast and syrups, the life rafts of the Prohibition days, continue to be flourishing Anheuser-Busch products now that Bevo, ginger ale and all the other "dry" concoctions are just an unhappy memory in the big brewery.

August A. Busch was not happy to hold people and plant together by turning out new products. He wanted to brew beer. He loathed Prohibition. Through Albert A. Lasker, chairman of the U. S. Shipping Board and formerly head of the agency which handled Anheuser-Busch advertising, he found out that liquor was sold aboard American-flag ships. He used this as an illustration of the hypocrisy of Volsteadism. Busch appealed for uniform and effective enforcement of the law as long as it was on the books. Senator Jim Reed of Missouri headed an investigation which not only disclosed the failures of law enforcement but also the graft in the Anti-Saloon League. Under Wayne B. Wheeler, this organization was no more than a self-perpetuating board and a gang of moneyraisers who exploited church people. The Reed Committee showed, for example, that Representative Richmond Hobson of Alabama, who introduced the League's antiliquor amendment in the House of Representatives, had received $170,000 for "dry" talks. He split these "contributions" with the League, fifty-fifty. William Jennings Bryan got $700,000 for a four-month speaking tour. Wheeler told the Reed Committee that up to the end of 1925 the League had spent $67,565,312.72. Wheeler made as good a thing of the campaign to keep the Eighteenth Amendment in the Constitution as he had made of the fight to have the amendment adopted.

Busch, through his attorneys, presented a simple argument to President Coolidge, to President Hoover, to Congress, and to the public: Law-abiding businessmen were being penalized while lawbreakers flourished, so long as Prohibition was the law of the land. People didn't want this legislation. A state prohibition amendment had been submitted in Missouri. Even with 150,000 men in uniform and unable to vote, it had been rejected by 73,694 votes. Yet the legislature, elected the same day, ratified the national prohibition amendment—obviously in defiance of popular sentiment. Figures from other states were adduced to show that, prior to ratification of the Eighteenth Amendment without a popular referendum, no more than two and one half per cent of the American voters had favored Prohibition. The Department of Justice admitted that it had been "called upon to prosecute a member of the judiciary, prominent members of the American bar, high officials of Federal and State Governments. The sordid story of assassination, bribery, and corruption has been found in the very sanctums where the law was presumed to be sacred." It is time, said Busch, to end this terrible nonsense. But President Coolidge only said "thank you," and President Hoover talked about a "noble experiment." So in 1928 Busch announced that "brewers certainly have as much right to support any candidate they like as has the Anti-Saloon League. For my part, I am going to support Governor Smith." Four years later Franklin D. Roosevelt was elected on the unequivocal statement that "your candidate wants repeal, and I am confident that the United States of America wants repeal." Repeal became fact on April 7, 1933.

Under a permit to brew beer in advance of the date for its legal sale, Anheuser-Busch had 250,000 barrels ready. It had planned to resume the business quietly. But the city's factory whistles greeted 12:01 A.M., April 7, as they had never greeted a new year. The Anheuser-Busch brewery was surrounded by a jubilant throng. The gates were opened and a fleet of trucks rolled out to deliver the first Budweiser to the city's crowded taverns. It was a great night for St. Louis—especially for the South Side. August A. Busch had brought the old brewery through from "doom to boom."

In the next twenty years almost $85,000,000 was spent to enlarge and improve Anheuser-Busch. Beer sales rose from 607,511 barrels in 1933 to the present output of more than 6,000,000 barrels. With new plants in Newark, New Jersey, in Los Angeles, and in Florida, Budweiser continued to be the first beer of the United States. Busch, however, saw just the start of the boom. He had suffered several heart attacks during the hard years. He suffered from gout and dropsy. He was a victim of claustrophobia, but could no longer go to his hunting lodge at St. Peter's, Missouri, to shoot snipe. Full of pain, he wrote a note—"Good bye, precious Mommie and adorable children"—turned up the radio, and shot himself on February 13, 1934. He was succeeded by Adolphus Busch III, known around the brewery as "the Third." A retiring man, he had to cope with the problems of keeping Budweiser up to standard, the depression, and the impact of World War II. He died in Barnes Hospital after a short illness on August 29, 1946.

August A. Busch Jr. took over, the fourth Busch to become president of Anheuser-Busch, with Eberhard Anheuser as chairman of the board. "Gussie" probably is closer to the pattern of his grandfather than his brother or father was. He is extroverted and colorful, loyal to the family and to the family brewery. He is fiercely jealous of its position and reputation. He lives with gusto at Grant's Farm, keeps up the roaming herds and the menagerie his father started, and drives, four-in-hand, the landaus, tallyhos, and phaetons on the place. He and his present wife, who likes horses as much as he does, enjoy the *Schlachtfest,* the butchering feast, held in the *Bauernhof,* the collection of farm buildings and stables on the estate. Busch "batched" in the *Bauernhof* while he was being divorced by Elizabeth Overton Dozier Busch and before he married Gertrude Buholzer of Lucerne, Switzerland. He likes the place, but smaller, more sedate parties are held in the big château-like house. In either place he entertains in his grandfather's manner—often the men who make and sell Budweiser.

Of all the Busches, Gussie is perhaps the most popular, for in 1953, when it seemed that the famous St. Louis Cardinals might be sold away from St. Louis, Gussie Busch wrote a check for $3,750,000, and bought the baseball team. He made old Sportsman's Park, now Busch Stadium, one of the handsomest baseball parks in the country. Gussie's worry now is the team. The Cardinals, let's face it, are not what they were in the golden age of Sam Breadon, Branch Rickey, and the "Gashouse Gang." Between 1926 and 1946, the Redbirds won the National League pennant nine times and the world's series six times—which is not bad at all. But after the Browns, the erstwhile St. Louis representatives in the American League who lost the world's series to the Cardinals in 1944, became the Baltimore Orioles, the Redbirds lost their batting eye and the ability to catch a corner of the plate with a fast-breaking curve. It may be that the depression years produced more talented recruits for Mahatma Rickey's farm system than the "bonus babies" now lined up with the help of Gussie Busch's open checkbook. Although Phil Ball, the Brothers De Witt, Bill Veeck and other owners of the Browns found that only winners would fill the ball park, the fans have remained remarkably loyal to the Cardinals in their lean years. They have not shifted all their interest to the Billiken and Hawks basketballers or the Kutis soccer champions. Nor have they deserted baseball for the horse racing at Fairmount and Cahokia Downs, the two East Side tracks in not-so-Puritan Illinois. By patching and plugging, "Trader" Frank Lane did put together a Cardinal team which finished a strong second in 1957. Since then, however, Stan Musial, the man with the Cardinal red "6" on the back of his shirt and for years the National League batting champion, has not been enough. And he has heard Time's winged chariot at his back.

Gussie wants a winner, and he has learned that it takes more than a check and a fountain pen to create one. Perhaps he should not have "blown his top" at one of the dinners of the Knights of the Cauliflower Ear, a group devoted to sports, food, and wine. Frank Lane was there to hear him order "a pennant next year—or else!" Lane rolled with the punch that night. He knew that the Cleveland Indians were in seventh place—just as the Cardinals had been a year earlier—and that they wanted help. So Lane went to Cleveland and raised the Indians to second place, just as he had raised the Cardinals and the White Sox before them. And the Busch team slid right back into seventh place. Of course that might have happened even with Lane around. At least Gussie is not crying into his beer. He has Bing Divine and Solly Hemus trying to bring back the grandeur and the glory, and he is confident that before long the team will need a bigger ball park to accommodate its followers. When it was suggested that the area south and west of the riverfront national park might be redeveloped with a stadium as its chief feature if St. Louis men would put up $20,000,000 in equity money, Busch promptly started the subscriptions with $5,000,000. (And on top of that, most of the money put into Busch Stadium probably will have to be written off.)

Naturally, this is more than a baseball matter. The redevelopment also involves new office buildings, ample parking garages, and a large motel. It is intended to replace more than twenty-five blocks of rather squalid lofts and parking lots, to beef up the downtown shopping district, and to extend the rehabilitation of the city. Yet the stadium would be out of the question without the Cardinals as chief tenants. So Gussie Busch has agreed to move in and to put up a large share of the needed capital too. He figures that what is good for St. Louis is good for the brewery. Anyway, what is a good South Sider doing in a North Side ball park? Perhaps moving the Cardinals nearer the South Side will move them nearer the pennant too. But that's a Busch-size job.

Stories about "the romance of business" became old hat when the *American Magazine*—anybody remember it?—went out of business. But if a market again opens up for such stories there are some good ones, other than that of Anheuser-Busch, to be written in St. Louis. The most up to date is that of McDonnell Aircraft, the largest employer in the area. The corporation "came from nowhere" to meet the wartime and postwar demand for military planes. It builds some of the fastest flown by the armed services, virtually its only customers. The "capsule" which is to carry the first American into outer space also is being built in its big plant at the Lambert-St. Louis airport.

The firm's remarkable development probably was enough to win for its president, J. S. McDonnell, the St. Louis Award for 1959. But that piece of framed parchment and the $1000 check that comes with it betoken public service rather than business success, and McDonnell showed that the award was merited on this basis too. At the presentation ceremonies he handed Mayor Tucker a check for $20,000 for the equipment of the new planetarium in Forest Park. Shortly thereafter he sent $100,000 checks to St. Louis and Washington universities— and one to Princeton as well—explaining that the corporation had decided to forego the parties, souvenirs, and publications planned for its twentieth anniversary. It would be better for the country and the company to send the money to the schools, McDonnell said. Other contributions, of course, have been made, especially in support of education. There is hope for St. Louis, great hope, so long as such checks go out to help meet its needs and not simply because "all gifts are tax-deductable." The Falstaff Brewing Company—as well as Anheuser-Busch, the department stores and the banks—is underwriting the downtown stadium, and helped to move the former Chicago Cardinals of the National Football League to St. Louis as a tenant. There is advertising here, but also enlightened self-interest.

A somewhat longer history than McDonnell's is that of the Monsanto Chemical Company. When John F. Queeny came to St. Louis in 1897 as purchasing agent for the now century-old Meyer Brothers Drug Company, he decided to provide some extra money for a growing family by grinding flowers of sulphur. With his life savings of $6000 he built a small plant in which he hoped to operate the East St. Louis Sulphur Company as a side line. It burned down the first day it was in operation. Two years later Queeny had saved another $1500. He had also persuaded Jacob Bauer, a soft drink manufacturer, to lend him an additional $3500. Then with the help of a Swiss chemist, Dr. Louis Veillon, and Dr. Gaston DuBois, who came to them from Zurich and Dresden in 1904, he began the manufacture of saccharin, up to that time a German monopoly. The new firm was called the Monsanto Chemical Company for Queeny's wife, who had been Olga Monsanto.

The new factory did not burn down, but neither did it set the world on fire. The German cartel met the new competition by selling saccharin in the United States at a price well below the cost of production. So Queeny held on to his job at Meyer Brothers. Meantime his Swiss friends found other chemicals for the company to produce. It earned its first profit, $10,600, in 1905. Queeny left his job, but he probably regretted this when the panic of 1907 threatened to wipe out Monsanto as effectively as fire had wiped out East St. Louis Sulphur. The firm did little more than survive until the war that came of the assassination in Sarajevo. With German chemicals no longer available in the American market, Monsanto flourished. Indeed its expansion seemed to have been too rapid when the depression of 1921 caught it with big inventories and bigger debts. Gaston DuBois was its president in those grim days.

By the middle of the decade, however, the company again was in good shape, and in 1928 John Queeny's son, Edgar Monsanto Queeny, took over. But Dr. DuBois remained in charge of research and development. Monsanto continued to grow even during the deep depression of the thirties. The period before the second world war was one of mergers and international expansion. Monsanto plants now are spread across the United States from Massachusetts to Texas, and others are in operation in Canada, Great Britain, Australia, Japan, Mexico, and South America. This giant—with its home plants on South Second Street, in the

County, and across the river in Monsanto, Illinois—surely is far bigger than the biggest dreams of John Queeny and his Swiss friends, Veillon and DuBois.

There also is good copy in Ralston-Purina. The red-and-white checkerboard pattern of this manfacturer of breakfast cereals and animal feeds has become almost the symbol of rural America. There are not many towns in which a feed store or elevator does not display it boldly. Founded by William H. Danforth in 1894, it has been under the active direction of his son, Donald, since 1932. Despite a loss of two thirds of the company's business during the depression, he kept its mills open and even built a new one in 1933, two more in 1934, and still another in 1935. He brought sales from $19,000,000 a year to more than $400,000,000 a year. Ralston-Purina now has almost fifty plants in the United States, Canada, and Latin America. Its St. Louis buildings, put up over the years near the municipal bridge, have been harmoniously remodeled. Together with a handsome new office building, they now form Checkerboard Square, one of the city's most impressive industrial groupings.

Also worth the business writer's attention are the stories of the Rands, the Johnsons, the Wohls, the Robertses, and the other pioneers in the mass manufacture of shoes in St. Louis. They brought the city the world's two largest shoe makers, the International Shoe Company and the Brown Shoe Company. There also is the story of Morton D. May, whose grandfather founded the chain of May department stores now close to fifty in number and with annual sales of $700,000,000 or more. The parent store in St. Louis is the Famous-Barr Company. With its outlying branch stores it is the largest of the city's three big department stores, the other two being Stix, Baer and Fuller and Scruggs, Vandervoort and Barney. Then there is the Emerson Electric Company, which was making motors and fans when Stuart Symington became its president in 1937. War contracts started its expansion. Its efficiency so impressed the Truman investigating committee that at the war's end, when Harry Truman found himself in the White House faced with the problem of war surplus disposal—a scandal-breeder if not managed with intelligence and integrity—he called Symington from St. Louis to do the job. That led to other Washington assignments, including appointment as the first Air Secretary, and eventually to Symington's decision to seek elective rather than appointive office. His campaigning for the Senate, incidentally, showed that it is not necessary to start as a precinct doorbell pusher to master the art of getting votes.

A small company which began to pick up speed after the war is the Orchard Paper Company. Firms like this are evidence enough that St. Louis businessmen are not devoid of the adaptability and ingenuity demanded by new conditions. Fortunately, some of the most hopeful among them are St. Louis-born. It is, of course, standard operating procedure for all business men to help in community fund drives and the like, but for the home-town men this is less a matter of routine. They are less impersonal. They are likely to have a deep interest in some particular institution as, again for example, Morton May has in the City Art Museum. Their benefactions need not be exacted by hard-working committees.

Frankly, this civic spirit sometimes has seemed low compared with its manifestations in other cities. There are those who theorize about the age of the community and the inevitable decline in venturesomeness. Yet there are signs of a reawakening as St. Louis nears its bicentenary. Civic Progress, Inc., and Downtown, Inc., may yet put up dollars as readily as they put out publicity. The Chamber of Commerce wants to develop a 5000-acre industrial park on Columbia Bottoms, a tract north of the city limits at the confluence of the Missouri and the Mississippi which the city acquired under Mayor Kaufmann as the site of a second airport. Since it is no longer needed for this purpose, the Chamber was able to obtain an option on the land. Then an Eastern consulting firm was asked to study the possibilities of the project. It stapled together a report which said: Thumbs down! The chances of attracting industries are slim chiefly because St. Louis lacks "a climate of success." Time was when this might have been accepted with a grave nod of a tired head as excuse enough for letting well enough alone. But in 1959 this superficial verdict was indignantly repudiated. Yes, plans for access highways and the like still need to be worked out in greater detail, but here is land ideally suited for planned industrial development. So the Chamber has renewed its option for another three years. The Missourian's "Show me" may yet become "We'll show you!"

XXIX. Strike and Riot

As it gradually turned from trade to industry, St. Louis developed a labor movement as much interested in long-range reforms as in immediate gains. On the whole, the unions have been responsible and somewhat conservative, but there was one strike during which the rest of the country was told that the city had fallen into the hands of Red Communists. That was the national railroad strike of 1877. It began in Baltimore. It was most destructive of property in Pittsburgh. It was most uncontrolled in San Francisco where it turned into an anti-Chinese race riot. But it was most nearly successful—and most significant for the time—in St. Louis.

Here it became the first general strike in American history. It was conducted not only for the restoration of railroad wage cuts, but also for fair treatment of Negro workers, for an eight-hour-day law, and for the prohibition of child labor. The St. Louis strikers offered Mayor Henry Overstolz several hundred men to supplement the police and federal troops in maintaining order, but they nevertheless produced the scariest headline: "St. Louis Under Communist Domination." But there was no such panic in the St. Louis press, not even in the *Republican,* which was most bitterly opposed to the men and their demands.

"The right of revolution is inherent in all people," said the *Journal.* Of the outbreaks in the East, it said that the strikers were not to be condemned "if they prefer war to starvation." The *Star* accused the railroads of attempting "to starve their employees into submission." It said that by halting passenger service, with which the strikers had not interfered, the roads were "incommoding the public so as to produce a revolution of the sentiment which now seems to be in favor of the strikers." And the *Times* said that "the railroads must yield because they are in the wrong." Nor did Mayor Overstolz at first seem especially disturbed. The first German to hold the office, he was a rather easygoing politician and despite the depression which began in 1873, he was more concerned with the separation of the city from the county, and the creation of a new bicameral Municipal Assembly, both made possible by the new state constitution.

The men of the East St. Louis Relay Depot were the first to stop working. In 1876 the Ohio and Mississippi had promised not to lower wages, but the following July it joined the Pennsylvania and other roads in doing so. Pay of brakemen, for example, was reduced to $30 a month —enough to allow them 25 cents a meal and another 25 cents for lodging. This meant worse depression in Clabber Alley and the neighborhood of the East Side tracks. So a mass meeting was held in the switching yards on Sunday, July 22. An empty freight car was used as the speakers' stand. In the audience were several hundred members of the four St. Louis branches of the Workers' Party of the United States— the German, English, French, and Bohemian branches. They were bakers, cigar makers, brewery workers, coopers, and representatives of other trades, a labor federation in embryo. The party had about a thousand members in St. Louis. The German branch had just held a successful picnic in Lindell Grove to raise money for a daily newspaper. The W.P.U.S. felt strong, and it pledged its strength to the railway strikers. One after another, the employees of the Vandalia line, the St. Louis and Southeastern, the Missouri Pacific, the St. Louis, Kansas City and Northern, and the rest went to Traubel's Hall and voted to join the walkout. As they did so, enthusiasm for their cause mounted on the west side of the river, especially in industrial Carondelet.

James Harrison Wilson, a Civil War cavalry commander who had been named one of the two receivers of the bankrupt St. Louis and Southeastern in 1876, was most determined not to yield to the demand for the restoration of pay cuts. He had a special reason. He had helped to build the road and he knew that it was again in good condition. So, on July 19—only two days before the East St. Louis mass meeting—he had written to Jacob Schiff of New York's Kuhn, Loeb & Company, asking him to buy debentures with a par value of $20,000 for $7000. He enclosed a check for $2000 as margin, and agreed to pay 7 per cent interest on the balance. Wilson was not using any of his own money, but he was to get half the profits of the deal, and he did not want it upset. So on the day the strikers held their meeting he wrote to Carl Schurz in Washington, saying "I shall certainly not permit my employees to fix their own wages nor dictate to me in any manner what my policy shall be."

He followed this with several telegrams to the Secretary of the Interior, asking for federal troops in St. Louis. Schurz passed these wires on to the Secretary of War, and Brigadier General John Pope was ordered to send some men to the city from Fort Leavenworth. On Tuesday evening 300 infantrymen under Colonel Jefferson C. Davis arrived, but their commander at once announced that they were there "merely to protect government and public property, not to quell strikes or run the trains."

Wilson was not happy. He wired for more troops, but he did not get them. After all, the army had been sharply reduced in numbers, and there were not many soldiers available for a coast-to-coast strike, not to mention duty in the Indian country. So Wilson was among those who urged President Hayes to call for 100,000 volunteers. But while the Administration was setting a precedent for intervention in labor disputes, it had no intention of plunging into folly. As Robert V. Bruce records in *1877: Year of Violence*, John Sherman told the Cabinet he had been warned that a call for recruits would "set off a revolution."

Other St. Louis railroad operators were not as adamant as Wilson. On Monday, on the suggestion of Mayor Overstolz that it might be wise to cancel the wage cuts, the Missouri Pacific did so. On Tuesday the St. Louis, Kansas City and Northern followed this example. But in each case strikers came over from the East Side and prevented the resumption of freight service. Relatively leaderless as the national strike was, there was a determination to make the tie-up total. That seems as big a mistake as any the strikers made.

It did, however, indicate their power. On the East Side, Mayor Bowman with a dozen policemen hardly could have done much against them beyond issuing an order on Monday for the closing of saloons. Further, he had been a rebel in Austria and in France and, so, sympathized with the men. He swore in some strikers as special police, and then became virtually their representative in discussions with the railroad managements. There were 325 policemen in St. Louis, but they were responsible to the governor's police board rather than to Mayor Overstolz, a somewhat timid man in any case, and they were quite supine. In the city, the strike was almost entirely in the hands of the leaders of the Workers' Party—Henry Allen, who was a sign painter with ideas galore for the cures of the ills of the body and of the body politic; Peter Lofgreen, a young Dane whose name really was Gronlund, and Albert Currlin, a twenty-four-year-old spellbinder from Germany. These men were inspired by the writings of Marx. So they were communists of a sort, but hardly of the contemporary, international,

Moscow-directed variety. When Marx read of their strike, he wrote to Engels that it surely would be crushed.

The leaders set up headquarters in the Turner Hall. There it was agreed to extend the strike to other trades, and to demand an eight-hour law and also a law forbidding the employment of children under fourteen. In rather short order some thirty factories were closed. Strict admonitions against violence were issued. A big parade was organized, and mass meetings were held in Lucas Market. Illuminated by torchlights, these attracted crowds of from 5000 to 10,000 excited men. The speakers also were excited, proclaiming in the name of Abraham Lincoln who had freed 4,000,000 black slaves, that labor must unite to free 9,000,000 white slaves. Congress was called on to relieve unemployment by setting up a program of public works. Governor Phelps was urged to call a special session of the legislature to adopt reform measures. Between stirring selections by the Centennial Brass Band and a Negro fife and drum corps, Currlin told the crowds that the colored men also must be given a chance. A representative of the Negro roustabouts on the steamboats was called to the stand.

"We work for $20 a month," he said. "Will you stand to us, regardless of color?"

"We will," shouted the crowd. "We will!"

The Negroes paraded along the levee from boat to boat, winning higher wages on every one of them.

By Wednesday, the 25th, the railroad strike had stopped all trains on 50,000 of the country's 75,000 miles of track. But on that day the strike also began to collapse. In St. Louis some businessmen had become alarmed by the cry that "capitalism has turned liberty into slavery." They feared a Red revolution such as those which had swept France. They raised $18,000 to arm the militia and obtained 1500 rifles from the Arsenal. (In Louisville, Louis D. Brandeis, a vacationing Harvard law student who was to begin his practice in St. Louis before long, joined in a similar law-and-order movement.) The Workers' Party, no longer regarded as a desirable tenant, was evicted from the Turner Hall and moved its headquarters to Schuler's Hall above a slum saloon. The leaders disavowed some of the shutdowns on which their followers had insisted. They even sent 200 men to reopen Belcher's sugar refinery. They obtained permission from the mayor to arrest possible troublemakers. Obviously, they were becoming afraid of what they could not control—even though there had been no violence, and no damage beyond the breaking of a few windows. When another big crowd gathered at Lucas Market on Thursday night, there were no Workers' Party speakers on hand. Sensing the "failure of nerve," many in the crowd went on to Schuler's Hall. They stood in the street, shouting derision. Enthusiasm had turned into disillusionment. The ebb of the tide was as fast as in the Bay of Fundy.

Friday afternoon the crowd again gathered in front of Schuler's, but now as spectators rather than as participants in a demonstration. The militia companies had formed with fixed bayonets. The police had come to life. Businessmen were ready to march. It was time for the last act. The crowd pressed back against the buildings to clear the street as a shout went up:

"Here they come!"

The militiamen with their bayonets charged up to the third floor of Schuler's. Workers' Party members scrambled out of windows and across rooftops. Seventy were arrested. No shots were fired. Colonel Davis finally was persuaded to cross the river and take over the railroad yards from the strikers in the name of the United States Marshal. He reported to Washington: "Occupied this place early this morning with U.S. troops without the least opposition." The "revolution" had been crushed.

But it was far from a failure. The Reverend Henry Ward Beecher, the *Congregationalist,* the *Presbyterian Journal,* and the *Christian Union* might cite the strike as an example of "social Darwinism, "proving that the propertied are destined to lord it over those for whom a dollar a day is not enough to support five children, if the man insists on smoking and drinking beer." Said Beecher: "A family may live on good bread and water . . . The great laws of political economy cannot be set at defiance." Said the Congregationalist *Independent:* "If the club of the policeman, knocking out the brains of the rioter, will answer, then well and good; but if it does not promptly meet the exigency, then bullets and bayonets, canister and grape." The survival of the fittest. The Abolitionist battle hymn had left some of the reverend clergy with a strangely strong taste for blood. Little wonder that many a workingman stopped going to church.

Most St. Louis clergymen and their parishoners, even if they had not yet heard much of the social gospel, did not see matters that way. As the newspapers had earlier, they now acknowledged that the strikers had not been without a cause. Things would have to be bettered. As a practical matter, one railroad man said that "it is clear that one may lose more money by cutting wages than by raising them." The leaders of the Workers' Party had been haled into court, but they walked out again when the state pleaded nolle prosequi. The eight-hour day was achieved. It took a little longer to outlaw child labor. But the labor movement grew in strength and acceptance. Its leaders, like bankers, now are pillars of the community. They serve on all civic committees. After all, labor may contribute both votes and money. Newspapermen go to Teamster cocktail parties. Oscar Earhardt, chairman of the AFL-CIO joint council, is regularly elected to the Board of Education. Some labor politicians even dream of a labor mayor in City Hall. But a dark chapter intervened between the crushing of the "revolution" of 1877 and present prospects.

The grievances of workingmen set off the East St. Louis race riots of 1919. Anti-Negro prejudice, of course, was more widespread. Suburbanites who contribute to the Urban League and deplore segregation in the schools somehow keep their swimming pools and country clubs "for whites only." And some of them still take a dim view of merger with the city, if the truth were told, because they hope to avoid social adjustments, not to mention taxes for welfare services. But the men who work in stockyards and steel mills live with what others only talk about. On the whole, they do so with grace and good will. But this was achieved with more difficulty on one side of the river than on the other. By and large, St. Louis has accepted its Negro citizens with genuine respect for their rights. The big subsidized housing projects are evidence of this, but the test of the 1919 riots showed it more dramatically. In the four days from June 30 through July 2, according to the St. Clair County, Illinois, grand jury, more than 100 persons were killed and 245 houses were burned on the East Side. During those days, the St. Louis police were on the bridges, protecting refugees and keeping rioters at a distance.

Negroes streamed across the bridges. More than 1000 of them found emergency accommodations in the old Municipal Lodging House on Twelfth Street. Mayor Aloe and Public Welfare Superintendent John Schmoll provided food and other necessities, while the Red Cross and other relief organizations mobilized their resources. The Negroes found the haven they expected, and it is not surprising that many never returned to the East Side to live. The Charlotte, North Carolina, *Observer* said of the two cities:

"Ordinarily it may be proper to treat one as the suburb of the other, but in the case of the riots . . . the two communities must be considered as widely apart—wider than the Mississippi which separates them."

Instead of becoming infected by the overflowing blood lust, St. Louis was appalled and indignant. Read Carlos Hurd* in the St. Louis *Post-Dispatch:*

For an hour and a half last evening I saw the massacre of helpless Negroes at Broadway and Fourth Street in downtown East St. Louis where a black skin was a death warrant.

I have read of St. Bartholomew's night. I have heard of the latter-day crimes of the Turks in Armenia, and I have learned to loathe the German army for its barbarity in Belgium. But I do not believe that Moslem fanaticism or Prussian frightfulness could perpetrate murders of more deliberate brutality than those which I saw committed in daylight by citizens of the state of Abraham Lincoln.

I saw man after man, with his hands raised pleading for his life, surrounded by groups of men—men who had never seen him before and who knew nothing about him except that he was black—and saw them administer the historic sentence of intolerance, death by stoning. I saw one of these men, almost dead from a savage shower of stones, hanged with a clothes line, and when it broke, hanged with a rope which held. Within a few paces from the telephone pole from which he was suspended, four other Negroes lay dead or dying, another having been removed, dead, a

* Incidentally, it was Hurd who seven years earlier had given the world the first detailed story of the sinking of the *Titanic*. He was aboard the *Carpathia*, bound for Europe, when the ship picked up the *Titanic*'s SOS and changed course to go to the aid of the big liner, which had struck an iceberg on its maiden voyage. The *Carpathia* picked up most of the survivors and turned back to New York. Hurd had time enough for interviews and to write his story, since there was no thought in 1912 of transmitting a long news story by wireless. He did, however, persuade the *Carpathia*'s captain to send a brief message to his paper. So a fast tug was sent out to meet the *Carpathia*. Hurd tossed his story, well wrapped in oilskins, from the ship to the tug's deck. It was on the street—in the Pulitzer New York *World* as well as in the *Post-Dispatch*—before he came down the gangplank.

The East St. Louis riots were covered in greater detail by a younger *Post-Dispatch* reporter, Paul Y. Anderson, then assigned to the East Side beat. Both in news stories and in lengthy testimony before a congressional investigating committee, by which he was highly praised, Anderson told the full story of the shocking corruption which was one of the root causes of the outbreak. Anderson's life was threatened repeatedly. Every possible obstruction was used to keep him from getting this knowledge. The revelations proved to be the first of his exposés, which included, after his transfer to his paper's Washington bureau, the unearthing of the Teapot Dome oil scandal of the Harding administration.

Among other newspapermen who distinguished themselves during the riots was Russell Froelich of the St. Louis *Globe-Democrat*. He was arrested by the East St. Louis police, but could not be intimidated.

short time before. I saw the pockets of these Negroes searched without the finding of any weapons. . . .

I saw Negro women begging for mercy and pleading that they had harmed no one, set upon by white women of the baser sort who laughed and answered the coarse sallies of the men as they beat the Negresses' faces and breasts with stones and sticks. I saw one of these furies fling herself at a militiaman who was trying to protect a Negress and wrestle with him for his bayonetted gun while other women attacked the refugee. . . .

It was not my idea of a mob. . . . The East St. Louis affair, as I saw it, was a man hunt, conducted on a sporting basis, though with anything but the fair play which is a principle of sport. The East St. Louis men took no chances, except the chances from stray shots. . . . They went in small groups. There was little leadership, and there was a horribly cool deliberateness and a spirit of fun about it. I cannot allow even the doubtful excuse of drink. No man whom I saw showed the effect of liquor. It was no crowd of hot-headed youths. Young men were in the greater number, but there were the middle-aged, no less active in destroying the life of every discoverable black man. . . . There were others who protested against the senseless slaughter. I would be ashamed of myself if I could not say that I forgot my place as a professional observer and joined in such protests. But I do not think that any verbal objection had the slightest effect. Only a volley of lead would have stopped these murderers.

" 'Get a nigger' was the slogan, and it was varied by the recurrent cry, 'Get another!' "

Policemen and Illinois National Guardsmen joined in the killing. Soldiers and policemen drove two Negroes out of a shed and shot them down. Fleeing Negroes were stopped by militia bayonets and forced back into the hands of the pursuing murderers. Some of the mob were arrested, but they were allowed to leave police headquarters by the back door as fast as they had been brought through the front door. Most of the police and militiamen were at best apathetic spectators.

Mayor Fred Mollman and other city officials did nothing while Negroes were killed on the City Hall lawn. Ambulances were turned back. Women and children were forced back into burning buildings. Bodies, some still half alive, were dumped into Cahokia Creek. Several Negro women actually were scalped. Interurban cars were stopped, their Negro passengers pulled off and slaughtered in the street.

Mrs. Lena Cook of St. Louis later told how her husband and her son were killed. The family was returning by streetcar from Eagle

Park when the car was stopped at one of the principal street intersections of downtown East St. Louis.

"All you white people get off that car," a man shouted. "We want to kill the niggers."

While her dress was being torn off, Mrs. Cook saw her husband killed in the street. The mob also seized her boy. (She later found him dead in an ambulance.) Pulled by her hair through a broken car window, she somehow managed to crawl into a store with the ruffians in pursuit.

"Leave that woman alone," the white storekeeper commanded. Mrs. Cook said "he took several cracks from clubs meant for me." But he did drive off her assailants—or perhaps in their cowardice they took after easier prey. Or they may have joined those who were smashing the windows of a pawnshop to arm themselves with pistols and revolvers.

Passions eventually spent themselves. Fires guttered out. The blood in the streets dried and then was washed away. But what had started the carnage?

An investigating committee appointed by Governor Frank O. Lowden of Illinois had trouble in finding causes. Not so the press, the St. Clair County grand jury, and the congressional committee under Representative Ben Johnson of Kentucky. Even one of the East St. Louis political overlords, Thomas Canavan, said:

"The prime cause of the trouble was the avarice of the manufacturers. They wanted to get rid of the white workers because they could not handle them. Negroes came in by hundreds, and there were many bad Negroes among them."

Canavan, of course, was trying to pass the buck, trying to cover up for the political machine of which he was a part, but he told some of the truth. Despite the war boom, or because of it, the absentee-owned East St. Louis industries were having labor trouble. Perhaps they invited it, since their pay for white common labor was 17 to 20 cents an hour, while in nearby Belleville it ranged from 30 to 35 cents an hour. Some of the employers also believed in a rapid turnover. As a result, many men kicked back 20 or 30 cents of a day's pay to their bosses for the privilege of working the next day. Union organizers did not have an easy time in East St. Louis, but there were strikes. A nasty one was long in progress at the Aluminum Ore Company. The firm had armed its guards. E. M. Sorrels of the East St. Louis Chamber of Commerce was in the employ of the company. As an officer of the

"East St. Louis Rifle Club" he borrowed 30 rifles and 10,000 rounds of ammunition from the government for the promotion of marksmanship. He turned over the rifles and the bullets to the company. There also was a threat of a streetcar strike. National Guards were housed in the carbarn. (Their commander refused to act when the rioting started, saying that he was charged only with the defense of property.) The unions were anticipating trouble and had appealed to Samuel Insull, chairman of the Illinois Council of Defense.

Labor unrest certainly was aggravated by the importation of Negro workers, recruited in the South especially by agents of the railroads. They were offered free transportation and promised as much as $4 a day. Most of them never were paid more than $2. Of course they were not told of the shortage of housing and sanitary facilities, nor of the gouging landlords and loan sharks many of them would encounter. So hundreds of them arrived in the railroad yards every morning to go to work in the big slaughterhouses or to spend twelve hours a day— from 7 A.M. to 7 P.M.—in front of the blast furnaces.

In the evening many of them wandered across Whisky Chute—St. Clair Avenue—which separates East St. Louis from National City, the town incorporated to keep the packers off the East St. Louis tax books. So they came into the notorious "Valley"—now wiped out—where flourished such institutions as "Aunt Kate's Honky-Tonk, Something Doing Every Minute." Few communities ever flaunted vice as brazenly as East St. Louis with its Commercial Hotel, the European, and the Star. The place was full of low saloons, barrel houses, and gambling joints. Since money did not last long in these dives, Negroes seeking night life were likely to wander to the "wine rooms" of nearby Brooklyn, Illinois—especially to one operated by the chief of police, Tony Speed. But about the best they or anybody else got was "twelve-block whisky." A barrel house proprietor explained the name to Congressman Johnson:

"You take a drink, walk twelve blocks, and fall flat on your face."

But who cared? Most East St. Louis workers, white or black, figured they were "two weeks ahead of the poorhouse." Yet the Negroes also were full of their particular joy of living. Groups would congregate near the Broadway viaduct. There old river roustabouts told tall tales for the edification of those newly arrived from the cotton fields. And these in turn sang plantation songs to the tune of a banjo. Always there were jokes and laughter.

The viciousness of East St. Louis was directly traceable to political corruption. Decent taxpayers, in despair, accepted this as inevitable. The city was largely in the hands of Locke Tarlton, his partners, and his stooges. Mayor Mollman was a stooge. Tom Canavan, the commissioner of public works, was a partner. Tarlton himself held the juicy chairmanship of the East St. Louis Levee Board. The three had offices in the notorious New Commercial Hotel in sight of City Hall. Naturally, they "passed things around." Dr. R. X. McCracken, the health commissioner, for example, owned a "house" in the "Valley," and he sold a 27-acre strip of land to the Levee Board for $21,600 after having bought it three months earlier for $5000. The Union Trust and Savings Bank paid no interest on public deposits, but the city borrowed money from the bank at 5 per cent. Former Mayor Henry F. Bader told how the Illinois State Bank raised a slush fund for Tarlton's election to the Levee Board. The East St. Louis *Journal* supported him as an able man, which, no doubt, he was. He got along very nicely with the St. Clair County State's Attorney, Hubert E. Schaumleffel, a Republican. Bipartisanship, it's wonderful! What if Schaumleffel was seen drunk in the streets? He had defended former City Treasurer Fred Gerold after the *Post-Dispatch* had exposed him as an embezzler, hadn't he? And when Father Christopher Goelz of St. Philip's Church had complained about the cockfights and other goings on in town, Schaumleffel had told him that "Illinois laws are too narrow-minded," hadn't he?

As a matter of fact, Father Goelz and the Reverend Mr. Alison were about the only consistent complainers in town—and the "boys" almost succeeded in framing Mr. Alison as a thief. There *was* the Committee of One Hundred; its members were Chamber of Commerce types who talked about reform. But they disbanded shortly after the riots. Their chairman told the congressional investigators that they really were not likely to accomplish very much. And Dan McGlynn, one of the Hundred, undertook the defense of three policemen accused of race killings. They were old friends, he explained. The corporations embarked on no crusades. Although the National City packers paid no taxes to East St. Louis, the city maintained one of its best fire companies near Whisky Chute at a cost of $10,000 a year, and it answered all National City alarms. City Treasurer S. J. Cashel had sharply reduced the tax bills of the Aluminum Ore Company, the Missouri Malleable Iron Company, the Eads Bridge, and the Wiggins Ferry Company, which owned virtually all of the East St. Louis riverfront.

Even the Negro "big shots" of the "Valley" turned out the vote for

City Hall. That is why they went unmolested. Negro bondsmen had no trouble in obtaining the release of pickpockets, thieves, and other unsavory clients of their race. Justice in East St. Louis at best was a so-so thing. (Paul Y. Anderson's reporting eventually brought about the impeachment of a federal judge.) The two busiest magistrate's courts in the city were on the second floor of a building across from City Hall. There hangers-on were impaneled as jurymen, or even called as witnesses. After rendering the services asked of them, they were taken to a saloon on the first floor and "irrigated." The saloon went by the name of The Court Bar.

East St. Louis was a simmering, rancid stew. The labor troubles generated enough heat for the mess to boil over. On June 25 at City Hall a mass meeting of Aluminum Ore workers was held. These men, according to the grand jury, in losing their strike had become aware of how they were disadvantaged by the importation of more than 8000 Negro workers. Some 1200 strong, they called on Mayor Mollman to stop this. The mayor, who himself had recruited Negroes in the South, promised to do what he could. There was inflammatory language. Alexander Flemming, described at the time as "a lawyer of some ability and no character," stopped just short of incitement to riot. He said that mob violence rarely was punished. The first trouble came within an hour of the report that two white men had been attacked by Negroes, and that the Negroes were talking of a Fourth of July massacre. According to the grand jury, this encountered only "the supine tolerance of indolent public officials overawed by cowardly inclinations."

Shortly after midnight on July 2, two policemen were shot by a group of Negroes, allegedly called into action by the sounding of a church bell. That night, whites in two cars had shot up a Negro neighborhood. The fire had been returned. The cars, full of bullet holes, were parked in front of the Commercial. The police asked no questions. After a meeting at the Labor Temple that morning, what had been at worst desultory fighting turned into a blood bath; what had started as a protest of workingmen called out the most vicious in the community.

About the only good thing that can be said about the riots is that the state authorities, notably Attorney General Brundage, moved with an energy utterly lacking in local officialdom. Brundage appointed deputy prosecutors who virtually superseded Schaumleffel. In less than six months the St. Clair County grand jury, sitting in Belleville, indicted more than 100 persons, black and white. In that time seventeen men were sent to the penitentiary in Chester, ten were jailed elsewhere, eleven were fined, and four were acquitted. The wheels of the law, for once, were spinning fast. It was made clear that white men are punished for killing black men. East St. Louis was about as well cleaned up as is possible where so much invites corruption. But the community's disgrace did bring an increase of tolerance. Knowing what did happen, there is caution lest it happen again.

xxx. Conversation Piece

Portland Place is the best address in the St. Louis society columns. It is one of a dozen or so private streets in the West End. Being closed to through traffic by heavy gates and chains, these streets do block speedy access to the suburbs, but their privacy, enhanced by stately trees and lawns, has been a strong defense against the blight which ordinarily spreads in the carbon-monoxide wake of the flight to suburbia. They have kept much of the West End as handsome a residential area as it was when it was developed more than a half a century ago—and only fifteen minutes from downtown. They are lined with the "palaces" Americans built when they were ready to show that they had culture as well as money. Here, side by side, are Tudor manor houses, Romanesque and baroque palazzos, down-scaled châteaux, up-scaled Swiss chalets, a miniature Gare d'Orsay, and less readily identifiable examples of architectural elegance. "Sedate" is not the word for them. Yet they are not nearly the incongruities they might be. Interiors have the marble floors, paneled walls, and crystal chandeliers more common before wars made the income tax groaning-heavy, but this aggressive elegance has mellowed.

Dr. Isaac D. Kelley, a nose-and-throat specialist, and his wife were reading comfortably beside the fireplace in the library of 32 Portland Place on the wet and stormy night of April 20, 1931. That was to become the most harrowing night in Dr. Kelley's life, the beginning of the most exciting of all St. Louis gangster-era scandals, the Nellie Muench case.

Dr. Kelley's telephone rang an hour or so after dinner. A man gave his name as Holmes and reported a child with a severe earache. He explained that he had just moved from Chicago to a Clayton subdivision called Davis Place. Dr. Ballinger of Chicago, he said, had told him to call Dr. Kelley in case of need. Dr. Kelley asked a few questions and instructed the man to call back. In another hour or so he did. Dr. Kelley put down the phone and told his wife he would have to make a night call. He put on his coat and drove off into the rain. As he stopped in Davis Place, another car pulled up. Two men stepped out and approached him. One of them displayed a pistol and ordered him to get into the other automobile. The doctor had been kidnaped.

In St. Louis, as elsewhere, Prohibition had ripened an unsavory crop of gangsters. There were Egan's Rats, the Cuckoos, the Hogans, the Russo gang, and lesser vermin. On the East Side the Bergers and the Sheltons fought for supremacy. Madison and St. Clair counties became notorious for their bootleggers, gamblers, and racketeers. Even today their taverns do not cater to Ladies' Aid fish fries. The story of hoodlumism in St. Louis is essentially what it is in other American cities. Young toughs, now called juvenile delinquents, coalesced in bands such as the old Bottoms Gang, which held sway in the vicinity of Washington and Jefferson avenues. Armed robbery became their line of work, and it involved callow killings. The old Lucas Avenue red-light district offered easy pickings.* Vigorous police officers, such as Captain Patrick Kirk, had relatively little trouble in rounding up these criminals. Prohibition brought "alky cooking," bootlegging, and hijacking, a rich field for the toughs. The public became acquainted with the names of more sinister gangs. The Italians of the Hill became involved. Factions developed. Gang wars broke out. Professional killers such as Monroe (Blackie) Armes of Herrin, Illinois, found careers. Armes was brought to East St. Louis by Carl and Bernie Shelton. He had so steady a hand on a Tommy gun even in a moving automobile that the close grouping of the bullet holes in a victim became for the police a trade-mark of his jobs.

Armes and his employers, the Sheltons, got their start in Herrin, in

---

* A century ago a rural legislature—either unusually naïve, or not unmindful that country lawgivers visit the urban fleshpots now and then—authorized St. Louis to control what are chastely, if not quite correctly, called houses of ill fame. So the municipal Assembly, with due deference to the pure and the Puritans, passed the Social Evil Ordinance, which simply introduced the European system of licensed prostitution. By and by, the reverend clergy called on the legislators, and the statute on behalf of the offending was repealed. It had much to do, however, with the origins of the legend of sinful delights in St. Louis and the alleged custom under which fathers introduced their sons to sex without so much as a single chat about birds, bees, or flowers, and without bringing home a copy of *What Every Young Man Should Know*. It is regrettable that the lately eminent Professor Dr. Kinsey of the state university in Bloomington was not on hand to avail himself of these splendidly furnished laboratories for the satisfaction of his scientific curiosity. No doubt he would have recorded for posterity the truth about the amenities in the era before the drugstore circulation of double-breasted paperbacks. Historians would have preferred the service of science to that of tradition, which, after all, may be stale gossip.

"bloody Williamson" County in the Klan and anti-Klan warfare of the early twenties. As Ted Link has pointed out, Tombstone, Arizona, was tame compared to Herrin. Half a dozen dead was about the average toll of a Herrin shooting affray in the days when S. Glenn Young walked the streets in semimilitary attire, carrying a pair of .45s, a pair of .48s, and a machine gun or rifle. Of course he did not live to a ripe old age. Shooting in Herrin was more or less for fun—or for hate. In St. Clair County and East St. Louis it was for profit. So the Sheltons fought a bitter war against the Bergers for dominance on the East Side, and won—for as long as they lived.

The dog-race track at Hanley Road and Olive Street Road in the County was a magnet for the toughs. They naturally dominated the "speaks" and "beer flats." Their business instincts were good enough to keep them from bothering the customers most of the time. The end of Prohibition meant that they had to find new activities. The infiltration of labor unions, especially in the building trades, began. Honest men like Oliver Moore of the East St. Louis Central Trades and Labor Union did not surrender, and died for their courage. Both sides of the street were worked. Industries hostile to unions hired gunmen guards. The Phillips Petroleum Company, building a $15,000,000 pipeline and terminal in 1932, employed Carl Shelton, who "had the softest tongue and the bloodiest hands of any gangster who ever operated on the East Side," to protect non-union workers. When Moore refused to "sell out" for $30,000, he was machine-gunned in front of his office. Said Carl R. Baldwin:

Officials of the oil-refining company, shocked at the death of Moore, came forward the next day and expressed their deepest regrets. The lesson of the Ollie Moore case is one all legitimate businessmen should have learned by now. It is: You cannot do business with a professional gangster without sharing his reputation. If he has blood on his hands some of it may come off on you. Yet men still go to the local rackets boss when they want a favor.

The contemporary racketeers—for example, Buster Wortman, successor to the Sheltons—is a smoother operator. There is no indiscriminate gunplay, perhaps because almost all of the gunmen fell as victims of gunmen. But while they were still developing new fields instead of inhibitions, the St. Louis gangsters took to kidnaping, which is, after all, one of the most ancient devices for levying tribute.

The abduction of Dr. Kelley was the gangsters' biggest coup, just as the attempted kidnaping of Oscar Johnson, a wealthy shoe manufacturer and for years the "angel" of the St. Louis Symphony, was their most daring failure.

The hoodlums had some respect for the St. Louis police and prosecutors. These might not have been too zealous in depriving people of a drink, but it would have been foolhardy to arouse them by unpopular lawbreaking. It was easier to "beat the rap" in the County. At least that's the way the criminals figured it. That is why Dr. Kelley was lured beyond the city limits. And that is why he was taken first to a farm in St. Charles County on which the bootleggers had for some years operated a sizable "moonshine" distillery. Then he was taken across the Mississippi, first to one hide-out, then another. In all, he was held for eight days. Obscene threats of mutilation were made. His guards turned their machine guns—"typewriters" and "choppers," they called them—on him, and warned him never to "open his trap." Yet it had been easier for them to make their "snatch" than to cash in on it. Finally one of Dr. Kelley's guards told the doctor that he was going to be turned over to "the only man in St. Louis who has done anything to help you, John Rogers of the *Post-Dispatch*." Rogers was the paper's ace crime reporter. More than once he had solved a case which baffled police. The underworld had a perverse respect for him. So Dr. Kelley was hustled into a car and dropped beside a lonely Illinois road. Soon thereafter another automobile pulled up, and the driver got out:

"Mr. Rogers?"

"Dr. Kelley?"

"Thank God!"

Rogers had received a phone call in the middle of the night, directing him to go to Grand and Finney avenues. There he saw a man whom he recognized and whom he believed. He was told where he could find Dr. Kelley. But O. K. Bovard, managing editor of the paper, and Ben Reese, its city editor, were not content to have one of their reporters serve merely as a blind agent in the return of an abducted citizen. They wanted a full story of the Kelley kidnaping. They had to work and wait from April 28, 1931, until February 7, 1934, to publish that story. But it was a bigger sensation than the abduction.

Adolph Fiedler was an enormous and unsavory character—he weighed more than 400 pounds—who ran a gangsters' hangout in the County. Reporters dropped into the place from time to time to learn what they could learn. When Fiedler offered the *Post-Dispatch* the Kelley story, Bovard and Reese were willing to listen, and to believe and to pay, after it had been checked by reporters. The story was developed by the paper and St. Louis County Prosecutor C. Arthur Anderson, who had been informed about it at once. It brought about the indictment of Felix McDonald, who was serving ten years for the attempted kidnaping of Johnson, Bart Davit, who had been acquitted in that case, Angelo Rosegrant, a shoe salesman with shady connections, Tommy Wilders, a Shelton gangster hiding in Florida, and John C. Johnson, the Negro tenant of the St. Charles County farm. Anderson also charged that the Kelley abduction had been master-minded by Nellie Tipton Muench, wife of Dr. Ludwig O. Muench, daughter of the Reverend William Tipton and sister of Judge Ernest Tipton of the Missouri Supreme Court.

(Three other men were implicated, but they had been killed in gangster fashion on the East Side April 15, 1932. They were "Pretty Boy" Lechler, "Willie Gee" Wilbert, and Tommy Hayes, a gang leader. Johnson, who turned state's evidence, was machine-gunned while in the protective custody of a deputy sheriff.)

Mrs. Muench and her husband were well known in the West End, especially in musical circles. The doctor played the violoncello and she played the piano. When entertaining, they often invited members of the Symphony to play with them. Mrs. Muench, a vivacious redhead, had been proprietor of the Mitzi Shop, one of the city's most expensive women's dress shops, a bower of floor-to-ceiling mirrors and gilt furniture, with unusually pretty models. Customers did not ask about prices —especially if they were men. Nellie Muench's shop had gone bankrupt in 1928 with a loss of $77,000 to the creditors. She paid off 15½ cents on the dollar. A rather fascinating description of her business was included in a book which appeared under her name about a year later:

To the sheltered and protected wives and daughters of the so-called socially and semi-socially prominent, I wonder if the idea ever occurs to them of some of the Bacchanalian orgies that take place behind closed doors in well protected spots in the city. . . . This type of man is in the minority, but he exists in the flesh. The Moody and Sankey type in the home and the *bon vivant* with a flare for wine, women and song when the desire or passion prompts him to raise hell. My shop, which was located at 392–394 North Euclid Avenue, was in close proximity and within plain view of several of the fashionable establishments of ill repute. It was a continual source of amusement both to myself and my employes to recognize some of the socially and semi-socially prominent faces coming and going. The "Mesdames" and the subjects who held themselves on call were patrons of my shop, as were many of the wives and daughters of their customers. . . .

Nellie Muench had had a litigious career. She was not unknown to the police. In 1919 she had been questioned about the disappearance of jewels from a hotel room. In 1925 Mrs. Muench herself was robbed of $12,200 in jewels. She was involved in a number of cases before justices of the peace. The proprietor of a rival shop once accused her of stealing several hundred dollars' worth of dresses. Mrs. Muench vainly sought to collect $17,000 from the estate of a businessman for finery which she said he had purchased before he died. She had been involved in a nasty dispute with Edward W. Foristel, a Republican politician, whom she accused of extorting forty-six per cent interest on a loan to her. All this she had winked away. But these affairs now popped out of newspaper morgues almost automatically. No doubt that is why her book—to which the printer would not put his name— is such an outburst against the press:

The great State of Missouri in 1932 conferred upon the Honorable Ernest M. Tipton, my brother, its highest honor by electing him to the Supreme Bench for ten years. Because of my brother's affiliation with Mr. Tom Pendergast of Kansas City, the *Post-Dispatch* did not relish the change of political complexion taking place in our Supreme Court. . . . Candidates selected by the Pendergast organization are pretty apt to be found lined up against monopoly and greed. The newspapers have incessantly carried on a warfare against this Democratic faction under a banner of "anti-bossism." By dragging me into this criminal plot, the name "Tipton" would also serve to seriously embarrass Judge Tipton.

But this is getting ahead of the story.

When Mrs. Muench was named in the Kelley kidnaping case, no fewer than thirteen lawyers undertook to defend her. A change of venue was obtained to Mexico, Missouri, not too far from Columbia, where her father had his church; where she and her husband had gone, respectively, to Stephens College and the University of Missouri, and where, in 1912, they were married. This is the Missouri bluegrass country, famous for its show horses, an area in which the Tipton name carried political weight. Yet confidence ebbed a bit when Angelo Rosegrant was convicted in October and sentenced to twenty years. And in January of 1935 Felix McDonald was convicted and sentenced to sixty years.

The defense tactics of a baker's dozen of lawyers might be enhanced if Mrs. Muench were to come into court as a mother, cradling in her arms a baby only a few weeks old. Or so she thought. Mrs. Muench was in her forties. She had been married for twenty-two years, and she still was childless. Yet on August 18 the Muenches announced the birth of a son.

The newspapers were skeptical about the "blessed event." Prosecutor Anderson also was skeptical. The sensations of the Kelley kidnaping and of Mrs. Muench's indictment were capped by a *Post-Dispatch* story that the "Muench baby" actually was born to Anna Ware, an unwed Philadelphia servant girl, in St. Louis a few hours before the Muench announcement. On September 18, 1935, the newspaper reported the discovery that a newborn baby, Arnold Frank Price, Jr., had been transferred from City Hospital to the Muench home on July 11. The child was seriously sick, so it was taken to Jewish Hospital, where it died on July 16. It, too, had been the child of an unwed mother, Estelle Oberg, a waitress in a Minneapolis night club. After this child's death, the Ware baby was substituted for it. The *Post-Dispatch* also reported that Dr. Marsh Pitzman, a socially prominent physician who shared an office with Dr. Muench, had been persuaded to open his purse to Mrs. Muench after being told that he was the father of her child.

Chagrined by this scoop, the *Star-Times* found Anna Ware and began publishing her story in serial form. She had been employed in a Philadelphia suburb by Mrs. Francis Giordan, a daughter of Mrs. Rebecca Winner of St. Louis. She admitted an affair with Mrs. Giordan's husband. When she became pregnant, Mrs. Giordan persuaded her to go to St. Louis to have her baby, telling her that it would be adopted by Giordan's aunt. She was met in the Union Station by Wilfred Jones, a lawyer, who took her to Winner home, where the child was born. Against the background of these stories, on October 3, 1935, Nellie Muench went to trial.

She was among friends in Mexico. Sheriff E. S. Haycraft treated her as an honored guest. He put only the names of his personal friends on the jury list. Supreme Court Justice Tipton sat beside his sister.

(She had brought the disputed baby to Mexico, but she did not bring it into the courtroom.) Her defense staff was an obvious reflection of Judge Tipton's influence. It was headed by Clay County Rogers of Kansas City, but the tone was set largely by Pross Cross of Lathrop, Missouri, a rather flamboyant character who reminded the jury that he was "just a country lawyer from a little town known only for its mules." He worked hard to create the impression that this was a case of the wicked city, its liquor-drinking rich, and its sensation-mongering press against the simple daughter of a simple rural community. Nellie Muench may not have helped him with her smart black costumes, her modish hats, her silver fox, and her mink. But then, she felt that the case was "in the bag."

Prosecutor Anderson put Fiedler on the stand to testify that Mrs. Muench had selected Dr. Kelley as the kidnapers' victim. She had learned, according to the witness, that Dr. Kelley, his wife, and some friends were to celebrate a birthday at the Coronado Hotel April 4, 1931. She had taken Rosegrant there, and they had danced by the Kelley table repeatedly so that she could point out the doctor to her accomplice. She had given the hoodlums the name of Dr. Ballinger of Chicago so that they could induce Dr. Kelley to respond to the false call in the night. Fiedler also said that she was known among her disreputable associates as "Goldie." Dr. Kelley on the stand testified that he had recognized Rosegrant and that he had heard his abductors talk of a "Goldie," but that he had not seen this woman.

Since the defense called no character witnesses, the prosecution was unable to introduce a mass of police evidence about the picaresque incidents in Nellie Muench's career. Defense objections saved her under cross-examination from answering questions about the presence of a child in the Muench house, so Anderson and Wolfe could not bring in the story of the baby hoax.

Mrs. Muench denied that she had ever seen Fiedler before he entered the courtroom. She denied that she had ever known McDonald or Davit. She said she had only seen Rosegrant once—and very briefly—when he paid Dr. Muench's bill for the treatment of his daughter. Asked where she was the night of April 4, 1931, she replied:

"I couldn't tell you, Mr. Wolfe."

"Do you know where Dr. Kelley was that night?"

"No." She spoke with a flicker of a smile.

That was about it. The trial ended on October 5, in its third day.

It did not take the jurors long to return their verdict: not guilty. Mrs. Muench embraced her chief counsel, and she kissed Sheriff Haycroft.

"You're a dear," she said to him. "You told me the truth."

"Didn't I though?"

The acquittal, however, was only the beginning of a sequence of court appearances for Nellie Muench. The exoneration was clouded by a habeas corpus petition filed by Anna Ware for the return of her baby. Hearings were started on October 15 before three judges of the St. Louis Court of Appeals, Judge William Dee Becker presiding. The outcome was foreshadowed October 29 when the Missouri Supreme Court, in a session from which Judge Tipton had excused himself, refused the Muench request to stop the proceedings, and even more clearly the next day when Judge Becker ordered her to bring the child into court.

The picture which was to have touched the jurors' hearts—Nellie Muench with a blanket-swathed baby in her arms—now produced a different effect. The spectators, mostly women, booed Mrs. Muench. After Anna Ware identified the baby as her missing child, Judge Becker announced that it would remain in custody of the court until the issue was decided. He sent it to the St. Louis Children's Hospital. When she heard this order, Nellie Muench lost control of her emotions.

"Nero," she screamed at Judge Becker. "You mean old brute!"

She pounded the table and had to be led from the room by force, shrieking and struggling. As testimony was to show, Mrs. Muench had apparently developed a genuine affection for the child. Helen Berroyer, her friend and also a respondent in the case, testified that Nellie Muench was "just crazy" about the baby. And Willa Mary Cobb, the loyal Negro maid, said that Mrs. Muench lovingly called the baby "Pudgy," and "little hog on a log," and "little fat pig on a lard bucket." The baby was swathed in finery.

The Solomon in this case was Rush H. Limbaugh of Cape Girardeau, Missouri, the special commissioner named to hear the evidence. Between October 15 and November 5 he heard eighty-six witnesses. Wilfred Jones, the baby broker, swore that he had obtained the Price and the Ware babies not for the Muenches but for "clients" in Memphis. Helen Berroyer, identified as the "nurse" who had helped Jones get the baby, swore that she was in the Muench house when the infant was born. Medical men cast doubt on Mrs. Muench's assertion that she was the mother of a premature baby. The star witness, however, was Anna Ware, the heroine of the spectators.

Anna, nineteen years old, hazel-eyed and full-lipped, told the court she was one of a family of two boys and three girls. She lived in Philadelphia with her mother and stepfather until she was fifteen. She left home because her parents no longer could keep her. In the fall of 1932 she got the job at the Giordans, through her mother. She was seventeen, she said, when the affair with Giordan began.

Her first suspicions were aroused in St. Louis when Jones took her for an automobile ride with a woman whom he introduced as "Mrs. Perkins." He told her of a baby he had obtained for "Mrs. Perkins." Unfortunately, the child died, and Anna's baby was wanted as a substitute. The woman was incapable of having a baby, Jones said, but she needed one "to come into some money." Asked whether she could identify this woman, Anna pointed to Mrs. Muench.

Her child was born at 5:45 A.M., August 17, in Mrs. Winner's home, without anesthesia. Anna said she asked Jones if she could keep her child if she raised the money spent in connection with its birth. His answer was: "No, not now."

The child was brought to her at 10 P.M. An hour or so later she heard the voices of Jones and a woman who was described as a nurse. They had come, Jones explained, to take the child to a Jewish hospital. She asked if she could see the child at the hospital and again the answer was: "No, not now."

"Why did you give it up?"

"I had to. What else was there for me to do? I had no money . . . to feed and clothe a child." Money was not easy to get in the summer of 1932.

"Isn't it a fact that you didn't want your baby, but only wanted to provide newspaper stories?"

"I didn't know anything about stories. I'd just as lief nothing was printed in the papers."

The *Star-Times* reporters had convinced her that her baby was the one in the Muench house. They had promised to help her get it back, if they could. That was her story. She stuck to it while the stories told by Helen Berroyer, Jones, and other Muench witnesses jibed less and less. Commissioner Limbaugh took a month to write his report—from November 5 to December 5. He concluded that Nellie Muench had obtained the Ware baby to influence the jurors in her trial in Mexico, and perhaps for "some other ulterior purposes." The Court of Appeals accepted the report. Marshal Joseph E. McDermott was instructed to go to Children's Hospital and to deliver the baby, now four months old, to its mother. This he did on December 19. And Anna Ware went —she would not say where—to celebrate Christmas with her child.

Details of the "baby-hoax" puzzle were fitted together more closely by the state when the Muenches, Jones, and Helen Berroyer went to trial in early April, 1936, in Kahoka, Missouri, again after a change of venue, on the charge of taking a child without the approval of the Juvenile Court. Newspaper readers got double measure because a mistrial was declared April 15 when a juror reported an attempt to bribe him. Some of the most significant testimony had been given by then, but all this had to be repeated in August before a new jury.

It was at Kahoka that Nellie Muench first swore that the baby was her own. It was at Kahoka that Dr. Pitzman first stated under oath that he had believed he was the child's father. He gave plain answers to plain questions, answers which showed that Nellie Muench had "worked" him for at least $16,000.

"I never had a more uneventful acquaintance than my acquaintance with Mrs. Muench," he testified. "Then (after her kidnaping indictment) she went to pieces and threw herself into my arms. For a long time I thought it was unfair. I didn't want to step across a line I had never crossed before."

"You really thought a great deal of her?"

"Yes, I did. One side of her was attractive. The other side I feared."

He broke off his visits to the Muench home for a while. But she called him on New Year's Eve and asked him whether he would meet her so they could begin the New Year as good friends. The following March, Nellie Muench followed him into a public garage, he testified, and told him that she was pregnant; that he was the father of her child.

"People are sometimes mistaken about things like that," he said to her.

"Time will tell," she said.

To speed time's disclosure, she showed him a convincing X-ray plate. This seems to have been an X-ray of Anna Ware and her unborn baby, obtained from the helpful Jones.

After the arrival of the baby, the doctor added a codicil to his will, providing that Mrs. Muench should get one third of his considerable estate, and the child another one third. He did this after Nellie told him that she felt quite secure while he was alive, but that she was worried about the baby's future in case he should die.

The story of the Ware baby, of course, was a shock to the doctor. He gave a last $2000 to Nellie Muench when she said she needed the money to get the real Ware baby from Memphis to disprove charges being made against her. But no baby was brought from Memphis.

"I am now completely confident that I was fooled."

Talk of an attempt to produce the "real" Ware baby brought Mrs. Grace Thomasson, a "butter blonde" friend of Jones, to the stand. She was the energetic type. She had a record of eight marriages and a dozen aliases. She had been married for a time to Hugh Thomasson, an elderly and wealthy St. Louisan. She had been accused of spending a holiday on a Colorado dude ranch with several St. Louis gangsters. Asked whether the men had not left the ranch long enough to rob a nearby bank, she refused to talk. She was much more willing to boast that she had retained eighty-four lawyers in litigation over the Thomasson estate. This explained, she said, why she sometimes was a bit vague about names. She was sure, however, that Jones had asked her to come from Florida for a "big deal." And she said that Nellie Muench had told her they would get $250,000. She also testified that she had helped Dr. Muench perform an operation on Nellie to create the impression that his wife had indeed given birth. Jones, to combat the testimony of this friend of his, told the court she was subject to mental illness and had been in half a dozen St. Louis hospitals.

Helen Berroyer, Nellie's friend, became uncertain of her role in the supposed birth. At first she said that she and the Negro maid were the only attendants. According to a later version, she was in the hall while Dr. Muench and a strange doctor delivered the child. And according to a still later version, she missed the "big moment" because she had gone down to the kitchen for a drink of whisky.

Even Nellie Muench became a bit wild in talking about her "gift from God," especially when she testified that she had been attended by a Dr. Ralph Williams. On being told that nobody by that name lived at the address she had given, she gave another address. But no Williams had lived there, either, for some years. In fact the only Ralph Williams licensed to practice medicine in Missouri up to that time had been dead for fourteen years.

Mrs. Muench had a rough time on the stand. She had to deny that she and her husband had ever extorted money from men who had been intimate with her; that she ever sent bills from the Mitzi Shop to widows for things she said their late husbands had bought for other women; that she had ever embezzled money; that she and her husband had played the "badger game"; that she had stolen jewelry; and that she knew Felix McDonald, Bart Davit, and other gangsters. It did her no good to say tenderly one day that her baby had been "born" exactly a year ago, and that she had been deprived of the child by a "crooked court." She and her husband and Helen Berroyer and Jones were convicted.

The hardest blow fell even before the Kahoka convictions. A federal grand jury accused the four of using the mails to defraud. St. Louis was so interested in the Muench case that this indictment got bigger headlines than another news event of the same day, the nomination of Franklin D. Roosevelt for a second term.

United States District Attorney Harry C. Blanton had a rather easy time outlining the case against Nellie Muench and her associates by the time they came to trial in November, 1936, before Federal Judge George H. Moore. The essential details of the baby hoax were now in the record, and postal inspectors had found evidence that the conspirators used the mails nine times. The federal trial took twenty-one days. At the end of those three weeks, on December 20, 1936, the accused were found guilty on five of the nine counts. They were brought before Judge Moore for sentencing the day after Christmas.

It was possible, of course, to impose a sentence of five years and a fine of $1000 on each count. As far back as could be remembered, however, such prison terms, when imposed in mail fraud cases, were served concurrently. But, as in a number of more recent income-tax cases, Judge Moore proved a stern judge. He sentenced Nellie Muench to ten years in the Federal Prison for Women at Alderson, West Virginia, and also imposed a fine of $5000. Dr. Muench was sentenced to eight years in Leavenworth. Helen Berroyer was sentenced to five years in Alderson. Wilfred Jones was sentenced to ten years in Leavenworth. Eyebrows went up in the courtroom as these stiff penalties were imposed. Nellie Muench turned to her husband and said, "Good-by."

Three days earlier Nellie had made a confession to John Rogers. She said that Grace Thomasson had had no part in the baby hoax, but that she, Helen Berroyer, and Jones were guilty. Her husband, she said, had been drawn into the scheme against his will.

"I have deceived everyone; disgraced my brother, Judge Tipton; ruined my husband. . . . I never gave birth to a child. The baby that was taken from me was procured by Wilfred Jones." Helen Berroyer was no conspirator, Mrs. Muench said. She had not been promised any money and had not expected any. She had gone with Jones only out of friendship. Mrs. Muench said that when she read of the Ware baby, she confronted Wilfred Jones:

"I told him that if I had the Ware baby, I wanted him to return it to that girl at once. He was evasive and quibbled. I seized from the wall a German Army bayonet Dr. Muench brought from France and threatened him with it. But he would not talk about the Ware baby. I stabbed him in the hand, and lunged again and again. He fell to his knees and begged: 'Oh, lady! Don't kill me.'"

She denied that she had intended to extort money. She denied that her husband knew of her affair before she confessed. She made the confession, she said, "but for one purpose: to do some good, if that is possible at this late day for the only innocent person convicted in this so-called conspiracy, my devoted husband."

Jurors, judges, and, in the end, even her husband did not see Nellie Muench as she painted herself. She was conditionally released from prison in April, 1944, the month and the year Dr. Muench divorced her. She moved to Kansas City, assumed a new name, and started a new life.

The name of Nellie Muench appeared again on the front pages of the St. Louis newspapers in the spring of 1960 when Carl Major of *The Globe-Democrat* disclosed that she was one of the stockholders, although a minor one, in a corporation which proposed to build a group of extraordinary skyscrapers at Kingshighway and Lindell—a forty-story hotel, a forty-story apartment building, and a twenty-five-story structure for offices and smart shops. But this hardly was necessary to recall the Mitzi Shop and Nellie Muench to St. Louisans. While most of the gangster stories of the speakeasy era—and the city had its share of them—were all but forgotten, tongues never really ceased to wag about the Muench case. It is the West End's number-one conversation piece.

XXXI. Muses and Attendants

Carl Milles probably was amused rather than annoyed by the renaming of his fountain in Aloe Plaza. Half a block long, it symbolizes the approach of the Missouri to the Mississippi, the one a comely woman and the other a virile man, accompanied by their retinues of nymphs, naiads, and other stream creatures. Milles called it, poetically, "The Marriage of the Rivers." But a few Mrs. Grundys blushed, fidgeted, and fussed. So it became "The Meeting of the Rivers." Oh, well, the fig leaf is merely verbal, as transparent as a bridal veil. It is more regrettable that on a windy day the many jets which throw a watery lace over the figures are turned down to spare motorists the hazard of a wet pavement.

On Grand Avenue, Prudery even set itself against the naked Truth, a fine figure of a brazen woman. But Truth, triumphant, still sits in full dignity in Reservoir Park. There was a rhubarb, all but forgotten, about the nude atop the fountain on Lindell Boulevard, opposite Forest Park. Then there was the case of the Egyptian Cat in the recession-harried middle 1930s. "What right," the indignant demanded, "does the city have to spend almost $15,000 for an old bronze, when unemployed people are being evicted?"

The art lovers also have been a little short of wit now and then—for example in their outbursts against the grotesque bronze of General Lyon, on the site of Camp Jackson, opposite St. Louis University. It never occurred to them that students, in the despair of exams, might glance at that improbability and smile again. And what cocktail battles have been waged over the destruction of plaster casts in the art school and the museum! This is vandalism, or is it getting rid of base imitations? It's all grist for city editors looking for a bright story for Page One! You can't tell them that the people should not be heard when they are most stuffy.

Actually St. Louis does rather well by the arts, especially in its tax-supported museum. This still is the only major one which gets public funds—even if the allotment nowadays barely meets the payroll, leaving little for acquisitions. The Friends of the Museum, who hold a masked ball in its galleries once a year, now help to make up the deficiency. Individual benefactors have been generous. And a municipal bond issue provided a new auditorium. Still, Charles Nagel, Jr., the museum's director, must keep his tin cup out just like a college president, unsolicited contributions being at least as rare as rare birds.

The museum's collections are exceptionally good by American standards. They are well balanced. A special show of "Fifty Masterworks from the City Art Museum of St. Louis" at the Wildenstein galleries in New York was made up of paintings by the younger Holbein, Tintoretto, Veronese, Rubens, Frans Hals, Zurbarán, Rembrandt, Gainsborough, Fragonard, Copley, Goya, Corot, Delacroix, Courbet, Manet, Winslow Homer, Cézanne, Renoir, Van Gogh, Seurat, Picasso, and others. It would be easy to argue that still other masters—El Greco, for example—were slighted. But a book should not be turned into a catalogue.*

Nor is there much point in declaring that the finest canvas in the museum is the "Portrait of a Young Man" attributed to Tosini, or Zurbarán's "Still Life" rather than his cowled monk, or Belotto's "View of Dresden" or Tiepolo's "Crucifixion." What about the magnificent Holbein? What about John Greenwood's amusing "Sea Captains Carousing in Surinam?" What of George Caleb Bingham's "Raftsmen Playing Cards?" (Missourians are almost obliged to favor that!) When it comes to paintings, unlike women, a man may love them all. But if he chooses one, the reason may be as unexplainable as "falling in love at first sight." This goes for sculpture, too, and for other art treasures. Among the museum's period rooms, he need not prefer the medieval chapel to the cool, sun-filtering Moorish gallery with its splashing little fountain. These things are for seeing and enjoying rather than for arguing about—or writing about.

St. Louisans know this, and they come to the big Cass Gilbert building on top of Art Hill in edifyingly large numbers. Few of them fail to go

* Vincent Price, movie star and former St. Louisan, writes that "for the children of our city, one frame alone contained the essence of our pictorial taste . . . a giant illustration of a gruesome scene, designed to make us shudder and have dreams. A tragic lady . . . must drink a glass of blood, the fresh blood of an executed Huguenot or else her father's blood is let. The shaggy executioner holds out the glass of blood, which the wonderful French painter couldn't resist making look like the best burgundy." Even those who complain most about non-representative art are not at all sure that they want that canvas back on the Museum's walls.

into the galleries west of majestic Sculpture Hall. In these the special shows are hung. Here is the chance to see something new, something different. Nagel has that touch of showmanship which makes a visit to the museum more lively than a duty call on old friends, even if that really may be more satisfying. One of the important special exhibits is the annual Missouri Show—not important in the sense that the great Van Gogh show, for example, was important, but because it is the function of a museum to foster art as well as to preserve it. The Missouri Show brings the artists of the area to the attention of the community. It is an opportunity for gaining recognition. It is a reminder to the public that art is a business of the living. Here is a chance for contemporaries to judge contemporaries—and perhaps to buy a picture at considerably less than an old master or a French impressionist brings at a London auction. The Artists' Guild and the People's Art Center, as well as a dozen or so small galleries, also serve to keep artists and other people in communion. These contacts may even be more immediate than those afforded by the museum, but the museum sets the tone. If it were to become an art mausoleum, art in St. Louis soon would be dead. It is far from that.

Another St. Louis collection which made an impression in New York —this time at Knoedler's—was a private one, that of Mr. and Mrs. Joseph Pulitzer, Jr., which was shown for the benefit of Harvard's Fogg Museum. Pulitzer began building his collection while an undergraduate in Cambridge. The real fun, however, began when he returned to St. Louis in 1936. Vladimir Golschmann was bringing a few paintings from Paris each time he returned for the Symphony season. Perry Rathbone, full of enthusiasm, was director of the museum. Edward Millman and Mitchell Siporin added to the excitement by painting the murals in the long lobby of the new post office. More than thirty men prominent in the city's history are pictured in these large wall paintings, making the post office a St. Louis Hall of Fame. Julio de Diego, Fletcher Martin, and other painters came to town frequently to observe their friends' work in progress. The ensuing storytelling and poker playing took all stuffiness out of high art. Kenneth Hudson was breathing fresh life into the Washington University art school, and Joseph Murphy was making the school of architecture exciting.

Morton May, Mrs. Mark Steinberg, the Sydney Shoenbergs, the Richard K. Weils, the Millard Waldheims, the William Bernoudys, Robert Orchard, and others were beginning to cover their walls with oils by Picasso, Utrillo, Renoir, Klee, Degas, Matisse, Monet, Roualt, Braque, Gris, Kokoschka, and Modigliani. Hitler's fulminations were forcing "decadent" works onto the market. Max Beckmann came to Washington University to teach. Europe's loss was America's enrichment. Of course, an older generation—Lionberger Davis, for example— had been collecting works of art and often had given them to the museum or the university. But the late thirties brought a remarkable quickening, handsomely illustrated by the growing collection of the Pulitzers.

It is generally vain to look for common denominators in groups of art works. This can lead to empty verbalizations, since one form of expression can be treated only weakly in another. Try to describe a marble Venus, or Botticelli's on the half shell. Try to define a color. Yet there generally is a basic idea which influences a collector's choices. In the Pulitzers' case it is Charles Eliot Norton's theory of salvation through taste. This comes rather naturally to one who grew up with Sargent and Rodin portraits of his grandfather. It also suggests the readiness with which Pulitzer paintings are made available to the City Art Museum. Many have been given to the community; eventually most of them will be in Art Hill. St. Louis collectors have been perceptive and discriminating. Aline B. Saarinen complained of a certain lack of daring in the Pulitzer collection. A matter of opinion. Daring can degenerate into the overindulgence of personal idiosyncracy. Perhaps the best of the St. Louis private collections, the Pulitzers', ranges from Van Gogh and Ingres through Roualt and Matisse to Klee, Tamayo, Beckmann, and Afro. Among its relatively few bronzes is Mary Callery's "Pyramid." Obviously the more than 150 works were not chosen with a director's compulsion to be "representative," to seek examples of every period and every school from the early Egyptian to the latest "discovery" of 57th Street. St. Louisans live with their pictures, yet these have been so well chosen that there can be no genuine appraisal of modern art without taking them into consideration.

Morton J. May, a pretty good "Sunday painter" who has had oils in four Missouri shows, also is an avid collector of moderns—from Chagall to Beckmann. He and his wife have given the City Art Museum an impressive number of paintings, old masters as well as contemporaries, together with examples of Chinese and pre-Columbian sculpture. Their private collection is to be "a legacy to St. Louis in the years to come."

As for St. Louis architecture, here is something of what was said by Louis LaBeaume, an urbane practitioner who had a hand in the building of the 1904 World's Fair and the Memorial Plaza buildings. He is a past president of the Art Museum's Board of Control, a member of the National Academy of Design, a man who can handle words as well as stone:

My interest in what we used to regard as architecture was awakened as a student in the old Manual Training School more than sixty-five years ago. The great H. H. Richardson of Boston had left his mark here in the fortress-like Lionberger residence in Vandeventer Place. There were two or three other Richardson houses, and a warehouse building on the corner of Eighth and Washington Avenue, still standing, but since badly mistreated.

We really had some local talent here among our painters and architects. Theodore Link was designing the Union Station, strongly influenced by Richardson, but with personal and romantic elements of his own. A group of younger men were beginning to make their mark. Eames & Young were designing the Cupples block for Robert Brookings, the Lorenzo de Medici, the Magnificent of that day. These were great brick, slow-burning warehouses cleanly and finely designed, although some of you now regard that period as "The Age of Innocence."

A competition for the new City Hall had just been held (this was in the early nineties) and had been won by an improvised firm called Somebody, Guissart and Ginder. Guissart was a Beaux Arts man and a real artist. His design for the City Hall was a typical French Hotel de Ville, but George Mann euchred the young firm out of the prize and brought Harvey Ellis down from Minneapolis to detail the winning parti. There it stands, the flèche removed, but revealing much of its original silhouette. Just about this time Link was rendering his own personal version of Richardson's Trinity Church in the design for the Second Presbyterian Church (still standing at the corner of Taylor and Westminster Place). Sometime in the middle nineties William B. Ittner had been appointed chief architect for the school board. He revolutionized our dreary old public school buildings, and laid the foundation for the success of the firm which still bears his name.

At about this time (1897 or '98) Mr. Robert Brookings decided to hold an architectural competition to select an architect for a greatly expanding Washington University. The firm of Cope & Stewardson of Philadelphia was selected, and buildings in the Tudor Gothic style, somewhat similar to this firm's work at Princeton, began to blossom from the barren soil. All of these intrusions from the outside were discouraging, but, at the same time, stimulating to our native practitioners. Later, James P. Jamieson, who had designed most of the University buildings, came out and took over on his own account.

Another very important intruder was Louis Henry Sullivan. Sullivan had distinguished himself as an innovator in Chicago, where he designed the Auditorium Hotel and the Transportation Building, one of the hits of the Columbian Exposition in 1893. Another Chicago architect, William L. B. Jenney, had developed the use of the steel frame to replace wall-bearing masonry. This system of construction permitted a new element of verticality and the accent of the pier, of which Sullivan quickly took advantage in the design of the Wainwright Building here in St. Louis. It still stands as a landmark in architectural history. About the same time ('94 or '95) Sullivan also built the Union Trust Building (now the 705 Olive Street office building) not as successful, but using the same kind of efflorescent and individually designed ornament. Sullivan also built the old St. Nicholas Hotel, at the corner of Eighth and Locust streets, since badly manhandled into the present Victorian Building.

As the University began moving into its new buildings about the end of the century, St. Louis was dreaming of a great World's Fair to rival and surpass Chicago's Columbian Exposition of 1893. The Directors formed a Board of Design, consisting of eight firms, four of St. Louis and four from elsewhere. The St. Louis firms were Eames & Young; Theodore Link; Widman, Walsh & Boisselier, and Barnett, Haynes & Barnett. The out-of-town firms were Carrere & Hastings; Cass Gilbert; Van Brunt & Howe, and Walker & Kimball.

Mr. Walker, knowing that I was from St. Louis, asked me to help him in the preparations of these drawings. C. Howard Walker was a very clever man, a scholar, an artist and a skillful draftsman, and he knocked out the design of the Electricity Building quicker than you can say Jack Robinson, or than a cat could walk on a hot tin roof. Of course, it wasn't well studied, but he and I, with a little outside help, made all the scale drawings, also in rather less time than it takes to tell.

The exposition people had organized a Department of Design under E. L. Masqueray, a Beaux Arts man. Masqueray had had an atelier in New York and brought out five or six of his pupils or protégés to help him. I joined this group and we had a merry time of it.

Howard Walker has generally been given credit for the main plan of the Exposition, the location of Gilbert's Festival Hall, the Main Cascades dropping toward the Lagoon, the Colonnade of States, with the circular Pavilion restaurants at each end, from which descended the Secondary Cascades. These and the bridges and the various decorative elements all over the place were all designed by Masqueray. Cass Gilbert designed the huge wedding cake called Festival Hall and the present Art Museum immediately south of it. The other main buildings were arranged along both sides of the Lagoon. All of this was a compact and orderly conception.

As all of the new University buildings were not yet occupied, the foreign buildings were arranged on both sides of the main Mall leading up from Skinker Road to the Administration Building. If the White City at Chicago could be called classic, Masqueray was determined to make our White City modern in the then French vogue, which had been born of the Paris Exposition of 1900. Masqueray's work was in the style of the Grand Palais, the Petit Palais, and the Bridge of Alexander III—florid, robust and unrefined, but bearing the stamp of its own originality.

Of course, the Fair was just a year late in opening, as the Chicago Fair had been. But the summer of 1904 was a glorious jamboree. The foreign exhibits were rich in interest and beautifully displayed. Alexander Guillmant, the great French organist, gave wonderful concerts in Gilbert's Festival Hall. We enjoyed German music and German beer under the stars in Tyrolean Alps, a beautifully conceived and executed concession that looked like a bona fide Austrian village nestling at the base of the snow-clad Alps. The food here was delicious, as it was in the official German restaurant in the Pavilion at the east end of the Colonnade of States. Gondoliers from Venice piloted their gondolas through the canals and under the bridges. The scene was bathed in moonlight, making a dream world full of song and silvery laughter.

Well, there is no denying that St. Louis had received a shot in the arm and things began to look up. Andrew Carnegie gave the town a million dollars to build a public library. A competition was held and won by Cass Gilbert. The ubiquitous Robert Brookings had badgered many of our leading citizens to contribute buildings at the University. The chapel, known as the Graham Memorial Chapel, was, as you know, modeled after Trinity Chapel at Cambridge. The Ridgley Library was rather closely modeled after St. John's at Oxford.

Our story up to this time might be entitled, "The Pre-Revolutionary Chapter." . . . For about ten years art and architecture in Scandinavia, Holland, Germany, Austria and Italy had been in a state of ferment. When this fermentation boiled over, nothing was left of anything that had gone before. The past, instead of being merely prologue, was *kaput*. America, which had boasted of it originality, bowed to Bauhaus.

In 1923 St. Louis, feeling the need of another shot in the arm, passed a large bond issue, in which a certain sum was set aside for the improvement of the Municipal Plaza, and the erection of the Civil Courts Building, Municipal Auditorium and the Soldiers' Memorial. The architectural revolution that was going forward in Europe really hadn't reached St. Louis and the conservative designs for the Plaza buildings had been approved. It was too late to change, so there they are to see, and to carp at.

The battle of styles is over, but it isn't quite safe to say that peace reigns either architecturally or politically. . . . The tall slab housing the offices and committees of the U.N. like a huge filing cabinet has served as a prototype for similar filing cabinets all over the United States. If the architects of an earlier day stole from the dead, may we not say that those of today plagiarize each other and pick each other's pockets? If Mike and Ike look alike, so do most of our contemporary buildings. Surely the older generations knew a richer store from which to steal.

The dissent to Louis LaBeaume's opinion may be read on the façades of new suburban churches, if they are churches. This, too, will pass.

Even before television went Western, one of the favorite haunts of St. Louis youngsters was the Missouri Historical Society in the Jefferson Memorial—half a mile down the hill from the art museum at the DeBaliviere Avenue entrance to Forest Park, which was the main entrance to the 1904 World's Fair. It is full of Indian tomahawks and regalia, George Caleb Bingham pictures of frontiersmen, and river-boat models, not to mention the Hawken rifles and dueling pistols in the Olin firearms gallery. Its greatest attraction, however, still are the "Lindbergh trophies," 15,000 medals and gifts showered on Colonel Charles Lindbergh, "the Lone Eagle," after his 1927 transatlantic flight in the *Spirit of St. Louis*. The Memorial consists of two wings flanking a loggia which canopies Karl Bitter's bronze of the seated Thomas Jefferson. Almost the whole first floor of the West wing is filled by the trophies. They are still fascinating in this day of space capsules.

Since the establishment of the Famous-Barr educational project, staffed with the help of the Junior League, youngsters may handle many of the objects in the museum. Their history teachers bring them by the busload. There are special programs during the summer, too, and they can always wander through the galleries—and usually do, after the "monkey show" at the zoo.

The Jefferson Memorial was built by the directors of the Louisiana Purchase Exposition as a gift to the city. It was completed April 13, 1913. It has been occupied since then by the Missouri Historical Society, a privately supported institution. The society has an unusually rich collection, and its archives are of major importance to historical scholars. They contain, for instance, more than 1000 documents and letters written by Thomas Jefferson, the reports of the Lewis and Clark expedition, and much material on the trans-Mississippi West, as well as many valuable books and files of early newspapers. Together with the Mercantile Library, the City Art Museum, and the Boatmen's Bank, the Society maintains for St. Louis an impressive group of paintings of George Caleb Bingham, who opened a studio in the city in 1833. There are also pictures by Carl Wimar, George Catlin, Charles Bodmer, Alfred Miller, Chester Harding, Thomas S. Noble, Sarah M. Peale, Edward Robyn, and other artists early in the region, who were the pictorial reporters of their time. They carried the story of the West to the East and to Europe.

Charles van Ravenswaay has been director since he put away his naval officer's uniform at the end of the war. With the support of Judge George H. Moore, chairman of the trustees, he has increased its dues-paying members from a few hundred to several thousand. The society also has the regular support of about a hundred St. Louis corporations. The museum has for years been under the curatorship of Miss Marjory Douglas. The pictorial gallery and files are in charge of Mrs. Ruth Field. In 1956 she discovered a method of restoring daguerreotypes. This method has been eagerly taken up by the Smithsonian Institution, the Library of Congress, and the British Museum. It has made available many old pictures after hope for their preservation had been given up. Mrs. Brenda R. Gieseker, the society's librarian, and other members of the staff have received many a grateful bow in many a preface.

The Mercantile Library is housed in the First National Bank Building at Broadway and Locust. It would be accurate to reverse this statement, since the library owns the building and the bank is its tenant, but some public misapprehensions are easier to accept than to correct. In any case, the rental received by the library has insured continuance of the service it renders its members. For $10 a year the Mercantile will deliver any books on its shelves—rare volumes excepted—to any address in the St. Louis metropolitan area and, later, pick them up. Some persons who use the library regularly never have been in its quarters. They simply telephone for the books they want. The City Assessor grumbles now and then about real estate beyond his reach, but he only grumbles. It is standard operating procedure in American communities to encourage education by the remission of taxation.

Established by James Yeatman and a half a dozen of his book-reading, self-improving friends, the Mercantile is rather like the Boston Athenaeum. In addition to housing an increasingly important collection of books, the old library hall was used for lectures in the pre-movie era, as well as for important meetings and public ceremonies. Wayman Crow, Carl Schurz, and other eminent St. Louisans met at the Mercantile before such encounters were shifted to the Noonday, the Missouri Athletic, the University, the Racquet and the golf clubs. The Mercantile also was the city's first art museum. It commissioned work by Bingham, Wimar, and others. Its favorite treasures still are two marble females by Harriet Hosmer, who was bold enough in the genteel era to study anatomy in old Dr. McDowell's medical college. This did "make Rome howl!" Another Mercantile treasure is Chester Harding's portrait of General William Clark. The present building was built in 1885. This once was a red granite and brick Romanesque-revival structure, massive but impressive. However it was modernized a few years ago and it now looks like another American box. Incidentally, a good many of the country's modern banks are designed in St. Louis. The Bank Building Corporation of America, on Hampton Avenue, has made a big thing of this specialty. It has a division called "Design" which does churches, colleges, office buildings, stores, warehouses, motels, anything.

In 1958 Mary Durward succeeded Clarence Miller as head librarian of the Mercantile. When he left, after more than sixty years in the job, he remarked that St. Louis had "turned its back on the river and had missed the train." He did not see much of a future for the place, but he did love the Mercantile's 200,000 books and its oak-paneled clublike atmosphere. The Mercantile owes Miss Durward to Charles Nagel, Jr. While he was director of the Brooklyn Museum of Art—between terms in St. Louis—she was put in charge of the museum library and really blew the dust off the shelves. When Nagel heard that Miller was leaving, he reminded Miss Durward of all his boasting about St. Louis. She came west and was convinced.

Always there have been at least a few St. Louis men hungering to make their city beautiful. Not the least of these was Hiram W. Leffingwell, who in 1869 launched the movement to induce the city to purchase from Charles P. Chouteau, Julia Maffit, and Isabella De Mun the 1326 acres which now are Forest Park. This plot of greenery along "the golden waters of the River Des Peres," now an underground sewer, was opened in 1872 with an old-fashioned St. Louis celebration—speeches by Schurz, Blair, and Blow, band music, fireworks, and all the crowd-pleasers of the last century. What has happened to the parades and spectacles of yesteryear? Time was when St. Louis missed no occasion for a celebration, be it the Fourth of July or the anniversary of the Battle of Lake Erie. Today only World War I veterans march on Armistice Day, and school children in the annual "Cleanup" parade, no great thriller. Yet the city is full of drum majorettes, horn blowers and *Glockenspieler*. Surely they need more occasions for self-expression, even if they do tie up traffic in the narrow downtown streets. Perhaps they should join the V.P. parade and give it some extra zip.

In 1850, before his interests had led him as far west as Forest Park, Hiram Leffingwell and his real estate partner, Richard Smith Elliott, laid out Grand Avenue on its high ridge in what still was fairly open country. They had a big idea: a street 120 to 150 feet wide and running from one end of the city to the other. Henry Shaw promised a park along this street on the South Side. Proud of the North Side, John O'Fallon gave the city what is now Fairgrounds Park. But the alderman could not match the imagination of these men. They refused to sanction a width of more than 80 feet for Grand Avenue. Perhaps they read a London report that a horse deposited 38 pounds, 2 ounces of excrement and 3 pounds, 7 ounces of urine on the streets each day and therefore decided not to provide too much space for horses. But how grand a 150-foot street would be! And how it would speed along the fin-tailed monsters!

Leffingwell was discouraged, but not Henry Shaw. He brought a bunch of roses from his garden to Leffingwell's office one day and began to talk of a new project: a botanical garden for St. Louis similar to London's Kew Gardens. He established the seventy-five-acre museum of plant life in 1858, and it was opened in 1860. Shaw named it the Missouri Botanical Garden, but St. Louis calls it Shaw's Garden. Shaw was one of those men of an earlier generation who believed that trade was not worth their time once they had accumulated an adequate sum of money. He did this about as quickly as possible. Born in England in 1800, he accompanied his father to Canada in 1817. Two years later he had set up as an independent merchant in St. Louis. In closing his books for 1839, he found he had made $25,000 that year chiefly in outfitting fur traders. To Shaw it was "more money than a man in my circumstances ought to make in a single year." So he sold his business and sailed for a vacation in Europe. He made a second crossing in 1851 to see the Crystal Palace, but by the year's end he was back in his town house at Seventh and Locust, and in fair weather riding out to his country place, Tower Grove. He bought this property because he long had enjoyed riding across it:

From the village of St. Louis I came through the bushes by a narrow path winding among the sink holes or natural depressions of the commons to the elevated ground now called Grand Avenue, where opened to view a beautiful prairie extending westward, uncultivated, without trees or fences, but covered with tall, luxuriant prairie grass, undulating in the gentle breezes of spring, not a tuft of which can now be found. I was informed afterwards by M. Lauderville, an old resident, that these lands, being fertile and productive, were the first selected by the colonists for cultivation; and were called *La Prairie de la Barrière à Desnoyer,* from Louis Desnoyer, a concessioner, who kept the gate or *barrière* of the fence by which the commons of the village of St. Louis were surrounded.

Leffingwell's partner, Richard Smith Elliott, recalled in his memoirs how Shaw walked into their office with the bunch of roses and quietly told them of his plan:

Looking at a map on the wall, he remarked, as if it were a mere common-place announcement, that he intended to have a Botanical Garden, with proper accessories, free for citizens and strangers to visit; and that he had in view the donation of a tract of land to the city for a public park, on condition that it should be properly improved. . . . There was no parade of generosity, or of unusual public spirit, but the statement was made as unpretentiously as if it involved nothing more than an ordinary act of daily life.

Fifteen years later—after the Civil War—he gave the city the park adjoining the garden, the park which was opened in 1870 under the name of his country place, Tower Grove. These considerable gifts, by the way, are evidence that the tall, handsome Shaw, although he had sold his business, had continued to increase his fortune—largely through the buying and selling of real estate in the growing city. Mrs. Dana O. Jensen of the Missouri Historical Society records that at one time he owned 32,000 acres. That is almost six times the acreage of the Mill Creek Valley redevelopment, of which contemporary St. Louis is so justly proud.

To plant his garden and to make it the heart of the school of botany at Washington University, which he endowed, as well as a pleasure for St. Louisans, Shaw needed the help of more than a few green-thumbed gardeners. And this help he got from Dr. George Engelmann. Born in romantic Frankfurt am Main, the son of a teacher, Engelmann was educated in the German universities and in Paris. He was an extraordinarily successful physician and a prodigious worker during cholera outbreaks. But he had a passion for botany, and except during epidemics he gave his time after nine o'clock to it every night. He became the outstanding authority on the gymnosperms, those cone-bearing plants which include firs, spruces, and pines. Cultured and sensitive, he was vastly enthusiastic about St. Louis. He wrote to Asa Gray at Harvard on September 27, 1843, that the city was "the center of North America, if not of the world and of civilization!—the great focus of the West and the Southwest. . . . We burn one third of our steamboats, destroy one tenth of the wealth of our citizens in one night, kill one tenth by cholera—try our hand in burning again—all only to show how much we can stand without succumbing."

Returning from a voyage to Germany in 1840, he had looked up Gray, the great botanist, in Boston and worked out the lines along which they co-operated for fifty years. In St. Louis, Engelmann recruited field workers, especially among the university-educated Germans, and helped them to join exploring, military, and trading missions into the wilderness. He received their specimens and sent most of these on to Gray, since he had "neither the leisure, nor books, collections, etc., sufficient to do the work [of classification] alone, or to do it so well as to be creditable." Here he was overly modest, yet his collaboration with Gray was richly fruitful.

Engelmann found Carl A. Geyer, Friederich J. G. Lueders, and Augustus Fendler especially apt for botanical explorations. Back East, Gray raised the necessary money, getting some of it from John Lowell, and more by selling specimens—$10 for one from the Rockies, $8 for one from Texas. There were disappointments of course. One or two of Engelmann's specimen hunters settled in the West instead of returning to St. Louis, and occasionally the work of a year or two was lost when a canoe overturned. Gray sometimes became impatient because field agents did not penetrate deeper into new territory or climb higher mountains. But Engelmann, closer to the frontier, understood the handicaps imposed by Indians and by Nature. Difficulties were overcome, however, especially by Fendler, who later went East to become curator of Gray's herbarium in Cambridge. To Engelmann, a Fendler's enthusiasm more than made up for the disappointments of a Frémont. In the winter of 1842–43 the doctor had generously coached the Pathfinder in how to collect growing things, but eventually he was forced to write to Gray that Frémont "appears to me rather selfish— I speak confidentially—and disinclined to let anybody share in his discoveries, anxious to reap all the honor, as well as to undertake all the labor himself."

Fendler, an experienced Western traveler, was manufacturing fuel for spirit lamps in St. Louis when Dr. Engelmann encountered him. He also had established a small herbarium and was trying to sell in the East specimens from the St. Louis area. Engelmann told him that he would find little profit in offering what was too familiar to be in great demand. Why did he not go collecting in virgin territory? This was in 1846, and the trouble with Mexico afforded unprecedented opportunities to join expeditions headed into the Southwest. As soon as Fendler was persuaded, Gray obtained contributions and enlisted the support of Secretary of War Marcy. So Fendler set out in August of 1846 with a cavalry regiment. He was cooped up in Santa Fe most of the winter and became "sick with scurvy and sick of matters in general," especially after he had to sell his watch and his gun. All this, however, was offset when he got back to St. Louis with his specimens. "They are beautiful," Engelmann wrote to Gray, "splendid, and a great many new things among them." Gray put other work aside and published *Plantae Fendleriane* before the end of 1848.

Even before the news from Sutter's fort, Fendler wanted to search for gold in California, but Engelmann and Gray persuaded him to go to the Great Salt Lake instead. Because of the ineptitude of a young army officer, all of Fendler's equipment was lost over the side of a steamer almost before he was well under way. Forced to return to St. Louis, he discovered that his herbarium and all else that he had left behind had been destroyed by fire. He never went West again. By now a confirmed botanist, he joined Gray in Cambridge.

The close collaboration of Engelmann and Gray was cooled a little by the Civil War. Gray, the New Englander, was dogmatic. Engelmann, the Democrat on the border between North and South, was sadly familiar with the human aspects of civil discord. "I believe in capital punishment," Gray wrote. "The life of the rebel is duely and justly forfeit." And Englemann wrote that Gray's letters, "I must confess, surprised, I might almost say, shocked me. I did not think you so bloody minded, harsh and one-sided, but I suppose, hearing and seeing only one phase, one aspect, and being far removed from the scenes and sorrows of fraternal war, you (and I mean all your people) can well afford to indulge in this way of thinking." It was a mild enough rebuke from the doctor whose heart had grown almost breaking-heavy as he tended the refuse of the battlefields in the St. Louis hospitals.

But the bond between Engelmann and Gray was too strong for breaking, and when Engelmann died in 1884, Gray succeeded him as adviser to old Henry Shaw. He found the first curator for Shaw's garden for him, William Trelease. The 1600-acre Shaw's Garden arboretum and wild-flower reservation, thirty miles west of St. Louis, is called Gray's Summit. But long before it was established, Dr. Engelmann had crossed the ocean time and time again to find rare specimens and rare books for the wonderful botanical institution on the South Side. After Shaw died in 1889, the well-endowed garden passed to a self-perpetuating board of trustees. Known only officially as the Missouri Botanical Garden, it flourishes as a monument to Shaw, Engelmann, and Gray. It contains Shaw's country home, Tower Grove. His handsome town house was rebuilt there and is now used as the administration building. It also houses the famous Botanical Library. Another structure that dates back to Shaw's time is the old Museum and Library Building which was restored in 1930 as a lecture hall. Still another is the Linnean House, an old-fashioned conservatory. Dr. Frits Warmolt Went in 1958 succeeded Dr. Edgar Anderson as the garden's director.

For green-thumbed St. Louisans, Shaw's Garden is a source of grass seed and plants adapted to the city's soil and climate. To the average visitor, it is a splendor of glowing color surpassing the "Jewel Box" in Forest Park. Four regular shows are held in the garden each year. Of these the most spectacular is the orchid display, which includes hundreds of varieties. A luxurious bouquet of the rarest of these flowers is made up each year for the Veiled Prophet's Queen. In accord with Shaw's will, a "flower sermon" is preached annually in Christ Church Cathedral. All the resources of the garden are used to decorate the church for this Sunday. Solomon, indeed, was not arrayed in glories such as these.

Newest of the major museums, not counting a planetarium to be built in Forest Park, is the Academy of Science. Founded in 1856, the Academy had a nomadic existence in its first century. Its library was sheltered successively by the Public Library, Washington University, and St. Louis University. Its collections were housed in unsatisfactory quarters on Olive Street and then on Lindell Boulevard. But in 1959 it moved into two large and handsome buildings in Clayton's Oak Knoll Park, thanks to the indefatigable efforts of Stratford Lee Morton. He also induced Mark Deusing, a veteran museum man and distinguished wildlife photographer, to come from Milwaukee as the academy's director. Under him it is anything but a conventional, haphazard collection of exhibits. Instead, objects are brought together in a coordinated display—for example, one illustrating the history and principles of flight ranges from birds through models of Leonardo's devices to jet engines. Youngsters have been known to pass up a ball game for a visit to either the Academy of Science or the Historical Society. There is so little distance between them now that a boy might also get to the Art Museum in the same day, and so cross culture off his list for a while.

A poll-taking outfit wanted to know awhile back whether the St. Louis newspapers paid more attention to George P. Vierheller or his performing apes. Silly! Neither is ever mentioned apart from the other. If he can help it, Vierheller—with the zoo for more than forty years—never misses a show in the chimp's gay outdoor theater. He is not quite as interested in the performing elephants or the trained lions and tigers, but he does not freely admit this. He is on such friendly terms with animals that he has shared a Pullman bedroom with a gorilla (a young one) and once had his car remodeled to accommodate a small elephant. But those chimps—they are wonderful. They know it, too, and are quick to prompt a slow audience to applause. They know that no circus ever put on an act as good as theirs.

All this makes Vierheller seem a circus man rather than the director of a zoological garden, and that is not true. Insofar as possible, he tries to have examples of all species of the animal world on display— and not in cages. He was one of the first to move animals into open, moated areas resembling their native habitat. He even trusts some birds not to fly away. "A zoological garden," he says, "should not be a penitentiary." The zoo on its eighty crowded acres in Forest Park is relatively new. It was not until 1913 that the St. Louis Zoological Society

—founded in 1910 largely through the efforts of Otto Widmann, Frank
Schwartz, and Julius Hurter—obtained the passage of a city ordinance setting aside the park area. The society also persuaded the Missouri Legislature to pass a bill which authorized St. Louisans to vote
a tax of one fifth of a mill for the zoo's support. George E. Dieckman,
president of the society in the 1920s, worked hard for the zoo's development. Vierheller's association with the zoo began when he became secretary of the Zoological Board of Control, which at that
time consisted of five city officials and four members of the society.
As he told Ellie Wehmiller, he "had the privilege, that falls to some
of us fortunate Americans, of starting as a raw recruit with an enterprise
in its infancy and of growing with it."

XXXII.   Wine—and Song

There has been an upsurge of culture in St. Louis ever since a saloon was devoted to its advancement. Some of the "unbeatniks" may ask what an accompaniment of jazz and "screwdrivers" does for poetry and painting, but it must be conceded that the fourth or fifth scotch on the rocks brings out nuances. The place to put this to the test is the Crystal Palace, which Jay Landesman, an antique dealer, and erstwhile publisher of *Neurotica,* opened first on Olive Street east of Grand and later moved into larger quarters on Olive near Boyle. This little neighborhood was tagged by its developers with the giveaway name of Greenwich Corners. Landesman and his talented wife, Fran, are trying to tune it down to Gaslight Square which, incidentally, sounds almost as contrived. But then, isn't all art really contrived?

The Crystal Palace, named for its huge, old, crystal candelabra, the more sedate Gaslight Bar, where customers play chess on Monday nights, the Golden Eagle saloon, meant to be a remembrance of the river packet that sank in 1947, the Eagle's Nest where Singleton Palmer's Combo sounds off, Smokey Joe's Grecian Terrace restaurant, and the newer institutions of the neighborhood, as well as the flats above them, reflect, more or less, the neighborhood's chief pursuit, antiques. Its twenty or so shops once were known as Secondhand Row. These places display not a bit of that shiny black porcelain-like stuff which, illuminated by neon, is supposed to constitute a stylish, up-to-date façade.

Jimmy Massucci, an antique scout who opened the Golden Eagle and its summertime sidewalk café in 1956, has sawdust on the floor and big brass chandeliers from an old Illinois church overhead. He has an old steam-operated popcorn wagon in one corner and a player piano in another. Walls are hung with the framed covers of old magazines, and partitions are embellished with hundreds of the song slides used when community singing—"Now everybody join in the chorus!" —was part of the entertainment in movie palaces. Dick Mutrux's Gaslight has made fine fun of stained glass and curious old oils from the mansions of Vanderventer Place, torn down to make room for the Veterans' Hospital. Mutrux likes flamenco music. If there is a competent Spaniard in town, he soon is playing at the Gaslight. But except on Saturday, "slumming" night, it is a relatively quiet place. Mutrux doesn't care how long patrons short of ready cash sit over a beer.

Massucci's father sold steamboat supplies on the riverfront, so it was natural for the host of the Golden Eagle to adopt something like the décor of the gay days on the Mississippi. The Landesman family has lived for years on Westminster Place. It's members have a legitimate interest in the neighborhood. It has attracted others more or less like them, all fresh, lively, and exciting.

In the good old days before the war, the section formed the last red-light district in the city. But before the first war it really reeked with culture, and color too. Helen Traubel, the baseball fan whose book revealed that she did not know too much about a game whose enjoyment depends on detailed knowledge of a vast lore, statistical and strategical, learned to sing in one of the studios in the Musical Arts Building at Boyle and Olive. There were private schools, dancing classes, and smart shops to serve the big houses on Westminster Place, a block south of Olive, and the other "West End private places."

After the Public Service Company concluded that it could no longer afford to run the Maryland Avenue cars all the way downtown just to serve the few blocks of Maryland Avenue between Boyle and Kingshighway, on the insistence of Governor Francis, who lived on Maryland, it placated old-timers by running the Maryland "dinkey," a two-car shuttle service from the Musical Arts building, at the junction with the Olive Street lines, to the Park Plaza Hotel at Maryland and Kingshighway. The democracy of the streetcar age—when the West End bluestockings as often as not went to parties and plays as well as to the marts of trade by public transit rather than by carriage—had a last fling on the "dinkey." Two conductors—one big and dour, and the other a cheery little Irishman who knew each passenger by name—started their cars at opposite ends of the line every seven and a half minutes, more or less. Stops were made, unofficially, in front of the passengers' homes, not merely at street intersections. Nobody who "belonged" read a newspaper on those two old wooden trolleys unless he was in a mood grim enough to spurn neighborly conversation. The Maryland-Lindell bus which replaced the "dinkey"— but only going downtown, not coming home—is not the same at all, even if it does assure its handful of Maryland Avenue patrons a choice of seats during the morning rush hour and has been accepted by such gallant elder statesmen as Judge Thomas Hennings, the senator's father, and Oscar Mullgardt, the architect. The trouble is that the buses become sardine cans soon after they turn into Lindell. Anyway, they turn away from Greenwich Corners and saloon culture, rather than toward, as the "dinkey" did. The popular vehicle of the Corners now is the sports car of the white-collar bohemians from darkest Ladue, in town for quickening of the spirit. This, Landesman provides.

As impresario, he naturally took to plush rather than sawdust. As a dealer in old busts and bric-a-brac, he went for crystal fixtures like a bear for a honey tree. He built his first Olive Street saloon around them. With black pseudo-velvety walls, a long bar, an equally long back-bar mirror, it was an intriguing place, and Landesman did a good business. Still, there was some space—very dark—beyond the bar, which invited exploitation. A chanteuse, pianist, and spotlight would have been standard, but Landesman came up with Theodore Flicker and the "Circle Theater," a small group which dramatized, extempore, themes suggested by the customers. Inevitably Flicker was drawn to New York. The Landesmans filled in with Kenneth Rexroth and Allen Ginsberg, the music-and-poetry "beatniks" from San Francisco's North Beach, as well as with *avant-garde* progressive jazz groups. Flicker returned to put on Samuel Beckett's *Waiting for Godot,* and the Crystal Palace was in the reserved-seat, cover-charge category. Also it was too small to accommodate its customers. So Landesman made the inevitable move to a larger saloon in the Greenwich Corners block—a red one, but with the same spangles overhead. The new place accommodates a larger stage, and Flicker has made the most of it, staging, among other productions, a beatnik musical, *The Nervous Set* written by Landesman and Flicker, with lyrics by Fran Landesman and music by Tommy Wolf, which soon was headed for Broadway's Henry Miller theater. It is a happy sign of the state of the arts in St. Louis that it should send a fresh show to Broadway instead of waiting for a stale one to come from Broadway.

Still, it has been done before—and more profitably. William Inge, formerly in the English Department at Washington University and drama critic for the *Star-Times,* staged his first hit, *Come Back, Little Sheba* (then called *The Front Porch*) in the Toy Theater in the Musical Arts Building. And a lot of good that did him. His friend,

Tennessee Williams, had to induce him to leave St. Louis to win recognition as an outstanding playwright. Landesman is sure that St. Louis again is friendly to creativity. He points out that people like Walter Barker, the painter, now live and work at Olive and Boyle. But it may be a matter of economics which induces artists to live where the slums and the mansions merge. And would a Barker be in St. Louis if the Washington University art school did not offer a steady job? For that matter, those two baseball intellectuals, Joe Cunningham and Al Blasingame, would not have lived in the neighborhood had they not had Cardinal contracts. But St. Louis does have the art school and the baseball team, while the stage of its legitimate theater is set very differently—as it is in all the cities of "the road."

St. Louis now supports one professional playhouse, the American, again handsomely housed downtown after a few years on Grand near Olive. It presents road companies, and now and then Katharine Cornell, the Lunts, and the few other stars who like to tour. There may be a week of Shakespeare or Gilbert and Sullivan when the Old Vic or the D'Oyly Carte tour for dollars. It is less than fully satisfactory to see a play about which one has heard for a year or two; and the radio quickly blares the bloom off a musical. Drama is in a bad way if its best is only for those who go to New York a few times a year. Attempts to put on repertory or semiprofessional performances generally meet with less than indifferent success in St. Louis. Myles Standish, the drama critic, blames this on the "star" system. No matter how good the play, it will not draw unless there is a well-advertised Hollywood or Broadway name on the theater front. That means bad economics for the local producer, since the star takes most of the ticket money. And more often than not it means a slipshod performance, since the star is not available for adequate rehearsals with a local supporting cast.

Even so, the decline of the theater in American cities other than New York—and perhaps in New York as well—has been explained only in part. It began before the movies reached their peak and before television was invented. While the attractions of the metropolis are obvious, why did the many who always have desired a career on the stage so largely lose the audiences of other cities? The first ambitious theatrical performances in St. Louis were presented a century and a half ago in a remodeled salt warehouse on Second Street. The actors were amateurs under the direction of William Turner, a professional from New Orleans who played the star roles. The town hardly could afford more. But in

1820 the Thespian Society was organized, and in 1835 General Clark and Colonel Charles Keemle headed a committee which raised $65,000 for the building of a theater. George I. Barnett was the architect. He later built other theaters, but did not improve on his first one, with its façade of massive Ionic columns. From dress circle to gallery, the house seated an audience of 1500. (Prices of admission, incidentally, ranged from fifty cents to a dollar and a half.) Other nineteenth-century houses included the Concert Hall, the Bates, the Varieties, the Grand Opera House—old and new—the People's, the Adelphi, Pope's, the Pickwick, the Olympic, the Odeon, and the old American. These were under the management of such men as Ben de Bar, J. M. Field, John McVicker, and that jack of all trades, Henry Boernstein. The star system, of course, got an early start, and all the big names came to St. Louis in due course.

In the carriage and gaslight days, people made a wonderful—and frequent—ceremony of dining out and going to the theater or the concert. Some still do, when they can. But in St. Louis, as in Chicago and so many other cities, the theaters were darkened one by one. Why? It seems a lame explanation to say that the cities grew too big, that it now is too much trouble to come downtown. After all, the automobile has minimized distance and time. Nor does it help to suggest that "the good old days" were not all that they are supposed to have been. For a time, St. Louis did have a number of theaters open. Now there is only the American. But what happened? There certainly has been a decline in the number of attractions. There also has been a decline in the number of patrons. But which is the hen? Which the egg?

Since the days of the old French fiddlers, music has been the liveliest of the arts in St. Louis. Its more ambitious performances began when Wilhelm Robyn took charge of the Old Cathedral choir about 1840, and with the organization of the Polyhymnia, the Arion Liederkranz, and Egmont Froelich's Philharmonic, almost a century ago. Today there is, first of all, the St. Louis Symphony Orchestra, which in its fourth quarter-century is the second oldest of the nation's major orchestras. It has just completed its second season under the young Belgian, Edouard van Remoortel. The first was not a happy year. Perhaps a little too determined to play "the new broom," van Remoortel made drastic changes in the orchestra's personnel and threatened so many more that the season almost came to a premature end when the musicians threatened not to play under his baton. Thomas Sherman, the *Post-Dispatch* music critic, described the concerts as "the product of unimaginative competence, neutral and colorless not because of any mistakes but because his readings were too literal." Yet Sherman conceded that "it is only fair to reserve final judgment for another year." The second one was better. Van Remoortel accepted a difficult assignment in taking over from the debonair Vladimir Golschmann, who had been the orchestra's leader for more than twenty-five years. Golschmann had occasional bad days, too, and sometimes was a little too easygoing; yet he had spirit which he imparted to his musicians. He was superb when playing the work of one of the friends of his youth in Paris—Ravel, for example—and with another of them— Robert Casadesus, for example—as soloist.

The orchestra's first professional conductor, Joseph Otten, took up the baton in 1881. He quit in 1894 when the number of concerts was cut back for lack of funds, an old Symphony bugbear. Alfred Ernst came from Germany to take his place. Even for a tyrant of the rehearsal, he had too sharp a tongue. Next came Max Zach, from the podium of the Boston "Pops." He demanded much of his players, and they respected him. He took a dim view of soloists and audiences who lost their hearts to them. When De Pachman, after a performance in 1911, played one encore after another—and apparently was ready to do so as long as the audience applauded—Zach put matters into correct proportion. He ordered a stagehand to close the piano, and then dismissed the orchestra. After Zach, the baton passed to Rudolph Ganz, the pianist who, when he lifted it for the first time, told the musicians:

"Gentlemen, this is an instrument I know nothing about."

To make up for the haste with which Ganz had been employed, the orchestra played for four years under guest conductors. One of these was Golschmann, who became the permanent conductor in 1931. Through tours and recordings he spread the Symphony's fame. But, in line with the common fate of orchestras, fame does not pay off sufficiently well at the box office. An annual maintenance fund drive is necessary. Another help is free use of the Kiel Auditorium concert hall in return for afternoon concerts for school children. Even if all 3000 seats rarely are filled, the Symphony concerts have a traditional place in the life of the community. There may have been a decline in the number of "after the Symphony" Saturday night parties because the exodus to the suburbs made concertgoing a little more difficult. But with the completion of the new Plaza apartments almost across the street from the auditorium, attendance is bound to increase.

Symphony musicians no longer play for $8 a concert and $3 a rehearsal. Zach introduced season contracts. Some supplement this income by playing in the Little Symphony concerts, given *al fresco* in the summer in the Washington University quadrangle. (Even more play in the big Municipal Opera orchestra pit.) The graceful colonnade of the Ridgely Library affords a congenial setting—Handel would have appreciated it—for the small orchestra assembled by jovial Max Steindel, cellist with the Symphony for more than forty years. There may be guest conductor after guest conductor, but Max always is on the podium for the last concert.

Older than the Symphony is the Philharmonic, an amateur orchestra which plays under professional direction with professional skill. Organized in 1860, it is approaching its 100th anniversary. In its early days, the Philharmonic was semiprofessional, but it soon dedicated itself to providing an opportunity for nonprofessional musicians to play symphonic music, and to providing experience for young, talented musicians. It operates under a not-for-profit charter. Its concerts, given in Kiel Auditorium, are free to the public. Its expenses, which run to something under $10,000 a season, are met by the dues of playing members and the subscriptions of patrons.

In recent years, the Philharmonic has been playing under guest conductors of a high order. Its first permanent conductor—from 1860 to 1867—was Edward Sobolewski, the friend of Robert Schumann and Richard Wagner. Others were Egmont Froelich, Abraham Epstein, Eugene Rantenberg, Alfred P. Hebard, Alfred Ernst, Ludwig Carl, Frank Gecks, Frederick Fischer, Alfred Hicks, Stanley Chapple, and Russell Gerhardt. The Philharmonic's weekly rehearsals are the big attraction for its members, whose enthusiasm has been especially high under the presidency of S. Carl Robinson, vice-president of the Public Service Company and an outstanding amateur musician since his student days at Harvard. The public concerts, usually four each winter, are well attended. St. Louis music critics invariably judge them by professional standards. That there are so many candidates for the orchestra is evidence of the community's grass-roots interest in music.

The real St. Louis summer favorite, however, is the Municipal Opera—which has nothing to do with opera, at least not grand opera. It presents twelve weeks of operetta and musical comedy in the 12,000-

seat amphitheater in Forest Park. Seen from the Crystal Palace, the "Muni Opera" is more corny than Iowa in July, but it is as popular as air-conditioning in August. Almost 26,000,000 persons have attended more than 31,000 performances of 425 productions. Critical wisecracks bounce off those figures. Frankly, there is little new about an evening at the "opera." The audience knows just what it is going to get—music, singing, and dancing in a familiar form—and that is just what it wants. President Harding stopped over in St. Louis a few days before his death in 1923 to attend a performance of *The Prince of Pilsen*. Between the acts he told the audience how delighted he was with the institution. "It is beautiful," he said, "a great credit to St. Louis." And anybody gazing at that sea of faces on the Forest Park hillside, if not at the stage, must be impressed.

Interest may be waning a bit. Attendance for the first season, in 1919, was 159,725. It passed 500,000 in 1926 and rose to more than 700,000 in the depressed 1930s. It was 811,513 in 1941 and reached an all-time high of 898,103 in 1949. Since then there has been a gradual decline. Attendance in 1957 was 637,050—which still is quite a crowd. Only the Cardinals, with an annual attendance of more than 1,000,000, outdraw the "Muni Opera," and Gussie Busch can seat twice as many people in his ball park—and he, by the way, does not offer anything new and original either. Perhaps the revival of band concerts in the city's parks, under Laurent Torno, may have reduced Municipal Opera attendance a bit. Nostalgia is a great drawing card. The band concerts are free. And there is that devil, TV.

The Muncipal Opera had its origin in the old beer gardens. More specifically, it stems from the *Pageant and Masque,* staged in Forest Park in 1914 to celebrate the city's 150th anniversary. (With a cast of 7500 and an attendance of 455,000 in five days, that was a real record setter!) As City Superintendent of Construction, Nelson Cunliff built the huge over-water stage at the foot of Art Hill for the pageant. This gave him the idea of a permanent outdoor theater in Forest Park. In 1915 the present site, a hillside with a graceful 53-foot slope to the stage, was used for singing performances under Frederick Fischer, and the next year for Margaret Anglin's production of *As You Like It*. With the Advertising Clubs of the World meeting in St. Louis in 1917, Cunliff persuaded the business community to subscribe funds for the improvement of the outdoor theater for a presentation of *Aïda* by stars of the Metropolitan and Chicago opera companies. The next year there was a patriotic pageant, *Fighting for Freedom*. With the coming of peace, Cunliff induced the somewhat reluctant Mayor Kiel to form a committee to see what could be done about "some form of public entertainment sponsored by a local group with sufficient money to put on a show that the entire city would be proud of." Max Koenigsberg of Famous-Barr, Arthur Siegel of General Outdoor Advertising, Ernest W. Stix, Isaac A. Hedges, Henry S. Priest, and G. A. Buder were especially interested. The Municipal Theater Association was formed in the spring of 1919. Its first season almost was its last. *Robin Hood* opened June 16, 1919, with the audience under umbrellas. *Bohemian Girl* was scheduled to open June 23, but the heavens opened instead. By noon, the stage was under the waters of the rising River Des Peres —now safely underground as a sewer. But the next night the show went on. That season closed with a $30,000 deficit. Never again was there red ink on the books. Profits have been regularly used to improve the theater, which now has even an outdoor air-conditioning system. It operates on a budget of $1,000,000—half of which represents the pay-roll of more than 400 employees.

The Municipal Opera policy sometimes is simply defined: Take no chances on anything new! Even slight departures from this have been reflected in a decline in ticket sales. So "Muni Opera" offerings in any season might almost be chosen from this list of all-time favorites compiled by Willie Zalken, manager of the Symphony and press agent extraordinary of the Municipal Opera.

Attraction	*Municipal Opera Performances*
Merry Widow	*1923, 1925, 1928, 1936, 1941, 1943, 1946, 1951, 1955*
Desert Song	*1930, 1932, 1933, 1935, 1941, 1943, 1946, 1950, 1955*
Rose Marie	*1927, 1928, 1929, 1931, 1939, 1943, 1947, 1952*
Chocolate Soldier	*1921, 1926, 1929, 1935, 1940, 1943, 1949, 1956*
Show Boat	*2 weeks each in 1930, 1934, 1938, 1942, 1947, one week in 1952*
Babes in Toyland	*1920, 1926, 1929, 1937, 1943, 1947, 1952*
Red Mill	*1926, 1927, 1936, 1941, 1944, 1949, 1954*
Rio Rita	*1931 (2 weeks) 1935, 1940, 1944, 1948, 1953*
Naughty Marietta	*1923, 1924, 1925, 1933, 1940, 1944, 1947, 1952, 1957*
New Moon	*1930, 1932, 1934, 1936, 1942, 1945, 1949, 1954, 1957*
Student Prince	*1928, 1929, 1930, 1933, 1952, 1956*
Three Musketeers	*1931, 1936, 1941, 1945, 1948, 1954*
Vagabond King	*1928, 1929, 1935, 1944, 1949, 1955*
Great Waltz	*1937, 1940, 1943, 1946 (2 weeks) 1951, 1956*
Bohemian Girl	*1919, 1924, 1929, 1936, 1944, 1951*

South Pacific, Oklahoma, Brigadoon, Carousel, Guys and Dolls, and *Kiss Me, Kate* have been put on several times, and *Damn Yankees* after only one listing seems sure to become one of the favorites. In the open air on a stage, 90 × 115 feet, these musicals take on different characteristics from those they had in an intimate theater. Settings costuming, music, and big singing and dancing choruses transform them into spectacles. But they are well done. Soft drinks or Mountain Valley water between the acts. And after the show, scotch and soda or bourbon and branch water at the Gatesworth, the Congress, the Chase, or the Park Plaza. St. Louis loves it!

XXXIII. A Poor Back Yard

By putting on smoked glasses, Hollywood style, or a pair of the rose-tinted kind which horse players wear, it is easy to see that St. Louis and its future are either as black as a flea in a tar bucket or as bright as a snow-covered alp in the morning sun. Both pictures do more for the emotions than the more or less gray, more or less mixed-up things as they are. Yet why do so many St. Louisans prefer the darker view? Tinsel and brightwork may be vulgar, but why a cult of the gloomy?

Chicago is largely to blame. After all, St. Louis was the metropolis of the western wilderness when the Indians massacred the Fort Dearborn garrison and left the town of the wild onion an empty and windy waste. Then Chicago took the "go" in its name seriously, while St. Louis slipped from fourth to ninth in the list of American cities. But if St. Louis lost that race, it lost neither population nor wealth. It does have a population of 856,796 (1950 census) within the sixty-one square miles to which it is constitutionally confined. And if there is not room for more in this small space, the metropolitan area has a population of 1,892,000 and no limitations. And the area is St. Louis —or nothing, no matter how the mayor of a speed trap may strut and puff.

There is a contemporary cult devoted to "the decline of the cities." Economists and sociologists as well as historians hold forth on urban decay, but they sometimes ignore the possibility of urban regeneration. True, Gopher Prairie's boosters never had a chance. Few cities fulfill the dream-promises of their founders by really growing into a new London or a new Paris. Many factors set limits on their development; yet they do continue to grow slowly instead of falling into ruin. Their decline is relative rather than real. It is rural America, not urban America, which is losing population.

"The city is the point of maximum concentration for the power and culture of a community," wrote Lewis Mumford, "It is the seat of the temple, the market, the hall of justice, the academy of learning. Here in the city the goods of civilization are multiplied and manifolded; here is where human experience is transformed into viable signs, symbols, patterns of conduct, systems of order. Here is where the issues of civilization are focused." The speed and reach of modern communications may help to concentrate some of these functions—or their more important aspects—in a megalopolis or two, but one may doubt that the radio voice of Big Brother ever will eliminate man's habit of coming together with his fellows to perform his labors, solve his problems, and celebrate his exploits. And not all of this can be done in New York.

So St. Louis still is growing, if not as sensationally as in the first half of the last century. Had they thought about it, Lewis and Clark, Zebulon Pike, or any of the old boatmen and mountain men could have explained that was how it was bound to be. They would have known that the St. Louis story was bound to be, in part, one of poor relations around the house while the young and rich "set up for themselves."

A century and a half ago, St. Louis was at the extreme western end of the string of settlements established beyond the Appalachians. Indeed it was remote even from this new territory, which consisted chiefly of western Pennsylvania, Ohio, and Kentucky. St. Louis had been settled earlier by way of French New Orleans, and to a lesser extent by way of French Canada. It was not a result of the *Drang nach Westen* from the Atlantic seaboard, but it soon became the chief beneficiary of that population movement, the economic capital of the frontier. It was the real take-off point for the settlers who came down the Ohio and up the Mississippi, even though many of these continued to travel by water to the present Kansas City and St. Joseph and points farther upstream on their way to the Oregon country. Passenger and freight for the Northwest had to be transferred at St. Louis from large steamers to the small ones which could navigate northern and western streams. The wagon trails to Santa Fe, Chihuahua, and California started at the levee. John Butterfield's famous Overland Mail—established in 1851 and under Wells-Fargo management after 1861—sent its nine-passenger stages or "celerity wagons" 2812 miles from St. Louis to Springfield, Joplin, Fort Smith, Fort Bliss, El Paso, Tucson, Fort Yuma, Los Angeles, and San Francisco. Farther to the north ran the Santa Fe and the Old Spanish trails. North of them, following the Platte to South Pass, was the route of the Pony Express; and beyond South Pass, the California Trail dipped down to Virginia City, and the Oregon Trail ran up to Portland and Fort Vancouver. Farthest north of all was the water route of the Missouri, dotted with such outposts of St. Louis as Fort Union, Fort Benton, and Fort Sarpy on the Yellowstone. The Missouri from St. Louis to Westport, established by François Chouteau of St. Louis and later called Kansas City, and St. Joseph, established by Joseph Robidoux of St. Louis, became the first leg of all these routes to the West, especially after the *Independence* proved the stream navigable by steamer. Many less well-known wagon trails also ran from St. Louis toward the sunset, while Tom Benton in Washington argued for national roads and then railroads to speed the opening of the West.

This was one of the most arduous and exciting phases of national expansion. The work of choosing routes, finding fords, establishing ferries, building bridges, opening inns, and providing for changes of horses every ten to fifteen miles was prodigious. Then, there were the Indians. They brought the army as well as the post office into the West. The work became even more important after the admission of California to the Union in 1850 and Oregon in 1859. The United States then consisted of an eastern and a western section, divided by the "Great American Desert." The distance from New York to San Francisco around Cape Horn was 15,348 seasick miles. By way of Panama—still without a canal—it was 6077 miles. Overland it was only 3256 miles, about two thirds of them west of St. Louis. Before the telegraph and the railroad, the horse was the quickest means of getting men, mail, and goods across the continent.

Between April 3, 1860, and October 24, 1861, seventy-five Pony Express riders—"Wild Bill" Hickock, "Pony Bob" Haslam, and other adventurers—covered 2000 miles in ten and a half days, each man generally riding from fifty to eighty miles. In their *mochilas*, or mailsacks, they brought to the West the news of Lincoln's election and of the outbreak of the war between North and South. Although carrying about 350 letters a trip at $5 an ounce, the Pony Express was a financial failure. The stagecoaches of such operators as Russell, Major, Waddell, Holliday, and Butterfield were compelled to charge fabulous freight rates. Yet in spite of raids by Indians and bandits, they had thousands of coaches and wagons on the trail—especially after the discovery of gold in the West.

Much of this freight came from St. Louis. The city was the logical source of supply for half of the country. This was changed by the railroads. The eastern lines had reached St. Louis—and also New

Orleans, Memphis, and Chicago—in the decade before the Civil War. The conflict slowed down the building of the heavily subsidized trans-Mississippi lines, and it pointed up the advantage of the northern route out of Chicago. Rails west from the head of the Great Lakes were inevitable. Rebellion in the South guaranteed that the Union Pacific—with all its scandals—should be completed before the Missouri Pacific, the Frisco, and other lines which connect St. Louis with its old markets, especially in the Southwest. The spending of some $180,000,000 in the city by Quartermaster General Meigs to supply the armies of Grant and Sherman, however, cushioned the blow. And by the time the Santa Fe became eager to come into St. Louis—only a decade ago—the city was so indifferent that the plan was not realized. By that time another revolution in transportation had occurred. More and more freight was being moved by truck. More and more passengers were traveling by plane. St. Louis had become the nation's second trucking center, as it had become the second railroad center. It had built its beautiful airport before the concourse of the big Union Station took on a deserted look. So it was not a lack of transportation facilities which slowed down the city's economic growth.

The slowdown was caused, inevitably if paradoxically, by the city's success. Men, money, and materials from St. Louis built the Southwest. They contributed to the growth of Kansas City, Little Rock, Tulsa, Oklahoma City, Dallas, Fort Worth, Houston, Galveston, and San Antonio and, in somewhat lesser degree, to the development of places like Omaha, Topeka, and Wichita, as well as Memphis and the other cities on the Mississippi. Chicago and the cities of the Northwest came into boom. And east of St. Louis there long had been Cincinnati, Louisville, and the other first fruits of the crossing of the mountains. St. Louis was encircled by growing communities. Its once vast market was cut back, and cut back to its poorest parts—Southern Illinois, the Missouri Ozarks, and Arkansas. This is reflected in the contraction of the city's wholesaling activities. But empty lofts and the disappearance of famous firm names such as Rice, Stix also indicate changing patterns —for example, selling by manufacturers directly to retailers, especially the chains. St. Louis, which once was primarily a huge mercantile establishment, is becoming a manufacturing center instead. On this its prosperity now depends.

The monthly review of the Federal Reserve Bank of St. Louis in the last few years has not cultivated a bouncy, hip-hip-hooray style. Its economists sometimes seem to be trying to turn the marble and bronze interior of the bank into the mausoleum it resembles, so gloomily do they explain what is happening to the Eighth Federal Reserve District—those sections of Eastern Missouri, Southern Illinois and Indiana, Western Kentucky and Tennessee, Northern Mississippi and all of Arkansas of which St. Louis is the official banking capital. The boundaries of the district reflect, if not quite accurately, the shrinking of the city's hinterland.

The birth rate of the region has gone up more slowly, and the death rate has gone down less rapidly than those of the nation as a whole. So it is declining in population. It has industrialized more slowly than the national rate. So it is more dependent on argiculture—and that is an aggravating story of rising per capita production and so of declining opportunities for employment, not to mention the economic problems of surplus crops. Here "American mobility" means leaving the farm. So in spite of the growth of the cities, the district has had more "out-migration" than the average. In the 1940–50 decade "only 27 of the 363 counties in the Eighth Federal Reserve District attracted more migrants than they lost in that period, and 11 of these were metropolitan counties," according to a Reserve Bank report. There is no great future for young men in "chopping" cotton, since the Missouri Division of Employment Security reports that the percentage of cotton harvested in the state by mechanical pickers increased from 7 per cent in 1952 to 30 per cent in 1955. In the not-very-long run, machines are cheaper than sharecroppers, and they make no complaints. War jobs had much to do with the 1940–50 exodus. The fact that this slowed down from 1950 to 1955, with sixty-two counties gaining more migrants than they lost, is attributable not only to the TVA boom in the Paducah, Kentucky, area but also to such statistical gimmicks as counting college students as residents of college towns and the enlargement of Fort Leonard Wood and other military camps.

The trek to the cities has confronted them with surpluses of unskilled and sometimes unemployable labor, while it has left the rural areas with relatively more old people. After all, it is the young—especially those between eighteen and forty—who move in search of economic opportunities. The population shift also has contributed to the growth of the suburbs at a rate seven times faster than the cities. St. Louis, with its copper-riveted boundaries, grew hardly at all, while other parts of the metropolitan area increased by 20 per cent. But this is a headache almost exclusively due to political balkanization.

Retail trade feels population shifts quickly and directly. In the Eighth District it rose 28 per cent while in the nation it went up 32 per cent. So for all their running, district merchants were falling behind in the race. Per capita income in the district actually went up 27 per cent compared with the national figure of 25 per cent, but there were only 3 per cent more "capitas" in the district while there were 10 per cent more in the U.S. of A. St. Louis was the bright spot of the district, with an increase in dollar volume of retail sales from $203,000,000 to $456,000,000, well above the national average. But sales in the city increased only 20 per cent while in St. Louis County they rose 80 per cent. The proportion of sales made by downtown department stores was about 90 per cent in 1946 and only 50 per cent in 1956. Here higher prices create a false impression, but the physical volume of downtown sales did fall about 25 per cent in a decade.

The prosperity of the metropolitan area, however, underscores the relative—and sometimes very real—poverty in the southern parts of the district. Per capita retail sales in Newton County, Arkansas, fell to less than $100 a year! Southern Illinois, with much of its land unsuited for farming and its soft coal less and less in demand, also is in relatively bad condition. Drought added to the hardships of the Missouri Ozarks. So it is understandable that some of the hill people should want the army engineers to dam such beautiful timber-bordered mountain streams as the Current River just for the jobs such work would create temporarily. It is questionable whether all the dams already built in the Missouri and Arkansas Ozarks are justifiable. Certainly a man-made lake is not an even trade for a mountain steam unless it means more than a small and passing increase in employment. No industrial region has sprung up at the base of Norfork, Bull Shoals, and Table Rock dams on the once magnificent White River, and motels and boat docks are not "keeping 'em down on the farm."

Unfavorable economic conditions in nearby areas mean a shrinking home market for St. Louis, a disturbing influx of unskilled labor, and also higher state taxes for the support of schools and other institutions in counties unable to maintain them. Above all, it means that St. Louis producers must look to the national market. Anheuser-Busch must sell more beer, International Shoe must sell more shoes, Monsanto more chemicals, and Ralston-Purina more feeds in other parts of the country.

Yet in the face of this necessity, St. Louis as a manufacturing center has fallen behind the national rate of growth in the postwar years. There are now about 275,000 manufacturing jobs in the area, but they represent an increase of only 5 per cent, compared with the national rise of 11 per cent. More alarmingly, St. Louis made its spurt in 1947–53. Since then employment in factories has fallen off a bit.

It is a question whether to use the dark or rose glasses in considering McDonnell Aircraft's increase in employees from 3300 in 1947 to 27,000 in 1957, which makes it the area's largest employer. It manufactures military aircraft, a field in which changes may be sudden and devastating. Construction of the huge wartime small arms ammunition plant, among others, made St. Louis an ordnance center. Employment was high during the war, of course, and got back to about 18,000 during the Korean War. It is now down to about 5000 and dropping. But this is a field in which the price of prosperity should be prohibitive.

Beer has done best by St. Louis, with Anheuser-Busch, Falstaff, Carling, and other breweries selling far and wide. But the shoe industry employs about 9000 fewer St. Louisans than it did in 1947. Low wages in small communities long have been an incentive to decentralization. This is not a total loss, since it adds an element of stability to the hinterland. And St. Louis still does produce about 16 per cent of the nation's shoes, a relatively small decline from its all-time high. To some extent the women's garment industry also has left Washington Avenue for the country towns. Once an important producer of railroad cars and other railroad equipment, St. Louis naturally has been affected by the plight of the railroads. The number employed in the manufacturing of durable goods has gone up almost 10 per cent since 1947, and there have been substantial gains in chemicals and petroleum products. In general the high-wage industries have shown the greatest gains. But especially since the demand for durable goods, not to mention military equipment, is variable, the St. Louis area is less stable economically than it used to be. It is no longer an economic Gibralter. It no longer has the home-owned economy which some regarded as the guarantee of stability and security and which others denounced as a parochial and primitive attempt to keep outsiders from making profits for themselves and the community.

"An important trend in St. Louis' industrial structure, not apparent from statistics, is the changing locus of ownership and management," according to the Federal Reserve Bank. "Mergers and acquisitions in recent years have made branch plants of many which were formerly owned or which had their principal management in St. Louis. The effect of such developments is not always unfavorable for St. Louis employment and income, but in some cases operations have been stopped or curtailed after the change."

It is a question whether such losses have been offset by the acquisitions of St. Louis firms in other cities. But the community is far from being an economic satrapy. When Chandler's Shoe Salon was opened on Fifth Avenue, New York, in 1958, it became the 332d retail shoe store opened in the last thirty-five years by Edison Brothers of St. Louis, the world's largest chain of retail shoe stores for women. The firm sells about 18,000,000 pairs a year in forty states. And there are bigger giants in St. Louis. Here are the top twelve, as listed by *Fortune:*

MONSANTO CHEMICAL CO.
Sales: $567,116,000; Assets: $633,050,000; Net Profit: $57,416,000 (9.6%); Invested Capital: $389,888,000; Employees: 19,076

RALSTON-PURINA
Sales: $438,262,000; Assets: $178,879,000; Net Profit: $14,570,000 (12.1%); Invested Capital: $120,781,000; Employees: 7500

McDONNELL AIRCRAFT
Sales: $335,288,000; Assets: $140,547,000; Net Profit: $9,672,000 (26.4%); Invested Capital: $35,130,000; Employees: 24,711

INTERNATIONAL SHOE
Sales: $266,073,000; Assets: $175,782,000; Net Profit: $9,577,000 (9.3%); Invested Capital: $102,783,000; Employees: 35,500

BROWN SHOE
Sales: $236,946,000; Assets: $104,552,000; Net Profit: $9,123,000 (14.5%); Invested Capital: $62,935,000; Employees: 21,500

ANHEUSER-BUSCH
Sales: $227,225,000; Assets: $167,321,000; Net Profit: $9,778,000 (7.9%); Invested Capital: $123,267,000; Employees: 8292

PET MILK
Sales: $184,602,000; Assets: $62,836,000; Net Profit: $2,604,000 (6%); Invested Capital: $43,683,000; Employees: 6000

GRANITE CITY STEEL
Sales: $123,763,000; Assets: $158,997; Net Profit: $9,984,000 (12.3%); Invested Capital: $81,207,000; Employees: 4943

BEMIS BROTHERS BAG CO.

Sales: $121,476,000; Assets: $66,658,000; Net Profit: $1,786,000 (3.6%); Invested Capital: $50,273,000; Employees: 8500

PEABODY COAL CO.

Sales: $104,588,000; Assets: $134,317,000; Net Profit: $9,593,000 (12.8%); Invested Capital: $75,103,000; Employees: 4500

FALSTAFF BREWING CO.

Sales: $97,093; Assets: $51,231,000; Net Profit: $4,079,000 (12.6%); Invested Capital: $32,263,000; Employees: 3217

WAGNER ELECTRIC

Sales: $95,143,000; Assets: $67,247,000; Net Profit: $5,997,000 (11.4%); Invested Capital: $52,730; Employees: 5305

"The metropolitan area will experience an encouraging rate of growth in the next few years," said A. J. Kaufmann after the Chamber of Commerce completed a survey showing that St. Louis still is the number two railroad center, served by eighteen trunk lines, four switching lines, and one short-haul line. Six of the rail lines have their headquarters in St. Louis. The city is at the heart of a 13,494-mile inland waterways system, and more than 6,000,000 tons of barge freight were handled in St. Louis in 1956. Eight air lines use the airport, at which there were more than 200,000 landings and take-offs in 1956. As for trucking, nearly 300 common and contract carriers—108 of them headquartered in St. Louis—operate out of the metropolitan area. The area also is served by twenty-two passenger bus lines. Other utilities are adequate and have plans for expansion. Water supply is abundant, with the Mississippi offering an average flow of 129 billion gallons per day. For financing, the metropolitan area has ninety-seven banks, with total resources of about $3,000,000,000. In addition to the Federal Reserve Bank there also is a Federal Land Bank. And the resources of the banks are supplemented by some forty savings and loan associations, with assets in excess of $400,000,000.

Some of the highlights of the Chamber's industry-by-industry survey show that with the completion of the big new Chrysler auto plant—supplementing the Ford and Chevrolet plants—St. Louis stands second only to Detroit in the production of automobiles. From 1918 to 1958, Chevrolet turned out 5,650,000 cars in St. Louis.

Grouping foods and beverages, the metropolitan area ranks fifth in the nation. In all, there are 428 firms in this field. The closing of the big Armour plant on the East Side in 1959, however, is disturbing. Only in the slaughtering of hogs, about 7 per cent of the national total, has St. Louis shown a gain in the postwar years. There has been a considerable decline in the slaughtering of cattle, calves, sheep, and lambs. Only in part can this be attributed to bad weather in the area from which St. Louis draws livestock. The feeding and finishing of cattle has been shifting westward, and it is becoming uneconomic to ship to the distant St. Louis stockyards. Chicago is losing the butcher trade more rapidly, but this is no consolation for the 58 per cent drop in employment in the local meat-dressing industry since 1950.

St. Louis has moved into sixth place in chemicals, probably its most rapidly expanding industry. There are more than 220 firms, with Monsanto as the leader. There also are four major oil refineries.

The area's furniture manufacturers, paper processors, and makers of stone, clay, and glass products stand seventh nationally in their respective industries.

Other outstanding industries are electrical equipment, metals, women's garments, and printing and publishing.

Like the *Federal Reserve Bulletin,* the Metropolitan Survey (made for the freeholders studying possible integration of the area) is less optimistic than the Chamber of Commerce. The report was made under the direction of Thomas H. Eliot of Washington University and Paul G. Steinbicker of St. Louis University under a $250,000 grant from the Ford Foundation and with supplemental help from McDonnell Aircraft. St. Louis is not exactly dying on the vine, the report concluded, in view of the metropolitan area's growth in population since 1900 from 800,000 to 1,892,000. But it adds that "the growth of industry and commerce has not kept pace with that of competing metropolitan areas. Compared to metropolitan areas in general, its development has been slower in the current century. Yet the innate economic strength of this community, grounded in its wide diversification of industry and commerce, remains. The future depends on whether the St. Louis metropolitan area, thwarted by regional factors beyond its control, shrinks weakly to a second-class economic area, or whether it chooses to make the most of its geographical and other advantages and to take all the steps necessary to foster vigorous and prosperous enterprise."

In blaming this on the St. Louis hinterland, the Metropolitan Survey does not see this area as primarily the Eighth Federal Reserve District but rather as the nine-state region of Missouri, Iowa, Illinois, Kentucky, Tennessee, Arkansas, Oklahoma, Kansas, and Nebraska. Thus it regards St. Louis as more Midwestern than Southern. Yet this area, too, has not industrialized as fast as the nation. In fact, it has been in a "relative economic decline for at least 85 years. Since 1929, for example, the region's share in the national business done by the retail, wholesale and service trades has experienced decreases ranging from 15 to 20 per cent." Since 1870, Missouri's share of the national population has declined approximately 44 per cent—a fact reflected in the state's reduced representation in Congress. Missouri's share in the national labor force is down 35 per cent, and its importance as a manufacturing area also has declined.

While manufacturing has become the most important segment of its economy, the growth rate in the St. Louis metropolitan area has been slower than that of New York, Chicago, Detroit, Pittsburgh, Cleveland, Dallas, Fort Worth, Minneapolis, St. Paul, Kansas City, Milwaukee, and some other cities. Substantial wholesale and retail trade still stood second in importance, with the service trades third, and transportation and public utilities in fourth place. Most of the employment, according to the Metropolitan Survey, was concentrated in seventeen industries: food products, primary metal products, chemicals, apparel, petroleum refining, machinery, electrical equipment, transportation equipment, leather and leather products, transportation, utilities, retail, wholesale, service, finance and construction.

Per capita income was estimated in the Survey at $1686, or 117 per cent of the United States average in 1950. The figures for Kansas City and Chicago were $1746 and $1994. Even more alarming is the fact that the per capita income in the St. Louis area as compared with the national average declined 10 per cent from 1929 to 1954. Yet many manufacturers are determined to keep their plants in the area. In 1954 they spent $51,000,000 for plant and expansion in the city and $11,000,000 in the County, and more on the East Side—the Illinois counties of Madison and St. Clair—than in the city and St. Louis County combined.

Interpretation again is a choice between the dark-making and the bright-making spectacles. Undoubtedly St. Louis has regional handicaps about which very little can be done—even by Senator Symington, hard as he may work for "dying towns" in Missouri. There is no excuse for the complacency which sometimes seems to be the community's besetting sin. Historic and geographic facts make it impossible for St. Louis just to "sit and grow" at the confluence of the great rivers, as it could when the whole West was its oyster. On the other hand it is not doomed to be a second-class market city for a third-class region. Its future is in being a manufacturer to the nation. Getting out of the doldrums is a matter of getting out of its own back yard. When he opened the 1904 World's Fair, David R. Francis said:

"St. Louis needed something like this. We are a peculiarly self-centered people. We need to be brought more closely in contact with the outside world."

Perhaps the powers that be in St. Louis should not have turned thumbs down on Stratford Lee Morton's proposal of another World's Fair after World War II. It might have been a potent stimulant.

xxxiv. Professor in Politics

The tight knot in his tie and the precise fold of his pocket hand-kerchief indicate that Raymond R. Tucker, Mayor of St. Louis since 1953, is an engineer. They are as exact as the principles of mechanical engineering, which he taught at Washington University. He would like to run City Hall with similar exactitude, but he has learned that aldermen are not reciprocal engines. Sometimes he is tempted to impatience—his lips tighten and his eyes flash. He is a politician by second choice, but one good enough to have been twice elected by record-breaking majorities. He was elected President of the American Municipal Association in equally impressive style. And he is the only mayor on Paul Butler's Democratic National Advisory Committee.

To political scientists, he is the very model of a model mayor. He is one of their kind even though he did not sit in their classes, joining them only belatedly as a lecturer. He went to South Side public schools, to St. Louis University High School, and then to the engineering school at Washington University. There he studied under Dean Alexander Langsdorf, a fine humanist despite his slide rule. Langsdorf made him an instructor; but since instructors' pay is bad pay, Tucker in 1923 went to work in the oil fields near Tulsa. Not cut out to be an oil Democrat, he was back at the university as associate professor in 1927.

Seven years later, Mayor Bernard F. Dickmann turned to the school for help against the sulphurous smoke which made St. Louis such a happy place for nose and throat specialists. Tucker went to City Hall and got his first whiff of politics. He made a preliminary smoke report and became the mayor's secretary, with smoke as his special assignment. The brain truster (nobody heard of eggheads in those pre-McCarthy days) was fascinated by politics. He became the leader of the Democratic organization in his ward, but it was engineering and not doorbell ringing which made him the city's best vote getter and the mayor who is transforming the appearance of St. Louis and trying, too, to transform its government.

Mark Twain thought that St. Louis water was as murky as St.

Louis air—not quite dense enough to grow potatoes but much too solid to drink. The water was made gin-clear (but not so tasty) by the opening of the Chain of Rocks filtration and pumping plant on the Mississippi, and a more abundant supply was assured by the construction of the big plant at Howard's Bend on the Missouri. The atmosphere, however, became ever more opaque and more acrid, due to the Illinois soft coal which Peter Lindell had first brought across the river more than a century earlier. Since Lindell also was a real estate operator, it should have occurred to him that coal profits could destroy property values. The heavy palls drove leading citizens out of the mansions which once lined the boulevard named for him. Smoke fouled the façades of buildings and killed plants in parks and gardens. Nurserymen would not sell evergreens for planting in the city. Combined with fog, the smoke actually filled the atmosphere with tiny globules of sulphuric acid. One could taste them. The United States Public Health Service pronounced the St. Louis smog worse than Pittsburgh's. It might have been picturesque—veiling ugliness, toning down the harshness of neon, and turning busy streets and plazas into mysterious and private places —had it not been so poisonous. It is a wonder that concerts and plays continued to be performed, since they went on to a steady accompaniment of hacking and coughing. The smoke plumes thickened as production picked up after the slowdown of the depression. There were days when even at high noon it was difficult to see the other side of a wide street. One discerned it only by the dim glow of a lamp or an illuminated sign. Motorists turned on their lights, yet drove more slowly than they would have had the streets been sheets of ice. The ensuing traffic snarls ruined the vestiges of equanimity not destroyed by the fumes and the unnatural dark. St. Louisans become a touchy lot.

Of course there had been anti-smoke campaigns before Tucker was given a desk at Twelfth and Market. In 1925, for example, the Citizens' Smoke Abatement League raised $200,000 and established a "firing" school. Staff members were sent out to show housewives how to bank their fires to avoid heavy smoke. Pamphlets pointed out that soot was costing each St. Louisan as much as $20 to $30 a year. This went on for two years. It had no noticeable effect. Enthusiasm waned, and by 1933 the city had only one Smoke Department employee to keep an eye on 150,000 smokestacks. In his very first report Tucker dismissed this educational approach as futile. Proper stoking was out of the question where furnaces and stoves were hand-fired. It was silly even to mention it in the Negro neighborhoods where people bought their fuel from "jaggers," men who took a battered old truck or an old wagon drawn by an older horse across the bridges to pick up a load of leavings at some nearby mine, and then hawked this stuff through the streets, a bucketful for a quarter. To prove that it would burn, the "jaggers" hung buckets of glowing coal and dirt from wooden arms nailed to the backs of their wagons. These coal peddlers added color to St. Louis streets as the successors of U. S. Grant, wood peddler. They also demonstrated the high cost of poverty. And they helped to create the city's "midnight noons."

Tucker reported that much of the coal being sold in St. Louis contained 30 per cent ash and from 5 to 6 per cent sulphur. Smoke might be reduced by washing this fuel. An ordinance was adopted in February, 1937. Scientific measurements showed less sulphurous smoke in the air, but the difference hardly was detectable by eye or nose. The chief benefit of this law probably was the establishment of the municipality's right of enforcement. The soft-coal interests attacked the ordinance in federal court as an illegal restraint of trade, but United States District Judge George H. Moore held it to be a valid protection of the community's health and welfare. The ordinance also created the office of Smoke Commissioner. Somewhat reluctantly Tucker took the job he helped to create. Nobody else wanted it. He started an enforcement program, concentrating on the railroads, industries, and large apartment buildings.

Tucker and the mayor, meanwhile, became the targets of a propaganda campaign eminating largely from those who had been selling 4,000,000 tons of dirty coal a year in St. Louis. A rumor was assiduously circulated that the officials received $10 for every stoker or oil burner installed in the city and 10 cents on every ton of approved fuel. The Department of Justice was induced to investigate, also the Federal Trade Commission. All charges fell flat. Another tactic in this guerrilla warfare was to keep Tucker's telephone ringing day and night. Cranks made their usual calls and threats, but all kinds of salesmen also were given his number as that of a prospect. It was funny—and annoying. Tucker went on enforcing the ordinance, sealing the furnaces of serious offenders. He and Mayor Dickmann appeared before the Illinois Legislature, which voted $300,000 for a study of ways of making Southern Illinois coal more acceptable. Nothing came of that. Billboards and radio were used in the campaign. Tucker spoke to one group after another. But the washed coal ordinance simply was not the answer to the problem, and he knew it.

St. Louis never fully accepted malodorous smoke as the inevitable accompaniment of prosperity. As other industries joined Anheuser-Busch on the South Side, housewives protested repeatedly against the soot which stained their curtains. Tucker was born a South Sider. But not only South Siders complained. Especially when the wind blew out of the East, a dense smoke shroud spread over the downtown area and far into the West End. All except the extreme southwestern portion of the city was held to be blighted and ineligible for government-insured building loans. An especially suffocating day in December of 1939—it came to be called Black Tuesday—brought a new outcry for relief.

Tucker had a simple answer: the city could get rid of smoke if it would stop burning the soft coal which produced it. Pass an ordinance prohibiting the hand firing of any fuel with a volatile content of not more than 23 per cent, he said, and the miracle would come to pass. This meant a ban against Illinois coal unless used with approved mechanical stokers. To many it seemed to mean only higher fuel bills. The Illinois producers feared the loss of a major market. But Tucker said that while coal acceptable for handfiring undoubtedly would cost more per ton, it would yield more heat, and many a householder would find his season's fuel bill no higher than before. The only real problem would be that of obtaining enough acceptable fuel.

Tucker convinced Mayor Dickmann that St. Louis could rid itself of smoke only by taking this radical step. The mayor foresaw more shortsighted, self-centered opposition, and the need for effective persuasion. So he appointed a Citizens' Smoke Elimination Committee, headed by the indefatigable James L. Ford, Jr., vice-president of the First National Bank. This committee was formed on December 11, 1939, and on February 24, 1940, came out in favor of Tucker's formula. Ford had enthusiasm and determination. With the wholehearted support of the press—the *Post-Dispatch* received a Pulitzer prize for its part in the effort—he launched a new campaign to end "midnight noons."

The first job was overcoming the propaganda of those who had a vested interest in the unrestricted use of soft coal. There was a hoopla against gouging the public, especially the poor. But since St. Louis still elected aldermen at large and the Merit System (civil service) amendment to the City Charter had not yet been adopted, the mayor could use patronage, if need be, to make them see the merits of the anti-smoke ordinance. Patronage, when not abused, is a sharp goad for the democratic mare. Even so, one of those slips 'twixt the cup and the lip was narrowly averted. At the very last moment an amendment exempting locomotives, among the worst of the smoke belchers, was adopted on behalf of the Terminal Railroad Association. That was on Friday, April 5, 1940. Mayor Dickmann was at lunch when he heard what had been done. He called the aldermen back into session Saturday morning, telling them the change was utterly unacceptable. On Monday, after a motion to reconsider, the ordinance was readopted without the wrecking amendment.

This victory might have meant next to nothing, since only about 250,000 tons of "smokeless" coal were available. At least another 1,000,000 tons a year were needed. Most of the processed Illinois coal which was offered did not meet requirements. But there was so-called "Arkansas anthracite." It came up to specifications, and it could be supplied at an acceptable price, except for the cost of hauling it to St. Louis. The Frisco Railroad offered to cut its freight rate from $3.05 to $2.75 a ton, and the Missouri Pacific offered to meet this rate. This still left Arkansas coal rather expensive. Then, with civic spirit as well as an eye to new business, the Frisco cut its rate to $2 a ton in trainload lots. The Interstate Commerce Commission gave its approval. And just in case St. Louis coal merchants might be reluctant to change their established business patterns, the aldermen authorized the city to go into the coal business, voting a $300,000 revolving fund for the purpose. It never was necessary to use that money.

Jesuit settlement-house workers among the Negroes established co-operatives so that the former customers of the "jaggers" could buy better coal. The stoker people enjoyed a boom. The Laclede Gas Company was inundated by applications for gas-heating installations, especially after a new Mississippi Valley Fuel Company pipeline made more cheap natural gas available. The Manufacturers' Railway Company was co-operative. It bought new diesel locomotives. It disclaimed praise, pointing out how economical they were. This turned Jim Ford into a railroad expert. He showed how substantial savings could be made by the stubborn Terminal by substituting diesels for the 113 coal-burners it was using to shunt cars from siding to siding. Tucker organized the enforcement of the anti-smoke regulations. A professional staff was recruited. Arrangements were made with the Department of Weights and Measures to obtain reports on the source and destination of all fuel brought into the city. Inspectors soon stopped the sporadic attempt to run bootleg coal across the bridges in the middle of the night. Inspectors riding in police squad cars photographed offending smokestacks. The Smoke Division was ready to help those with compliance problems.

The result was spectacular. One winter day followed another without a smoke pall. The air was as clear in January as in June. Fog, when it came, was fog and not smog. Inevitably there were days when a southeast wind carried some smoke across the river from the East Side. Fortunately the prevailing wind is from the southwest. Even so, the Union Electric Company, whose huge Cahokia generating plant was the greatest single source of East Side smoke, spent several million dollars to make its six giant stacks less offensive.

The official figures of the United States Weather Bureau, compiled under the direction of Harry F. Wahlgren, tell the story. Here they are for the heating season—September to March—before the ordinance went into effect and through the war years with their sharp increase in industrial activity.

Season	Hours of Moderate Smoke	Thick Smoke
1939–40	599:00	117:30
1940–41	178:00	19:15
1941–42	157:45	26:20
1942–43	127:10	14:50
1943–44	231:50	19:20
1944–45	156:38	33:20

Comparative daily observations made downtown and at the Shaw Arboretum at Gray's Summit, Missouri, thirty miles beyond the city limits, showed only negligible differences. The change was so dramatic that the figures were hardly necessary. Smoke-grimed buildings were cleaned everywhere and the community began to take on a bright look. No measurable smoke was reported in 1958–59.

Mayor Dickmann, however, came to believe that the anti-smoke ordinance cost him his office. Buttons lettered "Dickmann Coal" were distributed during his campaign for re-election. But the real reason for his defeat was the preposterous "Governorship Steal." This was a hare-brained scheme by which the Democrats in the legislature tried to keep the Republican governor-elect, Forrest Donnell, from taking office, and actually postponed his inauguration for more than a month. They outraged all but the blindest partisans. The mayor was a victim of party loyalty. He should have repudiated this scandal, with its overtones of comedy. But, like Harry Truman, Barney Dickmann believed that party membership, like matrimony, was "for better or worse."

In 1940 Forrest Donnell, a Republican comma-splitter, and Larry McDaniel, a rotund, outspoken Dickmann appointee, ran against each other for governor. The returns made Donnell the winner by 3613 votes. The margin was close enough to encourage the notion that recounts in a few counties might change it. Robert E. Hannegan, later head of the Bureau of Internal Revenue, Postmaster General, and Democratic National Committee Chairman, but at the time chairman of the party's city committee, called Democratic leaders to a meeting in the old De Soto Hotel* on November 13, 1940, a week after the election. Dickmann made an appearance. Others who were in that (naturally) smoke-filled room were Senator Bennett Champ Clark, Missouri Attorney General Roy McKittrick, State Senator Michael Kinney, Probate Judge Glendy Arnold, Charles M. Hay, Chairman of the St. Louis Board of Election Commissioners, and C. Marion Hulen, Chairman of the Democratic State Committee. Senator Clark said it was "just a gabfest."

Hulen told the group that he believed there had been irregularities in the voting in Republican St. Louis County and perhaps elsewhere in the state which warranted an investigation. He also said Donnell, meanwhile, might be kept out of the governor's office, which he was scheduled to take over on January 13, 1941. Donnell was not inaugurated until February 26—then only after an appeal to the Missouri Supreme Court. This delay was due to the refusal of the speaker of the lower chamber of the legislature, Morris Osborn, to announce the election of the new governor, as the state constitution required him to do, "immediately after the organization and before proceeding to other business." At least the germ of this scheme, if not all its details, was brought up at the De Soto, since Attorney General McKittrick warned the St. Louis Democrats how risky it would be for them.

"You have a city election coming up in the spring," he said to

---

* Purchased by the Archdiocese of St. Louis, the De Soto, at Locust and Eleventh streets, has been renamed the Hotel Alvernia and remodeled as a home for the elderly. Its guests are not confined to the usual rural or suburban institution in which they perforce are restricted to their own company, but live in a modern hotel within a block or two of stores and theaters. They are not removed from life, but are placed in the midst of it.

Hannegan, "while we country boys have two years to get over it before we have an election." And he told Hulen:

"You better get some money and some lawyers for your investigation. You can't drop it into my office. There are more reasons than one why I won't handle it."

Senator Kinney, the "Gray Fox" of the legislature, was cool to the idea. What was there in it for him? Hay said there had been no voting irregularities in the city. He advised that Donnell be seated and that any contest be taken to the courts. Mayor Dickmann, Senator Clark, and Judge Arnold did not stay long enough to hear of the plan. And McDaniel, its ostensible beneficiary, was not even at the meeting. In the end, matters were left to Hulen. He promised not to proceed without convincing evidence. He sent ten lawyers out to hunt for this. Then he called a meeting of the Democratic State Committee in Jefferson City on December 30. It was there that the plan was perfected.

When the legislature met on January 8, James T. Blair, Jr., the chairman of the Cole County Democratic Committee, who was elected governor in 1956, opened the contest. A joint resolution was adopted and an investigating committee of six Democrats and four Republicans was appointed. Democratic Governor Lloyd C. Stark, the man who helped to smash Boss Tom Pendergast's Kansas City machine after being elected with its support, vetoed the resolution. He said that the election could be contested after Donnell had been inaugurated. The matter was "dropped" into McKittrick's office, after all, when the legislature asked for an opinion on the validity of Governor Stark's veto. The Attorney General ruled that this was illegal, but he also held that the legislature and state officials could disburse no money without the governor's approval. So relief checks and all other state payments were held up. This probably caused even more indignation than the refusal to install the man who, on the face of the election returns, was Governor of Missouri. Donnell appealed to the Supreme Court. Hulen tried to take full responsibility, saying:

"I, and I alone, started this—no one else. If the Supreme Court rules against us, I will be the one who loses. I will have been in the wrong."

The Court kept the legislators from opening ballot boxes, as they had planned to do on Janurary 27, but they blocked Donnell's inauguration for another month. The responsibility for the continuing scandal rested on the Democratic majority. As Curtis Betts of the *Post-Dispatch* pointed out, five of the six St. Louis state senators and nineteen representatives continued to stand against Donnell. Hannegan and Dickmann might have "ordered" them to change their position. That word was not sent to Jefferson City. It was not Dickmann's fight, but he did not denounce the machinations of the party leaders. This—and not his battle against smoke—brought about his defeat in the April municipal elections by Judge William Dee Becker, the man who had restored her baby to Anna Ware. Indeed, Dickmann was almost alone in blaming the anti-smoke ordinance. Just about everybody in St. Louis was enthusiastic about that.

Tucker went back to Washington University as Chairman of the Department of Mechanical Engineering. But Mayor Becker soon asked the university for his services as smoke commissioner, as his predecessor had done. Chancellor Compton felt the university should help the community. So for a year Tucker met an eight o'clock class and then spent the rest of the day in City Hall. Back at the university in 1942, he was in demand as a consultant on smoke and air pollution in Pittsburgh, Los Angeles, New York, and a dozen other cities.

But after a taste of municipal government, the savor lingered on. The spring of 1949, Tucker was elected to the uncompensated position of chairman of a board of freeholders to draw up a new city charter. With certain restrictions, Missouri permits its larger cities to govern themselves under municipal constitutions adopted by their voters. St. Louis adopted such a charter in 1876, and a new one in 1914. But after thirty changeful years, revisions had become desirable. City departments needed functional reorganization. New sources of revenue had to be found. When the city divorced itself from St. Louis County, it had been saddled with so-called "county offices"—sheriff, collector, court clerk, and the like—which are regulated by state statutes. These had lost much of their usefulness. Their functions could be transferred to city offices with gains in efficiency and economy. It had been legally impossible to bring these offices under civil service when St. Louis added a merit system amendment to its charter. As a result, the sheriff, for example, had several hundred jobs, all political plums, at his disposal, while the mayor had given up virtually all patronage. So minor officials had—and still have—inordinate influence on election day. They were unwilling to give this up, so they defeated the proposed charter despite Tucker's work—and that, for a full year, added up to forty hours a week in addition to his university duties.

Unfortunately some of the state's provisions governing charters come close to being booby traps. Thus a city may impose only those taxes specifically mentioned in its charter. The freeholders, unable to anticipate what revenues might be needed in the future, felt obliged to authorize many forms of taxation, though there was no intention of imposing them in the foreseeable future. This made it easy for unscrupulous politicians to persuade a good many voters that every authorized tax would be levied as soon as the charter was approved. This misrepresentation defeated the proposal.

Mayor Becker was killed as a passenger in the wartime demonstration of a glider at the St. Louis airport—one of those meaningless activities demanded of public officials. He was succeeded by the President of the Board of Aldermen, Aloys J. Kaufmann, also a Republican. The "Governorship Steal" was recalled to insure Mayor Kaufmann's election to a second term, although he deserved re-election on his merits. As a wartime executive subject to overriding national necessities, he could do little more than plan for the future. Refusing to run for a third term, he was succeeded by Joseph Darst, a Democrat who found himself confronted by at least one World War II problem, civil defense. Again a call went out for the engineering professor. This time, as it turned out, Tucker left the campus for good. Joe Darst persuaded him to run for mayor in 1951. Despite the charter defeat, he was elected by a margin of more than 50,000 votes, by far the biggest in the history of St. Louis. He broke this record four years later by winning by almost 75,000 votes, with the practical politicians almost solidly against him.

His lack of ward-heeler support bolstered Tucker's independence. On the other hand, it did not make for easy relations with "organization" aldermen. In his first term the aldermen gleefully overrode his vetoes. They were reluctant to follow his advice on how to keep city expenditures within income, although St. Louis may not make appropriations in excess of anticipated revenues. But the professor-mayor learned about aldermen and they learned about him. With a notorious exception or two, Tucker defends the aldermen. They now are co-operative on major issues. He says they are jealous only where minor matters are concerned. The placing of a "Stop" sign is an important detail in their relations with their constituents. So is a "spot" zoning ordinance. Tucker believes that citizens have a right to seek such favors. He feels they will yield whenever they are convinced of the overriding importance of the general welfare. When they and their aldermen persist in having their way, the mayor believes there has been a "failure in communication."

By way of proof, he points out that the aldermen now follow the advice of the City Plan Commission on "spot" zoning.

St. Louis always needs money. It is a perfect illustration of Galbraith's theory of public poverty side by side with private affluence. There is money in St. Louis, and there is more St. Louis money in the suburbs. But the City Treasurer's pen always hovers over the red inkwell. The Board of Estimate and Apportionment is frustrated and bedeviled. Mayor Kaufmann found at least a partial answer in the earnings tax, levied on all who make their livelihoods within the city. It is fair enough that those who use the city's streets, are protected by its police and firemen, and enjoy its parks, its zoo, and its museums should pay at least a small part of the cost. But this earnings tax, first limited to one half of one per cent, could be imposed only if authorized by the legislature. And the Missouri Legislature is not noted for its friendly attitude toward St. Louis. It is inclined to treat the state's richest source of revenue as a stepchild. St. Louis County representatives regularly opposed the earnings tax until the authorization was made permanent. They saw votes in being niggardly. Some legislators feared that it would become a precedent for other cities. A special session refused to reauthorize the levy. This meant a loss to the city of $7,000,000 a year in revenue just as Tucker took office. So a fight for the tax became his first job. He and Kaufmann, a Democrat and a Republican, "took to the road" in the fall of 1953 and the early winter of 1954. Before the legislature convened, they called on member after member. Over the "blue-plate special"—there was no fancy wining and dining—they explained the city's plight. So in September, 1954, the authorization was renewed for a year with the stipulation that it would become permanent if the citizens of St. Louis voted to make it so. And in 1959 the voters were allowed to raise it to one per cent. This they did at once.

St. Louisans are as reluctant as anybody else to pay taxes. Yet they are rather good about approving needed increases. And the earnings tax has the added attraction of converting county residents from "free riders" to taxpayers. St. Louisans also have a good record of voting for public-improvement bond issues. Such an issue, involving $110,000,000, was one of the most important goals achieved by Tucker. It followed a $43,527,000 bond issue approved under the Kaufmann administration. The Tucker bonds covered twenty-nine projects, ranging from repairs of viaducts over the Mill Creek Valley to the construction of a planetarium in Forest Park, and the voters said "yes" to each of them. They also approved a $1,500,000 bond issue to cover the city's part of the cost of acquiring eight blocks between Aloe and Memorial plazas. These parks now have been connected by a block-wide strip of greenery. The remainder of this area was used to put up half a dozen apartment buildings under the federal urban renewal law, thus creating an attractive residential neighborhood on the fringe of the business district.

A few years later the city instigated a much more ambitious urban renewal project. Early in 1959 work began on the clearing of almost 500 acres of slum and semi-slum property between Eighteenth Street and Grand Avenue and Olive Street and the Mill Creek Valley railroad tracks. This is the biggest project of its kind in the United States. The land adjacent to the tracks is to become an "industrial park," given over to light manufacturing plants in a setting of lawn, shrubs, and trees. Most of the remaining land is to be covered with apartment buildings—some low, some tall—grouped imaginatively in a parklike setting. There also will be some shops. Five blocks at the western edge, along Grand and Laclede avenues, are being taken over by St. Louis University for an extension of its campus. When this so-called Mill Creek Valley project is completed, the slums nearest the city's heart will have been cleared away. New opportunities for industrial employment within the city will have been created. And a handsome residential neighborhood more than two miles long will extend from the downtown to "west of Grand."

This would not have been possible had not large areas north and south of this district been redeveloped for low-cost housing, chiefly under Mayor Darst. These made it possible to tear down slum property without depriving its occupants of shelter. The Mill Creek Valley project was started with $62,000,000 in loans and grants. Joseph R. Passonneau, formerly chief of design for the Tennessee Valley Authority and now dean of Washington University's school of architecture, has pointed out that in additon to providing 150 acres for industrial development, it will contain 2100 housing units in a pleasant, protected setting, "a five minutes' walk from schools, a ten minutes' walk to work, a five minutes' ride from the river, and a twenty minutes' drive from open country." Local real estate interests are handling the industrial area, and James Scheuer, of City and Suburban Homes, New York, made the best bid for the residential development. Mill Creek should spur on less ambitious urban renewal projects in other parts of the city.

The most spectacular change in the city's appearance, however, is the forty-block national park being developed on the downtown riverfront as a memorial to Jefferson's Louisiana Purchase and the westward expansion of the nation. The dominant feature of this tree-studded park is to be Eero Saarinen's 619 foot high, stainless-steel, parabolic arch symbolizing St. Louis as the Gateway of the West. The Old Cathedral and the Old Courthouse and two new museums also will be incorporated in the memorial. The State Highway Department is to build another bridge at its southern edge, which one hopes will be architecturally worthy of the Eads Bridge at its northern edge. Two other downtown bridges, the city's MacArthur Bridge and the East St. Louis Veterans' Memorial Bridge, are less than five minutes walk from the park site. Third Street already has been rebuilt as a super-boulevard. It will carry the traffic of the Mark Twain, Daniel Boone, and other expressways along the park. Plans for commercial and residential redevelopment of the west side of Third Street, facing the park, are being drawn.

Ray Wittcoff already has put up the sleek Thomas Jefferson Building, and he has remodeled the International Fur Exchange. The Peabody Coal Company has built an attractive office building. Lewis Kitchen is perfecting plans for a group of apartment buildings which are to occupy five blocks along the northern half of the memorial. Early in 1960, a Metropolitan Chamber of Commerce committee, headed by James Hickok of the First National Bank, raised $20,000,000 in equity money for a start on the redevelopment of thirty blocks south and west of the riverfront national park. This will link the park to Memorial Plaza, thus giving the city a new "core" from the river to Grand Avenue. The outstanding feature of this project will be a 55,000-seat stadium, designed for later enlargement. The stadium will be the home of the St. Louis Cardinals and a National Football League team which Joseph Griesedieck, president of the Falstaff breweries, helped to bring to St. Louis. It also will accommodate circuses and other outdoor events. The project includes ample garage facilities, which will greatly relieve downtown parking troubles. A riverfront motel and two office buildings also are included. All will be grouped around ample, landscaped plazas. The riverfront national park with its great arch, however, will be the crown of the new St. Louis.

This will not be an empty park. An observation platform at the top of the sixty-story arch, as well as the museums and the Courthouse,

will attract many visitors. Restoration of the Old Cathedral already
has been undertaken by Archbishop Joseph Ritter, and it will remain
in regular use. The archbishop, incidentally, also handsomely restored
old St. John's Basilica in the Plaza apartment area. The excursion
steamer *Admiral*—with five air-conditioned decks accommodating
4000 passengers, and with two ballrooms for 1200 dancers—will
continue to make its morning and evening trips from the levee. Captain
Billy Mencke no doubt will find a new anchorage nearby for his famous
showboat, the *Goldenrod*. And many of the workers in downtown
stores and offices will enjoy, whenever they can, a few minutes of sun in
the riverfront park.

St. Louis has been waiting a long time for this embellishment. The
old section along the riverfront—mostly warehouses—was cleared
twenty years ago, when Mayor Dickmann reached an agreement with
the federal government under which the city would contribute the site
and part of the cost of the development. The war, naturally, put the
plan on the shelf. After the war, Congress was reluctant to live up to the
government's obligation. Delay was encouraged by turning the area
into a parking lot for 4500 automobiles, and by the unwillingness of the
railroads to relocate tracks. Various interests made attempts from time
to time to obtain the site for almost everything from a housing
development to a baseball park. But they were blocked by a small group
of vigilant citizens, headed by the late Luther Ely Smith and William
Crowdus. It was Smith and his Amherst College friend, Jim Ford, who
raised $250,000 for the architectural competition which produced the
Saarinen design in 1948. Then Russell Dearmont, a public-spirited
lawyer, became president of the Missouri Pacific and broke the deadlock
over the railroad tracks. Senators Symington and Hennings and
Representatives Sullivan and Karsten reminded Congress that St. Louis
long ago had taken forty blocks of buildings off its tax books and voted
a $7,500,000 bond issue. So the federal money for the project—
$5,000,000 to start—was voted after two decades of frustrating delay.
Private enterprise, the affluent side of our society, now is beginning
to match what governments have started.

The bicentennary of St. Louis in 1964 is a considerable stimulant for
completion of the arch and the stadium, and for a general municipal
face-lifting. There will not be a grandiose world's fair such as that of
1904, which now lives on only in old scrapbooks. It has been decided
—and soundly decided—by the mayor's committee, headed by Charles

van Ravenswaay, that the celebration should center around what is permanent in the city. But surely there will be as much excitement and color as there was at the old Jockey Club, the Côte Brilliante track, the fairgrounds, or the most lavish Veiled Prophet visitation. There will be regattas and parades, fireworks and flags. But plans also are being made for an extraordinary Symphony season, special performances of the Municipal Opera, and notable displays in the City Art Museum and the galleries of the Missouri Historical Society. Learned societies—and others—will meet here in 1964. The city should be as attractive as it was when "Robert Owen used to come here to escape from the stagnant pessimism of his impossible perfection at New Harmony, and here he and Madame D'Arusmont (Fanny Wright) used to lecture and have seances, at which the most advanced radicalism was disseminated without . . . disturbing the general good humor any more than if rose water had been sprayed abroad on the tolerant air." John James Audubon used to come over from Louisville to quicken his spirit. Thomas Ford and Tom Reynolds and Ninian Edwards, in their years as Governor of Illinois, used to come down from Springfield. As in Mark Twain's "Gilded Age," people again are expected to come to St. Louis for more than business and baseball.

While Mayor Tucker has been successful in pushing municipal reconstruction, his desire for a modern city charter has been frustrated. Another board of freeholders was elected in his first term in City Hall. Under the chairmanship of George Stemmler, it submitted a new charter. Although strongly endorsed by the mayor, it was defeated by the same voters who a little later re-elected him. The ostensible reason for the defeat was a provision reducing the number of aldermen and providing that only half of them should be elected by wards and the other half at large. Tucker, however, was philosophic. Again he said:

"It simply was a failure in communication. We did not make the importance of a new charter clear enough."

Perhaps he is right. It also may be true that too many conflicting interests are involved in a charter to create a clear yes-or-no issue. It may be significant that in recent years several amendments to the old charter, presented one at a time, were adopted.

The heaviest burden on the conscience of the community undoubtedly is the care of its impoverished sick and aged. There never seems to be money enough to keep the city hospitals fully staffed and adequately supplied. The Chronic Hospital—especially its century-old, prisonlike West Wing—is more or less a standing scandal. It is over-crowded. Generally there are about 1500 patients in a building never meant to accommodate more than 1000. Usually there are a few hundred mental cases in the place who should not be there at all. They really are the state's responsibility, but the nearby St. Louis State Mental Hospital, the big red building with the dome that dominates the South Side skyline as it is seen from the viaducts across Mill Creek Valley, also is overcrowded and inadequately supported. Built for 1500 patients, it has for years accommodated 3000 or more. It is admittedly a firetrap. Its superintendent, Dr. Louis Kohler, is a competent man, but his reg-ular appeals to the legislature never are adequately answered.

This is not peculiarly a St. Louis story. Everywhere people avoid the rank smell of poverty and close their ears to the moan of pain. The afflicted become statistics, and their relief becomes a "long-range problem." The hospitals do get a considerable share of the city's tax dollar, but their budgets are pared, like those of all other departments. The rule is "a little for everybody." Some day it may be "first things first."

Political integration of the city and its satellites would create a more rational and economical community. At Tucker's suggestion and with Ford Foundation help, Professor Thomas Eliot of Washington Uni-versity and Professor Peter Steinbicker of St. Louis University directed a survey which brought the needs of the area into focus. They recom-mended the formation of a metropolitan district to take over some of the common concerns of city and suburbs. A board of freeholders was elected in 1958 to work out a specific proposal. Its members debated the merits of a city-county merger and of a district plan for ten months. Finally they decided in favor of the latter, by the narrowest of margins. So much time had been lost, however, that only a makeshift scheme could be thrown together. Under it, a metropolitan district, divided into eleven boroughs, would have controlled traffic and transit, some land-use planning, police communications, and civil defense, and it would have absorbed the existing metropolitan sewer district.

Mayor Tucker and most suburban officials opposed this scheme. The *Post-Dispatch* and the *Globe-Democrat* stridently supported it. So did the Metropolitan Chamber of Commerce. Most suburban papers were against it. Disagreement filled the air—as when the St. Louis CBS radio and television stations made this the occasion for taking their first stand on a public issue, and the radio station came out against the plan in the afternoon and the television station endorsed it that night. The sound and the fury were in vain. On November 3, 1959, the plan was defeated in the city, two to one, and it was beaten in the County, three to one. Among the No-voters were those who fear any change. Parochial suburbanites were determined to keep their communities "exclusive." (Only a few months earlier the consolidation of swank Ladue, Frontenac, and Huntleigh had been defeated.) Much of the opposition, however, was enlightened. Many voters felt with Mayor Tucker that the plan would create "an additional layer of government" which would produce new conflicts and few compensating benefits. To city voters, it seemed that the plan was concerned almost exclusively with better transportation for the suburbs. It assumed no responsibility for costly urban functions such as slum clearance, hospitals, and welfare services. "It should be bluntly stated," said the mayor, "that the core or central city in any metropolitan area performs certain functions which result from the existence of such an area. Upon these kinds of metropolitan problems, which tend to be physically located in the city, the district plan is silent. It would seem to be the implication of the plan that they are city problems which the city alone must solve, but they are as genuinely metropolitan as traffic control and planning." Despite its liberal supporters, the plan looked to city voters like a scheme to stick them with even more than they already were stuck with.

The outcome was disappointing to many, since it seemed to emphasize an insurmountable narrowness and selfishness which failed to apprehend the advantages in debalkanization. The test, however, may not have been a fair one, since the proposal was not broad enough. The debate has brought about a better understanding of urban-suburban relationships. There is a clearer understanding that any fresh proposal must be to the advantage of all. The difficulty is that so many of the problems of the city are not the same as those of the suburbs. Especially in the newer suburbs, the needs generally are elementary— sewers, paving, police and fire protection, and modern automobile highways to reduce the driving time between home and office. The city voter, with well-developed municipal services, may feel that he already has paid his share for expressways of which he makes relatively little use. His most expensive problems stem from neighborhoods more or less impoverished by the flight to the suburbs. There is nevertheless a mutuality of interest which was pointed out by Tucker. It will be recognized if the totality of the community is recognized. This recognition need not exclude respect for the identity of the lesser communities within the larger one.

The next initiative may come from the more mature suburbs. Among these are University City, the fifth largest municipality in Missouri, Webster Groves, Kirkwood, and Clayton, the county seat. With the exception of Florissant, settled by the French in 1785 and long an outlying rural community, all of them were incorporated after the Civil War. Most of the newer suburbs actually were formed after World War II. Ladue and Webster Groves once meant to St. Louis what Westchester meant to New York, the North Shore to Chicago, or the Main Line to Philadelphia. They were Suburbia with a big S, and that meant, more or less, estates, elegance, and wealth. The suburbanite's store or factory was on the city tax books, so the city did not need to tax his home. But suburbs mushroomed into a problem for cities with the coming of the automobile. Indeed, by simultaneously choking and dispersing our cities, the motorcar may be doing greater harm than it is by spreading its billboard-lined highways across a once charming countryside. It is rushing us into a motel culture, whose chief characteristics may be deadly speed and vapid rootlessness. For cities, it carries the threat of an ever increasing exodus of householders, with business and industry following in their wake. There is more than nostalgia in the pain which comes when once rich-respectable streets like Vandeventer Place or Washington Avenue go to seed while miles and miles of ranch houses sprout on soil freshly turned by the bulldozers, and TV antennae spring up like forests of wire sculpture to displace tall pin oaks, gums, and sycamores. The rickety little red-brick country courthouse in Clayton has been replaced by a high, massive, block-long structure. Around it, and almost overnight, sprang up blocks and blocks of "colonial" shops, including big branches of the downtown department stores. Office building after office building went up for doctors, dentists, lawyers, and insurance brokers. Hotels and motels were built. Industries sprang up. The big Ford and Chrysler plants are in the County. So are McDonnell Aircraft and the new Monsanto office and research "campus." Churches—fashionable St. Peter's, for example —moved from the city to the County. Even country clubs—topflight Bellerive, for example—have been moved even while new ones, like Old Warson, were springing up. The building industries boomed as the County's population passed half a million, and housewives took to saying:

"I never go downtown anymore."

Insofar as this represents growth—and much of it does—it is healthy and welcome, but insofar as it means merely the building of a new and less orderly community while abandoning the old city, it seems sheer waste. And the growing pains! The older suburbs just across the city line, part of the city in all but legal fact, suffered least. They have sidewalks. The new communities, if communities they be, which accommodate the automobile but not the pedestrian, emphasize the relation between "urban" and "urbane." What is to be said of a town which denies the walking man enjoyable prospects of avenues and squares, of plazas and promenades, the mingling of strolling people? Walking means talking. But to the creature on wheels the pedestrian is only a nuisance to be frightened by a blast of the horn. Perhaps the automobile is breeding a species with eyes only for the white line and the red light. Perhaps that is why the suburbs are encrusted with garish gas stations, corrugated-iron eateries, catch-as-catch-can stores, all jerry-built helter-skelter along the roadside. The motorists' attention can be caught only by the most frenetically vulgar neon. There can be no leisurely window-shopping at 60 m.p.h. There is comfort, often ostentatious comfort, along suburbia's "lanes" and "courts." Many of its homes, with their patios and pools, are handsome. There is St. Louis money in the suburbs. But so many of these homes are terribly private, self-centered. The absence of sidewalks is symptomatic. The incense of asphalt, however, is slowly pervading the County air. Boundaries between suburbs are becoming as undiscernable as the equator. As trade and industry grow beyond the city limits, the city and the satellites begin to look more and more alike. The difference is largely one of age. This, of course, is a big one. It would be minimized if the pace of urban rebuilding were as fast as the spread of blight. But in this race the cities are playing a long shot. Of course, they would have a cinch if money were poured into redevelopment as it is into rearmament. Modern man, scared creature, has a strange sense of values!

The Committee for Economic Development predicts that St. Louis —and American cities in general—in the future will consist of a modernized downtown shopping neighborhood with some offices and de luxe apartments attached. After a wide fringe of industrial slums and semislums will come the overgrown dormitory satellites with their big

new shopping centers and industries, often in a parklike setting. The
pattern is familiar enough, but St. Louis is rapidly breaking it by developing its new East-West axis. With the completion of the Mill Creek
redevelopment, this will extend from the river to Grand Avenue. New
building along Lindell Boulevard suggests that this axis of improved
property will be pushed to Forest Park and the city limits. The arrow
in the bow of St. Louis is being polished. It may, however, remain
as slim as it is bright, being narrowly confined between the factories
and railroads of the valley and the growing Negro neighborhoods of the
North Side. The West End and the sprawling South Side surely will continue to be attractive residential sections. Yet inevitably more and more
people will live in the County, not necessarily by choice but because
there is no room for them in the city. This became clear after the war,
when many young couples who would have preferred a city apartment
could find only a suburban ranch house. But these are essentially city
people. The suburbs are not changing them as much as expected. Instead, the people are changing the suburbs. St. Louis County no longer
is a Republican stronghold.

New residential communities are growing on the Illinois side of the
river and the meat packers are moving away. Ludwig Bemelmans
once described East St. Louis as "beautiful Dreck." Sherwood Anderson called it the city in which nobody lives. And for a long time it
certainly was the city nobody cared about—except as a source of money,
legitimate and not so legitimate. It was the city of Clabber Alley,
Whisky Chute, and the Valley, or railroad yards, slums, and dives. Its
political corruption incubated the 1919 race riots, and the shadow of
the 1877 strike overhung its factories. In fact, it was almost as bad
as its reputation. But roll the drums. Sound a fanfare of brasses. The
National Municipal Association and *Look* have named East St. Louis,
along with neighboring Alton and De Soto on the Missouri side of
the river, as one of the "All-America" cities of 1959. The community
has moved against vice and gambling. An improvement bond issue has
been voted. New health centers, schools, and parks have been created.
It is not yet the golden garden of the universe, but it is looking up,
and it is about to be linked to downtown St. Louis by yet another
bridge. And that means, incidentally, that downtown St. Louis still is
the heart of the metroplex—to use a new word introduced by educational television.

xxxv. Old City and New People

St. Louis is an old city full of new people. Only 38 per cent of the adults in the city, compared with 48 per cent in the County, were born there. One fourth of the people in the city and County have lived there less than twenty years. More than 10 per cent have lived there less than ten years.

If more than half of the population had its beginnings elsewhere, how much respect can there be for "old ways, old manners, old families?" Can the established customs, the remembered history of a minority dominate the community? Or are bygones strictly for the Historical Society?

Most American cities are largely contemporary phenomena. To the extent that they are, they are as alike as the standard-brand packages on chain-store shelves, the standardized cars and TV sets, the standardized and syndicated contents of most newspapers—and perhaps most minds too. We are a wandering people, conditioned to look for the same things everywhere. Yet St. Louis clings with more than ordinary tenacity to its singularities, its individuality. This must be attributed to tradition—to the devotion of old citizens to tradition, and to its appeal for new citizens. But change in the city and the pace of change must be attributed largely to the impact of its new people. Who are they?

There are the Negroes. There were 2000 of them at most in a city of 150,000 on the eve of the Civil War. Now they constitute 30 per cent of the city's population. One of the significant differences between St. Louis and the County lies in the fact that only 8.8 per cent of the County's residents were born in southern states, compared with 22.1 per cent in the city, and being born in a southern state is likely to mean being born a Negro. According to the Metropolitan Survey, 70 per cent of the neighborhoods in the city and in the County fall between the extremes of rich and poor, but the County has more of the rich, the city more of the poor. And many of the city's problems stem from the low-income neighborhoods in which most Negroes live. The problems range from substandard housing to crime. If the proportion of Negroes in the city's population increases, must the problems grow more serious? Or is there not hope in the fact that the Negroes soon should control half a dozen of the city's twenty-eight wards and assume responsibility commensurate with their authority? They have been represented from time to time on the Board of Education, usually because a mayor appointed a Negro to fill a vacancy until the next election. (No mayor would dream of appointing school board members as unqualified as those the voters often elect!) The Negro's surest way to public office still is by appointment, as it was when President Grant in 1871 appointed James Milton Turner, the son of a slave but educated by the nuns of the St. Louis cathedral school, consul general to Liberia because Turner was credited with swinging 20,000 Negro votes against Gratz Brown and Schurz. Negroes still tend to be bloc voters. Their best leaders, however, are less interested in winning office than in lining up votes as the most effective way of getting better schools and improved social services. Typical of these is the man of whom Ralph Coghlan wrote in the *Post-Dispatch:*

In my ignorance, I have just learned that a man named Jordan W. Chambers is one of the most powerful politicians in St. Louis. This confession of ignorance will amuse professional politicians, who have long known about the influence of the Nineteenth Ward Negro night club owner and undertaker. It will amuse the Negro population of St. Louis, who have for years looked to Chambers for guidance and for instructions as to how to vote on crucial issues. But I find my ignorance is shared by many people who think they know what goes on in St. Louis.

The former editor had met Chambers through H. Sam Priest, an old hand in Democratic politics, who remarked that "if he were a white man, he probably would be a national figure." Coghlan continued:

Like most other Negroes, Chambers used to be a Republican, but he made an abrupt switch to the Democratic party when Franklin Roosevelt came to power. In 1934, in the hard days of the Depression, he became a constable, a job he used to defend the poor from unfair evictions and the like. He quit being a constable in 1942. Since 1938 he has been a member of the Democratic City Committee. . . . Chambers is an organization man, or again, to quote Mr. Priest, a structural leader. He is very close to his people. . . . At his undertaking place (Cardinal and Franklin) he holds an open hour each day (usually between 6 and 7) when he listens to the troubles or ideas of his people. He may receive 10 or 15 each evening. Later on, he goes to the Riviera (considered to be the best Negro night club in the Midwest with name bands and good floor shows.) There, in a mecca of local Negroes, he sees many other people. The cocktail bar on the lower floor of the club is often turned into a kind of debating society. There "Pops," as the youngsters call him, listens to argument and dispenses wisdom. "Some nights," said Pops, "you might see three or four Negro Ph.D.s at the bar."

Obviously captivated, but not unaware of how Chambers combined profit and politics, Coghlan recorded a further observation: "One of his friends added that Chambers is a smart businessman who would not overlook the opportunity to 'turn a quick dollar,' though it was made clear that he did not mean dishonestly. However, if such a thing as a policy game were permitted in St. Louis, he said, Chambers would not hesitate at taking a cut. Chambers, as a matter of fact, told me he thought the police drive against policy was mistaken. He said it had been played here for fifty years and 'if you take everything away from the people . . . '"

Naturally enough, this businessman-politician, sipping mineral water in his night club, held forth on the need for "sound" men and the danger of "leftists." He deflated the Wallace boom and he is no enthusiast for such things as fair-employment-practice laws. He is no troublemaker. He is a little old-fashioned, but he is not the type that accepts appointments to Liberia or cares too much about being a trustee of a state college for Negroes.

But things are changing for the race in St. Louis—slowly. Negroes are better housed than they used to be. They are getting better schooling than they used to get. Better employment opportunities are opening up. Segregation in the schools was mandatory under state law until the Supreme Court struck it down in 1954. St. Louis was ready for that decision and welcomed it. St. Louis University already had opened its doors to Negro students and Washington University was doing so, first in its graduate schools and then in all divisions. The law school of the state university had been opened to them after an appeal to the Supreme Court. More dramatically, Archbishop Ritter desegregated the parochial schools in 1952.

There were no serious incidents when the public schools were desegregated. To permit orderly reassignment of teachers, this was done in two phases by School Superintendent Philip Hickey. In the September following the Court's order, the city's two teachers' colleges were merged and all high schools were opened without regard to race. The following September the grammar schools were opened on the same basis. Desegregation actually ameliorated some of the problems of the Board of Education. Under the state segregation law, there were half-empty schools in mixed neighborhoods. With integration, more efficient use of available classrooms became possible. In subsequent years a trend toward all-Negro and all-white schools again developed, but this is a result of "real estate" segregation. As more neighborhoods became exclusively Negro in population, their schools did too. Here is a tougher problem. Yet there have been no unseemly demonstrations against Negro "invasions" of white neighborhoods, even though there are the usual complaints about the deterioration of property values. In "exclusive" Windermere Place, an effort is being made to maintain high property standards while welcoming Negro residents.

There is no discrimination against Negroes in public conveyances, in stores, at the ball park, or Kiel Auditorium. It is gradually breaking down in hotels and restaurants, but the aldermen have not yet adopted the "equal accommodation" ordinance repeatedly recommended by Mayor Tucker. The division, however, is close, and failure to adopt the ordinance may be due to a feeling on the part of a few aldermen that they must vote not in accord with their own views, but according to the expressed desires of businessmen constituents. The majority actually may agree with the St. Louis *Review,* the Catholic archdiocesan newspaper, which said of Kansas City:

Their City Council passed a public accommodations bill by a stunning 3–1 majority. They said, in effect, that there would be no racial discrimination in their city. They said . . . that you can't expect a man to act like a civilized person unless you treat him like one . . . And they also have indirectly hinted that we in St. Louis will have a large concentration of population west of the city limits, and a stadium, and a bright, shiny downtown on the riverfront, and no-man's land in between—unless we morally grow up.

St. Louisans are trying to overcome vestiges of a stubborn old prejudice, and they are doing it in an environment in which they must practice what they preach. Increasingly accepted is the viewpoint of Robert Blackburn, of the mayor's brain trust. He is convinced that, far from being a handicap, the Negroes of St. Louis are becoming one of the strongest factors in the city's stability. Perhaps the Negro press —with a sensationalism in its news columns which hardly accords with its protesting editorials—is a major obstacle. Some people must grow up on both sides of the line.

Also among the new people are the "Hoosiers." In Missouri that name does not mean a gentleman from Indiana. It is applied to persons whom a Negro might call "poor white trash." But "trash" they are not. They are people with a rural background—many come from impoverished Ozark counties—who have given up trying to live on a submarginal farm and a relief check. The six-year drought of the mid-1950s —when it became impossible to keep farm animals alive without buying tank truckloads of water—drove many of them off the land. Unlike the prosperous farmer's son who comes to the city from the state university to start his career, these people are utterly unprepared for life on asphalt. They have little money, little education, and little of the skill demanded by urban industries. Inevitably they crowd into poor housing. Their only escape too often is a questionable corner tavern. Juvenile delinquency and worse are to be expected. Those who get to know these people best are the police and the social workers, and the managers of housing projects.

It may seem unfair that they should be a burden on the city, but St. Louis has broad shoulders and a pretty good heart. It has educated wave after wave of immigrant greenhorns and helped them to become prosperous citizens. "Exclusive" new suburbs can't do that. They do not begin to have the compassion and the resourcefulness of the old cities. So St. Louis may discharge this new task, too, and with means which seem inadequate. Maybe it will train "hoosiers" for the Yankee baseball machine or for nuclear laboratories. What's a city for? Cocktail parties and bridge games?

Not only the new elements, however, are sources of change. There is growth in the old stock, too. Mayor Tucker is a product of such change. He comes from the South Side, where the Republicans held sway for almost a century because the old Germans decided to "fight mit Lincoln und Franz Sigel" against Jeff Davis and Clai Jackson. They elected a fair number of fair mayors—men like Frederick Kreismann and Henry W. Kiel, men who were expected to bother less about national politics than about running a frugal, efficient city government. There always was a Democratic opposition on the South Side, but it was not too difficult for a man to make his mark in one of its sketchy

ward organizations south of the Mill Creek Valley. The Democratic
panjandrums recruited their strong battalions on the North Side, and
the South Side Republicans generally had to drum up considerable
independent support to beat them. (Al Kaufmann is an example of a
rare species, a successful Republican candidate from the North Side,
but he was elected president of the Board of Aldermen in a city-wide
election, and he had a good South Side name. And didn't he buy a
home on the South Side's Federer Place after he left City Hall?)

The closest thing to an old-fashioned political machine that St. Louis
has seen since Ed Butler's regime was the organization built in the
North Side wards by Sheriff Thomas Callanan with the financial support of his younger brother, Lawrence, then the "boss" of the steam
fitters' union. These two grew up in the North Side organization which
had as its most valuable asset the popularity of the late representative
Jack Cochran, known in Washington as the "watchdog of the Treasury."
Tom Callanan went into the coal business. He also was interested in
a saloon. When he ran for committeeman in 1936, he was defeated.
But he was appointed a deputy coroner and went about making political alliances, notably with State Senator Edward J. (Jellyroll) Hogan,
Jr. With Hogan's help, he sought to undermine Mike Kinney who,
according to some of the "boys," was losing his political touch. Callanan failed to drive Kinney out of public office, but for a while he certainly eclipsed him.

Callanan was the last of the bosses who threatened to dominate the
city and wield considerable power in the state too. He made his bid
after having been elected coroner in 1944 and announcing for the
sheriff's office (which he won) in 1948, after making an alliance with
Forrest Smith, the successful candidate for governor. Smith was known
as "Dear Pensioner" because as state auditor he sent a letter beginning with that salutation with every check that went out from Jefferson City, implying that it was a personal benefaction. His backers had
formed connections with Charles Binaggio, the gangster leader of a
remnant of the old Kansas City Pendergast machine, as well as with
Tom Callanan. Larry Callanan had vowed to "make his brother the
biggest man in the city." Perhaps he came closer than he knew. With
Smith in the executive mansion, the Callanans sought to control the
police board, the circuit attorney's office, and the Board of Election
Commissioners, the city's law-enforcement agencies and its election
machinery. These, plus the Democratic City Committee and the patron-

age of the sheriff's office, would have formed a strong base of operations. Sheriff Callanan acted like a man who had the feel of power and liked it. Typical of this were the annual Christmas parties he held in the big Civil Courts Building. Even the last of these, held after his power was broken and he was on his way out of office and his brother was headed for the penitentiary, was attended by 3000 guests who were served 100 roast turkeys, 200 pounds of ham, 200 pounds of sausages, 100 pounds of cheese, 16 cases of liquor, and 120 cases of beer.

But Callanan overreached himself. With the governor ready to name his police commissioners, the press disclosed that gamblers, racketeers, and gangsters were waiting for the green light in St. Louis. The city again was to be "wide open". This antagonized some of Callanan's strongest supporters, and the continued publicity forced Governor Smith to make more acceptable appointments. There was no doubt about the chagrin of the underworld. Binaggio, who had met with its agents and had made promises which induced the "Syndicate" to make expensive preparations for a rush of business, was murdered in Kansas City in the gangster manner!

Callanan's ambitions touched off a revolt among Democratic politicians. He lost nineteen of the thirty-two seats on the city committee. Kinney, always shrewd and now backed by the most conservative elements in the city, held his seat in the state senate in a close fight with Callanan's candidate, John L. ("Doc") Lawler, the steam fitters' business agent. The sheriff's candidate for attorney general carried St. Louis but lost in the outstate voting. His candidates for governor and circuit attorney were defeated in St. Louis. Yet Callanan tried to consolidate his faction as best he could. He talked of running for mayor in 1953 but finally backed Mark D. Eagleton, a respected lawyer and former president of the board of police commissioners, for the Democratic nomination. This Callanan support was a jumbo albatross around Eagleton's neck. He was defeated by Tucker. This really was the end of Callanan's attempt to build a machine. He did run against Tucker in 1957 for the mayoral nomination, but that was a pathetic anticlimax.

Callanan went from the sheriff's office in 1953 to the $150-a-week job of director of the Steam Fitters' Educational and Welfare Fund. Shortly thereafter his home was bombed, apparently a sign that the racketeers were in arms against him. The *coup de grâce* came when Federal Judge Rubey M. Hulen in 1954 sentenced Larry Callanan to twelve years in prison for conspiring to violate the anti-racketeering law. (He was paroled late in 1959.) Thomas Callanan died on April 4, 1959, at the age of fifty-nine after several heart attacks.

The South Side, like most of the city, now is almost solidly Democratic. In part this reflects the community's respect for Mayor Tucker and for Senator Hennings and Senator Symington. The Republicans in St. Louis and Missouri are a sadly divided party. Finding it increasingly difficult to beat the Democrats after the Roosevelt landslides (St. Louis and Missouri were for Adlai Stevenson), the Republicans took to fighting each other. And as Tucker points out, a divided party does not attract winning candidates.

He might well add that poor pay is not the best device for attracting good men to public office. The St. Louis delegation in the state legislature generally proves this conclusively. St. Louis—and Missouri too —can be too frugal. The city voters, for example, again have refused to raise the $10,000 limit on municipal salaries. This makes it difficult to employ a competent chief of hospitals or director of public works.

It would be preposterous to maintain that on election day or any other time St. Louisans, new or old, ask themselves what Tom Benton or Frank Blair, or Carl Schurz or Joe Folk would do. Many of them do not know too much about these worthies. Yet St. Louis does have a yeasty, living tradition. It is not ancestor worship, but an established attitude on fundamentals.

Why was state-imposed segregation ended so easily in St. Louis schools? Why are unpopular speakers not harassed by the police? Why did St. Louis and Missouri, too, so largely escape the inflammation of McCarthyism and the rash of right-to-work laws? Why does the community become so exercized about even petty graft? And why does it sometimes seem so self-satisfied, so smug?

It is largely a matter of example, of a point of view accepted by generation after generation. It started with Laclède's egalitarian village government and St. Ange's acceptance of this when he insisted that he would sign no order as an officer of the king until the men of the town had decided what should be done. The Spaniards in St. Louis were wise enough to accept this precedent. The "Bostons" naturally asserted this democratic spirit in the state constitution and the city charter. General Clark took it for granted. So did Benton, the old Jacksonian. So it has been. Departures from the pattern so far always have been corrected by a Joe Folk.

There is little talk about "the St. Louis tradition." But there is genuine regard for democracy, civil liberties, integrity, faithfulness to public trust, respect for public funds, a decent respect for the property of others and a decent concern for their needs, disregard for vaunting, a quiet self-respect, and an almost Athenian confidence in the ability to get things done in City Hall. Written out, all this is terribly hifalutin. With so much of the pioneers' down-to-earth language still on their tongues, St. Louisans expect only preachers, carpetbaggers, and commencement orators to talk this way. They affect a polite skepticism. They are not pompous—except at the Veiled Prophet's ball, which is something else again. Since St. Louis still is on the near side of the Pearly Gates, a man walking its streets will not be dazzled by halos or caressed by angels' wings. He will encounter mostly ordinary folks— housewives downtown for "Dollar Day," stenographers shopping on their lunch hour, lawyers or bookkeepers taking some rolls of colored home movies to be developed, policemen on the prowl for jaywalkers, horse players leaving a bet with the man at the corner newsstand.

For most of them old Cotton Mather would predict, with the self-assurance of the self-satisfied, a long future reeking of brimstone. And about some of them he might even be right. As any police reporter knows, there are characters around town who can be described only by the epithet which Harry Truman reserved for his favorite music critics and newspaper columnists. Why else does the police board need so much money for trained police dogs? And why would Mayor Tucker have approved a bond issue for a new workhouse? The human weaknesses, nice and not so nice, are just about as common along the Mississippi as along the Hudson, or the Euphrates. They are the most dependable of perennials.

The man buying a wrench at Central Hardware or a cheese in the Union Market may not keep a close eye on politicians, although he knows that they have let him down more than once. But he does expect the newspapers to sound the alarm, if need be. And if a legislator or an alderman is caught *in flagrante,* his constituents will be three-deep at the bar of the corner tavern, discussing his peculations like so many Schurzes or Pulitzers. But if the brouhaha about the missile gap gets too loud, a man can take a tranquilizer in St. Louis nowadays just as easily as in New York.

A good St. Louisan cannot be looking after such high matters personally all of the time. He has to take his children to the zoo to see the chimps. He has to take his wife to the Bevo Mill for supper. He has to drink a Bud or a Stag with his neighbor. He has to mulch the roses. He has to go to the ball park to watch the Cardinals and figure out how they can be in such a slump. But he can figure that things are working out all right. Aren't the Redbirds selling beer for Gussie Busch just as the city's first professional baseball team sold beer for Von der Ahe, Muckenfuss, Diddledock and Keck? So long as first things come first, a man can be true to the spirit of St. Louis; he can be *gemuetlich*.

He cannot be sure that things always will be that way—any more than he can say whether the Cardinals will win the pennant in 1964, or whether the city and County will get together so that they may grow in prosperity. For that he would need a ouija board as good as the one Patience Worth used. That Patience Worth! She is the strangest one in the whole St. Louis family album. She was not even rightly a St. Louisan, but a seventeenth-century Englishwoman—or so she said. But she took up one July evening back in 1913 with Mrs. John W. Curran of Vernon Avenue. Mrs. Curran was toying with her ouija board—has anybody seen one since the Kaiser forced St. Louis to change the name of Berlin Avenue to Pershing?—when this Worth woman introduced herself through the wooden contraption. She told Mrs. Curran to let the cat sleep, and then went on to dictate millions and millions of words—not all at once, of course. But for Mrs. Curran she spelled out novels, verse, epigrams, lectures, interviews, and even small talk. This went on for years until Mrs. Curran did not even need the ouija board to take down Patience Worth's somewhat Elizabethan outpourings. Quite proper persons—Caspar Yost of the *Globe-Democrat* editorial page, Mrs. Emily Grant Hutchings, a novelist, Clarence Miller of the Mercantile Library, and Dr. Walter Prince of the Boston Society for Psychic Research—were quite properly impressed. Henry Holt published the ghost-writings; and the *Literary Digest*, going strong at the time, said that "more than one critic has said plainly and clearly that Patience Worth or no Patience Worth, these lines have in them the quality of greatness seldom realized." The New York *Times* also praised the works. Even Carl Schurz would have had a doubt or two about Patience Worth, but nobody accused Mrs. Curran of out-and-out fraud; although in trying to understand her story a few were ungallant enough to say that she simply did not know enough or have enough literary style to be writing the stuff on her own. A Harvard gentleman simply said that Mrs. Curran was a case of multiple personality. Be that as it may, in 1929 she moved to Los Angeles, as might have been expected, and there she died in 1937.

Since then nobody around St. Louis has been much good with a ouija board. When it comes to predicting the future, people do little better than the eminent Dr. George Gallup. Judging by the past, there is not much truth in talk about a city dying on the vine. Right now things look good. Anyway, who wants to live in the future? A fine big catfish with beer—or sauerbraten, if you prefer—only can be enjoyed in the present. Nor is the meal spoiled because an old crystal chandelier or two have not yet been removed for something more modern. Crystal's nice.

Appendix A: Mayors of St. Louis

1823–28	William Carr Lane	1864–68	James S. Thomas
1829–32	Daniel D. Page	1869–70	Nathan Cole
1833–34	Col. John W. Johnston	1870–74	Joseph Brown
1835–37	John F. Darby	1875	Arthur Buckner Barrett
1838–39	William Carr Lane		(Died in Office)
1840	John F. Darby	1875	James Britton
1841	John D. Daggett	1876–81	Henry Overstolz
1842	George Maguire	1881–85	William L. Ewing
1843	John M. Wimer	1885–89	David R. Francis
1844–45	Bernard Pratte	1889–93	Edward A. Noonan
1846	Peter G. Camden	1893–97	Cyrus P. Walbridge
1847	Bryan Mullanphy	1897–1901	Henry Ziegenhein
1848	John M. Krum	1901–09	Rolla Wells
1849	James G. Barry	1909–13	Frederick N. Kreismann
1850–52	Luther M. Kennett	1913–25	Henry W. Kiel
1853–54	John How	1925–33	Victor J. Miller
1855	Washington King	1933–41	Bernard F. Dickmann
1856	John How	1941–43	William Dee Becker
1857	John M. Wimer		(Died in Office)
1858–60	Oliver Dwight Filley	1943–49	Aloys P. Kaufmann
1861–62	Daniel Gilchrist Taylor	1949–53	Joseph H. Darst
1863	Chauncey Ives Filley	1953–	Raymond R. Tucker

Appendix B: Queens of the Veiled Prophet

1878	Susie Slayback	1897	Jane Dorothy Fordyce
*		1898	Marie Theresa Scanlan
1885	Virginia Lee Joy	1899	Ellen H. Walsh
1886	Louise Scott	1900	Susan Larkin
1887	**	1901	Emily Catlin Wickham
1888	Louise Gaiennie	1902	Maude Wells
1889	X	1903	Lucille Chouteau
1890	Kate Hill	1904	Stella Wade
1891	July Thomson	1905	Julie Cabanne
1892	Ellen Sturgis	1906	Margaret Kehlor Tower
1893	Florence Lucas	1907	Margaret Cabell
1894	Hester Bates Laughlin	1908	Dorothy Shapleigh
1895	Bessie Kingsland	1909	Susan Rebecca Carleton
1896	Marie Louise McCreery	1910	Lucy Norvell

1911	Ada Randolph	1935	Lila Childress
1912	Jane Taylor	1936	Susan E. Thompson
1913	Adeline Capen	1937	Nancy Morrill
1914	Elsa Zeibig	1938	Laura Rand
1915	Jane Shapleigh	1939	Jane Howard Smith
1916	Mary Dee Jones	1940	Rosalie McRee
1917	***	1941	Barbara Wear
1919	Marian Franciscus	1942	****
1920	Ada Johnson	1946	Anne Farrar Desloge
1921	Eleanor Simmons	1947	Dorothy Clagett Danforth
1922	Alice Busch	1948	Helen Dozier Conant
1923	Grace Wallace	1949	Carol Moon Gardner
1924	Mary Virginia Collins	1950	Eleanor Simmons Koehler
1925	Maude Miller Street	1951	Mary Kennard Wallace
1926	Martha Love	1952	Sally Baker Shepley
1927	Anne Farrar Semple	1953	Julia Whitelaw Terry
1928	*	1954	Barbara Anne Whittemore
1929	Jean Ford	1955	Audrey Faust Wallace
1930	Jane Francis	1956	Helene Brown Bakewell
1931	Ann Ferriss	1957	Carol Lammert Culver
1932	Myrtle McGrew Lambert	1958	Carolyn Lee Niederinghaus
1933	Jane Johnson	1959	Laura Rand Orthwein
1934	Jane Wells		

* The Prophet's records are unavailable for these years.
** No Queen as President and Mrs. Cleveland were guests of honor.
*** No Queen, World War I.
**** No Queen, World War II.
X The Queen in 1889, according to the Missouri Historical Society, was "a Miss Wain of Cleveland."

Index